A New Look
at Guardianship

A New Look at Guardianship

Protective Services
That Support
Personalized Living

edited by
Tony Apolloni, Ph.D.
Executive Director
California Institute on Human Services
Sonoma State University
and
Thomas P. Cooke, Ph.D.
California Institute on Human Services
Sonoma State University

·P·A·U·L·H·
BROOKES
PUBLISHING C<u>O</u>

Baltimore • London

Paul H. Brookes Publishing Co.
Post Office Box 10624
Baltimore, MD 21204

Typeset by Brushwood Graphics, Baltimore, Maryland.
Manufactured in the United States of America by
The Maple Press Company, York, Pennsylvania.

Library of Congress Cataloging in Publication Data
Main entry under title:

A New look at guardianship.

Bibliography: p.
Includes index.
1. Guardian and ward—United States.   2. Developmentally disabled
children—Legal status, laws, etc.—United States.   I. Apolloni, Tony.
II. Cooke, Thomas P.
KF553.N48   1984   346.7301'8   83-23936
ISBN 0-933716-37-0   347.30618

Contents

Chapter Authors

TONY APOLLONI, PH.D.
Executive Director
California Institute on Human Services
Sonoma State University
Rohnert Park, CA 94928

MILTON BLACKSTONE
1301 Dellcrest Lane
La Jolla, CA 92037

JOEL R. CHRISTIE, B.A., M.S.W.
Public Guardian
Alberta Social Services and Community
    Health
Office of the Public Guardian
2nd Floor, Provincial Building
4920 51st Street
Red Deer, Alberta, Canada T4N 6K8

THOMAS P. COOKE, PH.D.
California Institute on Human Services
Sonoma State University
Rohnert Park, CA 94928

DANIEL GELLER, PH.D.
Associate Professor
School of Graduate and Continuing
    Education
Fairfield University
Fairfield, CT 06430

ERVIN J. LARSEN
Executive Director
Foundation for the Handicapped
1600 West Armory Way
Seattle, WA 98119

NANCY J. MARLETT, M.A.
Associate Professor
Rehabilitation Studies Program
Education Tower, Room 430
University of Calgary
2500 University Drive, N.W.
Calgary, Alberta, Canada T2N 1N4

LOUISE MONACO, J.D.
Monaco & Smilowitz
650 South Spring Street
Suite 807
Los Angeles, CA 90014

LLOYD MUNNEKE, M.A.
Executive Director
Crossroad Services
1311 Golf Course Road
Rock Valley, IA 51247

G. ALLAN ROEHER, PH.D.
Director of Human Services Graduate
    Studies
School of Environmental Studies
York University
Toronto, Ontario, Canada M2K 2G4

PAUL R. ROGERS, LL.B.
Editor
Guardianship News
30 Cottage Street
P.O. Box 674
Amherst, MA 01004

JERRY SMILOWITZ, J.D.
Monaco & Smilowitz
650 South Spring Street
Suite 807
Los Angeles, CA 90014

ALOYSIUS J. SOENNEKER, A.C.S.W.
Executive Director
Association for Retarded Citizens of
    Oregon
3085 North River Road
Salem, OR 97303

STEVEN R. SPROGER, M.S.W.
San Diego Regional Center
4355 Ruffin Road
Suite 206
San Diego, CA 92123

JAMES E. STUEMKE, J.D.., M.B.A. (Tax)
    C.P.A.
339 East Poppyfields Drive
Altadena, CA 91001

NOREEN VINCENT, J.D.
Executive Director
Mayor's Office for the Handicapped
200 North Spring Street
Room 2100
City Hall
Los Angeles, CA 90012

HENRY P. WIDRICH
Founder and Past President
Oakdale Guardianship, Inc.
President
Macomb-Oakland Guardianship, Inc.
29570 Sharon Lane
Southfield, MI 48076

Preface

The past several decades have produced a profound change in the perspective of North Americans toward persons with special developmental needs (mentally retarded and other developmentally disabled persons). These changes have been prompted largely by parental pressures. Until fairly recent times, parents had one of two choices: keep their child at home or place their child in an institution. The first parental efforts in the early 1950s simply focused on finding some place for their children to go during the daytime in order to have "something to do." Advances in scientific knowledge and changes in social attitudes, however, began to offer a more promising outlook toward the future potential of persons with special developmental needs. Parents began pressuring for meaningful educational, rehabilitation, social, and medical services. Today, the availability of these services is often taken for granted. Some services are even considered entitlements, i.e., services assured by government to persons in need of assistance due to disability or old age. It is assumed that developmentally disabled students will automatically receive needed services.

While many positive developments have transpired, the parents of highly dependent persons are still faced with the difficult task of deciding how to ensure the long term care and protection of their disabled child once they are no longer able to exercise personal oversight of his or her quality of life. Parents want assurance that someone will safeguard their child in a clean, wholesome setting and that he or she will be free from physical and psychological abuse. Parents need to know that the little things they do to improve their disabled child's life quality will continue to happen.

This book summarizes information on changes that have occurred in the area of legal and programmatic solutions to the "old-age" question. It is written to acquaint parents and professionals with emerging options for improving the security, stability, and continuity of services for dependent persons. The contents of the book are organized into two sections. The first includes chapters that convey general knowledge and opinions about the area of guardianship. The various chapters provide overviews of: 1) human services trends affecting guardianship, 2) recent developments in guardianship law, 3) a parent's perspective on the importance of guardianship services, 4) a counseling psychologist's perspective, 5) research on the determination of personal competence, and 6) questions parents must answer when making long term plans for their disabled child.

The second section reviews organizational models for delivering guardianship services. The section begins with a chapter that describes many of the existing corporate guardianship programs in the United States. Subsequent chapters offer detailed descriptions of two public guardianship schemes and four private guardianship corporations.

The parents of persons with substantial disabilities desperately want to feel secure about the future well-being of their dependent child. Increased emphasis on public and private guardianship models is thus inevitable. It is our fervent hope that this book will share knowledge and stimulate debate on this trend and that it will enable tomorrow's pioneers to actualize even more appropriate guardianship service models.

Acknowledgments

The editors express their appreciation to the late Dr. G. Allan Roeher for his guidance on the topic of corporate guardianship. Moreover, the California State Council on Developmental Disabilities warrants thanks for its support of the editors' preliminary research on the topic of corporate guardianship programs (Contract # 20500). The opinions expressed in this book represent the views of the authors and are not necessarily endorsed by the California State Council on Developmental Disabilities. Finally, Jane Wilder, editorial aide, deserves special thanks for her efforts in preparing the several drafts of each chapter.

Dedicated in Memory of

Dr. G. Allan Roeher

Visionary and Friend of People
with Disabilities
Throughout the World

A New Look
at Guardianship

ESSENTIAL FEATURES OF GUARDIANSHIP SERVICES

Guardianship Reconsidered

Tony Apolloni and Noreen Vincent

Because of mental and/or physical impairments, some developmentally disabled persons will always need help in order to maintain a decent quality of life. The issue addressed by this book is how parents and professionals may best ensure lifelong protection and advocacy for people who are diagnosed as "developmentally disabled." According to a federal definition:

"Developmental disability" means a severe, chronic disability of a person which (a) is attributable to a mental or physical impairment or combination of mental and physical impairments; (b) is manifested before the person attains age twenty-two; (c) is likely to continue indefinitely; (d) results in substantial functional limitations in three or more of the following areas of major life activity: (1) self-care, (2) receptive and expressive language, (3) learning, (4) mobility, (5) self-direction, (6) capacity for independent living, and (7) economic self-sufficiency; and (e) reflects the person's need for a combination and sequence of special, interdisciplinary, or generic care, treatment, or other services which are of lifelong or extended duration and are individually planned and coordinated (Welfare & Institutions Code, Statutes of 1980).

Many individuals with a developmental disability will never need to be placed under guardianship and their resources will never need to be controlled by a trustee. Some individuals, however, will need one or both of these services, partially or totally, throughout life or on a time-limited basis. The decision-making ability of the person with a disability is the deciding factor. Guardianship and trust arrangements remove decision-making power and thus are improper unless a dependent person's need for protection is more important for his or her welfare than is the maintenance of the person's right to make decisions for himself or herself.

The process of personalization allows for the tailoring of services to ensure the best possible match between needs and service resources (Apolloni, 1981). A

3

huge human services industry, primarily supported by federal, state and local government revenues, has emerged over the past 30 years to address the needs of people who are developmentally disabled. The components of this system have grown dramatically from small volunteer programs operated in church basements to complex corporations with multifaceted educational, habilitative, and medical services. One thing that hasn't changed much, however, is the locus of responsibility for ensuring the long term well-being of persons with developmental disabilities who are incompetent to manage their own lives and/or estates. Parents continue to be the "provider of last resort," i.e., the ones responsible to safeguard their child's quality of life. Yet, they are still faced with the difficult problem of planning an approach to ensure long term protection, advocacy, and personal attention to their dependent child/adult. In fact, parents must make provisions to support their severely disabled child even after their own death.

The long range planning problems that confront parents have intensified over the past several decades for a variety of reasons. First, the number of persons with developmental disabilities is greater than ever before. The longer life spans of disabled persons and the post–World War II population bulge mean that there now is a much larger population of severely disabled adults. Second, the movement to relocate persons from public institutions to community living arrangements has resulted in increasing numbers of dependent persons in living arrangements that do not provide the "security" formerly associated with public institutions. Third, the average age of members of major voluntary associations for people with developmental disabilities—the long assumed source of future advocacy—has steadily advanced over the past decade and the priority of these organizations has tended to shift away from advocacy and toward the management of direct service programs. Finally, the trend toward ever-expanding government responsibility for human services has begun to reverse (see Chapter 2).

Who then will take final responsibility to ensure the future well-being of people with developmental disabilities? Who will act as their "replacement parents"? To whom can parents turn for assurance of long range personal attention to their dependent child? This book addresses these questions. It moves beyond the traditional alternatives that parents are well aware of (relatives, friends, lawyers, and bankers) to describe an emerging trend: group guardianship models including public guardianship and corporate guardianship programs.

TRADITIONAL GUARDIANSHIP APPROACHES

Trusted relatives and friends are perhaps the most appealing and appropriate people who may serve as guardians. One limitation of using this approach, however, is that relatives and friends are often similar in age to parents and thus unlikely to outlive the dependent person whom they agree to assist. Moreover, relatives and friends, even if they are young, face competing personal and vocational priorities that interfere with consistent, face-to-face attention to a dependent ward, and they are unlikely to possess specialized information on how to optimally obtain and maintain needed services.

Lawyers and bankers as guardians offer the advantage of possessing the professional training and experience necessary to advocate effectively in formal proceedings. Moreover, their performance is regulated by a professional code of ethics. Lawyers and bankers, on the other hand, possess a number of weaknesses. They typically do not understand the service needs of disabled persons and the network of agencies that exists to address these needs. They may also lack the level of commitment that is necessary to ensure services, and their own services are costly. Most financial institutions refuse to administer trusts that do not exceed some minimum capitalization level (e.g., $50,000).

PUBLIC GUARDIANSHIP

Public guardianship programs (see Chapters 11 and 12) have been started in many areas over the past several decades. They offer the advantages of decreased dependence on extended family ties, the involvement of full-time professional guardians, the capability of providing services throughout the life of the ward, less likelihood of family-oriented conflicts of interest (as when a family member overly conserves a ward's estate in hopes of inheriting the remainder), and the authority and stability of a government-operated organization.

Public guardianship programs also manifest some problems, e.g., high job turnover rates, competing organizational priorities, lack of needed information, and outright conflicts of interest. The latter problem is perhaps the most vexing. Most existing public guardianship programs call for the appointment of an officer of the department or agency who is responsible for the delivery of direct services (case management, living arrangement, habilitation training, etc.) to act as public guardian. This results in potential conflicts of interest. The public guardian is responsible for monitoring the ward's access to services, care, treatment, and release from services in a manner that is in the ward's best interest. At the same time, the public guardian is responsible to ensure the stability of the ward's direct services in a manner that is not politically embarrassing. The heads of government are generally appointed by elected officials. The elected officials are very sensitive to any publicity that affects their political fortunes. The danger lies in the fact that the interests of the ward may sometimes be sacrificed to the interests of maintaining order and/or containing costs. It takes a courageous caseworker to go against the agency that pays his or her salary in order to advocate on behalf of a ward.

A related problem with public guardianship schemes is that wards with estates are sometimes required to pay ''reasonable fees'' for services. Many states are in dire financial straits and the costs of human services have skyrocketed over recent years. A potential conflict of interest arises when the director of the department or agency responsible for operating direct services on tight revenues is also responsible for fixing the level of fees that a ward must pay.

State officials who are appointed public guardian generally assign their responsibility for providing protection and oversight to social service personnel in local organizations or government offices. Problems arise when the number and competence of local caseworkers are not commensurate with the needs of wards. This method of assigning responsibility to social service personnel is followed in California, for example, where the ratio of clients to caseworkers is 67 to 1 and guardianship is only one of many caseworker responsibilities (see Chapter 11).

CORPORATE GUARDIANSHIP

Corporate guardianship programs represent the newest alternative for parents. A number of corporate guardianship programs have begun, mostly within the past few years, which serve persons with developmental disabilities. This book shares information on this trend in the interest of better equipping those who wish to consider developing similar programs. Chapter 10 describes the corporate guardianship programs that the authors are aware of in the United States. Subsequent chapters provide detailed descriptions of several of the more advanced programs (Chapters 12, 14, 15, and 16).

In theory, well-established corporate guardianship programs possess the same advantages of public guardianship models except for formal affiliation with government. In addition, they potentially hold advantages not found in public schemes: more individually tailored guardianship arrangements; improved caseworker-to-client ratios; direct affiliation, in many cases, with organizations that are committed to advocacy activities; and less potential for conflicts of interest.

The existing corporate guardianship programs unfortunately demonstrate a variety of drawbacks. First, none of the existing models appears to be adequately capitalized to ensure lifelong protection and advocacy. Second, the required endowment per client for an adequately capitalized corporate guardianship program is difficult to calculate but is almost certain to be prohibitive for the vast majority of families who need such services. Third, there is a very good likelihood that, over time, corporate guardianship programs will become bureaucratized and less responsive to individual needs.

ABOUT THIS BOOK

This book is a collection of information on the topic of planning approaches for assuring guardianship services to persons with developmental disabilities. It reviews current thinking on solutions to the "old-age question" (i.e., *What's after me?*) and summarizes the status of some recent efforts to implement public and corporate (private) guardianship programs. It is organized into two sections. The first (Chapters 2–9) is a review of theoretical and practical considerations that are involved in designing and delivering guardianship services. The second section (Chapters 10–17) consists of descriptions of corporate and public approaches to guardianship services.

Chapter 2 was prepared by Dr. G. Allan Roeher of York University, Toronto, Canada. Dr. Roeher, the founding Executive Director of the Canadian National Institute on Mental Retardation and the former Executive Secretary of the Canadian Association on Mental Retardation, was the President of the International Association for the Scientific Study of Mental Deficiency, and Distinguished Visiting Professor on the Faculty of Environmental Studies of York University. Dr. Roeher died in an airplane accident on June 9, 1983, just a few days following the completion of his chapter.

Dr. Roeher promoted the formation of a corporate guardianship program in Canada for many years. His chapter summarizes historical and contemporary trends in the provision of services to people with developmental disabilities that are likely to have an impact on efforts to formulate public and private guardianship strategies. He points out a number of factors that threaten the long term stability of services: a) changes in the roles and responsibilities of the public sector, b) the potential failure of the human services industry to effectively adapt to societal changes, c) the growing size and complexity of human service systems, d) the lack of effective coordination among service systems, e) the emergence of adversarial management-employee relationships in the field, f) the potential decline of consumer power, and g) cultural changes and increased competition for finite resources.

Chapter 3 was written by Paul Rogers, the editor of *Guardianship News*,[1] a monthly newsletter that reviews conceptual and practical developments in the law of guardianship and substitute judgment. Mr. Rogers is a practicing attorney in Massachusetts who specializes in handling guardianship cases. He has proposed a corporate guardianship model for serving indigent persons in several counties of Massachusetts. His chapter provides an overview of the meaning of the legal concept of guardianship and briefly discusses: a) how a person becomes a guardian, b) constitutional issues specific to court procedures, c) the duties of a guardian, d) limited guardianship, and e) substituted judgment.

Chapter 4 was written by Louise Monaco and Jerry Smilowitz, both attorneys who have specialized in protecting the civil rights of people with disabilities for over 5 years. Ms. Monaco is co-chair for the Southern California American Civil Liberties Union's (ACLU) Committee for Civil Rights of People with Disabilities and a former member of the Los Angeles City Council for the Handicapped. Mr. Smilowitz has served as a regional center civil rights advocate. Their chapter reviews constitutional and case law considerations pertinent to guardianship in the areas of marriage, child rearing, sterilization, institutionalization, employment, and general self-control.

Milton Blackstone, a leading parent advocate, prepared Chapter 5. Mr. Blackstone has served on the California State Council on Developmental Dis-

---

[1]*Guardianship News,* 30 Cottage Street, P.O. Box 674, Amherst, MA 01004; (413) 549-1409. Paul Rogers, Editor. Subscription rates: $48–one year, $86–two years; $38/year for automatically renewable continuous subscriptions.

abilities where he chaired committees on family support and community living arrangements. He has served on the boards of numerous community service agencies and has been the driving force in the development of many special education, habilitation, recreation, family support, and group home programs throughout California. He is the parent of a 22-year-old son who is brain damaged, blind, and labeled "autistic." Mr. Blackstone presents his thoughts on considerations that parents should take into account when planning for the future of their disabled offspring. The topics covered in his chapter include living arrangement options, the potential role of siblings, safeguarding entitlements to government benefits, and estate planning guidelines.

Daniel Geller is an Associate Professor, School of Graduate and Continuing Education, Fairfield University. Drawing on his counseling experiences with parents, Dr. Geller (in Chapter 6) describes the adjustment reactions that parents typically display as they rear a disabled child: grief, denial, anger, depression, and chronic sorrow. He also portrays how the reactions of family members and friends can have adaptive and destructive influences on parents' behavior toward their disabled child. Finally, he discusses the impact of a family's future vision on the way it treats a disabled member and the potential significance of corporate guardianship programs for constructively modifying future visions.

Nancy J. Marlett, in Chapter 7, provides a layman's description of the research that she has conducted on the question of how to decide if someone needs a guardian. Ms. Marlett is an Associate Professor in the Rehabilitation Studies Program at the University of Calgary (Alberta, Canada) an interdisciplinary program concentrating on the social and behavioral aspects within rehabilitation. She is a certified psychologist within the Province of Alberta and is involved in research, teaching, and consultation on decision-making. Her chapter includes checkpoints for parents and direct service staff to use in evaluating individuals' competence to care for themselves. Moreover, she summarizes state-of-the-art information for use by assessment specialists who must render professional judgments regarding individuals' competence.

Chapter 8, on estate planning, was authored by James E. Stuemke. Drawing on his wealth of experience in the area of counseling parents with disabled children, Mr. Stuemke defines and describes seven options: 1) guardianship, 2) trusts, 3) power of attorney, 4) concurrent ownership, 5) "secret trusts," 6) contracts for future services, and 7) inaction.

Steven Sproger is the Intake Unit Supervisor of the San Diego Regional Center. He counsels parents on a daily basis regarding how to make long range plans that will ensure the well-being of their disabled child. In Chapter 9, Mr. Sproger recommends that parents address the area of future planning by asking themselves three questions. He provides guidelines for parents to follow when answering them. The three questions are as follows: 1) Is guardianship needed at all? 2) If guardianship is needed, should it be guardianship of the person, of the estate, or of both the person and the estate? and 3) If guardianship is needed, who should assume the duties?

Most of the chapters in the second section of this book (Chapters 10–16) were written by individuals who direct group (public or corporate) guardianship programs (i.e., programs that provide guardianship services to a number of dependent persons). The section begins with a chapter that reviews important design features for group guardianship models and summarizes existing corporate guardianship programs vis-à-vis these features. This chapter is followed by two descriptions of public guardianship programs: the California system and the Alberta model. Most of the remaining chapters in the second section describe existing corporate guardianship programs in the United States.

Dr. Tony Apolloni prepared Chapter 10. Dr. Apolloni is the Director of the California Institute on Human Services, a research and development center that is located on the campus of Sonoma State University. He acts as conservator of the person (California terminology for guardian of the person) to his developmentally disabled sister. As noted above, his chapter delineates key elements of group guardianship programs, and describes the nature of the small number of corporate guardianship programs and corporations that do not act as guardian but provide similar services that he has been able to identify in the United States. This chapter should prove highly useful to those who are preparing to implement corporate guardianship models.

Chapter 11 describes the public guardianship program in California. It was written by Steven Sproger, whose duties at the San Diego Regional Center include the management of a large public guardianship program. This chapter covers two topics: 1) the distinction between plenary and limited guardianship, and 2) the history and status of California's public guardianship program.

In the next chapter (Chapter 12), Joel Christie, the public guardian for the Province of Alberta, Canada, describes the public guardianship program that he administers. Mr. Christie currently acts as guardian to over 1,000 persons, most of whom are diagnosed as "mentally retarded." Mr. Christie's chapter provides a detailed description of the Dependent Adults Act, the highly progressive legislative model that established the Alberta Office of the Public Guardian. He reviews the decision-making areas for which all guardians are accountable and the dilemmas that may be associated with making decisions for another person. He concludes with a summary of the lessons that the Alberta public guardianship model has for those who are interested in promoting similar public programs.

The first detailed description of a corporate guardianship program (Chapter 13) is supplied by Ervin J. Larsen, the Executive Director of the Foundation for the Handicapped. This program has operated statewide in Washington since 1963. It currently serves over 500 persons. Mr. Larsen describes revisions in the program that have occurred during the past 20 years and explains a master trust program that is administered by the Foundation.

A second corporate guardianship model is outlined by Mr. Aloysius J. Soenneker (Chapter 14). Mr. Soenneker is the Executive Director of the Association for Retarded Citizens, Oregon, a statewide association of parents who have mentally retarded offspring. In response to parental requests for help, the

Oregon ARC developed the GAPS (Guardianship, Advocacy, and Protective Services) Program. GAPS is a subsidiary of the state ARC and currently has long term responsibility for 35 persons and provides short term advocacy assistance or advice to approximately 350 persons each year. Mr. Soenneker describes the organization, personnel, services, and budget for the GAPS program and offers a series of recommendations to those who wish to develop similar guardianship programs.

The next two chapters (15 and 16) include descriptions of programs that were initiated by parents primarily to serve a more circumscribed client population, i.e., the persons residing in a congregate living arrangement. The first description (Chapter 15) was supplied by Mr. Henry Widrich, the Executive Director of Oakdale Guardianship, Inc. This program was begun in 1976. It was originally designed to serve the residents of the Oakdale Regional Center in Lapeer, Michigan (combined public institution and community services placement agency). Decisions to relocate clients to community living arrangements and to other public institutions in Michigan necessitated an expansion in the guardianship program's target population. Today, the program serves approximately 200 clients in seven counties of Southeast Michigan. Services are provided via a cadre of trained citizens called "volunteer monitors." Mr. Widrich provides a detailed description of the Oakdale Guardianship program including examples of the agency's activities on behalf of clients.

Mr. Lloyd Munneke, the Executive Director of the Crossroad Services program, summarizes the key features of this model (Chapter 16). The Crossroad model was begun in an attempt to address the concerns of parents of a single residential facility, Hope Haven, located in Rock Valley, Iowa, but has expanded to provide services to persons in five states. Mr. Munneke describes the three types of services that the corporation offers: 1) direct long term contractual services agreement, 2) family/guardian assistance contractual services, and 3) professional consultation. Copies of these arrangements are provided in an appendix.

CONCLUSION

A number of reforms in guardianship procedures have taken place across the past decade. They are:

1. More emphasis on functional definitions of legal incompetence (i.e., the person is unable to properly provide for his or her personal needs) and less attention to diagnostic labels
2. Attempts to limit guardianship provisions so that the power of the guardian does not exceed that which is in the best interest of the ward
3. The establishment of public guardians, and
4. The emergence of private corporations that provide guardianship services.

These reforms reflect efforts to modify the relatively inflexible concept of legal guardianship to better serve persons who are developmentally disabled. This book reviews these trends and, it is hoped, will aid those who are engaged in planning for the future security of dependent persons.

REFERENCES

Apolloni, T. Overcoming obstacles to the personalization of services. In: C.L. Hansen & N.G. Haring (eds.), *Severely handicapped persons in the community*. Seattle: University of Washington Program Development Assistance System, 1981.

Welfare & Institutions Code, Statutes of 1980, Chapter 1237, Section 6, Division 4.5.

Chapter 2

The Changing Context of the Human Services Movement

Implications for the Disability Field
and the Need for
More Adequate Backup Systems

G. Allan Roeher

The opening question for the readers of this book is, "Why are corporate guardianship programs needed, given the massive social legislation and support programs that have been developed over the last half century?" This chapter responds to the question by describing contextual changes in the human services[1] environment that planners, service providers, and consumers must take into account when determining appropriate protective mechanisms for at-risk individuals who are substantially physically and/or mentally disadvantaged. First, this

---

[1]The term "human services" is a common one; schools, colleges, daycare centers, hospitals and nursing homes, child-welfare and adoption agencies are among the more familiar examples. There are many more, especially for people with special needs. Social assistance programs, employment and immigration centers, family-planning programs, diagnostic centers for the disabled, "institutions" and group homes, and sheltered workshops for handicapped people are typical programs that exist in most communities. Human services represent a large and complex industry in our society. In the private and voluntary domain, the human services industry encompasses a wide array of individual and organizational relationships ranging from informal, small grass-roots, common-interest associations with close interpersonal membership involvement, to formal regional, national, and international bodies with complex legal corporate structures. In the public realm, agencies range from small assistance programs to bureaucracies of unmanageable magnitude. Services for special categories of handicapped people are part of, and typical of, the overall human services field. In the United States and Canada, there are over 200,000 registered voluntary organizations providing human services, exclusive of public (government) agencies. This industry absorbs the equivalent of over one-fifth of the gross national product in each of the two countries.

chapter reviews the complex dynamics, interrelationships and interdependencies that exist between the disability field and the larger human services environment. In the subsequent parts of this chapter, factors that threaten continuity and adequacy of services to handicapped people and the relevance of these factors to the need for improved group or corporate guardianship schemes are focused on more specifically.

DEFINING ADVOCACY AND GUARDIANSHIP

This chapter is intended to familiarize the reader with the nature of the human services field as it relates to advocacy and guardianship. It may be useful at the outset to clarify the definitions of the terms *advocacy* and *guardianship* since they are capable of many different meanings in their ordinary and technical usage. The term *advocacy,* as used here, refers to a person or group representing the interests of one or more handicapped persons to secure basic rights and services for him or her that other citizens enjoy. Advocacy, with classical origins as one of the essential components of the practice of law, has been widely adopted by the human services professions. Advocacy is variously defined to include consumer education, protest, evaluation, monitoring of services, social brokerage, and friend-to-friend support-type relationships. It can also include aiding groups to gain power for political or social change. Apart from self-advocacy, all advocacy efforts involve a relationship between a handicapped person and an advocate. The primary allegiance of the advocate is to the client or disadvantaged target group and their needs, interests, and rights. Some such relationships are:

The *natural advocate*—parent or near relative
The *volunteer advocate*—the friend or citizen advocacy concept
The *corporate advocate*—the society itself or a voluntary organization
The *public advocate*—a public official similar to an ombudsman or departmental official
The *professional advocate*—lawyer or social worker
The *court-appointed advocate*—guardian of person or property

In some ways advocacy can be viewed as the process of enabling special groups to express themselves politically and to help humanize bureaucracy. Contemporary forms of advocacy are as varied as people's creativity. Some advocacy organizations extend their activity to analysis of existing service systems and to organizing the community to bring about reform. Protege/advocate-type programs have recently gained momentum, for example, Big Brothers and Sisters, Citizen Advocacy, Parent-to-Parent, and Handicapped-to-Handicapped programs. Governments, moreover, have facilitated the advocacy process through the establishment of human and civil rights agencies, legal aid programs, and ombudsman offices. Various kinds of community crisis intervention groups exist. The most recent trend has been the emergence of clients forming their own local, regional, and nationwide organizational networks for more effective self-advocacy. These primary consumer organizations have begun to challenge service agencies, governments, and even the established consumer and citizen action bodies with which they may be directly or indirectly affiliated.

The term *guardianship* refers to a specific, formally structured form of advocacy wherein a court appoints someone or some group to take responsibility for making personal representation on behalf of, and/or financial decisions for, a dependent person. Family or friends usually act as guardians but provisions exist in many states and provinces for courts to appoint government officials as *public* guardians, and private agency representatives as *corporate* guardians.

It is widely accepted that guardianship should be resorted to only when other, less formal, advocacy relationships have proved unsuccessful or are inappropriate, because it transfers the affected individual's (ward's) decision-making power to another person. The great majority of handicapped people do not need a court-ordered guardian to protect their personal well-being and interests. It is important to remember that guardianship is only one form of advocacy and it is not an adequate substitute for the full range of advocacy arrangements that are needed in the field of human services, namely, increased self-advocacy, better services and improved public attitudes (Hanning, 1982).

THE POST-WAR HUMAN SERVICES ENVIRONMENT

The premise that we are in an era of rapid and unpredictable socioeconomic change is gaining popular acceptance among leaders in economics, social sciences, and governments. After an unprecedented period of growth since the Second World War, human services are entering a period of uncertainty, disillusionment, and perhaps even regression. This situation exists due to increased societal concern over energy-related resources, inflation that erodes personal income, unemployment, deteriorating environments, and more. The stable state of the past few decades, in which economic fluctuations always returned to normal, seems to have ended. The future is likely to be different. "Turbulence" has become the "in" term to describe the disruption associated with the transition from an industrial to a post-industrial era, with all the accompanying social and economic changes, and the human services field is directly affected by this turbulence (Roeher, 1981).

Residual Institutional Trends

Social science historians observing the cyclical changes in societal support for human services have formulated two metaphors or terms to describe the phenomenon. One is referred to as *residual*, the other *institutional*. The term "residual"

---

[2]The term "institution" has come to be identified as a large, generally undesirable, residential facility. Here, the term is used in its more general sense; namely, established pattern, attitude, or behavior that has become an accepted way of thinking, reacting, behaving, or doing, e.g., the institutions of the family, marriage, government, church, etc. The dual meaning and usage of the term in this chapter should not be confused.

describes a social attitude that public support of the needy is a privilege, not a right; while the term "institutional" describes the reverse. The residual formulation implies that support for human services is provided only when the family or individual develops a need. This usually occurs when the nation or society is in economic decline, or is responding to industrialization, urbanization, war, market breakdown, etc., when significant discontinuity disrupts the status quo. The residual concept focuses attention on helping only in times of need rather than on the basis of broader general social reform. It typifies the traditional "charity" notion or attitude toward people who become victims of societal change.[3]

The term "institutional" implies no stigma to such anticipated personal consequences of societal change. The turbulence, complexity, and dislocation caused by modern societal change is recognized as creating environments that have a more negative impact on some segments of citizens than on others—the old, handicapped, poor, and other minority groups. The technologically and socially changed society (as a product of the industrial revolution) is viewed as responsible for the disruption of people's fortunes, livelihood and social situations. Social and economic support measures are viewed as an inherent responsibility of society to its citizens (i.e., a citizen's right, rather than privilege).

Over the past century there has been a gradual shift from residual to institutional attitudes in both public opinion and social measures. In North American society, the *real* change emerged gradually from the days of the Great Depression, through World War II, and came into full "institutional" blossom in the post-war decade, reaching its peak about the mid 70s. Since then, sentiment toward the residual concept has once again begun to emerge and there are strong indicators suggesting that this may be a long term trend.

In reality, the two formulations overlap. Both have always been mutually operative: "hope, faith, and charity" has prevailed along with humanistic and progressive social legislation and practice. Even the most pessimistic social, political, and economic observers would concede that, at worst, the pendulum will not likely swing much past the center; that there will be some blend of residual-institutional patterns for responding to human services needs.

The Rationale Behind The Trends

The factors that motivate society's humanistic behavior toward its fellow citizens in need are varied, but there is both a logical and legitimate rationale for residual-institutional-residual trends or cycles. In the relatively simple rural frontier society, the spirit of primary self-reliance along with cooperation among relatives, neighbors, and local community members made the *residual* notion of help essential and appropriate. The Great Depression, however, heralded the effects of severe, large scale and long term problems of economic insecurity,

---

[3]Wilensky & Lebeaux (1966, pp. 138–140), Romanyshyn (1971, pp. 5, 38, 39, 79, 369) and Kahn (1969, pp. 178–179) all make this distinction in their conceptions of changes in welfare due to varying technological, economic and social changes.

deprivation, and a breakdown of social control. This, with the corresponding growing complexity of society (industrialization and urbanization), placed increased and unbearable demands on individuals, families, and helping (most often voluntary) organizations. The New Deal ushered in government intervention in human services and income security on an unprecedented scale for the unemployed, for the needy, and for child and family welfare cases.

While some services for handicapped people (deaf, blind and some "crippled children," especially those affected by poliomyelitis) existed in the pre-war era, the rehabilitation revolution is essentially a post-war phenomenon.

Growth and Prosperity Improvement in societal attitudes toward the needy was greatly reinforced by economic prosperity and a sense of affordability. The growth or decline of social and economic support for human need, especially in regard to those who are significantly impaired, is nearly always influenced by society's sense of being able to share its resources without the undue interference of other established (standard of living, quality and style of life) priorities. If these elements are threatened, society reduces or withdraws from its level of consideration for the needy.

Post–World War II economic growth and technological progress were accompanied by a corresponding growth and proliferation of private, voluntary, and public human services organizations, most relying for major support on the expanded public tax base that legislators favored due to the pressure of advocacy organizations and the opportunity to win votes.

In the pre-war era, financial liability for the provision of support services for handicapped people in Canada and in the United States was viewed as a shared responsibility among family, voluntary agencies, and public agencies. If the family elected not to place their child (or adult) in a public institution, the chances were small that a local (nonprofit) community service would provide the needed care. This bleak picture has changed dramatically during the past two decades. Not only is government playing a much more pervasive role in assisting families to care for their disabled offspring, but the notion that the taxpaying public has an obligation to assist and be responsible has gained widespread acceptance. The charity model of funding service programs has largely been abandoned by consumers and advocates. Indeed, the expansion of support at all levels of government (including generic voluntary and public agencies) has skyrocketed into a multibillion dollar developmental disability industry.

Rising Consumer Expectations for Service Provision Paralleling and exceeding this rapid growth were the rising expectations of consumers and providers. Expectations turned into demands first for permissive, then mandatory, legislation for expanding the service base. Primary consumers began to form organizations of their own (primary consumer advocacy movements, such as People First, speaking for themselves, living and acting independently—even practicing self-help and becoming political activists). Normalization became the guiding ideology and personal and group advocacy became the intervention strategy.

Litigation and Legislation Closely related to the growth of service provision has been the expanding impact of litigation and legislation for basic and equal human rights for handicapped people. Several sweeping declarations were adopted in the United States in the 1970s (PL 94-142, PL 95-602, and Section 504 of the 1973 Rehabilitation Act) that mandate government assistance to persons with disabilities relating to most aspects of human need—education, employment, marriage, reproduction, access, intervention, research (including experimentation safeguards), housing and zoning by-laws, etc.

The increasing demand by advocates to view services as binding legal rights rather than privileges has dramatized the claims of handicapped persons and resulted in more rapid expansion and integration of support programs over the past decade. These laws have also led to a major redistribution of authority and responsibility for delivering services, including vastly increased public influence over the manner in which they are delivered. Once free to exercise discretion in designing and delivering services, consumers and providers are now required to abide by an increasingly bewildering array of governmental rules, regulations, and standards. While the expanded role of government has resulted in more equitable distribution of services and almost eliminated grossly substandard programs, it has also increased program costs, stifled local and voluntary initiative, added frustrating rigidities, and allowed the public sector to have pervasive, far-reaching impact on such aspects as accountability and control of service provision. Moreover, it has also resulted in community service systems that are overly reliant on public legislative and fiscal support.

When legislation (and subsequent regulations and implementation) did not bring rapid enough change, recourse to the judicial process became a popular route, especially in the form of class-action suits (but not in Canada where the constitutional structure makes class-action suits against the "Crown" extremely difficult). Most court rulings have favored the plaintiff and there is little doubt that this has had a major influence on policies related to living arrangements and intervention procedures. Litigation, moreover, has dramatized decades of societal neglect and abuse and has forced state and provincial bodies to commit increased public resources to reduce longstanding deficiencies in large facilities, and increased community service and residential programs.[4]

---

[4]The long range consequences of the litigation are not yet known. When comparing Canada, where litigation has played a less significant role, to the United States, there is some indication that court involvement tends to obscure the action roles of both consumer and legislative bodies. It can also distort the allocation of scarce public resources. The energy and resources committed to engaging in the litigative process often detract from the capability of advocacy and state bodies to focus on, and improve, nonaffected components of the overall service delivery system. Opponents of judiciary intervention argue that court-imposed mandates cause delay, dislocation and polarization, thus impeding systemwide changes in services. Court-induced changes can subject "deinstitutionalized" citizens to inadequate alternatives in the absence of balanced funding policies and resources. Finally, judicial decisions superimposed upon the complex service delivery system tend to distort established lines of responsibility and accountability, thus actually impeding rather than expediting desired systemic reforms.

A Return to Greater Individual Responsibility

Most human services programs have become heavily tied to government funding and taxation and are being carefully scrutinized and even cut back. With growing economic constraints on governmental activity, attitudes toward the human services sector have recently begun to change. Political and civil service leaders are reversing the stance that has evolved since World War II. Spokespersons for governments now openly advocate increased roles for the voluntary sector as an objective that is desirable in its own right, as an alternative to public dependence on government services. Nonprofit agencies are encouraged to act in ways that encourage more independence from government (meaning less dependence on public taxation to fund operations) (Gettings, 1981).

The costs of this social enlightenment and generosity have begun to take their toll. Universal coverage programs are proving too costly a burden for government (Kettle, 1980).[5] Canada's health system, only fully in place for a decade and a half, is an example. It is currently undergoing budget cuts and provincial governments are gradually moving toward a modified form of privitization ("Hospital User Fees for Alberta," 1983). The Family Allowances program (under which *every* mother receives a nominal monthly payment from the federal government for each child under the age of 18, regardless of need or income), also has been cut back, as have unemployment benefits and other income security programs. The pendulum of sentiment is once again gradually swinging back to greater individual responsibility for health and social needs. Even though most such reductions attempt to be greater for upper and middle than lower income levels, all classes in effect experience reduced support or protection. One example of this is the growing reintroduction of "user fees" in health and other programs, which penalizes lower income groups disproportionately (Hartley, 1982).

In summary, the human services field in general, and services and social security needs for disadvantaged constituencies in particular, have come through a longterm cycle from a *residual* to an *institutional* ideology that has resulted in the most advanced social reform legislation in the history of both the United States and Canada. It has also resulted in unplanned and uncoordinated growth and proliferation of countless private, voluntary, and public agencies. These developments now constitute the largest (service) industry in both countries, equivalent in expenditure to over one quarter of the gross national product. Ironically, but understandably, consumer expectation and dissatisfaction has remained relatively high and is increasing. From the perspective of the elected public official, caught between the resentful taxpayer and angry consumer, it is a no-win situation; hence, the gradual readjustment to a blend of the two philosophical approaches. The net

---

[5]The underfunding of Social Security (in Canada, the Canada Pension Plan) and unemployment insurance schemes are examples of inadequately conceived systems that now threaten their own future as well as that of education, social and health schemes. A typical example of news reports on the subject is "Close Call for Social Security," *Time* (1983).

result is likely to be nongrowth, or slight decline, in public support for human services in the forseeable future.

FACTORS THAT THREATEN THE LONG TERM STABILITY OF SERVICES FOR PERSONS WITH DEVELOPMENTAL DISABILITIES

The disability field has fought its battles and prospered on the basis of two effective strategies. The first strategy was philosophical—it used education and political pressure to gain acceptance of the concept of right to treatment and opportunity (the "normalization" ideology). The other strategy produced successful results through the introduction of direct, usually segregated, services such as special (now increasingly integrated) education classes, vocational preparation via sheltered (now somewhat more integrated) work settings, housing, through special group (now often regular) homes, etc. Though these are only some of the essential components of a comprehensive services approach, the strategy proved so effective that it led to a growing conviction within the constituency of consumers and providers of services that essentially *more of the same* will result in the ultimate goal of community living, lifelong, for every disabled person, regardless of degree of impairment and according to the ideals of the "normalization" philosophy.

Some people recognized that the ideal alternate system involved a much more complex and complete approach. They undertook research and experimentation toward the development of a total community service *systems* approach that provides for the necessary *comprehensiveness* and *continuity* of care, and for *choice* of services (range of options), all according to the normalization philosophy. The results of these experiments also have fallen short even where projects were limited in scale, experimental in approach, and possessed better than normal levels of funding, staffing and organization.

Consumers and providers are currently divided as to whether the total community approach is a clear or *assured* alternative to the older segregated and/or "institutional" approach for all disabled people. This issue is uppermost in the minds of parents and relatives when they contemplate the future of their disabled persons beyond their own ability to be their protectors. It also concerns service planners who find it impossible to agree on realistic organizational, administrative, and political models that dispel the doubts of parents and others regarding continued need for "segregated/institutional" programs, at least for some disabled persons.

There is a small, but growing, network of people who believe that the community alternative is realizable through service provision approaches based on *open systems* theory, similar to the experimental programs that have been launched thus far (Apolloni, Cappuccilli, & Cooke, 1980; National Institute on Mental Retardation, 1982).[6] The concepts used in the experimental models appear to

---

[6]The approach is based on *open systems* theory in which all relevant factors or elements are viewed as interdependent and interactive at all times. *Closed systems* theory accounts for only some of the elements. The latter is also described as single-path, or simple cause-and-effect-type, problem-solving.

remain valid, but certain contextual factors led to problems that prevented successful attainment of major objectives.

The following are some of the relevant deterrent factors that undermine efforts to create comprehensive community service systems and threaten the stability of other services for persons with developmental disabilities. Some elements are broad and contextual in nature, while others are more specific.

Local-Central (Center-Periphery) Dynamics

Major shifts have occurred in roles and responsibilities in the public sector. Prior to World War II, local governments assumed major responsibility for addressing human service needs. The consolidation of central income-tax revenue by federal governments resulted in centralized control of a major source of public funds for health, education, and social needs in the post-war period. It also provided the federal governments in the United States and Canada with a degree of economic control over the state/provincial government programs, even when the direct operation of services or grants to local community delivery agencies was in the hands of the latter. In recent years, provincial/state governments have gained, or regained, more authority. The latter, however, vigorously defend their own central mandates over regional and community service agencies, contending that this is necessary in order to maintain order and effectiveness in the system (Birch, 1955; Simeon, 1979).[7]

In the private sector, most helping agencies began locally as voluntary societies that gradually federated into provincial/state and national movements. Many tend to retain local autonomy, with the central bodies serving in a complementary supportive role. Other voluntary movements started centrally, subsequently organizing and developing local units under a national charter, and hence retaining greater control by the central body. Neither approach overcomes the traditional local-central conflicts and resentments.

The centralizing process tends to breed bureaucracy, with budgeting, personnel practices, and program policies located at the apex of the structure. The proponents of decentralization maintain that since services must involve the client, good program policies derive from local decision-making. Moreover, recent consumer demand and program philosophy is toward greater comprehensiveness, more regionally systemized, community-based services, with normalization and integration as preconditions of service effectiveness; and toward alternative facilities and services that are less segregated and restrictive. These trends increase pressure on voluntary movements and governments for greater local self-determination. While the latter is constructive in many respects, experience shows that extremes in either direction lead to under-realization of objectives. The

---

[7]A paradoxical dilemma is emerging between the U.S. Social Security/Canada Pension Plan schemes, on the one hand, and the health and social services programs on the other. While all are underfunded, the social security programs' constituencies have more electoral strength. Social and health services support tends to be sacrificed (during periods of constraint) over social security requirements ("Close Call for Social Security," 1983; Kettle, 1980, pp. 211–213).

decentralist movement that is evident today may perpetuate fragmentation and discontinuity of services and/or undermine the potential for mobilization of economic and other resources.

Unplanned Change

Organizational change in services for people with handicaps is subject to a set of contingencies that are different from those confronting business and industrial organizations. The behavior of human service organizations is based on a fundamentally different model, necessitating both new organizational theory and different practice. Established human service organizations are generally comprised of three distinct domains—*policy, management,* and *service*—each operating under different and contrasting governing principles, success measures, structural arrangements, and work modes. The *policy* domain is occupied by elected or appointed representatives who govern by the consent of an electorate; the *management* domain mirrors the business model; and the *service* domain is client-specific with emphasis on quality of care and desire for self-governing professional modes. These three structures are organizationally discordant, which can result in a lack of cohesiveness, disharmony, tension, conflict, decreased central control, and an inherent interdomain struggle for control. What is good for one domain is not necessarily good for or acceptable to the others (Kouzes & Mico, 1979).

The domain theory helps explain some of the major problems that besiege service organizations. These organizations tend to either resist change in the face of shifting needs or change rapidly and dramatically in a fragmented manner. Some hold on to their old ways or slip into new forms of stagnation that fall short of needed change, and fail to maximize the organization's potential capability. On the other hand, others undergo precipitous change in response to ideological considerations and become unstable.

Size and Complexity of Human Services Systems

The service system for persons with handicaps is largely a twentieth-century phenomenon, having grown in an ad hoc fashion from individual and informal group charitable efforts into a monumentally large, bureaucratic, fragmented, and seemingly unmanageable industry. Problems arise when operations grow to extreme levels of scale and complexity. They tend to decline in performance and become increasingly incomprehensible, more vulnerable to disruption, and less amenable to democratic control. There is a diminishing relative capacity for the client to comprehend the operation, which results in consumers organizing into collective bodies around common interests to cope with their dissatisfactions. This, in turn, results in large service agencies interacting with large consumer-advocacy bodies, with the effect of diminishing the individual's (primary consumer's) chance of participation and direct access to decision-making. In contrast, there is increased participation and control by professionals and experts in the policy-making process. Coordination of the parts of the whole therefore becomes more difficult. Alienation increases between the provider (the operation) and the recipient (the consumer). Interaction becomes more dehumanized, system rigidity increases, basic value premises are compromised, the span of diversity and innovation narrows, and there is a decline in the overall performance of the system relative to changing needs and demands of the consumer (Elgin & Bushnell, 1977).

Operational Efficiency

Operational efficiency within an organization is more likely to occur when definitive and stable criteria exist for measuring the effectiveness of its operation. When, for instance, a system is guided by the rule of profit, recognized criteria, or yardsticks, exist against which to measure productivity and efficiency. The field of services to handicapped people, however, is faced with attempting to measure effectiveness through a number of qualitative, multidimensional, and often conflicting, changing, and ambiguous objectives. Few, if any, *adequate* measuring tools exist for this purpose. When a system's health is difficult to measure, its future also cannot be predicted with any degree of confidence. In the human services industry the problem is complicated by democratic "political" processes that pressure delivery agencies to respond to legislative edict or citizen concerns rather than relate to strictly consumer constituency needs. Operations grow, not by logic and long range objective planning, but in response to ever-changing sets of subjective influences and forces.

Fiscal support for specific causes is not generally in accordance with objective need but relative to subjective factors (such as attitudinal, image, or political influence). Competition for funds is another critical factor. The principal private (corporations and United Way) and public (governments) funding bodies have responded by trying to provide something for everyone. This tends to compromise quality for quantity of services for the individual cause or organization. The problem is likely to persist as taxpayers react to perceived excessive levels of taxation and solicitation for voluntary giving. The net effect is that continuity of services to clients cannot be assured beyond the present or short term future.

The Lack of Coordination Among Service Systems

The idea of coordinating activities between agencies in order to more fully achieve common goals remains popular. In reality, coordination is invariably approached with apprehension by agencies because it necessitates some level of consensus and compromise over ideological distinctions, jurisdictional power, and resource sharing. It also affects the relative power and status of agencies competing in the larger political-economic human services industry milieu. Coordination, therefore, is often viewed with uneasiness as limiting the capacity of stronger agencies to realize their goals. Hence, it is understandable that voluntary coordination efforts have generally failed, and that even mandated coordination has severe limitations.

"Neutral" or objective coordination can rarely be realized; even when the process results in mutual agreement on a policy matter or course of action, it inevitably advances some agency's self-interest at the expense of others. Indeed, some of the past consequences of the coordination strategy have resulted in strengthening the more established agencies, reducing competition, and giving some of the participating agencies a predominant role in determining resource allocation among others (Tucker, 1982).[8] The failure of coordination efforts to improve services to handicapped persons suggests that limits have been reached in contemporary approaches to managing large systems, or more correctly, the nonsystemic behavior of the human services industry.

Changing Management-Employee Relationships

The charitable origins, humanistic orientation, and nonprofit nature of human service organizations have tended to shield the field from the adversarial management-employee relationships intrinsic to the business sector. All this is changing because of the growing discrepancies in relative remuneration and working conditions in human service organizations, and because staff associations and professional organizations have proven to be less effective than organized labor unions in their negotiations. Grossly underpaid lower-level staff in human service organizations are demanding more equity with commercial industry. The fact that voluntary organization employers operate on a nonprofit basis is deemed irrelevant.

Public (civil) service workers led the way in becoming organized, but voluntary agencies are becoming the next mobilization target of labor unions. In addition, "clients"—blind, physically handicapped, and mentally retarded persons—in protected work settings are beginning to unionize.

One primary objective of organized labor is job security for its members. Traditional union philosophy and practice is to challenge the free enterprise-for-profit/competitive system. Applying the same concepts and practices to the competitive, nonprofit human services field can create unintended social and fiscal complications. For example, while the public and many governments are now working to alter or dismantle large, obsolete facilities, public service unions—representing workers—openly fight to keep institutions in operation (especially in small communities where such operations have become a major source of local employment). Union members can feel trapped between obligations to their fellow members and societal goals; the employee may be caught between societal goals and employment security; the public and governments are torn between economic and social objectives.

Until recently these labor-management conflicts affected primarily the large (bureaucratic) civil service operations. In the future even small community

---

[8]Others who also attest to the failure of (voluntary) coordination as an effective resource utilization strategy are Stanley Meyers, January, (1978) and E. Sullivan (1976).

programs (group homes and educational and sheltered work programs) will be affected, as service providers struggle between dedication to their work and satisfying their own needs, as primary consumer activism and advocacy become more organized, and as demands and pressures increase for improved services.

Declining Secondary Consumer Power

Most human services were pioneered by, or with, active citizen participation. Citizen activism has been an essential catalyst for transforming new knowledge and technology into general applications. Citizens resorted to pluralistic organizational structures to effectively represent their interests in complex democratic social systems. Inevitably such movements tend to stagnate and, by default, to stimulate the formation of new organizations reflecting newer needs. Thus, the field proliferates in an ad hoc fashion adding to the existing phenomenon of disparate, uncoordinated, overlapping, and wasteful "nonsystems." It is an ongoing birth-to-death cycle in which organizations emerge and plateau while others fade; some die out.

A study of past experiences and lifecycle patterns of voluntary organizations suggests that citizen-based movements change in relatively predictable ways. Young organizations and movements are innovative and flexible, but gradually tend to become unimaginative and rigid unless there are operating dynamics that keep movements revitalized. Membership within consumer-based organizations tends to become complacent and apathetic as the initial missions are accomplished, the visions realized, and the organization becomes professionalized or is taken over as a public service. Many pioneering movements have difficulty assuming new goals and atrophy into routine service delivery agencies (Wolfensberger, 1973).

Ongoing evaluation generally does not occur in organizations where membership change is slow. Change tends to correlate with new generations of membership. A movement that fails to achieve a gradual but ongoing change in membership stagnates. New troops are as vital to citizen movements as to any army in battle. Most voluntary organizations, not unlike cooperatives, unions, or political parties, tend to resist true revitalization. One result is the emergence of totally new and independent bodies that reflect changing times and needs. The older ones remain. Consequently, the proliferation and fragmentation of advocacy bodies increases, compounding self-defeating complexity. The clients become the victims. They need another advocacy and group protective vehicle to deal with such situations. While it is too early to predict the outcome with certainty, it appears that many of the leading consumer organizations in the field of developmental services are weakening and that adequate voluntary replacement bodies are not on the horizon. Those that do emerge compete with the residual organizations for limited resources, preventing the emerging entities from effecting optimal (or needed) change.

Cultural Changes and Increased Competition for Resources:
The Impact of the Baby-Boom-Baby-Bust (and "Me") Generations

No one predicted it, and society has not prepared itself for dealing with the upcoming changes created by the current, biggest single generation in the history of the United States and Canada. Only now is it becoming clear that these 75–85 million young men and women in these two countries represent, by their very numbers and their orientation, attitude, and expectations, what has been termed the "Big Generation" and the "Me Generation." They constitute a culture with quite different values and tastes, and they can be expected to respond differently to needs, crises, and obligations than did previous generations. For most, the issues of recent years—ranging from unemployment, economic and energy constraints, and housing, to different interpersonal (sex and marriage) and social relationships—are a letdown from the expectations with which they grew up. There are also unprecedented economic burdens this cohort will need to bear; supporting the increased numbers of dependent people; compensating for the consequences of past environmental abuse, natural resources depletion, defense costs, and public debt; and assisting the developing world with its exploding population growth. The views of futurists on this unprecedented post-war generation phenomenon portend significant changes in the competition for public funds—changes that will adversely affect the aged and disability populations. The "baby boom" or "big" generation is described as sharply differentiated from both its parent generation and from all previous ones. It is better educated but also more alienated from past value systems, more dependent on social support systems, and more demanding on the public sector. While the depression-born generation fought for an improved quality of life for its children, the contemporary generation is more "self-actualizing," viewing extraordinary obligations (such as supporting those who are less productive and more dependent on society) to be the responsibility of governments.

Whether or not such a generalization is totally valid, the possibility of it being so is undeniable. Facts about current phenomena reinforce the above, e.g., changes in women's place in the workforce and the growing desire and need for both parents to work; and the seeming instability of the family structure evidenced by recent data that almost half of (U.S. and Canadian) marriages are failing (approximately a 200% increase in the U.S. and a 500% increase in Canada since 1968) are forcing men and women to redefine the way they see themselves and each other (National Center for Health Statistics, 1983; "Statistics Canada Report," 1983). Whether this is one more sign of a fundamental and dangerous disintegration of traditional social values or evidence of a refreshing new honesty, with positive effects, the impact on the lives of children, especially disabled children, is likely to be negative and even traumatic.

The predicted greater future mobility of the "Big" generation and its adjustment to the postindustrial (information) revolution may further weaken the family (structural) stability and create even less certainty for those children who are dependent on their families. Vocational preparation and employment authorities predict that, on the average, people will change careers four to five times and move domicile more often than their predecessors (Kettle, 1980). If these trends prevail, dependence on state or community organizations to assure continuity of support for disabled people increases.

Not all forecasters are as pessimistic about the future. A minority are optimistic, at least with respect to the economy. They predict decline of the North American economy and the adverse consequences described above. Some view the present difficulties as a transitional adjustment, i.e., "downsizing" from the old industrial (the-bigger-the-better) preoccupation with giantism to the new postindustrial (the smaller-the-better) emphasis on scaling down (with the microprocessor as the leading technological change agent). They also view the downsizing of the population growth rate as a positive development. The "baby boom" of the late forties and early fifties powered much of the economic and human services (especially in education) growth of the sixties and seventies. For optimists, "the Baby Bust" (decreased birth rate) of the sixties and seventies means fewer young people, age 18–24, entering the work force, which is seen as helping to ease the unemployment problem in the eighties that has been a major drain on the economy and (competition for) public tax resources. (Cook, 1982).

Several trends appear to offset this optimism. First, it seems likely that the better educated Baby Boom cohort will result in a work force surplus in the more capital-intensive high skill and technology jobs and a shortage in the blue collar industrial and service areas. This could (and already has) lead to a trend for industries to move to developing countries where labor is plentiful and relatively cheaper. If so, this trend could compound the present problems of unemployment, particularly for developmentally disabled, aged and other persons with significant employment handicaps. For them, the future remains even less certain than for the able-bodied workforce.

Second, it is a generally accepted rule that growth and maintenance of the economy and social programs depend on the birth rate (including immigration of young people) remaining greater than the death rate. The trends are presently approaching reversal. The situation in Canada could remain more critical than in the United States. While both countries have constraints on immigration, the United States has a continuing influx of illegal immigration of significant proportions that could compensate for the decreased birth rate.

Third, an obvious but uncertain long term contextual influence is the changing economic scene brought on by the oil crisis of the mid-seventies, the world economic crisis, the growing industrial competition from Southeast Asian countries, the future stability of the monetary system (as a result of the indebtedness of the developing world), and the growing cost of military buildup and maintenance. These demands compete for the same tax base on which the human service industry depends for stability and even status quo maintenance. Human and social security expenditures do not generate products for the export market upon which both the United States and Canada are heavily dependent to maintain fuller employment and quality living standards. So, priorities are shifting in public and industrial policy thinking.

Finally, there are a host of economic and political pressures that influence the future: a) inflation, compounded by increased taxpayer and donor resistance, abnormal budget deficits, and consequent constrained (in real terms) public and voluntary support; b) transactional (between causes) competition for the available resources, particularly affecting constituencies of people who are handicapped and viewed as less productive; and c) consumer longevity (dependent persons are requiring more years of support services paid for by few productive workers).

Demographic, Bio-social, and Bio-ethical Dilemmas

The factors heretofore discussed are subject to change—for better or worse. One development that will almost certainly compound the threat of long term stability of service availability is the demographic reality of an increased ratio of disabled to nondisabled in the population. This is due to the cumulative effect of a continued decrease in the mortality rate of infants and children with birth defects at one end of the age spectrum, and increased longevity (of all people, including disabled) at the other. For example, conditions of premature senility (Alzheimer's disease) and senility are appearing as major problems because of medical science's progress in keeping alive people who ordinarily in the past did not reach the age where such debilitating mental and physical diseases of aging set in. The adage that progress in medical science and practice "compounds the felony" seemingly applies here. Given society's historic inability or unwillingness to deal adequately with these consequences, the magnitude of the economic costs and service-providing complexities of serving severely and multiply involved disabled citizens in the future, especially according to "normalization" ideology, has only begun to become manifest.

Management of these kinds of problems in family or group homes presents even greater (unplanned for) challenges. Even at present, without past and present efforts of advocacy and human services movements and professions, there would be even greater abuse and neglect of those that are deviant from the norm. Though religious, ethical, and moral convictions are powerful forces for maintaining a humane approach to treatment of less able individuals, there is growing controversy over the type and locale of care to be extended.

Recently, there has been much publicity about legal confrontations between relatives refusing authorization and advocacy bodies advocating lifesaving surgery ("Decisions about Life and Death," 1983). In two lower court decisions, the parents' position was supported, one of which was overruled in a higher court. Had it not been for strong advocacy in favor of the victims, the parents' position would appear to have prevailed, at least in some of the cases. This is an indication of ambivalent attitudes and feelings, reminiscent of other fluctuating societal attitudes, toward the sanctity of life. The case of capital punishment is another example.

This ethical chaos needs to be put in order ("Today's Dilemma," 1983). At least one prominent leader with a considerable following predicts that societal attitudes toward severely handicapped and terminally ill persons are becoming less humane (more evil), even moving toward the tolerance of euthanasia. He cites instances of proposed euthanasia laws in more than one state legislature.[9]

Unquestionably, the increasing power of medical science and practice to save and maintain life is ahead of societal acceptance, ability, or willingness to cope with the results. When families or service agencies cannot manage problems, neglect of the helpless individual follows—even cruelty occurs. Abuse of children and aged parents is not uncommon in family homes and community service facilities, as well as in larger institutions—often the consequence of family member or staff "burnout," inadequacy of fiscal and human resources, and/or sheer frustration. In spite of increased rights legislation, discrimination in employment and lifestyle is far from assured for those without strong and effective parental or advocacy support.

In summary, the present and foreseeable future service systems suggest a continuing scenario of discontinuity and uncertainty for, in particular, the moderate to severely involved disabled person ("No Room for the Disabled," 1983).[10] Clearly, some additional backup mechanisms are needed for the concerned parent, relative, or advocate—even for the responsible service agency ("Institution Is Not a Dirty Word," 1982).[11]

WINDS OF CHANGE: LONG RANGE IMPLICATIONS OF
PRESENT TURBULENCE IN THE HUMAN SERVICE FIELD
FOR HANDICAPPED PERSONS AND THEIR FAMILIES

Lifelong protection for persons with developmental disabilities involves long range plans and schemes capable of coping with unpredictable events and circumstances. Today's young adult of age 25 will only be 41 years old at the turn of the century. One age 40 will only be age 56. The child born this year with a substantial handicap may live to the year 2050 or longer. What conditions will prevail in the future? For what kinds of protection should plans be made? What

---

[9]The leading North American exponent of these beliefs is Wolf Wolfensberger, who documents signs, symptoms and factual situations in various issues of *TIPS*, The Training Institute for Human Service Planning, Leadership and Change Agentry, Syracuse University, and in his lectures and other writings.

[10]In a precedent-setting legal case, the Court ruled in favor of the plaintiff, a multiply handicapped 20-year-old man who took his father to court in order to gain the right for self-decision to discharge himself from a large residential facility ("institution"). He won his case, with the support of advocates and staff of the facility, to have the right to choose to live in a group home. The intended caregivers found, however, that they could not cope with his needs (the father's primary concern) and will require extraordinary special assistance. Without guardianship and assured lifelong protective advocacy, this person's future is unpredictable.

[11]This article reflects the growing split within both parent and service provider constituencies over the contention that community services can provide a full alternative to "institutions."

organizational vehicles are needed to assure parents that their children will be served after they are gone?

No one can predict the future with accuracy because the future evolves in a combination of both predictable and unpredictable elements. Nevertheless, it is important to attempt to ''crystal ball'' the future and to consider the types of actions that may maximize the security and continuity of services for disabled persons. As described earlier, prevailing and projected future elements suggest a long range countertrend that once again threatens to impose on individuals who are handicapped, and their families, a disproportionate share of the emotional burden and even a return to increased program and financial responsibility, and/or a trend toward re-institutionalization.

The following are some possible future changes in position, or directional shifts, that could occur:

1. Lawmakers and courts may become less willing to impose sanctions for failure to adhere to strict provisions of existing laws regarding mandatory services and rights for handicapped citizens. Indeed, attempts may be made to dilute or eliminate some statutory safeguards and regulations, and to limit enforcement activities.

2. Active advocacy for public responsibility will probably only succeed in protecting the gains that have already been made. If current trends prevail, governments will be reluctant to or will not improve and expand future services, human rights, protection and guardianship services aimed exclusively at developmentally disabled persons.

3. In view of the above (i.e., the public acceptance of less-than-hoped-for outcomes), sentiment of consumers and advocates for militant, proactive, judicial change-agentry to improved rights and services may fade. This will ease pressure on governments and public officials.

4. Greater protection and assurance of receiving services could occur for developmentally disabled persons through mandated generic services for which there are well established tax base structures, in contrast to the less stable supports for categorical services.

5. As citizen and political views harden, the emphasis may shift more to using public and private, including family, resources in a cost-effective manner by applying up-to-date management techniques. These include greater emphasis on design and implementation of comprehensive, long range strategies for the delivery of services, increased emphasis on involvement of local levels of government, generic agencies, and the private sector; advocacy for stronger working partnerships among local, state, and federal governments— partnerships that reach considerably beyond the rhetoric of the past; search for improved strategies and mechanisms for reconciling, on an interagency basis, contradictory or inconsistent goals and practices, and for eliminating unnecessary, duplicative and costly regulatory procedures.

6. Greater pressure may be placed on families to keep offspring with substantial intellectual and physical handicaps at home, and to assume a greater share of the emotional and other burdens associated with caring for their child.

7. There may be increased family interest in private arrangements to protect against extraordinary, lifelong protection, assistance, and guardianship. This book is an example of this trend. Corporate guardianship programs are likely to proliferate across the next decade because many families are desperately seeking assurance of services and protection for the long term well-being of their dependent, significantly handicapped child. Most are also unlikely to possess the knowledge, energy, or other resources to deal with the existing complex, uncoordinated, gap-filled system to obtain and maintain needed services in the future (Apolloni & Roeher, 1982; Roeher, 1978).

CONCLUSION

Public policymakers, service providers, advocates, and consumers are beginning to face issues not yet fully examined, understood, or accepted, but that will influence future developments in the field of services to persons with developmental disabilities. Most people have come to assume that the shift to government from family and charitable agency responsibility for human services in general, and for disabled constituencies specifically, was unidirectional. Yet, as the impact of the obligation mounted (described earlier), taxpayer and public-elected official alike are beginning to alter their views. The burden of the growing obligation in the face of rising costs and tax loads is helping to bring to the surface the long-standing public ambivalence toward government social programs and publicly financed services. While public support for those in need is likely to continue to be viewed as a legitimate, ongoing responsibility of government, societal reactions to consumer expectations that it be an almost exclusive role of the taxpayer, and hence government, are changing. A number of factors are contributing to such a countertrend:

1. The demands by advocates for services have resulted in categorical programs taking an increasing and significant share of public tax resources and this is placing them in direct competition with a myriad of other government programs. An example is the general public education system where regular education sectors feel threatened by the magnitude and cost of special education.

2. Advocacy movements are competing amongst themselves for the resource dollar, undermining the potential of even such desirable approaches as coalitions of common interest groups.

3. The public is increasingly frustrated by the unprecedented growth in the tax base in response to expanded public expectations for government to support human services. The public's dissatisfaction with the cost of human services

is compounded by its perception that human service programs are less than optimally efficient. The public is beginning to recognize that many social service bureaucracies have grown into monumentally complex operations, leading to deterioration and dysfunction, including the drift toward program rigidity and deterioration.

The effect of these developments is that during times of fiscal stringency and dwindling resources, there is a tendency for a sense of pessimism and gloom to pervade thinking, and for survival action strategies to emerge. Organizations hold on to what they have, resisting coordination and sharing, making the situation even worse. Another phenomenon is to hope for the past to revive in the not-too-distant future. It is believed that once the general public learns that reduced taxes mean inferior public services, the pendulum will swing back again. While this may happen, the indicators suggest a long range countertrend away from post-war prosperity and public human services support generosity. Parents and advocates of handicapped persons need to appreciate this trend and to participate in the development of backup strategies and mechanisms designed to safeguard their children's well-being. One such apparatus or change instrument to cope with this challenge is the concept of group or corporate guardianship, with its potential for increased and more potent advocacy, to assure lifelong protection for persons with developmental disabilities (Apolloni & Roeher, 1982; Roeher, 1978).

This chapter has been long on diagnosis of the human services environment—on analysis of the changing society with which citizens must cope. It has not attempted to provide detailed prescriptions. These follow in subsequent chapters. The intent has been to paint a mosaic depicting the complexity, uncertainty, and turbulence of the present and possibly future times and conditions. Extraordinary organizational and fiduciary models will be called for to deal adequately with the advocacy and guardianship needs of dependent persons if their rights to equal and humane treatment are to be realized. There is a light at the end of the tunnel, a silver lining in the clouds. Knowledge, experience, and the necessity to adapt are motivating an increasing number of advocates to develop improved and more powerful strategies to overcome barriers and constraints.

The program models and concepts detailed in this book are steps in this direction.

REFERENCES

Apolloni, T., Cappuccilli, J., & Cooke, T.P. (eds.). *Achievements in residential services for persons with disabilities: Toward excellence.* Baltimore: University Park Press, 1980.

Appolloni, T., & Roeher, G.A. Assuring continuity of services for dependent persons, Part I. *Guardianship News,* 1982, 2 (8), 57–58. (P.O. Box 674, Amherst, MA 01004.)

Birch, A.H. *Federalism, finance and social legislation in Canada, Australia and the United States.* London: Oxford University Press, 1955.

Close call for Social Security. *Time,* January 24, 1983, p. 16.

Cook, J. The molting of America. *Forbes,* November 22, 1982, pp. 161–167.

Decisions about life and death. *MacLean's,* March 28, 1983, p. 44.

Elgin, D.S., & Bushnell, R.A. The limits to complexity. *The Futurist,* December 1977, 337–349.

Gettings, R.M. Financing services and benefits. Draft manuscript produced for a proposed "White Paper," *Residential Services for Mentally Retarded Citizens in the 1980s.* Arlington, VA: National Association of State Mental Retardation Program Directors, 1981.

Hanning, J.D. Advocacy and guardianship. *I H Review* (Wellington, New Zealand), 1982, *22*(2), 2–3.

Hartley, V. *A community broker system for human service organizations in Ontario.* Unpublished master's thesis, Faculty of Environmental Studies, York University, Toronto, 1982.

Hospital user fees for Alberta. *Toronto Star,* March 29, 1983, p. 1.

Institution is not a dirty word. *Newsweek,* December 13, 1982, p. 17.

Kahn, A.J. Theory and practice of social planning. New York: Russell Sage Foundation, 1969.

Kettle, J. *The big generation.* Toronto: McClelland & Stewart, 1980.

Kouzes, J., & Mico, P.R. Domain theory: An introduction to organizational behavior in human service organizations. *Journal of Applied Behavioral Science,* 1979, *15,* 449–469.

Meyers, S. Wasted energy, wasted personnel, wasted resources. *Arise,* January, 1978.

National Center for Health Statistics, Public Health Service, quoted in *Newsweek,* January 10, 1983, p. 45.

National Institute on Mental Retardation. *Experimenting with social change: An interpretive history of the southern Alberta ComServ Project.* Toronto: National Institute on Mental Retardation, 1982.

No room for the disabled. *MacLean's,* March 28, 1983, p. 45.

Roeher, G.A. National Guardianship Foundation, Memorandum to Executive Committee of the Canadian Association for the Mentally Retarded, Toronto, May 1, 1978.

Roeher, G.A., Human service systems and turbulence. *Contact,* Journal of Urban and Environmental Affairs, Kitchener, Ontario, University of Waterloo, 1981, *13,* 37–51.

Romanyshyn, J.M. *Social charity to justice.* New York: Random House, Inc., 1971.

Simeon, R. (ed.). *Confrontation and collaboration: Inter-governmental relations in Canada today.* Toronto: Imperial Press Ltd., 1979.

Statistics Canada Report, quoted in *MacLean's,* March 21, 1983, pp. 38–44.

Sullivan, E. (*In Touch,* CBC-TV program). Ontario Institute for Studies in Education, December 1, 1976.

Today's dilemma: Live or die? *Toronto Star,* Insight Section, March 28, 1983, p. B1.

Tucker, D.J. *Voluntary auspices and the behavior of social service organizations.* Unpublished manuscript, McMaster University, Hamilton, Ontario, 1982.

Wilensky, H., & Lebeaux, C. *Industrial society and social welfare.* New York: The Free Press, 1966.

Wolfensberger, W. *The third stage in the evolution of voluntary organizations.* Toronto: National Institute on Mental Retardation, 1973.

Chapter 3

Understanding the Legal Concept of Guardianship

Paul R. Rogers

DEFINING GUARDIANSHIP

The concept of guardianship is very old. It is rooted in both Roman civil law and English common law. (See Brakel & Rock, 1971, and Custer, 1978.) There has always been an awareness that some persons, due to mental disability, simply cannot properly attend to their own self-interest nor exercise their legal rights. Therefore, as legal systems began to develop formal procedures and clearly defined personal rights, it became necessary to devise some means for taking account of those situations in which persons are unable to act for themselves. The result is the law of guardianship as it is known today. For an exhaustive treatment of the history of the law of guardianship and a penetrating analysis of the need for some fundamental reforms, see Frolik (1981).

The court has the duty of caring for persons who, due to mental disability, lack the capacity to attend to their own affairs in the ordinary ways most people do. Since the court cannot itself directly attend to all the details involved in caring for a ward, a person placed under the care of a court through guardianship proceedings (*Black's Law Dictionary*, 1979, p. 1420), the concept of guardianship has developed by which the court can carry out its responsibilities through an agent. As agent of the court, the guardian has a clearly defined role to play and certain specific responsibilities to discharge.

Before exploring various guardianship models and some of the more significant issues relating to the provision of guardianship services, it is important to have a good understanding of what a guardian is. The term ''guardian'' is used in different ways by different people. What is the legal meaning of the term? A "guardian" is a person lawfully invested with the power and duty of taking care of the person and/or property of another who, due to some defect of understanding, is considered incapable of administering his or her own affairs. The terms "committee" and "conservator" are sometimes used synonymously with the term "guardian " in some states. Under the civil law prevailing in Louisiana, the terms "curator" and "tutor" (used when the ward is a minor) are roughly synonymous with the common law term "guardian" (*Black's Law Dictionary*, 1979, pp. 635, 248, 277, and 1360, respectively).

Because a guardian is an agent appointed by the court, he or she is accountable to the court (*Estate of Guerra*, 96 N.M. 608, 633 P.2d 716 (N.M. Ct. App.1981)). Parents are "natural guardians" of their own children and do not need to be "appointed" by a court. By virtue of bringing a child into the world, parents are the natural guardians of the child up to the age of majority (see, e.g., Tenn. Code Ann., §§ 34-101, 34-103, and 34-105 (1977 Supp. 1983)). The same general considerations, however, relating to acting in the best interests of the child apply to natural guardians as well as to court-appointed guardians.

Courts with special limited jurisdiction over guardianship matters are known variously as "probate courts," "surrogate's courts," or "orphans courts." Sometimes courts of general jurisdiction, known as "superior courts," "circuit courts," or "district courts," handle guardianship matters (*Black's Law Dictionary*, 1979, pp. 1082, 1289, 220, and 427, respectively; see also "courts" at p. 318).

Responsibilities of the Guardian

There are two broad areas of responsibility either or both of which may be granted by the court to the guardian. First, certain *personal* affairs of the ward need to be taken care of, such as issues concerning where the home of the ward is to be located, what day-to-day supervision the ward needs, what nutritional and medical decisions need to be made and followed through on, and what the ward's needs for professional care and/or treatment are. A person appointed by the court to make such decisions as these on behalf of the ward is called a *guardian of the person*.

Second, there are often decisions that need to be made regarding the ward's *financial* affairs. How is his or her property to be safeguarded from waste and neglect? How should the ward's assets be used to benefit the ward? What bills need to be paid? What rights does the ward have regarding receipt of money or property from other persons? A person appointed by the court to make such decisions as these on behalf of the ward is called a *guardian of the property*. Sometimes a "guardian of the property only" is called a "conservator" (see, e.g., Mass. Gen. Laws Ann., ch. 201, §16 (West, 1958)).

Most of the attention devoted to guardianship duties has historically focused on managing the ward's property. But, increasingly, the importance of personal care of the ward is being recognized. Hence, guardianship of the person is getting more and more attention in the courts.

Usually, but not always, one person is appointed guardian both for the *person* and for the *property* of the ward. There might be, however, good reasons to separate these two areas of responsibility. If there is a close and caring family member, that person is usually the logical one to make personal decisions. But, if the ward has property of significant value, looking after it might require time and expertise that the personal guardian does not have. For example, a bank might, as guardian of the property, manage a stock portfolio much better than someone with no business experience. The personal guardian could then concentrate his or her time and efforts on improving the quality of the ward's personal life.

The crucial point to keep in mind regarding both guardianship of the *person* and guardianship of the *property* is that the duty of the guardian in making decisions and in taking actions is to act pursuant to the *best interests of the individual ward*, without reference to whether or not anyone else's interests are served. The guardian does *not* acquire any proprietary interest in either the personal or financial affairs of the ward. The guardian should not do what pleases himself or herself, or what pleases anyone else other than the ward. The guardian's duty is to do what the ward would presumably, if able, do for himself or herself, and to act in the best interests of the ward and *only* the ward.

ESTABLISHING GUARDIANSHIP

Having seen that a guardian is an agent of the court, one might ask how a person comes to be appointed guardian. Keep in mind, as noted previously, that parents as "natural" guardians do not have to be formally appointed as guardians of their children. When someone in need of a guardian does not have a natural guardian, then another person acquainted with the situation can petition the court to appoint a guardian.

The statute in some states provides that "any person" may file the petition. (See, e.g., Ark. Stat. Ann., §57-609 (1971); and Iowa Code Ann., §633.552 (West, 1964 & Supp. 1983).) In other states, the statute provides that specified classes of persons must file the petition. (See, e.g., Fla. Stat. Ann., §744.331 (2) (a) and (b) (West, Supp. 1983); and Mass. Gen. Laws Ann., §§6 and 6A (West, Supp. 1983).) The petition tells the court that the person alleged to be disabled needs a guardian but does not have one. Ultimately, if that is true, the court will appoint one. But the first procedural step that the court must take is to notify the allegedly disabled person (the prospective ward) that the petition has been filed so that he or she will have an opportunity to make a response.

Guardian Ad Litem

Usually, the court will appoint a *guardian ad litem* to represent the proposed ward, unless the ward is already known to be represented by counsel. A *"guardian ad litem"* is a person appointed to represent the interests of a mentally incompetent person in a *particular legal proceeding* (Black's Law Dictionary, 1979, p. 635). The *guardian ad litem* is usually an attorney, but this need not necessarily be the case. Depending upon state law and the language of the court order making the appointment, the *guardian ad litem* might function in a variety of ways (Baron, 1981a,b). Two of the most common roles (which, incidentally, are not compatible), are either *counsel* for the proposed ward or *investigator* for the court. As investigator, the *guardian ad litem* will investigate the facts of the situation, speak to the proposed ward, etc., and make a report to the court concerning the need for appointment of a guardian. As counsel, the *guardian ad litem* will not "report" to the court but will, within the usual attorney-client relationship, represent the interests of the proposed ward in the guardianship proceeding.

After hearing evidence, the court will enter a decree (or judgment) either allowing or disallowing the petition asking for a guardian to be appointed. If there are any limitations on the authority of the guardian, or if there are any other special conditions that the court wishes to impose, the decree will spell them out. (See pages 43–44 for a discussion of limited guardianship.) Otherwise, the guardian will have general authority regarding the personal and/or financial affairs of the disabled person.

Testamentary Appointment

One can also become guardian of another through a testamentary appointment. If, for example, the parents of a minor child wish to have specific persons become guardian after the parents have died, they can designate in their wills that such persons be appointed guardian after the parents' death. In some states, the law provides that the guardian becomes invested with authority immediately upon the death of the parent, subject to filing a notice of acceptance within a specified time period (see, e.g., Colo.Rev.Stat., §15-14-301 (1973); Minn.Stat.Ann., §525.6155 (West, Supp. 1983); and Miss.Code Ann., §93-13-7 (Supp. 1982)). In other states, the person named in the will as guardian must file a petition in court to be appointed, and simply has preferential status among potential guardians (see, e.g., Ill.Ann.Stat., ch. 110-½, §11-5 (b) (Smith-Hurd, 1978); Or.Rev.Stat., §126.035 (1981); and Wis.Stat.Ann., §880.09 (West Spec. Pamphlet, 1983)). In either case, the court can remove the named guardian, or not appoint him or her, if the court believes that the person is not suitable to be guardian.

Temporary Guardianship

A special form of guardianship is *temporary guardianship*. The purpose of temporary guardianship is to allow the court to appoint a guardian to deal with an urgent situation in the life of the ward. When circumstances have arisen that threaten imminent harm to the ward, the giving of notice to the ward and nearest relatives in the regular way will take so long (usually several weeks) that by the time the matter comes to a hearing the harm to the ward will have long since occurred. To avoid this life threatening situation, therefore, all states allow for the appointment of a temporary guardian in an emergency situation. (See, e.g., Cal.Prob.Code, §2250 *et seq.* (West, 1981).) The guardianship statute will require such notice to the ward and relatives as the court deems to be proper under the circumstances. If the court deems it necessary, a hearing can be held without *any* notice. Sometimes, either the statute itself or court rules will require that notice be given *after* the hearing if none was given beforehand (see, e.g., Mass.Prob.Ct.Rules 29B). Temporary appointments are ordinarily limited to a relatively short period of time (e.g., 30 days, 90 days, etc.), but they can usually be extended if another emergency requires it.

Unfortunately, temporary guardianships have been used too many times simply as a procedural shortcut when no real emergency actually threatened the ward. With no notice at all to the ward, all too often a guardian with general authority has been appointed and has promptly taken control of the personal and financial affairs of the ward, sometimes in ways that greatly displeased the ward.

The modern trend is for the guardianship statute to require proof of an *actual emergency* that threatens the ward, and to limit the authority of the temporary guardian *only* to that which is necessary to effectively handle the emergency. (See, e.g., Ga.Code Ann., § 49–608 (Supp. 1983); and Mass.Gen.Laws Ann., ch. 201, § 14 (West, Supp. 1983).) Thus, temporary appointments are available to the court to be used when the welfare of the ward is genuinely threatened. But anyone wishing to secure the appointment of a guardian other than for the purpose of dealing with a bona fide emergency is required to follow the usual procedures designed to protect the rights of the proposed ward.

CONSTITUTIONAL CONSIDERATIONS

Court Proceedings

Often those seeking the appointment of a guardian for someone else assume, because they are trying to "help" the person who is allegedly mentally disabled, that the purpose of the court proceedings is simply to permit them to do what they want to do, namely, secure the appointment of a guardian. Sometimes they become terribly impatient if the appointment is not more or less immediate.

Actually, the purpose of the court proceedings is to ascertain *whether or not* the court should do what it has been asked to do in the petition. The legal status of the person alleged to be mentally disabled will be substantially altered if the petition is allowed. On the other hand, as a practical matter, the person alleged to be mentally disabled may very well suffer severely if the petition is not allowed. It should be clear to anyone who reflects for a moment that the court simply *has* to ask the obvious question, "What should be done?"

That is what court proceedings are really all about—asking that kind of basic question in a structured way when someone wants the court to use its judicial power in a particular manner. Requesting a guardianship appointment is, in that respect, no different from asking that a neighbor be ordered to tear down a fence, or that someone be ordered to pay money for having caused an accident, or even that someone be imprisoned for the commission of a crime.

The formal judicial inquiry into "what should be done" is initiated with the allegations contained in the petition. Regardless of how the law may vary from state to state, basically the petition must allege *at least* the following: 1) that the proposed ward is within the territorial jurisdiction of the court; 2) that he or she is mentally disabled; 3) that because of the mental disability, he or she is unable to make the usual kinds of decisions that one's personal and/or financial affairs require be made; 4) that a guardian should be appointed to make such decisions; and 5) that a named person is suitable to be appointed guardian.

In addition to the issues already mentioned, some other important issues raised in a guardianship proceeding are:

1. How much authority should the guardian have?
2. Of all the possible guardians, which person or persons are best suited for safeguarding the interests of the ward?
3. How closely should the court maintain surveillance over the guardian's performance?
4. What are the personal needs of the ward for care and treatment?
5. Should the guardianship appointment be limited, either as to time or as to the scope of the guardian's authority?
6. Are any special court orders necessary to protect any civil rights of the ward that might otherwise be curtailed?

Concerning the exercise of broad jurisdiction in guardianship proceedings, see Rogers, 1982a, pp. 33–34; 1982b, pp. 41–43.

Adequate Notice

In any legal proceedings, all "interested parties" must be given notice that the proceedings have been instituted, some indication of the nature of what the court has been asked to do, and a chance to respond to the allegations made in the petition by which the proceedings were begun. Certainly, in guardianship proceedings, the proposed ward is an "interested party" (along with his or her nearest relatives). So, the first basic "due process" issue is the right of the proposed ward to receive adequate notice of the proceedings (*Covey* v. *Somers*, 351 U.S. 141, 100 L.Ed. 1021, 76 S.Ct. 724 (1956)).

Counsel for Ward

Another basic constitutional right of the proposed ward is the right to retain an attorney to represent him or her in the proceedings. But suppose the proposed ward cannot afford to hire an attorney. Or suppose he or she does not understand the implications of the proceedings and consequently does not appreciate the legal issues that need to be resolved nor the need to retain an attorney to represent his or her interests. Or, suppose the proposed ward *is* mentally disabled to the extent that he or she is unable to make informed decisions. That does not mean necessarily that all of the allegations in the petition are true, or that the persons filing the petition have disclosed all relevant information to the court (see Pecora, 1982, pp. 25–27).

The guardianship statute in some states *requires* the court to appoint an attorney for the proposed ward, unless he or she already has an attorney. (See, e.g., Kan. Stat. Ann., § 59-3010 (A) (3) (1976); and Wis. Stat. Ann., § 880.33 (2) (a) (1) (West Spec. Pamphlet, 1983).) In the absence of such a statutory requirement, appointment of an attorney for the proposed ward is usually considered to be *discretionary* with the court and within its inherent judicial power (*Guardianship of A Minor*, ____ Mass.App. ____, 419 N.E. 2d 1075 (1981), *further appellate review denied* July 15, 1981). Some statutes require the appointment of a *guardian ad litem* instead of counsel. (See, e.g., Ala.Code, § 26-2-42 (1975); and Tex.Stat. Ann., § 417 (Vernon, 1980). *Cf.* Wash. Rev. Code Ann., § 11.88.090 (2) (West Supp. 1983), providing that appointment of a *guardian ad litem* is *not* required when the petitioner is a parent of the proposed ward and the request for appointment of a guardian is based *solely* on minority.) Other statutes make even the appointment of a *guardian ad litem* discretionary. (See, e.g., Nev. Rev. Stat., §§ 12.050 and 65.010 (1979); and Vt. Stat. Ann., tit. 14, §§ 202, 2657 and 3066 (1974 & Supp. 1983).)

In this author's opinion, counsel should *always* be appointed, because it is simply too easy to confuse the interests of others with the interests of the proposed ward. The ward needs someone to represent his or her interests regarding the issues without compromising those interests by any obligations owed to other persons.

Burden of Proof

Another basic constitutional consideration relates to the burden of proof necessary to convince the court that a guardian should be appointed. The proposed ward does not have to prove that a guardian is *not* needed. Rather, the petitioners have the burden of proving that a guardian *is* needed. Some people might take offense at having to "prove" that their son or daughter is mentally disabled, when they "know" that to be the case from having cared for him or her for years and years. But allowing the legal status of the son or daughter to be drastically changed without requiring proof of its necessity would be a terrible affront to the civil rights and individual dignity of the son or daughter. Fortunately, the constitution makes no distinction in the Bill of Rights between those who are and those who are not mentally disabled.

While most states require the necessary allegations to be proven by "a preponderance of the evidence" (evidence that is more persuasive that a guardian is needed than that one is not needed), some states require that the evidence be "clear and convincing" that a guardian is needed. (See e.g., *Conservatorship of Sanderson*, 106 Cal. App. 3d 611, 165 Cal. Rptr. 217 (1980), *rehearing denied* August 6, 1980). The evidence presented is usually in the form of oral testimony by persons acquainted with the proposed ward and his or her behavior, and oral or written testimony by medical or psychological experts who have examined the proposed ward. If a *guardian ad litem* has been appointed as an *investigator* for the court, the report of the investigation will usually be introduced as evidence. Sometimes the *guardian ad litem* will also give oral testimony.

TRADITIONAL DUTIES OF A GUARDIAN

After the hearing has been completed, if the petitioners have proven the need for a guardian under the applicable standard of proof, the court will enter an order appointing the guardian. The guardian's duties then will fall into three general categories.

Preliminary Duties

First, there are a few preliminary steps that have to be taken in order to commence the guardianship in an orderly manner. The guardian will have to file a bond in court before exercising any authority granted by the court. A bond is a written instrument indicating that the guardian has accepted appointment and is legally liable to the ward (usually up to a specific amount, depending upon the amount of property owned by the ward) for any malfeasance that causes the ward's estate to suffer any loss.

The guardian will then have to prepare and file in court an inventory reflecting all property, including cash and bank accounts, owned by the ward. This might be easy if the guardian is a close relative of the ward. Conversely, it might not be so easy if the guardian is not already familiar with the ward's affairs. In any event, the guardian's duty is to make a diligent effort to locate and take control of all of the ward's property, and to list such property on the inventory. Thereafter, the guardian is responsible for prudently managing such property.

The guardian is then required to file annual accounts in court reflecting all additions to the ward's property (income) and all reductions in the property (expenses). Keeping proper records during the year so that an account can be prepared might be considerably time consuming if the ward's property is extensive. In most cases, though, this aspect of guardianship need not be particularly burdensome if the guardian uses common sense in keeping records. The "guardianship estate" can be thought of as an "account" to which deposits will be made and from which withdrawals will be made. The inventory will indicate the value of the ward's property, and this value can be thought of as the "opening deposit" into the "account." Each annual account filed in court will then simply be an "income and expense statement" for that year.

The ward's property should *always* be kept separate and distinguishable from the guardian's property, and should *never* be co-mingled with the guardian's property. If the ward's property is kept segregated, and if all receipts are recorded in a notebook in chronological order (with dates and sources noted), and all expenditures are recorded in a different notebook in chronological order (with dates and payees noted), then constructing the annual account will be an easily manageable task.

"Protecting" the Ward

Second, the guardian's duties involve "protective care" of the ward. After appointment, the guardian should make sure that he or she becomes familiar with the personal needs of the ward for food, clothing, medical care, educational or vocational training, and other appropriate services. Taking any steps necessary to assure that these needs are properly and consistently met is one of the main responsibilities of the guardian.

The ward's personal preferences about his or her personal care should be ascertained whenever possible. Communication should be established with staff who are caring for the ward. Plans should be worked out for the guardian to attend all relevant staff reviews concerning the ward's needs and programmatic services. In addition, the guardian should try to be aware of new approaches to care of the ward that might be possible but that simply might not have occurred to the staff.

Managing the Ward's Financial Affairs

Third, the guardian needs to begin managing the ward's financial affairs. This means that all proper bills owed by the ward should be paid. Financial arrangements should be made for all living expenses of the ward. Any property owned by the ward should be attended to so that it does not fall into disrepair or otherwise suffer diminution in value. Any money or property that the ward is entitled to receive must be pursued by the guardian until collected.

All expenditures should be for the *sole benefit* of the ward only, unless the court has given permission for expenditures that do not directly benefit the ward but that presumably are in accord with the ward's preferences and wishes. An example of such an expenditure would be payment of an allowance to a dependent of the ward, or a donation to a purpose that might benefit the ward only indirectly, such as an advocacy organization. Expenditures that do not *directly* benefit the ward should never be made without prior court approval. When the annual account is filed, any items of expense deemed improper by the court will not be "allowed," and the guardian will be personally liable to reimburse the guardianship estate.

LIMITED GUARDIANSHIP

A relatively new development in the law is the concept of "limited guardianship." Historically, when guardians have been appointed, they have had "general authority" over the ward's affairs and the ward has had no authority. Current insights into the nature of mental disability, particularly developmental disability, and the possibilities for treatment and habilitation, convince many that giving too much authority to the guardian can often work to the ward's detriment. When a person is denied the opportunity of making any significant decisions about his or her life even though he or she can do so adequately in some areas, it can cause a sense of powerlessness and lack of personal worth.

Therefore, efforts have been made to develop a form of guardianship under which the court would grant authority to the guardian only in those areas of decision-making that the evidence indicates the ward needs help. The authority of the guardian is "limited" in certain defined respects; hence the term "limited guardianship." Some states have adopted the concept of limited guardianship through legislation. (See, e.g., Conn.Gen.Stat. Ann., § 45-332 (West Supp. 1983).) Others have adopted the concept through judicial construction of existing guardianship statutes. (See, e.g., *Guardianship of Bassett*, 7 Mass. App. 56, 385 N.E. 2d 1024 (1979).)

Thus, the focus of guardianship appointments has begun to shift *toward* encouraging the personal development of the ward and *away* from merely protecting his or her person and/or property. Of course, not *all* developmentally disabled persons need a guardian. However, for those who do, the new concept of "limited guardianship" will significantly aid the court in taking a more active role in securing for them needed services. It is clear now to human services professionals that every developmentally disabled person has a unique potential for personal development, just as everyone else has. Special efforts are needed, however, to tap and develop that potential. With an individually tailored guardianship decree, the court has a means to help assure that those special efforts are undertaken. First, if areas in which the ward can function adequately are distinguishable from areas in which the reverse is true, it is likely that the ward's particular needs will be more clearly understood. In other words, if it is evident that the ward needs specific services but cannot personally seek them out, then there is a clear indication that the ward needs an *advocate* to seek those services on his or her behalf. Thus, the court can spell out with some specificity the things that the limited guardian is supposed to do, namely, to obtain necessary services for the ward and to see that they are properly maintained. (See Rogers, 1982a, 1982b.) That kind of advocacy by a guardian is quite a bit different from merely condoning "protection" of the ward through custodial care.

Second, the court is much better able to *monitor* how the guardian actually functions when there are specific things that the guardian is ordered to do. The whole point of appointing a guardian is that the ward is supposed to be better off *with* a guardian than *without* one. Rather than just assuming that to be the case, as has been done in the past, the court now has a basis for requiring periodic reports from the guardian as to what has been done to meet the ward's identifiable needs. If the guardian is doing nothing to see that those needs are met, or is functioning inadequately in other respects, the court can then enter more specific orders, which, if violated, will place the guardian in jeopardy of being held in contempt of court.

DOCTRINE OF "SUBSTITUTED JUDGMENT"

As has been previously noted, a guardian is supposed to make decisions and take actions "on behalf of the ward," except in those areas in which the court has denied authority to the guardian. That does not mean, however (and it has never meant), that the guardian has unbridled discretion over the ward's affairs. The exercise of authority by the guardian has always been limited by the requirement that the purpose can *only* be to serve the best interests of the ward. Personal wishes or biases of the guardian are no basis for decisions or actions.

Most day-to-day decisions require the guardian to simply use his or her judgment and common sense. Where is the ward to reside? What kind of diet is appropriate? What kinds of routine medical care are needed? Does some activity in which the ward engages present an unacceptable risk of harm? These are types of questions that require the guardian to use some degree of discretion concerning the ward's affairs. But in answering them, the guardian has the duty to honestly try and serve the *ward's* needs, not the wishes of the guardian or third persons. If the guardian is a vegetarian, he or she could not, for example, blithely assume that the ward also ought to avoid meats; that might or might not be consistent with the ward's nutritional needs. If the guardian "doesn't believe in doctors," that would be no excuse for denying the ward needed medical care.

Aside from these "routine" decisions, there are some decisions that have such a serious impact upon the ward that the guardian simply cannot make them without specific authority from the court. Sterilization of the ward is an example of action that the guardian has no authority to carry out or permit. If the guardian honestly believes this to be in the best interests of the ward, then he or she can and should seek court permission. (See *In re Grady*, 85 N.J. 235, 426 A.2d 467 (1981); and *In re Roe*, 385 Mass. 555, 432 N.E.2d 712 (1982). But cf. *Guardianship of Eberhardy*, 102 Wis.2d 539, 307 N.W.2d 881 (1981), holding that trial courts have both constitutional and statutory *jurisdiction* to authorize sterilization of mentally incompetent persons, but that they should not *exercise* such jurisdiction until the legislature has adopted "an authoritative declaration of public policy" that defines how the "best interests" of such mentally incompetent persons are to be determined.) That the guardian sincerely means well, however, simply does not justify imposing his or her judgment on the ward.

As to withdrawing or denying available medical treatment in the case of terminal illness, there are two basic schools of thought. One says that the guardian may decide the question "in consultation with the family and physician" without having to obtain court permission (*In re Quinlan*, 70 N.J. 10, 355 A.2d 647 (1976), *cert. denied* November 1, 1976, by the United States Supreme Court, 429 U.S. 922, 50 L.Ed.2d 289, 97 S.Ct. 319). The other more widely prevailing position is that the court must itself decide the question after a hearing in which the patient has had independent counsel (*Superintendent of Belchertown State School* v. *Sai-*

kewicz, 373 Mass. 728, 370 N.E.2d 417 (1978); *In re Severns*, 425 A.2d 156 (Del. Ch. 1980); and *Leach* v. *Akron General Medical Center*, 68 Ohio Misc. 1, 22 Ohio Op. 3d 49, 426 N.E.2d 809 (Ohio Com. Pleas 1980)).

What is at issue is the principle of *choice* as to when and how one's privacy is to be invaded. Everyone has the right of informed consent about bodily privacy, and so does the ward (*Harnish* v. *Children's Hospital Medical Center*, 387 Mass. 152, 439, N.E.2d 240 (1982); and *Saikewicz*, (1978). When the consequences of some proposed action are very serious, and especially when they are irreversible, the guardian must be very careful to respect the dignity of the ward as an individual person with legal rights that need to be recognized.

In making its decision, the court in most states will try to make a "substituted judgment" as to what the ward himself or herself would decide if able. (See *Saikewicz* (1978), Severns (1980), and *Leach* (1980).) This standard requires the court to ascertain not what the "average reasonable person" would want, but what the *particular individual patient* would want. This means that evidence of the patient's personal history and of any prior indications of his or her preferences regarding the decision to be made is of pivotal importance. (But see *Eberhardy* (1981), regarding "inherent limitations" on a court's ability to arrive at a "substituted judgment" without guidance from the legislature as to appropriate "public policy.")

There is no "list" of the kinds of questions that require judicial determination. The line of demarcation between those decisions that guardians have authority to make and those decisions that they do not have authority to make is often difficult to draw, but the line is there. Guardians simply have to remember that there *is* a point—somewhere—at which the consequences of a decision become so serious for the ward that guidance from the court is advisable.

CONCLUSION

Several fundamental considerations need to be kept in mind concerning the establishment of a program for providing guardianship services for developmentally disabled persons. The most important of these considerations is that the legal concept of guardianship exists for one purpose and one purpose only—enhancing the life experience of the individual ward to the fullest extent possible. When the need for appointment of a guardian exists, it is not difficult to bring that fact to the attention of the court. Parents can also plan for the future by providing in their wills for the appointment of a testamentary guardian for their mentally disabled sons and daughters.

In cases of emergency, the court can respond very quickly by appointing a temporary guardian. However, it will not (and should not) be easily rushed into appointing a guardian unless there is a bona fide need for acting quickly. As in any litigation, the court can only act when the appropriate issues have been established by evidence. The ward has the right to be treated fairly during the guardianship proceedings, because his or her constitutional rights are no less significant than those of anyone else.

Although the traditional duties of a guardian have focused on "protective services" and property management, the modern trend is toward using "limited guardianship" appointments in order to allow wards as much autonomy as possible. Guardians are increasingly being required to act affirmatively as *advocates*. In addition, courts are more closely monitoring the actual performance of guardians in order to try and assure that such appointments actually benefit the wards.

Finally, it is clear that the authority of a guardian is not without limit. First, the exercise of any authority by the guardian must be in pursuit of the ward's best interests, and must not be for any other purpose. Second, some decisions have such a profound impact upon the ward that the guardian may not use his or her judgment, even in the best of faith; these decisions require a hearing in court, and either a "substituted judgment" by the court itself or special instructions to the guardian as to what he or she should do. Third, in situations calling for a "substituted judgment," the court, either in making a decision itself or in giving instructions to the guardian, must strive to do what the individual ward would do if able himself or herself to make a decision.

In our efforts to enhance the lives and dignity of developmentally disabled persons, we have access to one of the oldest concepts in our legal system. Used properly, guardianship can help provide real advocacy for those in need of it.

REFERENCES

Baron, C.H., The mixed roles of the *guardian ad litem*. *Guardianship News*, 1981, *1*(3), 1–2. (a)

Baron, C.H. The mixed roles of the *guardian ad litem*. *Guardianship News*, 1981, *1*(4), 1–2. (b)

Black, H.C. *Black's law dictionary, 5th ed.* (J.P. Nolan, ed.). St. Paul, MN: West Publishing Co., 1979.

Brakel, S.J., & Rock, R.S. *The mentally disabled and the law.* Chicago: University of Chicago Press, 1971, pp. 250–265.

Conservatorship of Sanderson, 106 Cal.App.3d 611, 165 Cal.Rptr. 217 (1980); *rehearing denied* August 6, 1980.

Covey v. *Somers*, 351 U.S. 141, 100 L.Ed. 1021, 76 S.Ct. 724 (1956).

Custer, L.B. The origins of the doctrine of "parens patriae." *Emory Law Journal*, 1978, 27(2), pp. 195–208.

Estate of Guerra, 96 N.M. 608, 633 P.2d 716 (N.M.Ct.App. 1981).

Frolik, L.A. Plenary guardianship: An analysis, a critique, and a proposal for reform. *Arizona Law Review*, 1981, *23*(2), 599–660.

Guardianship of A Minor, ____ Mass.App. ____, 419 N.E.2d 1075 (1981); *further appellate review denied* July 15, 1981.

Guardianship of Bassett, 7 Mass.App. 56, 385 N.E.2d 1024 (1979).

Guardianship of Eberhardy, 102 Wis. 2d 539, 307 N.W.2d 881 (1981).

Harnish v. *Children's Hospital Medical Center*, 387 Mass. 152, 439 N.E.2d 240 (1982).

In re Grady, 85 N.J.235, 426 A.2d 467 (1981).

In re Quinlan, 70 N.J.10, 355 A.2d 647 (1976), *cert. denied* November 1, 1976, by United States Supreme Court, 429 U.S. 922, 50 L. Ed. 2d 289, 97 S. Ct. 319.

In re Roe, 385 Mass. 555, 432 N.E.2d 712 (1982).

In re Severns, 425 A.2d 156 (Del. Ch. 1980).

Leach v. *Akron General Medical Center*, 68 Ohio Misc. 1, 22 Ohio Op. 3d 49, 426 N.E.2d 809 (Ohio Com.Pleas 1980).

Pecora, A.K. The need for counsel in guardianship proceedings. *Guardianship News*, 1982, *2*(4), 25–27.

Rogers, P.R. The exercise of equity jurisdiction in guardianship proceedings. *Guardianship News*, 1982, *2*(5), 33–34. (a)

Rogers, P.R. The exercise of equity jurisdiction in guardianship proceedings. *Guardianship News*, 1982, *2*(6), 41–43. (b)

Superintendent of Belchertown State School v. *Saikewicz*, 373 Mass. 728, 370 N.E.2d 417 (1978).

Chapter 4

Legal Considerations Affecting Guardianship Relationships

The Constitution and Case Law

Louise Monaco and Jerry Smilowitz

**BACKGROUND ON LEGAL
CONSIDERATIONS AFFECTING GUARDIANSHIP**

However benevolent a guardianship may be in intent or design, the resulting loss by the ward of the right to make fundamental decisions (about the right to marry, to have and raise children, to live in residential communities, to make contracts, to vote, or to accept or refuse medical treatment) is, in constitutional terms, a devastating deprivation of civil rights. This chapter summarizes the status of legal opinion in several critical areas of personal decision-making, and advocates the expansion of the type of limited guardianship model that is currently in effect in California.

Due Process

It has long been an accepted principle of constitutional law that classifications based on ''immutable physical characteristics'' such as race will seldom withstand close scrutiny when they impinge on fundamental or basic rights. (See, e.g., *Yick* v. *Hopkins*, 118 U.S. 356 [1886]; *Korematsu* v. *United States*, 323 U.S. 214 [1944]; *Loving* v. *Virginia*, 388 U.S. 1 [1967].) Yet this principle has received minimal recognition in either statutes or case law where the ''physical characteristic'' at issue is the presumed inability of a person to function in a ''normal'' fashion.

Due process considerations enunciated in other contexts make clear the need for a stringent standard of proof when an individual's liberty interest is at stake (*Addington* v. *Texas*, 1979; *Conservatorship of Roulet*, 1979). (See also, *Vitek* v. *Jones*, 445 U.S. 480 [1980].) Constitutional considerations have also been used to invoke a right to treatment for one who is involuntarily deprived of liberty on the basis of incompetency (*Jackson* v. *Indiana*, 1972; *O'Connor* v. *Donaldson*, 1975; *Youngberg* v. *Romeo*, 1982). (Cf. *Pennhurst State School and Hospital* v. *Halderman*, 451 U.S. 1 [1981] and on remand, *Halderman* v. *Pennhurst*, 673 F.2d 647 [3rd Cir. 1982].)

> Although . . . the concept of "habilitation" for the retarded and "treatment" for the mentally and emotionally ill are separate and distinct concepts which should never be confused, in dealing with the question of the right of the retarded to adequate habilitation one must consider to the extent applicable, those cases which deal with the right to treatment of the mentally ill. [*Halderman* v. *Pennhurst State School & Hospital*, 446 F.Supp.1295 (U.S.D.C. E.D. Pa. 1977–78). See also *Kremens* v. *Bartley*, 431 U.S. 119, 135 (1977); *Wyatt* v. *Stickney*, 344 F.Supp. 387 (U.S.D.C. M.D. Ala.1972).]

Because the concept of guardianship has been historically viewed as an exercise of the *parens patriae* powers of the state for the "protection" of the ward, courts have made little effort to require a showing of a compelling need to deprive the ward of fundamental rights. (See, "Who Say's I'm Crazy?—A Proposal for Mandatory Judicial Review of Emergency Detention in California," 51 *So. Cal. L.R.* 695, 704, fm. 74.) Yet, as Justice Brandeis so aptly warned:

> Experience should teach us to be most on our guard to protect liberty when the government's purposes are beneficent . . . . The greatest dangers to liberty lurk in insidious encroachment by men of zeal, well-meaning but without understanding (*Olmstead* v. *United States*, 1928).

When the question of permissible abridgement of constitutional liberties is addressed, the Supreme Court said in *Shelton* v. *Tucker* (1960):

> Even though the governmental purpose be legitimate and substantial, that purpose cannot be pursued by means that broadly stifle fundamental personal liberties when the end can be more narrowly achieved. The breadth of legislative abridgement must be viewed in the light of less drastic means for achieving the same basic purpose.

A review of guardianship cases from almost any jurisdiction provides an "Alice-in-Wonderland" perspective of the rule of law. A person guilty of neither crime nor tort is nonetheless treated as a defendant who must prove his or her right to continued liberty in a forum where legal standards are a chimera of abstract (and often conflicting) phrases. (See cases excerpted in Leviton, 1980.) The guardian is routinely given broad powers, i.e., to decide where the ward will live; to define the nature and extent of his or her social and sexual relationships; and to regulate and determine the manner in which he or she can acquire or dispose of property. In short, the adult ward is reduced to the status of a child without being provided, in too many instances, the due process protections accorded children in juvenile court proceedings.

Parens Patriae

The power to impose this "benevolent dictatorship" has been claimed by legal authorities since at least the days of ancient Rome. The concept of *parens patriae* derives from the English constitutional system that allocated rights and powers to the king in his capacity as "father of the country." In the United States, the care of those deemed to be incompetent was originally given to the family. Generally, however, the states enacted laws delegating the guardianship power to particular courts (Burgdorf, 1980).

Guardianship of the Person or the Estate

Some states utilize a general guardianship concept, which grants to the guardian total control over the person and the property of the ward. Other statutes distinguish between a guardianship of the person and a guardianship of the estate (Burgdorf, 1980). The traditional focus of guardianships emphasized the preservation of property and estates, but seldom required an equivalent accounting for the "preservation" (much less enhancement) of the person of the ward. Even though statutes may distinguish between guardianship of the person and the estate, courts have all too often appointed guardians for both person and property without an adequate showing of the need for controls over the person.

Legal Models and Standards

In the face of growing enlightenment and recognition of the capacity of developmentally disabled persons to function as citizens, rather than wards, of the community, legal writers have increasingly pointed to the need to apply recognized constitutional principles to the development of appropriate social and legal models and standards (Burgdorf, 1980).

For instance, liberty, according to the United States Supreme Court,

> denotes not merely freedom from bodily restraint but also the right of the individual to contract, to engage in any of the common occupations of life, to acquire useful knowledge, to marry, establish a home and bring up children, to worship God according to the dictates of his own conscience, and generally to enjoy those privileges long recognized at common law as essential to the orderly pursuit of happiness by free men (*Meyer v. Nebraska, 1923*).

Various court decisions, drawing on a panoply of constitutional provisions, have affirmed a penumbral constitutional right to privacy, which similarly encompasses activities relating to marriage, procreation, contraception, family relationships, child rearing and education (see, e.g., *Griswold* v. *Connecticut*, 381 U.S. 479 [1965]; *Roe* v. *Wade*, 410 U.S. 113 [1973]). Following is a summary of constitutional provisions regarding fundamental decisions concerning marriage, child rearing, sterilization, institutionalization, employment, and general self-control.

MARRIAGE

Statutory prohibitions or restrictions on the right to marry have been struck down as violative of due process (*Loving* v. *Virginia*, 1967) and equal protection (*Zablocki* v. *Redhail*, 1978) rights. The general rule of law is that the state may not, without compelling reasons, say whether its citizens can marry, have children, use birth control devices, or undergo sterilization. See, e.g., *Eisenstadt* v. *Baird*, 405 U.S. 438 (1972); *Skinner* v. *Oklahoma*, 316 U.S. 535 (1942).

Most states have enacted statutes restricting those classified as incompetent (using such varied terminology as "idiot," "imbecile," "feebleminded," "mental deficients," "under guardianship," "legally incompetent," or "weakminded") of the right to marry. Few states, however, require any affirmative proof of competency before the issuance of a marriage license. Some applications do question whether the person has ever been adjudicated incompetent or institutionalized. Whether an affirmative answer merely precipitates a refusal to issue the marriage license or provokes further inquiry cannot be ascertained from available data. (See, Ogg, "Securing the Legal Rights of Retarded Persons" [Public Affairs Pamphlet No. 492, 1973] for examples of the results when such questions are answered "yes" [denial of license] or "no" [annulment proceedings brought]. Lawsuits in both cases won the retarded couples the right to marry. See also Wald, 1976.) Thus, these statutes not only discriminate on the basis of a physical characteristic, but are haphazardly enforced as well.

In a society in which one out of every four marriages ends in divorce, it cannot be said that we can safely predict how even so-called "normal" persons will function in a marriage. Current reporting of sociological data indicates an increase of the incidence of child and spousal abuse as the national economy worsens. If "normal" people are a danger to others (or themselves) in marital and family situations, but are allowed to marry without regard to such "dangerousness," where is the equity in prohibiting marriage of those assumed (but not proved) to be incompetent to carry out the legal obligations of marriage?

> Some evidence . . . indicates that many mildly retarded persons do marry and lead a self-supporting life in the community provided they are not faced with the stresses resulting from the care of children . . . Many persons who might be judged incompetent of adequate child care may well be competent in the other responsibilities and duties of a husband or wife. With effective methods of reversible and non-reversible contraception available, why should such individuals be prevented from obtaining the many benefits of marriage other than child-rearing? (Fotheringham, 1971, pp. 814–815).

No restrictions are placed on the right of poor and physically handicapped individuals to marry, even if they are not self-supporting. The devastating impact of alcoholism and drug addiction on marriage and child rearing is the subject of daily newspaper coverage and television fare. When laws are so haphazardly applied as to permit those known to be dependent or dangerous to marry at will, but prohibit those identified as "retarded" the same liberty, the concepts underlying those laws must be reassessed. (Cf., *Furman* v. *Georgia*, 408 U.S. 238, 306, 310 (1972), in which Justices Stewart and White concluded that a death penalty statute should be struck down as a violation of the Eighth Amendment proscription against cruel and unusual punishment because it was applied in an arbitrary, wanton and "freakish" manner and so infrequently that it served no justifying end.)

> The critical policy question is who among those who function at a lower intellectual and social level present such an intolerable risk to themselves or their mates that they should be forbidden to marry? Some mental retardation experts say categorically, none. Far more refined data than are available currently would be required to make a scientific differential diagnosis (Wald, 1976, pp. 7–8).

CHILD REARING

Although the Supreme Court has proclaimed that "the custody, care and nurture of the child resides first in the parents, whose primary function and freedom include preparation of obligations the state can neither supply nor hinder" (*Prince* v. *Massachusetts*, 1944) (see also, *Ginsburg* v. *New York*, 390 U.S. 629 [1968]; *Wisconsin* v. *Yoder*, 406 U.S. 205 [1971]; *Stanley* v. *Illinois*, 405 U.S. 645 [1972]; *Quilloin* v. *Walcott*, 434 U.S. 246 [1978]), the fundamental right to have and raise children has been denied to many handicapped parents.

The various reasons asserted for denying those deemed "mentally deficient" the right to bear and raise children (generally involving the asserted need to protect the health and safety of the child, or to limit the potential for significant social burdens) have been, more often than not, based on unprovable assumptions. The welfare of the child should be the paramount concern, obviously, when the state seeks to separate parent and child. What appears to be less obvious, from the cases, is the fundamental right to make decisions on an individual, case-by-case basis.

> In my 20 years of psychiatric work with thousands of children and their parents, I have seen percentually at least as many "intelligent" adults unfit to rear their offspring as I have seen such "feebleminded" adults. I have—and many others have—come to the conclusion that, to a large extent independent of the I.Q., fitness for parenthood is determined by emotional involvements and relationships (Bligh, 1965, pp. 1059, 1062).

Categorical assumptions about the capacities and competence of "retarded" persons—when the causes and results of retardation cover such a wide spectrum—run afoul of the doctrine of irrebuttable (or conclusive) presumptions enunciated in *Stanley* v. *Illinois*, 405 U.S. 645 (1972). There, the Supreme Court struck down a statutory presumption of parental unfitness, holding that such unfitness must be established on the basis of individual proof. (See also, *Vlandis* v. *Klike*, 412 U.S. 441 [1973]; *Cleveland Bd. of Educ.* v. *LaFleur*, 414 U.S. 682 [1974]. Limitation of the conclusive presumption doctrine was indicated in *Weinburger* v. *Salfi*, 422

U.S. 749 [1975], but the Court approved and distinguished the prior cases as involving fundamental rights of family and childbearing, *Id.*, at 771.)

> What is needed is empirical fieldwork to supplant general allegations that retarded persons are not competent to be mothers and fathers. What background characteristics of the retarded individual point to success or failure as parents? How do the children of retarded parents fare? What kind of help from relatives and the community affects success or failure? Without such data, judges and legislators work in the dark and make cruel mistakes (Wald, 1976, p. 15).

Unless we are willing to candidly concede that the ''status'' (cf., *Robinson* v. *California*, 370 U.S. 660 [1962], in which the Supreme Court set aside, on Eighth Amendment grounds, a statute which punished the ''mere status'' of being an addict) of a developmental disability operates to deprive a person of the prerogatives of citizenship and of his or her liberty, strict scrutiny must be required of the reasons advanced for curtailing the right of any individual to marry, have children and enjoy family relationships. Such vigilance may be especially necessary where developmentally disabled adults are living in group homes or are subject to group guardianships. Ease of administration should not be used as a justification to eliminate individual decisions, particularly where fundamental rights are involved.

> Guardianships should always be individualized and subject to the ''least restrictive alternative'' principle. A new role for a guardian . . . ought to be required . . . The object should be for the guardian to help the individual care for himself to the optimum degree and for the guardian to be held accountable on this basis (Wald, 1976, p. 20).

STERILIZATION

The right of developmentally disabled persons to engage in sexual activity outside of marriage is usually addressed indirectly, primarily in cases dealing with sterilization. In *Buck* v. *Bell* (1927), the Supreme Court upheld the right of the superintendent of the State Colony for Epileptics and Feeble Minded to require the sterilization of a ''feeble-minded'' white woman who was committed to the State Colony,'' with Justice Holmes observing,

> We have seen more than once that public welfare may call upon the best citizens for their lives. It would be strange if it could not call upon those who already sap the strength of the State for those lesser sacrifices, often not felt to be such by those concerned, in order to prevent our being swamped with incompetence (*Buck* v. *Bell*, 1927).

The principles of ''social Darwinism'' on which Justice Holmes' opinion was premised were repudiated by the court in *North Carolina Association for Retarded Children* v. *North Carolina* (1976). Yet, even here, the court took note of ''substantial medical opinion'' that sterilization may be ''occasionally'' desirable and indicated. The court construed the statute before it to limit sterilizations to those cases in which there is clear evidence of the subject's likelihood to engage in sexual activity without using contraceptive devices and to either bear a defective child or be unable to care for a child. In such instances, constitutional principles would seem to require that less intrusive measures—such as sex education—be resorted to first by the state (or a guardian) before authority to limit or prohibit the sexual freedom of developmentally disabled adults could be authorized or permitted.

INSTITUTIONALIZATION

The converse situation—routine institutionalization of retarded children—also bears reassessment in a constitutional context.

> Before a parent institutionalizes a retarded child, there ought to be a full judicial inquiry into: (1) the potential of the child to respond to other program alternatives; (2) alternative resources in the community that might be used to help the family care for the child; (3) conditions (personal care and programming) in the institution to which he will be committed; and (4) if the parents are adamant about removal from the home, whether foster homes or small-group setting are available in the community (Wald, 1976, p. 16).

Many courts have addressed the question of the nature and extent of the due process procedural prerequisites to commitment (*Addington* v. *Texas*, 1979) (see also, Burgdorf, 1980, pp. 632–640). In addition to the guarantees of notice, the right to be present and represented by counsel, and the requirement of "clearly convincing" proof or proof beyond a reasonable doubt, some courts are also explicitly imposing a duty to provide the least restrictive environment. In *Lynch* v. *Baxley* (1974), the court said that the state,

> acting through the probate court or whichever of its agents designates the place of confinement, shall have the burden of demonstrating that the proposed commitment is the least restrictive environment consistent with the needs of the person to be committed . . . . This duty of investigation and burden of persuasion derive from the general and well-recognized principle that ". . . even though the governmental purpose be legitimate and substantial, that purpose cannot be pursued by means that broadly stifle fundamental personal liberties when the end can be more narrowly achieved."

EMPLOYMENT

In the area of employment, the lag in application of recognized constitutional principles to the rights of disabled persons is also apparent. As of 1980, only 21 states had amended existing antidiscrimination laws to require equal employment opportunity for people with disabilities in public and private sectors. (See Burgdorf, 1980, at 331 *et seq.*) Even those laws that do exist are uneven in scope and quality. Some statutes (e.g., California Government Code 12940, *et seq.*) protect only physically handicapped persons. The definitions of disability contained in these statutes are often either vague or overly restrictive. The most significant difference between such statutes and other forms of employment discrimination prohibitions, however, is the number of exceptions that focus on disability as a classification to justify discrimination, as seen in the following statutory provisions:

> Nothing in this bill shall prohibit an employer from refusing to hire or discharge a physically handicapped person . . . where the employee, because of his physical handicap . . . is unable to perform his duties in a manner which would not endanger his health or the health and safety of others . . . (Cal. Labor Code § 1420 [West Supp. 1973])

> [Forbidding discrimination] . . . when the reasonable demands of the position do not require . . . physical handicap . . . distinctions. (Alaska Stat. § 18.80.220 [Supp. 1973])

> . . . unless it can be shown that the particular handicap prevents the performance of the employment involved (1 Ill. Ann. Stat. ch. 38, § 65-23 [Supp. 1974])

> There is no discrimination where . . . the handicap reasonably precludes the performance of the particular employment or where the particular employment may subject the handicapped or his fellow employees to physical harm (Mont. Rev. Codes § 64-301 [Supp. 1974])

> . . . unless the nature and extent of the handicap reasonably precludes the performance of the particular employment (N.J. Stat. Ann. § 10:4-4.1 [Supp. 1972])

The New Mexico statute provides: "An employee shall execute as a condition of employment a certificate of preexisting physical or mental handicap." N.M. Stat. Ann. § 4-33-7.1 (1974).

There has been, however, some affirmative action in the area of employment of developmentally disabled persons. The federal government, for example, sets aside particular civil service jobs for developmentally disabled persons. Certification by a state vocational rehabilitation agency substitutes for competitive examinations. In a period of approximately 8½ years, more than 7,000 appointments were made under this special procedure. It was reported in 1972 that over 3,000 persons had been so employed for at least 3 years. (See U.S. Civil Service Commission, *Handbook of Selective Placement in Federal Civil Service Employment* [1972].)

For those who can and do secure employment, the right to control and utilize wages is a paramount concern. "In general, the presumption should be that anyone who earns money can spend it. Voluntary counseling and consumer education should exist to help the retarded person in the community avoid exploitation and redress commercial grievances" (Wald, 1976, p. 19).

GENERAL SELF-CONTROL

With the advent of a growing movement to develop the capacity of developmentally disabled adults to live free and independent lives, some states have developed guardianship statutes that maximize the rights of such persons to exercise control over fundamental aspects of their lives. In California, for example, a guardianship is applicable only to minors. For adults or married minors, the applicable terminology is conservatorship. Moreover, a developmentally disabled adult may be subjected only to a "limited conservatorship." A limited conservator may be appointed of the person, of the estate, or both. The significance of the California model is that it explicitly recognizes the inherent right of the developmentally disabled adult to retain as many rights as he or she is capable of exercising. It also incorporates by reference the equal rights concepts embodied in the Developmental Disabilities Services Act.

> The intent of the Legislature, as expressed in Section 4501 of the Welfare and Institutions Code, that developmentally disabled citizens of this state receive services resulting in more independent, productive, and normal lives and that such services shall be the underlying mandate of this division in its application to adults alleged to be developmentally disabled (California probate code, § 1801 [d] [3]).

Section 4502 of the Welfare and Institutions Code makes explicit the recognition by the legislature that:

> Persons with developmental disabilities have the same legal rights and responsibilities guaranteed all other individuals by the Federal Constitution and laws and the Constitution and laws of the State of California.

The probate code reiterates that recognition:

> The conservatee of the limited conservator shall not be presumed to be incompetent and shall retain all legal and civil rights except those which by court order have been designated as legal disabilities and have been specifically granted to the limited conservator. (§ 1801 [d][2])
> Such limited conservatorships shall be utilized only as necessary to promote and protect the well-being of the individual, shall be designed to encourage the development of maximum self-reliance and independence of the individual, and shall be ordered only to the extent necessitated by the individual's proven mental and adaptive limitations § 1801 [d][1]).

The imposition of a limited conservatorship does not, unless specifically included in the court's order, limit the right of the conservatee to control an allowance, to control wages or salary, to make a will, or enter into transactions or types of transactions (Probate code § 1871, 1872, 2601).

The limited conservator is charged with the care, custody, and control of the limited conservatee, but may not exercise any of the following powers or controls over the limited conservatee unless such are specifically requested and granted by the court in its order:

1. The powers to fix the residence or specific dwelling of the limited conservatee
2. The right to have access to the confidential records and papers of the limited conservatee

3. The power to consent or withhold consent to the marriage of the limited conservatee
4. The power to deny the limited conservatee the right to contract
5. The right to deny the limited conservatee the power to give or withhold medical consent
6. The power to withhold the limited conservatee's right to control his own social and sexual contacts and relationships
7. The power to make decisions concerning the education of the limited conservatee (Probate code § 2351.5)

The limited conservator is charged, generally, with the obligation of securing for the limited conservatee such habilitation or treatment, training, education, medical, and psychological services and social and vocational opportunities as will assist the limited conservatee in the development of maximum self-reliance and independence (Probate code § 2351.5).

The powers granted to the conservator may be eliminated or augmented, as circumstances change, and may be terminated on petition by the conservatee (or someone acting on the conservatee's behalf) (Probate code § 2351.5[b]; 1860.5).

Two additional provisions are designed to ensure that the legislative intent is implemented. One requires the appointment of counsel to represent the limited conservatee (Probate code § 1471[c]). Compensation for such counsel is paid by the conservatee, if financially able, or by the county. Section 1827.5 requires the assessment of the proposed limited conservatee by a regional center serving developmentally disabled persons. The regional center is required to submit to the court, within 30 days, a written report of its findings and recommendations, including a description of the proposed limited conservatee's specific areas, nature, and degree of disability, if any (Probate code § 1827.5).

At the hearing on the petition, the court must do the following:

1. Inquire into the nature and extent of the general intellectual functioning of the individual alleged to be developmentally disabled
2. Evaluate the extent of the impairment of his or her adaptive behavior
3. Ascertain his or her capacity to care for himself or herself and his or her property
4. Inquire into the qualifications, abilities, and capabilities of the person seeking appointment as limited conservator (Probate code § 1828.5)

The court will also make a specific determination concerning the proposed limited conservatee's ability to vote.

If the court finds that the person has the capacity to care for herself or himself and to manage his or her property "as a reasonably prudent person," the court must dismiss the petition. If the court finds that the person has the capacity to perform some, but not all, of the tasks necessary for self and property management, the court must appoint the limited conservator (of the person, estate, or both), but must define the conservator's powers and duties so as to "permit the developmentally disabled adult to care for himself or herself or to manage his or her financial resources commensurate with his or her ability to do so" (Probate code § 1828.5[b][c]).

In practice, upon receipt of a petition for a limited conservatorship, the probate commissioner appoints a private attorney from the court panel to represent the proposed limited conservatee. That attorney will usually, though not always, visit the proposed conservatee and explain the impact of the proposed conservatorship and his or her rights under the law. The petition itself must be served on a regional center (as well as all relatives to the second degree). If the proposed conservatee is already a regional center client, the report submitted to the court will frequently be more sensitive to the ability of the conservatee to manage his or her own affairs.

CONCLUSION

Limited guardianship models, like the one in effect in California, have the advantage of explicit recognition of the right and ability of developmentally disabled adults to remain free from restrictions of their liberty. As with any new concept (or any bureaucratic system), old ideas resist innovation, and there is still evidence in the procedure of the outmoded "protectionist" system. Not every attorney appointed to represent the limited conservatee makes a diligent and thorough inquiry into his or her capacities and desires. Some appointed counsel rely far too much on the information provided by counsel for the proposed conservator, or meet their client for the first time only minutes before the hearing on the petition. The legal structure provided by the California model is sufficient, however, to accommodate the needs of developmentally disabled adults. The legislative intent is clearly and unambiguously apparent and provides ample grounds for a conscientious advocate to protect the constitutional rights of the developmentally disabled adult. The enactment and enforcement of similar laws in other states would greatly enhance the self-control accorded to persons with developmental disabilities.

REFERENCES

Addington v. *Texas*, 441 U.S. 418 (1979).
Bligh, R. Sterilization and mental retardation. *ABAJ*, 1965, *51*, 1059, 1062.
Buck v. *Bell*, 274 U.S. 200 (1927).
Burgdorf, R.L., Jr. (ed.). *The legal rights of handicapped persons: Cases, materials, and text*. Baltimore: Paul H. Brookes Publishing Co., 1980.
Conservatorship of Roulet, 23 Cal.3d 219 (1979).
Fotheringham, The concept of social competence as applied to marriage and child care in those classified as mentally retarded. *Canadian Medical Association Journal*, 1971, *13*, 814–15.

Halderman v. *Pennhurst State School & Hospital*, 446 F.Supp.1295 (U.S.D.C E.D. Pa. 1977–78).

Jackson v. *Indiana*, 406 U.S. 715 (1972).

Kindred, M. *The mentally retarded citizen and the law: The President's committee on mental retardation.* New York: Press, 1976.

Leviton, S.P. Freedom of choice: Competency and guardianship. In: R.L. Burgdorf Jr. (ed.), *The legal rights of handicapped persons: Cases, materials, and text.* Baltimore: Paul H. Brooks Publishing Co., 1980.

Loving v. *Virginia*, 388 U.S. 1 (1967).

Lynch v. *Baxley*, 386 F.Supp.378 (M.D. Ala. 1974).

Meyer v. *Nebraska*, 262 U.S. 390,399 (1923).

North Carolina Association for Retarded Children v. *North Carolina*, 420 F.Supp.451 (M.D. NC 1976).

O'Connor v. *Donaldson*, 422 U.S. 563 (1975).

Olmstead v. *United States*, 277 U.S. 438, 479 (1928).

Prince v. *Massachusetts*, 321 U.S. 158,166 (1944).

Shelton v. *Tucker*, 364 U.S. 479 (1960).

Stanley v. *Illinois*, 405 U.S. 645 (1972).

Wald, P. Basic personal and civil rights. In: Kindred, M. (ed.), *The mentally retarded citizen and the law: The president's committee on mental retardation.* New York: Press, 1976.

Youngberg v. *Romeo*, 73 L.Ed.2d 28 (1982).

Zablocki v. *Redhail*, 434 U.S. 374 (1978).

Chapter 5

Before I'm Gone
A Parent's Perspective

Milton Blackstone

I suspect that at least 50% of the people reading this book are parents, relatives, or guardians of dependent people. I also surmise that these same people are truly concerned about the long range future of their charges. My experience over the past 25 years has led me to draw certain conclusions and form opinions regarding how the system can be improved, altered, bypassed or simply used.

This chapter conveys the opinions of parents like me, who have sometimes been classified as "disgruntled." My study of the care, education, training, protection, and acceptance of severely disabled individuals, who until recently have been relegated to state-run institutions, has led me to design programs, devices, and techniques that have allowed my family and me to lead relatively happy, normal, and productive lives.

But what of tommorrow?

DEATH—LET'S TALK ABOUT IT

There is certainly no truer axiom than: "two things in life are certain—death and taxes." While there may be some variations on this theme when it comes to taxes, there is little hope that we will find a way to avoid death . . . at least in my lifetime. I know that the subject of death is one that few of us relish talking or thinking about, but being that it is inevitable, isn't it best that we not only talk about it, but plan for it?

I had a heart attack a few years ago and as I rested in my hospital bed in the intensive care room, all I could think about was, "Please not now, God, I'm not

---

Milton Blackstone has received the 1983 service award from the American Association on Mental Deficiency for improvement of services to individuals with developmental disabilities.

ready. I haven't made plans for my wife and children yet.'' Although I had thought about making a will many times, I did nothing formal about it, as I really couldn't make up my mind how I wanted things handled. The day after my heart attack, I wrote my will.

WHAT ARE PARENTS TO DO?

Some 25 years ago, not only did I realize that I had a handicapped child, but I was struck with the reality of having a son who was unique—being born blind, brain damaged, and having a number of other anomalies, including a bilateral cleft lip and palate. Little did I know then that I would virtually spend the rest of my life seeking appropriate services and having to be constantly concerned for his future.

The trauma at the time of my son's birth was aggravated by having doctors who, apparently having never seen such a child before, misdiagnosed his condition, not once, but on eight different occasions. Their well-meaning advice added to our confusion, as when they counseled us to ''institutionalize'' our son since he would most likely be a ''vegetable.'' His mother and I never gave any serious thought to these recommendations, however, and we have never regretted not doing so. What saddens me is that despite what society has learned in the past 15 or 20 years, many well-meaning but uninformed physicians are still offering parents similar advice.

In the days when my son was young, the thought of any agency assisting a child with multiple handicaps was an almost unheard of one. Agencies serving retarded persons referred us to agencies serving the blind since they considered our son's lack of vision to be his primary disability. Agencies serving the blind readily confessed that they did not know how to deal with his retardation. As a consequence, we found ourselves constantly in the position of being both grateful to anyone willing to work with our son, and at the same time compelled to withdraw him from program after program upon recognizing that each was indeed inappropriate.

The only alternative, it seemed, was to be experimental. We were willing to try any ''new'' approach, any new opportunity. Because most children with severe disabilities were placed in state hospitals, the number of such children in the community was miniscule. Support programs for multiply handicapped children were very hard to find. Only by locating other parents of children with equally severe impairments who were as desperate for help as ourselves did we finally manage to collectively finance a part-time program (2 hours a day, twice a week). After only 2 weeks, we realized that our program was beginning to show some promise of helping our son. With something so promising and miraculous in sight, how could we settle for just 2 hours, 2 days a week? We begged, borrowed, and scraped in order to obtain a site, get additional staff, and convince the director of the program to give up his regular job at a local school for the blind in favor of full-time attention to our program.

We managed to keep the program going for 11 months, while at the same time trying to convince the school system that our kids were worthy of support. Six parents each obligated themselves to $2,000 in loans to finance the program, which was now running 4 hours a day, 4 days a week. We were about to throw in the towel, having exhausted our small endowment, when the Department of Education informed us that it had reversed its determination that our children were "uneducable." We had convinced the Department that there was no such thing as an "uneducable" child and therefore won entitlement for state support. (I'm pleased to say that this program, now known as the Association for the Advancement of Blind and Retarded, is still ongoing, and that the organization that developed as a result of it is now the largest operator of services for the retarded and blind in New York City.)

Our son was doing well, but as often happens, other family considerations prompted a cross-country move, and our search for appropriate services began again. Each time he was placed in a program, it proved to be inappropriate for one reason or another, and each time, the system refused to correct it. Time and time again we were compelled to withdraw him. Each time, we had to struggle to get him into a new program, generally one that we helped to create.

Once he reached the age of 22 and was no longer eligible for public education, the battle continued to find an activity center program that would accept him. None would take him due to budget restrictions, inadequate staffing, or programmatic inappropriateness. Once again we had to be the instigators for starting a new activity center that could appropriately serve the many people like our son who were sitting at home eager to have someplace to go where they could do something.

Our quest for proper services for our son continues to this day. While we have finally achieved an appropriate day program that is producing positive results, state policy changes now threaten the program's continuity. Once again we are facing the possibility of having to seek new alternatives.

While we are here and able, the prospect of change no longer frightens us. We have learned to cope. Our primary concern centers on who will follow in our footsteps and how they will manage to maintain the level of care and attention that we have provided our son. What follows are some thoughts that might be helpful to others who share our concerns.

WHAT WILL HAPPEN TO MY CHILD AFTER I'M GONE?

With apologies to Sir Walter Scott, "Breathes there the man, with soul so dead, who never to himself hath said, . . . " what will happen to my child after I am gone? I think not!

Undoubtedly, the chief concern of all caring parents of disabled people is for the future of their offspring when they are unable to look after his or her welfare. Certainly, that's the way it is with us. The current system of "Regional Center case managers," "Department of Social Services social workers," and other "system" administrators who are supposed to be responsible for our son's welfare leaves much to be desired. From my perspective, these administrators frequently evidence conflicts of interest and generally do not remain in their roles long enough to truly become familiar with the needs of either clients or care providers. "What then?" "Who, then?" This is the problem that I have wrestled with for many years, and why I encourage new directions in guardianship planning.

Institutional Placement

Let's examine your child's options for out-of-home living arrangements. Obviously, the one area that offers "continuity" is state institutional placement. Until such time as the state offers protective care in a community setting that seems as secure as that afforded in state institutions, most parents who have not previously had their child in a community placement will not accept this alternative. I personally feel uncomfortable about state institutions. In my opinion they are impersonal and dehumanizing, even under the best of circumstances. Unfortunately, they are the only game in town for some people, i.e., people with severe health problems or behavior disorders. While this need not be the case (Apolloni, Cappuccilli, & Cooke, 1980; Human Services Associates, 1979), the fact remains that few appropriate community living arrangements exist for developmentally disabled people with these added problems (Bruininks, Hauber, & Kudla, 1980).

Group Homes

Perhaps the most popular community program mode is the group home that houses no more than six residents (and less if the residents' handicaps or behavior problems require added attention). This approach has generally been considered acceptable for many individuals. The primary problem with this arrangement, however, is that the administrators of such homes change readily and the stability of the home is often dependent on the whims of the current rate structure and the policies of the supporting state administration. Moreover, the residents are usually in the home of a "house parent" rather than in their own home and can be transferred from home to home whether or not they (or their guardian) approves of the moves. I prefer greater permanence for my son; his blindness makes it particularly important that he feel familiar with his surroundings. Frequent moves are very disturbing to him.

Foster Family Arrangements

The foster family arrangement is another popular model (Provencal, 1980). Again, this could be a fine arrangement, particularly if the individual is placed in a "small" family unit, with truly caring people who consider the child to be a member of the family rather than a temporary ward. Like the group home, the foster home model is not permanent. People who reside in foster homes are vulnerable to frequent changes for a variety of reasons.

Shared Living Arrangements

Being an adult and eligible for In-Home Support Services, a shared living arrangement, possibly with another disabled individual, might also be an acceptable arrangement for my son. Of course, he would require a full-time attendant, and so might his housemate. This is basically the formula outlined in a plan that I developed several years ago (Blackstone, 1982). Unfortunately, this plan also has weaknesses. While my son would be in his own home and would be the employer of his attendant, supervision and monitoring would still be required. Ideally, a family member who is familiar with his needs, personality, and behavior would handle this aspect. However, I, like most other parents, don't want to saddle my daughter or any other relative with this responsibility unless they voluntarily chose to accept it. Moreover, what if they do accept the role and later decided to leave the area? What alternative do we have? It is obvious to me that the current choices are not ideal. We need additional avenues to pursue if we are to find the peace of mind and security of purpose that we seek.

An organization composed of other parents and community advocates seems to me to be an avenue that warrants serious consideration. We need organizations, such as corporate guardianship programs, to assure a few of the extras that parents currently provide and want to continue to have provided, regardless of where their children end up living.

WHO CAN YOU TRUST?

In the previous section, I referred to a variety of living arrangement options. The ultimate selection depends a great deal on who can be relied on for oversight and supervision. Reference was made to Regional Center case managers and Social Welfare Department social workers, i.e., system representatives who provide some degree of oversight and sometimes act as guardian. Except for rather unusual circumstances, my general experience has been that "system guardians" are chosen as an alternative to "none."

If not the "system people," who are some of the others who might be your child's guardian? The logical order for consideration would be family members, generally siblings; family friends; legal advisors; and bankers.

Siblings

In considering the future welfare of your offspring, it is important to be cognizant of the feelings of other children in the family, even though the responsibility of your child's future rests solely with you.

The thoughts and feelings of a discussion group that included several adults who grew up with a handicapped sibling, and nine children (ages 10 through 18) who currently lived with a severely handicapped sibling may be beneficial in considering the possibility of siblings becoming your child's guardian (Bissell,

1976). The topic of the group's discussion was how they really feel about having a handicapped brother or sister. The adults said that as they grew older, they began to feel guilty over their own "normalcy," wondering why they had been spared. Those feelings were most intense when they participated in pleasurable activities that their handicapped sibling would never enjoy. The children admitted that they feel guilty about the resentment and hostility that they sometimes experience. They said that their parents continually remind them to be kind to their handicapped sibling, which makes them feel that it must be wrong to have negative feelings, even though similar feelings directed toward a normal sibling are acceptable. One adult said she often felt guilty when she refused her mother's request to take her handicapped sister to social functions although she would have felt no guilt at refusing to take along her normal sibling. Both the adults and children admitted to feelings of embarrassment when their sibling was stared at by strangers; the children were embarrassed for themselves while the adults felt more embarrassed for the sibling.

One man was embarrassed by his parents who were so mortified that they hid their retarded child in a back room whenever visitors came. Despite their actions, he did not in any way adopt his parents' attitude about handicapped children. Others said their parents paid so much attention to their handicapped siblings that the nonhandicapped children all feel resentful over what they felt was "favoritism." Additionally, many of the girls resented the additional chores they felt were imposed on them because of their handicapped brother or sister.

An area of annoyance expressed by both the adults and the children concerned the attitudes of relatives other than the parents. While some said that they felt the parents sometimes seemed overanxious and concerned, they all said that most other relatives were consistently oversolicitous, overattentive, and overprotective. Many people told of instances where relatives interfered in quarrels between the siblings and always defended the handicapped participant, whether right or wrong. One girl said that her main reason for annoyance at the excessive attention shown by some relatives was that she doubted they loved her handicapped brother as much as they professed, and were merely being patronizing. She perceived insincerity on their part and felt that her handicapped brother was equally aware of it.

One man felt guilty over a specific issue—the break-up of his marriage. Although his wife had known about his retarded brother before their marriage, it became a threat to her afterwards due to the possibility that genetic abnormalities might affect her children. After the marriage was dissolved, the man felt guilty, both because he felt that he had caused the break-up and because he felt angry and resentful toward his retarded brother.

Interestingly enough, both adults and children wanted their parents to share with them whatever information they had concerning the etiology of their sibling's handicap and information regarding his or her specific problems. Over the years, they had heard bits and pieces of discussions but were never told specifically what was wrong or what treatment was underway, and they sensed that their parents would be uncomfortable if asked. Their desire for information stemmed from their concern about what would happen to the handicapped sibling in the event of their parents' deaths. None of the adults or children had been told what, if any, arrangements their parents had made for the future care of the handicapped sibling and they assumed that the burden of care would fall on them. They were concerned about their ability to assume this responsibility.

I share this information about the feelings of siblings because they are all too often thrust in the role of guardian even though some other course of action might be more advisable. If your kids are anything like mine, chances are that you'll receive lots of advice when the subject of the future placement of your disabled child is brought up for discussion. And, if you feel anything like my wife and I do, you probably will feel very strongly that your other children shouldn't have to bear the burden of being responsible for their disabled sibling. They should be permitted to carry on "normal" lives of their own.

You are most likely saying to yourself, "Who else is there that we can trust, if not our own kids?" But unless your nondisabled children earnestly volunteer, to paraphrase an Old Sam Goldwyn colloquialism, I strongly recommend that you "include them out." By suggesting that you include them out, I mean that you should proceed in making your plans as though you had no other children. When the time comes to finalize your plans in some formalized fashion, make your decision known and gauge your children's reactions. Simply sit back and wait to see if there are suggestions or offers forthcoming. If there are, weigh them along with your insight of the personality and sense of responsibility of the maker. You may then wish to consider altering your original plan.

Others Who Can Help

Friends and Legal Advisors   Family friends and legal advisors are often thought of in lieu of family members. Serious thought should be given to the possible outcome of such a decision. What of the feelings of their spouse or children, to whom the responsibility might someday fall by default? What is their financial and family condition likely to be? And what of your disabled child's siblings who may be left out of future decisions?

Bankers   Another category that comes to mind is bankers. A bank is a safe place to go when money must be supervised, due to its fiduciary expertise. If this is a consideration, go see your friendly banker. Get his views on the future and who he sees at his facility as being ultimately responsible. What are their fees and how are they paid? There will be other questions that will crop up once you start thinking and discussing your plans. It's an important step and not one to be taken lightly, even though the actual changeover may be years away.

Even if you think you know someone well, you may not know how astute his or her judgment is, or if he or she is willing to invest time in enlarging his or her knowledge of areas in which he or she may be called upon to make important decisions concerning his or her charge. It is perhaps unrealistic to expect that he or she will have the experience that you have acquired over years of tending to the needs of your child, but if you are fortunate enough to have someone in mind to carry on after you, you have an exceptional opportunity to help sharpen his or her expertise in areas you deem important. Exposure to your perceptions now can go a long way toward assuring that your successor's future actions will coincide with your feelings.

Whenever you consider the possibility of allowing others to obligate themselves, it eventually becomes necessary to approach them to get their views on accepting the responsibility. The chances are that if you obtain their concurrence, it will be with specific conditions. If there are conditions, it is wise to try to meet them as quickly as possible, despite the natural tendency to delay preparations and the objections that may be offered by other interested parties. It's never too early to contact the people you have in mind in order to discuss your plans. If they are agreeable, get them involved in "learning the ropes" now, maybe even as an advocate, so they will have acquired some experience when the time comes for them to take over.

When No Choice Is Apparent

If you are not fortunate enough to have a choice, there are things that you can do to help find someone and to help prepare whoever is selected to make future decisions for your child. List all the people who have helped you to make the various decisions that you have had to make regarding your child. Write a few lines about each person (including what you expect of them—even if it is only that they share your philosophy). List also the various agencies and professionals you have had some association with and comment on them, or even grade them. Indicate who knows or has worked with your child and comment on the nature of the assistance that he or she has provided. The more information you can record, the easier it will be to convince the "guardian" of your choice that the role you are asking him or her to accept will not be as difficult as he or she is apt to suspect. Thus, you will not only be assisted in acquiring the help of those you select, but you will be assuring the guardian that he or she will have the ultimate assistance in making decisions comparable to those you would have made.

SAFEGUARDING ENTITLEMENT TO GOVERNMENT BENEFITS

There are actions that apply to your handicapped child's financial status that you should take now. As long as the individual who needs "protection" is insolvent, there often haven't been too many choices. However, is your handicapped offspring really insolvent? Let's examine the possible circumstances.

Assume that your adult child has never been gainfully employed and is receiving Supplementary Security Income (SSI) and other local benefits such as In-Home Support Services (IHSS). In California, he or she could be receiving assistance worth anywhere from $1,200 or $1,300 per month, give or take a little (depending on the degree of disability and current living arrangement). Additionally, he or she may be receiving "purchase of service" assistance from the Regional Center (or similar agencies in other states) that might also include transportation. Leaving it at that, we're talking about $1,500 to $2,000 per month that is or could be expended on behalf of your charge. Administered wisely, this sum should assure a variety of rewarding life activities. If the person responsible to help your child is as "entitlement knowledgeable" as he or she should be, other services such as housing assistance, Medi-Cal (or your state's equivalent), or therapy funding assistance might also be forthcoming. Thus, the question becomes not so much whether the person administering guardian-like oversight will "rip-off" your child, but will they take the time and interest necessary to assure that your child receives the most appropriate services that existing entitlements *could* provide.

ESTATE PLANNING GUIDELINES

There is no simple formula to use when planning for the future of a severely disabled child, and there is little information available to assist lawyers in counseling parents about the unique estate planning problems when there is a handicapped child in the family. Parents of mentally disabled persons should realize that most attorneys have little training in counseling parents of disabled individuals and parents must often guide the lawyer in applying known legal principles to the unique needs of their family situation.

Following is a brief overview of estate planning and a list of considerations that you and your lawyer will probably want to discuss before you decide on a particular estate plan. Think about these questions and the others I have raised before meeting your lawyer and be sure to bring them up if the lawyer fails to do so.

A person's "estate" is what he owns or possesses, like his home or his car, the money in savings or checking accounts, stocks and bonds, furniture, and all types of personal possessions. "Estate planning" is the process of planning how these possessions will be divided and distributed when you die. Parents must take care of the needs of their family by managing their income and assets, and they must also make plans for the time when each parent will die and how the needs of the family will continue to be met. Your estate plan should include at least your will and may include such things as trusts and insurance policies. The following constitutes a partial list of considerations that you and your lawyer will want to discuss:

1. What is the size of your estate? In what form is the estate—cash, savings, land, family business, etc? How much of the estate will be left upon the death of both parents? How much of the estate do the parents want to make available for the care and treatment of the severely disabled child?
2. What other children are in the family and what are their needs, e.g., college, special services, etc.?

3. What is your age, the age of your spouse and the ages of other family members?
4. Is the mentally disabled child a minor or an adult?
5. For what government benefits (Social Security, SSI, Medicaid, Medicare) is the disabled child eligible? (Parents will usually need to do their own research and may need to advise the attorney about availability and eligibility criteria for government benefits.) Be sure to find out how these benefits can be terminated or lost.
6. What are the disabled child's handicaps, both physical and mental? What appears to be the child's potential for self-support in the future? Parents should obtain a complete medical, psychological, and personal history for their child, along with a professional interpretation of the information.
7. What are the child's present and future needs for special services, such as special education, vocational training, recreational activities, etc.? Will these services necessitate placement in a residential facility? If so, will this facility be public or private?
8. What is your general attitude and what is the attitude of other family members toward the disabled person?

Parents should take to the initial conference with the attorney the names, ages, birthdates, social security numbers, addresses, phone numbers, and income of the parents of the disabled child. Parents should also be prepared to discuss and bring a list of all assets (such as their home, land, car, bank accounts, stocks and bonds, retirement benefits, life insurance policies, and other valuable personal possessions) and liabilities (such as mortgages, loans, other debts) for themselves and their disabled child.

The parents should also bring the following information in written form concerning their disabled child:

1. Degree of mental retardation, with copies of professional diagnostic reports
2. Educational background and level of functioning
3. Other physical and/or mental handicaps
4. Personality and behavioral traits
5. Capabilities and limitations (e.g., ability to read, walk, talk, toilet, dress him- or herself, take a bus, drive a car, make change, purchase items in a store, etc.)
6. Interests (e.g., enjoyment of music, television, radio, bowling, movies, reading, athletics, camping, dancing, swimming, others)
7. Work history and earnings (if any)
8. Other financial provisions, e.g., has anyone other than the parents of the disabled individual provided for the disabled person through will, insurance, or in any other way?
9. Personal legal status, i.e., has legal guardianship of his person or estate been established?

It is always important that each parent have a will. A will can be used to divide and distribute your estate as you wish. If you die without a will, the state laws will determine how your estate is divided and distributed. These laws do not take into consideration the special needs of your family.

There is no absolute rule to follow in deciding whether or not the severely disabled person should own property other than personal keepsakes. You should investigate the effect of eligibility criteria for governmental benefits and the payment for special services if the disabled person owns property. Be sure your estate plan does not result in depriving the disabled person of governmental benefits such as Social Security or SSI, and always get professional counseling.

If you have other children whom you intend to name in your will, you may very well have some guilt feelings if you were to leave your disabled child less than his or her share. However, be sure to consider the constraints placed on acquiring assets if your disabled child is to remain eligible for entitlement benefits. According to federal policy, an individual receiving SSI cannot have assets that exceed $1,500 in value ($2,250 if married and living with husband or wife), exclusive of his or her home and transportation vehicle, nor any item that has a cash-conversion value of $500 or more. In California, if one is receiving purchase of service assistance from the Regional Center, he or she must divest himself or herself of his or her cash assets by paying for these services before the Regional Center will assume the responsibility to (continue) purchasing these services or programs. Therefore, unless your heir will have sufficient assets to permit him or her to be independent of governmental assistance, it may be to his or her disadvantage to inherit what you might like to leave. There are alternatives that might solve your dilemma, however, in the form of trusts or other plans. An astute estate planner can assist you in this regard.

You should know that if you were to leave a burial plot to your child, it could be considered as ''convertible assets'' and could count toward the maximum assets he or she is permitted to acquire and still be eligible for benefits. Therefore, it would be wiser, if you have arranged for a personal or family plot, to be sure that it is not part of his or her estate. I am not an attorney but I'm sure any competent attorney could provide you with a trust plan or some alternative that would not jeopardize your child's benefits by exceeding the assets he or she is permitted to acquire. Although the preceding comments address his or her final resting place, the same would apply towards other prearrangements you may wish to establish or prepay for your child, such as services, casket, tombstone, grave care, etc.

The same advice would hold for gifts from your estate, be they material things or cash in some form. It would be wise to familiarize yourself with what is permissible for your child to own without risking his or her entitlements. I do not wish to be a ''doomsayer,'' but I am concerned about the prospect of the law being changed from administration to administration, as is being evidenced even now. For instance, one's home and automobile are excluded from the assets that are expected to be declared annually or whenever the ''payee'' or ''caretaker'' is audited by the Social Security Administration. What of the contents? Medically prescribed equipment is excluded, but in this age of everchanging Medicaid assistance, what does the future hold for a child who may be medically dependent? It is best to analyze your child's total future needs and attempt to foresee how those needs might be met without jeopardizing his or her government benefits.

Attorneys and other professionals should always be consulted before critical decisions are made. Many states have laws that permit a variety of trust exemptions from claims for support and maintenance in a residential care facility, as well as trusts for other types of care. Be sure to discuss this with your attorney. Finally, whatever the estate plan, review it periodically, especially when there are any important changes in the family situation or in the law.

CAN YOU REALLY HAVE PEACE OF MIND?

The formula that I recommend is:

1. Make your plans without necessitating the involvement of any of your other children.
2. Make your plans known to your children and consider what safeguards you would like in the event you alter your plans.
3. Leave room in your plans to accommodate any change of heart or unforeseen complications.
4. Formalize your plans in writing and name a third party to resolve any future differences or interpretations.

The act of putting it in writing and having it confirmed by the involved parties crystalizes everyone's intentions and doesn't leave anything subject to future misinterpretation. In addition, the obligation is recognized as though it were a contract, as opposed to a verbal promise. This may seem like a rather mechanical way to deal with what is most certainly intended to be a gesture of love and caring, but many changes occur in one's future life and circumstances. A businesslike approach may allow you to face your future a little more peacefully.

CONCLUSION

My comments in this chapter have focused on what you as an individual parent can do to safeguard the future of your dependent child. Most of the other chapters in this book focus on group strategies, an alternative that I have long supported and promoted in California. The research and study that have been devoted to the subject by the contributors to this book represents a tremendous step forward in resolving the "old-age question." I, for one, am convinced that a workable plan is feasible and that the recommendations found in these pages can provide guidance for those who are interested in designing group approaches for stabilizing the future of their disabled child. Your prompt action can mean peace of mind during the remainder of your lifetime. Don't forfeit your chance to succeed by postponing your personal and organizational plans.

REFERENCES

Apolloni, T., Cappuccilli, J., & Cooke, T.P. (eds.). *Achievements in residential services for persons with disabilities: Toward excellence*. Baltimore: University Park Press, 1980.

Bissell, N.E. *Communicating with parents (siblings) of exceptional children*. Cincinnati: University of Cincinnati, Department of Special Education, School of Psychology, 1976.

Blackstone, M. *Severely handicapped persons in the community*. Seattle: University of Washington, 1982.

Bruininks, R.H., Hauber, F.A., & Kudla, M.J. National survey of community residential facilities: A profile of facilities and residents in 1977. *American Journal of Mental Deficiency, 1980, 84*, 470–478.

Human Services Associates. *Personalized living: Homes for Californians with special developmental needs*. (T. Apolloni & T.P. Cooke, eds.). Sacramento: California State Council on Developmental Disabilities, 1979.

Provencal, G. The Macomb-Oakland regional center. In: T. Apolloni, J. Cappuccilli, & T.P. Cooke (eds.), *Achievements in residential services for persons with disabilities: Toward excellence*. Baltimore: University Park Press, 1980.

Chapter 6

Parental Dilemmas
Lessons I Have Learned
from Interacting with Parents

Daniel Geller

As a family therapist I have had the opportunity to work with parents and their children, one or more of whom is mentally retarded. Some parents have only recently received the diagnosis, while others have lived with it for years. They bring a variety of problems to solve, but the underlying problem they share is that, as a family, they must cope with the fact that a member of the family is mentally retarded. For some parents, the difficulty centers around their initial adjustment to having a retarded child and increased conflict between spouses. Others find it difficult to manage their child's behavior. Still others are struggling to deal with their child's emerging sexuality or the issue of fostering greater autonomy for their adult offspring by exploring group home facilities. And finally, there are those parents, well on in years, who have spent their lives caring for their retarded son or daughter and now are confronted with the issue they have repressed for so long—what will happen to their child when they die? This chapter has been written to convey my experience as a therapist and to define the role of corporate guardianship programs in terms of their importance for addressing family concerns.

INDIVIDUAL PARENT REACTIONS

"Every father's son must rise above his father before his days are done." These words written by Robert Tristan Coffin (1943) aptly reflect not only the uniquely American social assumption but also, to a large extent, people's expectations of themselves as parents and of their children. Becoming a parent is a major developmental step and an act of self-confirmation as well as self-perpetuation. It is an achievement in the eyes of society and a source of personal pride.

75

The period before a baby is born is one of expectancy, based both on one's experience and fantasized hopes. Visits to the obstetrician, changes in the mother's diet, the reading of infant care books, the purchasing of clothes and furniture, selecting a name, and preparing other children for the baby, all serve to create for the family an atmosphere of excitement and eager anticipation as they await the birth of a new human being.

Though these preparations may vary from one culture to the next, they usually culminate in the birth of, as expected, the healthy newborn with the attendant feelings of elation and joy. These feelings are shared not only by the extended family but often by the medical and nursing staff as well. Friends and co-workers all participate to some extent and share in the pleasure of the happy event. Fathers may pass out cigars and otherwise openly express their delight and exuberance. The common emotion for those who participate in various ways in this event is joy. All understand it and trust it, secure in the appropriateness of this feeling.

Grief

The reactions to the birth of a developmentally disabled child are markedly different. While the immediate family members may openly express their grief and profound disappointment, others, unsure as to how to respond, avoid the parents. A certain degree of emotional, as well as social, isolation results as sources of support awkwardly pull away. After the initial shock accompanying the shattering of their expectations, the parents may be feeling very ambivalent—experiencing joy in the birth of their child, as well as grief for the loss of their expected healthy child and the hopes they had for that child. They find little, if any, outside support for their feelings of joy; for, most commonly, others react to the birth much as they would to a death, with sympathy, sorrow, and awkwardness. In place of the periodic eager questions as to how the new baby is doing, parents encounter silence.

Medical personnel may actively encourage parents to emotionally distance themselves from their newborn child by recommending immediate institutionalization. When doctors lack current knowledge regarding the real capabilities of developmentally disabled individuals, their own pessimistic view of the child's future may reinforce the parents' fears about this issue. Overwhelmed and confused, the parents begin to mourn the child they lost. This grief reaction is similar to that delineated by Kubler-Ross (1969) with respect to persons who are dying.

Denial   The initial stage of the grief reaction is characterized by denial. Parents may reject the diagnosis and repress the hurt and guilt that accompany news of the diagnosis. Though this stage may persist for years, it does not necessarily mean that the child will not be well cared for by the parents. Rather, parents will deny those needs of the child that are based on the diagnosis, for denial is the refusal of parents to give up their initial expectations. Thus, while taking good care of their baby, the parents may refuse an infant stimulation program for their child on the grounds that he or she does not need it. Others may adamantly assert that their child will be roller skating by the time he or she is five when, in fact, the physical condition of the child might exclude ambulation. Denial is a necessary coping stage for the individual parent and is to be expected. It is functional to the extent that it reduces the initial shock to emotionally manageable dimensions for the parents, thereby enabling them to maintain some sense of stability and control. It is pathological only when it precludes the delivery of necessary services to the child for an undue length of time. Denial serves to protect the parents' self-esteem and self-image. It affords additional time for parents to become adjusted to the pain and disappointment that is attendant to changes in expectations. Case Illustration 1 is an example of the denial stage.

Anger When parents are able to relinquish their denial they are likely to become angry. It is at this point they ask, ''Why did this happen to me?'' They may choose to blame their spouse, who then becomes the object of angry feelings. When this happens, doctors and nurses frequently find parents extremely difficult to deal with. Unable to accept the anger and resentment they feel toward their child, parents often displace it onto others, such as medical personnel, who become convenient targets for their anger. They may think that their family, friends, and professionals are not sufficiently supportive or are only offering simplistic or patronizing solutions, and vent their rage at them. Finally, they may focus their anger at their child for failing to develop like normal infants or otherwise act as normal infants do.

Case Illustration 1

MRS. K's DENIAL OF HER CHILD'S DISABILITY

R is now 35 years of age, living at home under the supervision of his 76-year-old mother. He has Down's Syndrome. Mr. K died about 20 years ago. R is a very healthy young man who works every day in a sheltered workshop with 120 other workers. Mrs. K has had the sole responsibility for his welfare ever since Mr. K passed away. She has an excellent relationship with R, viewing her son as able to move toward more independent status. But it wasn't always this way.

R was the first male child and the second of two children. His progress was significantly slower than his agemates and sister in all areas of development. Nevertheless, Mrs. K was nurturant and patient. She didn't hear the doctors discuss the diagnosis, prognosis, and necessary management strategies a mother needs to incorporate into her daily routine. R was perceived by his mother as a baby who was slower than most. She was blind to R's limited ability. Mrs. K took care of R as she would any child. After 6 years of limited progress and with the beginning of school, Mrs. K heard the diagnosis for the first time: Down's syndrome, mental retardation. For the first time, Mrs. K cried and thus began the grieving process.

Case Illustration 2

MR. M's REACTION OF ANGER

Mr. and Mrs. M were a young couple who were not prepared to have a child, let alone one who was multiply handicapped by blindness, seizures, and mental retardation. Inappropriate patterns of communication had prevented them from establishing the necessary problem-solving strategies to deal with such a crisis. E's birth became confusing to the parents because he needed so much medical care for the first 6 weeks of his life. They were not given information about prognosis, nor was counseling about child care provided. When referred to me 6 months later, they appeared confused, fearful and angry. Mrs. M shared her feelings about being helplessly alone in performing daily child care responsibilities. Mr. M had distanced himself from the marriage and parental role. He was angry at all the people who tried to help. His anger persisted until he unfortunately fled, rejecting his role as husband and father.

Anger, like denial, is a necessary and normal reaction. It becomes a special concern when the parents' anger results in isolation from important sources of support—familial, social, and professional, or when it precludes bonding with the baby. An example of one man's angry reaction is provided in Case Illustration 2.

Bargaining Another aspect of the mourning process as presented by Kubler-Ross (1969) is bargaining. The term refers to the individual bargaining for more time before he or she dies. It is used here to describe the parents' search for a new diagnosis, the dissatisfaction with the original diagnosis, "shopping around." At this stage, like Kubler-Ross's dying patients, parents may begin to doctor-shop in the hope that a different doctor will have a different diagnosis, thus having a different prognosis. In their need to disconfirm what they have been told, parents may begin searching the popular press in an attempt to unravel the mystery of their child. This period is a preparatory stage for parents coming to view their child in a new way, arriving at new and hopefully accurate expectations for their child. Myths surrounding the diagnosis of mental retardation bring to the surface disturbing emotions for all involved, and many parents may have difficulty processing the meaning of the child's diagnosis. Because mental retardation is the most serious diagnosis to present to parents and certainly the most difficult one for them to accept, it is understandable that parents often search for a more hopeful label.

This period in the psychological adjustment of the parent must be distinguished from the search by parents who do not receive correct information from professionals. Misdiagnosis, misguided information and professional distancing also leads to doctor shopping. In any event, to treat parents who seek additional opinions as highly anxious neurotics only serves to further distance them from the professionals upon whom they must rely.

The search of one parent for more hopeful information and the adjustment that followed it are portrayed in Case Illustration 3.

Case Illustration 3

MRS. G's DIAGNOSTIC JOURNEY

J's parents were referred because of their inability to manage his home behavior. They were concerned about his inappropriate acting out in school, his difficulty with following directions both at home and in school, and his significant delay in academic progress and language development. The school tested and placed J in a resource room with other youngsters with similar difficulties. However, there was no diagnosis mentioned when his test profile and IEP were discussed.

We decided upon a course of treatment that would help the parents manage their 6-year-old son. Mr. and Mrs. G were very motivated to try interventions but were not committed to the treatment process. We discussed J's strengths and limitations and his diagnosis.

Mrs. G became psychologically deaf, while Mr. G felt relieved that the hidden fear of J's mental retardation was finally out in the open. When Mrs. G. needed to label her son, she used the label "learning disabled." For the next 6 months, training in parenting skills was significantly impaired. Mrs. G kept denying her son's limitations, forever getting angry at him for his inability to respond appropriately to her commands. She blamed Mr. G. for not reinforcing her. There were some very difficult times. Two side trips for second and third diagnostic opinions were made prior to continuing with the initial parenting program. With patience and reinforcement for her efforts, Mrs. G was able to respond to J more appropriately.

Depression   Once the parents acknowledge the reality of the diagnosis, they enter a period of depression during which they actively mourn not only the loss of the healthy child they expected, but also what they perceive their developmentally disabled child never having or doing. Parents may feel they have failed and blame themselves for their child's disability. It is during this period that the need arises to establish new expectancies. If these expectancies are accurate, parenthood may become reinforcing as parents become able to take pride in their child's accomplishments. This, in turn, enables the child to make a contribution to the family by reinforcing the parents' sense of their own competence in child raising. How one woman dealt with her depression is depicted in Case Illustration 4.

Chronic Sorrow

Even when parents are able to overcome their initial depression about their child's disability, they often still experience feelings of chronic sorrow (Olshansky, 1970). Chronic sorrow refers to parents' periodic mourning for the fantasized normal child their retarded child will never be. These periods of mourning are usually triggered by the child reaching significant ages associated with major milestones for normal children, such as reaching school age, entering the teens, or reaching college age. At these times, parents are more likely to compare their child to his age peers and be especially aware of their child's limitations.

Case Illustration 4

MRS. G's DEPRESSION

J's mother quickly applied a medical model to his mental retardation. She tended to view his problems as incurable and hopeless. This, however, did not last. Mr. G's patience and support during his wife's depression gave her the needed time to alter the way she was treating J. She soon found new sources of encouragement by focusing on the skills he was learning while she employed her own new skills. She stopped comparing J to his sister and to normal children his age. Thus, she began a new relationship with her son, one founded upon new goals, strategies, and expectancies. She began to accept his strengths as well as his limitations and successfully resist her desire to overprotect J to compensate for her feelings of sadness and disappointment.

FAMILY REACTIONS

Up until this point, individual parent reaction has been discussed. It is important to note that parents do not necessarily experience grief in the same way or progress through the stages of grief similarly. Thus, one parent may maintain denial longer while his or her mate is experiencing rage at the injustice of what has befallen them. The differences in their respective grief reactions can result in further stress for parents, as they may consequently feel misunderstood and unsupported by the person closest to them.

This leads to the impact of the birth of a retarded child on the family, for this event places stress not only on individual family members, but also on the family system. The stability of the family system can be looked at as a function of the marital relationship, the network of social ties, and the family's ability to allow their child the freedom necessary to learn and grow.

The Marital Relationship

Just as individuals vary in their ability to cope with stress, so do families. To a significant extent, the ability of a family to initially cope with the stress associated with the birth and parenting of a retarded child is a function of the strength of the marital relationship, of the mutual commitment of the parents to each other and the marriage. When such a commitment is lacking, parents may become emotionally estranged. There are a number of factors associated with raising a retarded child that can work to split parents and isolate them from one another.

The first is the fact that the major responsibility for child care traditionally falls on the mother, as it does with any child. Particularly during the early childhood period, mothers rely extensively on their husbands for emotional support. However, following the birth of a developmentally disabled child, both parents are experiencing a grief reaction and the husband may not be available to provide such support. Having a retarded child often engenders feelings of personal failure and inadequacy, which may seriously compromise parents' ability to support one another.

In addition, the traditional medical approach to serving infants and young children tends to exclude fathers and, in that way, support such defenses as denial and flight. What I am referring to here is the practice of medical professionals of dealing solely with the mother and child. This is not to say that fathers are actively and intentionally excluded, but rather that there is an assumption that care is primarily the mother's concern. Thus, check-ups are scheduled during the father's work hours and few doctors stress the importance of fathers participating in these visits. On the one hand, this can result in the mother feeling that she bears the major responsibility for the child. Mothers I work with frequently voice the wish that their husbands had been included more by medical personnel from the very beginning. On the other hand, fathers often feel left out. These visits afford the mother the opportunity to ask questions and voice fears, and it is not surprising that many mothers come to rely on their pediatricians as an important source of emotional support. The knowledge gained through such visits helps the mother relinquish denial and acknowledge the reality of the diagnosis. To the extent such visits enhance her sense of competence in mothering her retarded child, they also help her accept the diagnosis. When fathers do not participate in these visits, they do not have a similar opportunity to ask questions and share fears. It becomes easier for fathers to continue to deny the extent of their child's problems.

As a result, the mother may feel emotionally isolated from her husband, which may lead her to intensify her bond with her child at the expense of her bond to her husband. Feeling that only she understands their child, she may become enmeshed with and overprotective of the retarded child. The father's resulting feelings of exclusion may prompt him to take flight, either through work or other activities, or by actually leaving.

Another equally significant tension on the marital relationship is the fact that mental retardation is a presence in the life of the family that never disappears. The disability is not one that can be easily understood and accepted, but it must be confronted. It is not a symptom that can be alleviated by a pill. It is not a limitation that can be totally remediated through teaching or simply outgrown. It is both a label that is applied to an individual and a very significant social statement for the parents to confront. Nurturance, proper parenting, and teaching are among the many essentials necessary to the growth of a child who is labeled "mentally retarded," as they are to any child. Yet, the couple usually has no prior experience upon which to rely in parenting the mentally retarded child.

Therefore, all parents of developmentally disabled children can be expected to go through periods of confusion and isolation, and such feelings should not be viewed as pathological. Their ability to resolve these feelings, which tend to separate them, will largely depend on the degree of mutual trust, mutual empathy, and ability to resolve conflict that they established as a couple before the diagnosis.

The Network of Social Ties

Not only do parents at times feel isolated from one another, but they are also liable to feel isolated vis-a-vis their social network. In part, this sense of isolation may result from the family turning inward while their energy is focused on coping with the initial shock that accompanies the diagnosis. Feelings of shame may also prompt social withdrawal as parents blame themselves for their child's disability and shrink from anticipated social censure. Moreover, parental feelings of shame, embarrassment, or sheer physical exhaustion from the strenuous management regimen that is frequently associated with raising a disabled child may lead to decreased involvement with friends, family, and community. When this isolation is combined with feelings of hostility and resentment, available support systems are depleted at a time of greatest need. Mounting isolation from other supporting systems can impel the family to become solely reliant upon itself for emotional nourishment, at a time when emotional resources are drained. At this point, the need for family consensus is near absolute and any deviation by the members will tend to be perceived as rejection. In this climate, family members face great pressure with limited resources and tolerance. This is a crucial time in the life of the family.

Although the reaction of social withdrawal is not necessarily pathological, there is danger if the family experiences the increased stressors with feelings of helplessness and perpetual isolation. Social withdrawal is then prolonged, precluding healthy interaction with a significant social network. This increases the likelihood of both internal family breakdowns in the form of symptom development, and parent-child enmeshment reflected in an overly concerned feeling for the safety of the mentally retarded member.

LETTING GO

The process of letting go is a major issue for parents of retarded children that begins when the child is born, as it does with any child. Through this process, parents foster increasing competence, autonomy, and independence on the part of their child as they prepare him or her to become a responsible adult.

However, for parents of retarded children, this process is complicated by concerns as to what will eventually happen to their child. Perhaps it is, in part, this fear that makes it so difficult for parents of retarded children to let go, for the sense of immediate future raises this issue so early in the child's life and prompts such anxiety that many parents turn away from the issue altogether. Thus, rather than foster competence, autonomy, and independence, such parents strive to protect their child from the larger world.

Other parents, unable to accept their anger and resentment at having a retarded child, defensively become overly protective and devoted to their child. Caring for the retarded child becomes the focus of their time and energy, to the point where the needs of their other children may be neglected. Their lives revolve around their retarded child, and what socializing they enjoy evolves from the contacts they made while caring for their child's needs. For example, they may become active in the local Association for Retarded Citizens. When such activities constitute the parents' total social life, they risk coming to perceive themselves in very narrow terms. They are apt to see themselves solely as parents of a retarded child, rather than maintaining a more elaborated sense of self. For such parents, to let go of their retarded child is to let go of part of themselves because their identities have become so fused with that of their child. Just as the child has become their world, they see themselves as part of their child's world and are unable to envision their child as having a life of his or her own.

Other factors also contribute to the difficulty many parents encounter in letting go of their retarded child. The slowed skill development of the retarded child accentuates parental caretaking. Unable to rely on average developmental norms, parents are less likely to know when it is appropriate to expect more of their child.

In addition, parents' desires to pursue their own interests often go unrealized because of the limited availability of such external supports as respite care and transportation for their child to and from activities. In this respect, extended family systems can be of immense help in enabling the parents to have some life of their own by sharing caretaking responsibilities. Conversely, however, grandparents often undermine the parents' attempt to maintain their own interests and foster their child's autonomy and independence. In their grief over their retarded grandchild, they may accuse parents of being uncaring, and sabotage parents' behavior management strategies by spoiling the child.

Thus, both psychological and environmental factors complicate the process of letting go for parents of mentally retarded children. Many parents fail to plan for their child's future, for to do so necessitates that the parents can let go enough to at least envision their child as having a life without them.

PLANNING FOR THE FUTURE

A family's vision of the future is a major factor affecting its behavior toward a retarded child. As Sarason and Doris (1979) point out, parents of retarded children are concerned about what will happen to their child when they, the parents, die. Obsessed with thoughts of their child facing a difficult, complex, and often hostile world without them, some parents hope their child will die before they do. This sense of future forecasting is not present in families without disabled children.

The intensity of this future vision and the anxiety it generates vary depending on the parents' perception both of their child and of their own role. Normally, parents view their function as preparing their children to become responsible, capable, independent adults. In doing so, parents engage in many roles, such as provider, protector, teacher, manager, and friend. To protect and to nurture one's child are not only the first roles played by parents, but the most basic and elemental. The extent to which other roles also gain importance depends in part on parents' perception of their child's needs. Similarly, the extent to which protection remains a dominant parental role is related to how dependent the parents perceive their child to be. Many parents I have seen have underestimated their child's abilities and consequently overestimated his or her dependency and the need for parental protection. For these families, the vision of immediate future is accompanied by a considerable degree of anxiety as they can discern little life for their child, regardless of his or her age, other than that of which they provide for him or her. Their parental role has expanded little beyond that of nurturance and protection. Such a family is described in Case Illustration 5.

Of the parents I have seen, the P's are not atypical in their inability to plan for their child's future. Although parents' relative ability to let go of their child is certainly a factor affecting their ability to plan, other issues are also important. Parents often put off such planning because of the uncertainty as to what is really best for their child. Even parents whose retarded child has been institutionalized for years have considerable anxiety about their child's future without them, and question whether they've made the best decision. Until recently, options have been limited. Often, the only choice was whether a retarded child, not adult, would be institutionalized or live with a sibling.

The specter of one day being responsible for their retarded brother or sister has been a frightening inevitability for many retarded children's siblings. All too often, they are placed in the role of caretaker while still children themselves, with the result that they feel considerable anger toward both their parents and their retarded sibling. Guilt over these feelings may prompt them to assume lifelong responsibility for their sibling, even when they do not want to do so.

In the last 10 years, the options available to retarded citizens and their parents have increased dramatically (Apolloni, Cappuccilli, & Cooke, 1980). Parents are now confronted with the task of keeping informed of the many programs and services for retarded children and adults. To the traditional problems parents must wrestle with in planning for their child's future, they must now add the task of deciding which programs and services are most appropriate for their child, hoping that one day when they can no longer fulfill this function, someone else will. Parents worry about who this person will be.

It is to address the problem of present and future planning for retarded citizens that organizational guardianship models have evolved. These models, described in the second section of this book, conceptualize guardianship as a relationship between parents, an organization that acts as a guardian, and a retarded citizen. The organization becomes the family's ally and the child's advocate and works in tandem with the parents to ensure the child's best interests. This relationship can relieve parents of much of the anxiety that is associated with thinking of their child's future. They need not envision a stranger taking over responsibility for their child. By working with group guardianship programs, both public and corporate, and benefiting from their professional expertise, parents may become

---

Case Illustration 5

THE P FAMILY

The P family reflects the dynamics often found in families with a mentally retarded child. The P's have six children, the youngest of whom, V, age 15, is multiply handicapped, having cerebral palsy as well as being mentally retarded. They were initially referred because of V's markedly immature behavior. The first meeting was enlightening. As we entered the office to begin the interview, Mr. P took out his comb and proceeded to comb his son's hair. V politely lowered his head to help his father complete the task. Later in the interview, I asked V if he needed help in hygiene skills. He replied emphatically, "No." Despite this fact, V's father habitually combed his son's hair and tied his shoelaces. Mr. P's behavior was prompted not by V's needs, but by his own perfectionism and lack of patience. Mrs. P objected to her husband's behavior, but was unable to alter it. Mr. and Mrs. P had very different expectations for V and since they worked different shifts, there was significant inconsistency in their approach to managing V's behavior.

Mr. and Mrs. P had never discussed V's mental retardation, preferring to focus on his physical disability. They talked freely about his athletic activities and their fear of his falling and hurting himself. Mr. P in particular emphasized V's physical disability and had a great deal of difficulty permitting V opportunities for independent activities such as washing, dressing, and cooking. Mrs. P, on the other hand, expected V to perform these tasks. However, she could not get V to do them, since Mr. P's expectations would often be the deciding factor.

V's language skills were well developed and he was able to express his feelings about individual family members. He felt that his father worried a great deal about him and that this caused his father to have asthma attacks.

Over a period of 2 years, an enmeshed relationship between Mr. P and V was replaced by one that encouraged greater communication between father and son and more significant autonomous behavior by V. Mr. P's asthma attacks were reduced. Mr. and Mrs. P began to develop a social life, while V matured to the point of obtaining a part-time job stacking boxes in a factory after school and working in a sheltered workshop 1 day per week.

The P's obviously differ in the degree to which each can let go of V. Seeing her son as more capable, Mrs. P can envision greater autonomy and independence for him. Mr. P is not yet ready to perceive his son in this way, in part because he has always perceived him as less capable than has Mrs. P. It is also likely that Mr. P's perception of his son is largely determined by his difficulty in letting go of him, of seeing him as a separate individual who grows and develops.

The most sigificant conflict remains unresolved. Mrs. P expects V to eventually move into a group home, while Mr. P has not been able to discuss the issue. V shares his father's fear, stating vehemently that "I am not going into a group home. I'm going with my brother."

---

secure in the knowledge that organizations will continue to work for their retarded child after they are gone. Group guardianship programs can alleviate parents' sense of helplessness about the future because they can provide a vehicle for ensuring long term continuity of care for their retarded child.

REFERENCES

Apolloni, T., Cappuccilli, J., & Cooke, T.P. (eds.). *Achievement in residential services for persons with disabilities: Toward excellence*. Baltimore: University Park Press, 1980.

Coffin, R.P.T. *Primer for America*. New York: The Macmillan Publishing Co., 1943.

Kubler-Ross, E. *On death and dying*. New York: Macmillan Publishing Co., 1969.

Olshansky, S. Chronic sorrow: A response to having a mentally defective child. In: R. Noland (ed.), *Counseling parents of the mentally retarded*. Springfield, IL: Charles C Thomas, 1970.

Sarason, S.B., & Doris, J. The family's view of the future. In: S.B. Sarason & J. Doris, *Educational handicap, public policy, and social history: A broadened perspective on mental retardation*. New York: The Free Press, 1979.

Chapter 7

The Determination of Personal Competence
Important Considerations for
Parents, Service Providers, and Professionals

Nancy J. Marlett

A BRIEF HISTORICAL PERSPECTIVE

Guardianship is a legal mechanism wherein a substitute decision-maker is appointed by a court to act in the best interests of a person who is declared incompetent to make his or her own decisions (Burgdorf, 1980). It is uneasy legislation. A declaration of incompetence abrogates an individual's right to self-determination and denies unimpeded access to legal, medical and contractual services. Although twentieth-century democratic societies place great emphasis on the right to personal freedom of choice, this was not always the case. The recognition of the universality of rights to self-determination has occurred only recently and the historical evolution of trusteeship/guardianship has followed a similar trend, a systematic progression from sanctioned seizure of property, to the protection of property for heirs and family, and ultimately to the protection of the incompetent person's rights regardless of property.

While trusteeship "legislation" dates from 5 B.C., the first modern statute became law in Britain ca. 1300. *De Prerogativa Regis* enabled the king to legally acquire the property and land of persons who were declared incurably incompetent. It also allowed the regent to hold in trust the land and property of persons who were considered temporarily incompetent. Most mental illness was considered curable; mental retardation was not. Because of the potential for abuse inherent in such legislation, due process was initiated and committees were established to administer estates and to assume responsibility for the custody of incompetent persons.

The majority of North American legislation related to guardianship/trusteeship developed from this base. Statutory definitions of incompetence vary, but most include a combination of advanced age, mental retardation, mental illness and often intemperance, with a statement of degree of incompetence.

Procedures for establishing mental incompetence have usually been the responsibility of the medical profession with corroboration from a lay person who has personal knowledge of the individual alleged to be incompetent. In some Canadian jurisdictions the person whose competence is in question is given a court hearing but, more often, the declaration of incompetence is a perfunctory legal procedure. Often, a government official or a committee serves as trustee and is charged with conserving and protecting the mentally incompetent person's assets.

Twentieth-century society has begun to recognize the integrity of all individuals, with resulting benefits to mentally retarded persons. Before the 1950s, mental retardation was synonymous with incompetence. In the 1950s Clarke and Clarke summarized the scientific community's general perception of mentally retarded individuals as being incapable of adapting themselves to anything out of the ordinary . . . only capable of simplest routine tasks under constant supervision. This perspective of permanent incapacity changed in the 1950s when research demonstrated that mentally retarded people were capable of learning and performing manual tasks at a level close to ''normal'' expectations when learning principles were systematically applied (Clarke & Hermelin, 1955). Not only were retarded persons able to perform complex manual tasks, but their intellectual growth followed the same developmental stages as the normal child, albeit at a slower pace (Woodward, 1971).

The acceptance of the principle of normalization (Wolfensberger, 1972), a philosophy that affirms the rights of devalued people to live and to be accepted in their own communities, and the subsequent development of services delivery alternatives (family support, small residences, integrated schooling, workshops, and protected employment) have provided many opportunities for mentally retarded persons to learn new skills. The development of specialized vocational rehabilitation methods has shown that competitive skills are within the range of not just mildly and moderately handicapped individuals, but of severely handicapped persons as well (Brown, 1976; Martin & Flexer, 1976; Peck, Apolloni, & Cooke, 1981). Significant advances have also been made in residential and recreational domains (Apolloni, Cappuccilli, & Cooke, 1980; Beck, Possberg, & Brown, 1977; Marlett, 1979; Wehman, Blankenship, Edwards, Karan, Renzaglia, & Schutz, 1976).

As persons who have been isolated are allowed greater opportunities to become involved in the full spectrum of community life, new challenges are presented. Many have acquired the skills needed to live and work within society, only to be faced with subtle and ambiguous social or financial decisions that, due to their inexperience or lack of appropriate training, cause setbacks.

Both the civil rights movement and normalization have had a dramatic impact on society's acceptance of the legal rights of less able persons. As attitudes have changed, new approaches to the question of guardianship of mentally handicapped persons have been adopted. In the first of these, the Ohio legislature passed the *Protective Services Act* as an alternative to traditional legal guardianship for the mentally retarded or developmentally disabled person (Helsel, 1972; Hodgson, 1973). Three categories of protective service were established under the aegis of the Division of Mental Retardation: guardianship, trusteeship and "protector" to provide "guidance, services, and encouragement in the development of maximum self-reliance" (Helsel, 1972). This act is significant in three respects: first, it recognizes different degrees of guardianship; second, it removes the majority of guardianship cases from the court system to the social welfare system (McLaughlin, 1979); and third, it recognizes the rights of mentally retarded persons to be involved in both the selection of their guardian and the termination of guardianship.

The first Canadian act to reflect the movement toward protection of human rights for disabled persons through guardianship is the Alberta Dependent Adults Act (Government of Alberta, 1978). (For a full description of the act and its practice refer to Chapter 12). Instead of establishing degrees of support, it deals with the issue of the need for selectivity in guardianship by establishing full guardianship in specific contexts (e.g., where to live, licenses, medical consent, social activities.)

A guardian is instructed to exercise his or her power and authority: a) in the best interests of the dependent adult; b) in such a way as to encourage the dependent adult to become capable of caring for himself or herself and of making reasonable judgments in respect of matters relating to his person; and c) in the least restrictive manner (Government of Alberta, 1980).

The act supports the concept of "least restrictive alternatives," in that guardianship is viewed as the course of last resort. Partial guardianship is considered preferable to plenary guardianship, and other advocacy provisions are considered preferable to partial guardianship. The question becomes, "Could this person exercise his rights in these situations without guardianship, as long as supports such as advocacy or professional guidance were available to him?" The review process and the assumption of growth inherent in the act opens possibilities for including developmental expectations or goals in the guardianship order.

As this book testifies, human rights legislation in the area of guardianship of the person has progressed rapidly during the past 5 years. One basic issue persists, however; how is incompetency or the need for a substitute decision-maker determined?

The Alberta Act was a dramatic departure from existing guardianship legislation in which the need for guardianship was synonymous with diagnostic classifications such as "mentally retarded," "senile," "idiot," etc. These classifications were replaced with functional statements such as "unable to care for himself" and "unable to make responsible judgments in respect to all or any matters relating to his person.'' While reflecting a positive trend away from traditional labels, functional statements are open to interpretation and could potentially be applied to a much broader spectrum of persons than was originally intended. The Dependent Adults Act, conceived as human rights legislation to ensure dependent adults' rights to treatment, service, and legal support, could easily become a vehicle for denying the right of self-determination to persons who are ''undesirable'' rather than incompetent.

Issues of Competence

The majority of society's members are considered competent to make their own decisions. Their wishes are respected. A very small number of persons—those who are profoundly retarded or severely psychotic (e.g., catatonic)—are universally considered unable to care for themselves and hence incompetent. The reason for societal concern is the grey area between competence and incompetence where people are either temporarily or partially unable to make decisions for themselves (e.g., children, mentally ill individuals, and mentally retarded individuals). Within this grey area, scientific methods of assessment and a clear definition of competency are needed. In response to this need, the Public Guardian's Office of the Department of Social Services and Community Health (Alberta) commissioned a research study, ''Issues of Competence and the Dependent Adults Act'' (Marlett, 1980). The study sought to define competence in a way that would have meaning for parents, potential guardians, human services professionals, and the judicial system. The study also attempted to establish some insight into the nature of competence in the young mentally retarded adult.

This chapter reviews the outcomes of the Issues of Competence study and other related research. First, it provides an overview of the decision-making domains that are considered in judging an individual's competence. Next, it provides checkpoints for parents and direct service staff to consider when determining whether a person could benefit from the appointment of a guardian. The checkpoints were compiled from studies investigating the skills disabled persons need to make their own decisions. Moreover, these checkpoints may be helpful as instructional targets with mentally retarded individuals for avoiding the eventual need for guardianship. Finally, the chapter shares theoretical and technical information on the determination of incompetence with assessment specialists (physicians, psychologists, social workers, and psychiatrists) who must render professional judgments regarding individuals' competence.

DECISION-MAKING DOMAINS

In the eyes of the law, the term *competence* applies to decisions made regarding an issue at hand. The test of competence varies from one context to another (Meisel, Roth, & Lidz, 1977). A person may be competent in one area and not competent in unfamiliar areas or in making more complex decisions in the same area. For example, a person could be competent to buy records but not to purchase debentures, or competent to agree to a tonsillectomy but not to radical or experimental psychosurgery.

The predetermination of competence prior to an event presents serious problems. The ability to give informed consent, to give evidence, or to contract is determined largely by the individual's experience or exposure to the situation. Until the situation arises, it is almost impossible to determine whether the individual, given the circumstances and adequate training, would be considered competent or incompetent.

In some statutes, legislative reform has moved toward an affirmation of the presumption of competence for mentally retarded individuals by formalizing this principle of selectivity of incompetence, i.e., incompetence in some areas does not preclude competence in other areas.

While acts differ in the areas in which an adult is expected to take care of himself or herself and to make reasonable judgments, the following domains are generally accepted:

Living arrangements
Social activities
Work
Program/training
Legal action
Health care
Personal routines

It is important to understand the responsibilities of the guardian that are implied in each of these decision-making domains.

Living Arrangements

A guardian may be needed to choose where the dependent adult should live when the person is a victim of neglect, abuse, or overprotection, or if the person is unaware of his present living situation and cannot maintain personal routines with the supports available. Under these conditions, a guardian could help the dependent adult gain access to alternatives (e.g., residential training, group homes), monitor the suitability of placement, and ensure that the environment promotes growth and independence.

There are few legislative statements regarding attempts to gain access to less restrictive living conditions, but legal reviews have dealt extensively with involuntary commitment to mental health and mental retardation facilities (Meisel, Roth, & Lidz, 1977). Although many statutes grant the guardian permission to control his or her ward's environment, recent precedents and appeals raise questions regarding a guardian's right to commit a person to an institution.

Socialization

Socialization is a broad category that includes choosing social activities, roommates, friends, etc. Assistance may be indicated when the dependent adult is unable to recognize potential dangers in social situations, or is himself in danger of being exploited by "friends" or roommates. Support may also be useful for increasing the availability of social activities when the dependent adult lives in a situation where social activities are limited.

Although it is generally recognized that some mentally retarded persons may be subject to victimization because of their tendency to be overcompliant and nonassertive, guardianship is not warranted solely on this basis. In fact, most general descriptions of guardianship support the wards' rights to as much personal choice and lifestyle freedom as possible. It is also doubtful whether the guardian could enforce his or her personal choices in the area of socialization if his or her ward refused to be persuaded.

Factors such as the ability to identify one's friends or social activities, behavior consistent with personal standards, and assertion would appear to be important in assessing competence in this area. (Marlett, 1972; Rosen & Kivitz, 1973). Adherence to a specific set of values that agrees with those of the assessor should not be used as a determinant of competence to make choices related to friendships.

Work

A person who has the ability to secure and maintain a job usually cannot be considered incompetent, although there may be grounds for intervention when an employed person is in an exploitive situation and is unable to extricate himself or herself from it. The majority of guardianship actions, however, relate to structured work experiences such as work activity centers, sheltered workshops, group employment, etc. A guardian may be needed to speak on behalf of the ward in the negotiation of salary, working conditions, etc., and to ensure that the ward is covered by unemployment insurance and worker's compensation. A guardian may also facilitate alternatives for work activity and sheltered employment, and establish mechanisms for ongoing review of the ward's performance. It is not the role of a guardian to protect an individual from unrealistic vocational aspirations (inevitably these will be modified by the person's life experiences). The inconsistency of labeling a prospective employee incapable of handling his own affairs but capable of being competitively employed poses a serious legal dilemma, as does the inconsistency in the ability to earn wages without the right to spend without sanction (Kindred, Cohen, Penrod, & Shaffer, 1976; Swadron & Sullivan, 1976).

Measurement of ability to make work-related decisions should not be confused with measurement of potential for success. The issue is not the success of the dependent adult but whether or not he or she should be allowed to make decisions regarding his or her work and related activities.

Program/Training Decisions

The category of program/training decisions includes educational and vocational training as well as various therapies (e.g., physiotherapy, speech therapy, behavior modification programs). A guardian may be useful in a situation where the dependent adult is unable to gain access to an educational or specific treatment program. Guardianship may also be necessary when the dependent adult does not understand the purposes of the training (treatments) or is unable to evaluate either his or her present situation or his or her alternatives, e.g., a guardian may be required to give consent to behavioral control measures, or to advocate changes in the program proposed by the training facility. While the person may understand a behavioral system and, in fact, may use the system to personal advantage (e.g., breaking rules just before "graduation" in order to remain), the overwhelming effect of exposure to a behavior control program is loss of personal control. Behavior control programs are intended to suppress deviant behavior but in so doing they also suppress independent thinking and the ability to make decisions about the rules themselves. Assertion and self-control programs are emerging to address this problem. (See, Mahoney, M.J., & Thoresen, 1974.)

Numerous authors have addressed the issue of informed consent as it relates to treatment. To be considered valid, consent must be voluntary, knowledgeable, and competent (*Kaimowitz* v. *Michigan Department of Mental Health,* 1973; Turnbull, 1977; *Wyatt* v. *Aderholt,* 1974). Voluntary consent assumes an exercise of free will and clearly precludes the existence of overt coercion and force. It is difficult to determine the voluntary nature of consent where coercion is implied because of the dependent situation of the individual and the lack of realistic alternatives. Implied coercion overrules a written consent:

> Involuntarily confined mental patients live in an inherently coercive environment where indirect and subtle psychological coercion has profound effects upon the patient population. They are not able to give voluntarily informed consent because of the inherent inequity of their position (*Kaimowitz* v. *Michigan Department of Mental Health,* 1973).

Knowledgeable consent implies that the professional proposing the intervention has been responsible in presenting alternatives and disclosing risks in a manner that will be understood by the person, whereas competent consent relates to the person's evidenced understanding of the information. The test for competence in informed consent varies with the risk involved, i.e., the test for competence to consent to experimental procedures must be more stringent than that for routine intervention.

Legal Action

Tests of capacity to initiate action, withstand trial, secure defenses, or bring evidence are determined within the context of the case except in situations where, by reasons of insanity, the individual is considered mentally incompetent in all matters. The need for guardianship, in relation to legal action, is often assumed because of the seriousness and complexity of legal action. However, the judicial system has built-in mechanisms to protect those who are unable to instruct counsel or to understand the charges against them (e.g., in civil litigation there are precedents for someone speaking on behalf of an unable person—*amicus ad litum*).

Rights and privileges are meaningless unless they are complemented by an ability to enforce them through the courts. In order to be considered able to bring suit to recover damages, the mentally handicapped person must be able to explain the nature of his injuries and the facts surrounding the incident, and must be able to withstand cross-examination in court. In order to be considered capable of standing trial, a person must have ''sufficient present ability to consult with his lawyer with a reasonable degree of rational understanding and a rational as well as factual understanding of the proceedings against him'' (Roth, Meisel, & Lidz, 1977).

Some statutes also include licenses and contracts within the legal action domain. A contract, a legally binding promise, is an essential part of commercial and financial transactions—agreements to purchase, to lease, to provide service, etc. With few exceptions, contracts are considered voidable rather than void, and only under limited circumstances would the guardian be seen as the legal personality of the ward for the purpose of making contracts. Anyone may enter into a contract if he or she has the capacity to ''understand the nature of the promise made and the obligations arising out of it.'' Mentally handicapped persons are not, by law, considered incapable of contracting. If a mentally retarded adult signs an agreement to purchase a set of 20 platinum pots from a door-to-door salesman because he or she understood he or she was buying the two sample pots, and it is discovered that he or she owes $3,000, he or she has a number of alternatives to recourse. Most jurisdictions have an Unfair Practices Act that specifies when an unfair trade practice has occurred. For example, the Alberta Act declares a contract invalid when:

(i)   the consumer's ability was such that he was not reasonably able to understand the character or nature of that transaction;

(ii) the supplier took unfair advantage of that consumer's inability to understand the character or nature of that consumer transaction (Government of Alberta, 1980,§ 4[1]).

There are few rules or precedents to use in determining when the courts will set aside a contract on the basis of contractual incapacity. Instead, courts generally weigh all of the facts of the particular case and will support a contract even where the person is mentally retarded if he or she had sufficient capacity to comprehend the nature and consequences of the particular agreement.

Assessment of competence in legal areas must be tempered by the realization that the general public is largely unaware of the role of lawyers or the methods needed to make use of legal services. Assessment should therefore relate more to a knowledge of when one has been wronged and potential sources of advice, as opposed to the means by which specific redress may be secured.

Health Care

Health care covers decisions regarding medical, surgical, obstetrical, and dental treatments or procedures. Guardianship may be indicated when the client is unable to give informed consent to a specific treatment or where he or she inconsistently refuses to give consent to a necessary treatment or procedure. In order to measure competence in the area of health care, one must determine whether the individual has an awareness of his or her own health, and the routines and precautions that are necessary to promote and maintain it. It is difficult to measure comprehension of potential health care since most of us do not know the implications of various health care procedures until we have experienced them. We rely instead on a trusted physician to provide the information and advice needed. Those who have been healthy have had less opportunity to learn about health care than those who have had extensive problems.

Consent protects the right of self-determination to undergo or forego treatment. It also provides legal coverage for those offering the services. The need to validate a person's ability to give informed consent to medical treatment, or failing this, to provide alternative mechanisms to informed consent, has been a major impetus for enactment of guardianshp legislation. A variety of legal/medical tests of competency have been advanced (Roth, Meisel, & Lidz, 1977).

Evidencing a Choice   Evidencing a choice is a test set at a very low level and is most respectful of the autonomy of a person's decision-making. Criteria of competence relate to the presence or absence of choice-making behavior, not the quality of the choices that are made. During the research described later in this chapter, young adults willingly agreed to sign documents giving away $5,000 and their body parts on demand because they were asked to do so by a friendly stranger at their training center. For many mentally retarded persons, reliance on "evidencing a choice" as the basis for determining the person's competency is equivalent to carte blanche approval for virtually any procedure.

Reasonable Outcome of Choice   Reasonable outcome of choice is a test that evaluates the person's capacity to reach a "responsible" decision. The emphasis is on outcome, not on the actual decision or how it was reached. This is the test most often used when clear guidelines are not available. Because criteria for evaluation often depend on the personal philosophies and biases of the evaluators, inconsistencies can arise. To understand their own biases about what a mentally retarded individual "should want," evaluators must learn to listen to the person, not to interpret what he or she says in light of their own values.

Choice Based on Rational Reasons   The test of choice based on rational reasons relates to the quality of the person's thinking: is his decision due to, or the product of, irrational thought? It may be argued that this test is conceptually and legally unsound, and can too easily become a global indictment of the competence of mentally disabled persons (Roth, Meisel, & Lidz, 1977). Moreover, there is potential for abuse with persons who do not use sophisticated thought processes to reach decisions. Often, "reasonable" is inadvertently translated to mean abstract or logical reasoning. Many disabled persons think concretely, but this does not mean that the decisions that they reach are invalid. In fact, the majority of decisions are made using these same concrete processes. Evaluators must be careful not to use an overestimated standard when defining the term "reasonable process."

Ability to Understand The ability to understand the risks, benefits, and alternatives of a decision is the test that is most consistent with the law of informed consent. Decision-making need not be rational in either process or outcome, but the person must evidence sufficient ability to understand the information that is essential for making a decision. A major problem with this test is that it relies on unobservable and inferential mental processes rather than on concrete and observable elements of behavior.

One must make certain concessions when using this standard of informed consent. If the person can only work with limited amounts of information, one cannot expect him or her to weigh risks against benefits and consider alternatives at the same time. In order to implement this test of competence, one must be explicit and deal with alternatives systematically. Drawing diagrams, utilizing pictures, and using colored markers to delineate advantages and disadvantages can all help to make this alternative viable for those willing to break the decision down into manageable pieces.

Personal Routines

Guardianship may be indicated when the dependent adult is unaware of his or her surroundings or routine health care needs and appears unable to assert himself or herself in diet, dress, etc. A guardian may also be needed where personal routines are not being maintained or where the client is either completely dependent on established routines or unable to use day-to-day services. In these cases, a guardian might act for his or her ward to secure adequate or specialized routines.

LEGAL SUBSTITUTE DECISION-MAKING: CHECKPOINTS FOR PARENTS AND DIRECT SERVICE STAFF

Parents express a natural concern for the future as their mentally handicapped sons and daughters reach adulthood. While other children grow up, become independent, and establish separate lives, there is a tacit acceptance that mentally handicapped children remain frozen in time. Parents expect their nonhandicapped children to become independent, and accept their children's need and desire to do so. When their child is handicapped, however, parents often assume dependence and thereby may inadvertently shape their child's future.

The mentally handicapped young adult is entering one of the most dramatic growth periods of his or her life. Everyone tends to grow during periods of change and mild stress. Families grow during the preschool and early school years because of the additional stress inherent in raising a handicapped child, but once the hard-won routines of home life and school have been mastered, there follows a long period of relative stability. As the child leaves school, the stress associated with change emerges again. Many studies, including Issues of Competence, have shown that young adulthood is a time of "coming together," i.e., a period when the individual has learned many personal routines and is developing the cognitive skills necessary to meet the challenges of an expanding adult world. Gunsberg calls this growth period a "secondary learning spurt" (Gunsberg, 1973). In the Issues of Competence study, age was the single most important factor in the assessment of functional skills and decision-making ability. There was a dramatic increase in skills between the ages of 18 and 25.

Emerging adulthood must be recognized as a time for extra support and intervention, as is early childhood. As the young person leaves the familiarity and security of school and home and enters into an adult world, parents and direct staff must try to subdue their inclination to protect the young adult from failure and exploitation, and focus on enhancing his or her potential for change and growth. Growth requires some failure as well as the overt testing of established limits. It is normal for a nonhandicapped 12- or 13-year-old to test new ideas that may be contrary to those of his or her parents. But when these adolescent behaviors occur in a young mentally retarded adult, they are viewed as a loss of parental control. Often the parents' fear and dismay are translated into a need to control the potential for failure, to protect the young adult from himself or herself, to restrict and structure his environments. Guardianship is seen by many parents and guardians as the natural extension of this obligation to protect.

Guardianship is not a decision to be reached at age 18 and maintained for life. There is a lifelong process that must begin early in childhood. Handicapped people must be taught the skills needed to become less dependent, their families must be prepared to expect ongoing change and growth, and society must be educated to accept and support handicapped persons as adults who are capable, with some guidance, of making decisions for themselves. This does not mean that the guidance, support, and advocacy that parents provide will not continue to be needed, and limited term guardianship may often be required for a few years as skills are mastered. The following is a compilation of information from a number of studies that investigated the skills disabled persons need in making their own decisions.

Skills for Daily Living

The young adult living at home or in an institution has learned his or her place in the accepted routines. Parents or staff make decisions, as they have for many years, and the young adult with mental retardation is not expected to demonstrate independent routines. This does not mean that these skills could not be learned given adequate training and an environment that expects adult behavior. In fact, even the most seriously retarded person can learn the routines necessary to live, work, and play in the community. If your young adult son or daughter does not do the laundry, buy bread at the local store, make supper, or pay rent, don't despair. While it may be a little late to change your family's routines in order to teach these skills, it can and has been done. One example of a school responding to this need is the Oakley School in Melbourne, Australia. From the age of 12, students enter a school-run house for short respite periods as part of their curriculum (e.g., one weekend/week several times per year). Families see this as an accepted part of growing up and the young person learns with and from his peers. Families are constantly reminded that their child's skills are changing and find it easier to adapt their routines to allow for greater independence (P.M. Ellis, personal communication, September, 1982).

Teaching adult skills and routines may be easy compared to teaching adult attitudes of feeling competent and independent. Attitude change may take years to evolve but it is very important to a discussion of guardianship since it relates to the way in which the handicapped young person approaches life.

Awareness of Likes, Dislikes, and Choices

Unfortunately, home environments, group homes, and institutions frequently accommodate individuals' preferences and dislikes and, as a result, eliminate the need for ongoing choices or decision-making. The ability to choose is a skill that is difficult to acquire without practice. It can be uncomfortable to alter long-established routines in order to create situations where there is both a need and an opportunity to express likes and dislikes, but families and residential programs can teach mentally retarded persons to make reasonable choices by promoting and rewarding the types of behavior that are exemplified in the following questions. Fill in your son's or daughter's name in the blanks.

1. Does _____ express pleasure in certain aspects of his or her daily life? (_____ and _____ have met at the bowling league. They like each other. Does _____ mention his new friend and comment on what he likes about her?)
2. Is _____ able to indicate (perhaps nonverbally) his or her frustration, confusion or displeasure at something that is happening? (While _____ appears to be doing well in a work experience program, her fellow employees won't let her eat with them and she is thinking of quitting the placement. Does she recognize why she is distressed and can she tell you?)
3. Does _____ recognize changes in routines and comment on or question the change? (_____ is usually picked up by bus for school. Today there is a taxi instead. Does he question this?)
4. Does _____ realize when something is amiss and does he or she seek to correct the situation? (_____ dropped her lunch pail getting off the bus and picked it up. At lunch does she realize that there are glass fragments in her thermos?) (_____ is assembling electrical boards and the new batch of blue

wires are too long. Does he connect them anyway, or does he bring this to the attention of his supervisor?)

Establishment of Personal Routines Apart from Family Routines

Development of one's own routines signifies the beginning of independence. Breaking from set family routines usually occurs in late childhood or pre-adolescence, but with the mentally retarded young person, these "breaks" often need encouragement. Families are naturally resistant to change in a routine that has taken a long time to establish. If change is not encouraged, however, a mentally handicapped person will not see himself or herself as owning or controlling his or her own routines, and the routines are more likely to be lost when the familiar supports are not longer present. The following are some indicators of development in this area:

1. Does _____ maintain his or her own routines, e.g., getting breakfast, laying clothes out, etc.? While these routines required training, can he or she now accomplish them independently without being monitored? (_____ now gets up and off to school on her own.)
2. Does _____ change existing routines to suit his or her personal preferences? (_____ rearranged his drawers so that his socks and underwear were in the same drawer, because he always puts them on at the same time.) (_____ calls her friend in the morning and walks to his house so that they will be on the same bus.)
3. Does _____ establish his own routines within familiar situations? (_____ now waits for his friend and they go to Mac's for lunch rather than eat at the work cafeteria.)
4. Does _____ work out a routine to handle a new situation? (_____ has moved to a new group home and asks when the washer and dryer are free so he can always do his laundry on the same night.) (_____ decides to put all her tools in a case so that she doesn't lose them or forget to bring one from the tool room.)

Use of Time Concepts

Temporal anchoring refers to a person's awareness that he or she exists in time and can use past events as a resource when solving problems or making comparisons between present and past situations. It also includes knowledge that he or she will exist in the future and can plan toward it. The person can project hypothetical situations to test the probable outcomes of contemplated actions. The study found temporal anchoring to be the second most powerful factor in decision-making ability after age.

The development of an awareness of time is difficult to teach. There are two possible reasons for this. First, the mentally retarded person's life is full of routines controlled by others, and consequently a sense of time is not important. Second, the mentally handicapped person has a decreased ability to process information. In our study, most of the adults interviewed could simultaneously consider two or three ideas at a time, while those persons who were very handicapped could consider only one or none at all. This is compared with handling four or five pieces of information in the control group (persons who were marginally employed) and six to nine for university students.

Most routine or concrete decisions may be made if two or three ideas can be processed simultaneously, but some training is required. The following skills, if encouraged, should hasten the emergence of the effective use of time concepts and strategies.

1. Does _____ understand daily time sequence—morning routines, going-to-work routines, after-work routines, etc., and can he or she describe present routines, the one preceding and the next one to follow?
2. Does _____ relate what happened at school, at work, etc.?
3. Does _____ use time references in conversation (yesterday, today, later, now, last week, etc.)?
4. Does _____ make reference to similar past events when an event arises, or when making simple decisions?
5. Does _____ mention two or more alternatives when discussing his or her plans? (I'll either go bowling or for coffee tonight.)
6. Does _____ relate to schedules, e.g., find favorite show in "T.V. Times," find events on calendar?
7. Does _____ mention what he plans to do next?
8. Does _____ plan for future events, e.g. tonight, on the weekend, at Christmas break? This includes a range of choice, from "peas or corn for supper" to "which job to take."
9. Can _____ project a decision into the future to assess what might happen? (If I stay home to wash my hair and I don't go to choir practice, I'll look better tomorrow, but I won't know the anthem for Sunday. I would look foolish if I went into the choir or I could stay away from church. But then I'd miss coffee after. I'll go to choir.)

Self-Image as a Capable Person

In decision-making, the young person must see himself or herself as able to solve routine problems. This is a nebulous skill area but it is pervasive in the development of the ability to make one's own decisions. Most retarded young people reach adulthood believing that others will make all important decisions and will take care of them. They have inadvertently been taught to see themselves as incapable. The usual questions, "What would you do if . . . ?" remain academic exercises because they do not really believe that they will have to handle such situations. In fact, even graduates from residential training programs often express disbelief that they are expected to make decisions on their own; they wait for a worker to arrive, or failing this, seek out someone who will make the decision for them. The feeling of "being able" is unfortunately not an automatic result of mastering the skills needed to be independent.

As the young person grows, areas of self-control must be clearly identified and adhered to in order to learn, often from mistakes, that he or she can succeed independent of others. Young persons cannot assume control over all areas of their life at once. Small areas such as lunch making, choice of clothes on Saturday morning, and so on should be turned over gradually with the clear understanding that decisions in these areas belong to the young person. Mistakes made must not be "fixed" up by a well-meaning parent or staff person. This may mean mismatched clothes or lunch without juice, a fate often harder for parents to accept than for the young person.

The following skills will need to be developed before the young person can begin to take responsibility for his or her own actions.

1. Does _____ recognize that his or her actions had an effect on his or her environment? (I made my bed and the room looks different now.)
2. Does _____ recognize his or her part in accidents or mistakes? (I spilled the soup.) (I think this is wrong; the stitches don't look right.)
3. Does _____ recognize his part in doing well? (Look, I just made a house [rather than, did I make a good house, Mom?])
4. Does _____ recognize that he or she can correct mistakes? (Oops, I didn't clean the tub; I'll do it now.)
5. Does _____ take the initiative in routines? (My turn, I'll do it.)
6. Does _____ recognize that he or she needs help? (I did this but it won't work; can you help?) (Maybe Jane could help with my papers.)
7. Does _____ recognize that others like him or her make their own decisions?
8. Does _____ realize that he or she can make his or her own decisions, i.e., does he or she know that he or she is solving a problem? (Just a minute, let me think about that.) Note: This is called metacognition, or the knowledge that a solution can be reached by reasoning or thinking. It is a key indicator that the young person can learn strategies to make his or her own decisions.

Establishing a Support Network

Perhaps one of the most important skills for twentieth-century individuals to possess is the ability to seek out and maintain a support network. A support network functions as an extended family; it becomes the main source of friends and social activities, a haven, and an information resource.

Unfortunately, the long term stability of extended family networks is diminishing. Most of us find small, specific support groups to replace our families. Many elderly and disabled persons are placed in nursing homes because their networks fail (families and neighbors move on, old friends are unable to provide the same support they have given in the past). Mentally retarded adults frequently experience serious problems in developing and changing support systems.

It used to be that graduation from a training center meant graduation into loneliness and a loss of supports and friends. Over time, however, as graduates succeed, they begin to form networks in the community that can provide vital support for each other and new graduates. These networks may not be sanctioned or supported by parents or staff because the network does not reflect their notion of "what's best." Peer support may mean meeting in hangouts or associating with other "lower class" persons that do not reflect the values of staff or parents. But these networks can do what others often fail to do, i.e., provide teaching from a respected peer. Successful graduates should be encouraged to teach their peers, e.g., approved homes run by graduates, buddy systems with graduates, etc. It is important to draw attention to successful role models who are handicapped. Only when a young person knows that someone like himself or herself has been successful can he or she see himself or herself in that role. While a close peer group can provide emotional support, agencies should continue to provide counseling and followup if requested, with full use of generic services.

To prepare the young adult to access and maintain support systems, the following skills need to be cultivated:

1. Does _____ have a friend or friends who share feelings with him or her and do they help one another?
2. Does _____ have a family, school or work friend who is an adult and an outside support (such as a citizen's advocate)? (_____ and Ms. Jones have kept in touch since Grade 6. Now they go for lunch two or three times a year and _____ feels she can call her with problems she has difficulty talking about with her family or workshop supervisor.)
3. Has _____ established and does he or she maintain routine contacts with key resource persons, e.g., physician, social worker (re: finances), public health nurse, etc.? (_____ met Dr. Jones when he had an abdominal cyst while living in a respite care home. Dr. Jones took the time to explain the problem and suggested that _____ drop by in 3 months for a routine checkup. _____ now drops by regularly and _____ and his family feel secure in the knowledge that Dr. Jones knows _____'s history.)
4. Does _____ know others who have been successful in becoming more independent? (Michael has just moved to a supervised apartment. _____ met Michael before he moved and now calls him occasionally to see how he's doing. Michael has just invited _____ over for supper.)

Summary

The issue of guardianship has focused attention on new concerns regarding the ways in which young adults are prepared to live in the community. It is not enough to teach routines. If young people are to become part of the community, they also must be taught the skills needed to make decisions. This need places additional responsibility on families and agencies to work together to change expectations and encourage independent decision-making.

PROFESSIONAL ASSESSMENT OF COMPETENCE

Physicians, psychologists, social workers and psychiatrists are increasingly faced with the difficult task of assessing the need for guardianship under new legislation that incorporates the principles of partial or selective competence and functional definitions of competence. It used to be that the assignment of a diagnostic label of senile dementia, mental retardation, or psychosis was sufficient to designate someone incompetent. This is compatible with the medical interpretation of competence that is broadly based and considers "incompetence" a diagnostic label. If a person's past behavior or present thought processes are found to be irrational or lacking in terms of a designated ingredient, then the person is said to be, *in toto,* incompetent. The move away from "incompetent" as a diagnostic classification has been dramatic during the last 5 to 10 years as we recognized the prejudice inherent in predicting a person's functional capacities from labels.

The psychological perspective of competence shares similar problems with the medical model in that most psychologists have been trained to look for cognitive deficits and deviant thought processes instead of seeking out individual strengths and weaknesses related to decision-making. Undoubtedly, reliance on diagnostic categories has resulted, in part, from an inability to operationally define competence in a way that allows empirical study of situation-specific decision-making.

Global measurements of intelligence have traditionally been relied on to determine competence. Consequently, the notion that competence is synonymous with measured intelligence has been accepted. When assessing an adult who has already been labeled as deficient or deviant by the school system, there is a tendency to assume that these deficiencies will continue in adult environments. There is the potential of missing decision-making skills beneath the more obvious measurable IQ deficits.

Traditional Views of Intelligence

Before adequately assessing competence as it relates to emerging guardianship legislation, traditional views of cognitive processes as they relate to everyday decision-making must be altered, and new ways must be found to deal with the assumption of partial and selective competence. The traditional concept of intelligence derives in large part from the tests that have been used to measure it. Intelligence tests were initially developed to measure school performance, therefore theories of intelligence evolved from the understanding of "school intelligence." The majority of cognitive research continues to be done with university students—the "academic elite." The success of this comfortable, circular system of theory and research has hidden the fact that measured IQ may represent only one part of intelligent behavior, academic intelligence. This is not to say that IQ tests have not been effective in identifying children who perform poorly in school. There is, however, increasing doubt regarding the ability of IQ tests to provide valid information about the selective abilities of the "nonacademic adult."

One of the most dramatic reflections of the fact that IQ tests measure school expectations rather than life expectations is demonstrated in Figure 1, which depicts an internationally consistent pattern of the incidence of mild to moderate intellectual deficits (Marlett, 1979). As shown in Figure 1, there is a sharp rise in the incidence of identified impairment upon entering the school environment and a dramatic drop as the adolescent leaves school. This does not mean that youngsters become retarded upon school entry and are cured by the time they leave, but rather that the process of identifying "mental retardation" detects youngsters who do not learn in the prescribed academic manner. The highest incidence in identified problems occurs at the age of 11–15 when students are expected to reason deductively and perform abstract tasks. Academic problems typically place an emphasis on abstractness and speed of solution. "There is an attitude that there is at least one best answer that can be reached through rational processes based just on the information given in the problem" (Brown & French, 1979).

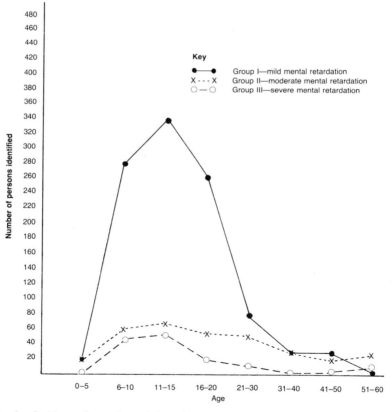

Figure 1. Incidence of mental retardation with no other handicap.

Decisions made in everyday life seldom allow the luxury or, in fact, possess the need for, such isolated problem-solving practices. Decisions are subject to social, personal and environmental pressures. Solutions are often concrete and based more on compromise, intuition, and expedience than on rational thought processes.

There is an increasing need for a more comprehensive psychology of reasoning based on the thinking processes of ordinary people. Concrete decision-making provides a way to prepare young people to use simple and realistic thinking strategies in their everyday decisions and assess their competence in this area. Acknowledgement of the need to broaden definitions from traditional cognitive measures is recognized in the AAMD definition of mental retardation that includes deficits in cognitive abilities and impairment in adaptive behavior (Grossman, 1977). There have been numerous attempts to identify personal competency related to adaptive behavior. Marlett (1972) identified situation-specific factors of residential functioning, vocational functioning, and social education skills. Reynolds (1981) identified three major factors in personal competency—adaptive, cognitive, and affective domains.

Everyday Intelligence

The Issues of Competence project discussed informally in this chapter allowed a unique opportunity to look at the components of everyday intelligence from the perspective of persons not skilled in academic decision-making. Four groups ($n = 25$) were assessed on a battery of tests:

> *Group 1* Mentally retarded adults randomly selected from groups identified by rehabilitation workshops staff as clearly in need of assistance in making day-to-day decisions
>
> *Group 2* Mentally retarded adults randomly selected from three rehabilitation workshops not necessarily in need of assistance in making decisions
>
> *Group 3* Mentally retarded adults who were randomly selected fron graduates of rehabilitation programs who were employed and living either on their own or in group homes
>
> *Group 4* Adults selected from persons who were marginally employed or on public assistance with eighth grade or less education who have not been seen by rehabilitation agencies, i.e., having no history of diagnosed mental retardation

The battery included skills relating to "unable to care for himself," skills relating to "unable to make reasonable judgments," and subject information.

Skills relating to "unable to care for himself" was further defined for the purposes of the study to be demonstrated underfunctioning in those skills necessary to participate in society at an adult level. The Adaptive Functioning Index (AFI) (Marlett, 1979) was chosen as a skill base and the most relevant items from the test were selected by a wide range of parents and staff (community workers, agency staff, public guardian's staff, nurses). Four new domains (*) were added to cover concerns expressed by parents and staff. The resulting skills or behaviors were compiled into a short functional checklist that was then marked by a person familiar with the subject and/or by the subject himself or herself. The skills covered were:

Self-care	Communication
Health care	Consideration
Time management	Handling problems
Housekeeping	Home management*
Transportation	Difficulties in memory*
Shopping	Difficulties in health care*
Budgeting	Difficulties in handling problems*

Part 2 of the test battery, skills relating to "unable to make reasonable judgments" is defined as the demonstrated lack of ability to process information and the inability to make choices and decisions based on that information and previous experience. The tests developed in this section evolved from a hypothetical model that identified four processes in making reasonable judgments: temporal anchoring, information processing, communication, and social judgment.

Temporal Anchoring   Temporal anchoring is the person's understanding of his or her existence in time, i.e., he or she is able to use past information for present and future decisions. It involves: a) short term working memory or memory capacity, i.e., the number of pieces of information that can be manipulated in memory at one time; b) intermediate (5–10 minutes) recall of familiar sounds and instructions; and c) general memory (long term), i.e., the awareness of a useful past, including personal and current information and orientation (where he or she is now, general information); logical memory (recall and comprehension of stories); metamemory (knowledge of what memory is and how to use/improve memory); and sequential memory (knowledge that events happen in a reliable manner).

Information Processing   Information processing is a concrete measurement of the ability to perform simple functional tasks (putting together a flashlight) and perform an unfamiliar task with instruction and demonstration.

Communication   Communication is the ability to make needs known and to understand and use language. This was tested by the subject's ability to express himself (nonverbally and verbally) throughout the test situation. The subject's degree of assertion was tested in a document-signing situation.

Social Judgment   Social judgment, the understanding of social consequences, was tested in a number of ways: a) the subject's ability to plan for the immediate and distant future, b) the subject's knowledge of the community as measured by response to pictures of community situations, c) the subject's response to hypothetical situations that reflect possible events within Section 9 of the Dependent Adults Act (1978), and d) the subject's response to a locus of control questionnaire—the extent to which the subject "chose" the alternative action that reflected accepting responsibility for his own actions.

The third part of the test battery was subject information. This was collected from the person identified as most familiar with the subject. Standardized forms were used as much as possible to facilitate coding of the data. Information was supplied on the level of handicap in five major areas: supervision and care, mobility, communication/socialization, developmental skills, and behavior, as represented in the Level of Handicap Grid (Marlett, 1978). Also supplied was a description of the type of residential, vocational, and leisure programs in which the subject was involved. Of primary concern was the degree of independence allowed and the types of training that were occurring. The Phases of Training form (Marlett, 1973) was adapted for this purpose. Clinical impressions of the need for guardianship in specific sections of the Dependent Adults Act (1978) were recorded by the interviewer based on the impressions gained from the interview and the functional data.

Figure 2 represents a model of competence that emerged from the statistical analyses (Factor Analyses, Discrimination Analyses) of the information gathered. It has three prominent factors: cognitive skills, social knowledge, and functional competence.

Cognitive Skills Cognitive skills include information processing and decision-making, including memory, verbal comprehension, and applied educational skills. The most significant short term working memory variables in this factor were temporal anchoring (understanding of past, present, and future), AFI reading, AFI money, socialization/communications in the Level of Handicap Grid (a quick screening device), and a Functional Checklist Assessment of Budgeting and Home Management. This factor comes close to describing "applied intelligence."

Functional Competence The factor functional competence refers to the ability to perform personal and community-related routines. This factor relates to the statement "unable to care for oneself" in the Dependent Adults Act. There was a little overlap between this and the other two factors. This may be related to the fact that even more severely handicapped individuals can learn routine skills by rote, without awareness of the routine or an appreciation of its purpose. It is also possible that, because this factor was largely based on third party observation, it may have been influenced by rater subjectivity and environmental opportunities. The most significant variables in this factor were self-care, health care, time management, housekeeping, shopping, budgeting, communication, consideration, handling situations, and home management.

Social Knowledge The social knowledge factor deals with how to handle everyday situations. This factor emerged as a hybrid of experience and personality factors. It is related to life experience and the ability to comprehend information and make decisions. Scores on the various sections of a structured interview

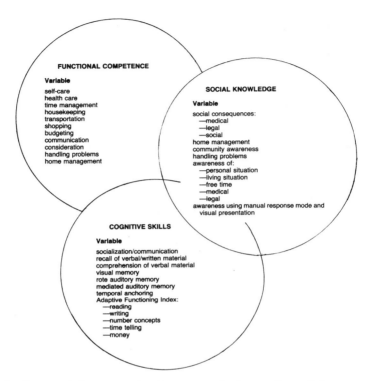

Figure 2. Factor analytic representation of competence for the mentally retarded persons studied in the Issues of Competence project.

relating to everyday situations weighed heavily on this factor as did the community awareness and functional assessment of home management and handling problems sections of the Adaptive Functioning Index.

The three factors identified provide a useful beginning for describing the areas of competence in decision making as they relate to new guardianship legislation, i.e., a) the cognitive skills that allow for information processing and adaptation; b) competence in functional skills; and c) social knowledge and basic decision-making skills. It was anticipated that a fourth factor, clearly related to personal style, i.e., locus of control, assertion, etc. would emerge, but the scores on these variables did not reach significant levels.

Traditionally, intelligence tests have been used to measure an individual's level of a cognitive ability, and they still have some usefulness in instances where formalized assessment is required for court purposes. However, it seems important, when dealing with competence in daily decision-making, to use more practical measures. The results of this and previous studies would suggest that the Social Education Test of the Adaptive Functioning Index (Marlett, 1971) can provide an alternative applied intelligence measure. The Social Education Test scores correlate highly with The Wechsler Adult Intelligence Scale (Wechsler, 1955) full scores but, unlike IQ measures, the Social Education scores correlate with success in training programs (Marlett, 1979).

Multivariate analyses (both discriminate functioning analyses and multiple regression analyses indicated that, of all the items in the cognitive skills factor, temporal anchoring emerged as the best single test of competence. There was a highly significant difference between mean scores in temporal anchoring for the four research groups identified earlier in this section. Temporal anchoring, unlike many of the other cognitive variables, correlated with almost all of the study variables indicating its primal importance in cognitive skills, functional competence, and social knowledge.

It is interesting to note that temporal anchoring correlates most highly ($r = 0.70$) with a standard test of memory capacity, i.e., short term mediated auditory memory. Memory capacity (M space) can be defined as the number of pieces of information that can be retained in conscious memory and acted on. In this study, two methods were utilized to measure memory capacity. The first consisted of repeating digits in backward order, and the second measured visual short term mediated memory.

There was a highly significant difference in the mean M space scores of the four research groups (Anova $F = 25.39, p < 0.0001$; e.g., mean of Group 1 = 1.7; mean of Group 4 = 3.9). The impact of the concept is most evident in the actual score ranges (Group 4 scores range from 3 to 5, whereas Group 1 scores range from 0 to 3 with no overlap).

This study afforded a unique opportunity to investigate the relationships between temporal anchoring, M space, and decision-making abilities. Responses to each of the 20 hypothetical situations (e.g., what would you do if your refrigerator stopped working?) were evaluated in two ways—adequacy of response (content of response) and style of response measured by the grid in Figure 3.

Based on a subset of 85 subjects, mediated short term memory correlated $r = 0.24$ with the volunteered responses, $r = 0.73$ with the ability to give alternatives, $r = 0.60$ with the ability to give integrated responses, and $r = 0.59$ with the ability to give a response that showed initiative on the part of the subject. There is a very strong relationship between the quality of the decision made (alternatives and integration) and mediated short term memory ($p < 0.01$).

It should be noted that while mediated memory has very strong connections with temporal anchoring, quality of decision-making, and other variables, the same does not hold true for rote memory as measured by the ability to repeat numbers in forward order. Repetition of material does not necessarily imply an ability to make relevant decisions.

It must be stressed that although cognitive ability is important in making decisions, it is only one component. Ability to perform functional routines and social awareness are equally important—the top 15 discriminating variables were equally distributed among the three major factors.

RESPONSE STYLE	Score 3 if response	Score 2 if response	Score 1 if response	Score 0 if response
Volunteered	was volunteered	needed to be encouraged	needed to be assisted	no response
Alternatives	provided alternatives	included alternatives with a prompt	was a single response	was irrelevant; not scorable
Integrated	was integrated	included both long range and immediate suggestions	was a rote response	N/A
Socialized	included socialized		was non-socialized	N/A
Initiative	presented initiative response		was a dependent response	N/A

Figure 3. Response style checklist.

Functional skills, the rising star in assessment and curriculum planning for slow learners, are skills that are demonstrated in natural settings and that are necessary (i.e., someone else will have to do them if the individual does not). While functional information is an important source in the determination of competence, it should not be used as the only indicator. There is a direct relationship between environmental encouragement to perform and the perception of ability. Functional assessments are best completed by informed third parties. The professional assessor must select the tool that best meets the needs within a specific act, drawing from the large number of adaptive tests available (Daucette & Freedman, 1950). It is clinically important to secure information from at least two different sources (home, work, group home, etc.). This will provide comparison data on the skills performed in different environments and will also give some idea of rater biases. Bias is an important source of information in that it often delineates expectations for the young adult. Staff marking the majority of items as non-applicable gives a clear indication of the restrictive nature of the program. The functional checklist that resulted from our research combined aspects of the present situation that indicated the need for intervention and a number of behavioral items that best discriminated between those who needed assistance in decision-making and those who were able to make their own decisions. The particular checklist was tailored to the specific areas identified in the Alberta Act (i.e., living arrangements, training programs, etc.); psychologists in other venues could also design reporting systems to reflect the domains identified in their legislation.

Measurement of social knowledge is in its infancy, and the methods that exist have been fraught with all of the rigidities of traditional IQ testing. Assessment of social knowledge should espouse a process rather than a product orientation. That is, instead of assessing adequacy of answers to set questions, the assessor should be free to probe limits and to identify the types of assistance that would be required to handle the situations presented. The structured interview, which is presently being field tested, provides a vehicle to probe decision-making capabilities. Each domain (e.g., living arrangements, social activities, program/training, legal action, medical care) is divided into two sections, as outlined below.

Awareness In the awareness section of each domain, the person is engaged in a conversation about his or her present situation in order to assess general awareness, his or her perception of allowed independence, and his or her ability to evaluate the present situation and its alternatives. The conversation also covers the person's willingness or ability to plan his or her own, and his or her desire for, or awareness of, the need for assistance. The interaction, while structured, allows for a natural, conversational progression and the client is encouraged to participate as fully as possible.

Comprehension Three standard hypothetical situations, selected because they evidenced good discriminative power in the research study, are presented to the client. The style of the response (i.e., alternatives, volunteered, initiative, etc.) and the type of assistance required in reaching a solution is recorded, along with the more traditional content analysis. This type of process assessment has long been advocated by Russian psychologist Vygotsky (1978) and more recently by Feuerstein, Rand, and Hoffman, (1979). The techniques of such assessments require further study but hold promise for measuring a dynamic social competence.

Summary of the Professional Evaluation of Competence

The goal of this section is to encourage professional evaluators to address the inadequacies in traditional assessment as they relate to new guardianship legislation. What is required is assessment of everyday intelligence as it relates to the ability to make decisions. A conceptual model consisting of three major components is proposed for further study. The model consists of tests relating to cognitive skill, functional competence, and social knowledge. This section also encouraged the use of altered testing formats, including the use of functional checklists to detect skills performed in different environments and to detect potential for skill development in those environments; and, the use of tests that would record not only the response but also the assistance required in reaching a solution to the problem. Above all, professionals need to involve the person directly in assessing his or her competence to seek assistance when needed and to make use of the assistance offered.

CONCLUSION

This chapter has discussed some historical and conceptual issues of the measurement of personal competence as it relates to guardianship legislation. The concept of personal competence acts as a lens to focus attention on society's prejudices about the potential of mentally handicapped persons in society. It provides a challenge to everyone—disabled persons, families, service providers, and professionals.

Professionals have been challenged by the abilities of persons with limited intelligence to function adequately within society. Their successes question the validity of traditional IQ intelligence testing. Families and service providers are challenged to re-evaluate their childrearing practices and training approaches in light of the increasing need to teach persons to make choices and to make relevant decisions rather than relying on the teaching of functional routines. The structured nature of teaching approaches needs to be altered, allowing young people to risk, to take chances, and to learn from failure as well as success.

Separately, an understanding of what personal competence entails cannot be reached. What is needed instead is a dynamic research partnership comprised of disabled persons, their families, and the professionals they work with. Within this partnership, the process of how decision-making evolves, particularly from adolescence into adulthood, needs to be studied, using longitudinal studies that have been so helpful in child development research. With the information gathered from longitudinal research, a base can be developed that will lead to greater understanding of the decisions that are required in everyday life. It will also lead to an understanding of how to realistically measure the acquisition of these skills. Measurement of personal competence within guardianship legislation may then achieve validity and thereby prevent unnecessary guardianship and conversely protect those persons who are indeed in need of a substitute decision-maker. The most important determination must be for those persons who are developing decision-making skills and therefore require only temporary arrangements.

The long range goal must be to look at innovative ways to encourage young people to exercise their developing decision-making skills while supporting families and service providers in accepting the mentally retarded young adult's competence to make choices and decisions. This will entail more creative teaching of decision-making strategies or adapting the decision-making process so that even more seriously disabled individuals can exercise control over their lives to the extent that they are able to manage.

Guardianship reform and the difficulties that the judgment of personal competence has engendered may be the impetus needed to force us to address honestly the issues of the mentally handicapped person's place in society.

REFERENCES

Apolloni, T., Cappuccilli, J., & Cooke, T.P. *Achievements in residential services for persons with disabilities: Toward excellence.* Baltimore: University Park Press, 1980.

Beck, V., Possberg, E., & Brown, R.I. Recreation and leisure time as an integral part of rehabilitation programming for the mentally handicapped adult. *REAP,* 1977, *3,* 153–168.

Brown, A.L., & French, L.A. The zone of potential development: Implications for intelligence testing in the year 2000. *Intelligence,* 1979, *3,* 255–273.

Brown, R.I., *The psychology and education of slow learners.* London: Rautledge, Kegan & Paul, 1976.

Burgdorf, R.L., Jr. (ed.). *The legal rights of handicapped persons: Cases, materials and text.* Baltimore: Paul H. Brookes Publishing Co., 1980.

Clarke, A.D.B., & Clarke, A.M. Cognitive changes in the feebleminded. *British Journal of Psychology,* 1954, *45,* 173–179.

Clarke, A.D.B., & Hermelin, B.F. Adult imbeciles, their abilities and training ability. *Lancet,* 1955, *ii,* 337–339.

Daucette, J., & Freedman, R. *Progress test for the developmentally disabled: An evaluation.* Cambridge, MA: ABT Books, 1950.

Feuerstein, R., Rand, Y., & Hoffman, M. *The dynamic assessment of retarded performers: The Learning Potential Assessment Device, theory, instruments, and techniques.* Baltimore: University Park Press, 1979.

Government of Alberta, Dependent Adults Act, 1978.

Government of Alberta, Dependent Adults Act: Chapter D-35 of the Revised Statutes of Alberta, 1980.

Grossman, J. (ed.). *Manual on terminology and classification in mental retardation.* Washington, DC: American Association on Mental Deficiency, 1977.

Gunsberg, H.C. *Social competence and mental handicap: An introduction to social education.* London: Bailliere Tindall, 1973.

Helsel, E.D. *A proposed protective service system for Ohio's developmentally disabled.* Paper prepared for delivery at the AAMD annual conference, Minneapolis, 1972.

Hodgson, R.J. Guardianship of mentally retarded persons—three approaches to a long neglected problem. *Albany Law Review,* 1973, *37,* 3.

Kaimowitz v. Michigan Department of Mental Health, Civil Action 73—19434—AW. (Wayne County, Mich. Cir. Ct., 1973).

Kindred, M., Cohen, J., Penrod, D., & Shaffer, T. (eds.) *The mentally retarded citizen and the law.* New York: The Free Press, 1976.

McLaughlin, P. *Guardianship of the person.* Toronto: National Institute on Mental Retardation, 1979.

Mahoney, M.J., & Thoresen, C.E. *Self control: Power to the person.* Monterey, CA: Brooks/Cole, 1974.

Marlett, N.J. Assessment, training and motivation of the inadequate young adult using the adaptive functioning index. *Western Psychologist,* 1971, *2,* 9–14.

Marlett, N.J. *Effects of discharging adults from Alberta institutions for the retarded to community living situations,* on request of Services for the Handicapped, Calgary, 1972. Unpublished manuscript.

Marlett, N.J. *Adaptive functioning index social education and administration manual.* Calgary: Vocational and Rehabilitation Institute, 1973.

Marlett, N.J. *Level of handicap grid in feasibility study.* Edmonton, Canada: Western Industrial Research Training Center, 1978.

Marlett, N.J. Incentive for independence in residential training for the developmentally handicapped. *Journal of Practical Approaches to Developmental Handicap,* 1979, *3,*(2).

Marlett, N.J. *Issues of competence and the Dependent Adults Act.* Alberta, Canada: Queen's Printer, Alberta Social Service and Community Health, 1980.

Martin, A., & Flener, R. *Three studies on training work skills and work adjustment* (Monograph No. 5). Lubbock: Texas Tech University, Research and Training Center in Mental Retardation, 1976.

Meisel, A., Roth, L.H., & Lidz, C.W. Toward a model of the legal doctrine of informed consent. *American Journal of Psychiatry,* 1977, *143,* 285–289.

Peck, C.A., Apolloni, T., & Cooke, T.P. Rehabilitation services to Americans with mental retardation: A summary of accomplishments in research and program development. In: E.L. Pan, T.E. Becker, & C.L. Vash (eds.), *Annual review of rehabilitation,* Vol. 1. New York: Springer Publishing Co., 1981.

Reynolds, W. Measurement of personal competence of mentally retarded individuals. *American Journal of Mental Deficiency,* 1981, *85,* 368–376.

Rosen, M. & Kivitz, M.S. Beyond normalization: Psychological adjustment. *British Journal of Subnormality,* 1973, *XIX,* 64–70.

Roth, I., Meisel, A., & Lidz, C. Tests of competency to consent to treatment. *American Journal of Psychiatry,* 1977, *134*

Swadron, B., & Sullivan, D.R. *Mental retardation—the law—guardianship.* Toronto: National Institute on Mental Retardation, 1976.

Turnbull, J.R. III. *Consent handbook.* AAMD Special Publication No. 3. Washington, DC: American Association on Mental Deficiency, 1977.

Vygotsky, L.S. *Mind in society: The development of higher psychological process* (M. Cole, V. John Steiner, S. Scribner, and E. Souberman, eds. and trans.). Cambridge, MA: Harvard University Press, 1978).

Wechsler, D. *The measurement and appraisal of adult intelligence* (4th ed.). Baltimore: Williams and Wilkins, 1955.

Wehman, P., Blankenship, N., Edwards, J., Karan, O., Renzaglia, A., & Schutz, R. *Leisure skills and recreation for severely/profoundly handicapped adolescents and adults.* Paper presented at the meeting of the American Association for the Education of the Severely and Profoundly Handicapped, Kansas City, November, 1976.

Wolfensberger, W. *The principle of normalization in human services.* Toronto: National Institute on Mental Retardation, 1972.

Woodward, in Stevens, B. *Teaching the developmentally young.* New York: Day, 1971.

Wyatt v. Aderholt, 368 F.Supp. 383, 1385 (M.D. Ala. 1974).

Chapter 8

Estate Planning for Families with Developmentally Disabled Children

James E. Stuemke

Estate planning is simply the process of establishing a plan to meet the goal of allocating one's financial resources now and in the future. This chapter acquaints parents with the major alternatives for planning their estates in a way that will be maximally beneficial to their disabled child. More detailed expositions on estate planning are available in the appendices at the end of this chapter.

One of the serious problems often raised by severe mental disability is the inability of the disabled person to handle his or her own finances. If action is to be taken, it must be by another person. The alternatives in this regard include:

1. Court appointment of a guardian
2. Creation of a trust based on a formal, written trust instrument
3. Use of a power of attorney
4. Use of forms of concurrent ownership, including the joint bank account
5. Outright transfer of the disabled person's property subject to the transferee's agreement to use the assets for the transferor's benefit
6. A contract for future services, usually for the care of the disabled person
7. Inaction

None of these recourses is an ideal solution in all cases. Each has some advantages and some disadvantages, which vary with the situation.

GUARDIANSHIP

In every jurisdiction a guardian can be appointed for a person who has become incompetent. If the guardian is responsible for managing a ward's resources in order to assure necessary personal care, food, shelter, clothing, medical attention, even recreation, he or she may be known as "guardian of the estate."

There are safeguards intended to protect the interests of the incompetent person. A court may appoint a guardian only after it has first determined that the grounds for appointment are present. Appointment by a court offers some assurance that unsuitable persons will not gain control of the person or property of an incompetent individual, since a guardian continues to be subject to judicial supervision.

Some objections to guardianship rest on the procedure used in the appointment of a guardian. In particular, the public nature of the filing of the required petition and the hearing before a judge can be unpleasant for the close relatives of an incompetent person. Their reluctance to proceed in this manner may be increased if the grounds for appointment are described in distasteful or epithetical terms ("insane," "lunatic," 'feebleminded," etc.) which, in their minds, attach a stigma to the determination of incompetency. They may fear, too, that the procedure itself, or the knowledge of it derived from the notice given, will have an adverse effect on a loved one. From this author's experience, this objection may be exaggerated. Appointment procedures are typically informal, relatively private, and conducted in the most sympathetic manner. Nonetheless, many families find the thought of formal guardianship proceedings unpleasant and wish to avoid them if possible.

The possibility that the court may appoint someone as guardian other than the person the family feels is the best choice can create a strong reaction against guardianship as a solution. Moreover, one of the most valid objections to formal guardianship has to do with the restrictions that are imposed on the actions of a guardian. A guardian's actions are limited by a set of statutory and court-imposed rules that apply to all guardians irrespective of the kind and amount of the ward's assets, the ward's wishes, or the wishes of his or her family.

The basic theory of incompetency, the *total* inability of disabled persons to act for themselves, also gives rise to objections to the appointment of a guardian. An individual may be able to perform the day-to-day acts of living (e.g., buying groceries or paying rent) while clearly needing help with more important matters. Therefore, family members may well be reluctant to have a member declared legally incompetent. Similarly, the need for protection may only be temporary.

THE TRUST

In comparison with the appointment of a guardian, the creation of an *inter vivos* trust (i.e., a trust established during life, as opposed to a testamentary trust that goes into effect after death) offers many advantages; e.g., it does not require the expense of probate fee or the time delay of probate; it assures privacy, in contrast to probate records, which are open; and it provides a period to evaluate the performance of the trustee. It can be established to serve as a standby vehicle to protect in case of disability, without interfering with the ability of the person who created the trust to control his or her property. Or it can be used to provide immediate protection. The creation of a trust is a voluntary action by a property owner. The fact that judicial action is not needed overcomes some of the objections alluded to above vis-a-vis guardianship. The person creating the trust must be competent at the time that the trust is created. However, unlike other alternatives discussed below, once created, the trust has a separate life of its own and doesn't depend on the continuing competency of its creator. This feature alone makes the trust device attractive in circumstances where the need for a protective arrangement arises due to the illness or declining faculties of the parent.

A second advantage of the trust is the opportunity it offers to prepare an agreement customized to the wishes of its creator, including care for others. Furthermore, flexibility and adaptability to future developments can be achieved by giving discretionary powers to others. For example, aspects of management and investment of trust assets are not necessarily predetermined by the creator. They may be left to the discretion of the trustees or to one or more advisors. Similarly, timing, form and amount of distributions and, to some extent, the identity of the recipients, may be made by others in the future. It is sometimes the case that only information that is available in the future allows decisions that more nearly achieve the objectives of the creator.

Parents frequently feel that they must omit their disabled child from their wills because otherwise he or she would lose entitlement to public benefits. It is possible, however, to draft trusts that do not interfere with public health and income maintenance payments. This may be accomplished by establishing a discretionary trust (i.e., all expenditures for the beneficiary are made at the discretion of the trustee) (see Appendix B of Chapter 13 for a model). Any funds held for an individual in a discretionary trust are not included in the $1,500 resource limitation, according to Social Security Claims Manual Section 12520, so long as the beneficiary is not able to revoke the trust or to control the amount or frequency of distributions from the trust. Added safety may be gained by utilizing the following devices.

Special Needs Provisions   It is good to formally inform the trustee that the purpose of the trust is to supplement, not supplant, the beneficiary's public benefits. The trustee may be directed to spend trust assets only for special needs, i.e., those requisite for maintaining the health, safety, and welfare of the beneficiary that are not provided by any public agency.

Sprinkling Provisions   Include several beneficiaries and authorize the trustee to "sprinkle" the funds of the trust among the various beneficiaries. This forces any creditor of the developmentally disabled beneficiary to contend with the interests of the other beneficiaries.

Charitable Remaindermen The government is less likely to challenge a trust if the funds that remain in it are passed to charity upon the death of the disabled person.

Safety Valve Provision The person establishing the trust may direct that the trust be abolished if the law regarding SSI eligibility changes in a way that makes funds in a discretionary trust a countable resource. Parents could direct that the resources in the trust be transferred to another and request that the person named keep and conserve the resources for the benefit of the disabled person.

The primary difficulty in utilizing a trust is the determination of a fiduciary who is both willing to serve and is likely to serve the dependent person. It is generally appropriate to name a succession of individuals backed ultimately by some financial institution. The difficulty lies in identifying someone who is willing to assume the personal responsibility (i.e., a trustee can be held liable if he or she violates certain fiduciary standards) and the administrative expenses (i.e., annual tax reports must be filed) that are associated with serving as a trustee. Parents usually must either find someone who is willing to serve without charge (e.g., a relative or close friend) or must create a trust with sufficient capital to permit the payment of administrative expenses.

THE POWER OF ATTORNEY

A power of attorney is nothing more than a written grant of authority by the person for whom action is to be taken (called the principal) to the person who is to act (called the agent or attorney-in-fact). Powers of attorney are widely used in all kinds of situations where one person wants to have another act for him. Like the trust, the power of attorney may be adapted to satisfy the needs of a particular user. This authority may be limited to a single act, or may be extended to include all legal actions that one person can perform for another. Likewise, it can be limited or unlimited in time. In short, the power of attorney can be as customized to the desires of the person to be acted for as can the trust to those of its creator.

However, in spite of its adaptability, the simplicity of its preparation, and its other advantages, the power of attorney has one major defect. Any authority to act for another person depends on the continuing agreement of that person to such representation. That agreement, in turn, depends on the existence of sufficient capacity to consent. Thus, the person giving the power must be competent at the time he or she originally gives the power to act and must continue to be competent as long as the agent acts. Loss of competency of the principal is said to terminate the agent's authority to act—even though the authority was in terms granted for a period that has not ended and even though the intent that such authority should survive the principal's loss of competency was clearly stated.

Another respect in which the power of attorney differs from the trust is that it can't be used to dispose of the principal's property after death. At the principal's death, his or her assets, including those held by the agent, will be administered as part of his or her estate. If one of the property owner's objectives is to avoid the difficulties of the posthumous disbursement of his or her estate, the use of an *inter vivos* trust, rather than a power of attorney, is needed.

CO-OWNERSHIP

Co-ownership can also be used as a protective device for a person who is or may become mentally impaired. Its use for this purpose rests on the power of a co-owner to act alone under certain circumstances. The terms may vary somewhat, but the term "joint bank account" is commonly used to describe a situation wherein two or more named persons or their survivors may withdraw any balance in the account.

The joint bank account offers several advantages. One of the principal advantages is familiarity. Joint bank accounts are widely used by married couples and others, so most of their characteristics are well known. They are created very simply by a deposit and signatures on the prescribed form. No expense is involved, there is no need for the services of a lawyer, and it is not necessary to go to court. Little, if any, explanation to bank officials of the reasons for opening of such an account is required. However, the joint bank account has limited use. The account gives one co-owner no authority over other assets of the other co-owner nor any role in managing the latter's investments or business transactions. Thus, if the impaired person's assets are extensive, the joint bank account may be a useful tool in performing certain tasks, but may not effectively meet other needs of property management.

Moreover, the joint bank account has some characteristics that can pose serious disadvantages. Its very looseness permits abuse. Either co-owner may withdraw funds at any time. Any understanding that the intended role of one is limited to that of a standby fiduciary is not evident from the terms of the signature card and does not affect the bank's legal responsibilities. If funds are improperly withdrawn and diverted to other uses, redress may be difficult to obtain.

Finally, there is the problem of competency. Establishment of a joint account and deposit of funds are voluntary acts dependent on the consent of a competent person. Once competency is gone, the creation of an account and the deposit and withdrawal of funds belonging solely to the incompetent person cannot be legally based upon his or her consent.

TRANSFER OF PROPERTY TO ANOTHER

Presumably, transfer of property to another is used principally between close relatives. The forms that document the transfer bear no evidence of the party receiving the money to care for the individual. Only where some objection is made, or where a dispute arises over rights in the transferred property or over the nature and extent of the obligations undertaken, does the existence of the arrangement and its nature come to light.

Perhaps because their experience is so largely confined to the unsuccessful use of the device, lawyers and other advisors are unwilling to consider these "secret trusts" as a serious alternative in planning. They are too familiar with the ways that such arrangements can go wrong. Disputes may arise over whether the transferee is or is not performing, or claims may be made to the property based on the transferee's apparent outright ownership. For example, the transferee's creditors may seek to seize the property to satisfy his or her debts or, after his or her death, it may be claimed as personal property and passed to his or her heirs, etc. If the transferee is unwilling or unable to reveal the limited character of his or her interest, the transferor and any other beneficiaries will find it difficult, sometimes impossible, to establish their rights.

As discussed above, the *inter vivos* trust offers many advantages for the management of assets of a disabled person. In comparison with its formal, written counterpart, the advantages of the secret trust are often outweighed by its major defects. The major advantage of the secret trust is that, since the funds in the trust are controlled by another, and thus not directly available to the dependent person, the dependent person may not lose access to government benefits (i.e., income maintenance and medical benefits).

CONTRACTS FOR LIFETIME PERSONAL CARE

Many of those wishing to prepare for the future of a disabled child are primarily concerned about personal care rather than property management. How and where will the loved one be cared for? Can I be sure that my funds will cover the expense of such care? Finding satisfactory answers to these and other questions is often much more important to parents than the question: Who will take over management of my property and finances? An alternative open to parents is to contract with a service provider for the lifetime care and supervision of their child. The primary difficulty with this approach is that the service agency may not outlive the dependent person. Contracts for lifetime personal care share one key weakness with all of the other devices considered so far. They create control over assets that can be used to procure needed personal care or other services for the disabled person. However, they leave the time, place, and manner in which things will be done largely to the discretion of the trustee, guardian, agent, or co-owner. While this may well be deemed sufficient, it is important to keep in mind that any contract that lasts for the life of another creates an open-ended commitment. This is doubly true where the contract imposes an obligation to provide personal care. Both the kind of care required and the length of the period are unpredictable. Thus, the terms of such an agreement demand special scrutiny by both parties.

INACTION

One method of handling the property and financial affairs of a severely disabled person is to do nothing; that is, to allow him or her to continue to act as best he or she can. Indeed, doing nothing may be the most frequent course taken, especially with respect to elderly persons of limited means. If the assets of the disabled person lend themselves either to purely passive retention or to informal management under some pre-existing arrangement, if the cost of care of the disabled person will be underwritten by others, or if the probable period of need is short, inaction is often the course that professional advisors will counsel.

CONCLUSION

The best plan for assuring the future of most disabled children may be a trust that benefits him or her but doesn't deprive him or her of government support because the trustees have complete control of the funds, i.e., a discretionary trust (e.g., see Appendix B and Chapter 13). The purpose of the trust would be to allow the disabled child some extras that government funds will not pay for, e.g., visits with distant relatives, a television, furniture, a trip to the zoo. Unfortunately, unless it is carefully designed, the establishment of such a trust carries with it the danger that the trustee will not appropriately apply the funds in the trust for the benefit of the disabled person. Moreover, when a trust is improperly drafted, it is possible that the assets of the trust may be erroneously included in the trustee's estate and thus subject to takeover by his or her creditors or heirs and thereby fail to accomplish the intended purpose. By far, the safest and most secure approach is the establishment of a discretionary trust, with the assistance of a competent attorney, particularly when the size of the trust is substantial.

Appendix A

RESOURCES FOR ESTATE PLANNING

The Association for the Severely Handicapped
Estate Planning for Parents of Handicapped Children
Foundation for the Handicapped
7010 Roosevelt Way, N.E., Seattle, Washington 98119
(206) 283-4520

"Journey's End" (film—16mm, color, 28 min). Encourages long range planning for death by the preparation of a will, acquiring a knowledge of probate procedures and in specifying funeral arrangements.
Mid-America Resource and Training Center on Aging, 5218 Oak Street, Kansas City, Missouri 64412   (816) 444-1121

Legal First Aid: Your Complete Basic Guide to the Law
By Henry Shain
New York: Funk and Wagnalls, 1975. 366 pp., $4.95, ISBN 0-308-10201-0

Legal Guide
Action for Independent Maturity (AIM), 1225 Connecticut Avenue, N.W., Washington, D.C. 20036

Understanding the Law: An Advocate's Guide to the Law and Developmental Disabilities
By Steven Taylor and Douglas Biklen
Syracuse, NY: Human Policy Press, 1980

"Estate Planning for Families with Developmentally Disabled Children"
Iowa Developmental Disabilities Council, 523 East 12th Street, Des Moines, Iowa 50319
(515) 281-3972

"An Analysis of Estate Planning Devices to Meet the Contingency of Incompetency"
By Professor David Weaver
Washington, D.C.: George Washington University School of Law

Appendix B

BASIC INVENTORY FOR FAMILY ESTATE PLANNING

ASSETS:
   Money—
      Cash on hand .... _____
      Checking account .... _____
      Savings account .... _____
      Certificate of deposit .... _____
   Real estate (appraisal value) .... _____
   Stocks (market value) .... _____
   Bonds (market or accrued value) .... _____
   Life insurance (cash value) .... _____
   Automobiles (market value) .... _____
   Personal property (household, jewelry, etc.) .... _____
   Other—
      _____ .... _____
      _____ .... _____

LIABILITIES:
   Credit cards .... _____
   Loans .... _____
   Home mortgage .... _____
   Others .... _____

As much of the following information as possible should be attached to the will:

Mother's Social Security # _____ Father's Social Security # _____
Military serial number or Veteran's "C" numbers # _____
Railroad retirement number # _____
Civil service employment number # _____
Banks, savings accounts, checking accounts (by location and number):
  # _____   # _____
  _____   _____
  # _____   # _____
  _____   _____

Saftety deposit boxes (locations and numbers of boxes)
  # _____   # _____
  _____   _____

List insurance policies—Life and medical (policy numbers)
  # _____   # _____
  _____   _____

List interested relatives:
Name _____   Name _____
Address _____   Address _____
Phone # _____   Phone # _____

Name _____   Name _____
Address _____   Address _____
Phone # _____   Phone # _____

Any other information that you feel would help an executor or guardian to do his or her duties in assisting a handicapped son or daughter:

_____
_____
_____

Appendix C

COMMON LEGAL TERMS
IN THE FIELD OF ESTATE PLANNING

Administration of estates   The management and settlement of an estate of a deceased or incompetent person.

Administrator   A person appointed by a probate court to administer an estate.

Adult   One who has reached the age of majority and full legal responsibility, as defined in state legal code.

Attorney at law   A person who is formally licensed to give legal advice and try cases in court. In the United States, the term "attorney at law" is synonymous with lawyer, counselor at law, and barrister.

Bequest   A gift of personal property in a will; technically the word "devise" means a gift of real property in a will, but "bequest" is often used synonymously with "devise."

Capacity   The legal ability to sue or be sued based on a person's presumed ability to exercise his or her rights. For example, minors lack capacity to bring lawsuits on their own behalf. A **guardian *ad litem*** may be appointed by a court to represent a person lacking legal capacity to sue or be sued. Capacity also refers to legal or actual ability to make other kinds of decisions.

Co-executor   A person named with one or more persons or corporations in a will to perform the duties of execution of the terms of the will.

Community property   Generally the property acquired by either a husband or wife during their marriage. Community property is only recognized in eight states.

Contribution   The reimbursement of a person who has paid a debt or judgment of others who are also responsible for its payment.

Dependent   A person who must depend on another for support.

Disinherit   To prevent an heir from obtaining possession of one's property after death.

Distribution   In probate this is the apportioning of property according to the will, estate plan or intestate succession.

Domicile   A person's permanent residence.

Emancipation   The independence of a minor from parental control and custody, when such independence gives the minor the legal status of an adult.

Estate   1) The property in which a live person has rights or interests; 2) the property left by a deceased or a bankrupt person.

Execution   1) The fulfilling of any and all legal requirements necessary to make a legal document valid; 2) the enforcement of a legislative or judicial decree or judgment.

Executor (m.) *or* **executrix** (f.)   A person who is appointed by a testator to execute the terms and provisions of the testator's will.

Fiduciary   A person who handles another's money or property in a way that involves confidence and trust.

Gift   The transfer of property from one person to another without any contract or consideration.

Guardian   The person who is legally responsible for the care of another person (and/or his or her property) who is incompetent to act for himself or herself. There are many types of guardians (sometimes also called conservators).

Guardian *ad litem*   The person appointed by a court to represent a person lacking capacity ("incompetent") in litigation.

Handicapped individual   According to federal law, specifically the nondiscrimination provisions of the Rehabilitation Act of 1973, a "handicapped individual" is "any person who (a) has a physical or mental impairment which substantially limits one or more of such person's major life activities, (b) has a record of such impairment, or (c) is regarded as having such an impairment."

Incompetent   A person unable to manage his or her own affairs and discharge his or her responsibilities.

Intestate   Dying without a will.

Joint tenancy   Property owned by two or more persons, all of whom have the right to automatically succeed to the ownership interest of a joint tenant who dies.

Law   A rule of conduct decreed by a judicial tribunal or a formal enactment by a legislative or executive body.

Life estate   The right of a person to use property for the duration of his or her life or for the duration of another's life.

Living trust   An *inter vivos* trust; a trust created during the lifetime of the person creating the trust.

Net   The gross amount of assets, recovery or income, less expenses.

Power of attorney   A written document that gives one the authority to act as another's agent. The power of attorney may be general, in which case the agent can act in all respects for the principal; or special, in which case the agent can only act in limited circumstances for the principal.

Probate   1) The judicial process that proves a will and oversees its execution; 2) the court that oversees the administration of the estates of persons who are legally incompetent—minors, incompetents, and the dead.

Real property   Land and whatever is affixed to it.

Spendthrift trust   A trust that provides for an irresponsible beneficiary to prevent creditors from garnishing any of the trust.

Testamentary   Pertaining to a will or an act that plans for the orderly passing of property at one's death.

Testator (m.) *or* **testatrix** (f.)   A person who makes a will.

Trust   The holding, managing, protecting, and disbursing of property by one person (trustee) for the benefit of another person (beneficiary). The person who creates the trust is called the trustor or a settlor.

Undue influence   That amount of improper influence that overpowers the will of another and induces him or her to act according to the wishes of the person who is exercising the undue influence.

Valid   Legally binding.

Ward   A person who is the subject of a guardianship.

Important Decisions when Planning for the Future Security of a Dependent Family Member

Steven R. Sproger

GUARDIANSHIP DECISIONS

This chapter examines the decisions that a family will need to make when considering guardianship. It appears that if the decision-making is done in a logical order, the first decision would be, "Is guardianship needed at all?"; second, "If guardianship is needed, should it be guardianship of the person, guardianship of the estate, or guardianship of both the person and the estate?"; third, once a decision is made regarding the form of guardianship that is needed, the parents must consider: "Who shall be the guardian—a friend, relative, bank, private agency, or public guardian?"

IS A GUARDIAN NEEDED?

Asking the above questions is easy; it is finding the correct answers that is difficult. The answers really depend on three variables: the mentally retarded individual, the philosophy of the family members, and the amount of money and property (to be) owned or (to be) held in trust on behalf of the mentally retarded individual.

The individual to be protected is the most important factor in considering how much protection is needed. The differences among people classified as "mentally retarded" are greater than the differences between that group and the group classified as normal. Many persons classified as mentally retarded are able to live independent lives, work in competitive employment, and live in their own apartments. On the other hand, there is a small proportion who need considerable help in most tasks of daily living. The latter individuals may need either a plenary guardianship or a limited guardianship with all of the possible powers allocated to the guardian.

Many moderately retarded individuals are in living circumstances where their needs are met and the decisions that must be made are such that the individual is capable of making them. For instance, an individual having seen Group Home A and Group Home B might easily be able to decide, based on his or her feelings for the individuals in the home, which of the two homes he or she prefers. If there is not a severe or chronic medical problem and there is no sizable estate to manage, such an individual may fare very well with merely a representative payee and a family member to advise the individual as needed, if there is an advisor to whom the disabled person will listen. The only difficulties that may be encountered might be in the area of medical care.

In many areas of responsibility, the parents of a profoundly retarded individual can act as if they have been appointed guardians since the community tends not to question the power of parents to make decisions on behalf of a profoundly disabled person. However, some problems exist in the area of medical care when physicians, afraid of malpractice or other suits because of lack of legal consent, refuse to perform a necessary procedure unless consent is legal. If it has been necessary for the parents to countersign or to sign medical consents in place of the retarded individual, it is likely that a guardian will be needed when the parents are no longer able to do so. The parents of a profoundly disabled individual should definitely consult an attorney concerning the needs of their son or daughter after their death since it is highly probable that some form of guardianship will be necessary.

The individual with mild retardation poses a complex problem. Although this person is by definition more competent than a moderately retarded individual, the reader must remember that the dividing lines between these categories are arbitrary. The mildly retarded person is placed more frequently in a position where the limits of his or her competency are tested. In the living situation, the mildy retarded individual may be in an apartment or a semi-independent living situation, while the individual who has moderate retardation is more likely to live in a more supervised setting. In the training or programming area, the person with mild retardation may be "mainstreamed" or integrated with nonretarded individuals for a greater percentage of time and with less supervision than the individual with moderate mental retardation. Here it is helpful to have a social worker, psychologist or other professional give some unbiased, objective view of the individual's strengths and weaknesses.

Parents must exercise caution when deciding whether their retarded child needs a guardian. Research by Kay, Farnham, Karren, Knakal, & Diamond (1972) indicates that despite the differences in the functioning levels of children, parents of retarded individuals tended almost uniformly to believe that their children cannot exercise their legal rights. While the parental desires to protect the retarded individual may be motivated by love and caring, the message that the individual receives is that the parent has very little faith in his or her ability. Parents should consider both the effects of instituting guardianship—including the negative effects—and the effects of not doing so, and determine whether the absence of guardianship will be permanently detrimental to the mildly retarded individual. If the absence of guardianship will merely cause inconvenience and discomfort, guardianship should not be established. Guardianship robs a person of certain rights to control his or her own life and can inhibit developmental growth and impair self-esteem. If, on the other hand, the individual is going down a path of self-destruction that is severe and/or permanent and guardianship might remedy the situation, the family should pursue this with their attorney.

Problems Guardianship Cannot Solve

It should be pointed out that there are some problems that guardianship cannot solve. For instance, guardianship will not instill a moral code if that has not previously been done. In addition, many of the powers given to the guardian presuppose the absence of active opposition on the part of the ward. For instance, in many states the guardian can designate where a ward will live. However, making the ward stay there is another matter, and many living arrangements will not accept an individual who does not want to be in their facility. Further, many states limit the discretion of the guardian in choosing the type of facility to which the ward will be sent. Often, public institutions are restricted to only those who are dangerous or who are profoundly retarded.

Another problem for which guardianship is not the solution is sterilization. The laws of most states and/or case law tend to forbid sterilization of individuals who are not competent to give informed consent themselves. If the court will not allow substitute decision-making for sterilization, it is even less likely to do so for abortion. Both the court and the Constitution of the United States agree that sterilization and abortion, and any area that is similarly personal and private, is not within the domain of a substitute decision-maker.

WHICH GUARDIANSHIP IS NEEDED?

Once it is decided that a guardian is needed, the next decision is to determine which form of guardianship is needed: guardianship of the person, of the estate, or of both the person and the estate. Of course, if the state in which the ward resides has a limited guardianship (only 16 states at this time have such a guardianship) then the powers needed by the guardian must be decided upon as well.

Guardian of the Estate

One of the first concerns in determining which type of guardianship is needed is defining the term "estate." If the ward only has some form of income such as Supplemental Security Income and does not possess a large amount of money or real estate, then there is no need to consider appointing a guardian of the estate. A representative payee can be selected for the Supplemental Security Income if the ward is unable to handle even that amount of money. Generally, a physician or psychologist may certify that an individual is unable to manage his or her Supplemental Security Income grant. If the Social Security Administration claims representative concurs, a person or organization may be selected to act as a representative payee. The payee must accept this responsibility with the understanding that the Social Security Administration will require an accounting of the money on an annual basis.

For a large number of people, their "estate" consists of a home, some savings, and life insurance. A question to consider might be: "Can the ward's share of the estate be converted into a lifetime income sufficient to sustain the ward in the type of living arrangement that he or she is likely to have?" There is also the question of whether to put the estate in a trust for the ward or to appoint a guardian of the estate. Further, consideration has to be given to the use of public funds to support the ward when the trust is unable to do so.

One of the primary advantages of guardianship of an estate can also be a disadvantage. The guardianship of an estate requires court approval prior to any major transaction such as disposing of property. This can result in significant fees for attorneys, but nevertheless, it can result in less cost to the estate than would a greedy guardian or dishonest executor of a trust. For those estates where legal fees may imperil the estate's ability to maintain the individual, careful discussions with an attorney will be necessary to determine the least expensive yet adequate means of protecting the estate.

If the estate is not likely to maintain the ward for the ward's lifetime, then consideration must be given to other sources of funds to support the ward. One government program that received considerable publicity in 1983 is the Social Security program. Under Social Security, certain individuals are covered if they have previously paid in a specific amount for a specific number of quarters of a year. Their dependents such as minor children or what the Social Security Administration calls "Disabled Adult Child" can also be covered if a parent is covered. It is important to know that if the "wage earner" who paid into the program is eligible to receive money from it, then the dependents are also eligible, regardless of any other income (except wages) or property owned by either individual. Amounts of benefits due the ward in the event of the disability, retirement, or death of the wage earner can be determined by the nearest Social Security office. (This coverage is to be distinguished from SSI, which can be received by the dependent adult during his parents' lifetime, but only if his assets—money and property—do not exceed a very low limit.)

Based on this information, the parents could take another look at the estate to determine if the combination of Social Security insurance benefits, private insurance, and the remainder of the estate will be sufficient to maintain the ward for life. The problems encountered by a family that has an estate that is not adequate to maintain their ward for life without public assistance programs are enormous. Parents must decide whether to disinherit the disabled child and leave the entire estate to a brother or sister along with a moral obligation to the disabled child, to leave an outright bequest for the disabled child knowing that for a period of time the disabled child will not be eligible for public assistance of any sort, or to find some other method of leaving money for the disabled child for those things that are not provided by public funds. There are benefits and disadvantages to each approach, again making the decision more difficult.

The advantages of disinheritance are that the family does not risk the disabled child becoming ineligible for public funding. The disadvantage is that the disabled child then is totally dependent on public funding and may feel that he or she was somehow slighted. The advantage of leaving the estate to the nondisabled child with a clear moral obligation to provide for the disabled child is that the disabled person's public funds are not endangered. Another disadvantage is that a moral obligation is not, in fact, binding on the nondisabled child after the death of the parents. One never knows when a case of ''acute greediness'' will set in. Further, as the nondisabled child's property, the bequest is subject to taxes at the income level of the nondisabled child. And if the bequest itself is not subject to taxes in the state where the nondisabled child lives, the interest on the estate is subject to taxes.

Another option to disinheritance is creating a guardianship or a conservatorship of the estate. The conservatorship of the estate has the advantage of having the court protect the expenditure of funds. It has the disadvantage of not allowing rapid sale or purchase of property and, therefore, not allowing the conservator of the estate to invest the principal to the best advantage. Another disadvantage is that since a hearing is generally required prior to expenditures, an attorney is also required frequently. This can be expensive and can slow the process of investing or devesting property of the estate to the maximum advantage. Finally, the guardianship or conservatorship of the estate does not protect the disabled person from having the estate considered a means of support and thereby making him or her ineligible for public assistance.

Trusts

The last choice, and one generally recommended by the majority of attorneys, is the *trust*. It has several advantages, one being that the developmentally disabled person is not slighted by being left out of the distribution. Second, a properly drafted trust generally does not jeopardize the individual's public funding. Third, a trust is generally less expensive to implement and to maintain than a conservatorship of an estate because of the lesser amount of legal fee involved. Fourth, a trust allows or can allow the executor necessary flexibility to act quickly to buy or sell property in order to invest the money of the estate in the best way possible. Fifth, the person for whom the trust is held can have funding set aside to meet the needs that are not met by public funding. Sixth, the purchasing power available on behalf of the disabled person protects him or her from the many changes that occur in the public systems. (For instance, the author was once employed by a county welfare department in California and recalls a time when the only dental work funded by the Medicaid program was extraction of teeth. No services to keep the teeth and repair them were funded by the program.)

The disadvantages of trusts are that trusts do not enjoy the same protection that conservatorship of estates enjoy because they are not closely monitored by the courts. Second, protecting the trust from attachment or use to meet the basic needs of the disabled person generally requires that the disabled person live at the same level of subsistence as a person receiving the public funds. While the provisions of a trust might protect it from attachment by the government to reimburse itself for the care of the disabled person, it is unlikely that any funds can be released to purchase better housing, for instance, without being deducted from the Supplemental Security Income grant.

Third, the trust that assures that the disabled person remains eligible for public funding relegates that disabled person to the status of "welfare recipient." Supplemental Security Income is a welfare program, funded by the taxpayers of the country and the state wherein the individual resides. It gives the person who is stigmatized by mental retardation a further stigma of being a welfare recipient.

The national Association for Retarded Citizens (ARC), in its brochure, "How to Provide for Their Future" (Association for Retarded Citizens National Insurance Committee, 1978) clearly recommends this approach and recommends numerous ways for families to be sure that they never reimburse the taxpayers for the care of their disabled person. The author suggests consideration of this approach as well as the approach of providing fairly for both the disabled person and the taxpayers. There are negative side effects to using public assistance funds, such as the emotional effect of being a public assistance recipient, particularly if the family has always stressed independence and self-sufficiency. Use of public funds may be unavoidable because of the extensive needs of the disabled person. In this case, it has to be accepted by the family and by the disabled person as a provision by the citizens of the country to provide for the special needs of its disabled population.

WHO SHALL BE THE GUARDIAN?

Once the decisions are made regarding the two questions, a) "Is a guardian of the person necessary?" and (b) "Is the estate in need of a conservator?", the next question is: "Who shall fulfill these roles?" The first thing one has to recognize is that the roles are different for a guardian of the person than for a conservator of the estate. The conservator of the estate needs to be astute in matters of handling funds, possibly in the matter of investing the money to maintain or increase the principal of the estate. At the same time, the conservator of the estate needs to be cognizant of the fact that the purpose of the estate is to maintain the ward and not merely to increase the assets for the benefit of the person who inherits the estate at the death of the ward.

The guardian of the person, on the other hand, has a very different role. The guardian must visit the ward regularly, regardless of where the ward lives, to assure that the ward has the best possible care, training program, recreational and social activities, and is able to exercise those rights within the ward's abilities that have not been removed by the court. In short, the job of the guardian is to assure that the ward has the best quality of life, the greatest opportunity for personal growth, and the maximum amount of independence possible given the ward's abilities and finances.

Both the guardian of the person and the conservator of the estate should have the least possible conflict of interest in their role. Reality usually does not allow the total absence of a conflict of interest, but it is possible to minimize these conflicts considerably. For instance, while a bank might manage an estate in a competent and honest way, the amount of payment that the bank receives is generally dependent on the principal of the estate, therefore creating a conflict between supporting the ward and adding to the estate. A relative attempting this same task might have a conflict of interest if he or she were in line to inherit the estate on the death of the conservatee.

Relatives as Guardians

The advantages of relatives acting as guardian are many. First, it is probable that the relative has considerable knowledge about the disabled ward. There is also a high probability that the relative has a longstanding feeling for and concern about the ward. Yet another advantage is the possibility that the relative is only responsible to serve as guardian to a single person and would, therefore, have the time and energy to attend to the ward's needs.

A disadvantage of a family member acting as guardian is the aforementioned possibility that there will be a conflict of interest between the ward's interest and the guardian's. This conflict could be more than financial. For instance, a ward in an institution poses fewer inconveniences for a guardian than does the same ward in a community residence. A ward in the community may need assistance with budgeting, medical decisions, even social decisions or may need protection from salespersons, while the ward in an institution may not require as frequent assistance. In many other ways, the use of more restrictive alternatives generally is easier than the emotional strain and worry associated with encouraging self-sufficiency and independence.

Another drawback of a family member acting as guardian is that the family member may not be aware of the various community programs, placement facilities, and other resources that could help the ward. This situation can be ameliorated if the guardian is able to find an agency that is knowledgeable of resources for persons with developmental disabilities or a knowledgeable professional to serve as advisor. California, for instance, has a system of regional centers that provide assessments and assistance with program planning for persons with developmental disabilities and their parents or guardians. The regional centers also assist with residential placements and monitor the quality of residential placements and programs for adults who are no longer eligible for public school programs. Because of their ongoing monitoring function, the regional centers have staff members who are very familiar with the facilities and programs in the centers' areas. Other states have similar services but the titles vary widely.

Public Guardians

For the purpose of this discussion, public guardians are employees of public organizations who become or act as the guardian. Only approximately one third of the states in the United States, and a few provinces of Canada (such as Alberta), have provisions for public guardians. The advantages of a public guardian derive from the professional staffing of such offices. The agency will continue to function even though the individual guardian may move to a different job, lending a certain amount of continuity. The records kept by the organization should allow the new person who will be acting as guardian to pick up where the previous person left off. Another advantage is the objectivity with which the staff person can view the individual who is the ward. Sometimes family members are not able to view the ward objectively, especially siblings who grew up with the ward and remember earlier problems. The objectivity that the professional maintains may make it easier for the professional to allow the ward to take realistic risks, furthering the ward's independence. Another advantage of a public guardian is efficient administration and greater expertise in the field of developmental disabilities. Family members serving as guardian may not know much more about developmental disabilities than their knowledge of the characteristics of their particular ward, while the group or organization that has been working with persons with developmental disabilities for years has acquired cumulative expertise that is difficult for any individual to duplicate. Yet another advantage of the public guardian is the ability to coordinate the guardian's services with the other social service programs that are available to the ward. Such a coordinated approach is not possible with fragmented private guardians. The final advantage of the public guardian is that, in fact, there may be no alternative. For individuals with limited estates, and families that have spread out geographically, there may be no available person or agency to accept the role of guardian except a public agency. As a matter of fact, most public guardianship services were envisioned as a last resort service and many have in their legislation a statement that the public guardian cannot be used if there is an alternative to public guardianship.

The disadvantages of a public guardian are many, and are similar to those of any group guardianship. In a sense, the advantages previously quoted have some double-edged kinds of disadvantages to them. For instance, the objectivity, which could be a great asset to a guardian, can be a great detriment if it means that there is complete anonymity and impersonal conduct. The National Center for Law and the Handicapped (1977) stated:

> Guardianship necessarily demands what is perhaps the most personal of human relationships—the exercise of one's decision making and individual rights by another individual or group. Recent exposure of the impersonality and dehumanizing aspects of mental institutions should provide sufficient warning that individual human needs cannot effectively be administered on a large-scale institutional basis. Personal interaction between the ward and the guardian is a prerequisite to the ward's mental and social functioning and growth.

In this age of fiscal constraint and shrinking public expenditures, the effects upon the persons served by public agencies are not always well considered when budget cuts are envisioned. The size of a public employee's caseload is generally inversely related to the amount of services that the public employee can provide to any one individual. As the workload of the person charged with actual responsibility for the ward increases, the tendency will be to do less and less for each individual. One possible outcome might be that the guardian would find it easier to manage a caseload if all of his or her wards were in institutions, where most of their day-to-day decision-making was delegated to the director of the institution. The other extreme is possible as well. An overworked public guardian, unable to respond to the needs of a ward, may inadvertently allow the ward to take excessive chances. Another disadvantage is the possibility that public guardianship may be "an all too easy short cut for an overworked and frustrated service provider who does not have the time, skill, or energy to obtain clients' consent and cooperation" (Frolik, 1981).

The most serious criticism of public guardianship revolves around the potential of conflicts of interest. In Chapter 12, goals that were proposed by the individuals who designed California's Public Guardianship program are listed. One of these goals was for the service provider and the guardian's office to be separate in an attempt to avoid conflicts of interest. Assuring that all service agencies provide the maximum appropriate level of needed services to the ward is one of the primary responsibilities of a guardian. The guardian cannot do this if he or she is employed by the agency that provides or funds direct services. A conflict will exist between the needs of the agency to save money and the needs of the ward to have the best possible services. For example, in California, the regional centers have been delegated the responsibility of guardianship by the director of developmental services. The director of developmental services is the administrator of both the state hospital and the community services systems, and a person may become a ward in either location. Since the regional centers provide funding to pay for services in the community but do not provide funding for services in the state hospitals, the guardian who is a regional center employee is in a conflict of interest between the interest of the ward and the interests of the regional center. The author has been in that position and has been able to successfully move numerous wards out of the state hospital, but not all regional centers are equally supportive of deinstitutionalization.

Another possible disadvantage is that when governments are seeking additional funds, they may seize upon the estates of the wards as a source for funding. Just as the costs of other state services have risen, so will the cost of guardianship services.

Corporate Guardians

Corporate guardians, generally chartered nonprofit organizations such as Associations for Retarded Citizens and private specially organized groups, are also capable of serving as guardians in most states. These types of guardians offer most of the same advantages of a public guardian with the exception of being less able to coordinate with public services. In addition, they may offer various other advantages dependent on such factors as the size of the organization, the staffing of the organization, and its administration, etc. These advantages, including objectivity, expertise, continuity, and ready availability, have been discussed in reference to the public guardianships.

The employee of a private organization can remain objective, just as the employee of a public organization can, because the employee does not have the emotional attachment to the ward that a family member would have. This objectivity can allow a private organization to help the ward to become independent by allowing the ward to take realistic risks. The employees of a corporate guardianship program can have the same expertise as those in the public guardian's office. As in the case of some public guardians, private guardianship organizations sometimes operate facilities and programs and thus have available knowledge of both residential facilities and training programs. Moreover, like the public organizations, private organizations offer continuity of services despite the resignation of any particular employee. Even when the director changes, the organization is likely to continue without any break in continuity. Again, agency records and supervisors' knowledge would allow a new guardian to take up the role of the old with no change in service.

The disadvantages of a group guardian also parallel the disadvantages of a public guardian. The objectivity that can be helpful in allowing the retarded person to take reasonable risks carried to an extreme would allow unreasonable risks. Continuity of the agency might not assure continuity of a specific guardian since, depending upon economic circumstances, employee turnover could be very high. Agencies' availability could become restricted due to funding cuts in both the public and the private spheres. Further, cuts in funding for a private organization could result in increases of the workload of the individuals who actually provide the guardianship services to unmanageable sizes, with the attendant risks of making the job easier by placing the wards in settings that are more restrictive than necessary. Overprotection could also occur for other reasons, such as a fear of liability or a misguided belief that institutional placement is appropriate for such persons.

Finally, the problem of conflict of interests cited in regard to a public guardian can be just as true of a private group guardian. For instance, if the local Association for Retarded Citizens acts as guardian of an individual who is living in a facility that is operated by the Association and attends a workshop program that is also operated by the Association, it would be impossible to conceive of the guardian as being totally free to advocate in the best interest of the ward. Most public guardians at least have the advantage of a civil service system that precludes loss of employment when they act as advocates for their wards. Private group guardians generally have no such protection, and could be readily replaced. Even if everyone involved was entirely ethical and there were no threats of termination, as is the case in most situations, there would still be the problem of loyalty to and lack of objectivity about the organization. To whatever degree the potential for conflict of interest exists, the family member planning for his other disabled relative's future must consider it and take steps to counter it.

SUMMARY

What is one to do? The author has posed more questions than answers since it appears that guardianship is a problem without a simple solution. But while it is true that there are no easy answers, some alternatives do exist. The reader has taken the first step by reviewing information on the subject. The next step is to seek individual advice. Since the issues that surround guardianship decisions are both legal and personal, the author suggests that both an attorney and a professional involved in the field of mental retardation be consulted prior to establishing a written plan. Some possible ideas for discussion might be: a) Is conservatorship of the estate or a trust appropriate for handling the finances? b) Is a guardian or conservator of the estate needed? c) Is there a family member or friend willing and able to be guardian of the person and/or conservator of the estate? d) If no relative is available to be the guardian of the person or conservator of the estate, is there a private organization that is not a service provider but has guardianship expertise and knowledge of resources for persons with developmental disabilities available to act as guardian and/or conservator? Finally, e) If no private sector alternative exists, is there a public guardianship program available?

It is hoped that these guidelines will assist families in planning for their children who have developmental disabilities. Although there is no absolute certainty in this world, thoughtful advance planning can account for most possibilities.

REFERENCES

Association for Retarded Citizens National Insurance Committee. *How to provide for their future*. Arlington, TX: Association for Retarded Citizens, 1978.

Frolik, L.A. Plenary guardianship: An analysis, a critique and a proposal for reform. *Arizona Law Review*, 1981 *23*, 600–660.

Kay, H., Farnham, L.J., Karren, B.D., Knakal, J., & Diamond, P.M. Legal planning for the mentally retarded: The California experience. *California Law Review*, 1972, *60*, 438–529.

National Center for Law and the Handicapped. *Guardianship of the mentally impaired; a critical analysis*. South Bend, IN: National Center for Law and the Handicapped, Inc., 1977.

GROUP
GUARDIANSHIP
PROGRAMS

Chapter 10

Design Elements of Corporate Guardianship Models

Tony Apolloni

The second section of this book was written to share information on emerging approaches to improving the provision of group guardianship services, i.e., public and corporate programs. It is widely accepted that relatives and friends should be the first choice when selecting a guardian. But there must be a guardian for every person judged in need of guardianship. Many potential wards lack relatives or friends who are willing to step forward and act as guardian and hence some other arrangement is needed. Public and corporate guardianship models offer alternatives when this situation arises.

It is not this author's intent to imply that public and corporate guardianship programs should or will totally replace traditional approaches to guardianship. Comprehensive guardianship services necessarily involve family members, friends, community professionals (e.g., lawyers and bankers), and public guardians. Group guardianship programs, which generally rely on paid staff, are not likely to fully replace the loving attention of family members and friends. Moreover, public and private agencies will find it difficult to afford the provision of guardianship services for the large number of orphaned and abandoned persons who cannot pay for such services. Public and corporate guardianship programs should be seen as supplementary, and in some cases complementary, to family and friends: group programs can serve as guardian when no other alternative exists, or they can advise family members or friends appointed to act as guardian. Both public and corporate models offer a number of significant advantages. The chapters in this section review these advantages (also see Chapter 11) and provide guidance to those interested in developing such programs.

GROUP GUARDIANSHIP SERVICES

At least 13 states currently offer some form of public guardianship. The first public guardianship program was begun in Minnesota in 1917 and over the years the public welfare department has acted as guardian to thousands of persons with mental retardation, both residents of institutions and those residing in local communities. Another early, comprehensive approach to public guardianship was implemented in California. Steven Sproger (Chapter 11) describes the history and current status of California's public guardianship program. His chapter is followed by Joel Christie's on the Alberta public guardianship model (Chapter 12), perhaps the most up-to-date public approach to guardianship.

The next four chapters, by Ervin Larsen (Chapter 13), Aloysius Soenneker (Chapter 14), Henry Widrich (Chapter 15), and Lloyd Munneke (Chapter 16), describe several of the more advanced guardianship models. Examples of corporate guardianship programs can be found in several locations across the United States. These programs generally consist of volunteer boards and paid staff. They provide protection and advocacy services to persons with disabilities (often in accordance with agreements that are made between the corporation and the disabled person's parents).

CORPORATE GUARDIANSHIP

This chapter focuses particularly on corporate guardianship programs since this phenomenon is extremely recent and little understood. There is considerable variety in the design of existing corporate guardianship programs and the entire field is too embryonic to make definitive statements on the best approaches for dealing with critical program features. It is possible, however, to categorize the most salient features of existing models and to relate options that warrant the consideration of those who wish to develop similar programs.

The purpose of guardianship corporations differs from that of most nonprofit corporations in one fundamental respect: corporate guardianship services must be planned to last forever, or at least until the death of the last remaining beneficiary. Unlike most human service programs, they are not limited term arrangements. Corporate guardianship programs make lifetime commitments to parents and their children. Some beneficiaries may well outlive their parents by 50 years or more. The requirement to design for long term existence makes it impossible to develop experimental prototypes that may be blithely dissolved if shown to be unsuccessful.

This chapter intends to be useful to those who are planning corporate guardianship programs. It begins by summarizing the major decisions that must be made by those who wish to initiate corporate guardianship services. These decisions are organized under three categories: organizational design decisions, service design decisions, and fiscal design decisions. The second part of the chapter summarizes the nature and status of the eleven programs that this author has been able to identify in the United States that act as corporate guardian for persons with developmental disabilities. Descriptions are also presented of five additional programs that do not formally accept guardianship status but nonetheless provide services to developmentally disabled persons that are very similar to those typically available from corporate guardianship programs. This information, augmented perhaps by direct communication with the programs (Appendix A), should give the reader a sound understanding of the alternative approaches to corporate guardianship that are currently in operation. It is extremely important for the reader to understand and comply with the legal requirements of his or her state, however. There is no substitute for competent legal advice from an attorney who is familiar with the prevailing guardianship law.

Organizational Design Decisions

Most corporate guardianship models are nonprofit organizations, but at least one existing program is a for-profit corporation (the Monitoring Council, Inc., of Pennsylvania). Regardless of its corporate status, the most important decision to be made regarding a corporate guardianship program is who shall serve on its board and how their successors will be chosen. The original board is usually a self-selected group that comes together due to a shared commitment to addressing the "old-age" question (i.e., what's after me?). The members of the board of directors are generally either a) the sole members of the corporation, with successors selected by original board members, or b) a broader group of people than those on the board, with the selection of board members made on the basis of a membership vote. The membership of guardianship corporations may include the families of service beneficiaries, volunteers who provide advocacy services under the auspices of the corporations, and members of the general public.

Organizational Questions The most essential questions for those who design the organizational structure of a corporate guardianship program are as follows:

1. *Corporate Status* What should be the organization's corporate status: profit or nonprofit?
2. *Board Membership* Who should serve on the board? What expertise should be represented? Should the board include persons with developmental disabilities, members of subscribing families, service providers, lawyers, trust management, and investment experts? Should there be a membership outside of the board? How many people should serve on the board? What offices are needed and what should be the duties and powers of officers? What committees are needed and what should be the roles and responsibilities of committees?
3. *Board Selection* How should board members be selected (membership vote; board member vote; appointment by outside bodies such as advocacy organizations, elected officials, judges, etc.)?

4. *Board Responsibility*   Is the organization the appointed guardian or should it merely facilitate the appointment of volunteers?
5. *Board Powers*   Which decisions should be made only by the board and which decisions should be delegated to staff?
6. *Service Region*   What geographic area will the corporation serve? Should it be totally administered from a central base or should it have a decentralized makeup (e.g., regional and local chapters)? If it has branch chapters, what should be the relative powers and responsibilities of its various levels of governance, administration, and service provision?
7. *Internal Development Requirements*   What self-renewal procedures will be mandated to assure that the governance board, administration, caseworkers, and volunteers are knowledgeable and sensitive to the needs of families and beneficiaries?
8. *Developmental Timeline*   What is a realistic process and timeline for instituting the corporation's program throughout its proposed geographic region? What observable milestones will be apparent to confirm that developmental progress is occurring in an orderly manner?

The answers to most of the above questions are usually stated in a corporation's by-laws. The by-laws for the corporate guardianship programs that are described in this section (Chapters 13, 14, 15, and 16) are included in appendices to each chapter.

Service Design Decisions

Corporate guardianship programs are generally developed due to parental concerns about the quality of life that their child (often an adult) will experience once the parents pass away. They help parents to ready themselves and their disabled child for the future and, once the last surviving parent dies, they act as a replacement parent to the disabled individual. Corporate guardianship programs are valid to the extent that they provide increased assurance of service quality once parents are no longer able to directly provide competent, personal representation for their disabled child.

Based on interactions with existing providers of corporate guardianship services, parents, persons with disabilities, and advocates, it would appear that those who want to develop comprehensive corporate guardianship models may wish to consider offering the following services.

Future Planning Assistance   Many families need professional help when making long term plans for their child with a disability. For example, guidance may be helpful in a) determining if their child should be placed under some form of guardianship (see Chapters 7 and 9), b) selecting an appropriate testamentary guardian and/or estate manager (see Chapter 9), c) establishing a trust arrangement (see Chapter 8), and d) making out-of-home placement decisions. A corporate guardianship program may directly deliver these services or may refer families to competent outside professionals. If directly delivered, the corporation may charge a service fee or may include this charge in an overall endowment requirement for subscribing families. Whatever the delivery and fee arrangement, parents frequently need competent professional advice when making long range plans for their disabled child, and all too often parents find this advice difficult to obtain. Corporate guardianship programs should help to satisfy this need.

Beneficiary Personal Services Many persons with disabilities need assistance in areas such as: a) life-quality monitoring, b) government benefit and service provision monitoring, c) making personal purchases and contracts, d) maintaining a suitable living arrangement, e) interpreting correspondence and confidential records, f) consenting or withholding consent to social relationships, sexual contacts, and marriage, g) selecting and arranging educational and habilitative services, and h) consenting or withholding consent for medical and behavioral procedures. Guardianship corporations may make formal agreements with parents to provide these services (see examples in Appendix B of this chapter and Appendices B and C of Chapter 16). Ideally, the agreement between the corporation and the parents will be in writing and will specifically delineate the corporation's responsibilities. The corporation will have maximum influence if it is appointed guardian by court order. Co-guardianship arrangements, wherein the corporation shares guardianship responsibility with a family member or friend, may sometimes be possible and desirable. The corporation may directly hire staff to exercise its guardianship responsibility, may utilize trained and supervised volunteers, or may contract with local voluntary associations. The latter alternative offers an exciting future possibility for changing the focus of parent organizations from direct services (i.e., providers of living arrangement, vocational training, and other developmental services) to protection and advocacy services such as corporate guardianship programs. Wolfensberger (1973) has argued that this shift is desirable since it would likely improve the stability of direct services.

Trust Management Services Corporate guardianship programs may act as trust manager and as representative payee for clients' government benefits. Master trust arrangements are sorely needed since many financial institutions refuse to manage small trusts (i.e., trusts under $50,000).

The appropriate investment and management of the estate of a dependent person requires specialized expertise that is uncommon among human services professionals. The corporation's decision as to whether it should directly administer trusts on behalf of clients depends upon several factors: a) the corporation's competence in this area, b) the size of the client's trust, and c) the self-support arrangement designed by the corporation.

Several alternatives exist. The corporation could require that parents recommend in their wills that it become trustee. Alternatively, the corporation: a) could mandate that an outside institution be used in all cases, b) could, by mandate or voluntarily, act as co-trustee with some outside institution or individual, or c) could require that it be appointed as trustee for all trusts or for small trusts (e.g., under $50,000) but that a trust institution be nominated for larger trusts.

Regardless of the trustee status of the corporation, it will often be required to assist clients when they make purchases. Moreover, guardianship operations sometimes will play a role in safeguarding clients' estates; i.e., oversee the behavior of outside trustees, institutions or individuals, to ensure that a client's estate is being prudently managed, and safeguard a client's right to government entitlements (see Chapters 8 and 9).

Universal Services Mature parents often play a role in helping to improve the life quality of all persons with disabilities rather than solely focusing on the status and needs of their own child. Similarly, some guardianship corporations may decide that a portion of their efforts should be directed toward improving the stability and continuity of existing direct services—public and private—for all persons with disabilities, both beneficiaries and nonbeneficiaries of the corporation. For example, corporate guardianship programs could: a) monitor the performance of government-supported agencies to assure compliance with legal protections for persons with disabilities, b) negotiate with agencies to correct deficiencies and provide technical assistance on service improvements, and c) engage in legislative and judicial oversight and public education to promote service improvements and expansions, including prevention programs. Corporate guardianship programs could directly deliver these services or could do so through contracts with existing organizations, such as government-supported protection and advocacy bodies, voluntary associations, university centers, and legal aid societies.

System Enrichment Services Corporate guardianship programs could provide training, consultation, and materials that strengthen the capacity of private and public sector entities to act on behalf of persons with developmental disabilities. Acting in cooperation with appropriate organizations, such as voluntary associations and/or institutions of higher education, corporate guardianship programs could support: a) dissemination of state-of-the-art technical information on guardianship and a wide range of related topics, b) systemic research to identify and plan needed service improvement, c) skill development training for the leadership of the voluntary movement, and d) public attitude-change programs to expand societal understanding of guardianship services and acceptance for persons with developmental disabilities. Again, these services could be directly delivered by a corporate guardianship program or delivered via contracts with appropriate entities.

Service Questions Those who are designing corporate guardianship programs would do well to determine answers to the following questions prior to recruiting subscribers for their program.

1. *Service options* What services will constitute the basic program unit that is provided to all beneficiaries?[1] Will all beneficiaries receive essentially the

---

[1]It is probably best that direct service and corporate guardianship functions not be mixed in a single agency. Corporations that administer guardianship services should not also deliver direct services since doing so could compromise the independence and objectivity of their advocacy activities on behalf of clients.

same service or will service variations exist due to clients' needs and/or prior agreements with parents? How will the corporation's services complement and relate to the existing advocacy and direct services for the target population? Will the program act as trustee and/or as representative payee?

2. *Onset of services* When will services to an individual begin: at the death of the last surviving parent? When living parents are unable to fulfill the parental role? When funding commences?

3. *Safeguarding entitlements* Are the corporation's services supported and provided in a manner that does not interfere with beneficiaries' receipt of government entitlements? If parents so desire, will the corporation directly pay, from monies supplied by the parents' wills, for services that would ordinarily be provided via government entitlements?

4. *Employees* What criteria will the corporation apply in selecting and training service delivery agents? What recruitment methods will be followed? Is it possible to use volunteers as sole or partial delivery agents? How should the performance of workers be evaluated? Is it possible to deliver local services to beneficiaries via contracts with existing advocacy organizations?

5. *Service evaluation* What form of internal and external evaluation procedures should exist to assure service quality and credibility?

6. *Target population* What criteria will be applied to determine client eligibility for the corporation's services? Is it possible and/or desirable to provide guardianship services to a wide range of persons who share the functional characteristic of being dependent (e.g., developmentally disabled persons, elders, physically and/or mentally handicapped persons who are not developmentally disabled, individuals with emotional handicaps, etc.)?

7. *Changes in client status* What will occur when a beneficiary later becomes sufficiently self-reliant to terminate guardianship status or to shift from plenary to limited guardianship status?

Fiscal Design Decisions

Corporate guardianship programs must have a stable source of income. Perhaps the most conservative approach is to require an endowment for all individuals served by the corporation, with individual endowments invested so that the corporation operates on the interest from each individual's trust (Chapter 16). This arrangement has the advantage of offering greater assurance of long term agency presence. The obvious disadvantage is that many persons will not have access to the corporation's services because their families cannot leave adequate estates. In theory, indigent individuals, i.e., persons who do not have resources to help capitalize an agency's endowment, will benefit from the corporation even if it does require substantial individual endowments because they will often be served in the same government-funded setting as corporation clients and will indirectly benefit from corporation-provided services such as on-site monitoring of life quality.

Another approach to supporting guardianship corporations is for clients to pay for services out of their support payments (SSI, Social Security Survivor's Benefits, etc.) or from payments made by a probate court (Chapter 15). This arrangement has the obvious disadvantage of overreliance on government good will. For example, the fact that the corporation could be weakened or eliminated due to government actions may adversely affect the corporation's advocacy on behalf of clients, particularly when the advocacy entails pressure on a government-sponsored program.

A third alternative source of support is private philanthropy. Most of the existing corporate guardianship programs receive substantial revenue from United Way and other private donors. This sort of support builds public confidence but, in turn, subjects the corporation to yet another form of potential pressure. Organized public charities such as United Way are sensitive to public opinion. Adversarial actions by the guardianship program may be viewed as too controversial.

The best support model for corporate guardianship programs is probably a combination of income from each of the above three sources, with emphasis on securing individual endowments and self-administered private fundraising efforts. In the final analysis, assurance of long term protection and advocacy services can be made to parents only when a sufficient endowment is established for each beneficiary to cover the costs of guardianship services. Even then, given the unpredictability of the future value of today's assets, assurances should be accompanied by recognition that unforeseen circumstances (e.g., the collapse of the monetary system) could weaken the corporation's capacity to act effectively or even possibly terminate its services.

In spite of the above, this author strongly recommends that corporate guardianship programs establish long term services on the basis of private, individualized endowments, and concurrently provide services to individuals without endowments on an as needed, interim basis via private fundraising efforts. The long term stability of a corporate guardianship program is its cardinal asset. Careful consideration must be given to maximizing the probability that the corporation's services will endure, while at the same time providing services to the greatest number of needy people.

Fiscal Questions   Those planning corporate guardianship models should determine answers to the following questions:

1. *Capitalization* How much capitalization will be needed to guarantee the corporation's essential services to beneficiaries on a lifetime basis? Is it possible to generate sufficient capitalization from family subscriptions? Will an initiation fee be charged? Will an annual membership fee be assessed? Will an endowment be required and, if so, what regulations will be mandated regarding the size and nature of endowments? What other sources of funding should be utilized?
2. *Options for indigent persons* Is it possible to design approaches that will permit indigent families to secure the corporation's services? Can a system be

implemented wherein indigent persons or probate courts may purchase the corporation's services without jeopardizing the security of the program's services to clients with endowments? Can a system be implemented whereby all or part of the principal endowment of deceased beneficiaries is used to provide services to indigent persons?

3. *Dispensing the trusts of deceased beneficiaries* What will happen to the endowment that a family invests in the corporation when the beneficiary dies? Will some or all of the unexpended capital remain in the corporation? If so, for what purposes will it be used? Will some or all of the unexpended capital revert to other survivors of the family or to other designees?

4. *Cost adjustments* Will it be necessary to regularly adjust the costs of the corporation's services to new subscribers? How often and by what method will these revisions be calculated?

5. *Fiscal accountability* What audit and other fiscal accountability procedures will be instituted to assure the fiscal integrity of the corporation?

6. *Withdrawals* Will subscribers be allowed to cancel agreements with the corporation? What penalties will be associated with withdrawals?

CORPORATE GUARDIANSHIP PROGRAMS

This author's research on the topic of corporate guardianship programs has led to the identification of 15 programs in the United States that provide all or some of the services listed in the first part of this chapter. Four of these programs are not technically corporate guardianship programs in that they do not assume the formal status of guardian. They provide services, however, which are very similar to those provided by the other agencies (either personal oversight or financial assistance) and they are therefore included in this review of corporate guardianship programs.

Table 1 summarizes the nature of the 15 identified programs in terms of a number of critical categories including organizational, service design, and fiscal features. As this figure indicates, most of the programs are freestanding (i.e., independent of a parent corporation), nonprofit corporations, which act as guardian of the person to developmentally disabled individuals. Other similarities among most of the programs include: a) involvement in monitoring wards'/clients' quality of life, b) involvement in planning to ensure that clients receive appropriate services, c) the provision of future planning services to families, d) court appointment of the board of directors as guardian, and e) insufficient endowment to ensure services on a lifetime basis.

The major differences among the programs pertain to: a) the extent to which they rely on professional staff versus volunteers to provide monitoring services, b) their association or lack of association with a formal parent organization, c) the nature of the client population that they serve, and d) their sources of startup and ongoing funding.

Table 1. Corporate guardianship programs and programs that provide similar services

Program characteristic	Guardianship Advocacy Program of New Mexico	Guardian Advocate Program of Dade County, Florida	Permanent Planning, Inc., of Waterloo, Iowa	Kindcare, Inc., of Milwaukee, Wisconsin	Foundation for the Handicapped of Washington State
Corporate status	Nonprofit; subsidiary	Nonprofit; subsidiary	Nonprofit; freestanding	Nonprofit; freestanding	Nonprofit; freestanding
Primary purpose	Act as guardian	Act as guardian	Acts as guardian	Manage program to ensure volunteer guardians	Act as guardian
Parent organization	Yes	Yes	Yes	No	No
Length of existence	5 years	6 months	10 years	5 years	20 years
Board composition	ARC board and guardianship committee	ARC board and guardianship committee	At least three of ten members are parents of beneficiaries	Representatives of participating churches	Community professionals and parents
Number of employees and volunteers	1 staff; 9 volunteers	2 staff; 15 volunteers	1 staff; 22 volunteers	1 employee; 50 volunteers	11 staff; 200 volunteers
Types of guardianship	Guardianship of the person: limited; plenary; temporary; testamentary	Guardianship of the person	Guardianship of person	Guardianship of the person; Guardianship of the estate	Guardianship of the person: limited; plenary; Guardianship of the estate: limited; plenary
Other services	Future planning assistance; Legal advocacy; Community education	Community education	Future planning assistance; Representative payee	Recruit, train, monitor, and provide follow-up support to volunteer guardians	Future planning assistance; Master trust workshops for parents and professionals; Representative payee
Number of wards/clients	46 wards	15 wards	22 wards	70 wards	500 wards
Nature of client population	Mentally retarded and developmentally disabled, 90% institutionalized	Mentally retarded and developmentally disabled	Mentally retarded and physically handicapped	Mentally retarded adults	Developmentally disabled, orphaned or abandoned; Elderly disabled
Entity of person(s) appointed guardian	Board of directors	Board of directors	Board of directors	Volunteers recruited by the organization	Board of directors
Source(s) of startup support	ARC fundraising	United Way	Private donations; Loaned staff	Private donations	Private donations
Current income and source(s)	ARC fundraising	United Way	Enrollment fee; Income from real estate	Private donations	United Way; Private donations; Fees for services

Program characteristic	Monitoring Council, Inc., of Pennsylvania	Oakdale Guardianship, Inc., of Michigan	Crossroad Services, Inc., of Iowa	Massachusetts Retardate Trust	Guardianship Advocacy, and Protective Services Program of Oregon
Corporate status	Nonprofit; freestanding	Nonprofit; freestanding	Nonprofit; freestanding	Nonprofit; freestanding; affiliated	Nonprofit; subsidiary
Primary purpose	Advocacy services to clients and their parents	Act as guardian	Skilled personal counseling to disabled persons and families	Master trust for MARC families	Act as guardian and other advocacy services
Parent organization	No	Yes	Yes	Yes	Yes
Length of existence	4 years	7 years	7 years	20 years	5 years
Board composition	Community professionals and parents	Community professionals and parents	Community professionals and parents	Community professionals and parents appointed by ARC board	ARC board and guardianship committee
Number of employees and volunteers	2 volunteer staff	2 staff 72 volunteers	2 staff	1 staff	4 staff
Types of guardianship	N/A	Guardianship of the person: limited; plenary	N/A	N/A	Guardianship of the person: limited; plenary; testamentary Guardianship of the estate: limited; plenary; testamentary Emergency guardianship of the person
Other services	Future planning assistance Visitations Attendance at planning meetings Advice to guardian	Future planning assistance Workshops for parents and professionals	Future planning assistance Oversight and advocacy to disabled person Advice to guardian	Trust management Advocacy Referral	Future planning assistance Advocacy Community and parent education
Number of wards/clients	107 families enrolled	200 wards	15 clients	82 clients	55 clients
Nature of client population	Developmentally disabled Mentally disabled	Severely and profoundly mentally retarded	Open	Mentally retarded	Mentally retarded and developmentally disabled
Entity of person(s) appointed guardian	N/A	Board of directors	N/A	N/A	ARC board of directors
Source(s) of startup support	Private donations	Parent group donations	Private donations	Private donations	Federal grants
Current income and source(s)	Enrollment fee Membership fee Required trust payments to organizations	Client fees Workshop income Private donations	Counseling fee Enrollment fee Required endowment	Enrollment fees Private donations	United Way Foundation grants ARC fundraising

Table 1. (*continued*)

Program characteristic	South Dakota Guardianship Program, Inc.	PACT of Chicago, Illinois	Protective Services of South Bend, Indiana	We Four, Inc., of Milwaukee, Wisconsin	Bridge Foundation of New York
Corporate status	Nonprofit; freestanding	Nonprofit; freestanding	Nonprofit; subsidiary	Nonprofit; freestanding	Nonprofit; subsidiary
Primary purpose	Act as guardian	Act as guardian and other advocacy services	Act as guardian and other advocacy services	Act as guardian	Providing for lifetime care of child after parents' death
Parent organization	No	No	Yes	No	No
Length of existence	18 months	3 years	9 years	10 years	18 months
Board composition	Community professionals and parents	Community professionals and parents	Council for the Retarded board appoints Protective Services board	Community professionals	Distinguished national leaders in the field of developmental services
Number of employees and volunteers	1 staff	10 staff 15 volunteers	3 staff 15 volunteers	7 staff	None
Types of guardianship	Guardianship of the person: limited; plenary; testamentary Guardianship of the estate: limited; plenary; testamentary	Guardianship of the person: limited; plenary; testamentary Guardianship of the estate: limited; plenary; testamentary	Guardianship of the person: limited; plenary; temporary	Guardianship of the person: limited; plenary; temporary	N/A
Other services	Future planning assistance Assistance to community attorneys	Future planning assistance General advocacy	Future planning assistance Representative payee	Representative payee Community education	Direct payment of a facility for services to a disabled person
Number of wards/clients	10 wards	10 wards	34 wards 300 clients	39 wards	9 families enrolled
Nature of client population	Developmentally disabled	Mentally retarded and mentally ill	Mentally retarded	Developmentally disabled, chronically mentally ill, elderly	Developmentally disabled
Entity of person(s) appointed guardian	Board of directors	Board of directors	Board of directors	Board of directors	N/A
Source(s) of startup support	Grants—state Fees for services Private donations	Corporate and foundation grants	United Way County grant	State government	The Mutual Benefit Life Insurance Co.
Current income and source(s)	Grant from the state Fees for services Private donations	Membership fees Corporate and foundation grants	United Way County grant	State government fees for services	Commissions from the sale of life insurance

The remainder of this chapter is a series of program descriptions that highlight critical features of each model. The address for each program is included in Appendix A and detailed descriptions of four of the more advanced models are included in Chapters 13, 14, 15, and 16.

Guardianship Advocacy Program of New Mexico

The Association for Retarded Citizens (ARC) of New Mexico's Guardianship Advocacy Program (GAP) serves as court appointed guardian for 42 and as court-appointed limited guardian of seven persons with mental retardation who do not have parents, relatives, or other interested persons willing to serve as guardian. The corporation has also agreed to be named as testamentary guardian for numerous other retarded persons after their parents' death. Most of the persons presently served by the program reside in public institutions. ARC is named guardian in court documents, and the responsibilities of guardianship are carried out under the supervision of the board and the guardianship committee. The board, by resolution, designates a volunteer advocate empowered to carry out duties and responsibilities as guardian. The membership of the guardianship committee includes the president and executive director of the ARC, a parent of a developmentally disabled person, a medical doctor, a lawyer, and a special educator.

The New Mexico guardianship program was begun in 1978. It operates on an annual budget of approximately $30,000, employs one staff person, and relies heavily on the services of volunteer advocates. The expenses of the program are paid by the ARC from its general fundraising efforts. The program does not rely on any funds from government sources. In addition to guardianship services, the program provides family-planning assistance and judicial and legislative advocacy. The regulations of the program specifically exclude it from consenting to marriage, adoption, sterilization, and to any therapeutic procedures that require a "treatment guardian" under the terms of New Mexico's Mental Health and Developmental Disabilities Code (e.g., psychosurgery, convulsive therapy, and aversive conditioning procedures).

Guardian Advocate Program of Dade County, Florida

The Association for Retarded Citizens of Dade County, Florida, is in the initial stage of implementing a corporate guardianship service called the Guardian Advocate Program. Similar to the New Mexico model, the Dade County ARC board of directors is the court-appointed guardian with guardianship services provided via volunteer monitors. The volunteers will periodically visit the ward's living situation and other direct service settings and will assure that the ward's needs are met on a day-to-day basis. Other responsibilities may be dictated by the court order and/or by the volunteer monitor's agreement with the ARC.

The Dade County program began taking wards in June, 1983. Fifteen persons have been identified who need the services of the program. There are two paid staff: a guardian advocacy coordinator, who serves as the program's director, and a secretary. Funding for the first year's activities is being supplied by United Way of Dade County. Wards who have financial resources are charged for program services in accordance with a fee schedule that is determined by the ARC, with court approval as necessary.

Permanent Planning, Inc.

Founded in 1973, Permanent Planning, Inc., is a single-purpose organization. The entire staff for the program consists of one part-time employee. Its income is derived from a $750 family enrollment fee and from income on 11 houses that are owned by the corporation and leased to group home operators. Permanent Planning acts as guardian of the person and occasionally as conservator of the estate, but does not serve as guardian of the estate or trust manager. Services are rendered in conformity with agreements between the agency and parents (Appendix B).

The membership of Permanent Planning is restricted to parents who have enrolled their children in the program, with the exception that nonparents with relevant professional expertise (e.g., bankers, lawyers, insurance agents) may be elected to the board of directors. The program currently serves 22 wards, individuals who are mentally retarded and/or profoundly physically handicapped. Services are primarily provided via volunteers who act as client advocates. Volunteers participate at individual planning sessions on behalf of wards, visit them on a weekly basis, and are responsible to ensure that wards are served in appropriate community programs. Guardianship services are limited to a six-county region due to a belief that it would be difficult to judge the quality of services in unfamiliar areas.

Kindcare, Inc.

Kindcare, Inc., plays a facilitating role in the area of guardianship by recruiting, screening, training, monitoring, and offering followup support to volunteer legal guardians of mentally retarded adults. It is an ecumenical organization sponsored by a host of religious organizations: the United Church of Christ, American Lutheran Church, United Methodist, Roman Catholic, Lutheran Church–Missouri Synod, United Presbyterian, Lutheran Church in America, Episcopal, and the American Baptist Churches in the greater Milwaukee area. The board of directors consists of representatives from each of these religious organizations and several members at large who do not represent specific religious denominations. The program currently serves 70 adults who have been diagnosed as "mentally retarded" and one individual who has been declared "legally incompetent." The annual budget of the program is approximately $30,000. The organization employs one staff person and relies on three committees: finance and resource development, program evaluation and planning, and parish action (to provide liaison with the participating churches). Fifty volunteers serve as legal guardians. The funding for the first five years of the program was supplied by a private family foundation. It is currently funded by private donations from individuals, corporations, religious groups, and individual churches. No fees are received from clients, and no government support is obtained.

Foundation for the Handicapped

Begun in 1963, the Foundation for the Handicapped (Chapter 13) is a freestanding nonprofit corporation with a paid staff of 11 persons. The Foundation, supervised by the board of directors, currently serves as plenary or limited guardian of the person and/or estate to over 500 wards. The population served by the program consists of persons who are handicapped due to sensory, intellectual, and/or physical disabilities and who have no other resource to help them, and elderly persons with no family or relatives to serve as guardian.

The Foundation manages a master trust (with current assets of over $3.5 million) but maintains a policy that large individual trusts (those greater than $100,000) must be administered by an outside fiduciary. The annual budget of the Foundation, approximately $189,497, is derived from United Way, private donors, and fees for program services.

Monitoring Council, Inc.

While it does not assume guardianship responsibility, the Monitoring Council, Inc., exists to provide advocacy services to persons with disabilities (mental and emotional handicaps) after the demise of their parents. Since its inception in 1979, 107 families in a five-county region that includes Philadelphia have signed agreements with the program. Parents must pay a $350 initiation fee and $50 annual membership fee. Moreover, they must agree to establish a trust outside of the Monitoring Council that guarantees the Council an annual payment that is equivalent to $2,000 of 1981 value. (The annual fee for 1983 is thus $2,175). The average trust thus far established by parents is $65,000. Trusts must require the trustee to either employ the Monitoring Council, Inc., or to employ some other independent advocacy service. The trustee therefore has the power to discontinue the services of the Monitoring Council and employ another service provider.

The services of the Monitoring Council will include: a) family planning assistance, b) at least two monthly visits to the persons's living arrangement and day program, c) representation at planning meetings, d) oversight of expenditures made by the trustee, and e) intervention, legal if necessary, to ensure appropriate services and trust management. As yet, none of the parents who have enrolled their children in the program have passed away, so no monitoring services are being provided. The program's board consists of six service professionals, three of whom are immediate family members of persons with disabilities.

Oakdale Guardianship, Inc.

The Oakdale Guardianship program (Chapter 15) was begun in 1976 to provide someone who could give informed consent on behalf of persons residing at the

Oakdale Regional Center. The service population of the program has since expanded to include 200 persons, some of whom reside at other state institutions and some in community living arrangements. Most wards are profoundly or severely retarded. The corporation's board of directors assumes guardianship but direct oversight of clients and personal representation is provided by volunteer monitors, community members who agree to assist one or more retarded persons. The finances for the program are obtained by charging clients a small monthly fee ($2.50). The average expenditure per client for services in 1982 was only $123.

Crossroad Services, Inc.

Like the Oakdale program, Crossroad Services, Inc., was initiated due to parental pressure at a community-based educational and rehabilitation agency for handicapped persons, Hope Haven. The Crossroad Services Program (Chapter 16) does not directly act as guardian, but rather serves as advisor to individuals with special needs and their families. Parents must thus nominate someone outside of the agency to serve as legal guardian. Two contract options exist. Under one arrangement, parents pay a $5,000 enrollment fee and a $50,000 endowment upon the death of the last surviving parent for direct, personalized oversight of their disabled child. The second arrangement does not provide services directly to the disabled person. Instead, Crossroad Services supplies information, advocacy, and assistance to the person's guardian. The charges for this service are a $500 enrollment fee and a $10,000 endowment.

Massachusetts Association for Retarded Citizens Retardate Trust[2]

The Massachusetts Association for Retarded Citizens Trust was established by the Massachusetts State Association for Retarded Citizens (MARC) to serve member families. The Trust program is incorporated separately from the ARC, and the Trust's board of trustees must be approved by the board of trustees of MARC. This program does not act as guardian. It currently serves approximately 80 mentally retarded persons. Yearly dues are $20 for a single parent and $30 for both parents. After the parents' death, a social worker visits the client and makes suggestions regarding placement.

A second option offered by the same organization is the MARC Friendship Trust. Here, the trust corporation will administer a gift of $10,000 or more for the benefit of the mentally retarded person, and will provide counseling. When the beneficiary dies, the remainder of the trust reverts to the Association's general fund.

---

[2]A similar master trust arrangement exists in Maryland but the author was unable to secure descriptive information. The contact information for this program is as follows: Ms. Marybeth Leopold, Maryland Trust for Retarded Citizens, Maryland Association for Retarded Citizens, 5602 Baltimore National Pike, Suite 200, Baltimore, Maryland, 21228.

Guardianship, Advocacy, and Protective Services Program

The Oregon Association for Retarded Citizens established a corporate guardianship program in 1978 (Chapter 14). Startup support from a 2-year federal grant enabled the Association to develop a comprehensive program model with professional staff and quality planning materials for use by parents and professionals (Association for Retarded Citizens, 1980). The program currently provides guardianship or supportive advocacy services to 55 persons whose parents have died. Services are delivered via local teams. Teams are geographically dispersed across the state and include a part-time employee, the team leader, and a cadre of volunteers, many of whom are parents of disabled persons. The program is governed by a committee of the ARC board and operates on an annual budget of approximately $100,000. A capital drive effort has been initiated to establish an endowment trust.

South Dakota Guardianship Program, Inc.

Begun in cooperation with the South Dakota Protection and Advocacy Agency in 1980, the South Dakota Guardianship Program, Inc., is now an independent corporation that provides future planning and guardianship services to persons with developmental disabilities and their families. The board of directors consists of seven statewide professionals, four of whom are parents of disabled persons. The corporation currently acts as guardian of the person and/or estate to 10 wards and anticipates adding an additional 30 wards during 1983, and approximately 30 more wards each succeeding year. Services are financed by a grant from the state office of developmental disabilities, private donations, and client fees. There is no current arrangement to administer clients' trusts. Work is currently being done to create a trust instrument appropriate to the needs of handicapped persons.

PACT

PACT began as a subgroup of the Illinois State Association for Retarded Citizens in 1980. Since 1981, PACT has operated independently of the ARC. It exists to provide advice and continuing personal assistance to disabled persons and their families. It employs 10 staff members, 8 professional workers, and 2 support staff, and receives assistance from 15 volunteers. PACT has 150 current enrollees in the program, and acts as guardian for 30 of these people. About half of the individuals are classified as developmentally disabled. The other half are considered mentally ill. Support for the PACT program is obtained from foundation grants and membership fees. The fee charged for guardianship services is $1,530 per annum. While the program does not currently administer clients' trusts, it is preparing to establish a master trust arrangement for the deposit of small trusts.

Protective Services

The Protective Services Program is a unit of the Council for the Retarded of St. Joseph's County, Indiana. The Council was originally a chapter of the Indiana

Association for Retarded Citizens but is now a freestanding advocacy corporation. The Protective Services Program provides personal and systematic advocacy to address parents' concern for the future security of their retarded children. It serves as representative payee for 80 people and as guardian to 34 people. In total, approximately 300 people are served in various advocacy capacities. The program's wards are mentally retarded and most live in nursing homes. The program is supported by grants from United Way and the St. Joseph County Council.

Lutheran Mission Society of Maryland

The Lutheran Mission Society of Maryland offered a program titled "Promise to Care" in the Baltimore area from 1973 to 1980. This program failed to survive due to its inability to attract subscribers. The Society offered to "sponsor" retarded individuals, not act as guardians, after the death of their parents. It received only one client and no one is presently enrolled. The services that were available included counseling for parents in the areas of legal concerns, medical concerns, and out-of-home placement; intervention to assure the appropriate placement of retarded persons when their last surviving parent died; monthly visits by a professional staff member; volunteer-led community experiences such as trips to ball games, shopping centers, theaters; and attention on special days such as Christmas, birthdays and other holidays. Interested parents were to pay for the program on the basis of individually negotiated plans, generally via life insurance with the Lutheran Mission Society designated as beneficiary.

The executive director of the Society believes that the basic problem with the program was that families wanted residency, not sponsorship. He feels that neither money nor staffing were important issues, but rather, the problem was the program's failure to address the strong desire of parents to assure their child's well-being through placement in a permanent residence. In his words, "We had a number of requests to provide a program that would assure such an arrangement. Of course, with the changing concepts in mainstreaming, this was not possible. So, the program was discontinued. I still believe the concept is very viable and maybe it was simply ahead of its time" (R.C. Alms, personal communication, April 19, 1983).

We Four, Inc.

Funded primarily by the Milwaukee County Department of Social Services, We Four, Inc., acts as guardian to 40 dependent persons, some of whom are developmentally disabled. It was begun in 1971 in response to the needs of older persons for an organization that could act as a substitute decision-maker. In addition to senior citizens, the program now serves people who are developmentally disabled and chronically ill. The program provides supervision and monitoring of nursing home care, and sometimes aids in placement of wards in independent living arrangements. The program acts as guardian of the person and estate and also serves as a representative payee for wards' government benefits. The board of directors consists of several senior citizen representatives, a bank trust officer, an insurance executive, an attorney, and a social service agency director. The executive director is also an ex-officio member of the board.

Bridge Foundation

The Bridge Foundation is a newly created national organization devoted to the development and administration of financial programs for disabled individuals. Its purpose is to: "provide a means of continuing care, as well as education, for developmentally-disabled people through private residential facilities, exclusive of public institutions, and a means for providing the various social benefits that the developmentally disabled people may be entitled to" (D. Laveman, personal communication, November 10, 1983).

The development of the Foundation was supported by the Mutual Benefit Life Insurance Company of Newark, New Jersey. Its board of governors is composed of nationally prominent people from the fields of education, health, business, and social services. The management and expenses of the Foundation are paid by a separate administrative agency, the C.F.G. group. Administrative costs are funded from commissions on life insurance policies.

The Bridge Foundation enters into a contract with parents of handicapped children wherein the parents agree to make annual, nonrefundable payments to the Foundation, and the Foundation agrees to reimburse the cost of up to $50,000 a year of all the necessary medical care and supervision of the children in an appropriate facility after the parents' death. The money is under the control of the child's guardian at all times and the money will always follow the child. All enrollees are making possible an endowment (in the name of the child) to the facility where the child resides in addition to the yearly reimbursements. The agreement provides that: a) the parent will apply for a life insurance policy with a face amount of $250,000, b) the policy will be owned by and payable to the Foundation, and c) the annual payments by the parents will be sufficient to maintain the policy in full force and effect. The agreement provides further that if the child predeceases the parent or if the parent fails to make any payment necessary to maintain the policy, all obligations under the agreement will terminate and the policy will remain the property of the Foundation.

One of the major advantages of the Bridge program is that the payments made by the parent are tax deductible. It has become well established that payments made pursuant to a legal obligation in order to secure medical services are deductible medical expenses despite the fact that the medical services are not to be performed until a future time. As yet, the IRS has not challenged the medical expense deduction of any of the Bridge Foundation's enrollees. Based on previous ratings, there appears to be a reasonable possibility of overcoming such a challenge should it occur.

CONCLUSION

As the foregoing program descriptions suggest, corporate guardianship programs represent an emerging trend in the field of services to people with developmental disabilities. Numerous models have been initiated but little information exists on their effectiveness or stability. The issue of their funding sources appears to be particularly troublesome. Since guardianship services for highly dependent persons means a long term commitment, corporate guardianship programs must be adequately endowed to assure continuity of service on a lifetime basis. Only three program models require an endowment prior to making service guarantees (the Monitoring Council, Inc., Crossroad Services, Inc., and the Bridge Foundation). The issue of designing support plans for corporate guardianship models that guarantee long term service continuity and yet permit service provision to families that cannot afford to establish substantial endowments is a major challenge. Future planners must successfully address this issue if the true potential of corporate guardianship programs is to be realized.

REFERENCES

Association for Retarded Citizens, Oregon. *Future planning on behalf of developmentally disabled persons—A guide for estate planners.* Salem: ARC, 1980.

Wolfensberger, W. *The third stage in the evolution of voluntary associations for the mentally retarded.* Toronto: International League for the Mentally Handicapped and National Institute on Mental Retardation, 1973.

Appendix A

CORPORATE GUARDIANSHIP PROGRAMS AND
PROGRAMS THAT PROVIDE SIMILAR SERVICES

David Laveman
Bridge Foundation
1790 Broadway Avenue
New York, New York 10019

Lloyd Munneke
Crossroad Services, Inc.
1311 Golf Course Road
Rock Valley, Iowa 51247

Ervin Larsen
Foundation for the Handicapped
1600 West Armory Way
Seattle, Washington 98119

Tony O'Shea
Guardian Advocate Program
Association for Retarded Citizens, Dade
County
8405 N.W. 66th St., Suite 100
Miami, Florida 33166

Aloysius J. Soenneker
Guardianship, Advocacy, and Protec-
tive Services Program
Association for Retarded Citizens,
Oregon
3085 North River Road
Salem, Oregon 97303

Bette Smith
Guardianship Advocacy Program
Association for Retarded Citizens of New
Mexico
8200-½ Menaul NE, Suite 3
Albuquerque, NM 87110

Sandra J. Cristensen
Kindcare, Inc.
611 East Wells Street
Milwaukee, Wisconsin 53202

Sally Miller
Massachusetts ARC Retardate Trust
217 South Street
Waltham, Massachusetts 02154

Henry Winkler
Nathan Goldberg
Monitoring Council, Inc.
310 South Easton Road, Suite A217
Glenside, PA 19038

Henry Widrich
Oakdale Guardianship, Inc.
P.O. Box 541
Lapeer, Michigan 48446

Kevin Breslin
PACT
6 N. Michigan, Suite 1700
Chicago, Illinois 60602

W.E. Brown
Permanent Planning, Inc.
2530 University Avenue
Waterloo, Iowa 50701

Sue Bowman
Protective Services Council for the Re-
tarded of St. Joseph's County
Logan Center
P.O. Box 1049
South Bend, Indiana 46624

Charlene Lund
South Dakota Guardianship Program,
Inc.
222 W. Pleasant Drive
Pierre, South Dakota 57501

Sister Margaret Underwood
We Four, Inc.
817 N. Marshall St.
Milwaukee, Wisconsin 53202

161

Appendix B

FORMAT FOR AGREEMENTS BETWEEN
PARENTS AND PERMANENT PLANNING, INC.

APPLICATION
PERMANENT SUPERVISION AGREEMENT

THIS AGREEMENT made and entered into in duplicate this _____ day of _____
_____, 19_____, by and between Permanent
Planning, Inc., an Iowa nonprofit corporation, located at Waterloo, Iowa, hereinafter
referred to as "PPI" and _____
_____ of _____ as natural parent,
legal guardian, legal custodian of _____
presently residing at _____ with
the former hereinafter referred to as "parents" and the latter hereinafter referred to as
"client"; witnesseth:

WHEREAS, THE PARENT IS desirous of applying to PPI for acceptance of client into the
lifetime supervision or parental substitution program being conducted by PPI; and,
whereas, the client is believed to be a fit and suitable person to receive the services of PPI
and said parent is and assumes the responsibility for said client;

NOW, THEREFORE, in consideration of the sum of _____ Dollars, the receipt of which is
hereby acknowledged and in the further consideration of the agreements, covenants
hereinafter set forth the parties hereto agree as follows:

I. PPI shall within _____ days hereafter conduct through a professional social
    work staff an in-depth study of the proposed client, client's needs and abilities, and
    the funds available to client with said study to include but not to be limited to:
    a) Evaluation of client's learning and educational abilities.
    b) Evaluation of client's physical and emotional needs and requirements.
    c) Home/institution/living quarters of the client. Determine financial assets
        available.
    d) Interview parents regarding parents' plans and desires for client. Provide
        parent a written evaluation and plan for client during parents' custodial control
        of client.

II. Parent agrees to execute all documents necessary to give PPI access to educational,
    medical, and financial records of client.

III. In the event the parents do not desire to implement the plan or acquire the services
    of PPI for client, or in the event PPI rejects the application of the parents, the sum of
    _____ dollars shall be retained by PPI and the remain-
    ing consideration returned to parent along with all records, plans, and executed
    documents of authority given PPI and this agreement shall become null and void.

IV. Upon parents' acceptance of the proposed plan of PPI, PPI agrees to accept or reject
    a client as an enrollee within _____ days thereafter; and upon acceptance
    of the client as an enrollee, PPI shall execute the agreement as proposed hereinafter
    and parents shall pay to PPI the balance due hereunder.

V. THEREFORE, upon receipt of an additional consideration in the amount of _____
_____, PPI and parents agree that client is
accepted as an enrollee of PPI and PPI agrees that said client is a lifetime enrollee of
PPI and shall continue to be an enrollee until such time as:
   a) He is withdrawn from the plan by parent.
   b) Client is withdrawn by enrolling guardian, legal custodian, or by judicial
      decree or by mutual consent of PPI, parent, enrolling guardian or legal
      custodian.
   c) By death of the client.

VI. Parties hereto further agree that upon acceptance of client as an enrollee the parent
shall become a member of the corporation and shall be entitled to one (1) vote for
each enrollee of the parent. PPI further agrees through its staff and/or volunteers
recruited and trained for this purpose to provide for enrollee until the removal of
parent created either through disability, death or other removal of the parent the
following:
   a) An annual re-evaluation of the enrollee and the enrollee's plan including an
      assessment of housing, schooling, employment, and facilities available to
      client.
   b) PPI will assist parent or parent's legal advisor with contents of Wills, Trust,
      etc., for benefit of enrollee.
   c) PPI will provide emergency consultation and assistance to parent.

VII. On the death, disability or inability of parent, PPI will:
   a) Provide immediate assistance to enrollee of enrollee's family and implement
      temporary plan for housing, care, and supervision of enrollee.
   b) Implement permanent living and care plans for enrollee as previously outlined
      by parent and PPI.
   c) Accept guardianship/conservatorship of enrollee upon proper judicial appoint-
      ment.
   d) Continue ongoing supervision of enrollee as provided in plan with parents.
   e) Provide emergency consultation and assistance to enrollee and/or enrollee's
      duly appointed guardian or custodian.

VIII. PPI agrees that upon proper judicial appointment of PPI as guardian/conservator of
enrollee to provide the following:
   a) Provide client with counseling and guidance to the extent necessary to enable
      client to obtain the highest degree of independence his capabilities will allow.
      This includes the areas of financial sustainment, employment security, struc-
      tured activity, living environment, and leisure time.
   b) PPI will give client guidance in the area of financial sustainment such as
      evaluating his earnings to determine if he is being treated fairly and in
      budgeting and managing his money.
   c) PPI will help the client gain security in employment and in progress towards an
      area of work which meets as close to maximum his capabilities as possible.
   d) PPI shall provide client with assistance in area of living environment, in-
      cluding proper supervision of the expenditure of available funds for housing,
      supervision of available housing to be sure that enrollee is being treated fairly,
      receiving proper meals and services, and that client is provided with oppor-
      tunities for social growth.
   e) PPI shall provide client with assistance in the area of leisure time. PPI, through
      its staff and/or volunteers, shall advocate for the establishment of an interest-
      ing and meaningful program during the evenings, weekends, and vacations.

f) PPI, through its staff and/or volunteers recruited and trained for this purpose, will watch over the client relative to his emotional and psychological happiness. Special attention will be given to the client for remembrances on birthdays, holidays, and PPI will provide parental care and advocacy on behalf of the client.

IX. It is understood by the parties hereto that PPI is not to provide funds for the housing, board and room, medical services, psychological services, or services required by emotional, mental, psychological or physical problems required by the client, but that PPI shall continually supervise the activities of the enrollee, the activities of the enrollee's custodian as related to the enrollee and shall advocate and insist that said enrollee client shall receive the best care available for the funds available to said enrollee.

X. It is specifically understood and agreed that PPI shall at no time become responsible for the acts of the client.

XI. This agreement contains the entire agreement of the parties hereto, and no agreements, warranties, or representatives have been made by either party unless set forth herein.

XII. In witness whereof, the parties hereto have executed this agreement on the day and the year first above written.

_____   _____
Parent/Legal Guardian   President, Permanent Planning, Inc.

_____   _____
Date   Date

Chapter 11

Public Guardianship in California

Steven R. Sproger

This chapter is written to satisfy two purposes. First, it provides an explanation of the differences between plenary (full) guardianship and limited (partial) guardianship and why these differences exist. To do that, a brief history of the guardianship laws in the United States is presented. Second, this chapter summarizes the history and status of the public guardianship program in California, including a description of California's decision to adopt a limited guardianship alternative.

PLENARY VS. LIMITED GUARDIANSHIP

Plenary Guardianship

Essentially, guardianship gives the guardian rights and powers that are similar to those that a natural parent has over a child. When an individual is appointed to be the guardian of a child, the guardian is expected to replace the natural parent in most ways. A parent is the "natural guardian" of a child and needs no court action to be such. Neither other family members nor organizations have such rights as the natural guardian unless the court gives the rights to them.

The power given the guardian of an adult is similar to that given the guardian of a child. Just as children are considered to be "incompetent" by reason of immaturity and inexperience, an adult ward is considered to be incompetent because of mental retardation (or other cause). As of 1979, the laws of 16 states require a finding of "incompetence" for a guardian or conservator to be appointed.

The difference between plenary (full) guardianship and limited guardianship results from the historical background of the two forms of guardianship. To understand this difference, which is more than just a variation in the *amount* of control given to a guardian, one must understand limited and plenary guardianship in light of their respective histories. Plenary guardianship evolved from the institutionalization movement and limited guardianship came into existence due to the deinstitutionalization movement.

Plenary (full) guardianship stems from English law transplanted to the United States with the colonists. During the colonial era, guardianship in England was part of the role of the manor lords. Later, it became a duty of the crown. English law, or common law, developed the concept of *parens patriae*, the state acting as parent to its citizens. Disadvantaged persons were thought of as objects of benevolent care who therefore did not need rights to exercise against the paternalistic state.

The trend continued with the institutionalization movement at the turn of this century in the United States. By 1900, every state had at least one institution for the "feebleminded." Guardianship laws were used to place individuals involuntarily in these state institutions. By the 1920s, a general fear of the "retarded" became prevalent and sterilization became an additional method of preventing the reproduction of retarded persons. Guardianship was used to permit sterilization operations and institutionalization.

As an outcome of this history, plenary guardianship results in almost complete control over another person. Even though a guardian may assist a ward in exercising some rights, the impetus for plenary guardianship has been to deprive wards of rights, not to implement their rights through informed representation.

The National Center for Law and the Handicapped, in a criticism of plenary guardianship, stated that a "ward under 'general' (plenary) guardianship is deprived of exercising the most basic and fundamental rights and decisions that all of us take for granted" (National Center for Law and the Handicapped, 1977). In essence, the guardian has *complete* power over the ward except those powers that are *specifically denied* either by the court or by case law (previous appellate court cases).

Limited Guardianship

In many ways, limited guardianship is the antithesis of plenary guardianship because it evolved from an opposite direction. Although there are limits set by state statutes and case law on plenary guardianship, limited guardianship gets its name from the fact that first and foremost it is limited. While a plenary guardian has full control of a ward except those powers specifically *withheld* by the court or denied by case law, a limited guardian has no control over a ward except those powers specifically *given* by the court.

As early as 1960, the White House Conference on Children and Youth published a paper titled, "Trends and Issues in Mental Retardation" by Gunnar Dybwad (Dybwad, 1960). He charged that legal planning for retarded individuals too often appeared limited to the appointment of a guardian, with consequent removal of the ward's civil rights. He challenged legal scholars to devise a way of making the degree of legal protection proportionate to the degree of handicap.

In 1962, President Kennedy appointed a President's Panel on Mental Retardation. The Panel's 1963 report confirmed Dybwad's ideas about the need for more legal flexibility. The report recommended a variety of guardianship plans for retarded individuals: a) limited "guardianship of the person" for mentally retarded adults wherein the scope of the guardian's authority would be carefully defined in the court's order, b) plenary guardianship for those persons incapable of basic self-management and routine day-to-day decision making, c) conservatorship of the property for those adults capable of conducting their own daily affairs but not capable of managing substantial business or financial interests, and d) public guardianship to make the above options available to those for whom private guardianship is unavailable. The Panel recognized that guardianship is a prerogative of the states and recommended grants to the states to help in legal planning. Congress subsequently authorized funds for this purpose.

Meanwhile, other events were shaping attitudes about mental retardation and the rights of persons with mental retardation. In 1969, the International League Committee on Guardianship met at San Sebastian, Spain, and made several recommendations (International League of Societies for the Mentally Handicapped, 1969). Many of the recommendations were later accepted by the United Nations as their "Declaration of Rights of Mentally Retarded Persons." The majority of the rights listed were related to basic human rights, many of which were denied to persons because of their retardation. One right listed was that "the mentally retarded person has a right to a qualified guardian, when this is required, to protect his personal well being and interests" (United Nations General Assembly, 1971). Other rights included the right to protection from exploitation and the right to legal safeguards when restrictions are placed on one's rights (as in the appointment of a guardian).

This was only a rudimentary beginning. Stating that a group of people have rights, without imposing an obligation on someone to implement the rights, is akin to making empty promises. To fulfill the promises, a plethora of litigation was followed by a mass of legislation. It took both court and legislative action to: a) accelerate the deinstitutionalization movement, b) change the attitudes of professionals and the community about persons with developmental special needs, and c) eventually change the guardianship or conservatorship laws in several states, including California.

The deinstitutionalization trend can be said to have started in 1968, the first year in which there was a *drop* in the institutional population. Over 60,000 persons have been relocated from public institutions to community living arrangements since 1968. The professional community in the field of developmental services and its legal associates began to question the need for placing many of the persons who were transitioning from institutions under plenary guardianships.

One of the first *court* cases concerning persons with mental retardation who reside in institutions was the *Wyatt* v. *Stickney* case (1971). The decisions in this case were some of the most far-reaching to date. They set standards for admission, program planning, care, and rights of persons with mental retardation in state institutions in Alabama. These standards were eventually applied nationwide. The following year, the *Mills* v. *Board of Education* case (1972) established the right to education for all handicapped children, and the *Lessard* v. *Schmidt* (1972) case established procedural protections for persons being committed to mental institutions. In 1973, *New York State Association for Retarded Citizens* v. *Rockefeller* (1973), commonly known as the Willowbrook cases, resulted in a right to protection from harm for the residents of state mental retardation facilities, including the provision of necessary training programs.

The early 1970s produced landmark legislation that formalized the trends of the late sixties and created obligations that fulfilled the empty promises. Some of the obligations were to honor the rights of persons with developmental special needs. Other obligations resulted in funding for school programs, for community residential alternatives, and for social services to assist persons with developmental disabilities in finding and using newly created services. And with these changes came attitudinal changes, some of which led to changes in conservatorship and guardianship.

During this same period, federal legislation provided for funding for non-medical residential care via Supplemental Security Income (Public Law 92-603, 1972). The Rehabilitation Act of 1973 (Public Law 93-112, 1973) required accessibility to buildings and public services for persons with handicaps and forbade discrimination against persons with handicaps. The Education for All Handicapped Children Act of 1975 (Public Law 94-142, 1975) established a requirement that states educate all children regardless of handicap, and provided grants to help states do so. Finally, the Developmental Disabilities Assistance and Bill of Rights Act (PL 94-103, 1975) enacted specific rights and required states to establish ''protection and advocacy'' systems to safeguard the rights of persons with developmental disabilities. It was from these changes in practice and law that the philosophy that resulted in limited conservatorship or guardianship evolved. A general shift began to occur in attitudes towards guardianship. It became accepted that:

1. People with mental retardation are people first with the *rights* and dignity possessed by all people and their *rights* cannot be removed except via the same process due every person whose rights are being denied.
2. No two individuals are alike and competencies vary from person to person. (Federal legislation and court cases in the late sixties and throughout the seventies resulted in requirements to individualize education and habilitation services and the planning processes used to define the services that each person will receive.)
3. Persons are *presumed competent* in all areas. The burden of proof is on proving the areas where the prospective ward is *not* competent.

4. The ward of a limited guardian retains all the rights not specifically given to the limited guardian.

5. The limited guardian should not overprotect the ward but should help the ward to receive training experiences that will eventually result in the ward attaining the maximum level of independence that is possible given his or her limitations. (Many of the states in the U.S. and provinces in Canada have this philosophy explicitly stated in their law pertaining to limited guardianship.)

Table 1 summarizes and compares the concepts of limited and plenary guardianship.

PUBLIC GUARDIANSHIP IN CALIFORNIA

In 1963, California established a study commission on mental retardation. California was the first state to establish such a legal planning commission (and to ask for federal funds). The commission recommended that public guardianship be available to every retarded person who needs it, and proposed a Mental Retardation Program and Standards Advisory Board (MRPSAB) to conduct a study and offer recommendations for making guardianship services available (Kay, Farnham, Karren, Knakal, & Diamond, 1972). The MRPSAB's Guardianship Subcommittee studied other state plans. The first public guardianship was created in Minnesota in 1917, and by 1967, 13 states had developed public guardianship

Table 1. Summary and comparison of limited and plenary guardianship

---

History
    Plenary guardianship derives from the old common law, poor houses (alms houses), and the institutionalization movement. Limited conservatorship derives from the de-institutionalization movement, rights movements, and the newer philosophy of respect for individuals.

Specificity of Power
    Plenary guardians' powers are generally not specified. They are, however, considered to be global and complete. Limited conservators tend to have specified powers listed in the court order.

Presumption
    Once found "incompetent," the ward of a plenary guardian is presumed to be *totally* incompetent. The ward of a limited guardian is presumed to be competent in all areas not listed as powers of the limited guardian.

Individual Differences
    Many states provide such a complete list of powers for "limited" guardians that, if the limited guardian were given all the powers, a limited guardian would have more *clear* power than most plenary guardians. This is as it should be if the courts review each individual's needs, since it allows tailoring the limited guardianship to each individual, from the most competent person who needs help in only one area of living to the profoundly handicapped person who needs total care.

---

statutes. The Subcommittee looked at Washington's Surrogate Parent Plan and Michigan's Public Guardian Program and found flaws in both, as well as in California's existing public guardian program.

The first Office of Public Guardian in California had been created in Los Angeles by the state legislation in 1945. By mid-1967, 45 of the 58 counties in California had established public guardians. Unfortunately, in California the Office of Public Guardian was authorized only to provide its service to persons who were recipients of public aid or were patients in a county facility.

The MRPSAB's Guardianship Subcommittee eventually defined seven principles that it felt should be embodied in new California legislation (Kay et al., 1972). Although the political processes precluded upholding all of them, they are important to keep in mind because they make sense. The principles are as follows:

1. There must be a social institution that is primarily directed to the needs of the person, not his or her estate.
2. There must be a public agency to assume responsibility when the family can no longer provide necessary protection for its retarded members.
3. The plan must be flexible enough to allow adaptation to each individual's degree of disability.
4. The protective function must be available to the retarded person regardless of where he or she resides (admission to a hospital, for example, should not terminate public guardianship services).
5. The public guardianship program must be independent of the agencies that provide services to retarded individuals.
6. The procedure for appointment of the ''surrogate'' should be respectful of due process and should seek ways to provide meaningful review of the individual's capacities.
7. Protective services should be available to all who need them, without regard to age or degree of retardation.

The outcome of the Subcommittee's work was legislation introduced on April 19, 1968 by then-state senators Claire Burgener, Donald Grunsky and George Moscone (Senate Bill 1159, April 19, 1968). It provided for guardianship of children and of adults with severe impairments and for conservatorship (the term applied to limited guardianships of the person and limited guardianships of the estate in California) of adults with less severe impairments. There were many similarities between guardianship and conservatorship with the major difference being that a conservatee would *not* have to be found ''incompetent'' in court nor lose all rights. This limited the effect of conservatorship on the conservatee's rights, at least in theory. In reality, the rights were not clear and the conservatee was often treated as if he or she were a ward and had been found incompetent by the court.

Public guardianship and conservatorship were established in the Office of the Director of Health (later the Director of Developmental Services). The law called for the appointment of the Director of Health to be the public guardian. He or she would assign day-to-day guardianship responsibility to a counselor in a to-be-created system of regional (diagnostic and counseling) centers for mentally retarded individuals. This arrangement did not totally satisfy the seven principles that the drafting committee had originally advanced. The proposed legislation did not provide for a limited guardianship, and part of the reason for this was the feeling of some of the drafters that persons with mental retardation could not use their rights anyway. It also did not provide for a guardian who would be independent of service agencies. Legislation is usually the result of compromise and the result is often quite different from the drafters' intent. Political processes being what they are, the drafters decided that the compromise legislation was better than none.

CALIFORNIA'S LIMITED CONSERVATORSHIP

Once California's guardianship legislation was implemented, problems developed that indicated a need for new legislation. The lack of clarity in the law about the powers granted the conservator and those retained by the conservatee caused much confusion and uncertainty, as well as legal battles. It became increasingly clear that many conservatees could do some things for themselves that only their conservators were allowed to do.

In 1980, a bill was passed to correct many of the difficulties in the 1968 law (Assembly Bill 2898, March 6, 1980). This chapter briefly summarizes the new law and then provides a more detailed description of each revision.

First, the 1980 law eliminated guardianship for *adults* with developmental disabilities. It provided that the existing guardianships would become conservatorships and that the conservatee would not be declared incompetent, retaining any rights that were not specifically given to the conservator. Second, the new law listed seven powers that could either be assigned to a limited conservator or retained by the conservatee. The presumption was that a proposed conservatee would retain all of the listed and unlisted rights unless the court was convinced that it should grant them to the conservator. Some of the rights that can be given to the conservator are listed below.

1. The right to decide where the conservatee will live (conservators cannot use locked facilities or state hospitals in California)
2. The right to have access to the conservatee's confidential records
3. The right to enter into contracts
4. The right to give or withhold consent to medical care
5. The right to give or withhold consent to marriage
6. The right to make decisions concerning education
7. The right to control social and sexual contacts and relationships

Third, the new law required that regional (diagnostic, counseling, and services) centers for developmental disabilities perform an evaluation of the proposed conservatee, with the proposed conservatee's consent. The evaluation report must be filed within 30 days and must describe the nature and degree of the person's disability and *recommend* which powers the limited conservator should have. Recommendations are not binding on the court. Judges can and do sometimes disregard them.

Appointment of a Conservator

According to California law, a conservator of the person may be appointed for a person who is "unable properly to provide for his or her personal needs for physical health, food, clothing, or shelter" (California Probate Code, Section 1801). A limited conservator of the person or of the estate or both may be appointed for a developmentally disabled adult. California defines a developmental disability as a

> disability which originates before an individual attains 18; continues, or can be expected to continue, indefinitely; and constitutes a substantial handicap for such individual. As defined by the Director of Developmental Services, in consultation with the Superintendent of Public Instruction, this term shall include mental retardation, cerebral palsy, epilepsy and autism" (California Probate Code, Section 1420).

Before addressing the method of petitioning, the California Probate Code states that the intent of the legislature is that disabled citizens of the state receive services resulting in more independent productive and normal lives and that such services shall be the underlying mandate of the law. The first step in most states, as in California, is to file a petition for limited conservatorship.

A petition for limited conservatorship, in addition to the common matters such as a description of income, property, etc., must also contain the nature and degree of the alleged disability, the specific duties and powers requested by or for the limited conservator, and the limitations of civil and legal rights requested to be included in the court's order of appointment. This means that the petition has to describe the alleged developmental disability and how it limits the individual's capacity to make decisions, and then list which of the seven powers should be given to the conservator. Notice of hearing has to be sent at least 15 days before the hearing to the proposed conservatee and to the relatives named in the petition. A copy of the petition also has to sent to the regional center that would serve the individual if the individual were eligible for the service. The regional center is then required, with the proposed conservatee's consent, to perform an interdisciplinary assessment of the individual. By California law this must include at least social, psychological, and medical assessments, and must be reported to the court within 30 days. The regional center must first determine if the individual is developmentally disabled and eligible for the services of the regional center and the limited conservatorship. Next, the regional center must indicate the specific limitations the individual has and make recommendations as to which of the seven powers should be granted to the conservator.

Rights of the Proposed Conservatee

The proposed conservatee has a right to be present at the time of the hearing, to oppose conservatorship totally, or to oppose any of the powers to be given to the conservator. The proposed conservatee has a right to select and to be represented by legal counsel, the right to have legal counsel appointed by the court if unable to retain an attorney, and the right to a trial by jury if he or she requests it. A court investigator is required to explain the petition to the proposed conservatee, including each power requested by the conservator and the effects of each limitation on the rights of the individual. The court investigator will answer any questions the proposed conservatee has and communicate to the court a report of the proposed conservatee's feelings about the conservatorship.

Court Hearing

At the hearing, the court will inquire into the nature and extent of the intellectual functioning of the individual alleged to be developmentally disabled and evaluate the extent of the impairment of the proposed conservatee's adaptive behavior. The court will determine his or her capacity to care for himself or herself and property if applicable. The court may use the regional center reports and will interview the proposed conservatee. The court will then inquire into the qualifications, abilities, capabilities, and motivation of the person seeking to be appointed as limited conservator. Finally, if the proposed conservatee did not consent to evaluation by the regional center, the court will inquire as to the reason for withholding of such consent and act accordingly.

Findings in Order

If the court finds that the proposed limited conservatee actually does possess the capacity to care for himself or herself or to manage his or her property as a reasonably prudent person would, the court shall dismiss the petition for appointment of a limited conservator. If the court finds, however, that the proposed limited conservatee does lack the capacity to perform some of the tasks necessary to provide properly for personal needs and health, food, clothing, etc., then a limited conservator will be appointed. In its order, the court will report the findings that the individual is developmentally disabled and the specific disabilities that result in limitations on the conservatee's rights. The order of the court will specify which powers are granted to and which duties are imposed upon the limited conservator, powers and duties that will not exceed the powers and duties applicable to a conservator under the code. The court will also specify the properties, debts, rentals, wages, or other claims due to the limited conservatee and obligations for which the conservatee may be liable.

Termination of Conservatorship

The limited conservator, the conservatee, or any relative or friend of the conservatee may apply to the superior court for termination of the limited conservatorship or to have specific powers and duties of the conservator revoked. In addition, 1 year after the appointment of a limited conservator and every second year thereafter, a court investigator will visit the conservatee and inquire as to the conservatee's wishes and the conservatee's abilities and disabilities as well as the performance of the conservator. The court then has the option to modify the conservatorship, change conservators, or terminate the limited conservatorship entirely.

Current Status

Since the passage of the first laws allowing the director of either health or developmental services to become the guardian or conservator of a person with a developmental disability, there have been over 650 petitions filed by the department. There are currently (as of March 16, 1983) 628 conservatees of the 60,000 clients on the rolls of regional centers (probably half of whom are adults).

To evaluate the effectiveness of California's revised guardianship legislation, readers may refer to the principles that the drafters of the earlier legislation labored to achieve and see if the principles were satisfied. The first principle was that there should be a social institution primarily directed to the needs of the *person*, not the estate. In California, the director of developmental services, acting through the regional centers, is directed primarily toward personal needs. The staff, either social workers or public health nurses, are trained for personal needs, not financial management. The services are part of a process that includes medical, psychological, and social assessments, 95% of which is concerned with personal needs and 5% with financial assessment to determine eligibility for public funds needed to support services. The management of the few estates for which the director of developmental services is conservator is accomplished by the headquarters of the department, not the regional centers.

The second principle was that there should be a public agency to assume responsibility when parents are no longer able to provide protection for their retarded offspring. Currently, the regional centers stand ready to provide the service of limited conservatorship on behalf of the director of developmental services. There is a qualification to their readiness, however. The staffing of regional centers is only as good as the legislature is willing to pay. As of this writing, caseloads average 70 or more per case manager and the state of California is proposing a shift that will increase the number of clients for each case manager by about one third. Since "there is no free lunch," one third more clients is tantamount to one third less service for each client. The minimal standard for most clients is to have a "face to face" visit quarterly from their case manager. This is not very often and the frequency may soon be reduced to 3 times per year. One must question the effectiveness of a conservator with 90 conservatees. The diligence and dedication of the case managers have prevented disastrous consequences and the availability of the service, albeit weakened by inadequate staffing, is certainly better than nothing.

The third principle was that the plan should be flexible enough to allow adaptation to each individual's degree of disability. With the advent of the limited conservatorship law, the conservatorship *can* be tailored to the needs of each individual by the judicious allocation of powers to the conservator and conservatee. The regional centers possess access to, but not always funding for, services ranging from state hospitals to apartment living programs to adult vocational programs. As previously indicated, the staff may soon begin taking longer to connect people with the programs and services they need, but the flexibility is there.

The fourth and seventh principles are related. The fourth states that the protective services of conservatorship should be available regardless of location. The seventh states that such services should be available regardless of age or degree of disability. The conservatorship of the person provided by the director of developmental services is through the regional center system, 21 centers that cover the entire state. The centers have access to state hospitals; however, there is a proposal as of this writing to eliminate staffing at the regional centers for the hospital clients since the hospitals have social workers. There is, of course, a problem with continuity when conservatees change location or type of living arrangement since such changes generally result in a change of social worker and/or a change of regional center. Thus, continuity is by transfer of records, not by maintaining the same person involved.

The director of developmental services provides conservatorship services to adults of any age but not to children (under 18). The main reason is that the needs of children for protection are the same regardless of the child's disabilities or lack of disability. A second reason is that the procedure of establishing conservatorship for an adult is time consuming since it is coordinated from the state capital regardless of the client's location. The counties all have child protective services with 24 hour "hot lines," and quick access to law enforcement officers and local courts.

The fifth principle was that public conservatorship/guardianship must be independent of the agencies that provide services to retarded individuals. Unfortunately, this principle was never upheld. The regional centers do provide services for retarded persons and do purchase other services. Both of these facts provide conflicts between client interests and agency interests.

The sixth principle was that the procedure for appointment of a "surrogate" conservator should be respectful of due process and should provide meaningful review of the individual's capacities. For the public (department of developmental services) conservatorship, the review is complete and multilayered. Each regional center has at least one or two layers of review. The department of developmental services, legal affairs section reviews each request for a petition and questions each carefully. The courts then review each petition before appointing a conservator. Thereafter, an annual report follows the same path with slightly less diligence since there are over 600 of them a year. There is a requirement that the regional center review all requests for private conservatorships and recommend to the court which powers the conservatee should keep and which should go to the conservator, if any. The courts seldom heed these reports and grant conservatorships exactly as petitioned despite the conservatee's abilities and needs. Conservatees of the director of developmental services have much more careful review.

In all, the services provided by the director of developmental services are useful, within limits. One limit, the worst, is the caseload size (not the conflict of interest). Even the most ethical, most dedicated regional case manager is only one person. The caseload size precludes the level of individualized *personal* services that could be given if a smaller number of clients had to be served. With 70 clients to serve, it is difficult to give truly personal services, but with 90, it is impossible.

Conflict of interest is a secondary problem. The built-in conflict between agency needs and client needs is usually reduced to a minimum by the regional center social work staff. Most of the regional center case managers are, as a group, especially dedicated, conscientious, and ethical. These traits follow people into administrative positions. There are, however, a few social workers who are just doing a job, but very few. Still, the possibility of having a conflict of interest is there.

Given the balance of positive and negative aspects, nomination of the director of developmental services to be the conservator of a son or daughter is still better than not having a conservator when needed. A good, willing relative is usually better. A private conservator with small caseloads and no conflict would be an excellent alternative if available.

REFERENCES

Dybwad, G. Trends and issues in mental retardation. In *White House conference on children & youth*. Washington, D.C.: U.S. Government Printing Office, 1960.

International League of Societies for the Mentally Handicapped (ILSMH). *San Sebastian Symposium on Guardianship of the Mentally Retarded.*, Brussels, Belgium: ILSMH, 1969.

Kay, H., Farnham, L.J., Karren, B.D., Knakal, J., & Diamond, P.M. Legal planning for the mentally retarded: The California experience. *California Law Review*, 1972, *60*, 438–529.

Lessard v. *Schmidt*, 349 F.Supp. 1078 (E.D. Wisc. 1972), 415 U.S. 473 (1974), 379 F.Supp. 1376 (E.D. Wisc. 1974), 95 S.Ct. 1943 (175).

Mills v. *Board of Education*, 348 F.Supp. 866 (D.D.C. 1972).

National Center for Law and the Handicapped. *Guardianship of the mentally impaired; a critical analysis*. South Bend, IN: National Center for Law and the Handicapped, Inc., 1977.

New York State Association for Retarded Citizens v. *Rockefeller*, 357 F.Supp. 752–762 (E.D.N.Y. 1973), 395 F.Supp. 715 (E.D.N.Y. 1975).

Public Law 92-603, 1972.

Public Law 93-112, Rehabilitation Act of 1973, July 26, 1973.

Public Law 94-103, Developmental Disabilities Assistance and Bill of Rights Act, June 26, 1975.
Public Law 94-142, Education for All Handicapped Children Act of 1975, November 29, 1975.
United Nations General Assembly, New York, 2027th Plenary Session, December 20, 1971.
Wyatt v. *Stickney*, 344 F.Supp. 387, 395, 1971.

Conservatorship: Protecting Well-Being while Promoting Self-Reliance

Laura White

Jane is an 18-year-old woman residing in a small group home. She has been in foster care placement off and on since early childhood. There are numerous documentations in the record outlining a somewhat tragic past.

Jane was born to a single parent. Jane's mother had a long history of psychiatric problems. During her early years, Jane had many "fathers," and there are several documented incidents of physical and sexual abuse. The family was receiving AFDC (welfare) payments. Neighbors would call in and report to the social worker that Jane was not being supervised, was dirty, or was observed being abused. Finally, at age 7, Jane was removed from the home and placed in foster care.

In the majority of cases, the Child Protective Services (CPS) department of the department of social services has a duty to try to reunify the family whenever possible. The mother maintained her contact with Jane and her CPS worker, cleaned up the home, and her then-current boyfriend moved out. So, after a few months, Jane was returned to the home. Things seemed to go smoothly without major incident until the mother was hospitalized after having what was, apparently, a psychotic episode. Jane was again placed in foster care and, after the mother was released from the hospital, Jane was again returned to her mother.

Her mother moved frequently, which made it difficult for an already over-burdened system to keep track of Jane. At some point, it became apparent to the school that Jane was not able to understand or retain information that was being taught. Through testing, Jane was found to be mildly mentally retarded and, at that point, became a regional center client. A transfer to special education classes proved to be helpful cognitively. However, about this same time, Jane began exhibiting some negative behaviors—screaming, self-abuse, extreme fearfulness. Further testing revealed serious emotional difficulties. Efforts were made to engage the mother in a treatment plan for Jane, but she proved unable to follow through. The added burden of having a child with special needs only worsened the mother's own problematic existence. Jane's behavior problems not only continued, but increased, until Jane was finally made a ward of the court and placed again in foster care.

The mother reacted violently to this situation, threatened legal action, became paranoid, and was eventually hospitalized for a short time once again. She continued contact with Jane on a sporadic basis, promising to come visit and then not showing up, or showing up several days later. Jane's foster care family found this a very trying time, especially since Jane's behavior problems continued and even escalated from time to time. The mother would take Jane home for weekend visits and Jane would return in an agitated, rebellious, and even aggressive state. Visits home were limited and, after another incident of sexual abuse by the mother's boyfriend, Jane was placed in a home out of the county, some 600 miles away.

For a time, the mother did not know Jane's whereabouts. Eventually, however, phone contact was resumed. The mother did not have the financial resources to visit Jane, who was then about 14.

It was apparent that Jane was very attached to her mother. She would talk about her mother frequently, whine and cry that she wanted to see her, etc. At this time, Jane's negative behaviors consisted of screaming, pulling her own hair out, and biting herself. There was one incident when Jane ran scalding hot water in the bathtub, then got in, burning herself severely.

Through documentation, it became apparent that Jane's self-abusive behaviors increased sharply following contact with her mother. Also, Jane would frequently become agitated during conversations with her mother. Finally, it was agreed by all parties (Jane, her mother, the Child Protective Services worker, the regional center worker, facility staff) that facility staff would monitor phone calls, and be able to interrupt them should Jane become overly agitated. Jane's behavior did indeed improve when this plan was added to the behavior modification program already in effect.

When Jane reached age 18, her wardship would come to an end and the California courts would have no way to protect her any further. Calls from her mother increased and were terminated more quickly as she "prepared" Jane for "coming home" when she turned 18. She told Jane that she was buying her favorite foods and making plans just for her. Jane, meanwhile, was torn. She was learning to care for her own needs, learning independent living skills, and learning to relate to other people in the group home. Her self-abuse had lessened and she was generally happy with herself and her achievements. But now her mother, whom she loved, was asking, even begging her to make a decision to come home.

The CPS worker was very concerned that Jane was not capable of making such a decision and it was her opinion that Jane needed continued protection of her rights. She asked that the regional center petition for limited conservatorship of the person. After consultation with facility staff, Jane's psychiatrist, and the CPS worker, plus interviews with Jane herself, and review of all past records, it was determined that conservatorship would, indeed, be appropriate.

Since there was no other interested relative who could act as conservator, the director of developmental services of the state of California was nominated for appointment.

It was explained to Jane, as clearly as possible, what a conservatorship meant and what would happen as a result. Basically, her life would remain the same; she could continue to grow and develop within the sphere she had come to trust and enjoy.

The mother was notified of the procedure and court date. She became hysterical; calls to Jane increased. She threatened facility staff. Jane became more agitated. Her mother stated she would retain a lawyer and contest the conservatorship.

Meanwhile, materials were gathered: reports, assessments, and interviews that would support Jane's need for conservatorship. On the day of the hearing, all was in readiness for a conflict. Jane was present, extremely anxious. The mother did not appear. She was not represented by an attorney. The conservatorship was uncontested and the director of developmental services appointed conservator with the local regional center director being designated as representative.

Jane's life didn't change much. The mother dropped her contact for a period of months. Jane was afforded the protection she deserves, and retained the human right to be free from harm and to benefit from the resources society has to offer.

Chapter 12

Guardianship in Alberta, Canada

Joel R. Christie

Alberta is a province in Western Canada with a population of approximately 2½ million. In December of 1978, this province proclaimed the Dependent Adults Act. This act, unique in Canada, offered an innovative legal means to provide support and protection for those adults whose disabilities are such that they cannot care for themselves and make reasonable judgments on their own behalf. It identified due process to be followed in obtaining orders specific to the individual, as well as granting powers of substitute decision-making to the guardian to allow him or her to make decisions for another adult.

This act is primarily human rights legislation. All Albertans over the age of 18 who meet the criteria of dependency are eligible to have a legal surrogate decision-maker appointed who is accountable to the courts for making decisions that are in the best interest of the dependent adult. This substitute decision-maker can provide a substantial measure of protection from abuse, neglect, or victimization. For those persons who do not have family members or an interested person who would apply to become their guardian/trustee, the act establishes an office of the public guardian as well as an office of the public trustee to make application and/or become that individual's guardian or trustee. Although some mention is made of the trusteeship portions of the act, the main focus of this chapter is on the guardianship provisions.

The primary objective of the guardianship provisions of the Dependent Adults Act is to provide a legal substitute decision-maker (guardian) who assumes legal responsibility for making decisions on behalf of the dependent adult according to the nature and extent of the court order issued. The guardian is expected to facilitate the development of an individualized support system that recognizes and respects the dependent adult's dignity and best interests, promotes the development of the dependent adult's ability to act independently, and utilizes the least restrictive alternative in the choices of decisions made.

This chapter provides a detailed description of the Dependent Adults Act and the office of the public guardian that was established to assure a guardian to all persons who: 1) require such services and 2) do not have a relative or friend who is appropriate and available to act as guardian. Before going into more detail, the background that led to the development of this legislation is examined.

LEGISLATION

In Canada, the law generally provides that upon attaining the age of majority (18 years of age in Alberta), a person is no longer under the guardianship of his or her parents. No other person has authority to make decisions or give consents on behalf of another person without a court order providing specific authority to act in that capacity. (For a review of the legal history of guardianship and trusteeship legislation, see, McLaughlin, P. *Guardianship of the Person.* Toronto: National Institute on Mental Retardation, 1979, pp. 35–46; and Burgdorf, R. L., Jr. [ed.]. *The Legal Rights of Handicapped Persons: Cases, Materials, and Text.* Baltimore: Paul H. Brookes Publishing Co., 1980, p. 528.) Prior to 1972, mentally retarded individuals, those suffering from chronic brain disorders, mentally ill persons, and those suffering physical brain trauma were often institutionalized and treated under the Mental Health Act. In Alberta specifically, the prevailing philosophy was to protect both society and the individual by removing persons in need of extensive treatment from the community and treating them within an institutional setting. Two pieces of legislation, the Mentally Incapacitated Persons Act and the Mental Health Act served as the legal base from which this philosophy was practiced. The Mental Health Act allowed the next of kin or the superintendent of a facility to consent to the treatment of a mentally incapacitated adult if that individual was not capable of giving his or her own consent for treatment. The rights of these persons to make decisions in any other areas of their life were not specifically mentioned in this act.

The Mentally Incapacitated Persons Act allowed the court to appoint a "committee" of the person and estate for those adults of unsound mind or mental infirmity. The act granted sweeping powers to the committee to handle any and all aspects of an individual's estate or life; however, the primary focus was on the management of properties and estates (trusteeship issues).

In 1972, a new Mental Health Act was proclaimed that limited the target population covered by that act to only mentally ill individuals. It also repealed the section of the act that allowed for the next of kin or the medical superintendent of a facility to consent to treatment. This created a gap in the legislation of the province as related to consent to treatment. Interim legislation, the Emergency Medical Aid Act, was passed that permitted ordinary medical/dental treatment without consent if: a) in the opinion of two physicians or dentists the adult person requiring ordinary treatment was incapable of giving consent and b) to the best of their knowledge this individual had not objected to such treatment in the past.

A "white paper" was then prepared and distributed to the public suggesting new legislation based on the guardianship principles proposed by the 1969 San Sebastian Symposium on Guardianship of the Mentally Retarded (International League of Societies for the Mentally Handicapped, 1969). This "white paper" proposed extending guardianship not only to mentally retarded individuals but to any adult who was deemed by the courts to be incapable of making reasonable decisions on his or her own behalf. During one of the public debates on this "white paper," it was suggested that guardianship should also be extended to those persons who had no one to act in their best interests. A "public guardian" was proposed to fill this gap. The current Dependent Adults Act evolved from these discussions and was proclaimed on December 1, 1978. The Dependent Adults Act reflects a change in treatment philosophy and the provincial government's social outlook that assumes that individuals should be moved out of institutions and treated within the community context wherever possible.

The Dependent Adults Act replaced and expanded upon the Mentally Incapacitated Persons Act (which is similar to most existing Canadian legislation in this area) as outlined in Table 1.

The Dependent Adults Act specifies the due process to be followed when an adult requires a legal substitute decision-maker and ensures that decisions made are regularly reviewed by the Courts. The act also distinguishes between "trusteeship" (the person's ability to handle his or her financial matters) and "guardianship" (the adult's ability to make personal life decisions excluding finances). Under the Dependent Adults Act, trusteeship and guardianship are dealt with separately. An adult person may have someone appointed to handle his or her financial or estate matters and continue to make his or her own personal decisions, or *vice-versa*. The primary focus of this legislation is on the dependent adult, his or her individual rights, and potential for development. Least restrictive alternatives are emphasized and guardianship decisions are to be made with the best interests of the dependent adult in mind. (For a review of current guardianship legislation in North America, see, Marlett, N. *Issues of Competence and the Dependent Adults Act*. Calgary: Vocational and Rehabilitation Research Institute and the Office of the Public Guardian, 1980, pp. B12–B21.)

Criteria for Guardianship

An application for guardianship must include not only diagnostic but also functional assessments. To ensure due process, and, as well, to verify the accuracy of this information, the act requires that a copy of the application be served on the potential dependent adult, the next of kin, the director of the institution (if applicable), the public guardian, the dependent adult's trustee (if applicable), and any other person the judge deems appropriate.

Table 1. Comparison of past and current Canadian law in the area of guardianship

Mentally Incapacitated Persons Act	**Dependent Adults Act**
1. Focused on estate	1. Focuses on the person (estate matters are separated from ability to handle personal matters)
2. Person declared totally incompetent when committee was appointed	2. Trusteeship separate from plenary/partial guardianship
3. No scheduled reviews	3. Regularly scheduled reviews, as well as dependent adult/''interested person'' review upon request at any time
4. Onus on mentally incapacitated person to prove he or she is competent	4. Onus on ''interested person'' to prove areas dependent adult cannot decide in his or her own best interests
5. Diagnostic evidence	5. Functional as well as diagnostic evidence
6. No guidelines for action	6. Guidelines for action: best interests, enhance well-being, least restrictive alternatives, access to court for advice
7. Broad range of unspecified power—authority of committee over personal matters uncertain, substitute decisions could only be made in institutions (1964 *Mental Health Act*) and thereby reinforced institutionalization	7. Tailor-made orders—promoting community living by dependent persons
8. Alberta Supreme Court	8. Court of Queen's Bench

Under the Dependent Adults Act, a guardian may be appointed for a dependent adult if the following conditions are met:

(1) When the Court is satisfied that a person named in an application for an Order appointing a guardian is:
    (a) an adult,
    (b) unable
        (i) to care for himself, and
        (ii) to make reasonable judgments in respect of all or any of the matters relating to his person, and
    (c) in need of a guardian, the Court may make an Order appointing a plenary guardian or a partial guardian.
(2) The Court shall not make an Order under subsection (1) unless it is satisfied that the Order would be in the best interests of the person in respect of whom the application is made.
(3) The Court shall not make an Order appointing a plenary guardian unless it is satisfied that a partial guardianship order would be insufficient to meet the needs of the person in respect of whom the application is made (Government of Alberta, 1980, p. 6).

The surrogate court judge considers the affidavit information in a chambers hearing. Anyone served with this functional and diagnostic information has a right to appear in court, as can any other interested person whom the court agrees to hear. The judge uses this information to determine whether or not the individual meets the above criteria for *each* of the following areas:

To decide where to live
To decide with whom to consort and live
To decide the nature and type of social activities
To decide the nature or type of work or conditions of work
To decide the type of educational, vocational, or other training
To decide to apply for any license, permit, approval, or other consent or authorization as required by law
To commence, compromise, or settle any legal proceedings that do not relate to the estate
To consent to any health care that is in the best interests of the dependent adult
To make normal day-to-day decisions such as diet and dress

If the court determines that the individual meets the criteria in one or more of the above areas, partial guardianship is granted (Appendix A). If the judge rules that the individual needs a guardian in all of these areas and, in addition, believes that the guardian should have the same authority as a parent in respect to a child under 14 years of age, then plenary or total guardianship is granted. It should be emphasized that before granting plenary (total) guardianship, the judge must be convinced that partial guardianship would not meet all of the needs of the dependent adult.

Since much of the information given to the judge is functional and somewhat subjective in nature, the office of the public guardian commissioned a study to identify which functional factors were highly correlated with a person's inability to make decisions. The resulting assessment instruments are currently being used to gather information to be presented to the court (Marlett, 1980). The outcomes of this study are presented in Chapter 7.

Decision-Making Areas

All appointed *guardians* are accountable to the courts for the decisions they make on behalf of the dependent adult. The Dependent Adults Act provides the principles upon which a guardian's decisions should be based.

A guardian shall exercise his power and authority:

(a) in the best interests of the Dependent Adult,
(b) in such a way as to encourage the Dependent Adult to become capable of caring for himself and of making reasonable judgments in respect of matters relating to his person, and
(c) in the least restrictive manner possible (Government of Alberta, 1980, Section 11, p. 13).

The principles involved in the implementation of the guardianship order parallel those involved in normalization (Wolfensberger, 1972). If the guardian is in doubt as to what would be in the best interests of the dependent adult in a specific situation, he or she may return to court to seek the judge's advice. The final decision, however, rests with the guardian. It may be instructive to review a number of the primary issues that the guardian may have to address in carrying out his or her responsibilities.

Place of Residence The order may give the guardian responsibility for where the dependent adult lives, whether temporarily or permanently. The dependent adult should have access to accommodation that will promote his or her growth and development as fully as possible; care for his or her physical and emotional needs; and resemble, as closely as possible, a normal living environment.

The place where a dependent adult lives should be the least restrictive environment possible. If care in an institution, nursing home, or auxiliary hospital is deemed necessary for medical services or other reasons, it is the role of the guardian to ensure that such accommodations are appropriate and as personalized or individualized as possible.

Social Contacts In this diverse society, how does one decide where a dependent adult should live, or with whom he or she should associate? It is the guardian's responsibility to ensure that the dependent adult is not exploited, victimized, or abused by others. A reasonable balance must be struck between allowing the dependent adult to grow, develop, and exercise the dignity of risk, and the need to ensure that the individual is not exploited.

Social Activities Social activities are significant as they encourage the development of a person's self-respect, allowing personal growth and a sense of identification with the community. A guardian should be aware of the activities in which the dependent adult is involved and of the activities in which he or she could further participate, whether he or she is in an institution or in the community. The role of the guardian in this area is to ensure that the dependent adult is engaged in activities appropriate to his or her interests and capabilities and that will help him or her remain oriented to, and active within, his or her community context. Are there any cultural, ethnic, or religious social activities that the dependent adult could be participating in with the help of his or her guardian?

Employment If employment is a reasonable and meaningful goal for the dependent adult, it is the guardian's responsibility to ensure that the dependent adult has the appropriate assistance to find a job that he or she is capable of doing, that offers him or her growth and development opportunities, and that does not have the potential to victimize or abuse him or her. Particular considerations the guardian may wish to give attention to are: the growth possibilities in the position, training programs, prevailing minimum wages, individualized safety devices or special work aids if necessary, and the usual employee rights such as health care or vacation benefits.

Education and Training Some of the most critical, and possibly the most difficult decisions a guardian must make, are in the area of education and training.

What are the best programs available? Where is the best place to go for advice and assistance? What are the goals of each program and what is each program going to do for the dependent adult? Does the program fit the needs of the dependent adult or is the dependent adult being placed in a program simply because there is available space? Has an assessment been done or counselling provided that indicates the capabilities and skills of the dependent adult and his or her training needs?

Probably the most important question is, "Can the dependent adult succeed in this program?" Usually, persons enter a program and either pass or fail, then go on to something different. Many dependent adults are channeled into programs that provide little opportunity for development, growth, and movement but are simply places to go to fill time. The guardian may have no available alternate program; however, he or she should understand the limits of this type of programming and should attempt to locate a more appropriate program.

Licenses and Permits   Is the dependent adult being denied a license or permit for which he or she qualifies? Does he or she receive goods or services that might involve signing an agreement? If this is the case, then it is the responsibility of the guardian to advocate on behalf of the dependent adult to obtain the license or permit and to ensure that the agreement is as favorable as possible to the dependent adult.

Is the dependent adult being victimized or abused by persons who may wish to take advantage of him or her? Is he or she being asked to sign a license, permit, or contract that is not in his or her best interests? If this is so, then it is the guardian's responsibility to protect the dependent adult.

Legal Matters   A mentally incapacitated person has the right to protection from exploitation, abuse, and degrading treatment. If prosecuted for any offence, he or she has a right to due process of law, with full recognition given to his or her degree of mental capacity. A guardian has a responsibility to ensure that the dependent adult obtains a lawyer, that the lawyer is properly instructed, and that the appropriate authorities are told about the nature and degree of the dependent adult's mental incapacity. The guardian is not responsible for any offense committed by the dependent adult unless, of course, the guardian is directly implicated in the offense.

The guardian must also ensure that all civil matters are taken care of in the dependent adult's best interest. The trustee would become involved in the solving of any financial matters.

Health Care   Health is one of life's most precious commodities. It is the guardian's responsibility to take both an active and a reactive role in the health care of the dependent adult. The active role would be to determine the present needs of the dependent adult and to advocate for such medically related treatments as physiotherapy, occupational therapy, speech therapy, and other medical programs the dependent adult may require.

The reactive role is giving informed consent for health care that the dependent adult needs. When a doctor or health care professional suggests that certain health care is needed, a guardian should ask himself certain questions before giving his consent:

What are the alternatives to this treatment?
What are the risks involved in this treatment?
What are the risks if the advised treatment is not carried out?
Is this treatment in the best interests of the dependent adult?
Is this treatment the least restrictive/drastic treatment possible?
How does the dependent adult feel about the procedure or treatment?
Is the treatment congruent with the dependent adult's values and beliefs?
What are the outcomes or consequences of the treatment?

If the guardian's answers to the above questions indicate that the health care procedures are necessary and in the best interests of the dependent adult, he or she may give consent for the treatment. If, on the other hand, the guardian believes treatment may be detrimental or unnecessary, he or she may ask for a second medical opinion. For very serious operations or situations, the guardian may ask the court for advice and direction as to what is in the best interests of the dependent adult.

Daily Decisions   The guardian may have one of two roles in daily decisions. If the dependent adult is a person who is going to grow and develop, the guardian should be asking such questions as: Is the dependent adult getting proper training to prepare him- or herself? Is the dependent adult being taught appropriate personal hygiene and life skills? Has an assessment been done and what are the goals of the residential training program? What steps are being taken to maintain the individual in the community?

If the dependent adult's disabilities are such that maintenance of his or her condition and prevention of further deterioration is of prime importance, questions that the guardian must ask are: Is the dependent adult getting a nutritious diet? Is the dependent adult wearing suitable clothing? Is the dependent adult's personal cleanliness being maintained? Is there any special food or clothing that could be obtained that would improve the dependent adult's quality of life?

The individual dependent adult's abilities and the nature of his or her dependency will determine the most appropriate goals for the guardian. The guardian should always remember that even though a dependent adult may need to live in an institution, he or she can be dressed normally, have living environments as personalized as possible, and can still live and act as everyone else does in their own homes.

Decision-Making Dilemmas

The dilemmas facing guardians in the exercising of their authority are great—especially if the value system of the guardian differs from that of the dependent adult. Dilemmas occur when one is faced with equally attractive or unattractive alternatives. Even when a decision or choice is made and resultant activities are undertaken, it is still difficult to determine if it was the "right" choice. Choices may be made more difficult by the realization that decisions are also reviewed on a regular basis by the courts.

It is difficult enough for thinking and reasoning people to utilize their own experiences, values, and ambitions when resolving dilemmas in their own lives. It is much more difficult to face and try to resolve a dilemma for someone else. Problems arise when one person makes a decision for another based on his or her own values. Decisions for dependent persons are sometimes made without taking into consideration the fact that they may be utilizing quite different values and assumptions to understand and resolve the situation. People automatically assume that their goals, ambitions, or way of reasoning is either the "right way" or is at least similar to those of others. It seems that it is on this assumption that self-help groups, such as "People First," concentrate. Their message (that as a consumer group, they know best for themselves) is met with parental attitudes based on the love a parent has for a child and the wish every parent has to protect his or her child from pain if at all possible. This, in turn, is met with the obective, scientific approach learned by professionals who are trying to intervene through the planned utilization of their professional skills associated with the ethics and standards of their profession. Everyone is trying to do "what is best" according to their own perspective. *But what really is "best"?* Who decides what is "best"? What gives that person the power and authority to make the decision? How will he or she resolve each of the dilemmas faced? What principles or guidelines should be followed?

If there is one answer to these questions, it appears to be "it depends." It depends on the history and experience of each of the persons involved. It depends on how they perceive the problem. It depends on the constructs or models they are utilizing to define the problem. It depends on the alternatives they have managed to develop and the resources available to realize them. It depends on the perceived risks involved, the consequences flowing therefrom, and the values and assumptions of the individuals involved. All of these must be looked at through the eyes of the dependent adult.

Court Review of Guardianships

The Dependent Adults Act allows any interested person to request a review of the guardianship order at any time. The court will review the dependent adult's situation and the guardian's decision at least every 3 years. If the judge feels that the dependent adult still requires guardianship in some areas, and that the guardian has properly exercised his or her power and authority, then a further order may be granted. This order again must be reviewed within a 3-year period (or sooner if specified in the court order).

During the review, the court can question the guardian as to how he or she believed his or her decisions to be in the best interests of the dependent adult. The guardian's actual decisions should be as congruent as possible with the dependent adult's value system and should take into account all the risks and alternatives presented to the guardian at the time the decision was made. As mentioned earlier, a guardian facing a particularly difficult decision can seek advice and direction from the court to help resolve dilemmas that arise.

Compulsory Care

After the act was proclaimed, it was recognized that the guardian had no authority to legally consent to the confinement of a dependent adult any more than a parent can legally confine his or her child for extended periods of time.

In October of 1981, the Dependent Adults Act was amended to include a compulsory care section. This section outlines the due process that must be followed and the regular reviews that must occur when a dependent adult is deemed to be a danger to himself or herself or others and requires confinement as the proper means of protection and treatment. It protects the dependent adult's rights by requiring a judge to review medical, psychological, and social evidence that supports the need for confinement. This section only applies to dependent adults who already have a guardian and/or trustee appointed. This is to ensure that the dependent adult's position is represented during the hearing. The section reads as follows:

> A Court shall only make a Compulsory Care Order if:
> (a) it has considered a medical, psychological and social assessment that shows the extent to which the dependent adult presents a danger to himself or others.
> (b) it is satisfied that it is in the best interests of the dependent adult that he be confined in a "Place of Care."
> (c) it is satisfied that the dependent adult is in a condition that presents a danger to himself or to others.
> (d) it is satisfied that a Compulsory Care Order is a proper means of ensuring the protection and treatment of the dependent adult (Government of Alberta, 1980, pp. 9–10, Section 10. 1[3]).

Once a compulsory care order is issued, a dependent adult can be confined to one of six "places of care" in the province. The person in charge of the "place of care" is required to provide any diagnostic and treatment services that the dependent adult needs (which have been consented to by the guardian and which the place of care can provide); a reasonable level of security; and must, at least once every 3 months, reassess the diagnostic and treatment service. In addition to these quarterly reviews done by the place of care, a ministerially appointed appeal panel, consisting of two physicians, a member of the general public, and an attorney, must review the dependent adult's situation annually.

If the appeal panel decides that the dependent adult no longer requires confinement, it notifies the public guardian, who must then apply to the court for a review. At any time, the dependent adult, or any interested person, can apply for a review of this order. The court must, however, review the situation at least every 3 years.

The dependent adult can obtain legal counsel to represent him or her at any hearings to ensure that his or her best interests are further protected.

IMPLICATIONS OF THE DEPENDENT ADULTS ACT

The Guardian's Role

As mentioned in the beginning of this chapter, the objective of the guardianship programs under the Dependent Adults Act is to provide legal substitute decision-makers who will facilitate the development of an individualized support system. This support system is to recognize and respect the dependent adult's dignity and best interests, utilize the least restrictive alternatives, and promote the development of the dependent adult's ability to act independently. The guardian, whether private or public, is the means through which this objective is achieved for each dependent adult. The functions of the guardian fall basically into three categories:

—Monitoring the direct services being provided to the dependent adult
—Deciding or consenting for the dependent adult
—Advocating for the services required by the dependent adult to realize his or her potential

The role of the guardian is separate from those of the service providers. His or her job is to ensure that the values and wishes of the dependent adult are being taken into consideration by the service providers. This is similar to the roles performed by a citizen advocate (Wolfensberger & Zauha, 1973) with the exception that the guardian has a legal authority and is accountable to the court rather than solely to a less defined contract with the protege. Ideally, the guardian becomes the means through which the dependent adult achieves his or her full potential. The principles inherent in the achievement of this goal include: 1) accessibility, 2) empathy, 3) availability of expertise, 4) continuity of care, 5) accountability, and 6) community-based setting.

Since the purpose of guardianship is to promote the development of the dependent adult, the guardian must be accessible to both the dependent adult and the service providers. This simply means that the guardian must make decisions, monitor guardianship, and otherwise assist the dependent adult. The type and duration of this accessibility must be determined by the needs and the situation of the dependent adult. If the guardian is to make decisions for the dependent adult as if *he or she* were the dependent adult, the guardian must be empathetic to the needs, values, and wishes of the dependent adult. It is only through understanding that the guardian can ensure that the decisions he or she makes are as individualized and as congruent with the dependent adult's value system as is possible. Moreover, if the guardian is to decide in the best interests of the dependent adult, he or she must be aware of all the risks and advantages of the various alternatives put before him or her (Wolfensberger & Zauha, 1973). The guardian's decision must be an individualized and informed decision. *To accomplish this, it must be specific, voluntary, informed, and competent* (Picard, 1978). To meet these criteria, the guardian must be able to seek out and receive adequate information from the appropriate experts involved.

Ideally, the same guardian will be responsible for the same dependent adult for as long as guardianship is necessary. This not only provides the dependent adult with a continuous source of personal support but also provides continuity in the decision-making for the dependent adult.

Under the Dependent Adults Act, the guardian is accountable to the court for deciding in the best interests of the dependent adult and in accordance with the criteria that are presented on page 187 of this chapter. Since the dependent adult is usually incapable of supervising the actions of his or her guardian, it is important that the decisions made by the guardian be reviewed on a regular basis. In Alberta, the review documents contain a brief outline of the type and nature of the decisions rendered on behalf of the dependent adult. They are reviewed to see if the decisions were in the best interests of the dependent adult, were made in such a way as to encourage the dependent adult to become capable of caring for himself or herself and making reasonable judgments on his or her own behalf, and were made in the least restrictive manner possible.

To be effective, guardianship must become part of the fabric of life of the community. It must be viewed as the last resort of the continuous protective services available to dependent persons. Guardianship should be viewed as a family and community responsibility before being perceived as a responsibility of the state. The role of the state is to provide the enabling legislation and the backup resources required to encourage suitable family and community persons to become guardians and to assume the role of guardian via the office of the public guardian only when absolutely necessary.

The Public Guardian

The Dependent Adults Act assigns a number of functions to the office of the public guardian. First, since the public guardian is served with all application and review documents, he or she monitors the guardianship system to ensure that the intent of the Dependent Adults Act is realized. Guardianship is sought only as a last resort and the office of the public guardian may intervene, formally or informally, where it feels that documentation to the courts is incomplete. Intervention may also occur when there are questions as to the nature and extent of the guardianship requested or when there are concerns relating to the suitability of the proposed guardian. The public guardian may intervene, as an interested person, whenever he or she feels it is appropriate. Secondly, as guardian of many persons, the public guardian monitors the service delivery system and can identify problem areas and service gaps from the dependent adult's point of view. The office of the public guardian may also help develop local guardianship support services through grants to community organizations.

Further, the public guardian's office encourages private citizens to apply for guardianship by providing information, by paying for the cost of private attorney applications (if the court determines the cost would be a hardship), or by making the application through Crown attorneys. Finally, the public guardian can become the dependent adult's guardian when no one else is willing, able, or suitable.

Structure of the Office   To help the public guardian carry out his or her responsibilities, a guardianship advisory committee has been established consisting of a lawyer, a psychologist, and two physicians. The ministerially appointed committee has the role of acting as a sounding board for the public guardian on ethical issues, as well as advising on guidelines and standards related to individual guardianship decisions.

As mentioned previously, the office of the public guardian is encouraging local community organizations to become more active in the guardianship process. A "community involvement program" has been established to set up a community-based guardianship support system in which the private and public sectors work in partnership to further the best interests of dependent adults. Meetings with provincial organizations dealing with potential dependent adults have already begun. This "community involvement program" is currently associated with the office of the public guardian to help plan realistic ways in which local organizations can become more supportive. Their relationship with the office is shown graphically in Figure 1.

Processes of the Office   Figure 2 summarizes the processes involved in making an application, carrying out guardianship services, and conducting reviews. Each component of the figure encompasses certain tasks, knowledge, and resources resulting in a number of issues that must be dealt with. The majority of these components within the model are encouraged to function at the community level through community agencies and other support systems. A typical scenario would go as follows:

1. The service provider (e.g., nursing home, group home, public health nurse, etc.) contacts the family stating that either the proposed dependent adult is reaching the age of 18 and is not capable of making reasonable decisions or is no longer able to give informed consents in certain functional areas.

2. The family is asked to contact their attorney to initiate a guardianship and/or trusteeship application. They are given the name of the local agency or agencies funded through the community involvement program who can provide them with further information and support throughout the application process.

3. If the costs of the application are a hardship to the applicant, or the estate of the proposed dependent adult, then the family is encouraged to have their attorney contact the office of the public guardian to discuss the situation and his proposed fee.

4. The attorney obtains a functional and diagnostic report from a physician or certified psychologist (see Appendix A) as well as any other functional

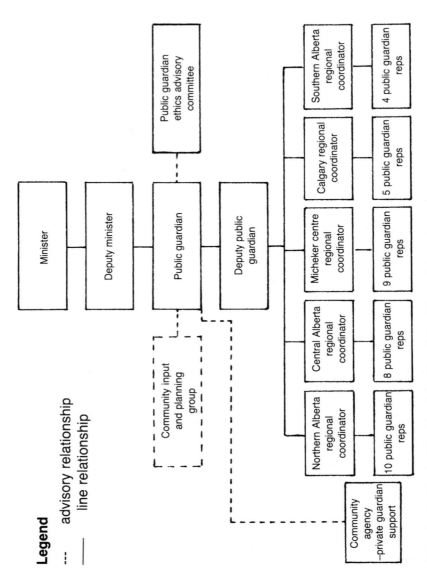

Legend

--- advisory relationship

— line relationship

Figure 1. Functional relationships of the office of the public guardian.

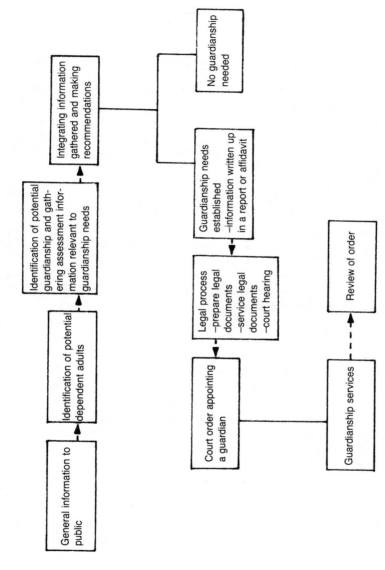

Figure 2. Guardianship process in Alberta.

197

      information from the family and other service providers who know the proposed dependent adult (see Appendix B for examples of functional assessment formats used to collect this information).

5.   The attorney examines diagnostic and functional data to identify areas, as stated in the act, in which the proposed dependent adult does not appear to be able to decide and the areas he or she does, utilizing the principle of least restrictive alternative.

6.   The petition, affidavits, and supporting exhibits are drafted and filed with the Court.

7.   A copy of this information is served on the proposed dependent adult, the director of the institution in which he resides (if applicable), the nearest relative (or the next nearest relative if the nearest relative is making the application), the public guardian, the proposed guardian and the trustee (if applicable), and any other person who may have a special interest in this situation.

8.   All of these persons, having been thus served with the documents, have a right to appear or have their attorney appear on their behalf at the hearing. If the proposed dependent adult is objecting and is unable to obtain a lawyer, the office of the public guardian will try to obtain a legal aid lawyer for him.

9.   When the order is issued, a specific individual is named as being responsible to make an application for review within the time specified by the Courts (which shall not exceed 3 years).

10.   At any time before this scheduled review, the dependent adult, the guardian, or any other interested person can apply to the court for review.

Statistics on the Office

The office of the public guardian originated in December of 1978 with 10 positions. Over the years, the office has expanded to its current size of 66 staff. It is expected that the office will remain at this number over the next 3 or 4 years with additional monies being put into the community involvement program for the development of local community-based guardianship resources. The operating budget of the office of the public guardian for the 1982–1983 fiscal year is just over $3 million. The program's activities from December 1, 1978 to September 30, 1982 are summarized in Table 2.

    The recent drastic drop in the number of crown solicitor applications (296) is a result of the new policy that allows the office of the public guardian to pay total rather than just taxed costs in applications made by private attorneys.

    Studies have shown that there may be as many as 15,000 persons in the province who could require some form of guardianship. Some 10,000 persons who appear to require some type of guardianship have already been identified.

    Of the 3,194 orders issued as of September 30, 1982, more than 90% were for partial guardianship. For the first few years, the majority of the guardianship applications (56%) were on behalf of senior citizens who were suffering from

Table 2. Activities of the office of the public guardian (December 1, 1978 to September 30, 1982)

Completed Guardianship Applications

	Private solicitor	Crown solicitor	Total
December 1, 1978–March 31, 1981	405	945	1350
April 1, 1981–March 31, 1982	291	1218	1509
April 1, 1982–September 30, 1982	226	296	522
	922	2459	3381
	27.27%	72.73%	100.00%

Guardianship Orders

	Private guardian	Public guardian	Total
December 1, 1978–March 31, 1981	942	359	1301
April 1, 1981–March 31, 1982	767	344	1111
April 1, 1982–September 30, 1982	578	204	782
	2287	907	3194
	71.60%	28.40%	100.00%

	Cases deferred*	Abuse investigations
December 1, 1978–March 31, 1981	99	33
April 1, 1981–March 31, 1982	191	30
April 1, 1982–September 30, 1982	64	2
	354	65

*Cases investigated—no guardianship required.

chronic brain disorders; 21% were mentally retarded persons, 9% were mentally ill, and the remainder were community cases. More recently, however, the diagnostic categories for the guardianship applications have been as follows:

Chronic brain disorders	42.7%
Mental retardation	41.9%
Mental illness	9.5%
Physical brain trauma	4.6%
Others	1.3%
	100.0%

The vast majority (approximately 90%) of those persons requiring guardianship were already located in institutions, nursing homes, or group homes. Only approximately 10% were living directly in the community.

THE UNITED NATIONS' DECLARATION

In 1971, the United Nations passed the *Declaration of Rights of Mentally Retarded Persons* (United Nations, 1971). This declaration was based primarily on the principles and recommendations arising from the 1969 San Sebastian Symposium on Guardianship of the Mentally Retarded (International League of Societies for the Mentally Handicapped, 1969). The Dependent Adults Act extends the rights presented in the United Nations' declaration to other mentally incapacitated adults. The following is a brief examination of how this occurs.

The mentally retarded person has, to the maximum degree of feasibility, the same rights as other human beings (United Nations, 1971).

The Dependent Adults Act has gone far toward affirming the presumption of competence by formalizing the principle of selectivity of incompetence. As mentioned previously, a person can be competent in one context but not in others.

The principle of "due process" is embodied within the act. This means that no person is to be denied a right enjoyed by other citizens except where, in an unbiased legal hearing, it is determined that the person is unable to exercise that right reasonably. Thus, functional information must be gathered regarding the adult's ability to take care of himself or herself and to make reasonable judgments within each of the guardianship areas mentioned in the act. This complements more global measures such as intelligence quotients and diagnostic categories that do not provide specific information. Finally, the person must be in need of a guardian and such an appointment must be in his or her best interest. Once the guardian is appointed, it is his responsibility to ensure that all of the rights of the dependent adult are respected.

The mentally retarded person has a right to proper medical care and physical therapy and to such education, training, rehabilitation and guidance as will enable him to develop his ability and maximum potential (United Nations, 1971).

The consent to treatment must be given by the guardian when the individual receiving the treatment is not capable of consenting and cannot authorize the treatment himself or herself. This legislation enables a guardian to give medical consent when the guardian is satisfied that such treatment is in the best interests of the patient. The guardian consents to one of the alternatives provided to him or her by the physician or other treatment provider after considering the value system of the dependent adult, the risks inherent to each alternative, and the risks involved in refusing any treatment and possible outcomes. Only after consent is given can a physician treat or authorize the treatment provider (e.g., nurse) to carry out the treatment.

The mentally retarded person has a right to economic security and to a decent standard of living. He has a right to perform productive work or to engage in any other meaningful occupation to the fullest possible extent of his capabilities (United Nations, 1971).

Guardians have a responsibility to ensure that the dependent adult is not exploited in the work place (i.e., wages, benefits, etc.) and that he or she is receiving all of the benefits of social assistance (i.e., pensions, subsidies, etc.) to which he or she is entitled. The guardian can also advocate for more appropriate work and work settings when these are required.

Whenever possible the mentally retarded person should live with his own family or with foster parents and participate in different forms of community life. The family with which he lives should receive assistance. If care in an institution becomes necessary, it should be provided in surroundings and other circumstances as close as possible to those of normal life (United Nations, 1971).

The guardian must try to ensure that the dependent adult is living in as normal a setting as possible. The Dependent Adults Act (1980) states that a guardian shall exercise his or her power and authority "in the best interests of the dependent adult; in such a way as to encourage the dependent adult to become capable of caring for himself and of making reasonable judgments in respect of matters relating to his person, and in the least restrictive manner possible" (p. 13).

The mentally retarded person has a right to a qualified guardian, when this is required, to protect his personal well-being and interests (United Nations, 1971).

The Dependent Adults Act specifies the due process required for the appointment of a guardian. Each potential guardian must show the court that he or she will "act in the best interests of the dependent adult, not be in a position where his/her own interests will conflict with the dependent adult's interests, be a suitable person to act as the guardian of a dependent adult, and be a resident of Alberta" (Dependent Adults Act, Section 7 (1), p. 7). During the regular reviews, the court reviews the decisions of the guardian to ensure that he or she is acting in the dependent adult's best interests.

The mentally retarded person must be protected from every kind of exploitation, degrading treatment and abuse. If prosecuted for any offense, he shall have a right to due process of law with full recognition being given to his degree of mental responsibility (United Nations, 1971).

The guardian must take steps to establish and protect the legal rights of the dependent adult. Rights and privileges are meaningless unless they are complemented by an ability to enforce these rights. The guardian has the power and authority to do just that for the dependent adult.

Whenever mentally retarded persons are unable, because of the severity of their handicap, to exercise all their rights in a meaningful way or it should become necessary to restrict or deny some or all of these rights, the procedure used for that restriction or denial of rights must contain proper legal safeguards against every form of abuse. This procedure must be based on an evaluation of the social capability of the mentally retarded person by qualified experts and must be subject to periodic review and the right of appeal to higher authorities (United Nations, 1971).

The Dependent Adults Act was designed to provide substitute decision-making for persons who were considered incapable of making reasonable decisions on their own. The act is significant in a number of aspects. First, it distinguishes between guardianship of the person and guardianship of the estate. Secondly, the act presumes that the individual is competent except in those areas where functional information is available that demonstrates incompetence and *a need for guardianship*. A guardian may be appointed in one area, allowing the individual to continue to make decisions in all other aspects of his or her life. Thirdly, there is a presumption that the least restrictive alternative must be pursued. This is recognized in that plenary or total guardianship is to be granted by the courts only when the judge feels that a partial guardianship order would not be sufficient.

The act makes the legal substitute decision-maker accountable to the court through regular reviews. During these reviews, the onus is again on the guardian and on the professionals to show where the person does not have the ability to make personal decisions. In addition, the court is made aware of and can examine the decisions made by the guardian on behalf of the dependent adult to ensure they were made in the best interests of the dependent adult.

Again, the act allows the guardian to seek the advice and direction of the court whenever he or she is not sure of what action would be in the best interests of the dependent adult.

What Has Been Learned

Experience has shown that there is a definite role for guardianship and trusteeship to ensure that the rights of dependent adults are protected in the delivery of human services. The skills and abilities required to handle financial matters may differ from those required to handle personal life decisions. Many persons have trustees and do not have guardians. Over 90% of the guardianship orders in Alberta are for partial guardianship; therefore, these individuals retain their rights to make decisions over many parts of their personal lives.

Guardianship and trusteeship protect the individual's rights if the dependent adult does not have the ability to make reasonable decisions. It is the author's experience that persons are not totally competent or incompetent but rather are open to abuse and victimization in specific areas of their life. In other areas, they have the ability to take risks and learn from their mistakes.

The need for and extent of guardianship depends not only on the dependent person's abilities and inabilities but also on his or her environment. Thus, as a person moves to a less restrictive and less structured environment, he or she may need guardianship in more areas (i.e., with whom to consort, social activities, etc.) until he or she has learned the required skills.

Guardianship must be seen as a right for all persons who required it and must not be limited to only those few who may be able to afford it. Allowing the judge to assess total costs against the crown when payment of these costs would be a hardship to the applicant or dependent adult's estate ensures that guardianship is available for all who need a legal substitute decision-maker.

In the view of most, any guardianship system should work in close conjunction with other service delivery systems. Whether a guardianship system is administratively integrated into other social service delivery systems or not, it is essential that conflict of interest be avoided, basically through terms of reference that give a degree of autonomy.

Although the office of the public guardian is located in the Department of Social Services and Community Health, it has been placed in a division that is responsible for planning, monitoring, and evaluating provincial programs rather than in the service delivery division. This has allowed the public guardian to remain at arm's length while still communicating and cooperating with the service delivery branches (i.e., in identifying service gaps).

It is very important that guardianship decisions be reviewed on a regular basis to ensure that the guardian is making decisions in the best interests of the dependent adult and to ensure that guardianship is still required. For example, in some cases the judge will include specific directions and guidelines to be followed by the guardian for the duration of the order, and in other cases guardianship will no longer be required or will be reduced.

A legislative mandate for guardianship should not only provide the basis for the right of a dependent adult to a guardian but should also state the principles to be utilized by the guardian when making decisions on behalf of the dependent adult.

Guardianship encompasses a protection service that extends not only to the dependent adult, but also to the service providers. On behalf of the dependent adult, the guardian ensures that he or she is receiving the services and treatment he or she requires to enhance his or her development. Conversely, guardianship also protects the service providers who can now approach the guardian to determine which alternative would be in the best interest of that particular dependent adult. If the service delivery agencies and organizations are dissatisfied with the values or assumptions utilized by the guardian, they can contact the office of the public guardian and ask that office to investigate to determine if the guardian is indeed acting in the best interests of the dependent adult. If the public guardian's office or any other interested person feels that the guardian is in a conflict of interest situation, is no longer suitable as a guardian, or is not acting in the best interests of the dependent adult, then that person can request an immediate review.

The demand for guardianship increased dramatically when the service delivery sector and consumers became aware of the potential within the human rights component of the act. This necessitated a drastic reconceptualization of how to deliver individualized services to persons while staying within cost limitations. The use of private guardianship was encouraged by arranging for costs to be paid by the office of the public guardian when it was a hardship, by increasing the outreach capacity of the office's staff on two occasions, by decentralizing the operation, and by encouraging community organizations to become more involved in monitoring and providing personalized support to persons who had a guardian.

Initial concern was raised regarding potential misuse of the compulsory care section of the act. Concern was expressed that this section might be used to unnecessarily confine dependent adults against their will. In practice, this has not occurred. Instead, this section has been used to ensure that due process and a thorough assessment occur before the person receives this type of care. It has also been utilized to ensure that those dependent adults who require compulsory care for their protection and treatment are not neglected by the service delivery system.

Within the model of guardianship, aging parents have two options to ensure continuity of care for their mentally handicapped adult child. The first option involves having a relative or trusted friend appointed directly as guardian. The second option involves appointing a family member or friend as alternate guardian. The alternate guardian takes over immediately in the event of the death of the guardian. In this way, an elderly parent can personally be the guardian, and can feel confident in the future of the dependent adult because of the guaranteed continuity of guardianship. This model also allows for children to decide who has the final say in what happens to their parents if, through the aging process, they lose the ability to make informed decisions.

One unanticipated consequence of this legislation occurred when parents, family members, and some physicians initially reacted to this act as if it abrogated some of their rights to decide for the dependent adult instead of perceiving it as protecting the rights of the dependent person. This misconception appears to have been corrected through public education programs conducted by the office of the public guardian.

Finally, and most importantly, the decisions made by the guardian must be as congruent as possible with the values of the dependent adult. In those areas in which he or she has power and authority to decide, the guardian's consent is deemed by law to be that of the dependent adult and the guardian must make decisions that are based on the dependent adult's value system. The guardian must individualize his or her own decisions and they must be as congruent as possible with the decision the dependent adult would have made.

SUMMARY

The model of guardianship that is being pursued by the Province of Alberta provides a legal basis for establishing accountable substitute decision-makers for those adults who are incapable of making reasonable decisions, unable to care for themselves, and in need of a guardian. The model incorporates regular reviews and emphasizes the use of the least restrictive alternatives for this purpose.

Initial statistical data appears to show success with this approach. Over 70% of Alberta's dependent adults have private legal guardians; more than 90% of the orders received are for partial guardianship.

Progress is being made towards involving local organizations in guardianship activities. Community organizations are being invited to participate more actively in helping both dependent adults and guardians through developing community support systems that assist dependent adults to remain active members of their community.

It is too early to determine the precise effect guardianship will have on the lives of dependent adults. This will be documented in the regular court reviews as they occur. It is clear, however, that changes are occurring and that the Dependent Adults Act will serve well as a vehicle to provide a voice for those who cannot advocate and care for themselves.

REFERENCES

Government of Alberta, Dependent Adults Act, Chapter D-32 of the Revised Statutes of Alberta, 1980.

International League of Societies for the Mentally Handicapped, *Symposium on guardianship of the mentally retarded: Conclusions*. Brussels, Belgium: International League of Societies for the Mentally Handicapped, 1969.

Marlett, N. *Issues of competence and the Dependent Adults Act*. Calgary: Vocational and Rehabilitation Research Institute and the Office of the Public Guardian, 1980.

Picard, E.I. *Legal liability of doctors and hosptials in Canada*. Toronto: The Carswell Company Ltd., 1978.

United Nations. *Declaration of rights for mentally retarded persons*, passed on December 20th, 1971, 2027th plenary meeting.

Wolfensberger, W. *Normalization: The principle of normalization in human services*. Toronto: National Institute on Mental Retardation, 1972.

Wolfensberger, W., & Zauha, H. *Citizen advocacy and protective services for the impaired and handicapped*. Toronto: National Institute on Mental Retardation, 1973.

Appendix A

FUNCTIONAL ASSESSMENT FOR GUARDIANSHIP

*(This assessment form is appropriate for use for
persons in extended care facilities only)*

Part One

Name of patient: _____

Date of birth: _____

Residence of patient: _____

Attending physician: _____

Date of assessment: _____

Physical condition (short summary): _____

_____

_____

_____

_____

_____

LIVING SKILLS:

	Needs no assistance	Supervision only	Partial assistance	Full assistance
Eating:				
Dressing:				
Walking:				
Wheelchair:				
Grooming:				
Bathing:				
Toileting:				

Continence:

Bowel: _____ None: _____ Some: _____ Frequent: _____ Total: _____

Bladder: _____ None: _____ Some: _____ Frequent: _____ Total: _____

SAFETY PRECAUTIONS:	Yes	No
Protective restraints:		

Please specify: _____

_____

_____

	Yes	No
Elopement risk:		

Other (describe): _____

_____

_____

LEVEL OF AWARENESS:

Alert: _____ Forgetful: _____ Periods of confusion: _____

Persistent confusion and disorientation: _____ Psychotic: _____

Examples:

_____

_____

_____

_____

EMOTIONAL STATE:

Stable: _____ Unstable: _____ Withdrawn: _____ Depressed: _____

Examples:

_____

_____

_____

_____

SOCIALIZATION   Check most appropriate description:

—participates on his or her own initiative: _____

—if taken to activity, will participate: _____

—does not participate but will observe: _____

—does not interact with others: _____

PROGRAMS:

Is involved in:

Occupational therapy: _____ Remotivation therapy: _____

Recreational therapy: _____ Other: _____

Is not involved due to:

Own choice: _____ Physical difficulties: _____

Behavior prevents participation (specify, i.e., cannot sit still, short attention span, etc.; give examples): _____

_____

_____

_____

COMMUNICATION SKILLS   Briefly describe ability to:

Read: _____

Write: _____

BEHAVIOR:

—are there any inappropriate and/or repetitive movements present (i.e., rocking, wringing hands, verbalization, etc . . .)? _____

—does this person relate well to others, _____ become suspicious or quarrelsome with little or no provocation? _____

—is this person capable of stating opinions or preferences about things in his or her environment, such as:

clothing: Yes _____ No _____   social activities: Yes _____ No _____

grooming: Yes _____ No _____   food: Yes _____ No _____

friends: Yes _____ No _____

EXPRESSIVE COMMUNICATION   Indicate most appropriate description(s):

—complex conversation involving abstract ideas: _____

—simple conversation involving routine matters: _____

—answers questions in monosyllables: _____

—answers by using gestures: _____

—answers questions but response is
irrelevant (i.e., off topic): _____

—does not respond to questioning: _____

RECEPTIVE COMMUNICATION   Indicate most appropriate description(s):

—can understand complex instructions
and directions and remembers them for at
least 24 hours: _____

—can understand simple two-step directions and
remembers them for over $\frac{1}{2}$ an hour: _____

—can understand simple one-step directions
but forgets quickly: _____

—does not appear to understand any verbal
communication but can respond to gestures: _____

—does not appear to understand even simple
gestures (i.e., come here, sit down here): _____

Examples:

_____

_____

_____

_____

_____

ORIENTATION:	Yes	No
—completely unresponsive to environment:	_____	_____
—needs to be led from place to place:	_____	_____
—can function within ward routine, i.e., can find bedroom, dining room, and bathroom:	_____	_____
—needs to be reminded of meal times:	_____	_____
—is appropriate for simple reality orientation such as being reminded of his or her name, the day, where he or she is, etc.:	_____	_____
—knows roughly what year and season it is:	_____	_____
—is "living in" the present and aware of his or her present condition:	_____	_____
—knows where he or she is, i.e., town & province:	_____	_____
—responds to own name:	_____	_____
—recognizes relatives or friends:	_____	_____
—knows their names:	_____	_____
—recognizes staff and knows which staff to go to for what:	_____	_____

—recognizes staff members: _____ _____
—knows some of the staff's names: _____ _____

Examples (If not living in the present or in contact with reality, describe patient's orientation):

_____

_____

_____

_____

_____

Would this person be capable of ensuring appropriate physical care for himself or herself if not in a supervised setting (i.e., does he or she need daily supervision of hygiene, need to be reminded to eat, etc.)? Give examples:

_____

_____

_____

_____

_____

HEALTH CARE: Yes   No

—reliable in regard to taking own
   medications: _____   _____
—knows when he or she has a health problem: _____   _____
—lets appropriate people know: _____   _____
—is able to indicate verbally or by gesture
   if in pain: _____   _____
—agrees to whatever treatment is suggested: _____   _____
—able to request medical, dental,
   and other appointments: _____   _____
—would require assistance in keeping
   medical or dental appointments (i.e.,
   time and transport):   _____   _____

INFORMED CONSENT:

—agrees to whatever treatment is suggested: _____   _____
—has a layperson's understanding of and is able
   to discuss alternatives to present and suggested
   treatment: _____   _____
—could remember alternative medical treatments
   suggested by doctor and could make a
   reasonable decision: _____   _____
—has a layperson's understanding and is able to
   discuss possible risks involved in suggested
   treatment: _____   _____
—can state his or her personal value system or
   preferences regarding treatment: _____   _____

Examples:

_____

_____

_____

_____

_____

_____

_____

_____

LEGAL MATTERS:	Yes	No
—would sign any document that someone he or she trusted presented to him or her:	____	____
—able to request the services of a lawyer:	____	____
—able to instruct counsel (being able to clearly define relevant legal problem and make a decision based on the alternatives that the lawyer may give):	____	____
—has reasonable skepticism of strangers:	____	____
—institutionalized or overly compliant:	____	____

Examples (Examples of behavior on a legal matter if there have been any, or examples of past victimization while the person was in the community):

_____

_____

_____

_____

_____

RESIDENTIAL ALTERNATIVES:

—is a change in residence recommended for this person: Yes _____ No _____

—what would be an appropriate alternative: Nursing home _____ Auxiliary hospital _____ Private residence _____ Other _____

—Could this person live in a noninstitutional setting: _____ If not, why? _____

_____

_____

BACKGROUND INFORMATION (If known):
Why was this person admitted to an institutional setting initially? (i.e., needed more nursing care than could be provided where he or she was, wandered, became confused, and forgot regular meals, etc.)

_____

_____

_____

DETAILS OF THERAPY PROGRAMS (Filling in this section is optional and at the discretion of the institution):

Rehabilitation: _____

_____

_____

_____

Occupational therapy: _____

_____

_____

_____

Social worker: _____

_____

_____

_____

Signature of person completing form: _____
Professional status: _____
Position: _____

Part Two

If this form is being sent directly to the office of the public guardian, please fill out Part Two. If this form is being sent to a private solicitor, send only Part One to the private solicitor.

VISITING:

—is there anyone other than staff persons who has shown an interest in this person: Yes _____   No _____

Name: _____

Relationship: _____   Address: _____

Phone number: _____

By visiting: _____   Writing: _____   Phoning: _____

Name: _____

Relationship: _____   Address: _____

Phone number: _____

By visiting: _____   Writing: _____   Phoning: _____

PERSON SUGGESTED TO BE THE MOST SUITABLE AS PROPOSED GUARDIAN:

Name: _____

Address: _____

ARE THERE ANY KNOWN FAMILY PROBLEMS: _____

_____

_____

_____

NEXT OF KIN:

Name: _____   Relationship: _____

Address: _____

Phone: _____

Name: _____ Relationship: _____
Address: _____
Phone: _____
Name: _____ Relationship: _____
Address: _____
Phone: _____

FINANCES:

Who manages finances of proposed dependent adult?
    Name: _____
    Address: _____
    _____
    _____
    Telephone: _____
Is this person the legal trustee?   Yes: _____   No: _____
Do you know the approximate size of the estate? _____

SOURCE OF INCOME:

Social assistance _____
Alberta Assured Income for the Severely Handicapped _____
Canada Pension Plan _____
Other (Please specify) _____

Signature of person completing form: _____

TO THE ATTENTION OF _____, PUBLIC GUARDIAN REPRESENTATIVE

Appendix B

EXAMPLES OF FUNCTIONAL ASSESSMENT FORMATS

FORM "A": FUNCTIONAL ASSESSMENT AND INFORMATION
RE: DECISION-MAKING AND SELF-CARE

PROPOSED DEPENDENT ADULT

Name: _____ Birthdate: _____

Address: _____ Telephone: _____

_____ Postal code: _____

Home address (if different from above):

_____

_____ Postal code _____

There are *two* sections to this information:

SECTION I: *A brief description of the person's specialized needs* in five general areas:
Supervision/Care, Mobility, Communication/Socialization, Developmental Skills, and Behavior.

In each area, check (√) the definition which most clearly describes the person's present requirements. In each of the areas, a level "0" represents no appreciable handicap and a level "4" represents extensive needs due to severe handicap.

SECTION II: *Assessment of the person's functioning in the major personal needs areas* as defined within the Act: 1) Where to Live, 2) Social Relationships, 3) Vocational/Education, 4) Legal/Licenses, 5) Health Care, and 6) Diet and Dress.

Where space is provided, briefly describe the proposed Dependent Adult's situation. In Section C, underline the trend(s) in parentheses that best describes the person.

N/A–Indicates the skill is not applicable in his present setting.

IMP–Indicates that the person is showing improvement in the skill.

213

SECTION I

Note: Please check the description that best fits the proposed dependent adult's level of handicap. Please respond to each category separately.

Level of Handicap

Category	Level 4	Level 3	Level 2	Level 1	Level 0
Supervision/ and Care	Extensive medical/physical care. Supervision and total care required because of multiple physical difficulties, e.g., body rigidity and fragility requiring positioning for congestion/ bed sores.	Regular medical nursing provision required because of multiple physical disabilities, e.g., supervision of staff in transferring patients, ileostomy/colostomy supervision, protection against self injury, brittle epileptic.	Some degree of nursing and medical backup required, e.g., supervision of drugs, protection against common danger, controlled epileptic, regular skin care.	Minor medical treatments carried out mainly by individual, e.g., regular medications, skin care.	No handicap
Mobility	Motor control severely affected due to spasm or limpness, e.g., few spontaneous movements, could be in wheelchair but must be propped or pushed.	Some mobility, e.g., in wheel chair with functional movement (lower/ upper limbs or head), needs transfer, crawls or walks with assistance, walks but sensory deficit makes unescorted travel difficult.	Generally mobile, e.g., walks alone but awkwardly or with cane/ walker, in wheelchair— self-propelled and self-self-transfer, blind but can travel in familiar terrain, gross or fine motor coordination difficulties, e.g., cerebral palsy.	General motor control. May have hand/eye coordination difficulties or some balance problems.	No handicap

214

Communication Socialization	Very difficult or impossible to understand, e.g., few spontaneous vocalizations apart from fear, pain, hunger, some awareness of environment apart from response to cuddling and sharp environmental changes, focuses on moving objects, becomes excited before regular events.	Can, with assistance, make needs known, e.g., has some clear words, gestures, or signals, understands some basic concepts, color, size, understands simple directions and responds to praise and censure, aware of surroundings but communication restricted, relates to others in structured setting.	Relates well to others in a familiar structured setting, e.g., communicates short sentences (tends to be rote language), adapts to new situations with assistance, understands most directions with practice, reads social sight words, can write name.	Good concrete language but with conceptual/abstract difficulties. Varied, spontaneous language. Good conversational skills, can read and write simple English and do simple arithmetic.	No handicap
Developmental Skills	Minimal skills in terms of eating, toileting or dressing, could help with feeding, dressing, etc.	Feeds, dresses and toilets self with assistance or close supervision. Could be in structured recreational or occupational day program.	Self-care with some supervision or special architectural assists.	Self-help generally sufficient. Community, residential, and vocational skills with practice but needs some assistance with budgeting and time management.	No handicap
Behavior	Dangerous toward self, others, or property and as a result cannot be handled in any existing program.	Unacceptable or disruptive behavior or complete lack of motivation.	Undesirable behavior, poor motivation.	No specific behavior problem although some inappropriate behavior is evident.	No handicap

SECTION II

1. ABILITY TO DECIDE WHERE TO LIVE:

 A. *Present situation* (Describe briefly the proposed Dependent Adult's present accommodation [e.g., home with parents, group home, institutional setting] and the programs or supports the proposed Dependent Adult is involved in [e.g., community training, cooking, Meals on Wheels]):

 _____

 _____

 _____

 _____

 _____

 B. *Environmental factors:* (Underline the circumstances that presently exist and add any others that may indicate that the person may require advocacy or intervention):

 Institutionalized for a long period of time   Overprotection

 Neglect   Lack of awareness of resources

 Abuse   Segregated from community

 _____

 C. *Awareness of abilities*

 1. Meets routine deadlines on his own—getting up, meals, bus, etc.
 (Always) (Sometimes) (Never) (N/A) (IMP)

 2. Is familiar with immediate neighbourhood services.
 (Yes) (Within close boundaries) (No) (N/A) (IMP)

 3. Knows about and can obtain immediate support from community—welfare, Handi-bus, emergency (911), police, fire department, etc.
 (Yes) (Only regular ones) (No) (N/A) (IMP)

 4. Demonstrates knowledge of safety and accident prevention in the home—combustible storage, separating foods from poisons, etc.
 (Yes) (With assistance) (No) (N/A) (IMP)

 5. Makes routine purchases such as groceries, clothing, etc.
 (Yes) (With assistance) (No) (N/A) (IMP)

 6. Knows whom to contact for routine repairs—phone company, appliance repairs, plumber, etc.
 (Yes) (With assistance) (No) (N/A) (IMP)

 7. Aware of other residential alternatives.
 (Yes) (Unrealistic ones) (No) (N/A) (IMP)

 8. Questions or effectively raises concerns about living arrangements.
 (Yes) (Sometimes) (No) (N/A) (IMP)

 9. Forgets or does not have his own personal routines.
 (Yes) (Sometimes) (No) (N/A) (IMP)

 10. Refuses help that is offered or refuses to seek help concerning upkeep of home or person.
 (Yes) (Sometimes) (No) (N/A) (IMP)

2. SOCIAL RELATIONSHIPS:

   A. *Present situation*   (Describe briefly his personal supports—who is available to give guidance related to social situations and activities):

   _____

   _____

   _____

   _____

   _____

   B. *Environmental factors*   (Underline the circumstances that presently exist and add any others that may indicate that the person may require advocacy or intervention):

   Is being exploited or abused by friends   Social activities are not available

   Leisure is controlled and planned, e.g., little choice in activities   Is in an isolated or segregated situation, e.g., friendship alternatives limited

   _____

   _____

   C. *Awareness and abilities*
       1. Has friends that he talks to and keeps in touch with.
           (Yes)   (With reminders or assistance)   (No)   (N/A)   (IMP)
       2. Chooses leisure—does things by himself, hobbies, TV, etc.
           (Yes)   (With assistance)   (No)   (N/A)   (IMP)
       3. Initiates leisure on his own—does things with friends, belongs to a group activity, hobbies, etc.
           (Yes)   (With assistance)   (No)   (N/A)   (IMP)
       4. Recognizes potential dangers in social situations.
           (Yes)   (When reminded)   (No)   (N/A)   (IMP)
       5. Interactions with staff or family show willingness to form friendships.
           (Yes)   (Sometimes)   (No)   (N/A)   (IMP)
       6. Shows interest in being with others by choosing whom to spend time with.
           (Yes)   (Sometimes)   (No)   (N/A)   (IMP)
       7. Has established leisure routines with someone—calls on same person for coffee, bowls with same person regularly.
           (Yes)   (With reminders)   (No)   (N/A)   (IMP)
       8. Gives personal belongings or money away or follows suggestions of persons who claim to be friends.
           (Yes)   (Sometimes)   (No)   (N/A)   (IMP)

3. VOCATIONAL/EDUCATION:

   A. *Present situation*   (Describe the present work or training situation, e.g., vocational training centre, sheltered workshop, work activity program. Include any other education/treatment programs, e.g., behavior modification training program, night classes, remotivation groups, etc.):

   _____

   _____

_____
_____
_____

B. *Environmental factors:* (Underline the circumstances that presently exist and add any others that may indicate that the person may require advocacy or intervention):

Denied access to job or training

Cannot initiate or terminate programs on his own

Is in exploitive situation and unable to remedy situation

In aversive behavior program without giving informed consent

_____
_____

C. *Awareness and abilities*

1. Shows basic understanding of work/training as opposed to leisure—that a "boss" instructs, that work must be done on time, etc.
   (Yes)   (Sometimes)   (No)   (N/A)   (IMP)

2. Questions or evaluates his program.
   (Yes)   (Sometimes)   (No)   (N/A)   (IMP)

3. Knows the dangers and rules of work and is aware of not hurting himself or others.
   (Yes)   (With assistance)   (No)   (N/A)   (IMP)

4. Shows interest in learning new things so that he can do things on his own.
   (Yes)   (Sometimes)   (No)   (N/A)   (IMP)

5. Knows what the result of his program should be and shows interest in his progress.
   (Yes)   (Some understanding)   (No)   (N/A)   (IMP)

6. Has an idea of what occupation he might like in the future—sheltered workshop, janitor, salesman.
   (Yes)   (Some understanding)   (No)   (N/A)   (IMP)

7. Does not understand concepts of wages or benefits.
   (Yes)   (Some understanding)   (No)   (N/A)   (IMP)

8. Is able to indicate (could be nonverbal) frustration, confusion, or displeasure at what's happening in his treatment/program.
   (Yes)   (With assistance)   (No)   (N/A)   (IMP)

9. Recognizes changes in treatment/program and comments or questions.
   (Yes)   (Sometimes)   (No)   (N/A)   (IMP)

4. LEGAL/LICENSES:

A. *Present situation* (Is he likely to need a license or permit, e.g., driver's license, marriage license? Has he been involved in legal actions?):

_____
_____
_____
_____

B. *Environmental factors* (Underline the circumstances that presently exist and add any others that may indicate that the person may require advocacy or intervention):

Compliant, will sign anything   Has been denied a license

Has been victimized   Has been charged with an offense

_____

_____

C. *Awareness and abilities*

1. Knows the "rules" of immediate environment—what is acceptable in the home, at work, etc.
   (Yes)   (With reminders)   (No)   (N/A)   (IMP)

2. Shows reasonable skepticism of strangers.
   (Yes)   (With reminders)   (No)   (N/A)   (IMP)

3. Understands implications of signing legal documents.
   (Yes)   (Some understanding)   (No)   (N/A)   (IMP)

4. Understands concept of legal/illegal related to theft and assault.
   (Yes)   (Some understanding)   (No)   (N/A)   (IMP)

5. Knows how/when to contact police and lawyers.
   (Yes)   (Some understanding)   (No)   (N/A)   (IMP)

6. Seeks assistance when wronged, e.g., aware that something is amiss.
   (Yes)   (Sometimes)   (No)   (N/A)   (IMP)

7. Able to relate what has happened to him when he has been wronged, e.g., could instruct counsel.
   (Yes)   (Some ability)   (No)   (N/A)   (IMP)

8. Aware of and stands up for his personal rights.
   (Yes)   (Some awareness)   (No)   (N/A)   (IMP)

9. Signs forms/documents when given to him by staff/family without question.
   (Yes)   (Sometimes)   (No)   (N/A)   (IMP)

10. Signs forms/documents given to him by relative strangers.
    (Yes)   (Sometimes)   (No)   (N/A)   (IMP)

5. HEALTH CARE:

A. *Present situation* (Describe the general health of the proposed Dependent Adult and need for ongoing or major medical intervention):

_____

_____

_____

_____

_____

B. *Environmental factors* (Underline the circumstances that presently exist and add any others that may indicate that the person may require advocacy or intervention):

Unable to give informed consent or objection   Is in an extended care institution without outside contact

Refuses to give consent   Presently being given care without his
                                           informed consent

_____

_____

C. *Awareness and abilities*
    1. Knows he is ill, and describes the symptoms—sharp stomach pain, hot,
        dizzy, etc.
        (Yes) (With assistance) (No) (N/A) (IMP)
    2. Cares for minor health problems, colds, menses, headaches, toothaches,
        warts, etc.
        (Yes) (With assistance) (No) (N/A) (IMP)
    3. Aware of medical problem and needed precautions—medications, seizure
        routines, alcohol limitations, wears medical bracelet, etc.
        (Yes) (With assistance) (No) (N/A) (IMP)
    4. Handles medications reliably on his own.
        (Yes) (With assistance) (No) (N/A) (IMP)
    5. Makes appointments on his own.
        (Yes) (Sometimes) (No) (N/A) (IMP)
    6. Consistently refuses to give health information or consent to treatment.
        (Yes) (Sometimes) (No) (N/A) (IMP)
    7. Neglects self by not following personal and health care routines.
        (Yes) (Sometimes) (No) (N/A) (IMP)
    8. Has let major medical concerns go, e.g., seems unaware of/ignores
        problem such as alcohol/drug abuse, dental decay, etc.
        (Yes) (Sometimes) (No) (N/A) (IMP)

6. DIET AND DRESS
    A. *Present situation* (Describe briefly the level of physical care or guidance
        required):

        _____
        _____
        _____
        _____
        _____

    B. *Environmental factors* (Underline the circumstances that presently exist and
        add any others that may indicate that the person may require advocacy or
        intervention):
        Unaware of surroundings   Unaware of personal needs
        Unable to use day-to-day services   Dependent entirely upon estab-
                                                lished routines

        _____

        _____

C. *Awareness and abilities*

1. Maintains basic personal hygiene and care.
    (Yes) (With assistance) (No) (N/A) (IMP)

2. Recognizes personal belongings.
    (Yes) (Sometimes) (No) (N/A) (IMP)

3. Makes preferences known concerning food, dress, etc.
    (Yes) (With assistance) (No) (N/A) (IMP)

4. Changes underwear and clothing as needed.
    (Yes) (With assistance) (No) (N/A) (IMP)

5. Wears the right kind of clothes for the weather.
    (Yes) (With assistance) (No) (N/A) (IMP)

6. Knows what a balanced diet is, e.g., not all one food.
    (Yes) (Some awareness) (No) (N/A) (IMP)

7. Monitors and ensures that he is receiving adequate personal care.
    (Yes) (With assistance) (No) (N/A) (IMP)

8. Forgets regular routines or personal information—where the bathroom is, where his bed is, when he had his last meal, etc.
    (Yes) (Sometimes) (No) (N/A) (IMP)

9. Must be reminded now to do things after a break (or a change) in routines—after a weekend visit.
    (Yes) (Sometimes) (No) (N/A) (IMP)

10. Becomes confused when out of familiar territory; forgets where he is going and why.
    (Yes) (Sometimes) (No) (N/A) (IMP)

People Served by the Alberta Office of the Public Guardian

Joel R. Christie

Lawrence was a man in his early thirties who had been receiving mental health intervention since his early teens. Previous to guardianship, he had never followed through with any therapy or program. A public guardian representative worked with Lawrence and the staff at his institution to identify four major problems he was having while in the community, to work out goal-specific therapy programs, and to obtain his participation in these programs. Eventually, Lawrence met the discharge criteria for his institutional placement and was discharged to the community. At the review of his guardianship order, he was doing so well that it was determined that he no longer needed a guardian. Guardianship was revoked. A short term guardianship intervention thus facilitated Lawrence's therapy programs and enabled him to stay in the community, whereas for the previous 20 years he had been unable to function for any length of time in a community setting.

Walter hadn't had any family contact since the early 1940s. His extended family had been told that Walter had passed away during the 1940s. The family had been given this information due to one member's concern over the stigma attached to having a member who was mentally ill. The office of the public guardian was eventually able to locate a grandniece who had not known that her uncle was alive. She was very interested in establishing a contact. After two visits, the niece decided that she wished to be Walter's guardian and family contact was re-established for a man who had no communication with his family for over 40 years.

223

Mr. Andrew's eyesight gradually deteriorated because of cataracts. As his vision became increasingly impaired, Mr. Andrew's complex delusional system and his withdrawal from his environment became more evident. His eyes were examined and a cataract operation was recommended, but Mr. Andrew refused on several occasions to have the operation. A public guardian representative was able to arrange for him to be moved to a new environment. Within this new environment, he received a thorough medical and psychological assessment. His medications were closely monitored and he became involved in special therapy programs. Mr. Andrew was again approached about having the cataract operation. This time he agreed to have the operation and he is now able to see. Since his eyesight has improved, his delusions have less impact on his ability to function. He has stated that he would like to live in an open space and as a result he is soon to be moved to a facility that is located in the country.

Olaf left his homeland, Denmark, when he was a very young man. He has no relatives in Canada and is now cared for in a senior citizen's facility and is under the responsibility of the public guardian. Through the public guardian's office, contact has been maintained with Olaf's sister in Denmark and pictures and letters have been exchanged. These letters not only brighten Olaf's days but also mean a great deal to the family. His sister wrote, ''It was a pity you could not see how high my spirit rose when a photo of Olaf came in(to) my hands and tears of joy came into my eyes . . . I wondered that he had so much hair left and looked so well in blue shirt and [his] face expression was so satisfied, it showed he is taken so much care of.''

Francis's only surviving relative lives in the Maritimes. Though she lives too far away to become a guardian for Francis, she is very concerned about his welfare. On Francis's 100th birthday, his niece made a trip to Alberta to celebrate the day with him. During that visit and in letters following, she has expressed how important it is to her to receive letters from the public guardian's office keeping her informed as to how her uncle is doing. She has written to say, ''It is so nice to hear that you have had visits with Francis. I do hope I will be able to visit him again on his 101st birthday . . . . Thank you again for your letters.''

Thelma is a 19-year-old woman who is severely mentally handicapped. She resides with her friend and guardian in an apartment in downtown Urban, Alberta. She attends a vocational rehabilitation program daily and is involved in many leisure pursuits such as ballet. At 18, following her graduation from a special education class, Thelma was at a very high risk for being removed from her home community and placed in an institution for mentally incapacitated people some 200 miles away. It was said that there were no services in the home community for a person as severely handicapped as Thelma, but her friend and guardian did not consent to such a move. She instead lobbied and advocated to have programs developed locally that would meet Thelma's needs without uprooting her from her home community. Thelma is no longer at risk for being institutionalized. She is leading a productive, satisfying, and secure life as a citizen of Urban. Guardianship in this instance made a dramatic difference.

Herbert is an elderly person who suffered a severe stroke that left him unable to care for himself, unable to make reasonable decisions, and unable to communicate. Herbert resides in a nursing home in a private room. He has no known family or friends. The court decided that Herbert was dependent and required a guardian. The public guardian was named. During the course of a regular visit with Herbert, a public guardian representative observed that he was in severe pain although he could not communicate his discomfort directly. He had a number of infected teeth that required examination and treatment. The public guardian brought Herbert's condition to the attention of the nursing home personnel, consulted with a dentist, and consented to the necessary examination and treatment. Although the efforts of the public guardian representative went virtually unnoticed by most people, they did make a great difference to Herbert.

Bess resides in a small town in northern Alberta. As a result of a drug overdose she sustained brain damage and subsequently attempted to commit suicide. The attempt was not successful and eventually the public guardian was appointed. Her lifestyle was rather questionable. She was frequently found in status epilepticus following weekends of heavy drinking and required hospitalization for several days to stabilize her condition. The police and the medical community in the town had reached the point where they were making arrangements to have her committed to a psychiatric facility. A public guardian representative became involved in an attempt to put more appropriate supports in place so that Bess could be rehabilitated and prevented from entering an institution. Through the advocacy of the public guardian's office, a placement was eventually found for her in a private residence where the landlady took her in as one of her own family. The results were dramatic. Within 1 month, her problems with alcohol abuse ceased, her problems with seizures requiring hospitalizations were greatly diminished, and she began taking her medications on a regular basis. It has been a year since this placement and Bess continues to show steady improvement. Agency staff involved with her have a hard time believing she is the same person.

Alice is a young woman who was diagnosed as being mildly mentally retarded. She became involved in a relationship with a man who was an alcoholic and eventually moved in with him. Staff from the workshop she attended raised concerns with the office of the public guardian claiming that she often failed to attend the program because she was staying home to nurse her boyfriend's hangovers. On other occasions she would come to work with black eyes or a swollen face and eventually would let the staff know that her boyfriend had been drunk and had struck her.

Following investigation, a public guardian representative was appointed as guardian for this woman. The representative met Alice on several occasions to express the concerns raised by staff persons about legal avenues that could prevent her from coming into further harm. After many meetings in which she denied that there was a problem in the relationship, one day Alice came into the office and explained that she felt life was too short and that perhaps it was not wise for her to be staying with this person. She went on to say that if he really cared for her perhaps he would be able to deal with his alcohol problem. She wanted advice as to what she should do. The public guardian representative supported her decision and recommended that she stay away from her boyfriend until he became involved in some form of rehabilitation program. She considered this and eventually agreed. The public guardian representative secured a restraining order to ensure that her boyfriend would not bother Alice while she attempted to set up a new life for herself.

Sam is a young man who is considered to be moderately mentally retarded. While living at home with his parents, he was coerced by them into committing several felonies for which he was arrested. The charges in this matter were eventually stayed as a result of his handicap and the public guardian was appointed to look out for his best interests. The representative involved arranged for the man to be placed in a group home and to attend a day training program. In the course of this assistance, it was discovered that a woman who had previously worked with the young man in a school program kept occasional contact with him. The representative contacted this woman and she became increasingly involved in Sam's life, attending case conferences for him and having him home on a regular basis for visits. When the guardianship order was due for review the woman applied and had herself appointed as his legal guardian.

Chapter 13

The Foundation
for the Handicapped

Ervin J. Larsen

BACKGROUND

The Foundation for the Handicapped is the largest and probably oldest corporate guardianship program in the United States. Since being established in 1963, it has handled over 500 cases. It was originally founded to provide an answer for the "ages old" question of parents, i.e., "Who will take a personal interest in my child after I am gone?" Since its inception, the basic tenet of the organization's philosophy toward guardianship has been to envision the steps that a parent or close friend would take and then act. For the first 7 years of its existence, there was no intent to directly enter into the guardianship relationships. The change in direction to accept guardianship responsibility was dictated by the real needs of the population that is served.

Parents concern for their handicapped children began increasing in the late 1950s as the professional community brought to light the deteriorated nature of living conditions in traditional state institutions, i.e., overcrowding and lack of suitable programs. Proposed changes included smaller, scattered institutions and community placement that utilized local resources. The presentation of such proposals often lacked easily identifiable systems for assuring service and supervision continuity for former institutional residents. Without assurance of a stable physical location (a primary feature of traditional institutions), parents visualized that their children might become misplaced and in danger of being ignored or forgotten.

As placement out of institutions became a reality, the issue of service continuity and security became a matter for extensive discussions among national organizations and their state and local chapters. Moreover, the question of

227

"personal interest," and all of its ramifications, became a paramount concern for professionals who were working with individuals who manifested handicapping conditions. It soon became very apparent, given the diverse nature of state laws and local services, that answers to the question of long term service stability had to be found on a state-by-state basis.

The first attempt to establish a corporate guardianship program was made in Massachusetts by a group of parents who joined together to form the Massachusetts Association for Retarded Citizens Retardate Trust. The concept was one of a mutual aid society created to give certain benefits to contracting members. The idea had merit for persons of means who could commit either funds or other assets to be used for the eventual benefit of their children. It lacked general appeal to the community as a whole, however, since services to an express group were specified. Perhaps the proposed exclusiveness of the program limited its growth. Another inhibitory factor was that a long term funding commitment was required of parents in the absence of a demonstrated performance capability on the part of the trust organization.

At about the same time, a number of persons in the state of Washington who were active in the national scene began to raise questions and to propose solutions to the question of how to improve the long term stability and continuity of services. Van R. Hinkle acted as catalyst among the various Washington parent organizations. He was then serving as director of the Division of Children and Youth Services with the Washington State Department of Institutions. Mr. Hinkle developed a working concept of a broadly based, statewide agency with a service goal of providing personal attention to ensure the welfare of all orphaned and abandoned persons with handicaps in the state of Washington.

After several years of building an awareness of the apparent need and a possible solution, Mr. Hinkle left the Department of Institutions and assumed the role of executive director of the Association for Retarded Children of Washington. It was agreed that he would be free to develop a protective services agency as he saw fit. The trust that the ARC board of directors placed in Mr. Hinkle was a key element in the subsequent success of the Foundation for the Handicapped. The decision as to whether to make the new concept an arm of the ARC or a separate organization was left entirely up to Mr. Hinkle and the concerned citizens that he recruited. This attitude engendered a broad base of community support and allowed for the development of a new organization (The Foundation for the Handicapped) with a single-purpose mission. This mission was eventually defined to be "personal interest in and concern for orphaned and abandoned persons with handicaps."

Among the early supporters recruited by Mr. Hinkle was John H. Hauberg, a businessman and philanthropist who had raised the match monies required to establish the University of Washington's federally funded Child Development and Mental Retardation Center. Mr. Hauberg, the father of a daughter with a learning disability, was fully capable of establishing a financial trust that would provide for the physical needs of his daughter, but he was still left with the problem of finding an agency to assure personal attention and interest. The answers to his and every parent's anxiety could be found only in a charitable, not-for-profit corporation that would combine parental concern with perpetual existence. Mr. Hauberg's generous financial backing was a determining factor in the early existence of the Foundation.

A key to the eventual success of the Foundation for the Handicapped was the caliber of persons who were invited to participate at organizational meetings. Both Mr. Hinkle and Mr. Hauberg had widespread contacts across the state. They carefully selected the original trustees, all persons of proven capability and community acceptance. The recruitment approach was an organizational masterpiece. Each person was individually briefed regarding specific reasons for being recruited. Incorporation papers were signed at a meeting that was held on November 26, 1963. The nine original trustees were Mr. Olaf E. Caskin, businessman and past Vice-President of the National Association for Retarded Children guardianship and insurance committee; Mr. John H. Hauberg, director of Weyerhauser Company, member of the Governor's Mental Health and Mental Retardation Advisory Council; Dr. Garrett Heyns, Director of Institutions, State of Washington; Mr. Raymond Howell, faculty member of Everett Public Schools, and Past President, Washington Association for Retarded Children; Mr. Frederick C. Jenner, Vice-President and manager, Ballard Branch of Seattle-First National Bank, and Past Chairman, Washington State Council for Children and Youth; Mr. John M. Nelson, Superintendent, Seattle City Light Company, and Past President, Washington United Cerebral Palsy Association; Dr. Willard B. Rew, pediatrician, and Past President, Washington State Medical Association; Mr. John N. Rupp, attorney, and Western Counsel, Pacific Telephone; and Mr. W.L. Thrailkill, Vice-President, Washington Water Power Company, and charter member, Washington State Council for Children and Youth.

With one exception, each of the original trustees continued with the corporation for the first 6 years. Mr. Hinkle was asked to serve as volunteer executive director. He continued in that volunteer capacity for 18 months until he accepted employment with a special national project. The board of trustees then appointed this author as the new volunteer executive director, due to his familiarity with the goals of the Foundation and his interest in the plans of the organization.

A continued commitment by the trustees to bring in interested replacements and recruit additional persons to serve on committees has been the basis for board renewal. The by-laws (Appendix A) currently permit a maximum board of 51 persons. This will probably be the permanent number since geographic coverage is easily maintained while still drawing an average quarterly meeting attendance of approximately 35 persons.

Funding

The funding of a new organization is always an interesting phenomenon to observe. Most new agencies require spin-off grants from parent organizations or a grant of some magnitude from either private or federal sources. Failure to receive a substantial grant often sounds the death knell for many very worthwhile concepts.

The Foundation for the Handicapped had no grant or written commitment of any kind. What it did have, however, was a board of such stature that no one questioned the capability of the organization to carry on its stated mission. Each trustee had the potential for tapping a series of resources and each was secure in the knowledge that collectively, the trustees could keep the agency expanding at a conservative rate until public support was available. Small grants were solicited at strategic times to support direct service expenses. The executive director and clerical workers served on a volunteer or contributed basis. Since there was little initial pressure to offer direct services, time was spent on defining the philosophies of the Foundation and on determining its general service pattern.

An operating budget was established in 1966 and the volunteer staff members were placed on salary. The initial services offered to the public were a speakers' bureau that made public presentations on the goals of the Foundation, counseling to parents or guardians on preparing a long range plan for their ward, and registration of those handicapped persons who someday would require the personal attention to be offered via the Foundation.

The future success of the Foundation was immeasureably assisted by a grant from the United Way of King County (the largest United Way in Washington State) in the fall of 1967. This assistance was the first of 12 United Way membership approvals. In addition to needed financial support, United Way membership approvals have served to assure the citizens of the state that the Foundation for the Handicapped has earned the support of its peers and is established as a permanent organization. As shown in Table 1, approximately 50% of the Foundation's current and annual budget is received from United Way and other private donors. The balance of the budget is derived from fees for services. The fee sources are discussed later in this chapter.

Registration

Registration was used in lieu of the traditional survey of need. A number of volunteer committees were set up and several work-study students were hired to compile and file the results. By the end of 1966, the Foundation had a roster of 1,700 persons. Over 400 of those registered were orphaned or abandoned with no person (other than public service staff) visiting them or taking a friendly interest in their well-being. These orphaned and abandoned persons were immediately enrolled as current clients and as such made up the first group of persons who were visited by the Foundation staff as well as remembered on birthdays and during the holiday season. The balance of the registry was made up of persons whose parents or guardians registered them for future service. The registration was stopped as a program component at the end of 1967 when the total roster had reached approximately 3,600 persons. The ratio of "orphaned" to "future" service had remained fairly constant across the registration period—about one to four. Since 1967, there has been no organized registration program, but the flow of persons wishing to be

Table 1.   The 1982 operating budget of the Foundation for the Handicapped

Income	
Contributions	$ 10,174
United Way	79,191
Program service fees & net incident revenue	78,205
Investment income	513
Miscellaneous revenue	8,414
Other	13,000
Total income	$189,497
Expenses	
Salaries	$ 95,636
Employee health & retirement benefits	1,879
Payroll taxes, etc.	14,644
Professional fees & contractual service payments	22,900
Supplies	2,230
Telephone & telegraph	4,637
Postage & shipping	3,332
Occupancy (building & grounds)	6,832
Rental & maintenance of equipment	5,487
Printing, art work, publications	2,935
Local transportation	8,714
Conferences, conventions, meetings	2,748
Specific assistance to individuals	1,965
Awards & grants	4,822
Miscellaneous	2,681
Depreciation	6,669
Total expenses	$188,013

placed on the roles has continued at a reduced rate. Approximately 4,700 persons are currently registered. It is interesting to note that in the past year there has been a new category of registrant, aged persons who, having outlived their closest relatives and peers, wish to assure themselves of personal interest and concern in the event of a stroke or disability.

The counseling activities of the Foundation soon developed into a consistent process for identifying common needs and goals with only minor adjustments to compensate for special situations. The typical steps in this process are: 1) ascertain the strengths and needs of the person with the handicap, 2) find out what the family visualized as an appropriate plan, 3) compile a list of the available long term resources, and 4) if the family intends to leave assets to the ward by bequest, review the will and trust documents to assure that the intent of the documents can be fulfilled.

ELIGIBILITY CRITERIA

The acceptance of the Foundation as a community agency with broad-based support required the publication of intake criteria. The initial efforts toward criteria were very simple. First, the person had to possess a long term disability (now known as a developmental disability), and second, the person had to be orphaned or abandoned. As these simple criteria were tested in actual use, each had to be reviewed and modified by the trustees. The current policy of the Foundation is "to serve those persons who are handicapped by reason of sensory deficits, mental retardation, or physical disabilities and who have no other person or resource to help them."

The priorities for client acceptance are:

1. Persons with a developmental disability who are orphaned or abandoned
2. Persons with a developmental disability whose parents or relatives are unsuitable or unable to assume guardianship
3. Elderly disabled persons with no family or relatives
4. Elderly disabled persons whose family or relatives are unsuitable or unable to assume guardianship
5. Crisis cases, i.e., accident victims with no relatives.

The Foundation does not knowingly accept mentally ill persons or persons with self-induced problems such as alcohol, drug abuse, etc. The magnitude and nature of the problems that are associated with mental illness and drug problems are such that a specialized agency offering a program similar to the Foundation's could well be established. There would be little possibility of service duplication.

GUARDIANSHIP OF THE PERSON

With the advent of stable funding and the capability of publicizing support services to parents and guardians of persons with handicaps, it became very obvious that many orphaned and abandoned persons needed guardians to truly represent them. The original intent of the Foundation had been to be a friend to those who were orphaned, but friends, while valuable to have, often are not accepted as legitimate spokespersons for individuals with mental retardation who may be legally incompetent. Although a fiduciary corporation could serve as guardian of an estate, the laws of the State of Washington were very clear that only a "person" could qualify to become a guardian of the person.

Through a series of seminars across the state, and the publication of several booklets on guardianship, the Foundation had some success in getting the parents of many persons with handicaps to see the necessity of assuming the role of guardian over their child. This still left the unresolved question of "Who will serve as guardian after I am gone?" All attempts to develop a consistent and accountable program of volunteer guardians met with little recruitment success. The concept also had little appeal to the family asking for help since it was quite apparent that there would be insurmountable problems for assuring continuity. The volunteer guardian approach was also unsatisfactory because it did not mesh well with the major potential strength of the Foundation, i.e., the ability to truly represent the orphaned or abandoned persons with handicaps by assigning a qualified guardian who is accountable to the corporation.

The first approach selected was to authorize staff persons, backed by the full resources of the Foundation, to assume the role of guardian for individual clients. The first such guardianships were processed in 1969 and (until the law was changed in 1975 to allow a not-for-profit corporation to serve as guardian) each guardianship was taken by a staff member, usually the executive director, with the knowledge and consent of the board of directors. A number of problems were encountered in using staff members as individual guardians, mostly in the area of court and public acceptance. For instance, the office of the Foundation was located in Seattle, 280 miles from the superior court in Spokane County. Initially, judges were reluctant to appoint the executive director as guardian since he did not reside in the same general area as the court. Assurances of local volunteer involvement usually resolved this concern.

The public often voiced another concern—"What will happen as staff changes?" Staff-change procedures were developed that were fairly easy to describe and were put to a practical test in 1971 when the first senior staff resignation occurred. An orderly transition to another staff member was managed with the 46 guardianships involved.

It soon became very evident that the proper approach was to work for a change in the guardianship statute. The change was accomplished in the 1975 session of the legislature, when not-for profit corporations with designated wording in their articles of incorporation and by-laws were authorized to serve as guardians of both persons and estates. All guardianships accepted since 1976 have been in the name of the corporation with appropriate board resolutions allowing certain staff members to serve as agent in signing the oath of guardianship. To date, the Foundation for the Handicapped is the only statewide organization that has qualified itself under this 1975 law.

The debate that surrounded changing this one section of the law in 1975 dramatized the need for total revision and "cleanup" of Washington's guardianship statutes. With the guidance of William H. Ellis and William L. E. Dussault, attorney members of the Foundation's board of trustees, the state's legislature completely revised the existing laws in 1977. This modern legislation provides for several stages of protective guardianships: full guardianships of the person and estate, limited guardianship of the person and estate, or any combination thereof. These options allow flexible tailoring of guardianship arrangements to match the characteristics of each person for whom guardianship is sought. Since the change of law in 1975 and the revision in 1977, the Foundation has assisted hundreds of parents to obtain guardianship status in relationship to their children. Morever, the Foundation has become guardian of the person, the estate, or both to over 500 persons who are orphaned and abandoned.

GUARDIANSHIP OF THE ESTATE

The second area in which the Foundation board determined that it must act as change agent was in the field of trusts. In its early attempts to establish long range plans for persons with handicaps, the Foundation learned that the protection and proper expenditure of handicapped persons' funds during their lifetime, and the distribution of any residue following their death, was a major planning hurdle. All major banks had minimum amounts for trust agreements. In 1969, this figure was usually $50,000. The banks felt that their management charges made it prohibitive to handle amounts less than this minimum. Any parent attempting to set up a trust for less than $50,000 thus had to turn to an individual for services. Choosing an individual trustee was often not a satisfactory solution because of the problem of lifespan and continutity.

The concern of the parent for the protection of funds placed in trust was not only in regard to the management and safety of the funds, but also to avoid loss of entitlements by the child-survivor. A scenario, too often played out to its end, usually took the following form: A trust beneficiary would be receiving care in a state institution or through some entitlement program. Upon activation of the trust, or upon receipt of an inheritance, all funds in the trust or inheritance would immediately be used to pay for care, including retroactive payments for care previously delivered. If there was no retroactive account, the funds would be disbursed for care over time until the amount of the trust or inheritance equaled an established minimum (usually $1,500). Once the trust or inheritance reached the minimum level, the beneficiary would be eligible for further entitlements. Understandably, parents considered it a futile gesture to arrange for a direct inheritance and were frustrated by the fact that there was no way to pay for the small, special needs of their loved one.

The solution to the above problem was the establishment of a specialized trust. Parents were instructed to include specific language in their wills that would restrict spending funds in ways that would cause a loss of entitlements. Moreover, they were told that their wills should include a spendthrift clause to prevent the ward from having any discretion over the expenditure of assets in the trust. The first trust incorporating these concepts was utilized by Leavitt and Maude Craven of Wenatchee, Washington. This approach has since become known as the "Craven" trust (see Appendix B).

The first proposed solution to the bank restriction on minimums was to develop a master trust. The laws under which nationally chartered banks are formed do not permit pooling of customer accounts. The Foundation then went to a state chartered bank, Seattle Trust & Savings, which did not operate under the national restrictions. Amounts as small as $500 were accepted and pooled together for management purposes. Separate accountings were available for each trust contract and earnings and costs were distributed proportionately. The trust allowed for a choice of secondary beneficiary and the trustors' choice regarding the distribution of any residual following the lifetime of the primary beneficiary. In spite of reasonable charges and flexibility, the pool trust was not popular, and the concept is no longer used but has been replaced with the present trust agreement system in which the Foundation assumes the role of trustee. It may be that lack of familiarity with the bank and its third party involvement put too much distance between parents and their trust arrangements.

In order to give the Foundation the capability of offering quality management to replace the pool trust concept, a special trust and investment committee was created. The first chairman was Harold A. Rogers, the president of People's National Bank, one of the eight major banks in the state. Mr. Rogers recruited trust officers from each of the major banks and added to the committee several attorneys and a superior court judge. The committee was staffed by Van R. Hinkle, the original force behind the Foundation, who had returned to the agency as a volunteer and consultant.

No attempt has been made to qualify the Foundation as a fiduciary under the law, since any agency can assume this capacity if it is a residual beneficiary of a trust. The requirement that the Foundation be named as beneficiary is clearly pointed out to anyone who wishes to have the Foundation serve as trustee. It has been arbitrarily determined that all trusts that are accepted must include the Foundation for at least 10% of the remainder following the lifetime of the primary beneficiary. Many parents have left all of the residual to the agency; others have left part to other charities or to surviving family members.

Policies and procedures have been developed that require each trust account to be reviewed by the trust and investment committee annually, and guidelines have been set forth for disbursements. Each account is handled on an individual basis. Expenditures vary depending upon the cash requirements of each individual. Long term monies are held in certificates of deposit. Intermediate funds are held in a cash management account or are invested in short term government paper. Short term funds are held in interest-producing bank accounts. At this time, there are no management charges for the establishment or holding of a trust until the Foundation is actively serving the beneficiary. Upon activation of the trust, charges against the individual trust are based on no more than 5% of the annual income, the same amount now allowed the Foundation in guardianship cases by courts, and the amount allowed by the Social Security Administration where the Foundation serves as representative payee. Close supervision of each trust beneficiary combined with staff time records document the service to each client. These steps assist in identifying the real needs of the client and point out the necessity of waiving the fee if it would deprive the client of needed support. Since the Foundation is always named as a residual beneficiary to some extent, it is the policy of the board to waive any fees that would place a hardship on the client.

One policy that has assisted in retaining the continued volunteer involvement of trust officers is that any account that goes over $100,000 must be assigned to a bank as agent for the Foundation. This procedure is incorporated in all trust agreements and allows for individual professional financial management of larger accounts. The Foundation, even though contracting with a trust agent, continues its role in monitoring the personal needs of the client as well as continued personalized interest.

At the present time, the Foundation holds over $3½ million in assets for clients. All such assets are under the immediate supervision of the trust and investment committee. Financial responsibility is a very necessary part of any guardianship program and probably the first area that the public will judge.

ORGANIZATIONAL DESIGN

A human service organization is not only legally, but also morally, accountable for a sensitive but sensible attitude toward the wards for whom it has assumed guardianship. The board of trustees must provide for a continuous evaluation and review of services. For the Foundation, the personal services and planning committee fills the role of monitor and evaluator of direct client service. The process starts with a review of all applications for service as measured against the previously stated criteria. The key question asked by the committee is, "Can we really help this person?" If the committee arrives at a "yes" answer, then the proposed plan of service is reviewed to determine if all resources are being utilized. Appropriate suggestions are passed on to staff.

In order to offer the best possible support to staff, the makeup of the personal services and planning committee is as diverse as possible. The present members include a medical doctor, a retired clergyman, an educator, an attorney, a registered nurse, a social worker, a bank trust officer, and an activist parent. This type of committee make-up provides a broad spectrum of viewpoints and attitudes. The committee meets regularly each month. In addition to reviewing service applications, it reviews a random sampling of case files.

The personal services and planning committee is the "heart" and "conscience" of the Foundation. It considers itself, in part, as a "composite parent" whose responsibility is to demonstrate concern for wards and to call for appropriate action. Without this continued input, it would be very easy for the agency's programs to become oriented toward convenience rather than personalized service. The personal service and planning committee is also responsible for reviewing the agency's staffing model. This added responsibility is employed to ensure that clients' interests take precedence when budgetary and personnel decisions are made.

While the personal services and planning committee is the heart and conscience of the Foundation, the staff of the Foundation is the body that carries out the daily functions of the agency. The staff not only is responsible for carrying out the service program, but must also serve as the sensory organs that bring back necessary information for use by itself and the board. The quality of this program, in the final analysis, is a direct reflection of the quality of the staff.

The Foundation's responsibility for statewide service makes it necessary to select staff who are versatile and can relate well to client needs and parent inquiries. As with any service organization, parents often make contact with only one staff person. Inappropriate conclusions may be drawn about the entire agency if a single staff member is unresponsive to a parent's concerns. The key criteria for staff selection are awareness, sensitivity, and adaptability.

The diverse nature of clients' needs requires constant adjustments. A staff member's role may change dramatically, depending on a client's needs and the circumstances in which the client lives.

Funding resources have always placed limitations on the size of staff. For the first 9 years, with the exception of a few work study students and a number of graduate students, the Foundation's staff consisted of an executive director and a secretary/clerk. All necessary roles were filled by these two principal staff and students, including counseling, volunteer coordinating, bookkeeping, and public relations. The next staff member added, due to expanded need for fiscal services, was a full-time bookkeeper. Concern for direct services made the fourth person a caseworker. Growth has continued with a reasonable balance maintained between the agency's support and service arms. At this time, there are, in addition to the executive director, five persons in the support area and five persons in the casework field services area. Special attention is now being devoted to the development of a volunteer corps in order to enhance personal services to clients.

The Foundation has always tried to maintain active volunteer involvement. At the onset of its volunteer program, it was proposed to volunteers that they establish "special friendships" with wards. In retrospect, it would appear that many persons, who may have otherwise made excellent volunteers, were unwilling to commit themselves to the role of "special friend." The use of the word "friend," before even meeting the disabled person, seemed to demand too large a commitment. The present volunteer recruitment program stresses the need for regularly monitoring clients' quality of life, immediately reporting any concerns back to the Foundation, and a commitment to serve in the volunteer role for an agreed upon length of time. While friendship is not being stressed, it appears that friendships develop as rapidly as when this was our emphasis. Much attention is given to matching the interests and personal preferences of volunteers and clients.

Care must be taken to ensure that staff and volunteers recognize the appropriate roles of other service providers. Most clients are recipients of services that are regulated, either directly or indirectly, by governmental agencies. It is now recognized that the representatives of these governmental agencies must be continually apprised of the role that is played by the Foundation. If the role of a corporate guardianship program, and its relationship to its clients, is properly expressed, it is highly likely that dialogue and actions between the corporation and governmental agencies will greatly benefit clients.

ADVOCACY ROLE

Unlike some concepts of advocacy, in which the prime tool may be confrontation, the Foundation has chosen to bargain, negotiate, and plead for the fair treatment of those whom it represents. It has taken an adversary stance toward governmental agencies on only two occasions. Recourse to lawsuits against individuals or corporations on behalf of clients has occurred more frequently, however. The most recent example concerned an accident victim for whom the Foundation negotiated a settlement of over $3 million.

The first case in which the Foundation challenged a governmental agency was a situation where it was felt that the civil rights of certain clients had been violated. The state of Washington had made retroactive collections of care costs from the clients' accumulated resources. Both the superior court and the supreme court of the state of Washington ruled that the rights of the citizens were improperly disregarded but no restitution has been ordered. This case is now being appealed before the United States Supreme Court.

The second case, which at present is on the appeals docket of the state supreme court, is on behalf of a man for whom the Foundation is guardian. The man in this case was admitted to a state university-affiliated hospital for care. While there, he suffered cardiac arrest but was resuscitated by the application of "heroic" measures. His continued existence, although his brain wave scans do not meet the legal definition of death, is totally dependent on life support systems. The Foundation has been asked to authorize the withdrawal of life support technology because of the excessive cost to the state of maintaining this retarded man. The attending physicians have rendered their opinion that he will have a poor quality of life even if he does recover. The board of trustees of the Foundation has refused to comply with this request for two reasons. First, the guardianship law is explicit that the guardian must "care for and maintain" the ward. Second, as a composite surrogate parent, the Foundation represents all parents and concerned persons, many of whom take a conservative position and maintain that life should be supported.

The attorney general's office of the state of Washington is representing the university-affiliated hospital and has sued the Foundation. The petition requests that the superior court order the Foundation to authorize withdrawal of life support systems from the ward. In a hearing, the judge found the petition reasonable and ordered the support withdrawn. The decision is now being held in abeyance pending appeal.

CASE EXAMPLES

Perhaps a better grasp of the Foundation's actual services may be gained by reviewing several examples of active cases.

In 1978, the Foundation was contacted by the 71-year-old mother of a 31-year-old retarded woman. The woman was living in a group home following placement from a state institution. After consulting with the Foundation staff, the mother made the decision to petition for guardianship over her daughter, with the Foundation being named as standby and successor guardian. In conjunction with the establishment of the guardianship, a "Craven" trust was prepared with the Foundation as trustee and having an initial funding of $500. A will was then prepared. It provided further funding for the trust from the mother's estate and stipulated that the daughter's share of the estate was to be spent at the discretion of the Foundation for her special needs over and above those that she was entitled to from other sources.

Two days following notice of the mother's death in 1981, a Foundation representative signed the oath of guardian. Regular visitation has occurred since that time, and, through the funding furnished by the trust, the Foundation has been able to provide for the special needs of the daughter, including participation in a closely supervised tour of Disneyland. Future unusual needs will be covered by the substantial trust. The concern of the mother as to "Who will take a personal interest in my child after I am gone?" has been answered.

From an agency standpoint this case is a perfect example of fulfilling the Foundation's role in the community. The needs of the daughter are being met as planned by the mother; the Foundation receives an annual guardianship fee; and the Foundation is reimbursed for any unusual expenses from the trust. Thirty or forty years from now, if there is a residual left in the trust following the lifetime of the daughter, the Foundation will have that money to help some other person who has a special need or to support its continued service.

Among those considered eligible for service by the Foundation are aged persons who have no relatives and who may develop conditions that make it impossible for them to manage their own affairs. A recent case involved the following steps. A call was received from a case worker in a local hospital. The 81-year-old woman involved had suffered a stroke and had been brought to the hospital for care. There were no relatives on record. Although Mrs. Doe had assets in several local banks, she could not be placed in a nursing home because she was unable to authorize the disbursement of funds for the payment of care.

At the request of the hospital, the Foundation petitioned for guardianship of Jane Doe. Upon appointment of the Foundation as guardian, Mrs. Doe's assets were gathered into a single account, her bills were paid by court order, and the Foundation was authorized to maintain Mrs. Doe in an approved nursing facility. For its services as guardian, the Foundation receives a court-established guardianship fee. Mrs. Doe is regularly visited by Foundation staff and volunteers.

If the assets of Jane Doe became exhausted, the Foundation will continue to take a personal interest in her welfare and will file for any entitlements for which she may be eligible. The guardianship fee will be waived if it places a hardship on Mrs. Doe.

A more out-of-the-ordinary case involves the 6-year-old victim of an accident. Negligence was involved in the accident so a substantial amount of money was paid in settlement. At the insistence of the Foundation, the funds received in settlement of the claim were placed by the court in a trust that incorporates the "Craven" wording. Since no one is able to predict whether the boy will recover his full faculties, the trust document also incorporates a clause that allows the Foundation to turn over a substantial portion of the assets to the young man at age 25, and the balance at age 40, if he has improved enough to manage his own affairs. In the meantime, the Foundation is responsible for his housing, the employment of suitable persons to give him care, his medical needs, and the selection of training and educational services. Fees for Foundation service are established on a cost reimbursement basis as long as there are available resources.

The cases described are only examples of the many serviced by the Foundation. A typical day at the main office (there are three branch offices) includes:

—One request for guardianship
—Three parental inquiries or interviews relating to long term planning or guardianship
—Three inquiries from either attorneys or trust officers for current information
—Activities pertinent to the management of the 500 clients now enrolled

Each request is considered on the basis of its merits and the human resources available to the person. Every effort is made to involve family and friends first. If a client is accepted and it is later determined that another appropriate guardian is available, the Foundation will withdraw in favor of any qualified person who is willing to serve.

While each case is substantially different, the persons who are accepted as clients share certain commonalities: no concerned person able to serve as legal guardian, the need for supportive visitation, and often the need for fiscal management. The board of trustees and the staff of the Foundation for the Handicapped are dedicated to fulfilling the role of substitute parent or family to orphaned and abandoned persons with handicaps.

LESSONS LEARNED

If ever again asked to develop an organization similar to the Foundation, there are a number of lessons this author would want to remember and review before opening the doors for the first client interview.

1. Get the strongest, broadest-based board that you can recruit. Previous track records are important; do not go by name alone.
2. Start with a specific geographic area and expand only as funded.
3. Select the type of client to be served and the public to be reached and then focus the program accordingly.
4. Plan for slower acceptance than anticipated. People do not easily give up

financial control, even in anticipation of death. It is the Foundation's experience that the preparation of a will, for instance, often has a gestation period of several years.

5. Families must be involved in all facets of planning. No planning can be done in a vacuum. It's a real world out there!

6. Stress that the agency be used as a last resort. All interested, qualified persons should have their chance to serve as guardian prior to agency involvement.

7. Don't try to do it all alone. Other resources are there to fulfill their role in society as well.

8. Stability is the reason people ask for help, so the stability of the program will be the key to its success. Program expansion must be accomplished in a manner that does not weaken the existing program base.

Sharing this history of the Foundation with the reader has been a privilege. No definite mention has been made of agency mechanics: the tedious hours of committee work, the endless memos and drafts, the juggled minutes, and the physical and mental stress on all concerned with making an agency a viable, living organism. These are givens, and most assuredly presumed by any reader who has earned the first scar at a board meeting. But the vision of service continuity for dependent persons is clearly a goal worth pursuing. The Foundation has made significant progress toward achieving this goal in the state of Washington. It anticipates similar progress in many places during future years.

CONCLUSION

The Foundation for the Handicapped was established almost 20 years ago to improve the long term continuity of services to disabled persons. It currently acts as guardian of the person and/or estate to over 500 Washington citizens who are handicapped and have no other person or resource to help them. The entire range of services offered by the Foundation includes:

1. Consultation with parents, relatives, and guardians concerning lifetime plans and protective services for their handicapped child or ward

2. Registration of all persons who may have a present or future need for the services of the Foundation

3. Providing trust services to families of handicapped persons; conferring with attorneys and trust departments regarding the Harold A. Rogers Memorial Trust and Investment Committee of the Foundation

4. Providing attorneys and trust departments with suggested forms of revocable trust instruments wherein handicapped individuals are the beneficiaries

5. Serving as trustee of funds for the use and benefit of handicapped beneficiaries

6. Serving as guardian, limited guardian, or standby guardian

7. Personal visitations, gift remembrances on birthdays, holidays, or other special occasions of orphaned handicapped persons
8. Serving as representative payee for Social Security, railroad retirement, and veterans' benefits
9. Safeguarding vital documents required by federal and state agencies and departments in order to establish entitlements for the disabled and handicapped
10. Maintaining current information on state and federal legislation affecting the financial interests of disabled and handicapped citizens
11. Liaison with other voluntary agencies in cooperative efforts to secure appropriate fiduciary and protective services for handicapped persons incapable of money management
12. Legal advice for handicapped individuals, their parents, guardians, or attorneys, when requested

The Foundation's success is due primarily to powerful, prestigious board leadership, a clear program focus, and dedicated staff. It strongly encourages parent associations and other advocacy organizations to consider developing similar program models.

Appendix A

ARTICLES OF INCORPORATION AND BY-LAWS FOR THE FOUNDATION FOR THE HANDICAPPED

ARTICLES OF INCORPORATION
OF
FOUNDATION FOR THE HANDICAPPED

I. NAME

The name of the corporation shall be FOUNDATION FOR THE HANDICAPPED.

II. DURATION

The duration of the corporation shall be perpetual.

III. REGISTERED OFFICE AND AGENT

The registered office of the corporation shall be 1600 West Armory Way, Seattle, Washington 98119, and the registered agent of the corporation at such address shall be Ervin J. Larsen.

IV. PURPOSES, LIMITATIONS AND POWERS

1. *Purposes.* This corporation is organized exclusively for religious, charitable, scientific, literary, or educational purposes within the meaning of section 501(c)(3) of the Internal Revenue Code of 1954, as amended. Without limiting the generality of the foregoing, the following purposes are specifically stated:

   a. To receive, hold, administer and disburse any moneys, securities or other property which may be transferred to the corporation by gift, devise, bequest or otherwise, and to invest, conserve, use and disburse such moneys, securities or other property, and the income derived therefrom, for charitable, scientific or educational purposes in serving the general area involving human mental and physical handicapping conditions, and for the support of other organizations and agencies of like character and purpose.

   b. To cooperate with and aid other organizations and agencies organized and operated for allied purposes, to the end of promoting the mental, moral, physical, social and vocational improvement of handicapped children and adults, without discrimination as to race, color, religious inclination, sex, national origin or age.

   c. To provide a counseling, visitation, supervisory and/or guardianship service for handicapped persons whose relatives are deceased or are otherwise unable to furnish such personal attention.

   d. To establish and operate residential facilities for the care, treatment, education, and vocational training of handicapped persons without regard to race, color, religious affiliation, sex, national origin, age or membership in or contributions to the corporation.

   e. To act as trustee of a living trust, a testamentary trust or any other trust authorized by law in which the corporation is named as a beneficiary of such trust; provided, however, that the corporation shall act as a trustee in any particular case only if so determined by the Board of Directors of the corporation or its Executive Committee.

    f.   To act as a guardian or limited guardian of any disabled or incompetent child or adult pursuant to the laws of the State of Washington applicable to the appointment and qualification of nonprofit corporations serving as guardians or limited guardians.

2. *Limitations.*

    2.1   This corporation shall have no capital stock, and no part of its net earnings shall inure to the benefit of any member, director, officer or any private individual.

    2.2   No member, director or officer of the corporation nor any private individual shall be entitled to share in the distribution of any of the corporate assets upon dissolution or final liquidation of the corporation or the winding up of its affairs. Upon any dissolution, final liquidation or winding up, all the remaining net assets of the corporation shall be distributed by the Board of Directors of the corporation to a nonprofit corporation selected by the Board of Directors which is organized and operated for purposes similar to those of this corporation and which qualifies at that time for exemption under the provisions of section 501(c)(3) of the Internal Revenue Code of 1954, as then amended, or any successor statute, or to the federal, state or local government for exclusively public purposes.

    2.3   No substantial part of the activities of the corporation shall consist of the carrying on of propaganda, or otherwise attempting, to influence legislation except as may be permitted section 501(c)(3) organizations by the Internal Revenue Code, and the corporation shall not participate in or intervene in (including the publication or distribution of statements) any political campaign on behalf of any candidate for public office.

    2.4   Notwithstanding any other provision of these Articles, the corporation shall not conduct or carry on activities not permitted to be conducted or carried on by an organization exempt under section 501(c)(3) or the Internal Revenue Code of 1954, as amended.

    2.5   The corporation is authorized to use, and it shall be the corporate policy to utilize in appropriate instances, the services of banking institutions, state or national, authorized to do trust business in the State of Washington as trustees, depositories or agents for the investment and reinvestment of corporate funds or for the safekeeping of securities and other property.

    2.6   Corporate funds shall be for use primarily within the State of Washington; provided, however, that when a donor so instructs, donated funds or property may be used outside of the State of Washington unless such use would be contrary to law or would impose a tax liability upon the corporation or the donor.

    3.   *Powers.*   Subject to such limitations and conditions as are or may be prescribed by law or in the corporation's Articles of Incorporation or Bylaws, the corporation shall have all powers which by law are now or may hereafter be conferred upon or allowed to any corporation organized for the purposes hereinabove set forth.

V. BOARD OF DIRECTORS

    1.   The number of directors on the Board of Directors of the corporation shall be as set forth in the Bylaws. The first Board of Directors upon the adoption of these Articles of Amendment shall consist of forty-three (43) directors whose names and addresses are as follows:

Name	Address
Henry A. Alkema	Peoples National Bank of Washington Trust Department 1414-4th Avenue Seattle, WA 98101

Name	Address
J. Scott Barron	c/o Whatcom Medical Bureau P.O. Box 937 Bellingham, WA 98227
W. James Bennett	Social Security Administration P.O. Box 36 Bellingham, WA 98225
Byron Berhow	1709 N.E. 78th #154 Vancouver, WA 98665
Philip S. Brooke, III	1400 Washington Trust Financial Center Spokane, WA 98203
Austin A. Burch	Vice-President Puget Sound National Bank P.O. Box 1258 Tacoma, WA 98401
George A. Cashman	Seattle-First National Bank 101 North Second Street P.O. Box 196 Yakima, WA 98901
Maurice C. Clark	1541 NE 76th Seattle, WA 98115
Donald E. Collins	First Interstate Bank of Washington Trust Department P.O. Box 21927 Seattle, WA 98111
L. H. Craven	201 South Elliot Avenue, #31 Wenatchee, WA 98801
George H. Dickson	3911 N.E. 100th Street Seattle, WA 98125
William L. E. Dussault	219 East Galer Seattle, WA 98102
Ronald W. Eaglestone	c/o Boeing Computer Services, Inc. 6510 Southcenter Blvd. Seattle, WA 98188
William H. Ellis	1111 Third Avenue Bldg. Seattle, WA 98101
Pat Fiske	P.O. Box 336 Mount Vernon, WA 98273
Robert F. Garing	Rainier National Bank P.O. Box 3966 Seattle, WA 98124
Chuck Gilman	Interlake Nursing Center 1640-148th Avenue S.E. Bellevue, WA 98007
Jerrold H. Goetz	P.O. Box 70587 5315 9th Avenue N.W. Seattle, WA 98107
John H. Hauberg	Grand Central on the Park #230 216 1st Avenue South Seattle, WA 98104
Lester W. Hein	3505 65th Avenue Court N.W. Gig Harbor, WA 98335
Van R. Hinkle	6223 Island Crest Way Mercer Island, WA 98040

Name	Address
Sherman Huffine	P.O. Box 304 Olympia, WA 98507
The Hon. David C. Hunter	10506 N.E. 46th Kirkland, WA 98033
Robert A. Hunter	901 S.E. 94th Avenue Vancouver, WA 98664
Arleigh T. Jones	Seattle First National Bank Bldg. 1114 Pacific Avenue Tacoma, WA 98402
Clayton J. Kick	5112 93rd Place S.W. Everett, WA 98204
John Kirby	United Cerebral Palsy Association 4409 Interlake Avenue North Seattle, WA 98103
Ernest LaPalm	Employment Security Department P.O. Box 367 Olympia, WA 98504
Dr. Jack Leighton	E. 1321 55th Spokane, WA 99203
Joseph S. Lemon	Bank of California Trust Department P.O. Box 3123 Seattle, WA 98114
Gerald M. Lorentson	Concepts for Independent Living 2450 Magnolia Boulevard West Seattle, WA 98199
Susan McKeehan	Lakeland Village P.O. Box 200 Medical Lake, WA 99022
Russell Mazzola	c/o Smith, Scott & Mazzola 314 North Second Street P.O. Box 1449 Yakima, WA 98907
Ivan E. Merrick	1522 Seattle Tower Bldg. Seattle, WA 98101
Ralph Munro	Secretary of State's Office Olympia, WA 98504
William Y. Nishimura	U.S. Department of Housing & Urban Development Arcade Plaza Bldg. 1321 Second Avenue Seattle, WA 98101
N. Frank Noren	P.O. Box 5301, NC Station Spokane, WA 99205
Leo S. Pavloff	Restorative Care Center 2821 South Walden Seattle, WA 98144
Dr. E. Louise Porter	1012 S.W. 296th Street Federal Way, WA 98003
The Hon. Yancy Reser	913 Bonnie Brae Walla Walla, WA 99362
Mrs. Harold A. Rogers	7849 S.E. 40th Mercer Island, WA 98040

Name	Address
Eloise Ross	1941 47th S.W. Seattle, WA 98116
Willard E. Skeel	Seattle Trust & Savings Bank 804 Second Avenue Seattle, WA 98104
Margo Thornley	W.I.S.E.R. Institute 16045 25th N.E. Seattle, WA 98155
Leslie Venables	5210 226th Street N.W. Stanwood, WA 98292
The Hon. Lloyd L. Wiehl	5211 East Sunset Drive Yakima, WA 98908

2.   The Board of Directors may remove any director from office as provided in the Bylaws of the corporation.

VI. MEMBERSHIP

The membership of the corporation shall be as set forth in the corporation's Bylaws.

The foregoing amendment was adopted at a properly called meeting of the members of the corporation on _____, 1982 at which meeting a quorum was present, and such amendment received at least two-thirds (2/3) of the votes of the members present at such meeting who were entitled to vote thereon.

FOUNDATION FOR THE HANDICAPPED

By _____
Henry A. Alkema, President

BY LAWS OF
FOUNDATION FOR THE HANDICAPPED
(A Washington Nonprofit Corporation)

ARTICLE 1–GENERAL

Section 1.   The name of this corporation as established by its Articles of Incorporation shall be the FOUNDATION FOR THE HANDICAPPED.

Section 2.   The Foundation for the Handicapped is organized as a corporation under the laws of the State of Washington. It is a nonprofit, non-sectarian and non-political corporation having no capital stock.

Section 3.   The principal place of business and registered office of the Foundation for the Handicapped is 4409 Interlake Avenue North, Seattle, Washington 98103, or at such other place or places as the Board of Directors shall from time to time determine.

Section 4.   If there be any net earnings from any of the corporation's activities, the same shall accrue solely to the organization and no part shall be for the personal benefit of any member.

Section 5.   The purposes of the Foundation for the Handicapped shall be: (1) To make the most effective use of moneys and property available to it for the benefit of orphaned and abandoned handicapped and disabled children and adults within the State of Washington; (2) To promote, stimulate and provide assistance to handicapped and disabled citizens through efforts to obtain suitable programs of training, education, recreation, employment, habilitation, and residential care; (3) To meet the concern of parents, relatives and the public for the supervision of and personal interest in the welfare of handicapped and disabled persons by serving as Personal Representative, Parental Successor, Guardian or Limited Guardian, Attorney in Fact under a Durable Power of Attorney, Personal Advocate, and Representative Payee; and (4) To act as Guardian or Limited Guardian of persons and/or estates under the provisions of Chapter 95, 1975 Session Laws of the State of Washington, 1st Extra Session.

ARTICLE II–MEMBERSHIP

Section 1.   Membership in the Foundation shall be classified into two categories, namely, (1) Active; and (2) Sustaining.

Section 2.   Application for membership as an Active Member shall be open to any natural person interested and supportive of the purpose of the Foundation for the Handicapped. Application shall be upon forms provided by the corporation and admission to membership shall be subject to election by the Board of Directors. Active membership shall continue until the death, disability or expressed desire of the member to withdraw from membership.

Section 3.   Sustaining membership shall be granted to any person, family or organization requesting such membership and submitting a minimum fee of Fifty Dollars ($50.00). Admission to sustaining membership shall be subject to election by the Board of Directors and shall possess all the rights of an active member.

Section 4.   Each active and sustaining member shall be entitled to one vote on each matter submitted to the vote of members at any annual or special meeting of the membership.

Section 5.   Membership in the Foundation shall not be transferable or assignable.

Section 6.   An annual meeting of members shall be held in the month of March in each year for the purpose of electing Directors and for the transaction of such other business as may come before the meeting. Notice of the time and place of such meeting shall be mailed to each member at least 20 days prior to the annual meeting.

Section 7.   Special meetings of the members of the Foundation for the Handicapped may be called by the President, the Board of Directors, or not less than ten (10) members. Notice of the time, place and purpose of such special meeting shall be mailed to each member at least 10 days prior to the date of such meeting.

Section 8.   A quorum of 25 members in attendance will be required.

ARTICLE III–BOARD OF DIRECTORS

Section 1.   The management and administration of the affairs and property of the Foundation shall be by a Board of Directors consisting of not less than nine (9) nor more than forty-five (45), who shall be elected by the membership, one third of them annually, to serve terms of three (3) years and until their successors are elected and qualified.

Section 2.   A quorum to transact business at any meeting of the Board of Directors shall consist of ten (10) or more trustees. A majority of such quorum shall decide any question that may come before a meeting of the board.

Section 3.   Whenever any vacancy shall occur among the directors or officers by death, resignation or removal from the State of Washington, or failure or refusal to serve following election, such vacancy shall be filled by action of the remaining members of the Board of Directors. Any director so elected shall hold office until the next annual meeting of the membership and thereafter until his successor is elected and qualified.

Section 4. Regular meetings of the Board of Directors shall be held quarterly, meeting at such times and places as may be designated by the Board of Directors or the President.

Section 5. Special meetings of the Board of Directors may be called by the Board of Directors by resolution duly adopted, the President, or on written request served on the Secretary by any five (5) members of the Board of Directors.

Section 6. Notice of the date, time, place and purposes of an annual or special meeting of the Board of Directors shall be mailed to each director at his or her last known post office address at least five (5) days prior to the meeting. Notice of any meeting may be waived in writing by any director at any time, either before or after the meeting, and attendance at the meeting in person shall constitute a waiver of notice of such meeting.

Section 7. Annual meetings of the Board of Directors shall be held immediately prior to and immediately following the annual meeting of members for the purpose of organization, election of officers, and transacting such other business as may come before it. The notice of the meeting shall include the report of the Nominating Committee and shall be sent to the directors at least five (5) days in advance of the meeting.

Section 8. The Board of Directors shall have the power to receive and utilize gifts and donations in cash or in kind to further the purposes of the Foundation.

Section 9. The Board of Directors may employ such staff, agents or representatives with such powers and to perform such acts and duties on behalf of the Foundation as may be assigned to them so far as may be consistent with these By Laws and to the extent authorized.

ARTICLE IV–EXECUTIVE COMMITTEE

Section 1. The Executive Committee shall consist of the Officers, the immediate past President, and the Chairpersons of all Standing Committees, at least two of whom shall be Board members. All meetings of the Executive Committee shall be open to any member of the Board of Directors who may attend and participate but shall have no vote.

Section 2. The Executive Committee shall, between meetings of the Board of Directors, have and is hereby granted all the powers and duties of the Board of Directors of this corporation that may be lawfully delegated to an Executive Committee under the laws of the State of Washington pertaining to non-profit corporations.

Section 3. The Executive Committee shall meet on call of the President as frequently as business of the corporation may require. Meetings of the Executive Committee shall be called upon five (5) days notice given to each member of the committee by mail or telephone indicating the date, time and place of the meeting.

Section 4. Four (4) members present shall constitute a quorum for the transaction of business at meetings of the Executive Committee.

ARTICLE V–COMMITTEES

Section 1.   The committees hereinafter set forth and such other committees as shall from time to time be established by the Board of Directors shall constitute the Standing Committees of the Foundation. The committee chairperson and membership shall be appointed by the President with the approval of the Board of Directors.

Section 2.   All Standing Committees shall serve for one year and until their successors are appointed following the next annual meeting of the membership of the Foundation.

Section 3.   Standing Committees and their functions shall be as follows:

A. TRUST AND INVESTMENT COMMITTEE.   This committee shall publicize itself and its services under the name of THE HAROLD A. ROGERS MEMORIAL TRUST AND INVESTMENT COMMITTEE OF THE FOUNDATION FOR THE HANDICAPPED. It shall have as its major responsibility the monitoring and supervision of the fiduciary responsibilities of the Foundation, except day-to-day bookkeeping of operational funds, and the determination of all policies with respect to the handling of securities, monies, trust funds, property, real and personal, held by the Foundation as owner or as trustee.

B. PERSONALIZED SERVICES COMMITTEE.   This committee shall have as its major responsibility the devising and directing of programs to provide services and personal support to Foundation clients, and shall administer any special projects established to provide such services by action of the Board of Directors, the Executive Committee, or the membership of the Foundation.

C. FAMILY COUNSELING COMMITTEE.   This committee shall have as its major responsibility the providing of counsel to parents, relatives and guardians or limited guardians regarding short and long term planning for their handicapped child or ward, including dissemination of information through a speaker's bureau, printed materials, or other means, relative to estate planning, insurance needs and residential care.

D. FINANCE AND BUDGET.   This committee shall be responsible for: (1) The preparation of the annual budget for each fiscal year and presenting the same to the Board of Directors for its approval; (2) Overseeing the day-to-day financial management and operational procedures; (3) Cooperating with the TRUST AND INVESTMENT COMMITTEE in monitoring and supervision of the fiduciary responsibilities of the Foundation; and (4) Arranging and carrying out any special fund raising plans and activities.

E. PERSONNEL COMMITTEE.   This committee shall be responsible for: (1) The establishment of professional requirements pursuant to which staff personnel shall be employed; (2) Recommending to the Board of Directors for its action the personnel policies applicable to employees relating to vacations, sick leave, hours of employment, reimbursement of expenses incurred by staff, etc.; (3) Interviewing of candidates for vacant staff positions; and (4) Recommending to the Board of Directors the salaries to be paid and increments, if any, to be awarded to employed staff, together with such fringe benefits as may be deemed appropriate.

F. MEMBERSHIP COMMITTEE.   This committee shall be responsible for: (1) The recruitment of new members; (2) Recommending any changes in qualifications and classification for membership that may seem warranted; (3) Reviewing and updating membership rolls; and (4) Maintaining an official roster of Active and Sustaining Members.

G. NOMINATIONS COMMITTEE. Not less than sixty (60) days prior to the annual meeting of the Board of Directors and the membership, the President shall appoint a Nominations Committee consisting of a chairman and at least two (2) members of the Foundation. In addition to the nominations to the Board of Directors submitted by the Nominations Committee, nominations may be made from the floor at the annual meeting of the membership.

H. PROFESSIONAL ADVISORY COMMITTEES. Such advisory committees may be appointed by the President, subject to approval of the Board of Directors, in special fields such as medicine, law, insurance or rehabilitation-employment for the handicapped and disabled. The members of such advisory committees shall be individuals whose professional or personal interests are in the field of activity of concern to the Foundation and the handicapped and disabled served by the organization.

I. STANDING COMMITTEES shall carry out those responsibilities and func-tions as may be delegated to them from time to time by the Board of Directors, Executive Committee, or the President.

J. SPECIAL COMMITTEES may be created from time to time for special tasks and assignments and dissolved upon the completion of their duties. Members of Special Committees shall be appointed by the President and confirmed by the Board of Directors.

ARTICLE VI–OFFICERS

Section 1. The officers of the Foundation shall be elected annually by the Board of Directors at its meeting immediately following the annual meeting of the membership at which directors are elected. If the election of officers shall not be held at such meeting such election shall be held as soon thereafter as can conveniently be arranged. Whenever any vacancy shall occur among the officers, such vacancy shall be filled by the Board of Directors. Any officers so elected shall hold office until the next annual meeting of the Board of Directors at which officers are elected.

Section 2. The officers shall be a President, a Vice President (elected from the directors residing in Eastern Washington), a Vice President (elected from the directors residing in Western Washington), a Secretary, and Treasurer.

Section 3. The President shall preside at all annual and special meetings of the mem-bership, and meetings of the Board of Directors and Executive Committee. He shall sign and execute instruments in the name of the Foundation as authorized by the Board of Directors, except in cases where the signing and execution thereof shall be expressly delegated by the Board to some other officer or agent of the Foundation. Generally, he shall perform all duties incident to the office of President and such other duties as may be prescribed by the Board of Directors.

Section 4. The Vice Presidents, one from Eastern Washington and one from Western Washington, shall perform such duties as may be assigned to them by the President or the Board of Directors. One of the Vice Presidents shall be selected to assume the office of President in the event of his absence from a scheduled meeting, temporary disability, or until a successor has been elected in the event of death, disability, or removal from the State of Washington.

Section 5. The Secretary shall cause to be maintained a minute book in which minutes of all membership meetings, Board of Directors' meetings, and Executive

Committee meetings shall be filed. He shall arrange for notification of members and directors of all meetings at which their presence is required. He shall assist the Membership Committee in maintaining an official roster of Active and Sustaining members.

Section 6. The Treasurer shall arrange for: (1) Payment of all proper invoices and expenses, and the salary drafts of the employees of the Foundation; (2) Maintain the corporation's financial records showing all receipts and disbursements therein; (3) Collect and receipt for dues of Sustaining Members, gifts and contributions; and (4) Prepare an annual financial statement for presentation at the annual meeting.

All checks, drafts or other orders for the payment of money, notes, or other evidences of indebtedness issued in the name of the Foundation shall be signed by the Treasurer and such other officers or agents as shall be determined by resolution of the Board of Directors. All funds shall be deposited to the credit of the Foundation in such banks or other depositories as the Board of Directors may select.

At the discretion of the Board of Directors, the Treasurer and any other officer or employee shall be bonded in such amount and with such bonding company or companies as may be directed.

Section 7. The Board of Directors shall employ such personnel as it may deem necessary to carry out the program of the Foundation, including an Executive Director who shall have charge of the business and office operations, record keeping, and internal management and administration of the Foundation.

ARTICLE VII–
ACTIONS AGAINST OFFICERS, DIRECTORS, EMPLOYEES, AND COMMITTEE MEMBERS

Section 1. Indemnification.   Any person who is made or was a party or is threatened to be made a party to any threatened, pending or completed action, suit or proceeding, whether civil, criminal, administrative or investigative, by reason of the fact that he is or was a director, officer, employee, or member of a standing or special committee of the Foundation, shall be indemnified against expenses, including attorney's fees, judgments, fines and amounts paid in settlement actually and reasonably incurred by him in connection with action, suit or proceeding, if he acted in good faith and in a manner he reasonably believed to be in or not opposed to the best interests of the Foundation and with respect to any criminal action or proceeding had no reason to believe his conduct was unlawful. In any action or suit be procure a judgment against such a person, no indemnification shall be made in respect of any claim, issue or matter as to which he shall have been adjudged to be liable for negligence or misconduct in the performance of his duty to the Foundation unless and only to the extent that the court in which such action or suit was brought shall determine upon application that, despite an adjudication of liability, he is fairly and reasonably entitled to indemnity for such expenses which such court shall deem proper. On request of such person who is made or threatened to be made a party to any such suit, the Foundation shall enter into an agreement confirming the foregoing indemnity subject to limitations as provided by law in such instances. The indemnification herein provided for shall continue as to a person who has caused to be a director, officer, employee, or member of a standing or special committee of this Foundation, shall inure to the benefit of his heirs, executors and administrators, and shall be in addition to rights of indemnification provided by law.

Section 2. Expenses. The Foundation shall pay expenses incurred in defending a civil or criminal action, suit, or proceeding against which a person shall be entitled to indemnification under the foregoing Section in advance of a final disposition of such action upon receipt of an undertaking by or on behalf of the person to repay such amount if the person is not entitled to indemnification as provided by law.

Section 3. Insurance. The Foundation may purchase and maintain insurance on behalf of any person who is or was a director, officer, employee or agent of the Foundation against any liability asserted against him and incurred by him in any such capacity or arising out of his status as such, whether or not the Founcation has or would have the power to indemnify him against such liability under law.

ARTICLE VIII–FISCAL YEAR

Section 1. The fiscal year of the Foundation shall be established by the Board of Directors and unless otherwise modified, shall be the calendar year.

ARTICLE IX–AMENDMENTS

Section 1. At any meeting of the Board of Directors at which a quorum is present, these By Laws may be altered, amended, or repealed by a majority vote of the Directors presented, PROVIDED that the notice of such a meeting shall set forth the proposed alterations, amendments or repeals.

ADOPTED DECEMBER 11, 1975

Appendix B

MATERIALS SHARED WITH PARENTS REGARDING ESTATE PLANNING

To: Parents of Handicapped Children
From: The Foundation for the Handicapped
Re: Estate Planning
The Importance of a Will
The Craven Trust Document

Concern, personal friendship, legal and social counsel and a number of special services are provided by the Foundation to meet the needs of orphaned and abandoned persons, and the parents and the relatives of the handicapped who seek the guidance and support of a responsive and caring organization.

This information is brought to you in memory of Mrs. Marjorie Lynch, a founder of the Foundation for the Handicapped.
Marjorie will long be remembered for her tireless efforts to assist our state and nations' handicapped children.

The Foundation for the Handicapped operates across Washington State. If you have a handicapped child or adult, or know of one, feel free to contact the Foundation for the Handicapped in planning for the future.

Volunteers and staff are available from the Foundation for the Handicapped to make presentations to local parents groups, bar associations, charitable organizations, and estate planners on "Planning for the Future of a Child, Wills, Trusts, Guardianship and Estate Planning."

Please contact the Seattle office for scheduling.

Every parent should have a will. This is especially true for parents of handicapped children. If a person dies without a will (i.e., intestate) his or her property is distributed to his or her heirs according to the laws of the state. Generally, under Washington law, when the first parent dies, the surviving parent inherits all the property. However, when the second parent dies, the surviving children share the family assets equally. State law does not take into account the fact of a disability.

Inheritance of property outright poses obvious risks to a disabled individual. He or she may not be able to handle the funds properly. If he or she is in a state supported institution, the state will bill the disabled child for the entire cost of stay in the institution from July 1st, 1967 on. In most cases, this will immediately consume all the assets that the individual has inherited. Moreover, the money collected by the state does not go into the budget of the particular institution, but into the general fund of the state.

Thus, the best way for you to insure that your desires regarding your child are observed, is by making a will. As you may have gathered in your will you do not want to leave property outright to your disabled child. What you will want to use in your will is a trust.

A trust is a relationship whereby one person (the trustee) administers property for the benefit of another person (the beneficiary) according to directions of the person who created the trust. There are several advantages to using a trust:

(1) Funds and property are managed to insure that maximum income consistent with protecting the principal is produced.

(2) A mechanism is established where the trustee pays bills, contracts for services, and if appropriate, gives the beneficiary spending money.

(3) The trustee has maximum flexibility in use of the principal and income by having broad powers of discretion and can tailor the use of the funds to the individual needs of the beneficiary.

(4) On termination of the trust the remaining funds can be distributed to other family members without incurring death taxes or expenses.

In addition, if the proper language is used in the trust document the assets of the trust will be protected from collection by the state. The reason that many parents are concerned about protecting the trust assets is the institutions usually do not provide full care and maintenance of their children. There are many expenses not covered, such as extra clothing, dental work, trips and outings, treats, cosmetic surgery, birthday gifts, etc.

Another consideration is that if assets are put in a properly worded trust for an individual, that individual is not considered to **own** the assets. This is extremely important in determining eligibility for medical assistance and S.S.I. These programs have a maximum amount of assets that an individual can own of $1,500. This same eligibility criteria is used by other governmental programs which cannot be purchased on the private market such as those services provided by the Department of Vocational Rehabilitation. Some examples illustrate these points:

1. John Smith is a retarded man, 32 years old, living at Fircrest School. He has lived there for 10 years. John's parents live in Vancouver, Washington, and are retired. Besides the home they own, they have very little property and did not think a will was necessary. John's parents visit him when they can, pay for all his clothing, summer camp outings, dental work, and send him phonograph records which he loves. When John's parents died, the home was sold for $25,000. John inherited the money. The state immediately billed John for the cost of his care at the institution at a rate of $57.27 per day for ten years. The money inherited by John was gone. In addition, there is now nothing available to pay for the items his parents previously purchased for John.

2. Jane Jones has severe cerebral palsy and lives in a nursing home. She has constant medical needs which are paid for by medical coupons for which she is eligible because she is unable to work. Before Jane's mother died, she prepared a loosely worded trust to take care of Jane. Her mother placed $40,000 in the trust. After her mother's death, the state was able to argue that these assets were available to Jane and cut off her medical coupons. In three years, the $40,000 was gone. All of it was used to pay for Jane's medical needs. Jane's trust wasn't worded correctly.

The . . . document [included on p. 258] is an example of the trust the Foundation for the Handicapped recommends be used. The language used is extremely important. A cover letter for your attorney is also attached. This trust was written for the Craven family in Wenatchee. They have agreed to give it to any family having a handicapped child.

The "Craven Trust" was written by a group of attorneys who serve on the Foundation for the Handicapped Board of Directors, several of whom are parents of handicapped children.

The "Craven Trust" is recognized as the safest document available to place your money in trust for the benefit of your handicapped child in the years to come.

The Trust and Investment Committee of the Foundation for the Handicapped administers numerous trusts for handicapped children across our state.

For further information call (206) 283-4520.

TRUST & INVESTMENT COMMITTEE

Henry A. Alkema, *Vice President and Trust Officer*
Peoples National Bank of Washington, 1414 Fourth Avenue, Seattle, WA 98101

Austin A. Burch, *Vice President and Trust Officer*
Puget Sound National Bank, P.O. Box 1258, Tacoma, WA 98401

Donald E. Collins, *Vice President and Trust Officer*
First Interstate Bank of Wash., Trust Department, P.O. Box 21927, Seattle, WA 98111

Richard R. Dunn, *Vice President and Manager*
Old National Bank, Trust Dept., Suite 800, 1111 Third Avenue, Seattle, WA 98101

William L.E. Dussault, *Attorney at Law*
219 East Galer, Seattle, WA 98102

Ronald W. Eaglestone
Boeing Computer Services Co., 6510 Southcenter Blvd., Seattle, WA 98188

William H. Ellis, *Attorney at Law*
1111 Third Avenue Bldg., Seattle, WA 98101

Robert F. Garing, *Vice President and Legal Officer*
Rainier Bank, P.O. Box 3966, Seattle, WA 98124

Van R. Hinkle, *Attorney at Law*
6223 Island Crest Way, Mercer Island, WA 98040

The Hon. David C. Hunter, *King County Superior Court*
Seattle, Washington

Arleigh T. Jones, *Vice President and Trust Officer*
Seattle First National Bank, 1114 Pacific Avenue, Tacoma, WA 98402

Ervin J. Larsen, *Executive Director*
Foundation for the Handicapped, 1600 West Armory Way, Seattle, WA 98119

Joseph S. Lemon, *Trust Officer*
Bank of California, P.O. Box 3123, Seattle, WA 98114

Ivan E. Merrick, *Attorney at Law*
1522 Seattle Tower Bldg., Seattle, WA 98101

Linda Newton, *Trust Department*
Wash. Mutual Savings Bank, P.O. Box 834, Seattle, WA 98111

Barbara Potter
Seattle Trust & Savings Bank, P.O. Box 12907, Seattle, WA 98111

Wayne A. Tavis, *Assistant Treasurer*
Boeing, M/S 10-20, P.O. Box 3707, Seattle, WA 98124

VITAL INFORMATION

If you have a handicapped child, the following information should be attached to your will:

Mother's Social Security Number # _____

Father's Social Security Number # _____

Military Serial Number or Veteran's "C" Numbers # _____

Railroad Retirement Number # _____

Civil Service Employment Number # _____

Banks, Savings Accounts, Checking Accounts.
(By location and number)

_____   # _____

_____   # _____

Safety Deposit Boxes
(Locations and Numbers of boxes)

\# _____   \# _____

_____   _____

List Insurance Policies
—Life & Medical (Policy Numbers)

\# _____   \# _____

_____   _____

List Interested Relatives

Name _____   Name _____
Address _____   Address _____
Phone \# _____   Phone \# _____

Name _____   Name _____
Address _____   Address _____
Phone \# _____   Phone \# _____

Any other information that you feel would help an executor or guardian to do his or her duties in assisting your child.

_____

_____

_____

_____

To: Interested Attorneys
From: Foundation for the Handicapped
Re: Trusts for Families with Handicapped Children

Estate planning for families with handicapped children is more complicated than planning for families with normal children. Two adverse consequences result if property is left outright to a handicapped person: Firstly, if the individual is involved in state-supported programs or living placements, the state will bill the person at high rates for the cost up to the date of that person's participation in the program. This bill will often wipe out the entire estate immediately. Secondly, if the individual is receiving any kind of government benefits, inheriting property or cash of almost any amount will render him/her ineligible to receive these benefits.

To avoid these adverse consequences, the Foundation for the Handicapped strongly recommends that attorneys use a trust similar to the one attached in preparation of will for families with handicapped children. Rather than leaving property outright, a trust is recommended for several reasons. Many handicapped individuals are unable to manage their own financial affairs. If the trust is properly restrictive, the assets will not be available to the beneficiary as his/her personal resource. Additionally, there can be advantageous tax consequences in using a trust. However, if a trust is used, it is of the utmost importance that the language below be used in addition to the language from the attached trust:

"The express purpose of this trust is to provide for _____'s extra and supplemental care, maintenance, support and education in addition to and over and above the benefits _____ otherwise receives as a result of _____'s handicap or disability from any local, state, or federal government, or from any private agencies any of which provides services or benefits to handicapped persons. It is the express purpose of the trustor to use the trust estate only to supplement other benefits received by the Beneficiary."

If this language is not used and if the trust only states that the funds are to be used for the care and maintenance of the handicapped beneficiary, several negative consequences may result. If the handicapped beneficiary resides in a state-supported institution, the state will immediately move to attach the trust to pay for the cost of maintaining the beneficiary. In most cases that action will consume the entire trust as the state will bill for the cost of care for the entire length of residence in the institution or group home. This is particularly unfortunate since the institutions are not funded to a level where they can provide full, complete care. Many parents, whose children reside in institutions continue to pay for clothing, some or all of their medical needs, outings and trips, prosthetic devises and special educational aids.

Many handicapped persons receive Supplemental Security Income. In addition to being disabled, the applicant must also not have resources in excess of $1,500. The eligibility criteria for SSI is used by other government programs. Some of these services cannot be purchased on the private market such as those services offered by the Department of Vocational Rehabilitation.

To date, none of the trusts that use the language in the attached trust have been successfully challenged. The Foundation for the Handicapped has received verbal indications of approval by the state and federal governments.

A recent case we lost illustrates the importance of use of correct language in the trust: A mother had established a trust for her handicapped daughter and had used the phrase ''for her care and maintenance.'' The lawyer who prepared the trust and another individual who had advised the mother both testified that the mother had intended the trust to supplement the benefits the daughter was receiving from the government. Not withstanding this testimony, the Court ruled that the assets of the trust were ''available'' to the daughter and allowed the trust to be invaded to pay for her care and medical needs. As the daughter is living in a nursing home and has considerable ongoing medical problems, the assets of the trust (totaling $90,000) will quickly be consumed.

In addition to using appropriate language in the trust, it is also important to include a spendthrift clause similar to the one in the attached trust. To emphasize that no assets are to go directly to the handicapped child, in the body of the will the handicapped child is specifically disinherited. The language we frequently use is: ''I specifically make no other provision than that made in this will for _____ except to leave him/her my love and affection knowing _____ will be cared for otherwise, nor any provision for any children hereafter born to or adopted by me.''

The Foundation for the Handicapped is a nonprofit corporation. Its purpose is to act as guardians and/or trustees for the handicapped people. Most trusts the Foundation handles are small. They usually do not exceed $50,000. The trusts are managed by a committee of lawyers and trust officers representing most of the major banks in Washington State. Some of these individuals are also parents of handicapped children. The Foundation charges no trustee's fees but is allowed to make a modest annual maintenance charge. The Foundation requests a percentage of the residue, if any remains, be left to the Foundation.

If you have any additional questions on the use of the trust, please do not hesitate to contact the Foundation for the Handicapped, 1600 W. Armory Way, Seattle, WA 98119. (206) 283-4520.

LIVING TRUST OF
LEAVITT H. CRAVEN AND MAUDE G. CRAVEN

THIS AGREEMENT made this 10th day of September, 1975, by and between LEAVITT H. CRAVEN and MAUDE G. CRAVEN, his wife, the TRUSTORS, and the FOUNDATION FOR THE HANDICAPPED, a non-profit corporation organized under the laws of the State of Washington with its principal place of business at 1600 W. Armory Way, Seattle, King County, Washington 98119 the TRUSTEE,

WITNESSETH:

The TRUSTORS have irrevocably conveyed, transferred and delivered to the TRUSTEE the property itemized on the Trust Schedule attached hereto. This property, together with additional property which may hereafter be added to this Trust, shall be held, managed and distributed by the TRUSTEE as hereinafter provided. The TRUSTORS further declare that all property placed within the Trust constitutes community property unless specifically identified as separate property in the Trust Schedule.

RIGHTS RESERVED BY THE TRUSTORS:

1.   This Trust shall be irrevocable but the TRUSTORS may add other cash sums or property acceptable to the TRUSTEE to the trust estate.

AUTHORITY OF THE TRUSTEE:

1.   Having confidence in the ability of the TRUSTEE to act for the best interest of MARY K. CRAVEN, daughter of the TRUSTORS, and not wishing to limit its ability to do so, TRUSTORS authorize and empower the TRUSTEE to manage and deal with the Trust Estate in all particulars in the same manner and to the extent that TRUSTORS could if living.

2.   TRUSTEE shall have authority to consolidate this Trust or any other Trust created by the TRUSTORS in which the FOUNDATION FOR THE HANDICAPPED has been named as TRUSTEE, in so far as the TRUSTEE shall deem appropriate and not in substantial conflict with the expressed terms of any instrument executed by the TRUSTORS, or either of them. The determination by the TRUSTEE as to any consolidation hereunder shall be conclusive on all parties interested in the Trust Estate.

3.   TRUSTEE shall have authority to determine what is income and principal; to pay such expenses, costs and taxes, if any deemed by it to be lawfully chargeable to the Trust Estate as well as reasonable compensation to itself as TRUSTEE in accordance with its regular schedule of charges then in force; to apportion all such charges between income and principal as it deems proper; to act without bond and without posting security of any kind; and to exercise all powers granted by law.

4.   TRUSTEE shall have authority to hold, manage, sell, exchange or otherwise dispose of the whole or any part of said Trust Estate upon such terms and conditions and for such price as it may deem best, and may invest and reinvest, loan and re-loan the whole or any part of the money in the Trust Estate, not necessary for the support of said beneficiary or other form of investment which TRUSTEE may deem prudent, whether or not the same may be permissible by law for the investment of trust funds, and in all respects the TRUSTEE may generally handle, manage and dispose of the whole or any portion of said Trust Estate in such manner and upon such terms and conditions as TRUSTORS might or could do had this Trust not been created.

5.   TRUSTEE shall have authority to employ such agents, attorneys, accountants or appraisers as to it may seem reasonably necessary, to rely upon their legal, tax or other expert advice and to pay reasonable fees for such services.

DIRECTIVES TO TRUSTEE:

1.   Upon the death of the TRUSTORS, the TRUSTEE, in its sole discretion, shall use the income and such portion of the principal as to it shall seem fitting and proper for the benefit, support, education, training and the maintenance of MARY K. CRAVEN.

2.   So long as the TRUSTORS may live, the TRUSTEE, in its sole and absolute discretion may accumulate income, and any Trust income which shall have been accumulated shall be distributed in accordance with the provisions of this Trust.

3.   In so applying the Trust Estate for the benefit of said beneficiary it is directed that provision be made for the needs of MARY K. CRAVEN over and above those paid for by the

Department of Social and Health Services of the State of Washington, and/or other state or federal agency or department, including those resources and experiences as will contribute to and make her life as pleasant, comfortable and happy as possible. It is the request of the TRUSTORS that the TRUSTEE make arrangements for our daughter, MARY K. CRAVEN, the beneficiary hereunder, to have vacation and recreation trips away from her place of residence, and the reimbursement of not only her expenses but also the expenses, if requested, of the person or persons taking her on such trips, be a proper expenditure from the Trust Estate. It is the further direction of the TRUSTORS, without limiting the use of the funds by the TRUSTEE on behalf of the beneficiary, that sums spent for medicine, surgical and dental care, clothing, recreation, entertainment and "treats" for our daughter, MARY K. CRAVEN, be deemed proper expenditures from the income and principal of the Trust Estate, PROVIDED, that the furnishing of such goods or services shall not be paid for by the TRUSTEE if in the judgment of the TRUSTEE such payment will jeopardize or reduce financial assistance from the Department of Social and Health Services of the State of Washington, and/or any other state or federal agency or department.

4.   No interest in the income or principal of the Trust Estate shall be liable for any debt of the beneficiary to the State of Washington or to any other creditor, or subject to the process of seizure of any Court, and the beneficiary shall not have the power to anticipate, alienate or encumber her interest in the Trust Estate or in the income thereof.

5.   It is understood the TRUSTEE undertakes to exercise no more than reasonable dilligence and shall not be liable for any mistake in judgment or decrease in value or loss in the Trust property, or for any acts or omissions done or permitted by it in good faith, but shall be liable only for any acts or omissions done or permitted by it in bad faith. Said Trust is to be administered free of the control and direction of, and without accounting to any Court or Courts, but complete and open records and accounts concerning such Trust and its income and expenditures shall be kept and maintained, subject to the inspection at reasonable times of anyone having an interest therein. The TRUSTEE shall make an annual accounting to the TRUSTORS, or in case they are both deceased, then to the beneficiary of the Trust, and the TRUSTORS specifically exempt the TRUSTEE from any requirement of any law of the State of Washington in force or which may hereafter be in force concerning the accounting by it to any Court.

6.   All discretions conferred on the TRUSTEE by this Living Trust Agreement shall be absolute and their exercise by the TRUSTEE shall be conclusive and binding upon all persons.

7.   TRUSTEE shall apply to the appropriate federal agencies and state departments for the payment of such disability awards as MARY K. CRAVEN may be entitled by reason of the handicapping condition with which she has been afflicted, such having been diagnosed and established by competent professional personnel, the records of which are available to such federal and state agencies and departments.

8.   The application of the Trust Estate shall continue as provided herein until expended as a result of disbursements by TRUSTEE on the behalf of the beneficiary, MARY K. CRAVEN, or until the death of MARY K. CRAVEN, whichever event shall first occur, and if funds remain in the Trust Estate at the death of MARY K. CRAVEN, the TRUSTEE shall immediately distribute such remaining funds and assets in the Trust Estate to the FOUNDATION FOR THE HANDICAPPED for its use in serving mentally and physically handicapped children and adults within the State of Washington.

IN WITNESS WHEREOF, the TRUSTORS have set their hands and executed this Irrevocable Living Trust on the day and year first above written.

§ _____

Leavitt H. Craven–Trustor

§ _____

Maude G. Craven–Trustor

Foundation for the Handicapped

§ _____

§ _____

§ _____

Acceptance Committee

The Garrett Heyns Memorial Trust Fund

Throughout our state there are many handicapped children and adults who have lost their families.

These "orphaned and abandoned" handicapped people do have a "family" at the Foundation for the Handicapped. The Foundation serves as guardian, representative payee, parent and friend for hundreds of handicapped children and adults, from Walla Walla to Bellingham.

The Garrett Heyns Fund has been established to provide for unmet needs of handicapped people. Needs that no other agency or organization will cover such as:

—Medical needs
—Surgical services
—Education programs unavailable otherwise
—Gifts, personal items
—Clothing, cosmetic needs
—Emergency food, housing or care
—These and other special needs where sources of private and public funding have been found unwilling or unable to provide assistance.

A special fund. At no time will these monies be used for ongoing operation of the Foundation for the Handicapped.

The Story
of Frances

Tom O'Brien

Frances was born in December, 1917. She is now 65. Frances has mild mental retardation but is able to live independently in her own apartment as long as she has support services. Frances has only a partial understanding of such things as money, contracts, and the like, and has never been able to manage her own affairs. She cannot read, write, or count money and has had difficulty learning such things as the use of the emergency 911 phone number. Frances' great strength is her verbal ability and her social skills. Although she sometimes shows poor judgment and becomes argumentative, on the whole she is very pleasant and easy to get along with.

Frances grew up in the Ballard area of Seattle. Ballard is a fairly close-knit and homogeneous neighborhood. Her father was a jeweler in Ballard until his death. In 1965, Frances's mother also died, leaving a trust fund for Frances with a couple who were close family friends acting as trustees. Over the next 14 years, Frances lived in an apartment in Ballard, with her living expenses paid out of her trust. She was able to have a highly satisfying lifestyle but by 1979 her trust was virtually depleted. She was then age 62.

Because of her skills and because she has spent her entire life in a community that she has come to know and come to be well known, Frances has been able to develop a strong support system. She is a church member and enjoys the social opportunities this provides. Moreover, because the clerks in the local stores know her, she is able to shop almost independently. She had thus succeeded in establishing a network of support, and, until 1979, the trustees of her trust account were perhaps the most important components of this network.

As is often the case, Frances was in a crisis situation when she came to the Foundation for the Handicapped. Her trust account was nearly depleted. The trustees of the account were unable to convey the nature of the problem to Frances, who decided that they had stolen her money. The question of how Frances was going to live, whether she would have to move to a group home or to a subsidized housing arrangement outside of Ballard, what public entitlements she was eligible for, and other serious problems, needed solutions. The trustees were unable to get along with Frances and were themselves incapacitated due to age-related conditions. They simply did not know how to help Frances solve her problems.

The trustees went to their own attorney. By good fortune, he was very familiar with the Foundation for the Handicapped. He contacted the Foundation and a guardianship was established. Sue Ralph, a Foundation caseworker, met with Frances and went to work on her problems. Within a few months, Sue, with some help from the attorney, established eligibility for SSI and food stamps, got Frances's apartment upgraded and certified for a federal Section 8 housing subsidy, obtained a chore worker to assist in her apartment, and recruited a volunteer from Frances's church to provide personal attention. Along the way, Sue patiently explained to Frances why all these changes were happening, and worked with her to accept new people and things in her life.

In the years since, Foundation staff have managed Frances's budget, have paid her bills, and have made sure that she maintains eligibility for the various benefits that she receives. Today, Frances has a new caseworker, Shelby Heimdahl. Shelby has made contact with the many people who in some small way are concerned with Frances's well-being. These include the landlord, doctor's office, pharmacist, chore worker, dentist, and church people. All of these people know that they can contact Shelby or other Foundation staff about problems or concerns.

Right now, Frances is doing extremely well. As time goes on, Frances, like all of us, will need to adjust to the problems of old age. Frances knows that she can rely on the Foundation to help her solve these problems in a way that is sensitive to her individual needs and preferences.

Chapter 14

Guardianship, Advocacy, and Protective Services (GAPS) Program

Aloysius J. Soenneker

The Association for Retarded Citizens (ARC) of Oregon is a private, nonprofit corporation dedicated to ensuring the social and personal rights of Oregonians who are mentally retarded. The Association, which is governed by a 21-member board of directors, was formed in 1954 by parents who were concerned about the unavailability of public services for their mentally retarded children. They believed that together they could make their voices heard by agencies, service providers, and the state legislature.

An affiliate of the Association for Retarded Citizens of the United States, the ARC of Oregon today enjoys a membership of over 2,300 parents, professionals, and interested persons residing in all areas of Oregon. Since 1954, the ARC has been instrumental in securing improved educational, vocational, residential, and other services for an estimated 50,000 mentally retarded Oregonians. The Association is active throughout the state through its 23 local affiliated units that represent 25 of Oregon's 36 counties. Its efforts include public education, legislative and governmental affairs, service system monitoring, prevention, development of housing and residential care, and advocacy services.

As one of its advocacy services, the Association sponsors a corporate guardianship program. This program, known as GAPS (Guardianship, Advocacy, and Protective Services), began in 1977 on a pilot basis, and has expanded to a statewide program with a network of local advocacy teams stationed in all major population areas. The purpose of this chapter is to describe how this unique program began, how it is structured, and the ways in which it can assist parents and their handicapped children.

THE HISTORY OF GAPS

The impetus for the development of GAPS came from parents who were searching for ways to ensure their handicapped children's future well-being. A small group of parents began meeting in 1974 to discuss what would happen to their sons and daughters after their own death. The parents felt that a program was needed to ensure that someone would take a parent-like interest in their handicapped children after they were no longer able to do so.

After meeting together for nearly a year, this group approached the Association for Retarded Citizens of Oregon with a request that the ARC assume a leadership role in establishing a program to address their concerns. The Association agreed to do so, and undertook a study of the problem and potential solutions to it. It examined existing programs in the states of Indiana and Washington and gathered information from other areas around the country.

By 1977, both a name and an overall format were settled on for Oregon's program. The ARC decided to develop a corporate guardianship program that would be available on a statewide basis to act as a successor guardian or advocate for retarded persons after their parents' death. In January of 1978, the board of directors of the ARC of Oregon formally recognized the program and authorized it to begin accepting clients. In October of 1978, the Association's local member units officially established the GAPS board in the ARC's by-laws as a permanent standing committee of the Association, and charged it to protect the individual rights and welfare of GAPS' clients (see Appendix at end of this chapter).

THE STRUCTURE OF THE GAPS PROGRAM

During the early phases of the program, significant attention was devoted to identifying an appropriate organizational structure. Initially, it seemed desirable to create a separate corporate entity. However, since the ARC in Oregon was already deeply involved in providing personal advocacy services and since it had a pool of volunteer resources available to it, the program was established under the corporate umbrella of the ARC. This was accomplished by installing an advocacy and protective services board as a permanent standing committee of the Association.

The wide variety of services available through GAPS have been designed to address the many difficulties that are encountered by handicapped Oregonians and their families. A great deal of care has been taken to prevent GAPS from becoming bureaucratic and out of touch with the needs of families. The GAPS board has sought to develop and maintain a parent-based approach to service delivery. GAPS relies heavily on a network of volunteers, many of whom are parents, to represent disabled persons in local communities. It is the belief of the GAPS board that parents make the best advocates. They have raised and lived with their handicapped children and thus bring a unique perspective that professional advocates cannot be expected to have.

The Board of Directors of the Association for Retarded Citizens of Oregon   The board of directors of the ARC is ultimately responsible for all activities that are undertaken in the name of the ARC which, of course, includes all GAPS activities. The ARC of Oregon board of directors, therefore, retains final legal and policy-making authority for the GAPS program. The board is also the legally constituted body that accepts guardianship, through its named agent, the executive director. The board of directors must approve all GAPS policies and procedures and retains general oversight of the program. The board meets monthly to plan and implement the goals and objectives of the Association.

The GAPS Board   Although the ARC board retains final authority for GAPS, the 15-person volunteer GAPS board has responsibility for developing and implementing all policies and procedures used to administer the program. The GAPS board meets monthly to review the program's progress and to make decisions in critical cases. Like the ARC board, the GAPS board is parent-based.

The Case Review Committee   The case review committee is critical to the delivery of GAPS services. Composed of five GAPS board members, the committee reviews each proposed GAPS case, and sanctions, with the assistance of GAPS staff, individual advocacy plans for those clients recommended for acceptance. Following its initial review, the committee recommends acceptance of the case and approval of the advocacy plan to the GAPS board. Once a case is accepted by the GAPS board, the case review committee is responsible for periodically reviewing and updating the client's advocacy plan to ensure that he or she continues to receive appropriate services.

The Local GAPS Teams   The nucleus of the GAPS program is a network of volunteer advocacy teams. These teams have been developed and trained throughout Oregon in areas where actual or potential clients are identified. A local team is usually composed of 5 to 10 volunteers who meet regularly to discuss the clients in their local community. It assists in investigating the specific needs of potential clients and helps in formulating service plans for those accepted into the program. In addition to these responsibilities, each local GAPS team provides support and assistance to individual team members when they act as personal representatives for GAPS' clients.

GAPS Personal Representative   Once a service plan has been approved by the case review committee and the GAPS board, it is returned to a local team for implementation. One team member is assigned as the personal representative and he or she accepts responsibility for the client in accordance with the specifications of the client's advocacy plan. Personal representative are volunteers, frequently parents, who assume individual responsibility for one or more of the handicapped persons who are served by the GAPS program.

GAPS PROGRAM COMPONENTS

The role of the GAPS program has evolved significantly during its first 5 years. Initially, its primary emphasis was to address parents' concerns for a mechanism that ensures the future welfare of their handicapped children. Accordingly, the initial focus was almost exclusively on future planning services.

As the GAPS board continued to meet and the program began to stabilize, the focus expanded from concern about the future to concern about the immediate plight of the large number of mentally retarded persons in state institutions and community facilities who have no family contact or involvement. Accordingly, the program developed the second capacity to assume guardianship responsibility in emergencies, or in particular cases where handicapped persons were subject to neglect, exploitation, or abuse.

The third stage in the evolution of the program was the addition of services to assist parents in carrying out their guardianship responsibilities in time of family illness, geographical separation, or personal hardship. Assistance to parents became a major component of the GAPS program.

The GAPS program today offers a variety of services and assistance that fall under three program components: future planning, intervention, and parental assistance.

Future Planning

The GAPS program has developed two documents that serve as the cornerstone of its future planning efforts. The first of these, designed to familiarize parents with the complex task of planning for the future of their disabled offspring, is entitled *A Future Planning Guide for Parents of Developmentally Disabled Persons* (1980). A second guide, *Future Planning on Behalf of Developmentally Disabled Persons—A Guide for Estate Planners* (1980), is designed to assist attorneys, trust officers, and other estate planning professionals in acquiring the specialized skills necessary to plan appropriately on behalf of developmentally disabled persons.

The purpose of the future planning component of the program is to provide information and assistance to parents and professionals who are developing comprehensive plans for the future of handicapped children. In addition to supplying written information and materials through the guides, GAPS meets individually with parents to discuss the specifics of their situation and to outline available options. Further, GAPS is available to consult with estate planning professionals, and to review wills and other documents created by estate planning officials.

The future planning component of the program also conducts systematic information seminars for parents throughout the state and holds training workshops for estate-planning professionals. In addition, the GAPS program is investigating the feasibility of creating special pooled trusts and other mechanisms that expand the options that are available to parents who are planning for the future of their developmentally disabled child.

Intervention Services

Future planning services are designed to help parents. Intervention services, on the other hand, have been created to aid developmentally disabled persons whose parents or other family members are no longer involved with them, or whose family involvement is inappropriate and detrimental to their welfare. To these persons the GAPS program provides a full range of advocacy services based on each individual's needs. Intervention services include short term intervention, consultation with service providers, and monitoring care through attendance at plan development and case review meetings. The GAPS program has the capacity to intervene as the representative payee or financial advisor, and in some instances as guardian of the estate (i.e., conservator) or trustee. The program's advocacy activities include nonlegal advocacy, temporary or limited guardianship, and longterm or plenary guardianship services. In addition, the program stands ready to assume emergency guardianship status in life threatening situations.

Parental Assistance

Even parents who are involved in advocating for their handicapped child on an ongoing basis recognize that unforeseen circumstances can interfere with their ability to act on their child's behalf. Family illness, geographical separation, or a host of other situations can arise that temporarily make it difficult or impossible for concerned parents to advocate for their child. GAPS recognizes this need. A third program component, called parental assistance, allows parents to contract with GAPS to obtain substitute advocacy on behalf of their child while a familial crisis is being resolved. Parental assistance contracts can be short term, as in the case of parents who must be out of town for a month and wish to arrange for substitute representation in their absence, or they may be agreements whereby GAPS agrees to act on behalf of parents for an extended period of time. The range of services that may be provided as part of a parental assistance plan include parent consultation, service monitoring, individual advocacy, assistance in financial management, and assumption of guardianship responsibilities through a power of attorney.

The role of guardian for legally incompetent persons is perhaps the most significant service offered by the GAPS program. The ARC's decision to accept guardianship responsibility was reached as a result of two factors. First, there are handicapped persons in Oregon who clearly need guardianship protection, yet lack the involvement of family or friends. Second, some parents wish to name a guardian for their children subsequent to their death, yet cannot identify a family member capable or willing to serve in this capacity. The board of directors of the Association for Retarded Citizens, through the GAPS program, accepts guardianship responsibility for mentally retarded persons who require protection and whose needs cannot be met through less restrictive alternatives. The Association is particularly attentive to situations that require immediate action by a legally empowered guardian to preserve life. Guardianship by a concerned family member or friend is clearly the most desirable alternative for handicapped persons, but corporate guardianship through GAPS is viewed as superior to guardianship by the state.

GAPS PROGRAM FUNDING

Funding a program like GAPS is, of course, not an easy task. Since the program is designed to affect the lives of mentally retarded persons both now and in the distant future, both short and long range funding strategies are needed. Like the GAPS program itself, plans for funding the program have undergone significant evolution during its first 5 years.

As previously indicated, when the GAPS program began, its focus was primarily on future planning and on services to developmentally disabled persons after the death of their parents. This focus led to an initial funding strategy that was based upon contracts with parents for future advocacy services. Under this strategy, parents were required to provide $10,000 to the GAPS program when they passed away, through a bequest or a gift of life insurance. In exchange for this financial gift, the Association, through its GAPS program, assured parents that it would play an appropriate advocacy role throughout the life of their disabled offspring.

While this funding strategy appeared attractive, it soon became apparent that its weaknesses far outweighed its strengths. The program rapidly became viewed as one that served only parents of some means. Those parents with few assets, particularly parents on fixed incomes who did not have $10,000 to give to the program, pressed for alternatives. In addition, the GAPS board struggled repeatedly with the question of whether $10,000 was an adequate gift, especially in highly inflationary times. While a $10,000 gift appropriately invested might provide sufficient principal, a deferred gift of $10,000, realized 20 or 25 years in the future, might buy little more than a dozen eggs. Thus, the board struggled with whether to require a substantial cash gift now, which could be invested, or whether to require a much more substantial deferred gift (i.e., $25,000 to $50,000) as a future bequest.

In addition to these concerns, several attorneys serving on the GAPS board cautioned that any agreement that involved financial consideration constituted a legally binding contract, enforceable irrespective of the availability of sufficient resources. The board received reports that indicated that many of the lifetime care schemes offered by both religious and nonreligious long term care providers have ultimately failed.

After struggling with these concerns for over 2 years, the GAPS board arrived at a decision to abandon any form of contractual scheme. Rather than entering into contracts with parents, the GAPS program provides extensive technical assistance to parents in developing appropriate future plans utilizing wills, trusts, and other existing legal instruments. As a part of such future planning, the GAPS program offers itself as a successor advocate or guardian that the parents may utilize. Those parents who wish to contribute to the long term stability of the program are encouraged to make current gifts or long term bequests but are advised that their donation does not constitute a contract for services.

In addition to funding services for handicapped persons for whom it might assume an advocacy role via the future planning program, the GAPS board faced the difficult question of whether it would assume any role with regard to handicapped persons already deprived of appropriate guardianship and advocacy support. As indicated earlier, this concern was the second stage in the evolution of the GAPS program. Several members of the GAPS board felt that the most appropriate way to measure the viability of a concept like the GAPS program would be to test its capacity to deal effectively with handicapped persons who are already victims of exploitation, neglect, or abuse as a result of inadequate advocacy structures. Such individuals typically have little or no resources to support services, since most are totally dependent upon the state for care.

The uncertainties about funding future services, coupled with the demand for immediate interventions, combined to suggest the need for a different funding strategy. Both problems suggested that the Association had to commit itself to the orderly development of a program that is capable of providing a broad array of guardianship, advocacy, and protective services to developmentally disabled persons both now and in the future. This commitment entailed the need to identify substantial resources at the present time and an approach to securing long term funding for the maintenance and growth of the program. Essentially, the Association concluded that if the GAPS program was indeed needed, worthwhile, and a high priority, then the Association must commit itself to raising the funds necessary to support the program. Although gifts, wills, and bequests from parents who might benefit from the program were one such source, funds from grants, foundations, United Way, and Association fund raising activities would also be needed.

With this change of direction, the Association began the task of securing the resources necessary to initiate and build a program. Initial funding to support professional staff came from a CETA grant in early 1978. This grant allowed the Association to pilot the program in three counties of the Salem area. In 1979, a grant of national significance from the Administration on Developmental Disabilities of the Department of Health, Education, and Welfare was secured. This grant was designed to extend the program on a statewide basis and to develop materials and training curricula for a statewide guardianship, advocacy, and protective services program. Although initially planned as a 3-year grant, changes in federal funding priorities required scaling down grant activities and completing it within 2 years. The reduced time frame placed extreme demands on project staff but the basic activities of the grant, as originally outlined, were completed. The loss of grant support required rapid diversification of funding in order to assure the continuity of the program.

Since October of 1981, the Association has secured $25,000 annually from United Way of Oregon to support the program. In addition, the Association has secured foundation grants of over $60,000 for the GAPS program. Finally, the Association provides approximately $25,000 annually from its general fund raising activities for GAPS.

Long Term Funding

In addition to its commitment to secure short term funding for GAPS, the Association recognizes the need to develop a long range plan that will ensure stable, orderly growth. To meet this objective, the Association has created an endowment trust fund to provide a stable, predictable income. This endowment effort currently provides approximately $7,000 annually. The endowment trust is a subsidiary corporation that is controlled by the Association for Retarded Citizens of Oregon, i.e., the Association has sole power to amend the by-laws and elect the directors of the endowment trust.

The principal of the endowment trust is being acquired through a capital drive aimed at the membership of the Association and others who may wish to contribute to such an effort. In addition, parents and others concerned about the welfare of mentally retarded persons in Oregon are encouraged to provide funds through bequests and other estate planning mechanisms. The principal of the endowment trust will be invested by its board of directors with the goal of securing maximum earnings. The earnings from the endowment will be used solely to benefit the Association and its GAPS program.

The board of directors of the endowment trust is composed of individuals who are highly skilled in financial management. They are primarily responsibile for ensuring that the assets of the endowment trust are secure, and that they provide a maximum of earnings to support the program. The board of the endowment trust will be free to utilize any appropriate investment sources to accomplish these goals.

The endowment trust will be established in such a way as to permit the pooling of small trusts that clients may have in order to ensure maximum return on the investment of their assets. The pooled trusts will be managed separately from the endowment trust in order to guarantee freedom from conflicts of interest and to protect against co-mingling of funds.

The endowment trust will remain closely tied to the Association for Retarded Citizens in order to ensure that its initial purposes are carried out. However, it will be structured to ensure that the assets of the endowment trust are protected from any potential creditors of the Association or its GAPS program.

GAPS PROGRAM BUDGET

The total annual budget for the GAPS program currently equals nearly $100,000. This allocation of resources includes two full time professional staff in the central office and 10 team leaders who are located in various communities throughout the state. The level of effort of the 10 team leaders is equivalent to one full-time position. The support services that are utilized by the program include clerical and accounting activities and program supervision by the agency's executive director.

For illustrative purposes, the budget of the GAPS program (Table 1) may be broken down into two major categories: 1) future planning, i.e., preparation for the long term future, and 2) case services, i.e., intervention services and parental assistance.

GAPS PROGRAM PERSONNEL

Staffing for the GAPS program has undergone significant changes during its first 5 years. Initial staffing including one professional staff person supplemented by related clerical support through CETA funding. This staffing pattern was expanded to include two additional full-time professionals during the period of the national significance grant. One of these positions was devoted to research, the

Table 1. 1982–1983 budget for the GAPS program

	Future planning	Case services	Totals
Expenditures			
Salaries	$23,750	$38,765	$62,515
Employee benefits	1,754	3,930	5,684
Payroll taxes	2,381	3,708	6,089
Professional fees	245	399	644
Supplies	622	1,010	1,632
Telephone	2,163	4,515	6,678
Postage	442	718	1,160
Occupancy	2,186	2,153	4,339
Equipment expenses	786	1,278	2,064
Travel	2,810	3,954	6,764
Conferences/conventions/meetings	300	400	700
Total expenses	$37,439	$60,830	$98,269
Sources of funds			
United Way of Oregon	$10,000	$25,000	$35,000
Foundation sources	22,300	22,700	45,000
Endowment earnings		4,000	4,000
Program service fees		1,000	1,000
ARC sources	5,239	8,125	13,364
Total revenue	$37,539	$60,825	$98,364

preparation of future planning materials, and the development and training of local teams. In the period since the national significance grant, the program has operated with as few as one professional staff position.

The current staffing of the GAPS program includes a full-time director, a full-time future planning specialist and ten part-time (10–30 hours per month) local team leaders. In addition, the GAPS program has the services of an attorney on retainer and part-time clerical and administrative support staff.

The director of GAPS is responsible for the overall operation of the program, including providing staffing support to the GAPS board and its case review committee. The skills that are viewed as critical for this position include substantial program experience in either a direct service or a case management capacity with persons who are mentally retarded. The director of the program must also have a demonstrated ability to supervise staff, to utilize volunteers in social services contexts, and must be familiar with the law, particularly laws affecting handicapped individuals and estate planning. Educational requirements include a bachelor's or master's degree in social work, special education, or a related field with advanced training or experience in social service programs and procedures.

The future planning specialist is responsible for the overall conduct of the future planning component of the program. The person in this position works extensively with parents, particularly older parents. As a consequence, the person should have social work or family counseling experience with mentally retarded/ developmentally disabled individuals and their families. At least a bachelor's degree in social work, special education, or a related field is required. Knowledge or an aptitude for learning estate-planning procedures for handicapped persons is also viewed as highly desirable. The individual in this position must be able to speak effectively to parent groups. Moreover, the individual must be able to communicate effectively with parents on an individual basis and assist attorneys, trust officers, and other professionals in creating legal mechanisms for implementing parents' future plans.

Local GAPS team leaders are primarily responsible for coordinating the activities of local community volunteers as they carry out individual advocacy plans for the wards of the GAPS program. They are responsible for assuring that individual volunteers carry out their responsibilities, assist volunteers when problems arise, and keep the director of the GAPS program informed of any problems that require intervention by the state office.

GAPS team leaders should have experience with MR/DD programs, either as a professional or as a parent. They should possess a demonstrated capacity to work with a variety of social services agencies as an advocate and facilitator. They are linked to the state office by a toll-free telephone.

CHARACTERISTICS OF THE POPULATION SERVED

The need for a program like GAPS within the state of Oregon is great. At the present time, it is estimated that GAPS reachs or is contacted by over 800 individuals and families annually. Requests for information or assistance are divided approximately equally between the future planning component of the program and the intervention services parental assistance aspects. The level of assistance provided, of course, ranges from merely disseminating information to extensive individual assistance.

The Oregon Developmental Disabilities Planning and Advisory Council, as part of its efforts to develop a 10-year plan for services to the MR/DD population in Oregon, recently completed a data-based survey of the known MR/DD population to assess their characteristics and needs. Among the characteristics studied were guardianship and competency status, frequency of family contact, level of retardation, and residential and day program settings. With an overall return rate of 73% on the survey, 1,965 over the age of 18 were identified as lacking effective capacity to make decisions in their own best interests and having no legal guardian appointed to do so. The data on this group indicated that 53% reside in state institutions and an additional 32% reside in other state supported residential facilities such as group homes, nursing homes, and homes for the aged. The data also indicated that 36% of this group are profoundly retarded and 22% are severely retarded. When frequency of family contact was studied, it was learned that 45% of the group had no reported contact with parents or families during the past year and an additional 28% had only sporadic family contact.

It would appear from this study that there exists a significant number of persons, at least in Oregon, who are profoundly or severely retarded, have no family contact, and have no one to assist them in making decisions regarding their lives or to make substituted judgments for them. The data also indicated that this group is deprived of day training services at a rate that is more than double that of the rest of the MR/DD population in Oregon. Other characteristics of this population include the fact that over 90% have a monthly earned income of less than $50 and more than 14% of the population are over age 55.

This group of handicapped persons is the primary target for the GAPS program. It is not the intent of the program to seek guardianship or some level of advocacy involvement in the lives of each of these nearly 2,000 individuals. Rather, the program's intent is to be available to assume guardianship or other responsibility when needed, particularly when crisis or life threatening situations arise.

At the present time, the GAPS program has long term responsibility for 55 individuals: 19 individuals in state institutions, 10 individuals in nursing homes, 2 in intermediate care facilities, 6 in foster care, 11 in group homes, 2 in homes for the aged, and 5 living independently or with their families. Of these 55 individuals, the program is legal guardian to 30 and uses less restrictive advocacy strategies for the remaining 25. In addition to these long term commitments, the GAPS program annually provides some form of short term advocacy assistance or advice to approximately 350 handicapped persons and provides future planning services to an estimated 450 families. These families represent all areas of the economic spectrum. Since 1981, over 2,000 copies of *A Future Planning Guide for Parents of Developmentally Disabled Persons* have been requested by parents in Oregon. The GAPS program has been notified by 72 parents that GAPS is designated in their wills to assume a future role on behalf of their children. Estate planners on the board estimate that only 20%–50% of persons notify those named in their wills to assume a given responsibility. Thus, it is estimated that 150–300 parents may have legally requested a future role for GAPS in the welfare of their handicapped children.

NATURE OF FAMILY INVOLVEMENT

The goal of GAPS, from its inception, has been to build a program that will earn the confidence and trust of parents and will provide a mechanism for parents to assure the future welfare of their handicapped children. What the parents want, more than anything else, is to ensure that someone will be there to take a personal and lifelong interest in the welfare of their handicapped son or daughter and to assist them in decision-making.

Though there is no ideal or perfect solution, the Association believes that a comprehensive guardianship, advocacy, and protective services program, operated under the auspices of a parent and consumer-based advocacy organization like the ARC, is among the best alternatives available. Such organizations have the capacity to deal with both the economic and personal concerns of handicapped persons, and have the backup of a comprehensive agency that is able to advocate in the legislative, administrative, and judicial arenas.

The Association strongly believes that parents must assume a leadership role in solving the problems that confront them. Parents are recruited to serve in a policy-making capacity on both the ARC board and the GAPS board. Additionally, every effort is made to encourage the involvement of families in the delivery of future planning and intervention services. When strong family ties exist, parents are encouraged to use GAPS as a secondary or backup guardian to available family members. In those cases when GAPS does assume primary guardianship or other advocacy responsibility, the program makes a particular effort to keep any known family members informed about the progress of their relative, at least on an annual basis. If families who have been uninterested for some time exhibit any interest in assuming a greater role in the life of their handicapped relative, all efforts are made to encourage them appropriately.

The GAPS program relies heavily on volunteers to serve as personal representatives for persons for whom the program has guardianship or other advocacy responsibility. A particular effort is made to recruit the parents of handicapped children. Indeed, parents who have come to the program for future planning services on behalf of their own child are frequently willing to assume a level of responsibility for another child in the program. The rationale, ''If I expect someone to look after my child after I'm gone, I should be willing to look after someone else's child now'' is the basis for this willingness.

TERMINATION OF GAPS SERVICES

The GAPS program, particularly its future planning aspect, is designed to ensure long term advocacy support for handicapped persons. Once the program has made a commitment to assume some level of involvement in the life of the handicapped person, it is anticipated that the program will almost always continue to maintain some level of contact in the individual's life. The degree of involvement, of course, may change as the needs of the handicapped person change. Once a year, the program re-evaluates the advisability of continuing each of its guardianship relationships and develops an individual advocacy plan for each client. If guardianship status is found to be no longer necessary, the Association will move to terminate its legal role with the person. The Association will continue its advocacy and monitoring roles, however. The only time a case is closed is when the parents of the handicapped person and/or the handicapped person request service discontinuation and: 1) the GAPS program can make no further contribution to the welfare of the individual, and 2) adequate alternative advocacy or monitoring mechanisms exist for the individual.

SERVICE EVALUATION PROCEDURES

The cornerstone of the service evaluation procedures of GAPS is the individual advocacy plan. Each client has an individual advocacy plan that is prepared by the case review committee with input from the local teams and the personal representatives responsible for individual clients. Advocacy plans delineate specific goals and objectives to be achieved with each client within 6-month periods. Plans address areas such as day program placement, residential setting, personal needs, medical needs, finances, and other considerations significant to the life of the client. They delineate the responsibilities of GAPS central staff, team leaders and personal representatives with respect to individual's goals and objectives.

The progress of clients with respect to their objectives is tracked by local teams during monthly meetings. Once each quarter a service evaluation report is completed on each client by the personal representative and local team. Once each 6 months the case review committee conducts a review of the individual advocacy plan for each client and prepares a new advocacy plan for the next 6-month period. The highlights of individual advocacy plans are reviewed and approved by the GAPS board at its monthly meetings.

In addition to these evaluation procedures, the GAPS program provides statistical information to the ARC board at its monthly meetings regarding: 1) the residential setting of each client, 2) how many clients are receiving antipsychotic medications, 3) how many clients are involved on a full- or part-time basis in an appropriate day program, and 4) how many clients have community access at least weekly. Subjective judgments are also rendered regarding the overall quality of life that is experienced by each GAPS' client. Semiannually, the GAPS program provides a detailed report to the ARC board of directors regarding its activities during the preceding 6 months. The semiannual review includes a comprehensive look at the current status of the GAPS program and its clients, and recommends service needs and policy changes.

SELF-RENEWAL PROCEDURES

Recognizing that a program like GAPS is relatively new, the GAPS board and staff have devoted significant time and energy to self-renewal procedures. Since its inception, the program has sponsored periodic retreats for the board and staff to reflect on progress and to chart future directions. The program has sought to grow in an orderly and systematic fashion and to carefully plan programmatic changes. This emphasis on systematic and orderly development has allowed the program to anticipate new service thrusts and to change policies and procedures when previous approaches have not worked.

At the present time, several significant changes are anticipated over future years. First, it is expected that the long term caseload of intervention and parental assistance services will expand from its current level of 55 to approximately 110 during the next 12–18 months. This increase will necessitate expanding local staffing support and extending services to two or three rural, sparsely populated counties.

A second major program thrust during future years will involve a highly concentrated effort to reach all parents needing future planning assistance and support. The materials that were developed as part of the national significance grant will be utilized to reach all known parents of MR/DD persons in Oregon. Intensive staff effort will be focused on assuring that parents follow through and complete the future planning process. Moreover, systematic training efforts will be implemented to reach large numbers of attorneys, trust officers, insurance personnel, and other estate-planning professionals. The Association anticipates creating a network of estate-planning professionals who will be available in every community in Oregon to assist parents.

Finally, the GAPS program is painfully aware that one of the major faults in advocacy services for mentally retarded persons is financial management assistance. Accordingly, the GAPS program anticipates devoting significant resources to the development of appropriate conservatorship and small trust mechanisms that assist families and handicapped persons in this difficult area. The program will seek to create appropriate fiduciary mechanisms, either as part of the GAPS program or independent of it, to ensure that clients' assets are competently managed in a manner that is free from conflict of interest. It is anticipated that the endowment trust fund will serve as a significant vehicle in this effort. The GAPS program is particularly concerned that it not enter into any financial management role in which its decisions regarding the allocation of clients' resources could in any way benefit or harm the GAPS program. An example of this conflict of interest would be a situation wherein GAPS acts as trustee for a client's funds during his or her life and is also named as an heir to the principal of the trust when the client dies.

RECOMMENDATIONS FOR STARTING CORPORATE GUARDIANSHIP PROGRAMS

It has frequently been stated that there is no substitute for experience. This is certainly true in an area such as the establishment of corporate guardianship programs. While 5 years of experience does not make one an expert, it provides at least a basis from which to make some tentative recommendations.

Don't jump in lightly. The establishment of a corporate guardianship or advocacy program like GAPS requires careful planning, both on a short term and a long term basis. Programs of this kind must be able to honor commitments. Guardianship is a legal relationship in which the guardian, in effect, becomes an officer of the court with legal responsibilities to assure the welfare of an individual handicapped person. Before agreeing to perform, a program must assure that it has the capacity to do so. This requires careful planning and deliberate, reasoned action.

Set up a sound decision-making procedure. Perhaps the most critical component of a corporate guardianship program is the establishment of a sound policy and decision-making structure. This structure should have clear lines of accountability and authority and should provide adequate checks and balances to ensure the quality of decisions. The establishment of a board or committee structure similar to the GAPS board is strongly recommended to provide oversight and collective decision-making. This is particularly critical when the program is called upon to make life and death decisions. The Association believes that the most critical factor in the success of the GAPS program has been the continuity and direction provided by the GAPS board. This guidance and continuity has occurred in large measure because of the balance of persons represented on the GAPS board. The Association suggests that the governing body of a corporate guardianship program for developmentally disabled persons should consist of one-third to one-half parents. The board should also include an attorney, a trust officer, one or more persons with expertise in medical areas, and at least one person with a strong professional background in mental retardation. In addition, an individual with a background in theology or ethics will prove very helpful when making difficult decisions that involve strong ethical considerations.

Involve parents heavily, and listen to them. Despite their individual strengths and weaknesses, parents of mentally retarded persons are more deeply committed to their children's welfare than any group of professionals or interested citizens. Moreover, they have a wealth of knowledge and good common sense about what is in the best interests of mentally retarded individuals. While they are sometimes inclined to be overprotective, parents have a unique capacity and perspective that professionals should value.

Don't set up highly improbable financial schemes. The GAPS program spent considerable time in its early stages attempting to design financial schemes that would guarantee the future welfare of handicapped persons. Such schemes invariably rely on procuring significant sums of money from large numbers of parents in order to ensure the future. These approaches make the program prohibitive for those parents who cannot afford it. Parents who can afford such schemes can afford to utilize generic estate-planning mechanisms and trusts to provide resources for their handicapped child with more certainty and more sophisticated financial management.

Avoid conflicts between clients' needs and agency financial stability. Whatever mechanism or structure for funding a corporate guardianship program is established, care must be taken to assure that it does not take funds that are necessary to support direct services. The program must be established in a way that does not detract from supporting the basic living needs of clients.

Approach funding the program as a fundraising task. The funding of a corporate guardianship program should be approached as any other fundraising task. The Association has found the program relatively easy to market to foundations and United Way. Whatever source of funds is available, the task should be approached in a manner similar to funding any other human services program. Begin the program, establish its credibility and quality, and then work on the long term funding rather than the other way around.

Don't try to guarantee the future. A critical mistake that absorbed considerable time in the early phases of the GAP program was the Association's emphasis on attempting to guarantee the future welfare of mentally retarded children. This guarantee was to be in the form of a legally binding contract between the program and parents. As discussed earlier, such mechanisms require a level of contribution from parents that is cost prohibitive and may deprive clients of needed resources during their lifetime. ARC believes that the strongest guarantee that a parent can have or anticipate is that a parent-based organization is deeply committed to guarding the welfare of their child through a program like GAPS.

Start small and build. The only way to begin a program is to begin. All too frequently, too much energy is devoted to designing perfect solutions to the problems of handicapped children and adults. In ARC's view, the way to begin a program like GAPS is to start with a few parents, a few persons for whom a guardianship responsibility is assumed, and limited staff resources. Once this base has been built, the program can grow in an orderly fashion.

Don't try to be all things to all people. There is no limit to the number of good things that you can conceivably do for mentally retarded persons. There is also no limit to the variety of good things you will be asked to do. Define clearly those activities and services that you can provide and clearly define the criteria that will guide client selection. Doing a good job of acting as guardian for 20 people is far superior to doing a mediocre job of advocating for a thousand.

Establish the program to serve all, not just the wealthy. Corporate guardianship programs should be established to serve all parents and all mentally retarded persons regardless of their economic situation. The poor and those who have been abandoned by their families through parental death or disinterest are frequently in the greatest need of advocacy support and assistance. Programs should be established to serve these persons, as well as families with means who wish to ensure the continuing welfare of their children.

Expect to get the tough cases. Corporate guardianship programs inevitably draw difficult, challenging cases. People will frequently turn to your program to assume guardianship and make the difficult decisions when all other mechanisms or systems have been unable to resolve a problem. This is particularly true in the case of medical decisions that involve extensive threat to life or the use of extraordinary medical treatment to sustain life. It is also highly true for cases involving the abuse of a handicapped person, particularly abuse by family members.

Make sure you have good procedures and that they are followed. The establishment of a legal relationship and the exercise of critical decisions places a great deal of responsibility on a guardian. While most state statutes indicate that a guardian is responsible for acting in a manner that is similar to a parent in relationship to a minor child, it is also clear that for corporate guardians, a higher standard of conduct is expected. For this reason, policies and procedures in critical decision-making areas such as consent to surgery and consent to litigation must be carefully defined and meticulously followed. The burden of documenting the reasonableness of decisions and the thoroughness of the decision-making process clearly rests with your program.

Carry adequate insurance. The GAPS program has not been sued for any of its actions during its first 5 years of operation and does not anticipate any suit in the immediate future. Nevertheless, it is acutely aware that the responsibility for making important decisions for persons makes it liable for errors. It is imperative that a corporate guardianship program carry at least $1 million in liability insurance and a similar amount of errors and omissions insurance for its officers and directors. Higher limits may be desirable.

Establish a clear policy on litigation. One of the major weaknesses of any program that retains legal guardianship of more than one person is the potential for a conflict of interest when litigation against a public official or private individuals seems warranted on behalf of a client. While some forms of litigation against private individuals have little opportunity to damage the interests of other clients (e.g., suing a convenience store operator for negligence regarding a client's injury), other decisions to litigate may have a significant impact. Particularly sensitive are decisions to sue physicians for medical malpractice on behalf of one client since the suit may affect the willingness of physicians to treat other clients in the program. Most sensitive are decisions to file litigation against state officials on either an individual or class action basis. Such conflicts are not easily resolved, but careful consideration should be given to the appropriate utilization of a guardian *ad litem* to assure that concerns regarding the welfare of other clients do not cloud a program's judgment.

A corporate guardianship program must, of necessity, operate in the real world. Communities of professionals do support each other, and you must learn to work with them. The medical community is but one example. Although it is frequently necessary to take firm action to assure appropriate services for handicapped persons, such action should be taken with appropriate sensitivity to the need to continue work with community professionals after a given crisis is resolved.

Do not assume the government's responsibility. The basic responsibility to care for those who are unable to care for themselves rests with the government. Some handicapped persons' needs for decision-making assistance are limitless. Resist the temptation to become overall case manager when the state has a case management program. Define the role of your program clearly, and stay within that role. Utilize existing services appropriately rather than assuming others' responsibilities.

Proceed cautiously, but proceed. The need for parents to have a program by which they can ensure the future welfare of their mentally handicapped sons and daughters is critical. Moreover, the need for quality advocacy and guardianship programs for severely handicapped persons who have no parents to advocate for them is overwhelming. The establishment of programs to meet these needs is not an easy task, but it must be done.

CONCLUSION

GAPS is designed to address the central concern of parents of handicapped children; namely, what will happen to their sons and daughters when they die. This concern is pervasive. Because they fear the future, some parents deny needed medical treatment, cause unnecessary and unwanted institutional placements, and even kill their children and themselves as solutions. This author has witnessed each of these reactions during his career in this field. Solutions to parents' fears, and mechanisms to assure quality representation and substituted decision-making for handicapped persons must be designed. The GAPS program represents one constructive response to parents' concerns.

Appendix

ARTICLE XIV
GUARDIANSHIP, ADVOCACY, AND PROTECTIVE SERVICES BOARD

Section 1   The Association for Retarded Citizens of Oregon will have a special permanent standing committee to be known as Guardianship, Advocacy, and Protective Services (GAPS) Board.

Section 2   The GAPS Board shall be composed of fifteen (15) members, appointed by the President of ARC-O initially. In addition, the GAPS Chairperson may appoint associate members. Associate members shall have the right to attend and speak at the meetings, but shall not vote.

Section 3   Regular members of the GAPS Board shall serve a tenure of three (3) years with five (5) members eligible for election each year. Members of the GAPS Board shall be limited to two (2) successive terms. If a GAPS Board Member resigns the Chairperson shall appoint an eligible individual to fill the unexpired term.

Section 4   The GAPS Chairperson shall appoint a Nominating Committee composed of five (5) members of the GAPS Board. The committee shall prepare a slate of eligible persons for consideration by the ARC-O membership at their Semi Annual Meeting. Nominations can be accepted from the general ARC-O membership at the time of the meeting.

Section 5   The GAPS Board shall elect its own Chairperson. If the GAPS Chairperson is not an ARC-O Board Member, he/she shall serve as a non-voting member of the ARC-O Board of Directors. No individual shall serve as President of the ARC-O Board of Directors and Chairperson of the GAPS Board at the same time. The Chairperson of the GAPS Board shall serve a two (2) year term with a maximum of two (2) consecutive terms.

Section 6   The GAPS Board shall be responsible to assure that proper legal, administrative, and procedural safeguards are available to protect the individual rights and welfare of the mentally retarded person that becomes a client of GAPS. The specific roles of GAPS shall include, but not be limited to, guardian, conservator, custodian of funds, representative payee, surrogate parent, personal advocate, protective intervention, estate planning, trustee of funds, and monitor of services for clients.

Section 7   A Case Review Committee shall be appointed by the GAPS Chairperson. The committee shall be composed of five (5) GAPS Board Members, who shall have responsibility to review all individual cases accepted by the GAPS Board, at least on a quarterly basis.

Section 8   All policies and decisions by the GAPS Board shall be subject to review by the ARC-O Board of Directors.

Our Need
for the Foundation

Lois Keelor

In 1951, shortly before our son's first birthday, our pediatrician diagnosed his delayed development as due to Down's syndrome. I remember thinking at the time, "How fortunate Ted and I are to have my large family to give us love and support." I little realized that the day would come when we would be alone, and very concerned about who would take a personal interest in Johnny after we were gone.

My husband Ted did not have the close family ties that I had since his father died when he was 4 years old. But I had six brothers and sisters. I remember the days, not so long ago, when the members of my family would come together. It was an exciting event. It feels funny now to be almost the last one left in our area of all those people. I feel totally alone. I cannot count on help from even my only surviving sibling, Helen, who is 4 years older than me and has had a heart operation as well as further problems that prevent most activities.

Things went well for Ted and me during the early years of our marriage except that we wanted a child. Finally, after 14 years of marriage we were able to adopt Johnny, who was born on October 10, 1950. It was a very happy occasion when we brought him home from the hospital. He was such a pretty baby, with such cute little hands and ears.

Johnny's development was slower than normal. Since there were no special early childhood programs in those days, we did not start him in the special education class at View Ridge until he was almost 8 years old. He did not do well in the classes. After much testing in school and at the Children's Orthopedic Hospital in Seattle, it was the unanimous recommendation of all the professionals that we should apply for placement at the Rainier School, our nearest institution for retarded individuals.

We went through some very serious soul searching but there were *no* alternatives. Finally, in November 1960, just after Johnny's 10th birthday, we made the 60-mile trek to Buckley, the setting for the Rainier School. Parting was hard, but we told ourselves it was for the best. We visited often, and in 1961, along with other parents who had children in Percival Hall, we formed a parents' club. I served as the first president and we continued to be active throughout Johnny's placement at Rainier School.

As Johnny matured, he tried various work stations available in the country setting of Rainier: barn work for the dairy, gardening, janitorial work, and clean-up man in the infirmary. In 1975, he was sent by bus each working day to the Industrial Skills Sheltered Workshop at nearby Enumclaw, with the obvious intention that he would eventually be placed into one of the group homes that were then being started in our state.

Ted and I wanted what was best for Johnny, but our concerns about his future became greater. During the years that Johnny had been in Rainier my parents had died. Where there once had been many family members, now all were either deceased, much older, or had moved away. If something happened to us, there would be no one except state employees to look after Johnny's welfare. We could not envision him being away from the protective custody of the Rainier School.

Then, in the fall of 1977, an announcement of a public seminar for parents, attorneys, and trust officers was made by the Foundation for the Handicapped. We had heard some things about the Foundation, and even received one mailing in 1968. But Ted and I had never really looked into the program. When we heard of the meeting in Bremerton, we went, very eager to find out all we could about this organization that claimed to take a personal interest in orphaned disabled persons.

The meeting was terrific and we immediately started our plan. By the following month, we contacted an attorney, established the Foundation as standby guardian and successor guardian for Johnny, and made up compatible wills for each of us with anything left by the survivor going into a trust with the Foundation. During Johnny's lifetime, the money will be used for things that will benefit and enrich his life. He loves music, and enjoys all types of entertainment. He will have funds to see and do the things that mean so much to him.

Johnny was placed in a group home near to us in May, 1980. He attends a regular workshop program nearby and makes his way to work and back, including a short ferry and bus ride. Each weekend he comes home to visit us so we keep his room ready. Although he cannot read or write, he has memorized our telephone number and can reach us either by dialing the operator or by getting someone to dial our number for him.

At this writing, I am 71 and Ted is 76 years of age. We don't know how much longer we have but we surely appreciate the peace of mind that our plan with the Foundation has given us. They contact us quite often to see how things are going for us and for Johnny and to assure us that the Foundation is ready to serve if we become unable to take care of his needs.

I never dreamed that I would not have family members to help Johnny. The Foundation has been a real answer for Ted and me as we make our plans for Johnny's future.

Chapter 15

The Oakdale Guardianship Program

Henry P. Widrich

Many of the clients who are served by the Oakdale Guardianship program have been deprived of personal relationships other than those with disabled peers and with staff assigned to care for them. In fact, some of the program's clients truly have been forgotten. Whether or not they have family, many have had no contact with the outside world for 10 years or longer.

This author once attended a meeting of parents and relatives at Oakdale Regional Center. One of the goals of the meeting was to determine how parents and relatives could best act as advocates for residents. Since most residents had had no visitors for years, it was decided that the best thing that could be done with the group's limited resources was to send a card and a small gift to each resident on his or her birthday. Names were drawn and I happened to draw the name of an old gentleman who had been living in the institution practically all of his life. He had never received any visitors, let alone correspondence. His birthday was a few days away. I sent him a tie and a birthday card. A week later, the tie and card were returned marked "deceased." I made up my mind that this should never happen again. No handicapped person should ever be so totally forgotten. Oakdale Guardianship was established to fulfill this goal.

The author is the past president of Oakdale Guardianship.

The author wishes to acknowledge, with deepest gratitude, Mr. Tom Trainer, the legal counsel for Oakdale Guardianship, for his valuable assistance in defining the various types of guardianships in the state of Michigan. Also, credit must be given to the staff of Oakdale Regional Center and its director, Dr. David A. Ethridge; to the staff of Macomb-Oakland Regional Center and its director, Mr. Gerald Provencal; and to Ms. Nancy Roseneau, the director of Admissions and Placement Services for the Macomb-Oakland Regional Center. Finally, appreciation is expressed to Mrs. Kathleen M. Diatchun for her help in typing and proofreading this chapter.

GUARDIANSHIP IN MICHIGAN

Webster defines a guardian as "a person who guards, or watches over, protects, cares for, or defends another person or property; a person legally placed in charge of the affairs of a minor or of someone incapable of managing his own affairs." Considered in this light, guardianship imposes an awesome responsibility.

Michigan law permits dual guardianships, namely guardianship of the person, guardianship of the estate, or a combination of both. There are three classes of guardianship.

Guardianship of a Legally Incapacitated Person   A guardian may be appointed for a person unable to care for himself or herself because of mental incapacity (other than mental retardation) or addiction to alcohol, other drugs, or gambling. The guardian has the same powers over the person that a parent would have over a minor child. The court may appoint a guardian of a legally incapacitated person with less than full powers, although in practice limited guardianships are seldom used.

Guardianship of a Minor   A minor, whose parents have died or who have lost their parental rights by court order, may have a guardian appointed. The guardian has the same powers over the minor that the parents had.

Guardianship of a Developmentally Disabled Person   A developmentally disabled person, who cannot protect his or her well-being, may have a guardian appointed by a probate court. The type of guardianship required by developmentally disabled individuals varies in relationship to their mental and adaptive limitations. The law requires use of the least restrictive form of guardianship. There are two types of guardianship in Michigan for persons with a developmental disability: plenary and/or partial.

Plenary Guardianship of The Person or Estate   When the court decides that an individual is totally without capacity to care for himself or herself or his or her property, a plenary (full) guardian is appointed. The guardian receives the same powers over the person that a parent has over a minor child.

Partial Guardianship of The Person or Estate   When possible, the court will only give limited and specific powers to a guardian, leaving the individual with all other rights.

The guardianship law in Michigan also permits the appointment of standby and temporary guardians. The court may appoint a *standby guardian* at the initial hearings or at a later date. The powers of a standby guardian become effective immediately upon the death or resignation of his or her predecessor. Also, the court may, for a short and definite time, appoint a *temporary guardian* who has specific powers and who acts until the court has a chance to schedule a full hearing on the guardianship petition. Finally, Michigan law permits the appointment of a *testamentary guardian*. Under this arrangement, the parents of minors and developmentally disabled persons may name a successor guardian in their last will and testament. When the parent dies, the person named in the will, called the testamentary guardian, has authority to act as guardian as soon as he or she files an acceptance letter with the court. This authority may be reviewed and cancelled by the court at a later date.

Michigan courts prefer that family members or close friends act as guardians. However, where this is impractical, any organization that is a legal entity, such as a corporation or association (including unincorporated groups) may act as guardian. Most courts also have one or more individuals, usually lawyers, who serve as guardians for persons without family, friends, or appropriate organizations to act on their behalf.

The primary objective of the activities at Oakdale Guardianship is to assure that the clients receive all of the services that they are entitled to under the law. Living conditions in and out of state institutions, medical services, educational programming, and the client's personal appearance are monitored. A client's written program is worthless unless it is implemented; therefore, Oakdale Guardianship works to assure the provision of agreed services in order to promote client's development.

HISTORY OF OAKDALE GUARDIANSHIP, INC.

Oakdale Guardianship was founded in 1976. The need for such a group was mandated by the state of Michigan's new mental health code. This law requires that mentally retarded individuals who are unable to give informed consent must have a guardian. Family members and friends are, of course, the first choice to act in such a capacity. Unfortunately, there are many persons with a developmental disability who either do not have family or have a family that does not express any concern for their well-being. This situation creates a void that Oakdale Guardianship tries to fill.

Oakdale Guardianship only accepts guardianships of the person, either plenary or partial. The determination of the guardianship type is the court's decision. Sometimes, the program is placed in the position of being appointed plenary guardian when it would prefer partial guardianship. If the organization feels that an appointment as plenary guardian is not needed in an individual case, it applies for a modification to become partial guardian. Plenary guardianships sometimes overly restrict a client's decision-making experiences and thereby may restrict his or her opportunities for personal development. There are, without a doubt, cases when plenary guardianship is needed, but these cases are few and far between. Each case must be judged on its own merits. It would be presumptuous on the organization's part to attempt to state normative criteria for partial guardianships. There is not and cannot be a convenient set of rules that apply to every individual with a developmental disability.

Oakdale Guardianship has declined to become representative payee, trustee, or guardian of the estate for its clients. These services require a full-time, skilled bookkeeper and a clerk, positions that would have to be funded. Being guardian of the estate would mean that Oakdale Guardianship is accountable not only to the courts (which it already is accountable to as guardian of the person) but also to state and federal agencies. Oakdale Guardianship may reconsider its present posture regarding the handling of clients' incomes and estates in the future if appropriate funding should become available to support these activities.

Oakdale Guardianship currently serves seven counties in southeast Michigan, with a total population of 2,691,961 as of January 1, 1983. It is estimated that approximately 3% of this total population has some degree of mental retardation. Of this 3%, 89% can be classified as mildly retarded, with an IQ between 51 and 70 (71,875 people); 6% can be classified as moderately retarded, with an IQ between 36 and 50 (4,845 people); 3.5% can be classified as severely retarded, with an IQ between 21 and 35 (2,827 people); and 1.5% can be classified as profoundly retarded, with an IQ of under 21 (1,211 people). The population served by the facilities located in Lapeer (Oakdale Regional Center) and Mt. Clemens (Macomb–Oakland Regional Center) is shown in Table 1. Oakdale Guardianship currently serves 200 of these individuals. The majority of its clients fall within the category of severe to profound mental retardation so the chances of completely discontinuing a guardianship are slight. Thus far, only two individuals have achieved sufficient independence to warrant cancellation of their guardianship status.

Oakdale Guardianship provides guardianship services via volunteer monitors, whose roles and responsibilities are described in a later section of this chapter.

The first four clients were assigned to Oakdale Guardianship by the probate court in 1977. It was the original plan of the organization to provide guardianship services solely to those clients who resided on the campus of Oakdale Regional Center in Lapeer, Michigan. By the end of 1977, it became apparent that this plan had to be abandoned. Some of the clients were beginning to move into community settings. These moves were welcomed by Oakdale Guardianship because of its belief that new, less restrictive environments would benefit clients by affording them greater opportunities for acquiring independent living skills. The extension of guardianship services to persons in the community, and later to persons at another institution (Macomb–Oakland Regional Center), greatly complicated the program, however.

It is important to note that without a guardian, an individual with a developmental disability generally has little control over where he or she lives or when he

Table 1. Population of regional centers served by the Oakdale Guardianship program

Agency	Institution	Community	Total
Macomb–Oakland Regional Center	97	1,103	1,200
Oakdale Regional Center	612	300	912
Total	709	1,403	2,112

or she is transferred to and from living arrangements. As guardian, Oakdale Guardianship has the right to object to transfers that are deemed inappropriate by filing an appeal. It does not make use of this prerogative very often since it is basically in agreement with the concept of deinstitutionalization. It does, however, object to transferring individuals from one state facility to another just for the sake of equalizing the populations of facilities.

As the caseload increased, more volunteer monitors were needed, and Oakdale Guardianship embarked on a recruitment program that included a direct appeal via public media. Radio time and newspaper articles were used to reach the public, but response was minimal. One additional approach that was intended to garner support involved discussing the program with officials of local school districts in an attempt to enlist their assistance. They were reluctant to formally participate but agreed to sponsor a meeting for addressing a gathering of teachers. This meeting was successful. Some participants were eager to become involved with Oakdale Guardianship as volunteer monitors. Even today, some of these teachers are among the group's most active members. As the number of clients continued to grow and more volunteer monitors were needed, the teachers and their aides embarked on a recruitment program of their own. They approached local churches and civic groups. Their success was limited but eventually people became aware of the organization's activities and more and more people became volunteer monitors.

At the beginning of 1980, some of the organization's clients were moved to Macomb–Oakland Regional Center, another state facility located in Mt. Clemens, Michigan. The director of this facility, Jerry Provencal, felt strongly that the Center needed a guardianship program. When requested, Oakdale Guardianship agreed to serve some of the clients at the Macomb–Oakland Regional Center.

In early 1981, Oakdale Guardianship obtained a much-needed office on the grounds of the Oakdale Regional Center. The caseload had grown to 140 clients, making it necessary to hire a part-time secretary. Prior to 1981, Oakdale Guardianship operated out of this author's basement. The whole operation, including all the paperwork, was handled by one person with limited help from members of Oakdale Guardianship. Little things meant a lot, however, for instance, when a copying machine was donated, saving an incredible amount of time and effort.

In the spring of 1982, many of Oakdale Guardianship's clients began to move into community living arrangements and into another state institution, the Mt. Pleasant Regional Center, located mid-state. Some of the clients were relocated more than 200 miles from the base of operations. A lot of traveling had to be done, which proved to be very costly. It was decided to form satellite groups: Northeast Michigan Guardianship, Central Michigan Guardianship, Livingston County Guardianship. At the same time, the client load at Macomb–Oakland Regional Center was steadily increasing. For practical reasons, it was decided to form still another satellite group: Macomb–Oakland Guardianship. Additionally, while Oakland Guardianship was the first volunteer guardianship group in the state of

Michigan, others began to follow its example. These groups are not necessarily affiliated with Oakdale Guardianship.

Beginning in 1983, Oakdale Guardianship hopes to have its satellite groups operating independently from it. It will petition the probate courts for guardianship modifications in order to transfer the corporate guardianship status of each client who resides in distant geographical areas to the satellite group that serves his or her region. Furthermore, it will consolidate all of the guardianship groups in the state under one federation, to be administered by a single executive director. Needless to say, these expansion plans will require additional funding. This problem is presently being confronted.

THE STRUCTURE OF OAKDALE GUARDIANSHIP, INC.

The structure of Oakdale Guardianship is simple but effective (see by-laws in Appendix A). The membership of the organization consists of a board of directors that consists of at least 12 members, and an assembly of the individuals who serve as volunteer monitors.

The volunteer monitor assembly annually elects a president, first vice president, second vice president, secretary, and treasurer. Two additional board members-at-large are selected by the president and submitted to the membership (volunteer monitor assembly) for approval.

The probate court recognizes the Oakdale Guardianship board as the official guardian when it makes guardianship appointments. Thus, only elected officers are allowed to sign documents concerning clients. Exceptions can be made in individual cases with the board's approval. For example, the geographical location of a client may necessitate delegating the board's signature authority to a volunteer monitor who lives in closest proximity to the client's domicile.

The board meets bi-monthly and the membership meets twice a year, usually in connection with training workshops sponsored by Oakdale Guardianship. The president has the prerogative to call board meetings and general assembly meetings whenever he or she sees fit.

Since many of the activities are repetitious, it is expedient to devise certain form letters, i.e., surgery approval, appointment of volunteer monitor, reminders to volunteer monitor. In the interest of time, such letters have been found to be helpful (see Appendix B).

A grievance procedure was developed as a guide for volunteer monitors to use when they observe problems. For example, if a volunteer monitor finds that a client is inappropriately dressed, this fact is immediately called to the attention of the service provider along with a request that this be rectified. If the service provider is evasive, unwilling, or tries to blame someone else, the volunteer monitor contacts the guardianship office. The next step is for a board member of Oakdale Guardianship to contact the building director (if the client is in an institutional setting) or the house manager (if the client is in a community setting). Usually these actions suffice and the problem is resolved. However, if these steps are unsuccessful, the matter is discussed by the Oakdale Guardianship board and an appropriate action is determined, including taking the matter to court if necessary. Volunteer monitors are kept advised of all procedures decided upon by the board.

The Volunteer Monitor Approach

As noted earlier, court orders name Oakdale Guardianship, Inc. as the guardian of its clients. This means, according to the by-laws (Appendix A), that the board of directors has sole responsibility for providing guardianship services. In practice, the organization exercises personal attention to its wards via volunteer monitors. These individuals receive training by the corporation on the rights of institutional and community-based residents and on how to advocate for these rights. It is important to remember that monitors do not have authority to provide any form of consent for wards. They refer needs for consent to an appropriate board member. The board is solely responsible for providing consent and for submitting reports to appropriate courts.

A volunteer monitor can be a member of an association for retarded citizens group or an interested person from the community. A minor cannot act as a volunteer monitor. Other qualifications are desirable but are not mandatory, e.g., experience with developmentally disabled individuals, and teaching, social work, or nursing experience.

A sincere effort is made to match each client with an appropriate person. Some prospective volunteer monitors express preferences regarding client charac- teristics, e.g., verbal or nonverbal, ambulatory or nonambulatory, male or female, age. Once an appropriate match has been achieved, volunteer monitors receive an identification card and background information on their client. Also, volunteer monitors are advised of any changes that are contemplated in their client's living arrangement and of any other relevant information concerning their client.

The purposes of the volunteer monitor approach are as follows:

1. To provide representation for clients
2. To provide each client with a friend as well as a guardian
3. To ensure that clients reside in the least restrictive environment appropriate to their needs
4. To assure the appropriateness of community homes prior to a client's placement
5. To help educate communities about the needs of persons with developmental disabilities and the services that are available to meet their needs
6. To promote the welfare of all handicapped individuals

A volunteer monitor is expected to visit with his or her client at least bi-monthly and to submit a report to the Oakdale Guardianship office following each visit. He or she can take the client off-campus, but not for an overnight stay. Whenever possible, volunteer monitors participate at interdisciplinary team meet- ings and at other staff meetings concerning their client. Such meetings are scheduled annually. Volunteer monitors cannot always participate. When this occurs, another representative of Oakdale Guardianship attends and shares the results of the meeting with the volunteer monitor and the staff of Oakdale Guardianship. A volunteer monitor has the right to look at his or her client's file.

The following guidelines have been developed regarding volunteer monitors:

1. The name of the volunteer monitor must be on file with the resident rights officer and the resident's building at Oakdale Regional Center.
2. At each visit, the volunteer monitor must present himself or herself to the person in charge of a building or ward. If he or she is visiting more than one person in a building, this fact must be pointed out to building staff.
3. The volunteer monitor must confine his or her interest to personal contact with the client and/or staff.
4. The volunteer monitor should take note of any problems or unusual situations concerning the client and report them to the guardian (board member) as quickly as possible.
5. Any attempt to badger a client or to inspect or search the client's body or personal possessions constitutes an invasion of privacy and is strictly prohibited. If a monitor suspects something suspicious, it should be reported to the guardian.
6. The volunteer monitor should make an effort to explain to the resident the purpose of visits and inform him or her that reports are made to the guardian.
7. The volunteer monitor should assure the resident that any personal message he or she has for the guardian will be kept confidential.
8. The volunteer monitor may take his or her client off the campus during the day but the facility may want to confirm approval in advance with an officer of Oakdale Guardianship.
9. When visiting clients in the community, it is necessary for the volunteer monitor to call the home ahead of time to make sure that the client will be in at the time of the visit.
10. The volunteer monitor must always wear an identification button when visiting with a client.
11. A seasoned volunteer monitor should accompany new monitors on their first visit whenever possible and/or the client's case manager/social worker should join new monitors on their first visit.

Overall experiences with volunteer monitors have been good. At this point in time, Oakdale Guardianship has 72 volunteer monitors. The annual turnover rate of volunteer monitors averages about 33%. One of the primary reasons for turnovers is transience. Volunteer monitors move, either to other parts of the state or entirely out of the state. Another primary reason for turnover is that some people seem unable, in the long run, to cope with the duties of a volunteer monitor. As stated previously, at minimum, bi-monthly visitations are required. If this expectation is not met, no other recourse exists but to replace a volunteer monitor.

It never ceases to amaze how many volunteer monitors become real friends to their clients. Many volunteer monitors take clients to their homes, out to restaurants, or to other social activities that occur in their communities. These experiences greatly contribute to a client's readiness to move out of an institution.

Having a volunteer monitor makes a client feel wanted and fills him or her with a certain amount of pride. Oakdale Guardianship is frequently told that clients like to talk about their friend, the volunteer monitor, to peers and staff where they reside. One volunteer monitor related an example. She had visited with her client, a young lady, for about 1 year and had found it very difficult to establish any kind of rapport. Then one day, while she was on a periodic visit, the client rushed up and threw her arms around the monitor. Not a word was spoken, but the perseverance of the volunteer monitor had borne fruit. While it is impossible to explain what goes on in the mind of a person with a developmental disability, one thing can be sure: clients have feelings like everyone else.

Certain individuals with developmental disabilities present behavioral problems. Acts of self-abuse, screaming, or other maladaptive behavior occur. Oakdale Guardianship makes an attempt to explain to prospective volunteer monitors that the behavior of some persons with developmental disabilities is emitted to draw attention. Appropriate training workshops moderated by people with expertise in the field of mental retardation are held bi-annually for volunteer monitors so that monitors can learn to deal with such behavioral problems.

The reports that volunteer monitors submit to the office are recorded along with the frequency of their visits. Once a year, citations are given to the most outstanding volunteer monitors. These awards are just pieces of paper, but they mean a great deal to volunteer monitors. This award program builds the morale of volunteer monitors and, in turn, builds their clients' morale. Without the help of the volunteer monitors, there would be no Oakdale Guardianship program.

Oakdale Guardianship has been told several times over the years that its activities should be carried out by people with the necessary professional expertise, i.e., those having degrees in social work, special education, psychology, etc. At least half of its monitors possess these requirements. Oakdale Guardianship feels strongly that degree requirements and payments to monitors are unnecessary and could be counterproductive. They could readily lead to the creation of a traditional, professionally dominated service model. Another costly bureaucracy would be created that sooner or later would lose the human touch.

Table 2 summarizes the activities of volunteer monitors for 200 clients over

Table 2. Activities of volunteer monitors over 2 years

Activities	1981	1982
Visits to a client's domicile	978	945
Home visits prior to a client's placement	30	26
Participation in team meetings	157	189
Miles driven by members of Oakdale Guardianship	21,209	22,100

the past 2 years. These activities on behalf of clients were conducted with total expenditures of approximately $36,000 during this 2-year period.

Family Involvement

Family members of individuals with developmental disabilities are probably the most qualified monitors. It is critical, however, that they be able to maintain objectivity when dealing with persons with developmental disabilities. While it certainly is necessary to bring a great deal of understanding and empathy to their activities, volunteer monitors must control their emotions. Whenever possible, family members should not act as volunteer monitors in the same location where their own relative resides. To do so causes disturbances in relationships between the family members and their disabled relatives. Moreover, not all of the volunteer monitors should be relatives of persons with developmental disabilities. Oakdale Guardianship believes that a healthy guardianship group includes a mixture of relatives and nonrelated persons from the general community.

There are instances when a family member is not permitted by a court to act as guardian. Should the court designate Oakdale Guardianship to become the guardian, the family member is not overlooked or ignored. Instead, he or she is encouraged to continue the relationship with his or her relative.

Upon petition by a social worker, case manager, or any other interested party, a court may order that a guardian be relieved of his or her duties. Any petition to the probate court for such an action must be accompanied by proof that the present guardian is unsuitable and/or unwilling to carry out the duties mandated by the law. A hearing will be called by the court and the judge will decide whether to grant or deny a petition. Should Oakdale Guardianship be appointed to become the guardian, it may wish to impose certain restrictions as to further contact between the client and his or her previous guardian. In certain cases where Oakdale Guardianship has reason to believe that contact would be detrimental to its client, it invokes the right to deny personal contact between the client and his or her former guardian. Oakdale Guardianship likes to cooperate with the families of its clients as much as possible, but the client's welfare must be the overriding factor in all dealings with others.

FUNDING AND BUDGET

As with any other volunteer group, funding presents a big problem. Oakdale Guardianship is perhaps more fortunate than similar groups. The Lapeer–Oakdale Parents Association has given Oakdale Guardianship financial support when needed, but the resources are limited. As a consequence, it is necessary to explore other avenues for obtaining revenues. The program's efforts to apply to foundations and for United Way supports have not been successful. In 1981, Oakdale Guardianship engaged in a small fundraising project that netted about $450. Its main source of revenue is a guardianship fee that is charged to clients. This is not done by choice, but rather out of necessity. After consultation with the clients' home facility and the probate court, Oakdale Guardianship arrived at a formula that meets its funding needs. Clients in the community and clients in a state facility who receive only SSI (Supplemental Security Income) are charged $2.50 per month. Clients in a state facility who receive other entitlements (V.A. benefits, pensions, social security, etc.) are charged 9% of the amount which they receive. In addition, Oakdale Guardianship has entered into a contract with the Michigan Department of Mental Health to fund services to clients who are under the jurisdiction of the Macomb–Oakland Regional Center.

In late 1982, the question arose as to whether it was legal for clients to pay a percentage of their income for guardianship services. This question is still pending a court decision and, in the meantime, contracts are being extended on a month-to-month basis. This is an unhealthy situation and has left Oakdale Guardianship with no other choice but to refrain from accepting additional clients. The program is currently petitioning the probate courts to establish a definite schedule of payments for services and is optimistic about the final outcome of this situation.

Based on the 1982 budget, the cost per client for Oakdale Guardianship's services was $122.65 annually or $10.22 per month. For 1983, the anticipated cost of services will increase to $131 annually per client or $10.92 per month. In addition, the program believes that the services of a paid executive director will soon be required in order to coordinate the network of guardianship groups that have been established and will be established in the state of Michigan. This change would substantially increase the per-client cost. The projected budget for 1983 does not reflect the executive director's position. It only allows for an additional part-time secretary at Oakdale Guardianship's new office in the Macomb–Oakland Regional Center.

Table 3 summarizes revenue and expenses during 1982.

ACCOMPLISHMENTS

The following examples of Oakdale Guardianship's activities on behalf of clients illustrate the impact of the program's services.

—A school district denied one of Oakdale Guardianship's clients the right to attend a school for handicapped individuals. The school district maintained that the client's records indicated that he was not trainable. Oakdale Guardianship had documentation in its files that he was "trainable." This information was given to the school district but their position did not change. Their attitude left no alternative but to resort to legal counsel. This client is now enjoying the benefit of a free public education and is doing well.

—Another client, a fairly high functioning woman in her early fifties, is wheelchair bound. She was unable to operate her wheelchair by herself. In order to get from point A to point B, someone had to push her chair. About a year ago, her physician prescribed an electric wheelchair, but nothing happened. When inquiries were made, Oakdale Guardianship was told that the state had no funds to allocate for this purpose.

Table 3. Funding and budget for Oakdale Guardianship, Inc. (1982)

Revenue	
Oakdale fees	$11,203.40
Community fees ($2.50 per month per client)	1,797.50
Macomb–Oakland Regional Center fees	7,352.61
Lapeer–Oakdale Parents' Association	4,337.50
Interest earned	105.10
Workshops	405.00
Donations	842.50
Total Revenue	**$26,043.61**
Disbursements	
Secretarial services	$ 6,450.70
Phone	2,292.61
Supplies	970.46
Mileage	5,466.69
Postage	525.12
Travel	320.19
Printing	199.27
Maintenance	220.00
Consulting	5,249.20
Legal	516.00
Association for Retarded Citizens/Lapeer–Oakdale	397.10
Refunds	70.00
Bank charges	17.93
Workshop (training volunteer monitors)	484.77
Macomb–Oakland Guardianship	736.22
Total Disbursements	**$23,916.26**

Subsequently, a recipient rights violation was filed with the Michigan Department of Mental Health. After months of waiting, Oakdale Guardianship finally received a reply. The Department claimed that there were insufficient funds for this purpose and cited a mental health code regarding freedom of movement to indicate that an electric wheelchair was not necessary to enhance the client's freedom of movement. The Department's decision was very upsetting, since Oakdale Guardianship did not understand its logic. On one hand, the law provided that everything has to be done to make an individual with a developmental disability as independent as possible. On the other hand, the state refused to make an expenditure needed to achieve this goal. As a last resort, Oakdale Guardianship contacted the local ABC network television station and gave them all the details. Two days later, it received a call from the station indicating that an appropriate electric wheelchair would be provided to this client and the chair subsequently was provided. Moreover, the whole story surrounding the incident was televised.

—There were two doors leading into the bathroom in a coed community home: one from the male residents' bedroom and one from the female residents' bedroom. Oakdale Guardianship complained about this situation to the home operator and due to this insistence one door was permanently locked.

—A group home operator, for religious and moral reasons, said clients could not smoke in her home. Arrangements were negotiated for a designated smoking area in the house.

—A regional center was having difficulty placing one of Oakdale Guardianship's clients in a community home due to his poor ambulation ability. After Oakdale

Guardianship successfully worked with a home operator to install a ramp, the client now lives in a community home.

—A doctor told one of Oakdale Guardianship's clients that he did not need glasses, even though the client could barely see. A second examination was done by another doctor at Oakdale Guardianship's request and glasses were prescribed for the client.

—A volunteer monitor suspected that one of Oakdale Guardianship's clients was being overmedicated. In a team meeting, it turned out that as many as seven doctors were involved in treating this client but no one doctor was serving as personal physician to coordinate the efforts of the other doctors. This was corrected immediately and the client's medications were adjusted to a proper level.

—A relatively independent woman whose front teeth were missing was placed in a group home. In order to improve her appearance, Oakdale Guardianship insisted that the client receive a permanent bridge. After a long struggle with the authorities, the bridge was approved. As a result, this client now looks and acts like a different person.

—In a case involving elective surgery, Oakdale Guardianship sought additional opinions from two physicians who both felt that the procedure recommended previously by another doctor was not necessary. The majority opinion was followed and the surgical permit was returned unsigned by Oakdale Guardianship.

Oakdale Guardianship strongly believes that there is a need, not only in Michigan but throughout the entire United States, for organizations such as its own to represent the rights of individuals with developmental disabilities. The clients described in the above examples may never have benefitted from improved services without the intervention of Oakdale Guardianship.

THE NEED FOR OTHER ADVOCACY GROUPS

Guardianship is not the only approach to the provision of guidance and protection to persons with developmental disabilities. Several alternatives exist:

1. *Citizen advocacy*—Citizen advocacy is a concept advocated by many local associations for retarded citizens. In essence, it is very similar to the Oakdale Guardianship concept and the services that it performs but without the legal rights and responsibilities of full-fledged guardianship.
2. *Foster grandparents*—The foster grandparents program is small in scope and limited to individuals with developmental disabilities from birth to 21 years of age. In Michigan, it is partially federally funded and partially state funded. The volunteers in this program must be senior citizens whose income falls below a certain level. They receive a stipend for their services.
3. *Civic groups*—While many civic groups are very sympathetic to the needs of persons who are mentally retarded, their efforts tend to be geared toward helping groups versus individuals. They sponsor picnics and Christmas parties, etc., but generally do not get directly involved with one handicapped individual.
4. *Protection and advocacy*—Protection and advocacy agencies are partially funded by the state and federal governments. They deal only with individual cases where there is evidence of a violation of a person's rights.

5. *Office of recipient's rights*—The office of recipient's rights is within the Michigan Department of Mental Health. It does deal with individual cases but its advocacy may be hampered by the fact that it is a part of the overall state system.

If Oakdale Guardianship were to take a global approach to the program's activities, its sphere of influence would be extended to mentally ill individuals, and to geriatric and juvenile populations. Providing manpower for such an operation might not be as difficult as one might think. There are many senior citizens or retirees who would very much like being involved in such a program. Also, there is no reason why colleges throughout the country cannot make serving as a volunteer monitor a curriculum requirement for students majoring in social services.

LESSONS TO SHARE

Do not rush into the provision of guardianship services until you have laid a proper foundation for action. One must be sure that adequate funding is available. It is helpful to have the cooperation of local authorities who are responsible for developmentally disabled individuals. The backing of a local Association for Retarded Citizens can also be of great assistance. It is very important to meet with local probate court judges to discuss your plan of guardianship with them. Media exposure can also be very helpful. Finally, acquaint local civic groups with your intentions.

It gives any new organization a great deal of prestige if local civic leaders can be persuaded to become members of the board of directors. These individuals do not necessarily have to be highly active board members, but they should be on the board.

Volunteer monitors should have some qualifications related to the field of mental retardation: either professional or experiential. It is advisable to have a mixture of relatives and nonrelated people.

Do not assign more than three clients to a monitor. In the formative stages, Oakdale Guardianship was pretty desperate for monitors. Once, a retired couple (parents of a mentally retarded person) asked the program to assign several clients to them. Over time, 20 cases were assigned to these individuals. They did a remarkable job, but they eventually both became very ill and had to abandon their activities with Oakdale Guardianship. This event left 20 clients without a volunteer monitor. It took a considerable amount of time to provide these 20 clients with new monitors.

It seems wise not to impose too many restrictions on volunteer monitors. Let them develop their own style in keeping with the general guidelines set by your group. Do not have too many meetings, and limit the amount of paperwork a monitor has to engage in on behalf of his or her client. Oakdale Guardianship attempted to make it as easy as possible for the monitor by providing preprinted forms to fill out after each visit (see Appendix B for examples). If at all possible, it is advisable to reimburse volunteer monitors for their travel costs.

Record keeping is very important. Volunteer monitors must be kept aware of all events concerning their clients. A volunteer monitor's client file should be a duplicate of the file kept in the main office. If a monitor requests that the board pursue a certain matter concerning a client, he or she must be kept posted of every step taken with regard to the request.

Finally, those who wish to create corporate guardianship programs should be aware that some conflicts with service providers are almost inevitable. When Oakdale Guardianship was originally conceived at Oakdale Regional Center, it received the full cooperation of the staff and the administration. Soon, it became apparent that both of us held a different interpretation of a guardian's primary function. Some direct care and administrative staff began to denounce the program as not really needed and as interfering with their work. They considered it audacious to question decisions made by the institution on behalf of clients. Oakdale Guardianship complained, for example, about clients being inappropriately dressed, i.e., wearing socks on their hands instead of gloves during the wintertime, and female clients with large feet being provided only men's shoes to wear. Social workers and case managers stated emphatically that they were perfectly capable of dealing with the needs of retarded persons. While Oakdale Guardianship has never disputed this fact, it insists on having a say about how its clients are treated.

The financial crisis that has hit the state of Michigan in recent years has had a tremendous effect on the way state facilities are operated. The budget of the Department of Mental Health has been slashed severely. It is very difficult to administer state facilities properly and to sustain services given the current political and economic climate. Oakdale Guardianship feels strongly that constant vigilance, such as that which it supplies, is essential to maintain the quality of life that clients experience.

SUMMARY

Oakdale Guardianship exists to act as a guardian to persons with developmental disabilities. The number of clients that it serves has grown steadily over the past 7 years and now totals 200 persons. It only acts as guardian of the person since its finances are not sufficient to provide estate management services. While the board of directors is technically assigned guardianship, most field services are delivered via a cadre of trained volunteer monitors. Oakdale Guardianship began as a program to serve the residents of one state institution. The communitization movement in Michigan has increasingly made the provision of services logistically more complex, and several satellite guardianship programs have been formed to address this problem. Efforts are underway to establish a statewide agency to coordinate these satellite programs.

Appendix A

BY-LAWS OF OAKDALE GUARDIANSHIP, INC.
(A Michigan Nonprofit Corporation)

ARTICLE I—*Repeal of Prior Bylaws*
All prior by-laws are hereby repealed except as to any unexpired term of office held by any officer thereunder.

ARTICLE II—*Name and Fiscal Year*
The name of the corporation is Oakdale Guardianship, Incorporated, and the corporation is a nonpolitical, nonsectarian organization. The Corporation's fiscal year is January 1 to December 31, inclusive.

ARTICLE III—*Board of Directors*
Section A.   The board of directors shall have the sole responsibility of providing guardianship services to those mentally retarded persons residing in an institutional setting (or community placement) when so appointed by a probate court.

Section B.   The Corporation can accept only the partial or plenary guardianship of the person of a mentally retarded ward in an institutional or community setting.

Section C.   The Corporation is prohibited from acting to provide consent in any of the following areas:
1. Sterilization, therapeutic or otherwise
2. Psychosurgery
3. Electro-shock treatment
4. Aversion techniques in behavior modification

Major surgical intervention shall require a second medical opinion and/or a letter of authority from the appropriate court, if deemed necessary by an officer of the Corporation.

Section D.   The number of wards the Corporation can serve shall be limited by the number of volunteer monitors trained by the Corporation. No volunteer monitor shall be assigned to advocate on behalf of more than ten individual wards of the Corporation.

Section E.   The Board of Directors shall have the responsibility of ensuring that each volunteer monitor is trained in the rights of institutionalized or community-placement residents as delineated in the Mental Health Code, and further, that each is trained in how to advocate for those rights.

Section F.   The Board of Directors shall require each volunteer monitor to make at least one visit every two months to each of his assigned wards, and subsequently to return a visitation report. Failure to comply properly with this requirement shall be reason for action by the Board of Directors.

Section G.   The volunteer monitors will not have the authority to provide any form of consent for any ward, but will have the affirmative duty to refer to an appropriate board member any need for such action by the Corporation. Exceptions can be made by the board.

Section H.   The Board of Directors will be responsible for submitting to the appropriate court the required reports.

Section I.   The corporate guardian shall strive for maximum normalization of each ward to ensure that each individual is in the least restrictive placement possible. To ensure this, the

Board of Directors will provide constant monitoring to ensure, first of all, that community placement is secured for all of those ready for such placement, the clients' wishes being considered, and in the alternative that each individual is receiving the proper treatment in the institution, and that all of those rights guaranteed by the state and federal constitutions and the Michigan Health Code are being met.

1. The Corporation presently serves the counties of Genesee, Lapeer, St. Clair, Oakland, Macomb, and Northwest Wayne (Northville).
2. In the event of a transfer to a county other than those listed above, the Corporation shall attempt to have guardianship responsibilities transferred to another person or body in the appropriate county of placement. In the interim, the Corporation will find a monitor for the ward.

Section J. A Director may be removed from office for cause deemed sufficient, after notice and hearing, personally or with counsel, by the Board of Directors, by a vote of at least seventy per cent (70%) of the membership of the Board, or seventy (70%) of the general membership.

Section K. Unless the bylaws require other notice, at least three (3) days of written or telephoned notice of all special meetings of the Directors shall be given in the name of the Secretary or other officer. No notice need be given of the annual or regular meetings unless the business to be conducted at such meetings shall, by these bylaws, require such notice. No notice of any meeting of the Directors or the purposes thereof need be given to any Director who attends such meetings in person, or waives such notice in writing, executed and filed with the records of the meeting either before or after the holding thereof. Notice by mail, telephone, or telegram to the usual business or residence address of a Director shall be sufficient.

Section L. Seven directors shall constitute a quorum for the transaction of any meeting.

Section M. Members are entitled to reimbursement for expenses incurred in performing their duties, with the exception of attending Board of Directors meetings and the visitation of a relative. Mileage shall be reimbursed after a minimum of ten miles at the current approved rate as set forth by the board of directors. Vouchers for reimbursement must be approved by at least one officer.

ARTICLE IV—*Amendments*

The by-laws may be amended or repealed by the majority vote of a quorum of the Board of Directors at any regular or special meeting thereof, provided that notice of such amendment or repeal has been given to each Director by mail at least two (2) weeks before such meeting, unless a Director not receiving such notice shall have waived such notice, or shall be personally present at such meeting as above provided.

ARTICLE V—*Structure*

Oakdale Guardianship, Incorporated, will consist of its general membership, officers, Board of Directors, and any other committees required to fulfill the Corporation's obligations as guardians for mentally retarded persons.

ARTICLE VI—*Officers*

Section A. The officers of this Corporation shall be as follows: President, 1st Vice-President, 2nd Vice-President, Secretary, Treasurer.

Section B. The officers shall be elected for a term of one year or until their successors are elected.

Section C. No employee of this corporation may serve as an officer, director, committee member or delegate.

Section D.   Vacancy or non-attendance of any officer or board member, for three (3) consecutive meetings, without just cause, may be filled by a majority vote of the remaining members of the Board of Directors voting thereon by ballot at any regular or duly called special meeting of the Board of Directors.

Section E.   Any officer or director may be removed from office for cause shown in a petition for such removal that is signed by not less than 25% of the membership of this Corporation, which petition when tendered to the President, the 1st Vice-President, or the 2nd Vice-President shall be notice for hearing thereon at the next general meeting subsequent to the next publication of the Corporation News. Said notice of hearing shall specify that a petition signed by not less than 25% of the members has been received for removal from office (naming the officer sought to be removed) from the office (naming the office from which removal is sought), and that the same will be brought to be heard at the (designate the next general meeting), which notice shall contain none of the facts upon which the petition is based. Said notice shall be given to the editor of the Corporation News, the printing of which said editor shall cause to be made. Said petition shall be read at the general meeting designated in said notice by the officer receiving same. Said petition shall be granted by a majority of the members voting by ballot at said meeting, after a hearing thereon by all members interested therein.

Section F.   The Corporation shall require a bond of its financial officers for the purpose of indemnifying the Corporation against loss or defalcation and shall pay the expense of procuring such bond. The amount of such bond shall be determined by the Board of Directors as necessary to protect the funds of the Corporation. It shall be delivered to the President and filed by the Secretary.

ARTICLE VII—*Directors*

Section A.   The Board of Directors shall consist of a minimum of twelve (12) members, these being the elected officers, the immediate past president, and the elected board members. An effort shall be made to include as board members two (2) residents of an institutional or a community-based facility.

Section B.   The directors at large shall be nominated by the nominating committee, based on interest, concern, potential service and contribution. They will be elected by the membership at the annual election in May. They will serve a one-year term or until their successors are elected.

Section C.   If for any reason a vacancy of a directorship occurs (example: resignation, lack of interest, etc.), this vacancy may be filled by appointment by the Board of Directors of the Corporation. This appointment will be for the remaining term of office of the resigning Director.

ARTICLE VIII—*Election of Officers*

Section A.   A nominating committee of not less than three (3) members and a chairman shall be appointed by the President and voted on by the membership not less than two (2) months prior to the annual meeting of the Corporation. The chairman of the nominating committee is to be appointed by the President and carry approval of the Board of Directors. The nominating committee shall, not less than two (2) months prior to the annual meeting, furnish to the President, the Secretary and to the editor of the Corporation News, a list of nominees for the various offices who have signified their consent to accept nomination. The list of nominees shall be published by the editor of the Corporation News one (1) month prior to the annual meeting.

Section B.   In addition to the nominations so submitted by the nominating committee, any member prior to the approval of the motion to close the nominations, may from the floor nominate at such election not more than one (1) candidate for each office as the member may desire, provided, however, the member has obtained the consent of the nominee to accept such nomination. In case of nomination from the floor, consent of the nominee must be in writing when nominee is not in attendance.

Section C.   A nominee shall not be a candidate for more than one (1) office at any one (1) election, and shall serve not more than two (2) consecutive terms.

Section D.   A husband or his wife is ineligible to hold office during the term of office of the other. If either of them should be nominated to a term of office contrary to the terms of this provision, the name of the one appearing second on the ballot shall be stricken therefrom and shall not be counted in the tally thereof.

Section E.   All officers and directors of this Corporation may be elected by written ballot. The candidate receiving the highest number of votes cast by the members at the annual meeting shall be elected to office and shall continue in such office for one (1) year unless a longer term is provided in these bylaws, whichever term of office may be the longer, or until his successor is duly elected and qualifies. Tie vote for any office will be resolved by written vote of the majority of the members in good standing in attendance at the annual meeting. The President shall appoint an election chairman and three (3) tellers who shall collect and tally the ballots and report the results to the membership at the annual meeting. After the results of the election have been declared, upon motion duly seconded and passed, the ballots shall be destroyed.

ARTICLE IX—*Duties of Officers*

Section A.   The regular term of all officers and directors shall commence upon election. At this time formal installation of officers and directors will be conducted.

Section B.   The duties and authority of the officers and directors shall be such as are implied by their respective titles, together with such as are specified in these bylaws.

Section C.   The President shall preside at all meetings of the members of the Corporation and all meetings of the Board of Directors, appoint all standing committee chairmen and special committees as required, subject to the approval of the Board of Directors, and be ex-officio member of all committees except the nominating committee. The President shall present an annual report and financial report to the membership following the close of the fiscal year.

Section D.   The 1st Vice-President shall assume and have all of the duties and authority of the President in his absence and shall aid the President in the performance of his duties. The 1st Vice-President will be responsible for the operations of the committees as assigned to him by the President.

Section E.   The 2nd Vice-President shall assume and have all of the duties and authority of the President in the absence of both the President and the 1st Vice-President and shall aid the President in the performance of his duties. The 2nd Vice-President will be responsible for the operations of the committees as assigned to him by the President.

Section F.   The Secretary shall conduct the authorized correspondence of the Corporation under the direction of the President and Board of Directors and shall take and report all minutes of the meetings of the members and Board of Directors and present a copy to the President.

Section G.   The Treasurer shall receive all revenues of the Corporation and shall maintain a complete and accurate account of all funds received and disbursed and send a copy of the report to the President. He shall deposit and disburse all such funds. He shall present an annual report to the membership after the close of the fiscal year listing all receipts and disbursements by budget categories. The Board of Directors shall have the authority to obtain services that may be required to help the treasurer perform his duties. All checks shall be signed by two (2) of the following officers: Vice-President, Treasurer, Recording Secretary, and President; or single signature checks may be issued only if a personal bond is procured for the Treasurer and alternate signee.

Section H.   The Treasurer shall make all tax reports as required by the State and Federal Governments.

Section I.   All officers and committee chairmen upon retiring from office shall deliver to the President all records, books, papers, and property belonging to the Corporation which are in their respective control.

ARTICLE X—*Parliamentary Authority*

Robert's Rules of Order shall govern the conduct of business in all cases in which they are applicable and not in conflict with this constitution.

ARTICLE XI—*Dissolution*

Upon dissolution of this Corporation any and all property of whatever kind of nature not theretofore expended for the purposes of this Corporation shall be transferred, assigned, delivered, and distributed to the Residents' Benefit Fund of the Oakdale Regional Center for Developmental Disabilities of the State of Michigan, absolutely.

SECRETARY'S CERTIFICATE

The foregoing by-laws were adopted by a majority of the members of Oakdale Guardianship, Incorported, a Michigan nonprofit corporation, voting thereon at the General Membership meeting on the ____ day of _____ , 1981.

Dated: Lapeer, Michigan

_____   _____
                                          Secretary, Oakdale Guardianship,
                                          Incorporated

                                          _____
                                          President, Oakdale Guardianship,
                                          Incorporated

Appendix B

SAMPLE FORMS USED FOR VOLUNTEER MONITORS

Date: _____

Re: _____

Dear Volunteer Monitor:

Our records show that no contact has been made with your client(s) for the last two months. Please advise at your earliest convenience.

Oakdale Guardianship must submit reports to the Probate Court on all our clients periodically.

This cannot be done without your help. Thank you for your past cooperation.

Sincerely yours,

President

HPW/ba

Date: _____

Re: _____

_____

_____

To whom it may concern:

Please be advised that _____ has (have) volunteered to be the monitors for the above clients. We know that your staff will extend every courtesy to the Volunteer Monitors. Further, please note that a Volunteer Monitor has the right to look at his/her client's file and has permission to take the client off the premises, if he or she so desires. Oakdale Guardianship also participates in any team meetings concerning our clients. Please advise at least a week in advance if and when such meetings are scheduled to enable us to make the appropriate arrangements. Thank you for your cooperation.

Very truly yours,

OAKDALE GUARDIANSHIP INC.

President

[continued]

In case of any emergency, please contact the following people who are all officers of Oakdale Guardianship Inc.

Mrs. Yvonne Weir, President, Lapeer, Michigan
Mr. Fred Ehman, Vice President, Lapeer, Michigan
Mrs. Dyane Moriarity, Treasurer, Columbiaville, Michigan
Mrs. Doris Roland, Secretary, Lapeer, Michigan

SAMPLE FORM FOR MEDICAL AUTHORIZATION

Date: _____

Dr. Isac O. Berker
Medical Director
Oakdale Regional Center
Lapeer, Michigan 48446

Re: _____

Dear Dr. Berker:

Upon the recommendations of Drs. _____,
Oakdale Guardianship, Inc., agrees to the suggested surgery and/or studies connected therewith.

Very truly yours,

OAKDALE GUARDIANSHIP INC.

President

SAMPLE FORM USED BY VOLUNTEER MONITORS

This form only to be used when client is in an institutional setting.

Please place checkmark in appropriate place. Thank you.

Name of client _____   Building _____

Volunteer monitor _____   AM _____   PM _____

Date _____

Client appearance: Dressed properly   Yes _____ No _____

Clothing clean   Yes _____ No _____

Visual body marks   Yes _____ No _____

Teeth   Excellent ____ Good ____ Fair ____ Poor ____

Personal health   Excellent ____ Good ____ Fair ____ Poor ____

Comments: _____

General Adjustment to Environment: Excellent _____ Good _____ Fair _____ Poor _____

Building Appearance: Clean _____ Fair _____ Poor _____ Dirty _____

Staffing:

How many attendants on duty: _____

Interaction with clients: Good _____ Fair _____ Poor _____

Comments: _____

Attitude of Client: Excellent _____ Good _____ Fair _____ Poor _____

Comments: _____

Client Verbal: Yes _____ No _____ Some _____

Staff Cooperation: Excellent _____ Good _____ Fair _____ Poor _____

Temperature: Normal _____ Too cold _____ Too hot _____

Restroom Appearance: Excellent _____ Good _____ Fair _____ Poor _____

Adequate Staffing: Yes _____ No _____

Privacy for Clients: Yes _____ Some _____ None _____ Overcrowded _____

Programming for Clients: Full _____ Some _____ None _____

General Information from Staff or Supervisor (especially if client is nonverbal):   *Use reverse side.*

My Experience as a Volunteer Monitor

Dyane Moriarity

I'm married to a very attentive man named Michael. We have two children, Greg, 16, and Shannon, 11. They are very active people, and at times are so involved with their peers and lives in school, sports, and ballet, that I feel lonesome. I'm not needed as much as I was when the children were small. I'm sure many mothers feel this way.

I was talking one day to an aide at Shannon's school about a child. The aide told me that she was his guardian, and I said, "Oh, that's great." I kept hearing other teachers and aides talking about being guardians to other clients. Finally I couldn't stand it any longer. I asked, "What are you talking about when you say you're guardians to so-and-so?" They told me about this organization called Oakdale Guardianship and the president of the organization, a man named Henry. "Go talk to Henry and he'll find you someone who needs a guardian, if that's what you want." Eventually, I went to see Henry. He gave me the details about the Oakdale Guardianship program and told me that I wouldn't actually be a real guardian *per se*. People who were with this organization are called "volunteer monitors." The clients of the organization do not have families for various reasons, either because they aren't wanted by their families or because some are too old to still have families.

My duties include visiting my clients at least once every 3 months, checking to see if they are bruised in any way and if so, why; checking to see if they have enough clothes and if they are clean; checking to see if they are getting good all-around treatment from staff and other clients, and seeing if they are happy in their environment. I wear a little pin to show that I am a volunteer monitor. It shows ward clerks, building staff, or anyone else that I have a right to check on the conditions of clients in this program, especially the ones assigned to me.

313

At first, Henry asked me to be a volunteer monitor to Theresa, a severely retarded, epileptic lady of 50, and Gladys, a severely retarded 81-year-old lady who had an IQ of 80 when she was admitted to Oakdale in her twenties. I became their monitor, and I enjoy them very much. My Gladie is full of rhymes she's learned over the years. She talks of chickens and what she feeds them. The first year I had Gladys, I bought her a toy stuffed chicken—this is the only stuffed animal she doesn't pull the strings out of to wrap around her fingers, one of her little habits. The chicken means something important to her.

I truly believe the two of them recognize me and my family. They know I'm theirs. At first, I was asked by the building staff not to bring my children with me to visit my clients. I immediately went to Henry expressing my views on this subject. I told him that if Theresa and Gladys were to be a part of me, then they will be a part of my family. My family should be allowed to visit them at any time with or without me. A notice was sent to the buildings by Henry stating this, and my children and husband are now welcome on the grounds or in any building. We have several dear friends at Oakdale, and we also visit other clients that aren't in Oakdale.

I also have one more client. She's also very special. Her name is Elsie. She walks with great difficulty. She has no use of her arms. She writes, colors, and eats, and does just about anything else you can think of with her feet! This precious little lady is 65 years old. Elsie has some family left; John, a brother-in-law is very good to her and still sends packages and cards to her, but is unable to be her guardian because of his age and the distance he'd have to travel. When Elsie comes home to our house on her birthday, we telephone John. This is a great feeling for her; it makes her feel that she has contact with the outside world besides us. I have to translate for Elsie what John says on the phone because she is deaf.

These people are like my children were when they were small. They are so loving and affectionate. I guess I do this for my own selfish reasons, as well as for them. I need that extra little love as well as they do.

I'm now on the board of directors of Oakdale Guardianship. I'm also a member of the Association for Retarded Citizens. I hold these two positions because having these two organizations behind me enables me to help my clients more.

Chapter 16

The Crossroad Services Program

Lloyd Munneke

HISTORY OF THE CROSSROAD PROGRAM

Parents of handicapped individuals were the instigators for the formation of Crossroad Services. Their children, many of whom are adults, were enrolled at a local provider of educational and rehabilitation services. This community-based program, known as Hope Haven, serves people from many geographical areas. As a provider of direct services, Hope Haven had no program of guardianship.

Parents expressed concern that after their death, someone else would need to continue doing the personal kinds of things for the children that their parents would have done. They asked, "What about our son or daughter after we die? Who will do those little things we do that he or she likes so much?"

Employees of Hope Haven heard the concerns of parents. Two employees, Mr. Paul Moos and this author, formed a planning committee consisting of themselves and five community members. They considered the question, "What can be done to assist parents of handicapped individuals achieve a sense of resolution to the 'What's after me' issue?" Guardianship arrangements, trusteeships, and advocacy programs were researched. The Iowa State Association for Retarded Citizens and the National Center for Law and the Handicapped assisted the research efforts. A good bit of technical information was unearthed, but nothing much of real significance regarding the parents' perspective was found.

Some of the parents were well informed about the technicalities and purposes of trusteeships and guardianships. They felt that traditional legal documents and legally defined arrangements that protect persons and their assets were well and good but that something more was needed. Some of them had already made traditional arrangements and their concern was now for the human element—the actual performance of parental activities instead of or in addition to traditional guardianship arrangements.

The planning committee listened intently and the attorneys on the planning group tried to capture the essence of what the parents wanted in the articles of incorporation for a new organization called "Crossroad Services."

> The purpose of this non-profit corporation shall be to offer and provide skilled personal counseling, guidance, and other services to individuals and families who have persons with special needs. This purpose shall include but not be limited to assisting parents or legal guardians in formulating and implementing plans for the care of these special individuals at such time as the parents or legal guardian shall no longer be able to provide guidance and assistance. These services shall be provided in a spirit of Christian concern and commitment based upon the Bible as the Word of God and the instruction provided in that Work concerning the command to love each other and to be stewards of God's Kingdom and all that is in that Kingdom. The purposes of this Corporation and all its activities shall be charitable and rendered regardless of race, color, or creed. The Corporation shall have all powers enumerated in the Iowa Non-Profit Corporation Act.

From this statement of purpose, it is clear that the program is not technically a guardianship arrangement but instead is intended to accomplish what parents want most from a guardianship arrangement, i.e., ongoing personal attention to their disabled child. The planning committee believes that Crossroad Services' program reflects the wishes of parents.

Crossroad Services was incorporated as a nonprofit organization in 1976. Guidance from a board of professionals and parents has continued. In 1982, this author was hired as a full-time paid employee to assume management leadership of the corporation.

ORGANIZATIONAL STRUCTURE

Crossroad Services is incorporated in the state of Iowa under Section 501 (c). A 21-member board of trustees controls the corporation. Members come from a broad geographical area: Minnesota, South Dakota, Montana, Iowa, and Colorado. The board is representative of parental, educational, medical, financial, pastoral, and mental retardation/developmental disabilities specialty areas. The board of trustees elects a seven-member executive board. Monthly meetings are held, and all of the trustees and board members serve without pay.

The affairs of the corporation are managed by the board of directors, whose members are also trustees. The board of directors consists of seven persons who are elected by the trustees at the annual meeting. The board of directors meets monthly to assure proper management of corporate affairs and to assure non-violation of the nonprofit status. Additional duties of the board of directors include the financial responsibility (approval of disbursements) and approval of applications for enrollment. The board of directors maintains the option to call upon other board of trustee members to perform specific duties. Any changes in the articles of incorporation are the responsibility of the board of trustees. (See Appendix A for the by-laws of the Crossroad Services Program.)

NATURE, SCHEDULES, AND COSTS OF SERVICES

Direct Long Term Contractual Services Agreement

Three distinct services have emerged during the corporation's short history of active programming. The original service is termed the "Direct Long Term Contractual Services Agreement." Under this agreement, Crossroad Services and the parents of a handicapped person attempt to put into writing the human element so that parental concern, responsibility, and involvement will be continued upon the parents' death. The format of this contract is shown in Appendix B.

The cost of the Direct Long Term Contractual Services Agreement is somewhat negotiable, depending on the parents' geographical location, the age of the parents, and the age of the handicapped family member. The base cost is $5,000 enrollment fee and $50,000 endowment upon the death of the parents.

Family/Guardian Assistance Contractual Services

The second type of service is termed the "Family/Guardian Assistance Contractual Services Agreement." This contract is less extensive. It is designed to assist a guardian as he or she carries out guardianship responsibility. In essence, this contract assures parents that the guardian will receive technical information, active advocacy, and personal assistance on behalf of the handicapped person upon the death of the parents. The format of this contract is included in Appendix C. The cost for this service plan is somewhat negotiable also, depending on the location and age of the parties. The base cost is a $500 enrollment fee and $10,000 endowment upon the death of the parents.

These two contractual arrangements establish workable agreements between the corporation and affected persons. Individual contracts can vary in terms of their exact content in order to meet the wishes and desires of those involved.

Safeguards are built into these contracts to help protect recipients. For example, Crossroad Services does not become the legal guardian of the person or estate. The parents must recommend another person or organization to the court to serve as guardian. This policy assures that Crossroad Services is accountable to someone outside of the agency. Furthermore, the contracts delineate procedures to be followed in the event of disagreement between the corporation and the guardian. Bonding options are available to protect an individual's investments.

While the two types of contracts are different, they both accomplish a common purpose: they assure parents that their child will receive personalized, "hands on" attention similar to that ordinarily shown by parents. The contracts differ in that one provides services directly to a handicapped person and the other directly to the guardian in the form of information, advocacy, and assistance.

In the event that the parents want to initiate services prior to the death of the sole survivor, an option exists for them. Upon payment of the endowment (generally received at the time of death), actual services can be started. Exercising this option allows the parent(s) to witness the performance of Crossroad Services as it carries out the terms of the agreement.

Professional Consultation

The third type of service is professional consultation. There is no contract involved with this service. Instead, it is a service that is available to any family with a handicapped member or to the handicapped person directly. The expertise and experience of Crossroad Services personnel are made available on an hourly fee basis. There is no obligation to enter into any contractual agreement for this service itself, nor is there any obligation to enter into either of the other services in order to receive the professional consultation. The cost of this service is $25 per hour.

FUNDING SOURCES

The funds needed to pay for the program's services are private monies. In a sense this is unfortunate. On the other hand, private funding has the advantage of allowing greater flexibility in meeting the wishes of parents. Every effort is made to facilitate participation in the program. For instance, the enrollment fees for both kinds of contract (Direct Long Term or Family/Guardian Assistance) can be paid in one lump sum or by installments, whichever is easier for the parents. The larger sum is not due until the parents' death. Parents can make financial arrangements through their estates, including the use of investment vehicles such as insurance policies.

Crossroad Services intentionally refrains from becoming involved with estate planning. Its purpose is to assist families with a handicapped member to design a long term approach to providing personal attention. It feels that becoming involved with estate planning complicates and taints its singular purpose. Crossroad Services personnel sometimes do take part in long range financial planning sessions involving parents and attorneys. Here, they serve as advisors on how the establishment of trust funds in estates may affect their child's receipt of government benefits.

PERSONNEL

Crossroad Services is a relatively new organization and presently employs only one full-time director and one part-time clerical worker. Additional personnel will be added as the program expands.

The director presently provides the services to clients. If distance between the director and the client would require a great deal of traveling, an individual geographically close to the client is hired as a Crossroad Services employee. The employee is supervised and directed by the executive director.

RELATIONSHIP TO GOVERNMENT-PROVIDED SERVICES

Crossroad Services has established professional liaisons with various government programs but it does not formally contract with any governmental agency. There have been discussions with government-operated guardianship programs to define the respective roles of the public guardian and Crossroad Services. Public guardians provide legal guardianship services while Crossroad Services provides the ''hands on'' kinds of things that are needed by handicapped persons in the absence of their parents. These ''hands on'' kinds of things include taking the person on vacation, attending staffings, being available as a parent would be, etc. These services are delineated for each individual beneficiary in his or her contract.

INVESTMENT OF ASSETS

The enrollment fee is not invested. It is used for up-front administrative expenses. The principal, which is paid upon the death of the parents, becomes the property of Crossroad Services. It is invested. The contract between the parents and Crossroad Services requires that monies provided by the parents will be invested in non-speculative investments. The income from this investment is used to pay the costs of providing Crossroad's services. Each family's bequest is used exclusively for their son or daughter. Upon the death of a handicapped person, Crossroad retains the principal in order to cover the costs of services to other disabled people whose estates are insufficient to obtain Crossroad's services.

The contract is legal and binding. While it is perpetual, there is ongoing opportunity to modify contracts. Additional services may be stipulated. Any increase in the amount of funds that may be necessary to fund service additions is negotiated when a contract change occurs.

NATURE OF FAMILY INVOLVEMENT

The intent of Crossroad Services is to involve the family and to maintain family relationships. Experience has shown that parents become concerned about who's to do the little things for their son or daughter that they have always done. Many parents are hesitant to place this responsibility on other family members.

The family and the handicapped person are usually both included in the planning process. Their needs are addressed in the part of the planning process that involves contract writing. The contract content consists of basically two parts: a) a section that is common to all contracts such as name, intent, etc., and b) an individualized section related to fulfilling the desires of the family and handicapped person. Upon completion of some initial discussion as to what the parents want Crossroad Services to do upon their death, a draft agreement is written. The family can then study it, have an attorney or someone else review it, make corrections or additions, and change it in any way they want. When the parties are in agreement regarding services and an exact cost figure is agreed upon, a contract is signed.

Crossroad Services finds that parents usually desire to have some trusted relative or friend serve as guardian and that person is usually also involved at planning sessions. Any request for someone to be the guardian in the future is the responsibility of the parents. Experience indicates that people, usually another family member, are more willing to become a guardian when they know that someone else, namely Crossroad Services, will be responsible for much of the involvement with the handicapped person.

Stipulations concerning the involvement of family members such as siblings with the handicapped person after the parents' death can be explained in the contract. For example, one contract requires Crossroad Services to assure that the handicapped person gets an annual vacation to see a sister in another state.

The parents and the handicapped persons meet with Crossroad Services' board of directors so that each gets to know the other. During the time the parents are still living, a representative of Crossroad Services makes periodic contacts with their handicapped child to establish a relationship and to allow parents an opportunity to interact with the representative.

SIZE AND COMPOSITION OF POPULATION SERVED

The target population of Crossroad Services is open-ended. The determination to contract or not to contract with a particular family is made on a situation-by-situation basis. For example, in a family where there are extreme intrafamily conflicts, great caution would be exercised. There are no geographical limitations. Judgment is used in determining Crossroad Services' ability to carry out the responsibilities that are stated in contracts upon the death of parents.

Crossroad Services does not apply rigid criteria regarding which population is served. Most service requests involve families with a child diagnosed as mentally retarded. However, there has been an inquiry by a family whose parents both travel extensively. They are concerned about protection services for their two normal children in the event of their own death due to accident, especially simultaneous death. It appears that family situations dictate the nature and degree of concern by parents. The willingness of a brother or sister to act as a parent substitute appears to be a major factor. Another factor seems to be the extent to which the parents want to place the responsibility on their other children.

Because the organization has just been in operation since June, 1982, Crossroad Services is proceeding cautiously. Each situation is considered individually with all ramifications taken into account. Referrals are recruited via churches, generally upon referral from Reformed denominations.

ENSURANCE OF LONG TERM STABILITY

It is the opinion of the board of trustees that there is no absolute means to ensure permanent stability. Crossroad Services has taken precautions to maximize the probability of its success, however. First, the composition of the board of trustees is important. They are selectively appointed since ultimate responsibility rests in the hands of the board. Board members include parents as well as people with particular kinds of expertise, e.g. medical, financial, investment, legal, psychological, and spiritual experts. Each represents a particular interest and a balance is maintained to assure proper representation of various areas of people's lives. Of particular emphasis is the parents. They are viewed as the dominant experts because they know what it means to be a parent. Moreover, board members are encouraged to demonstrate flexibility so that the services of the corporation are less likely to become obsolete.

There is also flexibility in the financial design of Crossroad Services. The organization is intended to maintain itself based on the fees that it charges for its services. Moreover, it has developed a working relationship with some foundations and promotes itself through organized churches of various denominations. Its location in northwest Iowa is an area wherein a great deal of financial support is channelled to nonprofit corporations through churches. In addition, it is an area that is characterized by substantial public awareness of the needs of handicapped persons.

PROVISION FOR DISCONTINUING A SERVICE RELATIONSHIP

If the handicapped person becomes self-sufficient prior to the parents' death, Crossroad Services would view this positively. If the decision was mutually agreed upon by the parent, the handicapped person, and the Crossroad Services, it could be decided to terminate the contract. The parents would not be credited for the enrollment fee and there would be no need to return the service fee because Crossroad Services will not have received it. If the independence comes after the death of the parents and consequently after a period of service, the service fee would still be returned to the handicapped person. There is a provision in the contracts that states that Crossroad Services may keep the service fee (the principal) only upon the death of the handicapped person. The decision to terminate a contract must be mutually agreed upon by the guardian, Crossroad Services, and the handicapped person. There is a provision in the contract to resolve disagreements that may arise.

LESSONS TO SHARE

This author's experience in developing Crossroad Services makes it possible to share a number of lessons. First, it is important to understand that corporate guardianship fulfills only a part of the need that families express. For the most part, it is the organization's assumption that corporate guardianship or any guardianship is something that protects the handicapped person's finances, and sometimes a few other things, such as entering into contracts and medical permission. These things are important to parents; that's why they enter into such agreements. Parents, however, are conscious of other needs that may not be satisfied through traditional guardianship relationships. Primarily, they are concerned about ensuring the replacement of their personal attention to their child when they die.

Another lesson is that corporate guardianship programs need to be developed with the motive of becoming partners with parents and families. Professional expertise and professional training do not necessarily meet the qualifications expected by parents. Corporate guardianship programs hire people to perform the functions of the guardianship. The "people's" ability to empathize with the family and particularly the handicapped individual is a major concern of parents and families. Limiting hours that employees are available, insisting on meeting at a guardian's office, or a hurried attitude cause suspicion. Likewise, parents and families generally are unfamiliar (or are not totally familiar) with the professional language that is commonly used by human services workers. True partnership with families and parents requires the use of language that is understood by parents.

Finally, guardianship models meet the needs of the handicapped population best when they do so within the private sector as a private enterprise. Government programs, while well intended, present too many bureaucratic entanglements and generally fail to express human, personalized concern.

Appendix A

BY-LAWS OF
CROSSROAD SERVICES, INC.

I. PREAMBLE

The purpose of this nonprofit corporation shall be to provide skilled personal counseling, guidance and other services in lieu of parents or guardians and accept the responsibility of planning for the needs of these special persons at such time that the parents or legal guardians are no longer able to provide guidance or assistance. This corporation shall use as its standard and basis Christian love and concern for the needs of others.

II. MEMBERSHIP

A. Composition: The membership of this corporation shall consist of twenty-one persons who shall be known as the Trustees. These Trustees shall be selected from a broad geographical area and shall be persons who are interested in and who agree with the concepts set forth in the Articles of Incorporation and in the Preamble of the By-Laws of this corporaton.
B. Trustee Meetings:
    1. The annual meeting of the Trustees shall be held during the month of February of each year at a time and place determined by the Trustees. Special meetings of the Trustees may be called by the President of the Board of Directors of this corporation, by the majority of the Board of Directors, or by the majority of the Trustees.
    2. Notice of all meetings of the Trustees shall be given to the Trustees at least two weeks before such meeting is called.
    3. Each Trustee shall be entitled to one vote in respect to all matters which the Trustees decide. No voting by proxy shall be honored.
    4. Any action which may be taken at a meeting of the Trustees may be taken without a formal meeting if there is unanimous consent by the Trustees and if such consent is confirmed by a writing setting forth specifically the action to be taken and such consent is signed by all Trustees.
C. Selection of Trustees:
    1. The initial Trustees shall be appointed by the initial Board of Directors of the corporation as shown by the Articles of Incorporation. Seven of the initial Trustees shall be appointed to a one-year term, seven of the Trustees shall be appointed to a two-year term, and the remaining seven Trustees appointed to a three-year term.
    2. The successors to the initial Trustees shall be selected by the Trustees at their annual meeting with the term of new Trustees beginning immediately after the annual meeting in which they are selected. All Trustees shall be appointed to a three-year term. The Trustees shall select at each annual meeting a sufficient number of new Trustees to fill any vacancies. Successor Trustees may be nominated by any Trustee with the Trustees then elected by the existing Trustees. The Trustees may also elect a number of substitutes to serve if any of the elected Trustees decline to serve. All vacancies which occur shall be filled no later than the next annual meeting at which time a new Trustee should be elected to fill the unexpired term. No Trustee shall be appointed to more than two consecutive terms.

323

III. BOARD OF DIRECTORS

A.   Composition and General Duties: The affairs of this corporation shall be managed by a Board of Directors elected by the Trustees at their annual meeting. This Board of Directors shall consist of seven persons who are also Trustees. The Board of Directors shall be responsible for managing the business and the affairs of this non-profit corporation and shall have authority to do all acts necessary to manage the affairs of the corporation so long as these acts preserve the non-profit status of the corporation and such acts do not violate the Articles of Incorporation, By-Laws, or laws of the State of Iowa.

B.   Election of Directors:
1.   The initial Board of Directors shall consist of Paul Moos, Lloyd Munneke, Ronald Oostra, Ken Sabers, Ken Veltkamp, John H. Van Holland, and John Van Zanten. Individual members of the Board of Directors shall serve one, two, or three years with the term of each initial Director decided by resolution of the initial Board.
2.   Subsequent Board members shall be elected to three-year terms and shall serve until their successors are elected. No member of the Board shall succeed himself for election after two consecutive terms. Vacancies occurring in the Board of Directors shall be filled by the Board until the next annual meeting of the Trustees at which time the new Director shall be elected to fill the unexpired term.

C.   Meetings:
1.   In addition to an annual meeting held immediately after the annual meeting of the Trustees, the Board shall also hold regular monthly meetings at a time and place determined by the Board. Special meetings may be called by the president or by a majority of the Board of Directors.
2.   Each member of the Board of Directors shall be entitled to one vote in respect to any matter decided by the Board. Four members of the Board shall be considered a quorum. No proxy vote shall be accepted in respect to any action taken by the Board.

D.   Committees: The Board of Directors may designate that committees be appointed. The Board of Directors shall upon creation of a committee outline the duties of the committee and the number of persons to serve on such committee. All committee members shall be appointed by the president subject to Board approval at the next regular or special meeting.

E.   Informal Action: Any action which may be taken by a meeting of the Board of Directors may be taken without a meeting if there is unanimous consent by the Board of Directors and if such consent is confirmed by writing setting forth specifically the action to be taken and such consent is signed by all Directors.

IV. OFFICERS

A.   The Board of Directors shall at its first regular meeting in each year elect from its own membership a president, vice-president, secretary, and treasurer. Each officer shall serve for a one-year term or until their successors are elected.

B.   Duties of Officers:
1.   President: The president shall preside at all meetings of the Trustees and of the Board of Directors. He shall determine the time and place for Board meetings. He shall also assume all other duties delegated to him by these By-Laws or by the Trustees or Board of Directors.
2.   Vice-President: The vice-president shall preside at all meetings which the president is unable to attend. The vice-president shall also perform all other duties that may be assigned to him by the president or by the Board of Directors.

3. Secretary: The secretary shall keep minutes of all meetings, give notice of all meetings to the Trustees or to the Board of Directors, conduct the correspondence for the corporation, prepare reports for presentation to the Trustees at the annual meeting, and perform all other duties that may be required of him by the Board of Directors.

4. Treasurer: The treasurer shall take charge of all funds of the corporation, disburse such funds as directed by the Board of Directors, submit periodic financial reports to the Board of Directors, submit an annual financial report to the Trustees, and perform all other duties that may be required of him by the Board of Directors.

C. Assistance to the Officers: The Board of Directors may appoint any assistance they may deem necessary to assist any of the officers in the performance of their duties.

V. FINANCIAL MATTERS

A. The Board of Directors shall prepare and submit to the Trustees of the corporation at the beginning of each year a budget estimating all corporation expenditures to be made during the year. The Trustees of the corporation shall approve this budget.

B. The books of the corporation shall be kept on a calendar year basis and shall be open to all Trustees upon any request to examine the books of the corporation.

C. The treasurer shall disburse funds on behalf of the Board of Directors. The Board of Directors shall be authorized to set limits on the maximum dollar amounts that can be paid in respect to any bill without prior consent of the Board of Directors.

D. The treasurer shall upon motion of the Board of Directors be covered by a bond in an amount deemed necessary by the Board.

E. The Board of Directors shall appoint auditors to examine the records of the corporation and the treasurer's report once each year with said auditors reporting directly to the Board of Directors.

VI. OWNERSHIP OF PROPERTY

A. The corporation may own, sell, hold, lease, and furnish any real or personal property as may be necessary to carry on the functions of this corporation.

B. All instruments concerning the conveyance or incumbrance of any real estate shall be signed by the president and the secretary upon resolution of the Board of Directors approving such action.

C. The Board of Directors may authorize the president and secretary to borrow money in any amount and to pledge or mortgage the assets of the corporation as security.

D. The private property of the Trustees or of the Board of Directors of the corporation shall not be liable for debts of the corporation.

VII. DISSOLUTION

In the event of the dissolution of the corporation, all properties and moneys belonging to the corporation shall be distributed in accordance with Article VIII of the Articles of Incorporation.

VIII. BY-LAWS

The By-Laws of this corporation can be amended by any duly called meeting of the Trustees after at least two weeks notice has been given to all Trustees. Notice of this meeting shall set forth the substance of the proposed amendment. The By-Laws shall be amended by a two-thirds vote of a quorum of the Trustees.

Adopted by the initial Board of Directors this _____ day of _____, 1976.

Adopted by the Trustees this _____ day of _____, 1976.

Attest:

President	Secretary

ARTICLES OF INCORPORATION
OF
CROSSROADS SERVICES, INC.

Article VI
The date on which the Corporate existence shall begin is that day on which the Secretary of the State of Iowa issues the Certificate of Incorporation of this Corporation.

Article VII
The names and addresses of the incorporators are:
Lloyd Munneke, Rock Valley, Iowa
Ken Veltkamp, Rock Valley, Iowa
John H. Van Holland, Rock Valley, Iowa

Article VIII
No officer or director or member of this Corporation shall benefit financially in any manner or form upon dissolution of this Corporation. No part of the net earnings of the Corporation shall inure to the benefit of, or be distributable to its members, trustees, officers or other private persons except that the Corporation shall be authorized and empowered to pay reasonable compensation for services rendered and to make payments and distributions in furtherance of the purposes set forth in Article III hereof. Upon the dissolution of the Corporation, the Board of Directors shall after paying or making provision for the payment of all the liabilities of the Corporation, distribute the assets of the Corporation to another non-profit organization dealing with persons having special needs, if such can be found. Any such assets not so disposed shall be disposed of by the District Court or the county in which the principal office of the Corporation is then located, exclusively for such purposes to such organizations as the court shall determine, which are organized and operated exclusively for charitable, educational, religious, or scientific purposes as shall at that time qualify as an exempt organization or organizations under Section 501 (c) (3) of the Internal Revenue Code of 1954.

Article IX
The purposes and objects of this Corporation as set forth in Article III shall not be broader than the definitions and purposes encompassed by Section 501 (c) (3) of the United States Internal Revenue Code.

Article X
The private property of the officers, directors, and members of this Corporation shall be exempt from liabilities for the debts and obligations of the Corporation.

Article XI
The Corporation may make and amend By-Laws at its pleasure and may authorize the Board of Trustees to do so subject to restrictions as may be deemed advisable.

Dated this _____ day of _____ , 1976.

_____   _____

Lloyd Munneke   Ken Veltkamp

                                      _____

                                      John H. Van Holland

STATE OF IOWA, SIOUX COUNTY, SS:

On this _____ day of _____, 1976, before me, the undersigned, a Notary Public in and for the State of Iowa, personally appeared Lloyd Munneke, Ken Veltkamp, and John H. Van Holland, to me personally known and who, being by me duly sworn, did say that they are the persons named in and who executed the foregoing Articles of Incorporation and acknowledged the same as their voluntary act and deed.

                          _____

                          Notary Public in and for the
                          State of Iowa
                          (W. C. Anderson)

Appendix B

THE FORMAT OF DIRECT
LONG TERM CONTRACTUAL SERVICES AGREEMENTS
(Sample Draft)

AGREEMENT WITH CROSSROADS SERVICES, INC.

THIS AGREEMENT made and entered into this _____ day of _____ , _____ , by and between _____ of _____ herein referred to as "parent" and Crossroads Services, Inc., herein referred to as "Crossroads" WITNESSETH AS FOLLOWS:

WHEREAS, _____ as the parent(s) of _____ hereafter referred to as "Client" and,

WHEREAS, said Client has special needs for which there is a concern and desire to gain assistance to assure that these needs are met presently and in the future, and,

WHEREAS, Crossroads is willing and desirous of providing needed services to the benefit of the client,

IT IS THEREFORE AGREED that Crossroads will deliver services and accept responsibility in accordance with the terms, conditions and stipulations outline below:

ARTICLE I
Policy

By this instrument Crossroads makes a commitment to assume a role that is not easily described with words. Crossroads is committing itself to recognize the needs of the client as would a parent; to provide the human element of concern; to assure the Client that she/he does not face human existence alone. Crossroads *does not* promise to provide the actual services themselves. Rather Crossroads promises to use compassion in recognizing the Client's needs and to see to it that those needs are met. Though the services below are enumerated with particularity, Crossroads does not intend to limit the Client to those services.

ARTICLE II
Services

[The following section is adjusted to meet each particular family situation.]

1. Crossroads Services, Inc. agrees that for the consideration set out in this agreement, it shall provide the Client parental-type counseling, supervision, guidance, and advocacy necessary to assure the client the following: (Upon the fulfillment of the terms of Article III and the financial satisfaction of Option B.)

   A. Access to regular social involvement and daily activity.
   B. Access to health service and medical care as needed.
   C. Guidance in money management and assistance in acquiring grooming and care items.
   D. Guidance in legal advocacy, as needed.
   E. Access to immediate aid and assistance if there are special needs due to an accident, death, or any special event affecting the Client, his/her next of kin or friends.

328

F. Access to spiritual nurture and attend a _____ Church on a scheduled basis.

G. *The following individual requests:
 1. Opportunity to visit his/her parent(s) in the event of the parent(s) disability.
 2. When appropriate provide work opportunity to make available funds to be used for requests in Article III, Section G.
 3. Opportunity to participate in a planned vacation separate from his/her place of residence and separate from his/her place of employment.
 4. Arrange holiday stays at private homes, so that he/she can have a diversion from his/her everyday activity.
 5. Arrangements for attendance at athletic events which constitute a specific favorite pastime of Client's.

H. Placement in good living arrangements that are adequate, dignified, and as private as possible.

I. Placement in employment positions that are suitable to the needs and ability of client.

J. To assure good communication for client, a respected person to his/her liking is to be present when a Crossroads Services' representative contacts him/her relative to arrangements and scheduling to carry out the terms of this agreement.

2. The above counseling shall include providing Client with a person or persons who shall contact the Client at least monthly and be available when needed. Crossroads realizes the highly subjective nature of the above services and hereby promises its utmost good faith in selecting services needed by the Client and in carrying out the terms of this agreement. Crossroads agrees to maintain and provide staff sufficient to provide the above counseling, supervision, guidance and advocacy.

ARTICLE III
Options and Considerations

1. Option A: _____ declined the need for Option A, which included the purchase of monthly responsibility at a prearranged monthly fee.

2. Option B: Client will receive all of the services enumerated in Article II, except individual requests (Section G) for the remainder of his/her life upon the absolute gift of _____ to Crossroads Services. The gift is to be paid to Crossroads at the death or the inability to execute (as determined by the court) _____ responsibility. Funding vehicle for this option is to be established in _____ will with Crossroads being the beneficiary for the agreed amount. (A copy of that portion of parent(s) last will and testament attached). This option is NOT subject to a revision in price and exercised at the death of _____ who signed this agreement.

   With the _____ gift under this option, Crossroads will establish an account in the name of the Client. The gift will be invested in Certificates of Deposit or similar non-speculative investments whose income will supply Crossroads' general operating fund; but whose principal may not be invaded during the life of the Client. Upon the death of the Client, all unused funds or interest of unused funds shall become the absolute property of Crossroads to be used for the benefit and assistance of persons who need the services provided by this organization.

3. As consideration for this agreement, the parent whose signature appears below agrees to pay Crossroads _____ as an initial enrollment fee upon the execution of this agreement. This enrollment fee does not pay for the above counseling,

---

*All the requests in Article II Section G are to be provided when the appropriate funds are available.

supervision, guidance and advocacy and is not refundable. The enrollment fee does entitle those signing this agreement to exercise Option A and freezes the cost of Option B at _____ .

For the purpose of establishing a working relationship between Crossroads and _____ it is hereby agreed that Option A will be utilized for zero months before any right to exercise Option B arises. At the end of said zero months period, the parent of the Client shall have the right to continue exercising Option A or to exercise Option B. If, at any time, the parent of the Client wishes to withdraw from Crossroads, he/she may do so; but there will be no refund of the enrollment fee or any other amounts paid under either Option A or B. Should the parent of the client wish to resume utilizing Crossroads, having previously withdrawn from them, he/she may do so without paying an additional fee.

4. Option C: _____ reserves the opportunity to recall the use of Option A at any time prior to the implementation of Option B.

ARTICLE IV
Reports and Grievances

1. Crossroads agrees to provide monthly reports to the legal conservator named upon death of the parent. Such reports shall provide information as to the services Client was provided and Client's condition, needs changed, or any other specific information requested in respect to the Client.

2. PLEASE NOTE that Crossroads will not act as either trustee or legal conservator for Client. Should Crossroads' Board of Directors decide Client is in need of legal conservator, they shall require the party signing this agreement, or other interested party, to petition the proper District Court for appointment of a conservator, but Crossroads will not act as such nor accept appointment as conservator.

3. Since there may be differences of opinion at a future date as to whether Crossroads is providing adequate services as promised in this agreement, it is hereby agreed that disputes shall be resolved by arbitration.

If disputes remain unresolved after a good faith attempt has been made by both parties to resolve them, arbitration proceedings shall be conducted in the following manner:

Crossroads shall select an arbitrator, conservator of Client shall select an arbitrator, the two chosen arbitrators shall select a third arbitrator. The panel of three arbitrators shall immediately study the dispute and may require testimony and evidence from the interested parties as they deem necessary. The dispute shall then be decided by a majority vote of the arbitrators whose decision shall be binding.

ARTICLE V
Approval

1. This agreement is SUBJECT TO THE APPROVAL OF THE BOARD OF DIRECTORS OF CROSSROADS.

IN WITNESS WHEREOF, we have signed this Agreement this _____ day of _____ , _____ .

CROSSROADS SERVICES, INC.

BY: _____   : _____
    Mr. Paul Moos, President   Parent

BY: _____

Appendix C

THE FORMAT OF FAMILY/GUARDIAN ASSISTANCE CONTRACTUAL SERVICE AGREEMENTS
(Sample Draft)

AGREEMENT WITH CROSSROADS SERVICES, INC.

THIS AGREEMENT made and entered into this _____ of _____
_____ , by and between _____ of _____ herein referred to as "Parent" and Crossroads Services, Inc., herein referred to as "Crossroads" WITNESSETH AS FOLLOWS:

WHEREAS, _____ as the parent of _____ and,

WHEREAS, has special needs for which there is a concern and desire to gain assistance to assure that these needs are met in the future, and

WHEREAS, Crossroads is willing and desirous of providing needed services to the benefit of _____

IT IS THEREFORE AGREED that Crossroads will deliver services and provide assistance in accordance with the terms, conditions and stipulations outlined below:

ARTICLE I
Policy

By this instrument Crossroads makes a commitment to assume a role that is not easily described with words. Crossroads is committing itself to recognize the needs of _____ _____ as would a parent; to provide the human element of concern; to assure _____ that he/she does not face human existence alone. Crossroads *does not* promise to provide the actual services themselves. Rather Crossroads promises to use compassion in recognizing his/her needs and to see to it that those needs are met. Though the services below are enumerated with particularity, Crossroads does not intend to limit them to those services.

ARTICLE II
Services

[The following section is adjusted to meet each particular family situation.]

1. Crossroads Services, Inc. agrees that for the consideration set out in this agreement, it shall provide _____ professionally related services as consultant to the guardian to assure _____ the following: (Upon fulfillment of the terms of Article III.)

2. A. Access to VOCATIONALLY RELATED activity including:
    1. those established to meet the need of _____ such as work activity or activity center placement.
    2. those innovative programs which may be established in the future directed toward meeting the vocational needs of handicapped individuals.
   B. Access to LIVING arrangements including:
    1. those which protect the dignity and safety of _____
    2. those which provide the level of care to meet _____ _____ needs.

C. Access to SOCIAL activity including:
    1. those that are planned as part of the program at the facility ⎯⎯⎯⎯⎯ is attending.
    2. those which may be considered optional such as camping experiences or spiritual retreats.
D. Access to MEDICAL treatment including:
    1. those which are preventive in nature.
    2. those which relate to his/her disability or those unforeseen.
E. Access to FINANCIAL resources including:
    1. those which presently exist.
    2. those which may be legislated or established by volunteer groups.

3. Crossroads shall provide a person or person to assist the guardian to assure ⎯⎯⎯⎯⎯ the above opportunities. This assistance shall include providing:
    A. *Technical Information* in areas unfamiliar to the guardian.
    B. *Active Advocacy* as a partner to the guardian on behalf of ⎯⎯⎯⎯⎯ .
    C. *Personal Assistance* to the guardian in the guardian's monitoring of vocational, living, social, medical, and financial aspects.
    These are intended to assist the guardian in the guarianship responsibility for ⎯⎯⎯⎯⎯ .

4. Crossroads realizes the highly subjective nature of the above services and hereby promises its utmost good faith in helping each one and in carrying out the terms of this agreement. Crossroads agrees to maintain and provide staff sufficient to provide the technical information, advocacy, and personal assistance.

ARTICLE III
Considerations and Options

On behalf of ⎯⎯⎯⎯⎯ the guardian shall receive the services enumerated in Article II throughout ⎯⎯⎯⎯⎯ life time.

As consideration for this agreement, the parents whose signatures appear below agree to pay Crossroads $500 as an initial Enrollment Fee upon the execution of this agreement. The Enrollment Fee does not pay for the above services and is not refundable.

As consideration for this agreement, the parents whose signatures appear below agree to pay Crossroads ⎯⎯⎯⎯⎯ for the services enumerated in Article II. This amount is to be paid to Crossroads upon the death or incapacity of the mother. Funding vehicle for this contract is to be ⎯⎯⎯⎯⎯ in the amount of $ ⎯⎯⎯⎯⎯ . This amount entitles ⎯⎯⎯⎯⎯ to the services as enumerated in Article II. He/she has access to these services, with the degree of utilization of these services to be determined by the guardian. Crossroads will establish an account in the interest of ⎯⎯⎯⎯⎯ and invest the funds in a Certificate of Deposit or similar non-speculative investments which income will supply Crossroads' operating fund to provide the enumerated services, but which principal may not be invaded during the life of this contract.

Upon the death of ⎯⎯⎯⎯⎯ , all unused funds or interest of unused funds shall become the absolute property of Crossroads to be used for the benefit and assistance of persons who need the services provided by Crossroads.

ARTICLE IV
Reports and Grievances

1. Crossroads agrees to maintain records to verify actual services provided. Such records shall provide information as to the services ⎯⎯⎯⎯⎯ was provided and ⎯⎯⎯⎯⎯ condition, needs changed, or any other specific information. Such reporting shall be done a minimum of once a year.

2. PLEASE NOTE that Crossroads will not act as either trustee or legal conservator/guardian.

3. Since there may be differences of opinion at a future date as to whether Crossroads is providing adequate services as promised in this agreement, it is hereby agreed that disputes shall be resolved by arbitration.

   If disputes remain unresolved after a good faith attempt has been made by both parties to resolve them, arbitration proceedings shall be conducted in the following manner:

   Crossroads shall select an arbitrator, the guardian shall select an arbitrator; the two chosen arbitrators shall select a third arbitrator. The panel of three arbitrators shall immediately study the dispute and may require testimony and evidence from the interested parties as they deem necessary. The dispute shall then be decided by a majority vote of the arbitrators whose decision shall be binding.

ARTICLE V

Approval

1. This agreement is SUBJECT TO THE APPROVAL OF THE BOARD OF DIRECTORS OF CROSSROADS.

   IN WITNESS WHEREOF, we have signed this Agreement this _____ day of _____ , _____ .

CROSSROADS SERVICES, INC.

BY: _____   :   _____
     Mr. Paul Moos, President   Parent

BY: _____
     Mr. Ken Sabers

I have read the foregoing Agreement, understand its terms, and as a potential guardian of _____ , I hereby consent to the terms of this Agreement.

_____

_____

_____

Guardianship Isn't Right for Everyone

Karin Melberg

This is the story of a young man named Justin who opposed his parents' guardianship petition.

Justin was born on September 21, 1962. He was cyanosed at birth, necessitating resuscitation. He had a convulsion 3 days after birth; his development was abnormal, and cerebral palsy, hydrocephalus, and mental retardation were diagnosed by the Hospital for Sick Children, Toronto. Justin was admitted to the Rideau Regional Centre on October 22, 1964. On admission, he was diagnosed as severely retarded and suffering from cerebral palsy. Today, Justin is confined to bed and a wheelchair. He cannot speak. His muscles are quite rigid, and coordination of all movements is poor. The muscle rigidity has not been improved by drug treatments as it is too severe to be overcome by medication.

It was not until September, 1974, just before his 12th birthday, that Justin was provided with a key to a whole new world; a world of communication. He was introduced to Carol Ann McLaughlan, a highly qualified instructor in the communication system known as Blissymbolics.

"He taught me . . . a lot more than I ever taught him initially and that continued over the years we worked together. He was like a sponge," McLaughlan said. "His progress in terms of cognitive development, his development in terms of perceptions of things was really quite amazing. He had many, many, many questions that had obviously been stored up for a lot of years."

Judge Matheson noted that those questions revolved around what went on outside of Rideau Regional; how other people lived; about his own family. "He

This text was reprinted from *SAMR Dialect,* February, 1983, with the permission of the author.

had a great interest in people's families; how they lived together and related to one another,'' said Matheson, ''and the positions of rooms in the house; those kinds of day-to-day things that we take for granted but were virtually unknown to him. We almost have the picture of a little extra-terrestrial being.''

In October, 1980, Felicity Khan, a medical social worker of wide experience overseas and at the Rideau Regional Centre, was assigned to prepare an individual program plan for Justin. The purpose behind this move was to develop some long term objectives with Justin and an interdisciplinary hospital team.

''I found him a very quiet, gentle person who related easily,'' said Khan. ''I thought he was quite a bright young man and a mature young man with a great deal of insight. He said he wanted to leave Rideau Regional Centre, and he asked if he could go to Hamilton for 3 weeks. There is a participation house at Hamilton, and several of his friends from the ward where he resided had gone [there] . . . He had been identified as a suitable client for the community,'' continued Khan. ''Way back in '75 at the review conference, he had been recommended as a prime candidate for the community (which means outside Rideau Centre) and possibly an approved home . . . When Participation House opened it was felt this was an ideal resource. . . .''

This review conference concerning Justin's long term future, chaired by Khan, was attended by the chief residential counselor and his physiotherapist and a representative from the school. It was suggested that a preplacement visit be arranged and the possibility of the now 18-year-old giving his own consent be examined. This recommendation was unanimously adopted, and an informative letter was sent to Justin's parents. There was no reply.

In due course, consent was obtained from a psychiatrist at the Center and Justin's ward physician. Justin was sent for referral to Dr. Sprecko Pregelj, M.D., F.R.C.P.(c), Ph.D. After an examination was conducted, it was certified that Justin was capable of giving his consent and authorization for the release of information, for community placement, for outings, activities he would like to be involved in, treatments, etc. Dr. Pregelj testified during the court case that he had found Justin to be ''quite versatile, quick, maintaining an intelligent conversation through Blissymbolics, giving appropriate answers and expressing his wishes well.''

''This, of course,'' said Judge Matheson, ''was an immense personal achievement. Justin had come of age and had become a man of some personal responsibility.'' Dr. Pregelj placed Justin at the ''borderline range of mental retardation.''

Approval of the 8-day trip for Justin with Normand Pellerin, a former teacher, was given by the senior program director and hospital authorities.

Suddenly Justin's trip was cancelled. Although his parents had reportedly not visited him during most of his teenage years, they said no to the trip. Authorities complied with their wish, despite the unanimous approval which had been given Justin.

"Justin was very upset, frustrated, confused, and angry," said Matheson. "Felicity Khan, Robert Curzon (his counselor), and Penelope Deering (his social worker) gave evidence with respect to Justin's hurt, humiliation, and continuing anxiety. This case," added the judge, "in Justin's mind, revolves around his right to make a decision about friends he chooses to have, where he wishes to live, and how he chooses to lead his life."

Matheson added that Dr. Pregelj had emphasized the need in Justin's life for a progression and spoke of the devastating psychiatric effect that would flow from a finding that he was "stupid." The result, he predicted, would be surface despair, depression, and a loss of the abilities that he now can exhibit. "He is incompetent for athletics; he is incompetent for toilet independency," said Pregelj, "but he is not incompetent to understand."

In commenting on the testimony offered by expert witnesses called by the applicant for guardianship, Justin's father, Judge Matheson made comments such as that the testimony of the institution's doctor "sheds very little light on the issue to be determined." The doctor "did not appear to remember the boy, nor could he offer any explanation as to why he had been assigned to write an opinion." The judge described the examination conducted by Dr. Bruce McCreary, a consulting psychiatrist and affiliated with Ongwanada Hospital, to be "a physically painful ordeal for Justin . . . I felt his approach to the examination to be tendentious and unsympathetic." Matheson added, regarding the psycholinguist who was critical of Justin's skills with the Bliss Board, that "she fails to take into account the horrendous physical effort required of a cerebral palsy victim and the ever-present need to employ muscle-saving strategies and shortcuts."

Matheson indicated he was impressed with the witnesses who appeared on behalf of Justin. "They had the incalculable advantage of personal knowledge of Justin and proved to the court they knew him as a person." Regarding testimony of the experts Dr. Frederic Grunberg, psychiatrist; Dr. A. D. Bower, psychologist; and Jane I. Staub of the Ontario Crippled Children's Centre in Toronto, Matheson said all "were noteworthy for insight, approach, common sense. Philosophically, these three were ideologically committed to what is called the 'normalization principle.'"

Matheson complained of the Ontario Mental Incompetency Act. Under the 1937 statute, the judge was required to either rule Justin competent or incompetent. "There is no middle ground," he said, "which might envisage a limited guardianship."

The Outcome

The final words in Matheson's "Judgment with Reasons" followed wrenching arguments which were shot back and forth across the courtroom for nearly a week. Matheson, himself crippled by injuries he received in the Second World War, watched as Justin took the stand and said simply, through his Bliss Board, that he would "like to go out—that's what I want to do." His parents said they did not rule out Justin's leaving Rideau Regional, but said they wanted to choose the time and place he would go.

"With incredible effort," said Matheson, "Justin has managed to communicate his passion for freedom as well as his love of family during the course of this trial. We have recognized a gentle, trusting, believing spirit and very much a thinking human being who has his unique part to play in our compassionate, interdependent society."

And on November 25, 1982, while friends and spectators cheered and Justin "screamed with joy" Matheson concluded his judgment with the following:

"So, in the spirit of that liberty which Learned Hand tells [us] seek to understand the minds of other men, and remembers that not even a sparrow falls to earth unheeded, I find and declare _____ Justin _____ to be mentally competent."

Index

DATE DUE

HIGHSMITH 45-220

MAPPING
MULTICULTURALISM

MAPPING
MULTICULTURALISM

AVERY F. GORDON AND
CHRISTOPHER NEWFIELD,
EDITORS

© 1996

UNIVERSITY OF MINNESOTA PRESS
Minneapolis / London

Published by the University of Minnesota Press
111 Third Avenue South, Suite 290, Minneapolis, MN 55401-2520
Printed in the United States of America on acid-free paper

Library of Congress Cataloging-in-Publication Data

Mapping multiculturalism / Avery F. Gordon and
Christopher Newfield, editors.
p.   cm.
Includes bibliographical references (p.   ) and index.
ISBN 0-8166-2546-8 (hc. : alk. paper)
ISBN 0-8166-2547-6 (pbk. : alk. paper)
1. Multiculturalism—United States. 2. Minorities—United States—
Social conditions. 3. Pluralism (Social sciences)—United States.
4. United States—Ethnic relations. 5. United States—Social
conditions—1980– 6. Multiculturalism.   I. Gordon, Avery F.
II. Newfield, Christopher.
E184.A1M29   1996
305.8—dc20   95-39877

The University of Minnesota is an
equal-opportunity educator and employer.

Contents

v

Part II. Rethinking the Political Subject

Part III. Reading Multicultural Narratives

Preface

This book grew out of a large conference, "Translating Cultures: The Future of Multiculturalism?" organized by the two editors and held at the University of California, Santa Barbara from November 11 through November 14, 1992. In addition to those included here and a couple of conference attendees who are not present in the volume, the conference included a wonderfully engaged and provocative panel on Women Rebuilding Los Angeles with Cynthia Hamilton, Shirley Kennedy, Angela Oh, and Esther Valadez. Film screenings and a concurrent exhibition at the University Art Museum, *Mistaken Identities*, were also part of the event. The audiences were memorable from beginning to end. The papers included in this volume have been substantially revised since the conference, although a few contributors have maintained the character of their conference presentations.

A project of this scope requires the generous support and assistance of many people. For help in making the conference possible, we would like to thank our valuable graduate assistant Julia Garrett, as well as the other UCSB students who helped us with everything from publicity to student outreach to ushering to cleaning up: D. A. Dixit, Crystal Griffith, Patty Ingham, Helen Quan, Chivy Sok, Suran Thrift, and the women of AKANKE. Special appreciation for all their energetic efforts on our behalf go to Barbara Harthorn of the UCSB Interdisciplinary Humanities Center, and Zaveeni Khan, Director of the UCSB Multicultural Center. We would also like to acknowledge the kind assistance of Marla Berns, Director of the University Art Museum, Roman Baratiak and Susan Gwynne at Arts & Lectures, Corey Dubin and Kris Peterson of Coyote Radio, Randi Glick and Linda James at the UCSB Interdisciplinary Humanities Center, Elizabeth Robinson and Jamon O'Brien of KCSB, and Michael Young, Vice-Chancellor for Student Affairs. For chairing panels and hosting our guests, thanks to Tomás Almaguer, Kum-Kum Bhavnani, Yolanda Broyles-Gonzalez, Sarah Fenstermaker, Gerald Horne, Shirley Kennedy, Shirley Lim, Charles Long, Constance Penley, Judith Raiskin, Beth Schneider, Denise Segura, and Mayfair Yang. For sending his film when he couldn't be there, we are grateful to the late Marlon Riggs. For our beautiful poster, we thank Karen Shapiro, its designer, and Jimmie Durham for allowing us to reproduce his work *New Clear Family*. For their conversations during the planning stage, we would like to thank Elliott Butler-Evans, Antonia Castañeda, Ward Churchill, Rosa Linda Fregoso, Herman Gray, Carl Gutiérrez-Jones, Barbara Harthorn, Wahneema Lubiano, and Gerard Pigeon. Financial support came from the UCSB Interdisciplinary Humanities Center, the University of California Humanities Research Institute's Minority Discourse Initiative, the Chancellor, the Vice-Chancellor for Academic Affairs, the Provost of the College of Letters and Sciences, the Affirmative Action Office, the Academic Senate, the Office of Research, the departments of Sociology, English, Asian-American Studies, Chicano Studies, Film Studies, and Women's Studies, the Center for Black Studies, the Multicultural Center, and the Women's Center, all at UCSB. For financial support in preparing the book, we thank the UCSB Academic Senate, the UCSB Office of Research, and the UCSB Interdisciplinary Humanities Center. Darryl B. Dickson-Carr has been an invaluable and professional assistant to us and we thank him for all his efforts in making this book possible. Rachel Luft stepped in during the final stages of manuscript preparation, and for her talented perseverance we are very grateful. Finally, we would like to extend our appreciation to all the contributors to the volume for their hard work and patience in creating this book.

CHAPTER ONE

Introduction

AVERY F. GORDON AND CHRISTOPHER NEWFIELD

Multiculturalism has established itself as a major framework for analyzing intergroup relations in the United States at a time when it seems more obvious than ever that we cannot advance one inch as a society, or even remain where we are, without major changes in race relations in all their dimensions and new confrontations with racism. Yet as the term "multiculturalism" has appeared more and more frequently in current social and cultural debates, its meanings have become less and less clear. It acknowledges cultural diversity, but what else does it do? For some, it means renewed demands for assimilation in disguise. For others, it means a rejection of all the good things about "Western culture" that made America great. For still others, it is a simple descriptive fact about U.S. society that could serve as an everyday term for the interaction among the country's five major "racial" or "panethnic" groupings: African Americans, American Indians, Asian Americans, European Americans, and Latino Americans.

The term "multiculturalism" has become current in the last five years, but little has been resolved about its meanings and effects. Why does multiculturalism still produce so much simultaneous rejection, ambivalence, and interest? How do its meanings vary? What cultural and political traditions is multiculturalism replacing or displaying? What are the promises and limitations of multiculturalism as a rubric for new knowledges? What prospects

1

does it hold for racial reconstruction as the United States enters a period of general economic and geopolitical restructuring?

Mapping Multiculturalism is occasioned by these kinds of pressing questions as they surround the increasing ubiquity of the term. The essays collected here map the terrain of multiculturalism in its varied dimensions and effects and discuss its future. They question and challenge the coherence, value, and current uses of multiculturalism as a concept and practice. They engage in the debates over the term. They analyze and criticize. In many cases, they propose alternatives to the priorities that multiculturalism encourages.

Mapping Multiculturalism convenes a range of scholars and artists working, regardless of their formal affiliations, in sociology, history, film, literary criticism, inter-American relations, popular culture studies, political economy, critical legal studies, industrial and labor relations, Women's Studies, Chicano Studies, African-American Studies, Asian-American Studies, and American Indian Studies. One hallmark of the volume's contributors is that they link race's complex cultural questions to questions of power and institutional authority. They see race and racism not only as intricate cultural issues that involve all aspects of individual and group life, but as immersed in economic, international, political, and policy dynamics. These scholars and artists not only connect dimensions too long separated by the artificial boundaries and restricted missions of academic departments. They also put culture at the center of politics and society and thus change what culture itself means for the humanities and social sciences. Their endeavors suggest the prospect of the wholesale restructuring of social and cultural knowledge—including the establishment of alternative methods, histories, and future projects—to better fit the often suppressed actualities that are the United States.

Multicultural Dilemmas

Since multiculturalism resurfaced in the late 1980s, commentators have offered a series of conflicting accounts of the term's basic meaning. The authors of the present essays came together for a conference called "Translating Cultures: The Future of Multiculturalism?" at the University of California, Santa Barbara in November 1992, and since that time the debate has only become more involved. As background for the following essays, we offer here a short outline of some of these accounts. We proceed two by two for the sake of a little exaggerated clarity, and we do not hereby imply a consensus among the contributors about the meaning or the value of the term multiculturalism or their agreement with our description of its most commonly expressed internal conflicts.

1. *Is multiculturalism antiracist or oblivious to racism?* Multiculturalism in the 1980s sponsored renewed protests against white racism, and yet it appeared to replace the emphasis on race and racism with an emphasis on cultural diversity. Multiculturalism rejected racial subordination but seemed sometimes to support it.

On the one hand, multiculturalism was a delayed antibiotic to the race trends of the 1970s and 1980s, but better late than never. This period's attacks on various uses of civil rights gave certain kinds of white racism a new lease on life. The official doctrine of these attacks was not white supremacy, however, but color blindness. The backlash against civil rights achieved its greatest gains not by celebrating white racial consciousness but by officially restricting the relevance of race. It did not defend white racism but claimed that racism had passed from the scene.[1] Conservatives had contended that all Americans were living in a postracist era, and their strong attacks on multiculturalism suggested that the latter had indeed contested this claim. Multiculturalism, to the contrary, implied that race is everywhere. If you thought there were mainly two races, multiculturalism insisted there are at least five. If you thought race was a function of economics, multiculturalism told you race is also central to your personal identity. If you let policy talk convince you that race had been taken care of with antidiscrimination statutes, multiculturalism reminded you that it constitutes all social relations. If you were led to assume that American culture would be better if color-blind, then multiculturalism shocked you by showing that color consciousness *is* American culture. And if you came to believe that avoiding race meant peace, multiculturalism implied that avoiding it meant war. The dispersed and complicated presence of what Michael Omi and Howard Winant call "racial projects" suggested that racial thinking, including the white racist variety, had to be examined with a renewed intensity. Multiculturalism underwrote this broadened investigation.

Well, maybe. For, on the other hand, multiculturalism often avoided race. It designated cultures. It didn't talk up racism. It didn't seem very antiracist, and often left the impression that any discussion of cultural diversity would render racism insignificant. It was ambiguous about the inheritance and the ongoing presence of histories of oppression. It had the air of pleading for a clean start. It allowed "culture"'s aura of free play to attribute a creative power to racial groups that lacked political and economic power. It was propelled by culture's traditional belief in its ability to transcend social forces such as racial discrimination or class antagonism. It often played into the view that became backlash orthodoxy in the 1980s—that whites, in Charles Murray's terms, should "abandon the tenet at the core of liberal racial orthodoxy, that white racism explains black problems."[2] In an era in which the evasion of civil rights proceeded by asserting the already existing equality of all individuals and groups under law, multiculturalism chimed in with a similarly idealized equality, an equality among multiple cultures.

2. *Is multiculturalism cultural autonomy or common culture revisited?* Multiculturalism was an *attack* on America's putative common culture, descended from Europe, and yet it was also regarded as this common culture in drag. It was anti-Eurocentric *and* neo-Eurocentric. It promised independence to various cultures to negotiate their own relations to the national whole, *and* it looked like a cornerstone of national union in a more flexible guise. It underwrote alliances among racial minorities grounded in resistance to Euro-American norming, and yet also it gave white people a new way of horning in on the action.

The Canadian philosopher Charles Taylor, on behalf of the first possibility, wrote that "the demands of multiculturalism build on the already established principles of the politics of equal respect. If withholding the presumption is tantamount to a denial of equality, and if important consequences flow for people's identity from the absence of recognition, then a case can be made for insisting on the universalization of [equal respect] as a logical extension of the politics of dignity."[3] Equal respect would replace common culture as a nation's social cement. It would cope with the divisiveness so greatly feared by the common culture crowd, yet would do so by ensuring communities of color a position of independence and strength. Governance would flow from free cooperation and negotiation rather than from coercion or from traditions of white preeminence.

On the other hand, many noted that multiculturalism had a secret longing for the kind of commonality it pretended to replace. Liberal multiculturalism, in particular, had a very difficult time keeping its abstract principle of egalitarian plurality from becoming a set of shared values whose core components were to remain unspoken rules. Proponents sometimes blurted out things like, "If multiculturalism is to get beyond a promiscuous pluralism that gives every thing equal weight and adopts complete moral relativism, it must reach some agreement on what is at the core of American culture."[4] But a good deal of what is "core" to American culture, including the beneficence of capitalist democracy, was unchallenged by multiculturalism's emphasis on cultural respect. In general, granting reciprocity and diversity was compatible with insisting on some underlying cultural unity, as the history of cultural pluralism attests. Behind the celebration of diversity, then, lurked an ambivalent attachment to *e pluribus unum*, with *unum* regaining command when white-majority rule was disrespected or challenged.

3. *Is multiculturalism grounded in grassroots alliances or diversity management?* Multiculturalism sponsored contacts among people of color that avoided white mediation and oversight by white opinion. And yet, it became a popular term in managerial circles for controlling a multiracial and gendered workplace.

Sounding relatively upbeat, Kobena Mercer wrote that while the British version of multiculturalism was a Thatcherite tillering through the shoals of minority demands, "in the United States in the 1980s, against the background of neo-conservative hegemony, [multiculturalism's] connotations suggest a breakdown in the management of ethnic pluralism and draw attention to the question of possible alliances and coalitions between various groups."[5] Multiculturalism might not only support coalitions between groups but could also explore how intermixed and hybrid these groups were in the first place. As Trinh T. Minh-ha put it, "Multiculturalism does not lead us very far if it remains a question of difference only between one culture and another. Differences should also be understood within the same culture ... Intercultural, intersubjective, interdisciplinary. ... To cut across boundaries and borderlines is to live aloud the malaise of categories and labels; it is to resist simplistic attempts at classifying, to resist the comfort of belonging to a classification, and of *producing classifiable* works."[6] Or in Lisa Jones's terms, "First I arrived, fatter than an A&P chicken, just another black child in New York City born to a Jewish woman and a Negro man. ... For many years I thought the entire world was a band of Latin, black, and Chinese children dancing around the maypole and singing 'Qué Bonita Bandera' and the few Ukrainians who served us lunch."[7] Moving from fixed to mixed, multiculturalism sponsored an official identity that seemed to reflect social reality, and that enabled alliances to emerge from everyday life. The crisscrossed and in-from-everywhere things you do already were a better frame for coalitions than the formal categories of institutional processes, multiculturalism suggested. Hence so many explosive developments in concepts like the boundary-shattering borderlands, biraciality, and intersectionality. Multiculturalism reflected how coalition politics and even personal identity itself could evade the regulating effects of official procedure.

But at the same time multiculturalism was another name for that regulation. Driven by the imperatives of "global competition" and "changing demographics," diversity management arrived on the corporate scene to help business get, in R. Roosevelt Thomas's words, "beyond race and gender." Putting a spin on a Taylor-type liberalism of recognition, he argued that the "recognition of the uniqueness" of all individuals and groups could be a boon and not a hindrance to the corporate mission. Diversity management explicitly dehistoricized culture, race, and gender in order to offer *management* itself as the instrument for organizing differences. Employee differences would be encouraged but employee sovereignty over the use of difference would not. Multiculturalism alternately encouraged and suppressed the use of cultural difference to expand political democracy.

4. *Does multiculturalism link politics and culture or separate them?* Multiculturalism reinjected culture into politics and politics into culture, and yet it seemed just another page in the book of cultural substitutes.

Although acknowledging that cultural and political activity are by no means interchangeable, many thought multiculturalism might be a way of clarifying the broad sociopolitical relations that are woven into the ties among different cultures. This did not necessarily mean less attention to cultural artifacts themselves but more attention to their stakes. Cary Nelson noted that while "inclusion in an anthology is not equivalent to wielding effective political power," a multicultural anthology's "role in promoting core values that are . . . inclusive, in valuing . . . minority cultures, in familiarizing readers with different traditions, and in imaging a multicultural body politic can be significant."[8] Multiculturalist educators often saw cultural change leading to political change. "One of the central ways power is exercised in democratic societies," wrote Theresa Perry and James W. Fraser, "is in structuring discourse." By "defining a new conversational terrain," multiculturalism can "fundamentally reorder the ruling definitions of culture" and the distribution of power and resources.[9] Perry and Fraser's book on multicultural education has a number of chapters devoted to teaching, to the curriculum, and to "Shifting the Power, Shifting the Players" in school structures. Even Diane Ravitch, best known for her attacks on what she viewed as politicized, race-conscious education—especially the Afrocentric kind—argued that multiculturalism should pay attention to issues like "intergroup conflict" and "liv[ing] together in peace," although these are as political as they are cultural.[10] Multiculturalism regarded these as systematically interlinked.

But it also separated them. Multiculturalism sometimes celebrated cultural diversity while preserving a political core from being affected by this diversity. Gary Nash argued that "*pluribus* can flourish in these ways only if *unum* is preserved at the heart of the polity—in a common commitment to core political and moral values."[11] Cultural diversity often regarded culture, in Chandra Talpade Mohanty's terms, "as noncontradictory, as isolated from questions of history," as a realm of individual attitudes in which diversity leads to the reduction of prejudice but not to any change in the relative positions of various groups.[12] Cultural diversity noted differences in values and outlooks while ignoring the differences of social position that influence those values. Commentators on multiculturalism have repeatedly warned that it teeters on the brink of lapsing into insipid encouragement of variation with little idea of what difference it makes, like quality-of-life rankings that give more points to the city that has all four kinds of major-league sports teams rather than just two or three. Multiculturalism seemed torn between demanding and avoiding the full conjuncture of political, social, and cultural elements that affect our racialized everyday lives.

Some of these conflicts over the basic meaning of the mere word "multiculturalism" follow from the remarkable range of uses to which it's been put. It has indeed referred to "the life of various ethnic groups, racial diversity, gender differences, international issues, non-Western culture, cross-cultural methodologies, sexual preference, and the physically challenged."[13] But the term also manifests mainstream American irresolution about these four conflicts. Does a democratic United States require orderly racial hierarchy or racial equality? Does American society have one or many centers? Will the bottom or the top control intergroup conflict—will control be relatively popular or relatively elite? Finally, is cultural knowledge intrinsic to or outside of social relations and political life?

Obviously actual choices are not as binary as these heuristic questions suggest. There are combinations, and these vary from place to place. But the elements of these combinations are often at odds with one another, and reflect a profound and gendered ambivalence about these issues. It is simply not possible to invoke an "American Creed" of equality and democracy that rejects racist and exclusionary attitudes, for any such creed is in fact divided within itself. The creed is itself incessantly dubious about the benefits of racial equality, a nonhierarchical society, grassroots control of intergroup relations, and culture's influence on politics. Multiculturalism was hatched into an ambiguous relation to a "post-civil rights" white racial consensus that does not oppose but instead produces the Janus-faced—or Hydra-headed—contradictions around race, racism, and culture. Were there indeed a set of "core American values" ready to assert unambivalent antiracism and democratic equality against their opposites in American life, we would not be in our fourteenth decade of working toward racial Reconstruction of an America without slavery. Multiculturalism, adopting something like the eight stances we've described, has not escaped the conflicts within the consensus it attempts to revise.

The end of the Cold War has not brought the openings for national redevelopment that many hoped for. Part of the reason has been the successful replacement of the communist threat with equally global "ethnic threats" in the minds of many important opinion makers. The columnist Charles Krauthammer fired an early shot against an "intellectually bankrupt 'civil-rights community,'" which he claimed "poses a threat that no outside agent in this post-Soviet world can match"—"the setting of one ethnic group against another, the fracturing not just of American society but of the American idea."[14] Economic and social decline have been attributed not to inefficient and inequitable domestic policy but to allegedly uncontrollable international forces such as world wage competition and ethnic hatred. As we complete this introduction, anti-immigration sentiment in California has managed to link a pervasive sense of economic disintegration to undocumented minimum-wage laborers rather than, say, to avoidance of urban investment or the investment strategies of aerospace firms.

Current trends are tipping ambivalence into retrenchment and restriction. We recur to the four dilemmas listed earlier. First, around the pursuit of antiracist projects, the dominant tendency has recently been to define race not as a social force flowing from center to margins, from the powerful to the less so, but as the threat of chaos wielded by the margins and the powerless against the center. Mainstream common sense in post-Cold War America increasingly ties race consciousness not to First World sovereignty over other peoples (including others within) but to the others' power to transform the globe into a smoldering ruin.[15] "Race" and ethnicity are being radically remodeled into synonyms for the weak's senseless and self-destructive threats to the strong.

Second, recent years have enhanced the prestige of common culture as the primary defensive barrier to the dangers posed by the existence of ethnicity and race. Plurality is increasingly seen as a dangerous thing. Although Lynne Cheney, once christened by George F. Will as the "secretary of domestic defense," has temporarily shed her armor, excessive domestic differentiation remains a threat.[16] Cheney's liberal replacement at the National Endowment for the Humanities, Sheldon Hackney, was unable to devote his confirmation hearings to a theme like increased independence of and representation for "minority" cultures. He was instead compelled to denounce that form of "political correctness" that is "overly solicitous of minority groups and fashionable and trendy concerns."[17] Common values, shared principles, core beliefs, national purpose, bringing people together—all these, in this prescription to transcend actual economic and political processes, are invoked repeatedly against a nameless but standing threat of civil war.

Third, the post-Cold War policy mainstream traces domestic and international poverty and war to excessive local control. It rarely blames histories of excessive management or current top-down alliances of international and local officials. Manufacturing failures are attributed to union demands in a global economy rather than to the international institutions and behaviors that comprise that economy itself. Or trouble in the Los Angeles Unified School District is attributed to disruptive teachers, students, and unions rather than to funding decisions in Sacramento. Diversity management is thought to balance impartial and uniform structure with inclusion and openness; it supposedly offers the best virtues of moderation, in which the clash of vibrant, creative energies can be organized and reconciled by the comprehensive and balanced overview provided by the leadership above. Direct coalitions, on the other hand, attempt to make a supervisory wisdom amongst themselves. In the last few years, they have been repeatedly castigated as at worst divisive and at best antiquated in today's interconnected and transnational flows of resources and information.

Finally, the post-Cold War period has seen a circling of the wagons around increasingly ossified political processes, defending them against direct forms of participation and expression. One famous symptom was the attack on "political correctness," which amounted to an attack on the relevance of cultural identity, experience, and history to the governance of institutional affairs. Culture would be encouraged when controlled by a resurgent emphasis on "Western culture" as a repository of unchanging values, a giant "book of virtues." This meant keeping politics out of culture. Culture would be discouraged when it represented a local, changing, spontaneous, unregulated compilation of historicized individual perspectives. This meant keeping culture out of politics. Strong forms of multiculturalism see culture as expressing and changing how people see their place in the world. The aftermath of the Cold War tends to make the logic of the world invincible. The political process becomes inaccessible to everyday culture and the latter's insights into desire and need.

So we could end up with this conglomeration of the restrictive side of these four dilemmas. American society declares itself postracist and blames all racializing stigma on its targets, declaring exclusions to be the benefits of a common culture while managers supervise a self-perpetuating political and economic process in the name of diversity. That would be terrible. On the other hand, we're used to it. It's what's been going on, and for quite some time. Too many other countervailing things are happening in every kind of community in the United States for these four developments to achieve any simple success.

The essays in this book, though fully aware of problems like these, attempt to circumvent their conditions and outcomes. The essays have been grouped under general rubrics intended to highlight the ways in which they are *not* confined by the dilemmas we've been outlining here.

Overview of Organization

The book is organized into several sections.

Part I, "Mapping Multiculturalism," situates the concept in connection with a range of related discourses about race, culture, and power. It offers essays that link multiculturalism to existing race-based and/or oppositional discourses. How does multiculturalism connect to the history of antiracist struggle in the United States? How does its structure and efficacy compare to the oppositional narratives of postcolonial discourse? Does it build and improve upon Marxist notions of the liberation of oppressed groups, or does it reject (or sidestep) Marxism? Would such a sidestepping be helpful or not? Does multiculturalism continue civil rights protests, or is it a characteristic product of the post-civil rights period? How does it aid or hinder the civil rights effort to establish party-based social movements? Does it successfully expand race-based political activism into the cultural realm?

In "From Farce to Tragedy," Jon Cruz considers multiculturalism's relation to Marxist and post-Marxist forms of social critique. What has multiculturalism given up through its distance from Marxism? What role does multiculturalism play as it negotiates between global capitalism and the fiscal crisis of the state? Angela Y. Davis's "Gender, Class, and Multiculturalism" asks whether multiculturalism hasn't traded in the critical insights of the distinguished histories of antiracist and antisexist struggle for the dubious prerogatives of diversity management. She suggests that multiculturalism cannot accomplish the necessary transformation of social relations, and falls far short of the coalition work performed by women of color. M. Annette Jaimes Guerrero argues in "Academic Apartheid" that multiculturalism develops its notions of multiracial cultural interaction by ignoring the specifically colonial history of American Indian subjugation. She explores the reasons why decolonization remains the necessary theoretical and political model for the liberation of Native peoples. In "Like Being Mugged by a Metaphor," Wahneema Lubiano analyzes the role of state narratives in cultural projects of dominance and resistance. She makes a case for a radically transformative version of multiculturalism that, critically engaging the intersection of race, class, and gender, addresses the state directly. In "Multiculturalism's Unfinished Business," Christopher Newfield and Avery F. Gordon analyze multiculturalism as part of cultural pluralism's erratic attempts to diverge from white-norm assimilationism. They argue that if multiculturalism can build on the overlapping antiassimilationist insights of pluralism and nationalism, it can serve as a useful *starting point* for multiracial, democratic initiatives. Finally, Cedric J. Robinson's "Manichaeism and Multiculturalism" situates the current multiculturalism debate in the history of Western "specular imaginings" of racial difference. Focusing on the politics of knowledge, he argues that Manichaeism has produced atrocities *and* underwritten countervailing understandings of oppression; multiculturalism, Robinson suggests, has the potential to go beyond it.

Part II, "Rethinking the Political Subject," inquires into the ways that politics forms subjectivity and subjectivity informs politics. It brings both empirical and theoretical vantages on gender, class, and sexuality to the analysis of racialized and oppositional subjects. These papers ask a number of questions: How are contemporary events forming new types of collective political subjects? What are the effects of multiculturalism on established and newer modes of identity? What is a "minority" in a multicultural society? How does multiculturalism affect the ongoing projects of recovering historical and cultural identity in nondominant cultures? Are women of color a political class? Does multiculturalism reinforce traditional identity politics and individualistic political modes, like resentment? What are the current relations between theories of the subject and ethnic and gender studies?

Naming the impulse for a different world, Norma Alarcón calls it women of color. In "Conjugating Subjects," she describes how the concept "women of color" establishes a paradigm of multiple determinations and incommensurability for the project of coalition politics. By offering a form of affiliation that has shifted from sameness and commonality to the recognition of distinct social histories, such a concept goes beyond multiculturalism's merely pluralistic "politics of difference." Wendy Brown's "Injury, Identity,

Politics" elaborates, through reconsideration of Nietzsche's genealogy of the logics of *ressentiment*, the ways in which some of the emancipatory aims of politicized identity are subverted not only by the constraints of the political discourses in which its operations transpire, but by its own wounded attachments. Less a critique of identity politics than an analysis of its investments, Brown's essay calls for a reevaluation of the relationship between pain, political recognition, and the agonistic theater of forging alternative futures. In "Multiculturalism as Political Strategy," Cynthia Hamilton discusses the history of the manipulation of racial and ethnic identity as a management tool in the workplace. She argues that multiculturalism fails to see how multiracial workers are made political citizens of U.S. capitalism's "work culture," and thus can't imagine how racial or cultural differences might offer a real alternative. In "Racialization in the Post-Civil Rights Era," Michael Omi notes that in recent years the racial dimensions of political and social life have expanded rather than declined in significance. Omi identifies three key examples of this trend—the development of new racial subjects as a result of panethnic consciousness, the emerging crisis of white identity, and the increasing racialization of electoral politics—and discusses their implications for mainstream politics. "Screening Resistance," a conversation between filmmaker Lourdes Portillo and scholar Rosa Linda Fregoso, situates the formation of Latina/o identity in an international Latin American context.

Part III, "Reading Multicultural Narratives," examines already existing descriptions of U.S. culture as multicultural. These narratives have been around for a long time—they have played a central role in the survival of nondominant U.S. cultures. What do their readings of the country's multicultural past say about the uses of multiculturalism as a guide to the future? Do accounts of the U.S.-Mexico border imagine a multicultural entity? Does multiculturalism add to or detract from the realities of cultural conflict? How do these narratives locate individuals in racial groups? Does a "border" sensibility improve interaction across cultures and teach cures to fear and loathing? How has linguistic and cultural translation served as a paradigm of multiculturalism? What do existing narratives say about improving cross-cultural relations within and across national boundaries?

In "Language and Other Lethal Weapons," Antonia I. Castañeda examines the experience of children, principally Tejana farmworker children, as translators of culture. Basing her analysis on interviews with women whose families lived in various labor camps in the state of Washington during their childhood in the 1950s, Castañeda examines the cultural and political effects of that experience, suggesting that such translation is a process so fraught with conflict, subordination, and pain that it may not be understood by multiculturalism's notions of enlightening cultural exchange. Angie Chabram-Dernersesian's "The Spanish Colón-ialista Narrative" discusses an international form of multiculturalism, Spain's "Colón-ialista narrative" of 1992. Chabram-Dernersesian offers a multinational analysis that demonstrates how the Colón narrative enlists subjugated U.S. identities to develop a fully Eurocentric paradigm of Hispanic multiculturalism. In "Multiculturalism and Racial Stratification," Neil Gotanda reads Judge Joyce Karlin's sentencing colloquy in the widely publicized case of *People v. Soon Ja Du*. Gotanda shows how Karlin, justifying probation in the shooting of African-American teenager Latasha Harlins by Korean grocer Du Soon Ja, used multi*cultural* techniques to establish a racial hierarchy of model and monitored minorities. Ramón Gutiérrez's "The Erotic Zone: Sexual Transgression on the U.S.-Mexican Border" argues that many borderland Americans use negative sexual stereotypes to suppress the dependence of white middle-class prosperity on the intimate presence of Mexicans. Gutiérrez suggests that "multicultural" contact easily coexists with polarizing domination and paranoia, leaving the conjunction of sexuality and economics untouched. In "Site-seeing through Asian America," Renee Tajima explores the complexities of Asian-American identity across the major changes in Asian-American social positions over the last four decades. The themes of her partly autobiographical narrative include the decline of Asian-American assimilation and the continual interaction between Asian- and African-American histories of protest.

Part IV, "Multi-Capitalism," connects group and individual identity to recent changes in national and international economics. The section brings diverse expertise to bear on concrete questions of the relation of culture to political economy. Multiculturalism arises in a context in which culture is a commodity to be bought and sold in a multinational marketplace altered by the globalization of production, the rapid development of international finance, the simultaneous advance of high-tech and sweated labor in the United States, U.S. domination of cultural markets, and the hybridization of nearly all cultures around the world. How does multiculturalism translate this rapidly changing political economy? What is the future of local culture in the context of the internationalization of culture and economy? Can local cultures resist transnational capitalism without directly confronting it? Does connecting culture to economics improve the opportunity for cross-cultural alliances, or not, and why?

Richard P. Appelbaum, in "Multiculturalism and Flexibility," reviews Marx's arguments about globalization in order to investigate the emergence of new transnational forms of labor exploitation, the "information-based economy," and the meaning of flexibility. Drawing on his study of apparel production in Los Angeles and Asia, he reflects on multicultural capitalism. In "The Class Question in Global Capitalism," Edna Bonacich argues that class remains a life-threatening aspect of social organization and social dynamics in the profoundly racialized manufacturing sectors that thrive in Los Angeles. She suggests ways multiculturalism might link race and gender to union struggles and other kinds of worker response to the ongoing consequences of the capital-accumulation process. Appelbaum and Gregg Scott's "Travelogue" offers a short visual essay on the factory districts in Los Angeles and various Asian cities. In "Unified Capital and the Subject of Value," Paul Smith explores the meaning of German reunification. Focusing on the rise of racism and xenophobia and the struggle over the stakes of an authentic German culture, Smith argues that these are aggravated by factitious unifications of capital and labor; the need to oppose these while opposing white supremacy may be a major lesson for U.S. multiculturalists. Patricia Zavella's "Living on the Edge" examines the problems of Chicano families living in poverty in the American Southwest. Arguing against "culturalist" arguments that attribute Chicano employment patterns to having better work attitudes than African Americans, Zavella indicates how culturalism, in conjunction with American family ideology, veils institutional discrimination and exclusion, and ignores the differences between the specific situations of different communities of color.

Part V, "Multiculturalism and the Production of Culture," explores artistic production as a type of social movement that can not only represent traditionally marginalized groups and individuals but refashion public policy. Here, the papers address such questions as: How can multiculturalism be reworked to more closely suit the needs of the cultures it claims to defend? What lies beyond multiculturalism? What will the future of cultural self-determination look like? How do nondominant cultures define winning cultural contests? How do we define a cultural community? What are the histories that have created cultural identities and movements? What is an artistic coalition, especially across cultural difference? How is multiculturalism produced by cultural institutions?

Steve Fagin's "Machine Talk" reflects on his experiences with presenting his video on the overthrow of Philippine president Ferdinand Marcos in 1986, *The Machine That Ate Bad People*. Fagin discusses his efforts to enact political expression through televisual fragmentation rather than coherent metanarratives and interacts with a UCSB audience that is sometimes critical of his format. In " 'It's All Wrong, but It's All Right,' " George Lipsitz explores the question of what popular culture consumers and artists do not know, and the "mistakes" they make while trying to figure things out. He suggests that "mistaken" ideas often contain crucial insights about the social construction of identity and the unreliability of surface messages. Lisa Lowe's "Imagining Los Angeles in the Production of Multiculturalism" analyses how the Los Angeles Festival of the Arts (1990) obscured the divergence between the aesthetic representation of cultural difference and differences in material resources. She identifies multiculturalism's tendency to produce consensus by homogenizing differences while also identifying oppositional moments in the festival, ones growing out of juxtapositions of different cultures that acknowledge contradiction without asserting generalizable oppressor/oppressed relations. And in "A Style Nobody Can Deal With," Tricia Rose investigates the postindustrial urban context of hip-hop culture and the political implications of hip-hop style. Analyzing the South Bronx as a critical symbol for urban ruin in the United States, Rose shows how hip-hop artists, who were designated as surplus labor, instead transformed obsolete vocational training skills in such fields as printing, drafting, electronics repair, and auto mechanics into the basis for artistic commentary on the crossroads of lack and desire in African-Diasporic communities.

These essays explore the contradictory and powerful meanings of the concept of multiculturalism and reject its terms altogether when that becomes necessary. Above all, the forces they describe, and the force of the work itself, suggest a comprehension, a momentum, a passion that means come what may, there shall be no going back.

Notes

1. Joe R. Feagin and Melvin P. Sikes recall that "in a 1981 book *Wealth and Poverty*, once called the 'Bible of the Reagan-Bush administrations,' economist George Gilder declared there was no need for government action to assist black Americans because it was virtually impossible to find a serious racist in a position of power and because major discrimination had been effectively abolished in the United States" (*Living with Racism: The Black Middle-Class Experience* [Boston: Beacon Press, 1994], 6).

2. Charles Murray, "The Reality of Black America," *Times Literary Supplement,* 22 May 1992: 10. Murray, reviewing Andrew Hacker's *Two Nations*, is claiming that "white upper-middle-class society" is in the process of abandoning this tenet.

3. Charles Taylor, *Multiculturalism and "The Politics of Recognition,"* with commentary by Amy Gutmann, ed., Steven C. Rockefeller, Michael Walzer, and Susan Wolf (Princeton, N.J.: Princeton University Press, 1992), 68.

4. Gary B. Nash, "The Great Multicultural Debate," *Contention* 1:3 (spring 1992): 24.

5. Kobena Mercer, " '1968': Periodizing Postmodern Politics and Identity," in *Cultural Studies,* ed. Lawrence Grossberg, Cary Nelson, and Paula Treichler (New York: Routledge, 1992), 449.

6. Trinh T. Minh-ha, *When the Moon Waxes Red: Representation, Gender and Cultural Politics* (New York: Routledge, 1991), 107–8.

7. Lisa Jones, "How I Invented Multiculturalism," in *Bulletproof Diva: Tales of Race, Sex, and Hair* (New York: Doubleday, 1994), 7.

8. Cary Nelson, "Multiculturalism Without Guarantees: From Anthologies to the Social Text," *Journal of the Midwest Modern Language Association* 26:1 (spring 1993): 48.

9. Theresa Perry and James W. Fraser, "Reconstructing Schools as Multiracial/Multicultural Democracies: Toward a Theoretical Perspective," in *Freedom's Plow: Teaching in the Multicultural Classroom*, ed. Perry and Fraser (New York: Routledge, 1993), 18.

10. Diane Ravitch, "In the Multicultural Trenches," *Contention* 1:3 (spring 1992): 31.

11. Nash, "Multicultural Debate," 25.

12. Chandra Talpade Mohanty, "On Race and Voice," in *Beyond a Dream Deferred: Multicultural Education and the Politics of Excellence*, ed. Becky W. Thompson and Sangeeta Tyagi (Minneapolis: University of Minnesota Press, 1993), 56.

13. Jerry G. Gaff, "Beyond Politics: The Educational Issues Inherent in Multicultural Education," *Change* (January–February 1992): 32.

14. Charles Krauthammer, "An Insidious Rejuvenation of the Old Left," *Los Angeles Times*, 24 December 1990: B5. Conservatives frequently attack women's studies programs in tandem with ethnic studies. Culturally conservative journalists, during 1990–92, seemed more wary of the danger to national unity posed by multicultural programs, but this does not imply reconciliation with women's studies in the least. For an interesting set of responses to the PC-bashing rejection of feminism, see the *Women's Review of Books* for February 1992.

15. For the matching graphics, see the punctured and burning beach-ball globe illustrating Robert D. Kaplan's cover story, "The Coming Anarchy," *Atlantic Monthly* 273:2 (February 1994): 44–76.

16. George F. Will, "Literary Politics," *Newsweek,* 22 April 1991: 72. As a paranoid rapture, the passage stands the test of time: we must attend, Will wrote, "to the many small skirmishes that rarely rise to public attention but cumulatively condition the nation's cultural, and then, political, life. In this low-visibility, high-intensity war, Lynne Cheney is secretary of domestic defense. The foreign adversaries her husband, Dick, must keep at bay are less dangerous, in the long run, than the domestic forces with which she must deal. Those forces are fighting against the conservation of the common culture that is the nation's social cement."

17. Sheldon Hackney, quoted in Adam Clymer, "Clinton Nominee Defends Himself," *New York Times,* 26 June 1993: A6.

PART I

Mapping Multiculturalism

CHAPTER TWO

From Farce to Tragedy

Reflections on the Reification of Race at Century's End

JON CRUZ

This essay is about multiculturalism. But it is not written in the spirit of benevolent engineering, or as a celebration of ethnotourism, or as added applause to cultural pluralism as a goal in itself. These sensibilities have their virtues and champions. What I propose is that we step back and look at multiculturalism as part of a *social logic* of late capitalism and as a cultural feature at the intersection of economic globalization and the fiscal-domestic crisis of the state. This conjuncture is culturally charged, and part of this new charge is conveyed in the promises and the antagonisms surrounding multiculturalism. As a term that hosts competing claims, multiculturalism is more than a cultural site for pluralism; it is also a cultural fact under siege. There are many ways to approach multiculturalism. The one offered here evaluates multiculturalism as *symptomatic* of our particular historical conjuncture within the social formation of late capitalism.

To present this perspective I have chosen to return first to some well-worn—and, many might argue, worn-out—issues that are central to Marx: *fetishization, reification,* and the importance of *critique.* I proceed with some trepidation since so much of contemporary cultural theory frames itself as "post-Marxist." Plagued by its own history, Marxism is in disrepute, and so to draw on Marx is a troubled and troubling enterprise these days. Marxism's problems are numerous, but there are two very general and overlapping developments, one worldly, the other quite academic, that compromise any use of Marx. In the first case, the humanist and emancipatory vision that oriented much of Marx's writings, meant to flourish in proportion to the withering away of the state, instead atrophied into authoritarian statism. Accompanying the rise and fall of Stalinism is a history of ideas quick to argue that Marx authorized the politics and practices of Stalin. Conflation aside, for those who detest any aspect Marxism as an interpretive tool, the withering away of the Soviet superpower is seen as a glorious testimony to the triumphant virtue of a corporate capitalism that is now even more free to move beyond its national confinement to an even larger global reach.

Joining the recoil from Marxism is the much larger intellectual indictment of the entire epistemological and ideological underpinnings of the Enlightenment in which Marx's writings are embedded. In this criticism, the roots of rationality have been argued to be nothing more than a set of moral fictions that underwrite power and domination. In the interrogation of the Enlightenment, the rationalist table has been turned: Descartes's *Discourse on Method* has been overtaken and inverted by the methods of discourse; Kant's *Critique of Pure Reason* has been undermined by the dismissal of Reason. Certainly the theoretical moves have been significant. In its classical conception, Reason was to have purged metaphysics; at least that was the dream of rationalism. But Reason turned out to be just another metaphysical facade. We have come to distrust the not-so-hidden hands of essentialism, universalism, patriarchy, sexism, and racism that prop up modernity (inasmuch as they prop up social formations in general). In the new spirit of antiuniversalism and antiessentialism, we have moved away from Grand Reason and Big Truth in exchange for multiple, increasingly proliferating, and characteristically embattled arenas occupied by lots of little reasons and little truths. In the process, the notion of a post-Enlightenment antiuniversalism has fostered a new notion of reason (spelled with a small "r"), and endorses a sense of epistemological safety in the turn to local knowledge in the present. Theoretical downsizing appears to compete in the atmosphere of a new and peculiar uneasiness, and in a world of flux where few things come with guarantees. The lesson is registered in the most reflexive theorizing, which displays a shrewd wariness for the metaphysics residing in all rational fronts.[1] In this larger scenario of epistemological crisis, Reason has been strip-searched to reveal the naked profile of patriarchy behind the ideological fig leaf and the justifications used to hold up class, racial, and cultural domination have been rendered visible. This critical assessment has been carried over ecologically to Marxian theory and has, in some cases, warranted Marx's total dismissal. Today we are awash in the glee of market vindication touted in the references to a "new world order" and "globalization," while the best and brightest seek an interpretive haven in cultural identities and cultural fragments. Yet it is precisely because of the new developments tying capitalism and cultural forces together that Marx's insights warrant revisiting.

As capitalism expands, so too do new identity formations. Both work within newly expanded political economies of money and meanings. But as long as there is the perception of open territory for the movement of economic capital and symbolic capital, and where money and identities can be made and allowed to circulate, there is a sense of progress (understood as economic and psychocultural growth). Both logics thrive on the achievement of something tangible and substantial. But what if we view these as two social constellations yoked to a deeper ideology of the marketplace? For if liberal democracy can be likened to an open market that sells investment stock in the new currencies of political pluralism, then it would appear that multiculturalism is part of a paid dividend to be enjoyed collectively by civil society. Market metaphors aside, there is perhaps much wishful thinking here.

I am sympathetic with and yet troubled by the theoretical predicaments and the societal contexts in which multiculturalism is currently configured. Coming together in both are mixtures of emancipation and paralysis, and a sense of intellectual freedom accompanied by political default. In the contemporary context, capitalism and social identities tend to appear as separate and distinct realms with little to tie them together. But perhaps multiculturalism is this link. This proposition deserves to be examined. I will argue that, in the American context, multiculturalism now mediates capitalism and modern social identities, and these spheres, in turn, are connected in a conjuncture that was first opened by the political liberalism of the civil rights era but is now being joined by a deepening fiscal crisis of the state associated with large-scale social disinvestment over the last two decades. Understanding this connection may also give us a way to assess (borrowing from Raymond Williams) the structure of not-so-good feelings in which multiculturalism takes on a double life of troubled parentage.

I turn to Marx in order to bring these mixed sensibilities associated with multiculturalism into a particular kind of focus. The premise is that some aspects of Marx's analytical vision are helpful in framing and elucidating problems that come with identity formations and multiculturalism. Given what I've already said about the critique of Enlightenment, I confess in advance to indulging in what some might call the temptation of retrograde humanism and unoriginal sin.

Retrieving Critique: An Excursus

Two concerns need to be raised. First, the kind of *critique* carried out by Marx—specifically the attempt to interpret the modern social formation we call capitalism—seems to have atrophied within contemporary cultural theory.[2] The result appears as an erosion of the interpretive will to think through the fragments of modernity and to forge linkages between cultural forms and sociohistorical formations. In some cases this abandonment of critique is condoned through selective interpretations of poststructuralism.[3] This move is not innocent or naive in associating the theoretical framing of "structures" with a teleologically contaminated *structuralism* (and, by extension, essentialism). In some cases, essentialism is avoided by a retreat from systems and histories to the present and the local. There are analytical virtues to this move. It has restored the problem of meaning, retrieved the value of hermeneutics, and brought social and cultural analysis back to an appreciation for the nuances of flesh-and-blood subjects who must negotiate through sensuous knowledge-making the conditions of everyday life.

My second concern is that there are also costs in the move to jettison Marx as damaged progeny of the Enlightenment. One such cost is that the insights made possible by Marx's notions of *fetishization* and *reification* under capitalism have been eclipsed.[4] I want to retrieve some of these insights because I think they are needed in order to bring some important aspects of multiculturalism into relationship with economic globalization and the new kind of cultural work facilitated by the state. To do this requires a brief excursus into some key aspects of Marx's concepts of *critique, fetishization,* and *reification.*

For Marx, the rise of capitalism was more than an economic system; it was fundamentally a new, socially organized form of life. Understanding capitalism as a social system required an analysis of the commodity, the most discrete but analytically crucial *fragment* within the capitalist social formation. What is pertinent in Marx's starting point is how commodities as the keys to the social could be *thought*—not simply as distinct and discrete items or things in themselves, with self-enclosed identities and essential attributes, but as embodiments of practical human activity. As moments within a larger continuum, commodities refracted human practices enmeshed in historically specific social relations; commodities functioned as *social hieroglyphics*.[5] Individuals, groups, and classes, however, are seldom able to comprehend themselves as embedded in the larger web of social relations, or to grasp critically the modes of domination that hold and shape these relations in their social form. What reigned instead was the triumphant effect of the market conceived as a natural and autonomous reality. Under capitalism and commodity production, the social identities of individuals were increasingly mediated by commodity production and regulated, too, as if they were *things*, reified along with commodities. Marx called this fundamental misrecognition *commodity fetishization*. Understanding and grasping the conditions that generate specific social relations and the forms that they take—commodities, value, production, circulation, identity, and so on—is included in what Marx meant by *critique*.

Weberian and Western Marxist social theory from Lukács and Gramsci to Adorno and Althusser expands upon these insights, though with different accents. By blending Marx's method of critique, Weber's theory of rationalization, and Freud's contributions to the problem of the unconscious, Western Marxism, while not a unified theory, was able to think through the processes of modern capitalist bureaucratization and the further developments of social fragmentation and atomization. With the growing emphasis on the cultural sphere, Western Marxism identified ways in which an expanding and changing capitalism was able to create new requirements of knowledge and specialization, including more distinctive and specific mechanisms of identification. Individuals under modernization (though still conceptualized in the framework of class reductionism) also became increasingly more *reflective* and *contemplative* of their own particular activity.[6] This activity, however, was not based on a consciousness that grasped the wider, underlying, and systemic social relations that generated one's identity. On the contrary, as capitalism penetrated deeper and deeper into the social formation, modern consciousness was increasingly pushed away from the capacity for critique. Driven to the surfaces as a *social effect*, the contours of consciousness through individuality became increasingly fragmented.[7]

This kind of perspective is like salt in an open wound. It is disconcerting to think that we have such little autonomy and self-control. It grates against and casts aspersions on the civil religion of individualism (American or otherwise). But while it has its problems, the concept of critique is a tool we can use to help us think through the fragmented surfaces of cultural forms that we inherit, and in which we live out our lives. It can give us ways to pose and grasp the links between different social sites, and see them as relations. Most important, it helps us come to terms with the historically specific and materially grounded modes of *power* and *inequality* that condition social relations and underwrite ostensibly distinct and discrete cultural forms—like identity formations and multiculturalism.

I do not want to suggest, however, that simply stepping back to Marx is enough. There has been and there continues to be great debate around what should be jettisoned as well as retained and reconstructed in Marx's very sweeping notions of historical materialism. Marx may have criticized religion, but the presupposition that human history has a transcendental telos that unfolds initially with the transgression of innocence through alienation is a variation on the thesis of original sin, and the idea that the human predicament is eventually to be overcome by final redemption shares an eschatological vision as much as any great religion. The inherent teleology and appeal to transcendentalist solutions places *part*—but not the whole—of Marxian theory squarely in the larger tradition of Western Judeo-Christian metaphysics. Marxism is also shaped by the Romantic movements of the late eighteenth and early nineteenth centuries. From these layered teleological legacies it takes on the dual pressures of dread and euphoria that mark the transition from modernity to postmodernity. Furthermore, race and gender, now recognized as major social, cultural, and historical mountains, were barely envisioned due to the peculiar blind spots induced by the privilege of what C. W. Mills called the "labor metaphysic."

The theory of reification is just as much a way of seeing as it is a crude overstatement. Indeed, overcoming reification is precisely what is attempted in the critical self-reflective dimensions within identity formations where individuals reject the inherited categories and social classifications that are structured in domination and marginalization. This is particularly the case in the United States for racialized groups. These problems and limits noted here mark many of the tensions that run through the whole of Western Marxism, and much of poststructuralism, postmodernism, and feminist and race theorizing. Such theoretical developments represent, in part, a series of complicated and overlapping moves that use as well as reject Marxian notions. These problems aside, historical materialism suggests a way to decenter everyday consciousness by rethinking the immediate, practical, experiential, and concrete in relation to social and historical developments. And this angle of analysis is where Marx suggested we should hedge our analytical bets about where things might matter.

Multiculturalism as a Social Hieroglyphic

I go through the motions of this perhaps tedious retrieval because we have moved lately into new modes of theorizing that restore what Marx tried to reverse. For in cultural analysis today there is an end-of-century intellectual nervousness that seeks a presumed epistemological safety in the ahistoricism of the temporal, the turn to the *local*, and the *cultural fragment*. In essence, cultural fragments—abstractions—have been exonerated as the sites of new (misplaced) concreteness. The surfaces of the social have been restored with a new sense of cultural depth. These theoretical sensibilities sometimes overlap the anguished struggle over the meanings *inside* identity formations. To be safe, to avoid metaphysical contamination, there is sometimes comfort in being wary of the global, the historical, and the structural. This, I think, is one of the conditions we must acknowledge and work to contextualize if we are to begin a critical assessment of the tensions associated with identity formations and multiculturalism, especially when the latter involves the evacuation of any critical reflection on the social formation.

Identity formations are not strictly comparable to commodities. Yet they come into being as political, social, moral—and classed, raced, and gendered—currencies; they draw their value not in and from themselves as isolated entities, but from within a socially and historically embedded grid of meanings and multiple powers of investment, brokerage, and exchange. Their values are not fixed and frozen, but subject to shifting configurations of power and multiple modes of appropriation that refract underlying social relations. This is so, not because social identities are distinct and unique, or based on pristine and preformed essences, but because they are constructed in the shifting field of historically constituted social relations. Governed by *socially embedded transactions*, cultural distinctions through difference function as temporal, transient elements. This means that identity formations are not the result of autonomous, self-fashioning subjects engaged in a pluralist field of options. Theoretical reflection might enable us to generate great inventories of existing and possible combinations of identity formations, but situated subjects are not necessarily free to pick and choose among the cornucopia of options to make themselves anew. (The desire to make the world anew, to scrap bad histories and begin over again, with the belief that this involves not much more than self-willed redefinitions of identity, is fundamentally American. This is as much a part of John Winthrop's vision in 1630 of a Puritan-inspired "city upon a hill" where a new liturgy could be practiced, as it is of the most recent notion of dramaturgy where new selves can be self-fashioned through conscious, reflexive performativity.)[8] On the contrary, social identity formations are subject to the conditions of social surroundings and are traversed (unevenly, of course) by various institutional forces and relations. Identity formations are shaped not by fiat but by social limits and determinations. This underscores the importance of assessing *identity formations* as *social hieroglyphics.*

If the commodity as a social hieroglyphic refracts *class* formations, identity politics under late capitalism refracts the field in which antagonistic relations orbit around struggles over social and cultural—hence political—*classifications* as well as class relations. The analytical sensibility inherent in Marx's notion of critique, however, is not what characterizes the debates and analyses surrounding multiculturalism. Instead, what seems to be more common are frameworks of fragmentation, particularization, fetishization, and reification. In the absence of attempts to ground these developments in the context of historically specific social formations, analyses too frequently begin—and end—with invoking yet abandoning the social through identity politics. Here, Lukács's claim that reification is tantamount to forgetting comes back to haunt.

Economic Globalism versus the Cultural State

What kind of social formation is useful for assessing multiculturalism in the contemporary American context? I would like to sketch an analytic framework that begins to frame just how and why reification and fetishization capture much of the contemporary terrain upon which our understanding of multiculturalism and identity formations unfolds. Let me begin with *race* and the American state. It cannot be denied that race in the United States is a state-constructed and state-sanctioned mode of institutional materiality anchored in the fine print of juridical-legal language and shored up by apparatuses of what Weber called *legitimate force*. Let's just quickly recap the longer legacy. The state stood firmly behind slavery until the Civil War fractured the juridical-legal basis for the "peculiar institution." But even after abolition, the state turned its back to the systematic practices of social control exercised (de facto as well as de jure) over African Americans through institutionalized terror and violence. It was in the name of the state that the military conducted the ethnic cleansing of American Indians and the installment of the reservation system; we still have racial *nations* within the state. It was military conquest and then the imposition of the juridical-legal courts that rationalized the expropriation and transference of Mexican-held land out of Mexican hands. With the Chinese, the state denied citizenship to and excluded already emigrated people, by a series of acts culminating in the Chinese Exclusion Act of 1882, a policy that was modified and extended in various ways to Japanese, Filipino, Korean, and Asian-Indian immigrants in the United States. And many states enforced antimiscegenation laws well into the twentieth century. These examples all hinge on highly institutional-ized and formalized juridical-legal racial codifications that operated as state law (which is precisely why "race" and "ethnicity" should not be conflated as interchangeable terms, a tendency common in the social sciences).

But shortly after mid-century a qualitatively and formally new *cultural transformation* of the polity took shape. With the African American-led civil rights movement during the 1960s—a mere thirty years ago—and the ensu-ing "rights" legislation, the state began to alter substantially its long history of much older racializing strategies that predate the modern national for-mation and reach backward some three centuries. What is interesting about this modern conjuncture is that the state began to adopt, rather feebly, what we might call an ideological-culturalist realignment in terms of *race,* by re-coding and reframing the meaning of race with the rise of "rights" rhetoric and legislation.[9] It is in this conjuncture that the rhetoric and symbols of egalitarianism, long a site of deep contention, were given greater ideological weight, were thrust into broader circulation, and were invested with a new sense of cultural and political capital for *raced* groups and new sociopolitical social alliances (e.g., the New Left vis-à-vis "free speech," and what was ini-tially called the "women's movement"). None of these groups looked like the classic proletariat, a fact that also quickened the broader cultural turn in Marxian theory. These new groups and their affiliated social movements in-terrogated not just corporatism and the bourgeois social contract, but the entire institutional infrastructure of civil society.

Emerging in tandem with the impact of the civil rights movement was the politicized reemergence of additional raced groups—Chicanos, Native Americans, and Asian Americans (hitherto "Orientals")—each holding to, and in some cases making for the first time, their historical memories and raced identities in more reflexive ways. This cultural development is also im-portant because it marks the high point of modern democratic liberalism. The state's response to political struggles over the Enlightenment-rooted bourgeois social contract altered the *political surfaces* of the social terrain and made possible—indeed began to sanction—the modern framework within which identity formations took shape in dialogue with state power. This process has since expanded into multiculturalism. Of course American society (not the polity) has always been "multicultural," but only recently has this been recognized and *named* as such in the context of the modern state's attempt to work with a politically pragmatic blend of cultural benevolence and statecraft to configure its own legitimacy. In negotiating radical egalitarian struggles launched by raced and gendered constituents, the "racial state" took a significant cultural turn.[10]

Centrifugal Capitalism and Centripetal Culture

But there is more to the conjuncture. Just as the cultural dimensions of the state opened up new spaces for raced and gendered identity formations to be understood as such—that is, *in themselves* and *for themselves*—the fiscal crisis of the state began to register. At this point two antagonistically spiraling dynamics began to expand. On the one hand, a *centrifugal capitalism* began to push outward, disengaging from domestic commitments in pursuit of transnational strategies. On the other hand, a *centripetal culture* shaped in part by political developments and aided by new tiers of internal mass-media development augmented the process of identity formations. But key in this conjuncture was the beginning of a significant social split between global forces and domestic developments. It is with the deepening antagonisms as well as intimate ties between *global capitalism* and state-sanctioned *domestic culturalism* that the problems of racial reification—first as historically constructed farce, and now as deepening tragedy—begin to unfold along modern fetishized and reified lines. For as the polity began to give racial groups the recognition of political subjects with civil rights, the economy began to move in directions that would quite quickly strip away the political resolve to underwrite this important cultural turn. As capitalism began to spin centrifugally outward, dispersing and dispensing more and more of its material resources to maintain *transnational trenches and alliances,* liberal democracy was challenged by conservative realignments, and in some spheres became increasingly frail, embattled, and brittle, particularly over public expenditures associated with fiscal liberalism. Deindustrialization began to take its toll in the 1970s and throughout the 1980s. With the Reagan-Bush administration, economic deregulation promoted and intensified capital flight. But coupled with this is what we might call *social deregulation*—best understood as the *deregulation of the bourgeois-liberal social contract.* Many analysts have noted the ties between deindustrialization, capital flight, and the erosion of jobs and tax bases, all of which have been increasingly linked to the globalization of late capitalism. But social deregulation entails increasingly the shriveling of the state's commitment to domestic support, including the domestication of social conflict through public spending. The surplus populations of abandoned social zones have expanded with the deterioration of capital investment. These developments reflect the erosion of the state's capacity to keep capital investment at home.[11] In this dystopian scenario, the logic of law and order surges to the forefront of public discourse as the primary form of legitimate social spending and as the fiscal policies of domesticity under siege. Today, the construction of prisons outpaces that of schools and universities, and the expansion of the carceral society signals the response of power to social change through state intervention and the necessity of "policing the crisis." In this framework, the massive conflagration in South-Central Los Angeles that came on the heels of the Rodney King verdict was not simply about the perception of a miscarriage of justice, but signaled instead the subterranean mass frustration of those social sectors most bypassed by the new globalism's obvious disinterest in them, and the failure to include them in the cornucopia of late capitalism's new worldly post-civil rights, post-Cold War prowess. Rage, the fruit of long, structural disenchantment, seizes opportunities to engage in what is left of a rapidly contracting public sphere. Incidently, the chants in the streets of "No justice, no peace," in the context of the largest urban upheaval in postwar American history, should be read against the erroneous postmodern claims that grand narratives no longer exercise their ideological grip and collective affect has withered.[12] That such social conflagrations stop short of what Hobsbawn called "collective bargaining by riot" aids the hasty and ahistorical analysis of these actions as nothing but mass criminal hooliganism. The poorest of the poor are too quickly conceived of as primarily a symptom of demographic mobility,[13] and come to signify the worst-case scenario of the arrested development or collapse of traditional communitarian morality.[14] In the process, the social deregulation of a society paralyzed by fiscal hemorrhage and the multiplication of "cultural differences" lends itself to the political opportunism of quick fixes.

The crisis in which we are now steeped is shaped by a deepening contradiction. On the one hand, there is the growing refusal to pay for the egalitarian reformism of the culturalist move launched and sanctioned during the civil rights movement with the state's attempt to amend the history of racial exclusion through policies addressing class, racial, and gender inclusion. On the other hand, there is the globalizing pressure of capitalism to *abandon the will to social investment within the national-domestic sphere.* It is in this conjuncture that neoconservatism as a post-civil rights-era discourse emerged to broker this crisis in the form of conservative populism. From the rise of the Moral Majority to Rush Limbaugh's mass-mediated conservative forum, conservative populism has moved forward with an interrogation of what Samuel Huntington some time ago called the "democratic distemper," by which he meant the state's willingness to *tolerate* the civil rights movement and related liberalist-driven cultural aberrations of American politics.[15] In the conjuncture, the academic squabbles over "political correctness" take on their amplified sound and fury, but are seldom understood as skirmishes in the shadow of what has come to matter much more: the apparent triumph of the new and deepening refusal of liberal democracy to embrace and pay for its own social ideals. In essence, any ideals outside of individuals in the marketplace appear in eclipse. A most revealing symptom of this junctural crisis is the rhetoric of "privatization," the lingua franca of social deregulation.

In the conjuncture, numerous clever diatribes in the form of misplaced concreteness chastise the academy for the decline in intellectual property values induced by too many resident aliens in the academy.[16] Here lies the rub: the academy is one of the only places left in modern civil society where reason, power, and tradition are supposed to be interrogated, examined, made transparent, and held accountable to publics in whose name they purport to operate. And not every voice in the academy is willing to sing praise to either statecraft or the now globally shaped forces of technocratic rationality. The flash points appear, not surprisingly, around themes of institutional contamination—and nothing these days grounds debates quicker than racialized topics like multiculturalism. Behind the manifest argument that "diversity" promotes a decline in standards, a falling rate of intelligence, and thus an increasingly dulled faculty, is a more latent realization: the academy's *critical* faculties have expanded in their sharpness as they take on increasingly more democratic representation. New angles of vision, additional and competing interpretations, and expanded debate give a vibrancy to democratic institutions, and democratic vibrancy is, by definition, hard to manage. The harangues against the academy, which too often pivot on multiculturalism, convey a nostalgia for cultural boundaries that were once less pervious. In this regard, the voices against multiculturalism echo with what they purport to detest: *tribalism*. It is through modernity's transformations that an older "insiders" tribalism of the *familiar,* hitherto beyond reproach, is being challenged by the new and problematic tribalism of social and cultural "outsiders."

The Social Logic of Multiculturalism

But multiculturalism is by no means a panacea. Ironically—and tragically—the ideology of privatization permeates the reification of identity formations: social groups are increasingly compelled to define their identity boundaries, which locate them and mark them as distinct. Moreover, these boundaries of distinction have to be increasingly defended. Multiculturalism is, in part, about groups struggling to achieve moral solidarity, a precious good in an era of profound transformation and instability. But there is a deeper social logic to this development that makes the antagonisms of identity formations much more complex than being composed simply of self-willed acts of collective volition or cast in terms of misguided "tribalism." Stripped of more and more of its resources, the cultural state has been left holding the bag, a bag stuffed mainly with symbols and sound bites for managing diversity as a rhetoric of moral consent, but backed (feebly) by state sanctions. What is key here is that the state contains precious little domestic fiscal capital. And under the new centrifugal flows of capital, the state is increasingly threatened with being reduced to a shell within which the politics of culture and the contentious ground of sprawling and multiplying identity formations become the major forms of symbolic and political capital in a context in which the notion of nation is what remains up for grabs—after capital flight. Culturalism becomes one of the few weapons of the weak,[17] but within an economically abandoned and fragmented civil society. In this dystopian scenario, symbols and the busywork of social differentiation and distinction fill in where money and social institutions cannot, and groups hailed by the new multiculturalism chase after their own interests in a domestically receding economy. As capitalism takes on a new worldly "postfordist" flexibility,[18] American civil society takes on an increasingly illiberal and intolerant moral ecology, and with signs of a growing populist inflexibility.

It is in this conjuncture that identities take on their signs as social hieroglyphics and where multiculturalism is formed and caught in crossfire. For in this conjuncture multiculturalism appears as both a surface promise and a deeper symptom. Multiculturalism signals a concession to earlier modes of exclusion and a cashing in on long-held promissory notes—back pay, if you like—as it gives us currencies that are seen internally as precious to those who have struggled to "own" the notes with their own names and pictures on them. For this is certainly part of what takes place in the struggle over the retrieval of "culture" and a usable past for a troubled present. None of this is trivial. The educational system—from kindergarten classes to the universities—has manifestly entered the important promotional work of encouraging toleration, pluralism, and diversity. But in a latent sense, this work is simultaneously engaged in rearguard damage control, juggling the domestic tensions brought by the post-civil rights legacy that now reaches into the dovetailing developments of centrifugal capital flight and centripetal cultural crisis.

If economic capital seeks flight, cultural capital seeks stable moorings. What we call "culture" in identity formations and multiculturalism operates as a kind of psychosocial currency—or, better yet, as multiple currencies. These currencies, however, are *not* meant to be recognized as equivalent. On the contrary, identity currency has value for its possessors precisely because of its distinctiveness and, in some cases, its purported and cherished incommensurableness. Identity is about own-ness, owning, possession, and not about dispossession. In some cases, identity struggles are responses to dispossession. In addition, *difference* signifies an expanded notion of *cultural freedom.* Yet cultural distinctions operate upon a social terrain that is encircled by conditions of exchange; as currencies, they are limited in both their purchasing power and their circulation. Distinctions are meant to be particular, not universal (even though they unwittingly invoke universalisms).[19] However, there are now lots of newly minted currencies vying for circulation and exchange: like economic capital, such forms of symbolic capital expect to flourish in a restricted public sphere where they struggle in the context of a shriveling domestic realm that is crisscrossed by more and more trenches.

Multiculturalism is thus much more than "identity politics." In the disjunction of economic expansion and cultural compression, multiculturalism becomes a new and profoundly contentious social mixture that is not captured—indeed it is obscured—in the framework of pluralism. On the one hand, it appears—and rightly so—as a settling of accounts, a return of the repressed, an admission of diversity, a deepening of tolerance, an expansion of social membership, and an empirical sign of an enlarged civil society. Within the framework of liberal democracy, the ideology of egalitarianism positions us to applaud the expansion of the social bases of identity as important, overdue, and progressive. For as promise, multiculturalism has the potential to manifest its best political moments by allowing raced groups to move beyond the show-and-tell domestication of late nineteenth-century folklore and the externally imposed caricaturizing of people into cultural texts and artifacts. It does this by bringing into political discourse the promises dangled in the ideology of a larger equality enshrined at the core of bourgeois liberal democracy, by giving groups a sense of place in society and in history, by offering the comfort that comes (tendentiously) in being able to say something about who they are, by attempting to rethink morally and reconstruct institutionally the meanings behind egalitarianism, and by insisting that social power be truly empowering, enhancing, and protecting for all.

On the other hand, it indicates just as much an unsettling of the presumed homogeneity of American society, signals a call for more cultural repression to nip an emerging "tribalism" in the bud, and equates the renewal of civic virtue and a return to *traditionalism* with an antimodernist intolerance articulated in the shadows of a receding American dream. As the conservative populist Rush Limbaugh sums it up, multiculturalism is the label for all those groups who have failed to make it in America.[20] The sensibility behind Limbaugh's diagnosis feeds into and off of a "differential racism" that substitutes "culture"—and by extension ideology—for "biology" by insisting on insurmountable "cultural differences" for those who imagine a social order in which undesired "mixing" can be prevented by the dismantling of the liberal state.[21]

Taken together, all of these aspects enable multiculturalism to register the full gamut of appropriations—from celebration to demonization. No wonder multiculturalism reverberates antagonistically across virtually every major social institution. It is an overloaded term, a symbolic container that is not capable of containing the range of investments that it attempts to carry. If it is a social hieroglyphic, it is one that is in the process of rupturing under the pressure of multiple conflicting meanings. The strains are now acutely visible. In the conjuncture between economic globalism and cultural crisis, we might begin to look at multiculturalism in two ways: in terms of its own *internal identitarian logic* and as a *symptomatic condition of the disjunction between global and domestic realms within the social formation of late capitalism*. Multiculturalism operates simultaneously as *identity politics* and as *sociosystemic politics*. Both are intimately entwined. As identitarian logic, multiculturalism locates the internal, psychic, and culturally collective desires for, and contestations over, a sense of social place—an arena of protection—in an increasingly turbulent social formation. Here—which is where the term "identity politics" takes hold—piecemeal meanings are fought out, lines of identity demarcations are struggled over. For here is where identities mirror to an extent the identifications imposed from above and outside, and juggle the fact that they are not self-made, but "constrained to see themselves as a community."[22] On the terrain of racialization, gender, and sexuality, we call these *social places* Asian American, Chicano, African American, Native American, feminist, lesbian, gay, and so on. Certainly the list expands with decreasing social stigma beyond the raced and gendered frameworks to include ethnicities and political orientations. Moreover, as dimensions within a social spectrum, none of these sites are airtight and hermetically sealed (even though, upon closer internal examination, they can include, but are never totally encompassed by, wrenching schisms along micromanaged lines of hyperidentified demarcations and over criteria of authenticity, taking on a spirit kindred to nationalism but without reference to a state). In a sense, these identity demarcations are more like landmarks that are erected upon and driven into a social chunk of very sprawling terrain; they attempt to capture and mark the vast surroundings and the deep layers of social lives as *categorical imperatives* (just when Kantianism was thought to have been abandoned). Nonetheless, they overlap and move outwardly and unevenly across institutions and in relationship to various social movements.

It would be the height of arrogance to dismiss as socially constructed moral fictions the meanings that are charged in the identities we inherit and inhabit, for it is in these cultural interstices that we live our socially and institutionally marked everyday lives. On the surface is where we do the bulk of our thinking, swim in our emotions, navigate with our institutionally traversed common sense. We dwell in the inner logic of these surface spheres, our modern social cells; they govern experience and enable us to feel so deep. Historical forces much larger than our individual or collective selves compel us to take on our raced, gendered, and classed places, and to adjust to the fields in which these identities are located. We live and act in their names, working with the combination of plus or minus signs that accrue around them. As modernity churns on, new identity formations hitherto nonexistent, or previously denied, denigrated, devalued, undermined, punished, and repressed, continue to emerge. They register, understandably so, as major psychic as well as social victories. The indulgence in identity politics afforded by multiculturalism can make us feel more whole, more like subjects than objects. Yet could it be that our sense of the social whole may be shrinking? For multiculturalism also appears now to be the latest unfolding of a half-gratifying, half-debilitating social logic. It functions in the contemporary context as a political-demographic fix, and as a patching of fissures that have opened on the social surfaces over the last quarter century. Inheritors of this cultural logic speak in a language of subjectivity and place, and are busy maintaining popular memory; overseers of the new multicultural workforce speak of diversity management. These seem to be the preferred views that embrace the notion of social autonomy and domestic(ated) pluralism.

From Farce to Tragedy?

As with all social identities, raced identities—those that are probably most associated with the term "multiculturalism"—are the result of historical constructions. Marx once suggested that history first unfolds as tragedy, and then repeats itself as farce. In rethinking the historical development of *race* as an organizing operation configured in power relations, we might reverse Marx's summary statement: race as a social category emerges first as a fabricated symbolic construction (farce), and then operates through objectified and mediated institutional practices as social "truth effects" (tragedy). Once put into motion, the fabrications of racialization take on the power of truth as they wind along socially tragic paths. Farce has taken on great power. Through it we are forced to squeeze symbolic virtues out of historical, social, and institutional coercion; we are compelled to weld *artificial* identities into *natural* ones. But we work with raced identities on already reified ground. In the context of domination, raced identities are imposed and internalized, then renegotiated and reproduced. From artificial to natural, we court a hard-to-perceive social logic that reproduces the very conditions we strain to overcome. When most effective, ideology *dehistoricizes* historical developments and fixes through *naturalization* what is historically constituted. Multiculturalism refracts both the attempt to overcome historical fixity and naturalization, and the seduction of reification.

There is, it seems, another potentially tragic outcome. The multiplication of identity formations can also purge the desire for something bigger, and *bigger for all*. As localized identities become more numerous and compressed, the capacity to achieve a larger social identity appears to be compromised. In building more and more symbolic arenas filled with more and more symbolic strategies of distinction, the vision of a transformed society that is substantively better for all atrophies against the velocity and force of the superficial and feebly institutionalized identities. What is troubling in the conjuncture is how *surfaces* of culture in general, and multiculturalism in particular, seem now more capable than ever of continued expansion as our "preferable" identity locations begin to compress and contract. This development is likely to be the most pressing challenge to a radical democracy, for the very principles of a shared framework of political universalism that protects the raison d'être of particularisms are in the process of cultural eclipse. Ironically, with the critique of reductionism, the distaste for the structural side of things, the disdain for universalism, and the dismissal of history as a narrative trope, we seem all too tempted to adopt a reduced if not pulverized notion of the social contract. What is more salient is the growing urgency of patrolling the borders of besieged identities. And as our general, worldly political horizons shrink, our internal identities compress more and more along aestheticized—and ascetic—lines of meaning and distinction, where a sense of certainty and place can be had in a world in which uncertainty and dislocation deepen and intensify. In this regard, there is a disturbing parallel, or kindred cultural spirit—notwithstanding the blatant contradictions here—between the deepening *psychic interiorization* that characterizes identity politics and the fear of the *national interior* being threatened by unwanted, border-crossing immigrants.

Conclusion

If the globalization of late capitalism continues to develop in ways that strip liberal democracy of the domestic capacity to maintain a vision of the social, of "society," while eviscerating the will to use social resources to mitigate the social conflict rooted in the seeming intractability of inequality, then the cultural trenches will likely multiply, deepen, and widen. As corporations rush to secure new positions of strategic power in the global economy (a "strategic essentialism" for the transnational capitalist class willing to forsake domestic peace!), and the draining of fiscal resources for the domestic-national sphere continues, the work of bridge building across the social fissures of *socioeconomic classes* as well as *cultural classifications* will grow in urgency precisely because such *social work* is just as likely to shrivel in importance as it becomes overwhelmed by the decomposition of the economic infrastructure and the spiraling inflation of symbolic capital. The hand-wringing over essentialism and metaphysics that surrounds us and from which we have learned much also tends to abdicate the political challenges over the larger social contract to forces inimical to the egalitarianism that drives the most important facets of multiculturalism and its important place within an expanding democracy.

I want to underscore the need for taking our location in the academy seriously—for this is where we work. We are linked intimately to the problems I've sketched. There is no avoiding them. It is the fate of our work— whether we work with or ignore the larger fate of modern American civil society. I suspect that the split will deepen between the culturalist state and economic globalization, and this will make our work as critical intellectuals within the academy increasingly charged. If I understand our historical context and our institutional location correctly, we, as *cultural workers* working in the cultural infrastructure, have to see to it that the road signs that help us map out the emerging struggles surrounding identity politics and multiculturalism do not point toward our own little Sarajevos. We are nowhere near this dismal example. But it would be quite unwise for us to think that we are exempt from such possibilities.

We live in the conjuncture. It is also our context that presents us with a window of opportunity in which to rethink and rework new social possibilities for a greater social contract, one that builds from multiculturalism toward substantive egalitarianism and political protection for cultural, racial, gender, and sexual differences. The challenge is to recognize that the identity formations that have come about are important. But if we are to weather the crisis between globalization and domestic erosion, such identity formations simply will not be enough to ensure the greater collective forms of engagement in the critical transformation of civil society. Put another way, multiculturalism is necessary but not sufficient. Multiculturalism is not enough. It has to be reconceptualized as *means* rather than *ends*. This is where we might begin: as a key element in our social formation, multiculturalism presents new challenges for us to see to it that the fetishization of identities and the reification of differences do not take hold in ways that deny us *in our partial differences* the mutually enhancing chances to reconfigure the crisis-ridden social contract.

Notes

1. See Stuart Hall, "The Problem of Ideology—Marxism without Guarantees," in B. Matthews, ed., *Marx: 100 Years On* (London: Lawrence & Wishart, 1983); Ernesto Laclau and Chantal Mouffe, *Hegemony and Socialist Strategy: Towards a Radical Democratic Politics* (New York: Verso, 1985); Pierre Bourdieu, "Objectification Objectified," in *The Logic of Social Practice* (Stanford, Calif.: Stanford University Press, 1990), 30–41.

2. But see Frederic Jameson, *Postmodernism, or, The Cultural Logic of Late Capitalism* (Durham, N.C.: Duke University Press, 1991), and Anthony Giddens, *Modernity and Self-Identity: Self and Society in the Late Modern Age* (Stanford, Calif.: Stanford University Press, 1991).

3. Bryan D. Palmer, *The Reification of Language and the Writing of Social History* (Philadelphia: Temple University Press, 1990).

4. Karl Marx, *Capital*, vol. 1 (New York: Vintage Books, 1977), 163–78; Gajo Petrovic, "Reification," in *A Dictionary of Marxist Thought*, ed. Tom Bottomore (Cambridge: Harvard University Press, 1983), 41–43.

5. Marx, *Capital*, 167.

6. Georg Lukács, "Reification and the Consciousness of the Proletariat," in *History and Class Consciousness: Studies in Marxist Dialectics* (Cambridge: MIT Press, 1971).

7. For Lukács and Gramsci, this was registered as the fragmentation of the historical subject. Lukács and Gramsci are perhaps the last of the major Western Marxists to hold firmly to the notion of the proletariat as the historical subject. In the context of an expanding mass culture, the emergence of fascism underwritten by working-class populism was enough to install a deep distrust in the belief that exploited classes occupied the most privileged social location for the development of critical subjectivity. This indeterminacy of class undermined the Marxian prop of the labor theory of value and the automatic and unproblematic reliance on economism. From here on, social and cultural theory register this unraveling of economic reductionism through the increasingly focused lenses of "ideology," "discourse," and "culture."

8. Judith Butler, *Gender Trouble: Feminism and the Subversion of Identity* (New York: Routledge, 1990).

9. I am not suggesting that the state took on a cultural dimension in the context of the civil rights movement. As a primarily political institution, the state is by definition a cultural enterprise and is deeply enmeshed in the making and brokering of cultural relations. Politics is thus never an arena removed from questions of culture; rather, it is a key site that registers and hosts cultural as well as other struggles.

10. On the "racial state," see Michael Omi and Howard Winant, *Racial Formation in the United States*, 2d ed. (New York: Routledge, 1994). Here, it needs to be pointed out that the problems associated with what could be called the "cultural turn" in the social sciences and the humanities are not simply the creations of schools of thought (e.g., British Cultural Studies, deconstruction, or feminist theory). More consideration deserves to be given to how we might situate theoretical shifts and new social knowledge formations in the junctures of social change. Theoretical shifts are thus more than cases of intellectual innovation unfolding as paradigm shifts.

11. Robert Reich, President Clinton's secretary of labor, views global capitalism as based in the forms of transnational tiers of management, and these forms operate beyond the notion of traditional state boundaries. According to Reich, in the modern economy there is little government can do to stem the flexible mobility of corporate investments from one country to another. Global multinational corporatism transcends the state. In Reich's view, there "will be no national products or technologies, no national corporations, no national industries. There will no longer be national economies, at least as we have come to understand the concept. All that will remain rooted within national borders are the people who comprise a nation" (*Los Angeles Times*, 12 December 1992: A22). See also Robert Reich, *The Work of Nations* (New York: Alfred A. Knopf, 1991).

12. On the withering away of grand narratives, see Jean-François Lyotard, *The Postmodern Condition: A Report on Knowledge*, trans. Geoff Bennington and Brian Massumi (Minneapolis: University of Minnesota Press, 1984). The thesis on the waning of affect can be found in Jean Baudrillard, *Simulations*, trans. P. Foss, P. Patton, and P. Beitchman (New York: Semiotext[e], 1983), and *In the Shadow of the Silent Majorities . . . or the End of the Social and Other Essays*, trans. P. Foss (New York: Semiotext[e], 1983).

13. William Julius Wilson, *The Declining Significance of Race: Blacks and Changing American Institutions* (Chicago: University of Chicago Press, 1978).

14. Amitai Etzioni, *The Spirit of Community: Rights, Responsibilities and the Communitarian Agenda* (New York: Crown Publishers, 1993); Robert N. Bellah et al., *The Good Society* (New York: Vintage Books, 1992).

15. Samuel Huntington, "Chapter III: The United States," in *The Crisis of Democracy: Report on the Governability of Democracies to the Trilateral Commission*, ed. Michel Crozier, Samuel P. Huntington, and Joji Watanuki (New York: New York University Press, 1975).

16. Cf. Alan Bloom, *The Closing of the American Mind* (New York: Simon and Schuster,

1987); Dinesh D'Souza, *The Politics of Race and Sex on Campus* (New York: Free Press, 1991); Jon Weiner, "Campus Voices Right and Left," *Nation*, 12 December 1988: 644–45.

17. I draw the phrase from James C. Scott, *Weapons of the Weak: Everyday Forms of Peasant Resistance* (New Haven: Yale University Press, 1985).

18. David Harvey, *The Condition of Postmodernity: An Enquiry into the Origins of Social Change* (Cambridge, Mass.: Basil Blackwell, 1989).

19. Ernesto Laclau, "Universalism, Particularism, and the Question of Identity," *October* 61 (summer 1992): 83–90. See also Joan Scott, "Multiculturalism and the Politics of Identity," *October* 61 (summer 1992): 12–19.

20. Rush H. Limbaugh, *The Way Things Ought to Be* (New York: Pocket Books, 1992).

21. Etienne Balibar, "Is There a 'Neo-Racism'?" in Etienne Balibar and Immanuel Wallerstein, *Race, Nation, Class: Ambiguous Identities* (New York: Verso, 1991), 21–23.

22. Ibid., 18. Cf. also Joan W. Scott, "Experience," and Jane Flax, "The End of Innocence," in *Feminists Theorize the Political* (New York: Routledge, 1992).

CHAPTER THREE

Gender, Class, and Multiculturalism

Rethinking "Race" Politics

ANGELA Y. DAVIS

Last week, during the television coverage of election night, I saw a black and white choir singing black gospel music at the Arkansas state capital. Just then, something struck me about the multicultural veneer of the Clinton victory, and the use of the televisual presence of black people to create an illusion of victory over racism. Considering the virtual absence of discussions on racism (outside of Clinton's encounter with Sister Souljah in which she was portrayed as an archetypal racist), this not only camouflaged the persistence of anti-black racism, but it effectively rendered more palatable the absence of Latino, Native, and Asian Americans. In fact, many of the current strategies that propose to make marginal cultures visible and accessible tend to reproduce ideologies of racism, as well as male dominance and middle-class privilege. I therefore want to suggest a number of ways we can look critically at multiculturalism, not in order to adopt a general position against multiculturalism, but in order to predict and identify possible strategies of containment and co-optation. This will hopefully enable us to move toward a vision that incorporates multiculturalism within a context of powerful political resistance to racism, as it is informed by and in turn informs economic exploitation and male dominance.

I will begin by sharing with you an excerpt from an article that recently appeared in the *Kennedy Career Strategist* by Linda Mitchell entitled "Get Ready to Manage a Salad Bowl":

> In the past, managing a labor force really meant managing white males. However, experts tell us we have jumped out of the "melting pot" and into the "salad bowl." The once-homogeneous workforce is becoming decidedly heterogeneous, and the parts of the whole are determined to retain their own cultures and customs. . . . Some African-Americans will "signify" when they are curious, but their etiquette prevents them from asking a direct question. . . . Some Asians may prefer not to speak unless thoroughly knowledgeable about the subject—research first, then talk—and even then, only when invited to speak. . . . How is corporate America dealing with this? A number of megacompanies have complex training programs. . . . These multicultural programs generically are termed "workforce diversity management." . . . Progressive firms want every employee to receive diversity training.[1]

Of course, the most obvious flaw in this notion of corporate multiculturalism is the assumption that until recently the U.S. workforce consisted primarily of white men. But what I want to suggest is that the concept of "diversity management" may not merely reflect the way multiculturalism is being translated into corporate workplace strategies. Additionally, it may reveal the potentially problematic character of the popular presentation of multiculturalism discourse as an overarching strategy for putting racism to rest. "Diversity management" assumes that a racially, ethnically, and culturally heterogeneous workforce needs to be managed or controlled in ways that contain and suppress conflict. This process is precisely a means of preserving and fortifying power relations based on class, gender, and race. Such disciplining of diversity is, in fact, a strategy for more exhaustive control of the working class. Recall the debates during the last century on the abolition of slavery. Northern industrialists foresaw the end of slavery as providing conditions for a more effective exploitation of the entire labor force, black and white alike.

In the debates around workplace multicultural strategies, there is little discussion about persisting economic inequities, dead-end jobs, unemployment, job hazards, environmental disease, and sexual harassment. Although these may be acknowledged as problems, they are rarely presented as integral to "multicultural programs."

Looking at another constellation of institutions, the so-called correctional system, strategies explicitly named multicultural are even more unabashedly subordinated to the discipline process. Because of the pervasiveness of "racial conflict"—between white and black, white and Latino, and Latino and black prisoners—current multicultural programs (which aim �458 prevent the violent explosions in which guards and administrations are often implicated) strive for ways to reestablish control over inmate populations. Since jail and prison populations are represented as increasingly more racially and culturally heterogeneous, efforts are under way to reorganize them as racially and culturally harmonious institutions. Actually, we are confronted with increasing racial homogeneity in the incarcerated population. It is fairly common knowledge that young black men are more likely to be found in jails and prisons than in colleges and universities. In a way that parallels the corporate compartmentalization of multiculturalism, correctional institutions rarely if ever address the underlying reasons for vast increases in the incarcerated population and for the ideological process of criminalization that leads so many people of color into the jails and prisons of this country.

I have alluded to workforce and prison strategies for the purpose of suggesting ways of looking at multicultural educational practices in terms of the power relationships they may implicitly affirm, conceal, or reconfigure. Ultimately, I want to pose the question of whether, or what kind of, multicultural approaches can potentially take on the political task of challenging the gender, class, and race hierarchies that continue to shape the institutions of this country.

Progressive approaches to nonracist education that attempt to contest white monocultural dominance are generally referred to as multicultural. The debate around multiculturalism has unfolded within the United States around such notions as "diversity," "political correctness," "pluralistic multiculturalism versus particularistic multiculturalism," and so on. As progressive students, staff, and faculty, we generally have positioned ourselves as advocates of diversity and multiculturalism, in opposition to the defenders of a monolithic notion of education that privileges a white Western intellectual tradition. In the process of fighting these battles around elementary, secondary, and higher education, and specifically around the most immediate policies implemented in these institutions, we sometimes ignore the historical and political context within which these debates and campaigns have taken shape.

In thinking about multiculturalism, I found it helpful to revisit some of the more salient moments in the recent history of race discourse and in a relatively unsystematic way I want to evoke some of the terms that have been used over the course of the last half century or so to represent challenges to the persisting problem of racism: "Assimilation," "Cultural Pluralism," "Desegregation," "Integration," "Black Nationalism," "Black Power," "Chicano

Power," "Puerto Rican Independence," "Indian Sovereignty," "Affirmative Action," "Reverse Discrimination," "Difference," "Diversity," "Multiculturalism."

With some obvious exceptions that represent the input of militant oppositional movements, what these terms have in common are implications of "overcoming" racism without necessarily shaking up the power structures that are expressed through and that constitute the social context of racism. In the 1960s, Malcolm X made the observation that integration demands, as advocated by the early civil rights movement, did not take into consideration the fact that we might well be fighting for embarkation onto a sinking ship. What they all have in common, however, including the slogans addressing issues of power, independence, and sovereignty, is a failure to address the ways in which gender, race, and class intersect and inform each other in complex, mutating ways. As Kum-Kum Bhavnani and Margaret Coulson have asked, "How do ['race,' class, and gender] combine with and/or cut across one another? How is gender experienced through racism? How is class shaped by gender and 'race'?"[2]

I am not suggesting that we throw out all these concepts. As historical evidence of important contestations around demands raised by social movements, they reveal the extent to which what we count as victories often challenge us to rethink and reorganize the terms and terrain on which battles against racism, sexism, and class exploitation are fought.

"Race" has always been difficult to talk about in terms not tainted by ideologies of racism, with which the notion of "race" shares a common historical evolution. The assumption that a taxonomy of human populations can be constructed based on phenotypical characteristics has been discredited. Yet we continue to use the term "race," even though many of us are very careful to set it off in quotation marks to indicate that while we do not take seriously the notion of "race" as biologically grounded, neither are we able to think about racist power structures and marginalization processes without invoking the socially constructed concept of "race." Obviously, there is a reason we are stuck with the term "race," and that has to do with the persistence of racism and processes of racialization that perpetuate race-based oppression, even as they appear to move beyond it.

I am convinced that the category "race" is so laden with contradictions that it no longer works in the way it used to, at least within the context of radical theories and practices. Until the fifties and sixties, one way of indicating one's opposition to policies of segregation in the black community was to identify oneself as an upholder of the "race." Billie Holiday, for example, referred to herself as a "race woman." That this has become an obsolete way of identifying oneself is also indicative of the fact that many of us find the term "the black community" problematic in ways that could not have occurred to us thirty or forty years ago. That "race" no longer works as a focus of resistance organizing does not mean that racism has become obsolete and that we should discard it as a concept. I certainly do not wish to associate myself with those who claim that a rising importance of class relations has led to "the declining significance of race" or with those who see no other way of moving away from victimization paradigms than by means of individualistic notions like the precedence of character over race.

But many of us who persist in raising charges of racism—whether in relation to the configuration and exploitation of labor, the educational system, housing, health and welfare issues, or the legal, law-enforcement, and penal systems—are regarded as relics from the past. Even within progressive movements around reproductive rights, sexual harassment, gay and lesbian rights, and trade-union campaigns, charges of racism are often viewed as old and tired arguments. The arguments may be old—and certainly those of us who propose them are tired of always having to point to racism—but there is a sense in which the term "racism" still maintains its ability to ruffle people's feathers. There is a persistently piercing character about the term "racism" that is one sign of the perseverance of power relations based on race.

The term racism itself sharply calls for redress of historical and current grievances. It places blame in institutional structures and policies as well as in attitudes and behavior. But what happens when we shift our arguments away from charges of racism and begin to talk about difference, diversity, and multiculturalism? "Difference" and "diversity" are descriptive: people are different; cultures are diverse. In this context, we must be aware of the fact that multiculturalism can easily become a way to guarantee that these differences and diversities are retained superficially while becoming homogenized and harmonized politically, especially along axes of class, gender, and sexuality. Although this is not an inevitability, multiculturalism can become a polite and euphemistic way of affirming persisting, unequal power relationships by representing them as equal differences. Somehow, I get more excited at a Public Enemy concert when I hear young people chanting "Fuck racism" (even though I might find problematic moments in the performance) than in a discussion on "recognizing diversity."

These unequal power relationships are not only those based on white supremacy. Sexism is often glossed over or even justified by invoking multiculturalism. Nira Yuval-Davis argues that in Britain, various kinds of funda-

mentalism have been "the main beneficiaries of the adoption of multiculturalist norms." Multiculturalism, she argues, "has provided [fundamental-
ism's] chief ideological weapon. . . . The multiculturalist consensus . . . sees
racism not as a form of institutionalized inequality, but as a matter of different mutually exclusive ways of life which must be preserved." She continues
to point out that "Women's demands for freedom and equality are seen as
being outside 'cultural traditions' (often themselves only half understood),
and therefore not legitimate. The most conservative versions are often considered to be the most 'authentic.' Appeals to culture and tradition have been
used to attack women's autonomous organizing."[3]

Multiculturalism often emphasizes what Barry Troyna calls "the expressive features of ethnic minority cultures" and is thus associated with what he
calls "voyeuristic imperatives."[4] In Canada, where multiculturalism has a
history that defined it as a strategy for containment of the separatist demands of the Front de Libération Québécois during the late 1960s, it is often
referred to by community activists as "multivulturalism." In Ontario, the
most visible face of the federal multicultural policy is a caravan that is organized each year in which each "culture" has its own float—to use Faith
Nolan's words—"for the Wasps to gaze upon, for the vultures to devour." Interestingly enough, last year a memo from the Ministry of Multicultural Affairs—where the minister, by no coincidence, is white—circulated among
the provincial offices declaring that gay and lesbian projects were not to be
funded, because they do not represent cultures and therefore are not to
be included under multiculturalism. This meant, for example, that if a
Jamaican lesbian project applied for a grant, it would not be considered
fundable as multicultural. In a related move, indigenous peoples' projects
are not funded by the Ministry of Multiculturalism because there is a
Department of Indian Affairs. Needless to say, there is a great deal of progressive grassroots opposition to the multicultural policies of the Canadian
government.

Multiculturalism has acquired a quality akin to spectacle. The metaphor
that has displaced the melting pot is the salad. A salad consisting of many ingredients is colorful and beautiful, and it is to be consumed by someone.
Who consumes multiculturalism is the question begging to be asked. This
leads us back to the corporate multicultural strategies, wherein the purpose
of acknowledging difference is to guarantee that the enterprise functions as
efficiently as it would if there were no cultural differences at all. As R. Roosevelt Thomas put it in an article in the *Harvard Business Review*:

The correct question today is not "How are we doing on race relations?" or "Are we promoting enough minority people and women?" but rather "Given the diverse work force I've got, am I getting the productivity, does it work as smoothly, is morale as high, as if every person in the company was the same sex and race and nationality?"[5]

Thomas is the executive director of the American Institute for Managing Diversity, Inc. at Morehouse College in Atlanta. As this approach discards the melting pot analogy in favor of the "unassimilated diversity" of the metaphorical salad, the assumption is that not only is it not necessary to be a straight white male in order to participate in this process, you need not even pretend to be one. Yet, although you are permitted to be an "other," you must work "as if" you were not a member of a marginalized group. Corporate culture, Thomas argues, should not attempt to "assimilate diversity into the dominant culture," but rather should "build a culture that can digest unassimilated diversity." But the end result should be the same as if racial, gender, and sexual homogeneity prevailed. Workers may look different and talk (even signify), eat, dance, and act differently from one another, but they will be expected to be as productive "as if" they were all the same. This is a process reminiscent of the Hegelian Idea that externalizes itself and unfolds in wondrous historical heterogeneity, but in the final analysis, it returns to itself and remains its unified self.

Diane Ravitch's defense of cultural pluralism in opposition to cultural particularism has a similar ring. Pluralists, she claims, seek a "richer common culture," while the particularists insist that "no common culture is possible or desirable." While she opposes reconfiguration of school curricula, she applauds such celebrations as Black History Month and Women's History Month: "The point of those celebrations is to demonstrate that neither race nor gender is an obstacle to high achievement. They teach all children that everyone, regardless of their race, religion, gender, ethnicity or family origin, can achieve self-fulfillment, honor, and dignity in society if they aim high and work hard."[6]

Both of these conceptions imply that difference doesn't make any difference, if only we acquire knowledge about it. If our difference is understood, consumed, and "digested," we simultaneously can be different and perform "as if" we really were middle-class, straight white males. Difference as object of "distaste," "dislike," or "hate" must be transformed into difference as object of knowledge. In other words, the locus of racism is in the attitudes of individuals. White racists "hate" Latinos, Native people, Asians, and black people because they have internalized negative stereotypes of our respective cultures. And we, as people of color, have internalized negative stereotypes of each other. Although it is certainly the case that racist representations inform attitudes of hostility, the notion that if we simply correct those stereotypes with knowledge of the "true" cultures, we will no longer be hated and will no longer hate each other, is extremely dangerous. I am certainly not opposed to enlightenment, but policies of enlightenment by themselves do not necessarily lead to radical transformations of power structures.

In fact, some of us already have learned how not to hate each other. There are now harmonious multiracial formations that continue to develop and implement antiracist projects in the context of the law. Here I cannot resist the temptation to evoke Clarence Thomas. Not that I claim a relationship with Clarence Thomas, even though we are racially marked in the same way and to a certain extent share a common historical culture. For example, he claims a relationship to Malcolm X. So do I. He claims a relationship to the Black Panther Party. So do I. But there is a political demarcation that defines my relationship to that political culture in a way that is very different from his. Cultures are not politically neutral. A multiculturalism that does not acknowledge the political character of culture will not, I am sure, lead toward the dismantling of racist, sexist, homophobic, economically exploitative institutions.

As a black woman, I am aware of the extent to which the politics of "race" have evolved around black-white constructions: black versus white or white versus black or black and white. These binary constructions tend to ignore everyone who does not fit into them. Since women, gay men, and lesbians have not been historically acknowledged on the black side of this binary, not even all black people get included. But what I want to refer to here is the way in which relationships among communities of color are being crowded into this paradigm as the object of multiculturalism's reconciliation. Relationships between Asian and black communities, for example, are currently represented through the media in simplistic terms that draw upon the antagonistic representation of black-white relationships, with black people occupying the "white" space and Asians occupying the "black" space, or vice versa. The cover of the October 1992 issue of *Atlantic Monthly* depicts two faces in profile confronting each other, one colored black and the other brown, with the bold caption "Blacks vs. Browns." This is the way the cover advertises a disturbing article by Jack Miles entitled "Immigration and the New American Dilemma." To criticize this rigid way of thinking about relationships among people of color across racial boundaries is not to deny the real conflicts and the all too prevalent racist attitudes in many of our communities. Rather it is to say that a multiculturalism that posits itself as the solution to racial conflict, based on the black-white model, will hardly move us forward.

If multiculturalism is to be liberated from historically outmoded ways of conceptualizing race, it may be helpful to consider some of the theories and practices associated with women of color over the last decade. Departing from the publication of *This Bridge Called My Back*, a great deal of work on class, gender, and sexuality has emerged in relation to women of color feminist theory.[7] The political construction of women of color as a new historical subject has served as an important rallying point for new social movements. Among others, Avtar Brah's notion of "differential racialization" and Chela Sandoval's theory of "differential consciousness" may be helpful to those of us who want to build upon what Wahneema Lubiano calls a "strong multiculturalism."[8] This conclusion is, of course, a point of departure. I will simply say that the kind of multiculturalism that makes sense in 1992 is a multiculturalism that, in Manning Marable's words, not only informs but transforms: a multiculturalism in which difference does make a difference.[9]

Notes

1. Linda Mitchell, "Get Ready to Manage a Salad Bowl," *Kennedy Career Strategist* 5 (January 1990): 3.

2. Kum-Kum Bhavnani and Margaret Coulson, "Transforming Socialist Feminism: The Challenge of Racism," *Feminist Review* 23 (May–June 1986): 81–93.

3. Nira Yuval-Davis, "Fundamentalism, Multiculturalism and Women in Britain," in *"Race," Culture and Difference*, ed. James Donald and Ali Rattansi (London: Sage Publications, 1992), 284.

4. Barry Troyna, "Can You See the Join?: An Historical Analysis of Multicultural and Anti-racist Education Policies," in *Racism and Education*, ed. Dawn Gill, Barbara Mayor, and Maud Blair (London: Sage Publications, 1992), 70.

5. R. Roosevelt Thomas Jr., "From Affirmative Action to Affirming Diversity," *Harvard Business Review* (March–April 1990): 109.

6. Diane Ravitch, "Multiculturalism: E Pluribus Plures," *American Scholar* (summer 1990): 340.

7. Cherríe Moraga and Gloria Anzaldúa, eds., *This Bridge Called My Back: Writings by Radical Women of Color* (Watertown, Mass.: Persephone Press, 1981).

8. Avtar Brah, "Difference, Diversity and Differentiation," in *"Race," Culture and Difference*, 126–49; Chela Sandoval, "U.S. Third World Feminism: The Theory and Method of Oppositional Consciousness in the Postmodern World," *Genders* 10 (spring 1991): 1–24; Ted Gordon and Wahneema Lubiano, "The Statement of the Black Faculty Caucus," in *Debating P.C.: The Controversy over Political Correctness on College Campuses*, ed. Paul Berman (New York: Laurel, 1992), 249–57.

9. Manning Marable, "Multicultural Democracy: The Emerging Majority for Justice and Peace," in *The Crisis of Color and Democracy: Essays on Race, Class and Power* (Monroe, Maine: Common Courage Press, 1992): 249–59.

CHAPTER FOUR

Academic Apartheid

American Indian Studies and "Multiculturalism"

M. ANNETTE JAIMES GUERRERO

Sweet America . . . To me I see you Naked,
While Others see just what they want to See.

Buffy Sainte-Marie, "Sweet America"

Multiculturalism or Decolonization?

It is an unfortunate state of affairs that ethnic scholars, as well as nonethnic academicians and educators, are advocating a "multicultural" vision for American education without challenging the paradigmatic status quo that creates such problems as educational disparity and social hegemony in the first place. These well-known and respected educators are aware of the racism and sexism rampant in our social institutions, but are still advocating accommodationist resolutions to those with a non-"ethnic" and even anti-"minority" mindset, a mindset that perpetuates these social ills, Euro-American privilege, and the presumed superiority of "Western civilization."

For American Indians, there is a substantial case to be made for the necessity of *decolonization before any genuine multiculturalism* can take place. Decolonization is a necessary first step in countering the relations of subordination imposed on Native peoples and established by U.S. colonizers through federal Indian policy. Putting decolonization before multicultural-

ism would ease the tension produced by the mandated policies of assimilation *and* marginalization to which Native peoples have been subject in the
process of their colonization. It would allow for compensatory reparations
to be made to be used for educational restoration and preservation programs. This would, in turn, counter the hegemony that perpetuates the
myth of the intellectual superiority of "Western civilization" at the expense
of indigenous peoples, our cultures and contributions to modern society,
and our sophisticated *traditional* knowledge bases. Such an educational plan
would have to be community-centered, and concerned with providing survival skills for employment and opportunities for academic and intellectual
endeavors. Such a plan would be conceptualized from an indigenous worldview of balance with and within the natural order, what some active scholars
are calling *Indigenism.*

American Indian Studies solutions to the problems wrought by U.S. colonization will have to address, therefore, the cultural, economic, and environmental spheres with sociopolitical agendas from Native peoples, and will
have to challenge the conventional wisdom of academic dogma and orthodoxy that has institutionalized a kind of *academic apartheid.* These challenges require an indigenous interpretation of knowledge bases that is predicated on indigenous experiences of both animate and inanimate phenomena,
access to funding and accreditation, and consideration of the rights and national responsibilities of indigenous peoples in an international context and
within international forums such as the United Nations. In short, American
Indian Studies helps begin the work of decolonization that must take place
before a genuine multiculturalism is established.

Colonization and Indian Education

In 1792, Benjamin Franklin recorded the reply of Cornplanter, a Seneca
leader, to Thomas Jefferson in response to Jefferson's overture to provide
free education for selected Iroquois youth:

> You who are wise, must know that different Nations have different Concep-
> tions of things; and you will therefore not take it amiss, if our ideas of this
> kind of Education happens not to be the same as yours. We have had some
> experience of it; Several of our young people were formerly brought up at the
> Colleges of the Northern Provinces; they were instructed in all your Sciences;
> but, when they came back to us, they were bad Runners, ignorant of every
> means of living in the Woods, unable to bear either Cold or Hunger, knew
> neither how to build a Cabin, take a Dear, or kill an Enemy, spoke our Lan-

guage imperfectly, were therefore neither fit for Hunters, Warriors, nor Counsellors; they were totally good for nothing. We are however not the less oblig'd by your kind Offer, tho' we decline in accepting it; and to show our grateful Sense of it, if the Gentlemen of Virginia will send us a Dozen of their Sons, we will take great Care of their Education, instruct them in all we know, and make *Men* of them.[1]

Contemporary Native American scholars, the most prominent being Vine Deloria Jr., have built upon Cornplanter's diplomatically expressed critique of why Euro-American educational ways are not appropriate for a traditionally proper "Indian education"—an education that is community-oriented, predicated on cultural traditions, and focused on survival skills. Deloria even went so far as to call the Euro-American indoctrination of Indian youth in the U.S. school system a form of "cultural imperialism" intent on eradicating Native cultures and belief systems.[2] From the infamous mission and boarding schools to the present-day situation of Indian students denigrated in U.S. public schools, the historical record of federal Indian policy has substantiated the charge of cultural imperialism.[3]

The history of colonialism in North America, the expropriation of Indian lands and resources, parallels the history of U.S.-Indian relations in education and in related areas such as health and social services. As Jorge Noriega has pointed out, from the mission schools of the sixteenth century to the block grant system of today, despite the variation in educational policies and levels of federal funding, these policies have pursued assimilationist goals at the expense of indigenous cultures and belief systems.[4]

As shown by Felix Cohen, author of the seminal treatise that laid the legal ground for tribal sovereignty, *The Handbook of Federal Indian Law* (1941), the original relationship between the Treaty Indians and the early American colonialists was meant to be a bilateral arrangement and was understood by Indians to be such. But major court decisions in the 1830s comprising the Marshall Doctrine revised this arrangement into a unilateral one that enabled the United States to subordinate Indian nations (called tribes since the 1903 *Lonewolf* decision) into what John Marshall called "domestic dependent nations."[5] Initially through this doctrine, the U.S. government constructed a unilateral relationship with Native peoples as tribal groups that established a wardship, or what is often called a "trusteeship." First established after the Indian Settler Wars through the Office of War and later implemented by the Department of the Interior via the Bureau of Indian Affairs (BIA), the authority to act "on behalf" of Indian groups' "best interests" created what I call a dominant-subordinate construction in U.S.-Indian relations. Operated at Indian people's expense, the assumption of U.S. "eminent domain" to Indian lands led to the expropriation of land and resources, the diversion of water, and the later devastation of reservation-based communities.

Federal policies toward Indian education have historically taken place in this colonial context and have been a major part of its organization. Included in certain treaty agreements between Indian nations and the U.S. government were educational appropriations to build schools and services for Indian youth. Indeed, as Jorge Noriega points out, "the real contours of what might be described as the U.S. model of colonialist education began to emerge" in the early nineteenth century with the Civilization Fund:

> In 1819, Congress established the "Civilization Fund," an annual appropriation of $10,000—in addition to those monies already allocated for the purpose—for "education of the frontier tribes." This was followed, in 1820, by acceptance of a proposal by Secretary of War John C. Calhoun that future treaties with indigenous nations be required to directly incorporate provision of additional cash annuities for instruction so that Indians might "be initiated in the habits of industry, and a portion taught the mechanical arts." For delivery of the intended program, the government relied primarily on missionaries supplied by the American Board of Commissioners for Foreign Missions, established collectively by the Congregational, Presbyterian, and Dutch Reform churches in 1810.[6]

The nineteenth century saw the further elaboration of these policies and their combination of coercion and assimilation. With the endorsement of President Teddy Roosevelt, leading intellectuals of the nineteenth and early twentieth centuries called themselves "Friends of the Indians." Several of these educational leaders were also members of his cabinet that gathered in upper New York State in 1889 to discuss the future of educational opportunities for American Indians.[7] The members of the Mohonk Proceedings, a public policy forum, believed their intentions to counter the harsher years of the so-called Indian Wars and the containment of Indian peoples on reservations were honorable and good. However, the history of the boarding school system tells a different story. During the years of the boarding school system, Indian children were kidnapped from their communities by the military and taken to faraway places where they were punished for being "Indian," for speaking their native languages, or for practicing their cultural traditions. In these schools, infamous schoolmasters, men and women of missionary zeal, used Indian youth as factory and farm labor to pay for their upkeep. This was the case, for example, in Chico, California, where a school for Native young women turned out to be a textile factory. One of the particularly pathological headmasters was Eleazar Wheelock, founder of Dartmouth College, who attempted to induce Indian youth to become Christians and missionaries, in effect using them as psychological guinea pigs. Overall, these military-regimented institutions implemented punitive corporal punishment when Indians resisted, often leading to early death and a high incidence of suicide among Indian youth. A gruesome sign of these schools' true nature was the adjoining cemeteries where Indian youth were buried.

The late nineteenth and early twentieth centuries witnessed the popularity and implementation of "scientific racism," manifested in, among other things, U.S. laws against miscegenation and for the protection of the "purity" of the "white" citizen-race, incorrect assumptions about the unified racial nature of all Native groups,[8] and perhaps most pointedly, the racist pseudoscience, *Crania Americana*. "Selected" Indian skulls were compared and contrasted with other "racial" groups and the results were used as a rationale to substantiate the biologically grounded "inferiority" of American Indians as a race. What's more, the Indians were sometimes compared with the African "race," so that white scientists could determine which was considered the more inferior.[9] These race scientists were extremely influential in establishing the scientific grounds for the eradication of "Indianness" that so characterized the concerted federal policy campaign to assimilate Indian students. This assimilationism was the preparation for their return to the reservations as second-class citizens or for their role as a labor force for a first-class citizenry in the predominantly Euro-American society.

Continuing distortions and bias in academic scholarship on American Indians is a direct result of this early colonizing history and the attempts to justify it. The manipulation of demographic data to establish the minimum presence of indigenous peoples prior to Columbus and European conquest, the perpetuation of stereotypes of Indian primitiveness, especially with regard to European standards of civilized agriculture, engineering, metallurgy, and religion,[10] and the marginalization or outright rejection of the Native nations' contribution to democratic governance, particularly the role of the Iroquois Confederacy,[11] all contribute to the legitimacy of the "rights of conquest" by Euro-Americans.

Only in recent years has Native scholarship made inroads into correcting this version of American history. These scholars have sought to counter what Ward Churchill calls these "sins of omission and commission." Alternative facts about the extent of indigenous occupancy in America and about the role of disease in decimating Native populations, the critique and inversion of the judicial theory that underwrites the Discovery Doctrine, and the debunking of Indian stereotypes in history and in contemporary popular culture[12] have sought to challenge the outright denial of inconvenient patterns of events, to reject the "both sides were guilty" rationalization, and in general to reject the standard methodologies in assessing the motives, policies, and impact of Euro-American conquest and colonization on Native America.

The Modern State of Affairs and the Politics of "Indian Identity"

The modern years began with the systematic campaign to mandate American education in public school systems for all Indian students. The 1928 Snyder and Johnson-O'Malley Acts established Indian education programs and provided for federal funds to go directly to school districts for the express purpose of servicing this new student population. At first, Indian youth and their parents resented and resisted this new education mandate and there was a high truancy rate among Indian students living on reservations. In addition, before more watchful oversight by the school and district administration was implemented under pressure from Indian parent committees, there was considerable mismanagement of funds designed for library acquisition and gym equipment. Overall, by the 1970s, federal Indian education policy had become more liberal, reflected in, among other things, the recognition of the growing population of Indians in urban metropole areas. The liberalization of federal Indian education policy was a direct result of the activities and leadership of the American Indian Movement (AIM) across the country in the 1970s. Particularly in the aftermath of the Wounded Knee occupation by AIM in 1973 on the Pine Ridge Reservation in South Dakota, considerably more attention was paid to quelling unrest among Indian peoples in the United States.

The legacy of coercive benevolence is nowhere more apparent than in the debates over federal Indian identification, a highly political issue for American Indians today. All those who claim Indian identity have to have a tribal enrollment number or BIA certification in order to be considered a federally recognized Indian or tribe. In order to receive federal monies and services, the state requires such certification. Prior to the 1970s, the tribes themselves determined who were members and thus would receive educational services as federal benefits. But during the 1970s, legislation was introduced that resulted in the infamous 506 forms, which were used to certify proof of tribal membership. This process was regulated by the BIA and required considerable paperwork for Indian parents and the tribes.[13] Certification demands have created serious problems for younger generations of Indians who have what are called "pending enrollments" for closed tribal rolls. These pending enrollments were exacerbated by a series of termination cases in the 1950s when the federal government declared whole tribes, as well as individuals, "extinct" and removed others from its list of those federally recognized. More recently, the Bush administration announced that the federal government has the power to "declare any Indian tribe in the nation extinct, even if the tribe has been recognized by a congressionally ratified treaty."[14] To make matters worse, the BIA is again being threatened by closure, this time, by Senator Daniel Inouye from Hawaii, who chairs the Senate Select Committee for Indian Affairs. Despite numerous complaints by Indians about the BIA and despite the fact that state certification of identity does not promote tribal self-sufficiency, Indians have generally held that a federal bureau to represent Indian peoples is better than none at all.

The political struggles and dealings around federal Indian identification policy have an important impact on educational policies since they affect the hiring of Indian faculty, administration, and staff to meet ethnic/minority quotas and affirmative action guidelines, as well as who will qualify for educational services and fellowships. Federal Indian identification policies have also contributed to the production of what I call the cloning of "Indian Identity Police," those who circulate in institutional settings, usually behind closed doors rather than in face-to-face interactions, to denounce the hiring of others who are not "real" Indians because they can't produce their certification cards or tribal enrollment numbers. Today, one finds professional Indian organizations and professors claiming "ethnic fraud" among those suspected of not having the proper pedigree or papers to call themselves American Indian or Native American.[15] This has encouraged the "Indian Identity Police" to instigate "hit" lists and "witch-hunts" on university campuses, accusing selected individuals of impersonating or masquerading as Indians. In my view, this "ethnic fraud" is at best a premature assessment and is at worst motivated by self-interest and other personal agendas, including tribal partisan policies in the Indian communities that have little to do with "genuine" Indians or cultural integrity. There are, in reality, many historically grounded reasons why Native peoples do not have BIA certification, reasons that do not generally involve their choice in the matter. Indeed, there are exceptions where individuals have made the choice not to register, but in many cases, this choice is based on the view that the U.S. government should not interfere with the internal affairs and sovereignty of tribal membership. Rather than pursue divisive strategies that ultimately presume that the fewer Indians there are, the more federal support there will be for the remainder, I would propose that the various tribal groups reestablish their traditional kinship systems to determine their tribal membership based on traditional cultural criteria and in this way counter the prevailing federal control of and regulation in this area. This is especially needed in light of the fact that the terms "American Indian" and "Native American" are state constructions that began with the Columbian invasion. The reappropriation of these terms, particularly in the context of an increasingly acknowledged pan-Indian experience, is an ongoing process that must be led by considerations of tribal sovereignty and cultural integrity.[16]

The political difficulties surrounding the role of the state in Indian identification are a sign of the ongoing coerciveness in what are now liberal education policies that encourage assimilation. This assimilation is often promoted as multicultural education. But the history of federal Indian education policies demonstrates the need for a decolonization of prevailing Euro-American rules and norms through a more genuine self-determination of ethnic/minority experiences, or, what I prefer to describe as the experiences of peoples of culture among indigenous groups.

American Indian Studies: Indigenism and Multiculturalism

Multiculturalism favors treating American Indians as ethnic minorities, rather than as descendants of indigenous peoples and members of tribal nations, whether the latter have federal recognition or not. But the history of indigenous peoples in the United States is, as I have shown, one of colonization. Although multiculturalism offers access to new knowledge bases, only a decolonization approach can link the critique of Eurocentrism to the particular experiences of Native peoples. And it is the displacement of Eurocentrism and its replacement by an indigenous worldview that must guide the radical work that some multiculturalism claims to want. To the extent that multiculturalism fosters the assimilation of American Indian Studies into the academic mainstream as a polite pseudo-intellectual vehicle maintained for purposes of providing the appearance of "ethnic diversity" on campus and for providing "Indian validation" to the supposed insights and conclusions of Euro-American academia, it hinders the crucial task of American Indian Studies. That task is to build an autonomous Indian tradition of scholarship and intellectualism that carries a viable conceptual alternative to Eurocentrism and its institutions.

The central dilemma of American Indian Studies was summed up neatly by Marlys Duchene when she observed that the designers of standard academic curriculum were/are Euro-Americans. "This resulted in academic curricula that embodied beliefs and routines that were strictly Euroamerican, the basis of which provided the 'object' for self-reflection."[17] For Native peoples who want to preserve and restore cultural traditions and belief systems that are different from the prevailing Eurocentric ones, any educational reform must challenge, at root, this dominant-subordinate construction. This construction is a social hegemony and moral philosophy that perpetuates the myths of Euro-American superiority at the expense of Native cultures/cosmologies and at the expense of the indigenous worldview, which holds that all living entities are interrelated and integrated for the whole of the universe.

The problem at hand was perhaps most profoundly described by Ward Churchill when he articulated the nature of the "educational imperialism" inherent in the contemporary functioning of the academy, a condition he terms "white studies." Within Churchill's schema, the "linear conceptual model" marking European culture dominates modern U.S. academic life, extracting conformity to its structures and conclusions as the price of intellectual legitimacy. American Indian intellectualism, which he defines as being structured in a "circulinear" fashion and belonging to the tradition of "the relational indigenous worldview," is thus excluded by institutional mandate.[18] Churchill observes that,

> as currently established, the university system in the United States offers little more than "white studies" to students, minority and mainstream alike. This is to say that curriculum is very nearly monolithic in its focus upon European conceptual modes as being the "natural" formation of knowledge/means of perceiving reality. In the vast bulk of curriculum content, Europe is not only the subject (conceptual mode; process of learning to think), but the object (subject matter) of investigation as well.[19]

Nowhere is this more evident than in the epistemologies of Western philosophy that permeate most academic disciplines and define our conventional notions of truth. Significant in this regard are the time/space/place constructions as human-derived.[20] By contrast, indigenous knowledge and traditional practice emphasize natural and seasonal rhythm. Native scholars like Churchill highlight the Eurocentric bias that is upheld by linear modes of thinking that rationalize an ideology of Indo-European and Euro-American superiority over indigenous reality and approaches or lifeways. The presumed universality and universal beneficence of the Western scientific and philosophical paradigm is Eurocentrism and it remains, for Native peoples, the dominant example of the power of knowledge to determine reality and to secure the subordination of Indian peoples. *Not all people "know" the same way.* As many have suggested, "superior" reasoning does not determine whether one group's way of thinking dominates another's. Rather, control over institutions and socioeconomic resources usually determines the ability to rule. But Eurocentrism, the ethnocentrism of European-descended populations, plays a part in creating hierarchies of social knowledge and in creating inequalities in resources and in institutional power. Historically, the ideological rule of Anglo-Saxon ethnocentrism was a major force in the European colonization of nonwhite populations and in the resulting inequalities in the distribution of resources and privileges. Increasingly sophisticated versions of Eurocentrism assist in smoothing the transition from traditional colonialism to Third World neocolonialism.[21]

It is difficult to imagine a way of looking at and relating to the world more antithetical to the holistic totalism marking indigenous worldviews than Eurocentrism, which forces American Indian Studies to be evaluated by conformity to conceptual standards and methods that are patently in opposition to Native American realities. What ethnocentrism has wrought in academic institutional settings is a form of *academic apartheid* that marginalizes Ethnic Studies or American Indian Studies or Gender Studies as fringe programs of less merit and credibility. This determines its overall status in hiring, course development, departmental determination, and budgetary allocations. Indigenous knowledge is contrasted with Eurocentric knowledge, and the subordination of the former is justified when it doesn't meet the tests of "rigorous" science and "objective" standards.

Efforts to correct this situational and institutionalized academic apartheid are being undertaken by Native scholars and some non-Native academic allies in all disciplines, from both a historical and a contemporary perspective, and with alternative ethnic as well as interdisciplinary approaches. Hence inroads are being made in demographics and education, in sociology and indigenous ("ethnic") studies, in anthropology, in religious studies, in history and politics, in American studies, in law, in environmental studies and ethics, in cultural philosophy, in art, poetry, and literature.[22] These efforts are driven by a basic fact of American Indian life:

> If, as they say, knowledge is power, then American Indians in the U.S. have been very thoroughly disempowered. Outside a relatively narrow range of traditionalists, mostly on a handful of reservations, our knowledge of ourselves, our histories, our cultures, and the nature of the process by which we

have been subordinated, has been appropriated by the dominant society for its own purposes. Knowledge not just of who we are, but of the nature of the system which dominates us, is consistently denied us, leaving us in near total ignorance of our true situation, more-or-less permanently at the mercy of our domination. In order to change this condition for the better, we must first and foremost recover the knowledge which has been taken from us and our ability to put this knowledge to use. In effect, we must regain our ability to think clearly, and to share this power with others. This, more than anything, is the "mission" of American Indian Studies.[23]

A good deal remains to be accomplished before a viable canon of American Indian Studies can emerge as a coherent whole. American Indian Studies will need to be able to stand on its own as a fully accredited discipline with departmental status and even with a broader institutional standing. Before this can happen, however, institutional standards that support structural barriers and preserve academic apartheid must be challenged. Questions about what kinds of models will prevail (multiethno program centers, autonomous departments, subordination to conventional disciplines, or some combination) will need to be answered. So too issues of hiring, promotion, and tenure, and the composition of degree-granting programs, require careful consideration. American Indian Studies usually gets the short stick in any multiethnic program or center, and often attention is focused on the hiring of "big guns" at the expense of programmatic development; issues of equity will require hard discussion. In addition, gender parity will need to be dealt with. Ethnic women in the academy are the last to be hired in Ethnic Studies and Women's Studies programs; Native women find themselves at the very bottom of a hierarchy that displays little interest in our experiences or perspectives, much less in the wherewithal to initiate permanent faculty positions for us. In addition, any viable American Indian Studies will need to reassess the publish-or-perish structure that consumes academics. In general, we will need to make decisions about how best to disseminate indigenous research and scholarship to the academy and the larger public— whether to operate within mainstream presses and media or whether to seek out alternative enterprises or establish independent Native-determined journals and book publications.

American Indian Studies will also have to take a global perspective so that it can incorporate the experiences of all indigenous peoples. Inter-American Indigenous Studies or Indigenous Global Studies would provide a broader international and interdisciplinary foundation for a more enlightened comprehension of the affairs of humankind. The global reconceptualization of the discipline can help counter the parochialism and ethnocentrism that abound and that perpetrate political factionalism and divisiveness within ethnic communities, reservation-based communities, and American society as a whole.

Most important, the indigenous worldview of American Indian Studies is grounded in the principles of intellectual decolonization long espoused by such theorists as Frantz Fanon and in the more recently emerging perspective of Indigenism elaborated by writer/activists such as Guillermo Bonfil Batalla.[24] As Vine Deloria puts it, "Indian Studies programs should ... define their goals as encompassing all the relevant knowledge and information concerning the relationship between American Indians and the rest of the world, be it the federal government, other religions, the world of art and music, or international and domestic economics."[25] To decolonize Eurocentric knowledge, American Indian Studies approaches these tasks through the deployment of the "Native American Conceptual Mode" itself:

> With such a conceptual structure ... there is really no compartmentalization of "spheres of knowledge." All components or categories (by European definition) tend to be mutually and perpetually informing. All tend to concretize human existence within reality (nature) while all are simultaneously informed by that reality. This is the "Hoop" or the "Wheel" or "Circle" of life referred to within the (continuing) oral traditions of so many indigenous peoples. Reality is not something "above," but an integral part of the living/knowing process itself.[26]

What both Deloria and Churchill are insisting on is not merely the inclusion of Indians and Indian programs in academia (although both certainly demand these), but a fully interdisciplinary approach to American Indian Studies as a discipline. This involves reaching a coherent *Indian* understanding of law or political science with a firm grasp of the spiritual principles governing Indian life. These spiritual principles can only be apprehended via a grounding in the Indian relationship to the environment. Indian philosophy cannot be approached without a solid appreciation of all these elements.

In its global context, this approach has led some Native scholars to call for Indigenism, a liberation movement and a worldview that provide an integrated orientation to life with nature.[27] This worldview sees an indigenous "Fourth" or "Host" world on the planet, composed of a multitude of distinct peoples ranging from the Indians of North and South America to the Inuits and Samis of the Arctic Circle, the Maori of New Zealand and the Koori of Australia, the Karins and Kachins of Burma, the Kurds of Persia, the

Bedouins of the Sahara and onward, the Zulus and Bantus of southern Africa, and many others. Even in contemporary Europe, peoples such as the Basques of Spain and the Gaels of the Scottish Highland region may be viewed as indigenous nations. The modern, industrialized and industrializing states of the First, Second, and Third Worlds are seen as sitting squarely atop the Host World.[28] The perspective of Indigenism presumes that indigenous peoples share a common experience of colonization and incorporation into a modern nation-state, a shared interest in the rights of all indigenous people to the right of sovereign nationhood, and a nondisruptive way of relating to the habitat.

This vision of American Indian Studies presumes the necessity of decolonization and seeks universal truths from the contributions of indigenous knowledge and the ancient wisdom that has been passed down through the ages. It is a positive alternative to a multicultural movement that has not yet done what it needs to do to challenge the denigration of ethnic/minority populations who still are forced to meet Euro-American standards and be ruled by Euro-American values for educational and life success. The indigenous worldview of American Indian Studies recognizes collective commonalties with each other at the same time that it acknowledges and respects our differences so that a rich cultural diversity and creative expression of individuality can flourish without sacrificing our universal holism. This is what is meant by the Lakota blessing *metakuyeayasi*, "All My Relations."

Notes

1. Excerpted in Leonard W. Larabee et al., eds., *The Papers of Benjamin Franklin* (New Haven: Yale University Press, 1961), 481–83.

2. Vine Deloria Jr., "Education and Imperialism," *Integrateducation* 19 (January–April 1981): 58–63.

3. See M. Annette Jaimes, "American Indian Identification/Eligibility Policy in Federal Indian Education" (Ph.D. diss., Arizona State University, August 1990).

4. Jorge Noriega, "American Indian Education in the United States: Indoctrination for Subordination to Colonialism," in *The State of Native America: Genocide, Colonization and Resistance*, ed. M. Annette Jaimes (Boston: South End Press, 1992), 371–402.

5. For the Marshall cases, see Vine Deloria Jr., "Trouble in High Places: Erosion of American Indian Rights to Religious Freedom in the United States," in *The State of Native America*. For the *Lonewolf v. Hitchcock* case, see Ward Churchill, "Perversions of Justice: Examining the Doctrine of U.S. Rights to Occupancy in North America," in *Struggle for the Land: Indigenous Resistance to Genocide, Ecocide and Expropriation in Contemporary North America* (Monroe, Maine: Common Courage Press, 1993). For a deconstruction of the original meanings and contemporary terminology of "tribe" and "nation," see Ward Churchill, "Naming Our Destiny: Towards a Language of Indian Liberation," *Global Justice* 3 (summer–fall 1992): 22–33.

6. Noriega, "American Indian Education in the United States," 377.

7. See Alexandra Harmon, "When Is an Indian Not an Indian? 'Friends of the Indian' and the Problem of Indian Identity," *Journal of Ethnic Studies* 18 (summer 1990): 95–123.

8. The myth of Native peoples being a single "race" of people actually began with the Bering Strait theory, which purports that all indigenous peoples are relative newcomers to the American hemisphere since we are presumably all Asian immigrants. Such Eurocentric hype, which tries to make indigenous peoples into immigrants, is now being supported by geneticists who claim to be deconstructing DNA in various racial groups. See Tim Friend, "Genetic Detectives Trace the Origin of the First Americans," *USA Today*, 21 September 1993: 5D, and Russell Means and Ward Churchill, "About That Bering Strait Land Bridge (Turn the Footprints Around)," statement by American Indian Movement leaders (1993).

9. See Stephen J. Gould, *The Mismeasure of Man* (New York: W. W. Norton, 1981), 20–60.

10. See M. Annette Jaimes, "Re-Visioning Native America: An Indigenist View of Primitivism and Industrialism," *Social Justice* 19 (summer 1992): 5–34.

11. See Bruce E. Johansen, *Forgotten Founders: Benjamin Franklin, the Iroquois and the Rationale for the American Revolution* (Ipswich, Mass.: Gambit, 1982); Donald Grinde Jr., *The Iroquois and the Founding of the American Nation* (San Francisco: California Indian Historian Press, 1977); Donald Grinde Jr. and Bruce E. Johansen, *Exemplar of Liberty: Native America and the Evolution of Democracy* (Los Angeles: American Indian Studies Center, 1991); and Donald Grinde Jr., "Iroquois Political Theory and the Roots of American Democracy," in *Exiled in the Land of the Free: Democracy, Indian Nations and the U.S. Constitution*, ed. Oren R. Lyons and John C. Mohawk (Santa Fe, N.M.: Clear Light Publishers, 1992), 227–80.

12. See M. Annette Jaimes, "False Images: Native Women in Hollywood Cinema," *Turtle Quarterly* (fall 1993).

13. See Jaimes, "American Indian Identification/Eligibility Policy in Federal Indian Education," chapter 1. This situation has escalated dramatically. The Indian Arts and Crafts Act of 1990, signed into law during the Bush administration, requires certification of Indian artists. It states that it is now a criminal act to proclaim oneself an "Indian" artist if one is not able to show BIA certification. Uncertified individuals can now be fined and jailed for impersonating an "Indian," and galleries that sell their art as "Indian" can be fined into bankruptcy. This certification is based on a race formula in contrast to the cultural criteria that has traditionally determined one's membership in a tribal group.

14. "BIA Can Declare Tribes Extinct," *American Indian Anti-Defamation Council (AIADC) Newsletter*, Denver, Colo. (July 1992): 13. "The new policy is stated deep in the text of a (BIA) decision last month denying recognition to the Miami tribe of Indiana. The BIA . . . says it has no plans to use the power to disqualify already-recognized tribes, though it claims the right to do so if they fall short of agency requirements on continuing existence" (ibid.). It should be noted that an Indian community can petition the Congress for federal recognition or for reinstatement of past recognition, but it is a long and expensive process, with no guarantees that the goal will be attained.

15. Elisabeth Lynn-Cook, "Meeting of Indian Professors Takes up Issues of 'Ethnic Fraud,' Sovereignty and Research Needs," *Wicazo Sa Review* 9 (spring 1993): 57–59.

16. See Robert K. Thomas, "On Pan-Indianism," in *The Emergent Native Americas: A Reader in Culture Contact*, ed. Deward E. Walker (Boston: Little, Brown, 1972), 741–76.

17. Marlys Duchene, "Problems in Curriculum Development in Indian Community Schools," paper presented at the Western Social Science Association Annual Conference, Albuquerque, New Mexico, 1980: 3.

18. Ward Churchill, "White Studies: The Intellectual Imperialism of Contemporary U.S. Education," *Integrateducation* 19 (January–April 1981): 51–57.

19. Ibid., 51.

20. See Vine Deloria Jr., *God Is Red: A Native View of Religion*, 2d ed. (Golden, Colo.: North American Press, 1992), 62–77; M. Annette Jaimes, "Native American Identity and Survival as 'Indigenism': Environmental Ethics for Economic Development" (forthcoming). See also the non-

Indian authors Anthony F. Aveni, *Empires of Time: Calendars, Clocks, and Cultures* (New York: Basic Books, 1989), and Michael O'Malley, *Keeping Watch: A History of American Time* (New York: Viking Press, 1990).

21. See Edward Said, "The Politics of Knowledge," in *Debating PC: The Controversy over Political Correctness on College Campuses*, ed. Paul Berman (New York: Dell Publishing, 1992), 172–89.

22. See, for example, work by George Moriega, Antonio Barriero, Vine Deloria Jr., Jimmie Durham, Ward Churchill, Louise Erdrich, Jack Forbes, Donald Grinde Jr., Joy Harjo, Linda Hogan, M. Annette Jaimes, Clara Sue Kidwell, Hans Koning, Winona LaDuke, John Mohawk, Glenn Morris, Jorge Noriega, Simon Ortiz, Rebecca Robbins, Wendy Rose, Kirkpatrick Sale, Leslie Marmon Silko, David Stannard, Lenore Stiffarm, Ines Talamantez, Russell Thornton, Dagmar Thrope, George Tinker, Haunani Trask, Laurie Whitt, and Winona Stevenson.

23. Ward Churchill, quoted in M. Annette Jaimes, "American Indian Studies: Towards an Indigenous Model," *American Indian Culture and Research Journal* no. 3 (fall 1987): 1.

24. Frantz Fanon, *The Wretched of the Earth* (New York: Grove Press, 1965); Guillermo Bonfil Batalla, Utopia y revolución: *El pensamiento político contemporáneo de los Indios en América Latina* (México: Editorial Nueva Imagen, 1981).

25. Vine Deloria Jr., "Indian Studies—The Orphan of Academia," *Wicazo Sa Review* 2 (fall 1986): 6.

26. Ward Churchill, "White Studies," 54.

27. See M. Annette Jaimes, "Native American Identity and Survival as 'Indigenism,'" and Ward Churchill, "I Am Indigenist," in *Struggle for the Land*. Churchill was perhaps the first to begin to employ this term with consistency in the United States. For example, see his "The New Genocide: An Indigenist Perspective on Native American Environments," *Akwesasne Notes* 18 (1986).

28. The World Council of Indigenous Peoples was one of the first entities in North America to start using this terminology with regularity. See, for example, J. R. Diabo, "The Emergence of Fourth World Politics in the International Arena," paper presented at the Western Social Science Annual Conference, San Diego, 1984.

CHAPTER FIVE

Like Being Mugged by a Metaphor

Multiculturalism and State Narratives

WAHNEEMA LUBIANO

Recently, I have been thinking about political subjects as subjects who imagine their position in the world and act, but who are also subject to state power. I have been thinking about the way the state manifests its power, especially when it does not call attention to its presence.[1] My title, then, was inspired by my interest in the presence of the state in the cultural narratives with which we imagine the world and the social constructions that act as mystifications. Some mystifications can kill or maim us. "Like being mugged by a metaphor" is a way to describe what it means to be at the mercy of racist, sexist, heterosexist, and global capitalist constructions of the meaning of skin color on a daily basis. Whether or not I am a card-carrying believer in distinctions of racial biology, I am nonetheless attacked by the hegemonic social formation's notions of racial being and the way those notions position me in the world. Like a mugging, this attack involves an exchange of assets: some aspect of the social order is enriched domestically and internationally by virtue of material inequities stabilized and narrativized by race oppression and I lose symbolically and monetarily. Further, I am physically traumatized and psychologically assaulted by an operation that is mystified. It goes on in the dark, so to speak—in the dark of a power that never admits to its own existence.

Michael Hanchard has argued that the analytic space between names and

64

appearances and "real problems" is socially traversed by collective and individual narratives.[2] He builds on Raymond Williams's assertion that "the conventional distinction between the material and the symbolic does not correspond to the social reality of language and signification as indissoluble elements of material process."[3] Hanchard makes this argument to remind us that changes in name, in construction, are contextual and not necessarily—but they can be—the mystification of other operations. For example, take the nineteenth-century use among Black people of the sign "American." The construction of Black people as Americans signified a specific refusal to go back to Africa at the urging of white people. It is true that some Blacks were also interested in emigration, but here Hanchard is referring to a set of polemics directed against white supremacists who insisted that Blacks go back to Africa. He is arguing that U.S. race relations have been a dance of meanings not necessarily about, but not excluding, pigmentation. In a similar vein, Michael Omi and Howard Winant argue, along with Stuart Hall, that race is "an unstable and 'decentered' complex of social meanings constantly being transformed by political struggle."[4] Furthermore, they argue that the U.S. state is a racial formation, part of an entire social order equilibrated unstably to preserve the prevailing racial order, and that race is neither an illusion nor an essence that an ideal social order would eliminate. Thus, while there is no universally accepted definition of race, nor a universally accepted position against racism, race can simply be thought of as any group of people generally believed to be, and generally accepted as, a race in any given arena of ethnic competition. As the sociologist Oliver Cox put it, if a person looks white but is in America called a Negro, that person is a Negro American.[5]

This understanding of race has all kinds of ramifications for state deployments of narratives that ensure a particular global economy. Within the terms of race relations in the United States, the tendency, then, of a white bourgeoisie is to proletarianize the whole racial group "Black" or "African American" so that it functions socially and politically as a *class*. In other words, there appear no easily discernible class differences among a racialized group's members in the eyes of the dominant group. Of course, this does not mean that there is no class stratification within the group, but rather that the state's narratives of power empty the meaning of the effects of class stratification on racially marked groups. I mention this as background because I am interested in under what circumstances, for whom, and to do what in the world the political subject is constructed. In other words, the state thinks the subject too. Thus, to some extent, what we think of ourselves in relation to the world, what we imagine ourselves to be in relation to the world, is also, under most circumstances, at least partially a state project. In my discussion of multiculturalism here, I am going to suggest what it means to be an intellectual affiliated with the university system; in doing so I want to remind us of the relationship of that work to the larger operations of state power.

What political work does insistence on a difference, on an identity, do? What political work does staging, performing, foregrounding, articulating, or criticizing recognition of an identity do? In a recent article entitled "Critical Multiculturalism," the Chicago Cultural Studies Group wrote: "What do subalterns have in common except that somehow they are dominated?—a statement so general as to be nearly useless."[6] The statement they sneer at is so important that I am amazed that they could not see it. *What do subalterns have in common except that somehow they are dominated?* "Somehow they are dominated" is the simplicity that is supposed to render the statement itself useless, when in fact it is that statement that signifies what subalterns have in common as individuals in groups attempting to project some form of political agency for themselves. Domination may not determine the specificity of a particular cultural, racial, gendered, sexualized, or classed group, but domination has everything to do with how we think about the internal complexities of those groups and their relationships to larger dominating groups. Somehow the statement "all they have in common is domination" empties out the very thing I want to focus on: what it means to be dominated. Domination is complicated and varied. But domination is so successful precisely because it sets the terrain upon which struggle occurs at the same time that it preempts opposition not only by already inhabiting the vectors where we would resist (i.e., by being powerfully in place and ready to appropriate oppositional gestures), but also by having already written the script that we have to argue within and against.

Part of that script includes what counts as "authentic" opposition, a partial result of that tendency to proletarianize the whole group I mentioned earlier. Our political imaginary always focuses on the non-middle-class person of color, and this focus is part of the reason why I want to highlight the university and the role of the activist intellectual there: one place the state makes its presence felt, but is not necessarily named, is the university. We need to articulate a political imaginary for the middle-class person of color in the university, where we still have a form of political agency, despite the onus that is demonized under the name of "elite intellectual activity." When I am accused of that, on my home ground, I say, "Yes, indeed. There's no getting around it. I not only occupy this hybrid, historically produced position of being an intellectual of color at an Ivy League university, but I'm not leaving it either. And I am not leaving it precisely because it seems to me that if we are willing to have the stain on our honor as people of color who are not 'authentic' political subjects, then there is a certain kind of work we can do there." I also admit to enjoying being in these places because part of what I have learned is that as incredibly corrupting as power is, there is something about it that we can use to help us stave off those corruptions if we are willing to be tainted by them. In a way, this work is another form of rugged bourgeois individualism, instilled in me by virtue of my great training in the U.S. educational system. But part of the impulse for this position comes from growing up in a particular set of circumstances. When I was six years old and I saw someone stomped to death in front of me as a result of a gang war, then I thought I knew what goodness was and what badness was. In the community's response I thought I saw that power was something you used in order to make sure that everybody was good in your imagining of what the good could be. Over the years, I've been traumatized in other more subtle ways and always my response to it has been that you must get in and grapple with the trauma, as opposed to allowing yourself simply to feel the injustice of it, or feel your own implication in the exercise of it. In other words, my complicity in the production of an elite research university system is not all I can be or do.

My understanding of multiculturalism against this context is guided by my troubled response to two questions: Can we affect any change in institutions aimed at the state through education? and Haven't some of us, to some extent and in some places, already begun to try to, if not transform the academy, then at least stage an opposition from within it? Haven't some of us also tried to stage opposition from within our entire educational system, including the K-12 schools? Haven't we tried to extend the knowledge that is produced and disseminated from the agreed-upon but inadequate re-creations of the status quo and its world dominance to something better? My response to these questions is always "yes and no." This double-edged response is true for multiculturalism as well. Can multiculturalism be reduced to cultural relativism, to an empty noncritical pluralism, or to an intellectual and social smorgasbord offered to particular clients by elite institutions or corporations for the purposes of elites, elite institutions, or corporations? Of course it can. But part of the work of those who have been and are engaged in radical multiculturalism is to keep it from being reduced to slogans, to meaning things like "Different strokes for different folks," or "To understand all is to forgive all," or "All we need is peace, love, and understanding."[7]

Within the parameters of the present hierarchical structure of the university, multiculturalism can be and has been in some places and in many ways thoroughly appropriated, diluted, and neutralized so that the domination of Eurocentric knowledge remains completely unchallenged. More to the point for my purpose is the connection between Eurocentric knowledge and the operation of international economies in the name of multiculturalism. For example, any university can simply continue business as usual by making available a selection of ethnic or racially specific courses without ever addressing the ways in which the focus of what we understand as Western culture is itself incomplete and distorted and has a political relationship to the ways in which our world is constructed. Nonetheless, to some limited extent, many universities and colleges are already multicultural. The constituencies that represent the marginalized multiplicity of U.S. culture are present there in some numbers, but—and this is a huge "but"—neither their presence nor the specific knowledge that inheres within the terms of those constituencies has any real curricular or institutional presence or force. Therefore, in order for multiculturalism to be something other than an empty abstraction used by administrators to take the political heat off their institutions, those of us interested in transformative multiculturalism must insist that it cannot be held to exist within dominance at the same time that we use multiculturalism as a way to intervene in that dominance. Multiculturalism is, then, an organizing principle, a tendency to use the space opened up by discussions under rubrics previously marginalized, or not known at all, to do particular work for particular people, including the middle-class intellectuals of color, who have not known previously to think of themselves as operating within a political imaginary.

Multiculturalism is a deliberate attempt on the part of the historically marginalized to reconstitute not simply particular curricula, but the academy itself as part of what George Lipsitz has called "the enormous industry of meaning making."[8] The pressure that is organized under the sign of multiculturalism and placed on universities, colleges, and the public school system to change curricula, admissions, and faculty and staff composition, has forced such institutions to respond, in however inadequate and attenuated a fashion, to the demands of traditionally marginalized cultures for the inclusion of individuals, for group power, and for some reorganization of these institutions. It can be made to do more. But why would we want to make a sinking ship do more? Apart from the fact that the ship is something that is going to pull us down if it doesn't transform, if it isn't made to transform, we will have abandoned it to others. To abandon the university as a site for this kind of work is to abandon the incredibly powerful if co-effected relationship between the university system, the primary and secondary educational system in the United States, and a military and international global economy.

I am not only referring to public relations assistance to the movement of global capital that depresses the wages of labor everywhere to bring you baskets and blouses from Thailand and Buicks from Mexico, and which sends fuel air explosives from the United States to the rest of the world. Nor am I referring only to liberal tolerance of difference, necessary for discussion, but insufficient to effect change. Instead, I am trying to describe a field of inevitable ongoing contestation, argument, and reformation. In regard to the particular criticism that multiculturalism can assist the perpetuation of Western dominance through the creation of a new pluralism to be consumed by elites, I suggest that we remember that even without multiculturalism, other forms of state and elite management continue business as usual. If elites manage business as usual and can't call it multiculturalism, they will simply call it something else. We cannot give up the ground because of what they can do in the name of the ground on which we have chosen to fight. The process of normalization or the work of oppositional gestures is an ongoing dynamic of our system and, of course, multiculturalism can be used to continue such management. Radical multiculturalism, however, turns its attention to demystifying just such management and to fighting it. Contestation is the driving force of such a dynamic. As David Lloyd has argued, "Culture is the ground for both accommodation to and contestation of state desires."[9] As such, it's an important ground for the work of those of us who think of ourselves as progressives engaged in both domestic social justice and international economic justice.

I want to be specific about the complexities of multiculturalism and its negotiation of politics and epistemology. For instance, radical multiculturalism is not just an attempt to make sure that the estimates of genocidal oppression are correct. The work of revising our notions of New World discovery in order to include the knowledge that the North American Indian population was decimated by 1900, and that the twelve million slaves shipped to the New World by 1870 represented less than a third of those captured, is important work, not only for reasons of intellectual accuracy, but also because the work of de-aestheticizing the myth of a glorious New World (or a New World Order) has something to do with establishing the cost of imperialism, including the cost to the peasants back in the Old World of the skewed fifteenth-, sixteenth-, and seventeenth-century conquest economies.

This work has something to do with influencing how priorities are set by the state and with articulating how the U.S. national subject understands the nation's place in the world and its history. De-aestheticizing the myth of America is one of the means by which we do cultural work to oppose the incredibly powerful state myth of a romantic and conquering American past.

But multiculturalism's work is not just epistemological. Universities are corporate in their very structures. They are workplaces for hundreds of thousands of workers and they are legitimation factories at the same time. What kind of work can and ought those of us engaged in radical multiculturalism do in these places? Universities are in the business of investments, of initiating and cooperating in corporate business projects, and are producing research that contributes to the way in which the United States shapes and controls the world economy. It is important, therefore, that we target for pressure the makeup of decision-making bodies in that corporate university, and that the new knowledge produced by multicultural intellectualism be used as part of that pressure. Radical multiculturalism, for example, can include attempting to influence decisions such as whether to focus on high-tech military research, Department of Defense contracts, or fuel air explosives instead of contributing to research based on meeting housing needs. It can influence decisions on whether to reconsider not only lopsided hiring practices at all employment levels in the university, but also the means by which the marginalized are represented in the policy-making entities of the university.

Multiculturalism can of course be appropriated. It can be normalized in ways that lend themselves to static and conservative politics. So can democracy, or the discourse of democracy, or specifically deployed uses of democracy. At the sound of the word "democracy," for example, some people in different parts of the world, including parts of the United States and its sphere of influence, either reach for their wallets or their guns or duck and cover while they grab their loved ones. Yet, both of the academic organizations established over the past three years to oppose "political correctness" bashing and assaults by conservatives on the generation of new knowledges in the academy have made the word "democratic" part of their names: the Teachers for Democratic Culture and the Union of Democratic Intellectuals. Those of us who are part of either or both of those organizations, or those of us who are determined not to let democracy stand for the operation of laissez-faire capitalism, have a stake in claiming the word, its meaning, and its vision. Within the terms of this vision of democracy, multiculturalism is a term worth fighting over also. The analogy to democracy is meant to demonstrate that multiculturalism does not have to displace other ways of describing the projects outlined within the terms of this essay, but neither is it dismissable on the basis of its appropriability by corporations or even by sites within the academy that are hostile to its political force.

By the time I came to undergraduate study at Howard University, being a Black Studies major meant, among other things, studying slavery in a two-semester comparative course so that we could see American slavery in a world context. When we studied imperial American cultures, it meant thinking about movements through history and within race differences. We studied Black history not simply to understand what was left out of many American history books—Black relations to whites, for example—but to understand Black relations to other nonwhite groups. Doing so meant facing up to what was painful for a lot of the students, facing up to what the Western frontier meant to Blacks, for instance. The Western frontier meant, on one hand, escape from the South after Reconstruction failed. On the other hand, it also meant participation for some Blacks in the wars against the Native peoples and the massacres of those peoples. Conquest, then, was not just something that Euro-Americans did to other people. Blacks, too, had a complicated and sometimes complicitous relation to that conquest. I use that as one small example of what radical multiculturalism can make its object of business.

Although multiculturalism cannot fix all that ails the U.S. polity in general, or the education system specifically, it is a way to intervene at the site of education and in the tensions that tie larger structural global concerns and policies to intellectual and cultural work. We should remember that the military and prisons, for example, places where the state is present, both create and rely on knowledge produced by universities about marginalized groups. Radical multiculturalism offers the possibility of countering the state's use of the intellectual and cultural productions of and about marginalized groups and thus offers institutionally transformative possibilities for middle-class people of color affiliated with universities who, as I've suggested, are also themselves bound up with this state-sponsored knowledge.

What is involved in imagining the university's relationship to an international military capitalist economy and a domestic prison economy? What role do culture and cultural opposition play in this imagination? Remember that I have been arguing that the state is involved in these imaginings. One job of the state is to make its manifestations of power in the operation of the economy culturally acceptable. Part of the way the state accomplishes this acceptance is to make culture the terrain, the place, where we imagine our relationship to the world. When we think of state power we do not tend to consider gender socialization and homophobia as constitutive to the way in which the state authorizes itself, partially because the effects of class are obscured, and partially because our gendered and sexualized identities are often the means through which we imagine ourselves outside of the purview of the explicitly political. But, imagining ourselves to be outside of the purview of the explicitly political allows us to participate in concrete ways in an international military economy and a domestic prison economy.

Consider Black males in prison, who are visible and overwhelmingly identified as Black men, as racial subjects. Ninety-three percent of the Black male prison population is comprised of people who were poor, unemployed, or underemployed. Of those who were employed, their average incomes were less than ten thousand dollars a year. Among all people in prison, roughly 85 percent are poor.[10] Black male prisoners or those who will be in prison (or could be as a result of their participation in illegal alternate economic activities) are not identified as poor: they are identified as a Black transgressive outlaw group. The state's identification of them as such and the generalization of that identity are an imposition, a means by which the state dominates culturally, you might say. But it is also the case that Black male prisoners or those who will be in prison or could be in prison internalize a warrior ethos, with its attendant homophobia and patriarchalism, that is relayed elsewhere. This is in large part a result of the invisible cultural hand of the state, which imposes upon the most imposed group its own ethos, an ethos that seems to exist as if it did not have state sponsorship.

This dynamic has implications for Black women who are, as a group, dominated economically and politically regardless of whether each woman or all women are always at the mercy of the same types and degrees of oppression. Black women must function within the Black community where the warrior ethos finds its cultural expression. The warrior ethos remains unchallenged partially because the state seems so absent at its most local articulations. The inability to challenge the state sponsorship of the warrior ethos leads the community as a whole, including those not explicitly engaging in a warrior ethos, to reproduce patriarchal relations that cannot be recognized as state-sponsored. An example: gangs are not only the means by which the drug economy organizes itself ostensibly outside the realm of the state, they are also concentrations of gender socialization and one means by which the drug economy romanticizes itself in the community at large. Women become, willy-nilly, part of this cultural economy that perpetuates a warrior ethos through their roles as socializing agents. This socializing takes place not only in the context of the attenuated history of patriarchy within the community, but within the constraints imposed on Black women to prove to the state that they are not "culturally poor" mothers and can produce "strong" men.

In other words, the constructions of our various beings as a group are both material and cultural. The material and the cultural are neither completely separate nor do they operate autonomously. The idea "Black people" is a social reality. Black people are a dominated group politically and economically, even if every member is not always dominated under all circumstances. Individuals who think themselves part of the social and historical consciousness of the group are claimed by that group and/or accused by others of being part of the group. These claims to group membership, or accusations of group membership, whether imposed or voluntary, function as cultural narratives that make the operation of a political economy possible. Insofar as these narratives are tied to a prison economy, a warrior ethos, and a patriarchal structure within the community *that makes itself known to the community as part of an empowering device for the group as a whole, the cultural apparatus of the state is doing its work.* To put it bluntly, Black people who consciously think of themselves as part of a Black group often think of themselves as oppositional at the very same time as they are internalizing precisely the state's most effective narratives, narratives that are the medium by which the state dominates the group in ways the group does recognize.

Black men and women as an outlaw group: this metaphor is part of a cultural narrative that builds a domestic economy. Think of the prison economy as a capital investment project that rests on the particular manipulation of a group of people. Think of the drug trade as posing such a necessity for disciplinary measures that the whole group's identity is wrapped in this disciplinary necessity. Think of the "culture of poverty" and its ethnographic knowledge as the grease that makes the engine of the United States' racial imagination run more smoothly. Think about how the international circulation of all these narratives forces those of us who are temporarily not in prison, or temporarily not being targeted, but who are concerned about the drug trade's ravaging of our neighborhoods, to participate in the state's disciplinary apparatus, sometimes without our even knowing it.

What does a prison economy have to do with an international military economy, and what does that have to do with selecting the university as a site for radical multiculturalism? In the dominant imaginary, the United States is threatened from within by Black men and the drug trade and by Black women and their culture of poverty. The threat from within prepares the ground by which the American public recognizes the threat from without. And how do people learn something new? By analogy, by reference to what is already understood. The bogey man in the closet is prepared for by the various fears already available to us. Black men and Black women are highly visible in the media, but they are also highly visible *to themselves as metaphors for deviance* and for transgressiveness. These metaphors are so visible within the group that they function as the grid through which we check our concrete reality. Consider how many times certain Black intellectual work has been dismissed because (*a*) it won't save crack babies in the ghetto, or (*b*) it won't reach the brother on the street corner selling crack. This dismissal depends on the renarrativization of all possible effects of epistemological change by virtue of a larger narrative that is so highly visible before us that we think everything through that narrative. The socially, economically, and politically constructed issue of Black pathology becomes, then, the extended metaphor that explains the world and delimits what we could do to change it. That metaphor prevents us from seeing how Black pathology as an explanation is state-derived. But it also prevents us from understanding *the general power of the state to provide, to the public imagination, metaphors for explaining how the world works.*

What does this have to do with multiculturalism and the university? Over the past 250 years, university scholars have created and legitimated the knowledge that has justified the particular oppression I have been discussing. University scholars have provided the necessary cultural justifications for the movement of capital and for state imperatives and policies. University scholars have provided fodder for the cultural narratives that tell the stories of Black people. The university generates and disseminates the metaphors and narratives that thoroughly imagine our world. Those metaphors and those narratives are the very stuff of our educational system, our media representations, our state policy, our individual lives. Black pathology is a thoroughgoing and useful academic production for the state.

I have five brothers. All five have been in the military, four of them in the Korean War, one in the Vietnam War. Their military participation is not at all unusual for working-class Black families. The military is one of the ways that one ensures oneself a job for the time being and possibly the chance at a better job afterward. But the military is also the romantic manifestation of a warrior ethos for individuals concerned that their position within a socially and politically dominated group means that somehow they're female and not male. I have a seventeen-year-old niece who is a community college student. She tells me, "I want to become a prison guard." She tells me, "The prison system is the fastest growing sector in the U.S. economy." She tells me, "I want a job with some chance for career advancement." She tells me, "I do not want to just work in McDonald's. I do not want to just have babies like my friends. I do not want to clean anybody's house like Grandma did." She tells me, "I don't understand why you're so upset." Part of what I have said to her in response I have been trying to convey here. The water is being poisoned right here at the epistemological well. It is important to make a stand right here at that well. These life-directing narratives are produced by a political economy and by an educational system where the state's presence is most dangerous because it is where it is most unnamed.

Notes

This essay includes some material previously published in *Concerns: Women's Caucus for the Modern Languages* 22, no. 3 (1992): 11–21, and in *Debating P.C.: The Controversy over Political Correctness on College Campuses*, ed. Paul Berman (New York: Dell, 1992).

1. See, for example, Wahneema Lubiano, "Standing in for the State: Black Nationalism and 'Writing' the Black Subject," *Alphabet City* 3 (1993): 20–23.

2. Michael Hanchard, "Identity, Meaning, and the African-American," *Social Text* 24 (1990).

3. Raymond Williams, *Marxism and Literature* (New York: Oxford University Press, 1977), 99.

4. Michael Omi and Howard Winant, *Racial Formation in the United States: From the 1960s to the 1990s*, 2d ed. (New York: Routledge, 1994): 55.

5. See Oliver Cox, *Caste, Class, and Race* (New York: Monthly Review Press, 1970 [1948]).

6. Chicago Cultural Studies Group, "Critical Multiculturalism," *Critical Inquiry* 18 (1992): 543.

7. For a program of radical multiculturalism, see Ted Gordon and Wahneema Lubiano, "The Statement of the Black Faculty Caucus," in *Debating P.C.: The Controversy over Political Correctness on College Campuses*, ed. Paul Berman (New York: Dell, 1992), 249–57.

8. George Lipsitz, discussion at the "What Is an Oppositional Left?" conference at the University of Vermont, March 8, 1991.

9. David Lloyd, discussion at the "Americanist Vision of Cultural Studies" conference at Columbia University, March 7, 1992.

10. See *The Fortress Economy: The Economic Role of the U.S. Prison System*, Alexander C. Lichtenstein and Michael A. Kroll (Philadelphia: American Friends Service Committee, 1990), 6–12.

CHAPTER SIX

Multiculturalism's Unfinished Business

CHRISTOPHER NEWFIELD AND AVERY F. GORDON

Contrary to its media image, multiculturalism wasn't born yesterday. Its most important but largely forgotten development took place in the early and middle 1970s in work on primary and secondary education. This earlier work was developed far from the newly multicultural humanities programs at highly selective private universities like Stanford that received most of the coverage in the late 1980s. As expressed in statements by the American Association of Colleges of Teacher Education or in articles in the *Journal of Teacher Education*, 1970s multiculturalism was a grassroots attempt at community-based racial *reconstruction* through that vital local institution, the neighborhood public school. It attempted a multidimensional approach relatively foreign to the compartmentalized knowledges of universities, addressing institutional factors along with questions of personal identity, bi- and tricultural relations, community culture, teacher attitudes and behavior, school administrative structures, and local politics and economics, among others.

In its strongest 1990s versions, multiculturalism continues to have a similar potential to reform racial inequalities within existing institutions. As we mentioned in the Introduction, the meaning of multiculturalism remains varied and often vague despite its growing presence as a policy rubric in schools, businesses, arts and other cultural institutions, the military, and various local and national political organizations. In this essay, we don't survey all the possible meanings of multiculturalism or its institutional practices. Instead, we focus on a general conceptual source for multiculturalism's limited but positive potential to describe one of the baseline conditions necessary for the establishment of multiracial democracy in the United States.

The prominence of multiculturalism in the late 1980s and 1990s can be traced to many complex economic, political, and cultural factors, some of which are discussed by the other contributors to this volume. From the point of view of the popular imagination, multiculturalism's most insistent reason for being is a recognition, however belated, of the fundamentally multiracial and multiethnic nature of the United States. This recognition, though often divorced from the long-standing and broader struggles that produced it, is occurring in what is now called a post-civil rights context, a context in which most Americans believe themselves and the nation to be opposed to racism and in favor of a multiracial, multiethnic pluralism. Whatever delusions and contradictions attach to this belief, and there are many, it nonetheless remains a deeply held structure of feeling. It is in this environment that this essay offers a conceptual source for multiculturalism's potential to describe how to achieve even the limited result of a true cultural pluralism. True pluralism is the surprisingly rare precondition for the democratic debate of a range of economic, political, and cultural problems. It involves taking the widely accepted notion of cultural pluralism and divorcing it from its longtime companion, *assimilationism*. It involves rejecting assimilationist forms of pluralism, particularly what we'll call the supremacist and unionist variants that use pluralism to conceal repressive effects.

Problems and Limits

Multiculturalism's most general goal in the 1970s was to reorganize education for the benefit of minority students. Its proponents saw it as an idea that supported other everyday work toward antiracist social and cultural life. Multicultural education served as an umbrella term for a variety of racial equity projects. It did not envision revolutionary change, but did seek to dismantle white-majority control of schools and the use of white backgrounds and values as the sole yardstick of excellence. It sought to recover lost knowledge and thereby produce new understandings of U.S. history and social life. At its broadest reach, multiculturalism imagined the building of racial democracy through popular pluralism. Its cultural pluralism was popular in that it imagined ways in which intercultural rules would be drawn and re-drawn by those affected by them, particularly by people of color, rather than by experts, bureaucrats, and managers, particularly white ones.

Multiculturalism sought the means through which, in Manning Mar-able's phrase, "people of color [could] radically redefine the nature of democracy."[1] But there are good reasons to be suspicious of multicultural-ism's ability to perform such a redefinition of the national framework. Many of this volume's contributors see multiculturalism as obstructive or irrele-vant to the progressive work they deem most essential. We heartily share their concerns. Marable himself, who defends multiculturalism as an ally of genuine and multiracial democracy, calls for an interconnected set of pro-jects that does not obviously need the concept of multiculturalism, even though expanded multiculturalism needs them: the completion of civil and human rights movements, the enactment of feminist visions, opposition to homophobia, international resistance to tyranny and exploitation, ex-panded critiques of capitalism, and situation-specific cross-racial alliances among people of color.[2] Each of these crucial projects has a life of its own as well as numerous practitioners, and each seems like exactly the kind of po-litical and social movement that is doing just fine without multiculturalism's *cultural* focus.

Multiculturalism's cultural turn has been highly significant in advancing our understandings of race, power, identity, and social institutions. It has helped to displace biological notions of race and is compatible with anti-essentialist notions of racial, ethnic, gender, class, and sexual identity, in which one's identity is real and determinate without being fixed or defined by inherent properties supposedly shared by every member of the group. It has allowed us to focus on how internal differences comprise a group with-out undermining that group's reality. It has helped us to see how porous and flexible group boundaries are, allowing for explorations of hybridity, bor-derlands, and imaginative coalitions, while at the same time helping us to understand how intersectional identities are both constrained and creative. The turn to culture has fostered the exploration of identity as a process of identification, a partly voluntary, partly contradictory, always constructed set of multiple ties to a group or groups. Culture has also shown how per-sonal identity and group formation are themselves political, being directly involved in the application of resources and power. In short, the turn to cul-ture has given us a whole new vocabulary for describing the experiences, ar-tifacts, values, struggles, and history of various groups who are marked and subordinated by race, gender, and sexuality. And, it has, of course, been an important component in the extraordinary efforts to redefine the nature and content of knowledge itself.

But culture has its own history of dubious battles. Although the concept of culture can insist on the sociocultural reality of race and racism, it doesn't always do so. The culturalism of multiculturalism threatens to shift attention from racialization to culture and in so doing to treat racialized groups as one of many diverse and interesting cultures. This makes racism more difficult to acknowledge and control: phenomena that might be at least partially attributed to racism, such as crime in racially segregated, low-income neighborhoods, can be attributed in a culturalist approach to the deficient, or just different, values of the sufferers. Seeing whiteness as cultural produces a complementary blindness. While the attention to whiteness as a cultural system has been a very important move in the reconceptualization of race problems, it downplays the ongoing existence of white supremacy as a system of privilege, favoritism, discrimination, and exclusion. Indeed, given existing racial inequalities and the continuing segregation of most social institutions, the reduction of all racial groups to a nonexistent level playing field poses serious problems. Multiculturalism has also been very uncertain about where gender and sexuality fit into its notion of cultures. When the culturalization of race meets up with a de-gendered and de-sexualized notion of race, the cultural move takes us two steps backward in our efforts to develop complex understandings of intersecting identities and social power.

The most severe problem with multiculturalism's culturalism is that it can be satisfied with bracketing or avoiding institutional and structural determinants of inequality. Social scientists, in particular, are very familiar with the ways in which cultural emphases have mistaken symptoms for causes and promoted an individualized understanding of advantage and disadvantage. For example, explanations of urban poverty that invoke a culture of poverty have allowed researchers to ignore poverty's institutional causes. Ignoring factors such as the loss of urban industry to cheap labor zones abroad, culturalists have blamed poverty on the unemployed and underemployed's bad attitudes toward work (see Zavella in this volume). At the most general level, multiculturalism's culturalism can allow for the segregation of culture from systematic social relations of power like capitalism, patriarchy, and neocolonialism. This segregation both subjectivizes the concept of culture, treating culture not as a structure but as an "ephemeral set of behavioral attitudes and values,"[3] *and* de-culturalizes economic and political structures, treating the latter as transparent objective forces.

Multiculturalism is plagued with doubts arising from these weaknesses and others superbly analyzed elsewhere in this volume. Whether it will be able to provide the conceptual and practical tools necessary for a multiracial democracy is uncertain at this time. What multiculturalism does do is address the need to avoid even benevolent white oversight over the process by which various groups reconstruct democracy and social justice. Multiculturalism's tradition does specifically challenge the most lethal *cultural* aspect of white rule—assimilationism—which allows the mere presence of white people to be a form of control. As we'll try to suggest, a strong multiculturalism can at least extract cultural equity out of the pluralism such a multitude of Americans claim to favor.

Assimilationism

Multiculturalism arises largely from the tradition of cultural pluralism. Although it might seem surprising, cultural pluralism has frequently been a determined opponent of white-norm assimilationism. By assimilationism we do not mean *assimilation*, the means and ends pursued by immigrants or marginalized citizens who wish to join the existing economic and political mainstream. Wanting assimilation often indicates a desire for the kinds of interesting jobs, pleasant neighborhoods, home ownership, financial security, personal leisure time, good health care, vacations, community influence, and other benefits that in the United States are reserved for the proverbial middle class. We are not here passing any kind of judgment on the wish to assimilate in this sense. We are instead criticizing the *terms* that *assimilationism* extracts from those who need and want its rewards. Assimilationism likes to portray itself as nothing more than the innocent desire for a good life, and indeed this is the foundation of its social influence. But as we use the term here, assimilationism refers to a specific ideology that sets the fundamental conditions for full economic and social citizenship in the United States. It is this ideology that we criticize here, and that multiculturalism and cultural pluralism have often pointedly opposed.

Assimilationism has three main features, all of which are contested by the genuinely pluralist traditions we will discuss. Assimilationism requires adherence to core principles and behaviors. It rejects racialized group consciousness. And it repudiates cultural equity among groups. These three features are profoundly interconnected. The demand for a common core displaces both demands for equality and the effects of racial difference. Lacking any notion of cultural equality, assimilationism encourages functional ranking of various cultures. Downplaying the effects of racial marking, assimilationism ignores the way supposedly neutral institutions are pro-white.

Through the interaction of these features, assimilationism continually militates against demands for enhanced equality. It declares these a threat to social harmony and peace, and requires instead the kind of individual upward mobility that, though individually beneficial, does not challenge unjust ground rules since it is contingent on obeying them. Assimilationism requires different groups to follow standards they had no share in making and that they may dislike, even as it presents these requirements as the bedrock of orderly freedom. These standards are very difficult to criticize because they seem inclusive, neutral, and unifying rather than racial and divisive. Assimilationism is the general operating system for everybody's different software of cultural interaction. And it is an immensely powerful opponent of all kinds of equity movements in American life.

Assimilationism is compatible with pluralism, but it is *antipluralist* in a fundamental sense. Pluralism, in the words of one college dictionary, holds that "no single explanatory system or view of reality can account for all the phenomena of life."[4] In the United States, pluralism has been translated as *e pluribus unum*, meaning that multiple groups are subsumed into a single whole. But the strong version of pluralism *rejects* what goes by its name in the United States, since it denies that the many are finally united by the one. What we usually call pluralism in this country is a pluralism of form leading to a monism of rules. It should be called *assimilationist pluralism*, where the outcome is not actually irreducibly plural, but a union or core. Assimilationist pluralists continually insist on conformity to this core even as they profess their belief in plurality. This assimilationist-pluralist position is contradictory, and yet it forms a pillar of the American Creed, standing next to its fellow pillars "democracy" and "free enterprise" and transforming these into elements of a core political culture. Strong versions of cultural pluralism, like the 1970s multiculturalism developed largely by people of color, tried to rehabilitate pluralism as an *alternative* to assimilationism.

The contrast between the two is not so easily sustained. Assimilationism generally tries to endorse pluralism and accuses its adversaries of failing to do so. It charges those who attack the inequalities of assimilationism with attacking pluralism itself.

The recent multiculturalism debates provide an excellent example of this dynamic, which has typified post-World War II racial discourse. One side— call them race progressives—challenged multiculturalism as Eurocentric assimilationism in disguise. It believed that multiculturalism tolerated harmless kinds of diversity while continuing to enforce Euro-American norms. This side called for rejecting weak multiculturalism in favor of cultural equal time and a redistribution of institutional space and power. A second group treated these criticisms of assimilationism as an (ironically, "multicultural") attack on pluralism itself. Group two denounced multiculturalism as a stalking horse for cultural separatism, which it believed to be perennially responsible for civil unrest and national decline. Thus "multiculturalism" in the 1990s came to denote not so much any particular position in an argument about race relations but the argument itself.

This argument has a general postwar form: An opposition group suggests that beneath the borrowed mantle of pluralism is the old emperor of assimilationism militating against cultural and social equality. The emperor says that his critics are not really complaining about the alleged assimilationism beneath his pluralist mantle, but about his pluralist skin itself. His skin, he says, is not merely white, but a neutral tone that harmonizes many colors. Asserting his nakedness, he continues, is a cheap way of denying his ingrained pluralism. As soon as his opponents are successfully branded separatist or nationalist or otherwise blind to pluralism, they lose. This outcome remains a major media hit. Much of the media seems convinced that multicultural research, teaching, and art that put racial power and inequity on the table undermine not so much the wrongs of assimilationism but the rainbow harmonies of a post-civil rights pluralism. Social unrest is traced to calls for racial equity rather than to the emperor's efforts to contain them.

We side with those who are wary of anything that seems like assimilationism in disguise. Many versions of multiculturalism have indeed been this. Even at its closest approach to the popular pluralism we will elaborate, multiculturalism is not likely to be a radical force that undermines the existing ensemble of social relations. It is reformist, and its reforms, though they go beyond a narrow definition of culture, cannot substitute for other kinds of political and social activity. Nonetheless, multiculturalism has the crucial job of constructing a new nonwhite majority without the assimilationist premises being so warmly defended today. Multiculturalism has at times been very good at making white people mean the good things they say about pluralism. Fortifying itself with various race-based nationalisms, and retaining its interest in antiessentialist and hybridized forms, strong multiculturalism can continue to develop its long-standing *rejection of assimilationism from within cultural pluralism itself.* Pluralism remains something like a majority ideology in the United States. Reconditioning it could link large numbers of people to pluralism's most important idea—the never-ending designing and redesigning of "America" out of the *equitable* interaction of its multiple and racialized centers.

Our essay, then, investigates this imperfect tradition within cultural pluralism, from its 1920s roots to its development in the 1970s as "multiculturalism" on through its most hopeful elements today.

Kallen's Pluralist Attack on Assimilationism

Multiculturalism is saddled with the weight of its major precursor, *cultural pluralism*. Cultural pluralism has come to signify cultural "multiplicity in a unity," in the phrase of the term's official source, Horace Kallen, writing in the *Nation* in 1915.[5] Defined in this way, cultural pluralism redivides the public along familiar lines. Some stress multiplicity and some stress unity. The former are wary that pluralist *unity* is a nice word for the assimilation of all U.S. groups to Euro-American or even Anglo-Saxon norms. The latter insist that *pluralist* unity can dissolve our national institutions into partisan tools of interest-group bickering and even civil war. The former group worries about cultural *autonomy;* the latter is preoccupied with cultural *commonality.* The former denounces the cultural *dominance* of the majority, while the latter rejects the cultural *separatism* of the minority.

This argument has gone back and forth for most of this century, with each side laying claim to the mantle of pluralism, though always a pluralism fortified with some other principle (like a core American "creed"). This kind of bipolar arrangement tempts people to split the difference and say the truth lies in the middle, in a combination of autonomy and commonality, of multiplicity and unity. Recently, for example, the respected sociologist Troy Duster, drawing conclusions from the University of California, Berkeley's "Diversity Project," invoked Horace Kallen as a forebear of a kind of third way (a "third experience") of diversity between the untenable poles of separatism and assimilation: "In a pluralist society, ethnic and racial groups can maintain distinctive cultures, organizations, and identities while they participate in the larger community. Individual members of ethnic and racial groups may choose to live in delimited communities, marry within their own group, . . . [but] they also relate to others."[6] Multiculturalism needs to update Kallen's "differences in a symphonic blend or harmony" to acknowledge more conflict and ongoing difference. But it remains tied to the project of balancing independence and interaction.

But cultural pluralism, in Kallen's usage, was something more precise than multiplicity in unity. It was formed in opposition to some subtle updates of the stress on "unity." We can clarify the current dispute somewhat by noting that Kallen defined cultural pluralism in *opposition* to one kind of thought that currently claims the name. His most lasting contribution to pluralism is not his encouragement of a third way that balances difference and unity, but his strong tilt away from unity, which writers like Arthur Schlesinger Jr. ignore.

In his later elaboration of cultural pluralism, Kallen makes clear that the idea came into being as the enemy of assimilationism. At one time, he claims, "Americanization" sought "cultural monism" as its outcome: "Any immigrant on whom difference from the natives lays a burden of inferiority will take Americanization for identification, for digesting differences from them into sameness with them. From this point of view equality *is* identity"—no actual equality between different groups exists, for difference is replaced by emulation and replication.[7] Kallen periodically casts doubt on phrases like "the union of the diverse" and the "American Idea" in distinguishing pluralism from monism, which of course raises the prospect of a subtler kind of assimilationism happening all over again.[8] How does Kallen draw a line between his version of pluralism, always flirting with unity, and the kind of unity denoted by traditional assimilationism?

Three features are particularly important. First, cultural pluralism opposes the idea of a *core culture*, one that defines a true national identity. Kallen traces this notion to what he calls "cultural racism":

> A new sort of racism emerged [in the late nineteenth century] to segregate and account for the American past and to rationalize present claims. This has its analogies with the racism of Kipling's "white man's burden." But it was not a racism of color as in imperial Britain and America's Southern states. It was a racism of culture. It claimed that the American Idea and the American Way were hereditary to the Anglo-Saxon stock and to that stock only; that other stocks were incapable of producing them, learning them and living them. If, then, America is to survive as a culture of creed and code, it can do so only so long as the chosen Anglo-Saxon race retains its integrity of flesh and spirit and freely sustains and defends their American expression against alien contamination. Universal suffrage, for example, *is* such a contamination [in this view].[9]

Kallen rejects what he takes to be a biological claim that "Anglo-Saxon" honesty and so on arise from its "stock." But his major complaint is with the identification of the American Way with one particular group. Such a view acknowledges U.S. diversity while identifying the real national culture with the culture of only one group. No less dangerous than biological racism is a cultural racism that assumes that institutions pervaded by Anglo-Saxon persons or ideas can stand for the American Idea. For Kallen, an institution can be "American" only when it is *not* Anglo-Saxon. The American always includes the plurality of America's actual groups. Whatever Kallen means by the unity of diversity, this unity cannot have any one cultural center. The grounding of the American in an Anglo-Saxon or other core is not only monoculturalism; it is cultural racism or what we might call *cultural supremacism.*

Second, Kallen's cultural pluralism insists on the irreducible social reality of *group life.* He rejects the idea that one's group identity must finally dissolve into a larger whole or that one's "individuality" is separate from one's membership in a group. A "group-life prolongs and redirects the lives of the individuals whose association generates, sustains and impels the formations of the group. Individuals not only live and move and nourish their being amid traditions, they are themselves traditions."[10] Kallen is not what we would now call an essentialist on groups: they overlap, move, and mix. Even the word tradition itself, he says, means "a carrying on, a continuous ongoing—but a carrying on, or ongoing, as any person's life goes on, not changelessly, but as a process of changing."[11] Nor is he a determinist: "In freedom, commitment and withdrawal are collaborative decisions of the individual, not compulsions of his group or of any of its institutions."[12] Groups are a fundamental feature of American life, and indeed of culture itself. Cultural groups cannot be dismissed as artificial political factions or as corruptions of the American Idea, because they are the American Idea itself.

Third, many of Kallen's "unifying" moments demand equality among diverse cultures. Cultural pluralism marks "an orchestration of diverse utterances of diversities . . . each developing freely and characteristically in its own enclave, and somehow so intertwined with the others, as to suggest, even to symbolize, the dynamic of the whole. Each is a cultural reservoir whence flows its own singularity of expression to unite in the concrete intercultural total which is the culture of America."[13] Kallen retains concepts like the "whole," although these concepts will betray his better purpose. But orchestration does not necessarily mean the subordination of lesser cultures to one with a broader perspective or higher wisdom. "Note the word 'intercultural.' . . . The intent is in the . . . prefix: *inter,* which here postulates the parity of the different and their free and friendly communication with one another as both co-operators and competitors."[14] *Equality precedes "unity,"* and the unity is the "total" outcome of these interactions, a result that follows from independent *cultural* activities encountering each other. Unity thus does not guide these encounters.

Writers who summon Kallen's cultural pluralism as a mainstream of racial thought are not, whether they know it or not, authorizing diversity subsumed by cultural union. They are also, whether they mean to or not, conjuring some pretty specific criteria for genuine pluralism: a *multicentered* national culture, which cannot be identified with the values of a dominant group or groups; the inevitability of *cultural groups*; and *cultural parity* among these different cultures, rather than implicit hierarchy. Kallen's cultural pluralism has some serious deficiencies, which we will discuss. But it comprises a much more rigorously democratic model of multigroup negotiations than do most that go by its label today.

In fact, it was precisely this kind of cultural pluralism that came under fire in the 1980s in the name of pluralism. With Kallen's efforts in mind, we can find choicer names for these recent detractors.

The Struggle for Pluralism (1): The New Supremacists

Kallen's work on cultural multiplicity perpetuated some serious flaws. One appeared in his silence on the difference between white ethnic and racialized groups.[15] Taking white ethnics as his standard, he overlooked the importance of racial exclusion and subordination in American life. Complacent about the increasing political equality among whites, he did not explore the dependence of genuine cultural pluralism on political and economic parity. He assumed that American capitalism was not subject to the diversity principle and would foster the economic mobility required to integrate ethnic groups into a culturally variegated society. He was also so drawn to concepts of union, harmony, and the One that there was plenty of room for later writers to read him, as Schlesinger does, as grounding plurality in a higher unity. Nonetheless, subsequent theorists of pluralism could have attempted to refine Kallen by eliminating his residual Eurocentrism. Instead, although he launched cultural pluralism as an attack on assimilationism, the bulk of the white pluralist thought that has followed Kallen has attempted to *reconcile* pluralism and assimilationism.

When multiculturalism began to hit the news in the late 1980s, it seemed a relatively mild reform movement. It was pro-diversity *and* it defined diversity not in racial or political but in cultural terms. Although it was enacted, often with the encouragement of radical student protest, it took such forms as Stanford's "Western Civilization" courses, now revised to include "non-Western" or "minority" materials, or the University of California, Santa Barbara's "ethnicity requirement," or New York State's report on the schools, "A Curriculum of Inclusion," or the University of California, Berkeley's "American Cultures" sequence, whose innovation stemmed from the pluralization of American "culture." Such changes were a real improvement at schools where student bodies, curricula, and faculty were disproportionately white and casually segregated. But this multiculturalism looked like curricula reforms and not at all like a social movement. One assessment, by Arthur Levine and Ette Cureton in early 1992, expresses the calmness of multicultural reality: "The sheer quantity of multicultural activity . . . belies the belief that the traditional curriculum has been largely impermeable to, or has simply marginalized, diversity. And the character of the change—principally add-ons to, rather than substitutes for, existing practice—makes untenable the notion that multiculturalism is replacing the historic canon."[16] Much criticism centered on multiculturalism's ideological timidity: since nonwhite materials were "add-ons" to white structures, they did not address the centrality and dominance of the latter. As we've noted, multiculturalism seemed to many a kinder, gentler form of assimilationism, with some expansion of a commitment to a mostly cosmetic pluralism. Levine and Cureton called this the "quiet revolution," quiet like the tenth draft of a committee memo coming out of a laser printer.

Real noise came instead from those proclaiming that this multiculturalism had already gone too far. Some amazing statements were made.

> Counterposed to the traditional idea of American culture—"the melting-pot"—is multiculturalism, the United States as a cartel of tribes, of separate cultures existing side by side. Accordingly, individual rights in civil society must yield to group or corporate rights—the citizen related to the state and society through his ethnic or interest group. Though it would come as a surprise to the trend-setting multiculturalists, their true ideological forefather is not Gramsci but Mussolini.[17]

Here, multiculturalism is fascist because it opposes American pluralism. In Roger Kimball's words, "'Multiculturalism' as used in the academy today is not about recognizing genuine cultural diversity or encouraging pluralism. It is about undermining the priority of Western liberal values" on which real pluralism rests.[18]

Attacks like this were so common that Burger King could have used them as hamburger wrappers. But though they tended to substitute hyperbole for evidence of their clear and present dangers, their targets were precise. Both of the passages just cited are attempting to recover the meaning of a true pluralism. The first claims that the "traditional idea of American culture" is assimilationism (the "melting pot") rather than separate cultures. It goes on to subordinate group to individual rights. The second bases pluralism on "the priority of Western liberal values" to others. Taken together, these passages reject all three of the features we extracted from Kallen's strong version of cultural pluralism. They deny the multicentered structure of American culture, the irreducible reality of group identity and social life, and the presumptive equality of different U.S. cultures. Crucially, these statements also claim the title of pluralism. They reassert the unity of pluralism and assimilationism that they find besieged by multicultural tendencies.

The attractions of this pluralism-assimilationism alliance are not limited to the political right, but cut across the political spectrum. The most famous example is probably the longtime liberal Arthur Schlesinger Jr., whose 1991 book *The Disuniting of America* rendered him the theoretical mastermind of those that feared that renewed civil unrest could spring from excessive race consciousness. Schlesinger admits the reality of America's diverse "ethnic" cultures but insists on the need for these to subordinate themselves to an overarching American Creed. The three key ingredients of assimilationist pluralism are there well expressed. First, he calls for a return to George Washington's ideal of a "new race" forming "one people" in the New World.[19] This depends on ending "the attack on the common American identity" and on respecting "the assimilation process" that produces "an acceptance of the language, the institutions, and the political ideals that hold the nation together."[20] Second, American values place the individual above and apart from group life: we must remain aware that "individualism itself is looked on with abhorrence and dread by collectivist cultures in which loyalty to the group overrides personal goals."[21] Finally, cultural equality is bogus; the West is Best. "Whatever the particular crimes of Europe, that continent is also the source—the *unique* source—of those liberating ideas of individual liberty, political democracy, the rule of law. . . . There is surely no reason for Western civilization to have guilt trips laid on it by champions of cultures based on despotism, superstition, tribalism, and fanaticism."[22] Schlesinger's pluralist sense that there are indeed other systems of values that might be (or might seem to be) better for other people easily coexists with his belief that ours *are* "absolutely better."[23] The highest payoff of this strain of cultural pluralism is that it combines tolerance and hierarchy, difference and inferiority, into a pluralist, democratic supremacism.[24]

The assimilationist pluralists veer quite close to what Kallen called the "racism of culture." Other groups are not biologically but culturally inferior.

These pluralist supremacists do not favor racial segregation and skin-color exclusion, and on this point their sincerity need not be doubted. But their sense of the superiority of a consensual creed that they insistently associate with Euro-American ways underwrites a sense of the historical fitness of white or European rule.[25] A "racism of culture" justifies the de facto priority of white concerns and values in U.S. society, including ostensibly neutral institutions. Indeed, it defines this de facto priority of white concerns *as* neutrality itself, where whiteness is nothing other than American standards of democracy and procedural fairness. Cultural racism allows political and economic factors to seem irrelevant, since they merely reflect the relative strength of different cultures. It depicts criticisms of the impartiality or equity of these preponderantly white institutions as the product of inferior cultural values. The absence of de jure white control is touted as evidence of genuine neutrality. So is white indifference to the racialized dimension of this neutrality, an indifference sometimes called "color blindness."[26] Such supremacism, calling itself pluralism, has tremendous influence. Its trinity—one-culture national unity, individualism, and a supremacism cleansed of biology and Jim Crow—forms the intellectual baseline for race talk today.

The Struggle for Pluralism (2): Cultural Unionists

But what about the moderates who seek a balance between assimilation and pluralism, interaction and autonomy? The recent multicultural debates featured a number of writers who reject the visible chauvinism of the emperor mentioned earlier. They are closer to Kallen's original position, as we noted regarding the remarks of Troy Duster. Do they avoid assimilation and find a genuine third way between it and separatist nationalism?

One test case is "The Great Multicultural Debate," whose author, Gary B. Nash, is a nationally renowned historian of American colonial and antebellum history who has placed race at the center of his research for at least twenty-five years.[27] He has more recently served as general editor of a series of systematically multicultural history textbooks for California schoolchildren that has taken a critical and revisionist stance toward earlier, Anglocentric versions of history. He is also director of a congressionally mandated National Standards for the Teaching of United States History, which as we write is pending certification. Nash speaks as a proponent when he says, "Multicultural curricula, 'stressing a diversity of cultures, races, languages, and religions,' and eliminating 'ethnocentric and biased concepts and materials from textbook and classroom,' have been adopted by school systems throughout the United States" (11). He argues that the history profession has often disseminated misinformation about the racial past, and sees multi-culturalism's ongoing task as criticizing this ethnocentrism in order to tell a larger truth about such issues as Anglo-Mexican and European-American Indian relations and the centrality of cultural and racial diversity to the creation of the past.

Nash rejects one of the assumptions of assimilationist-pluralism: its individualism. Groups are also important actors in history, which cannot be reduced to the tale of various individuals succeeding or failing on their own personal terms. Unlike Schlesinger, he makes allowances for the fact that many of these groups are racialized instead of "ethnic," which alters their relations to the white cultures they encounter. In order to understand these groups, one can legitimately be "race-conscious"; that is, one must *not* be color-blind in order to understand the place of Mexican Americans or Korean Americans in the past and present United States, for so much of that past and present has been affected by racial difference. Individuals have a group life that, for Nash, must be considered through race consciousness.

Nash also avoids white cultural supremacism even as he avoids endorsing Kallen's cultural parity or equality. He does *not* associate preferred American values with the "West" or the "European origins of American civilization" that Schlesinger claims.[28] But he does denounce "a promiscuous pluralism that gives every thing equal weight."[29] Henry Louis Gates Jr., writing in a later issue of *Contention*, also opposes the thesis of "cultural equity," which holds that "as people enjoy equal standing under the law, so too must the cultural products of different groups be considered both as representative of those groups and as of at least equal value to those other groups."[30] But Gates regards the likely hierarchy of cultural products as something to be mutually established through "the contraposition of different interests, different perspectives," rather than as a rank already known via an artifact's culture of origin. Sharing Kallen's rejection of cultural supremacism, these writers nonetheless do not insist that the best alternative is cultural parity. They endorse multisided cultural *interaction* as a kind of middle way between hierarchy and equality.[31] Interaction suggests two-way contact without making any assurances about the relative positions of the parties involved.

But these writers reject the principle of a multiple core culture in favor of a single, unifying center. Nash's vexed encounter with his version of Afro-centrism leads him to conclude that we need to teach students "the common humanity of all individuals while discovering the historical relevance of gender, race, religion, and other categories that help shape their identity."[32] He explicitly replaces cultural equality with a cultural core: "If multiculturalism is to get beyond a promiscuous pluralism that gives every thing equal weight and adopts complete moral relativism, it must reach some agreement on what is at the core of American culture."[33] "Pluribus can flourish in these ways only if unum is preserved at the heart of the polity—in a common commitment to core political and moral values."[34] In Nash's view, diversity and egalitarian negotiation among various groups do not make common culture unnecessary, but require a common culture to furnish appropriate ground rules. Common or core culture *transcends* cultural difference. It manages diversity via a set of principles that is neutral to the distinctive qualities of the various cultures it manages. The core culture is not, in this view, undergoing continual modification at the hands of everyday group life, but is the unchanging heart that regulates diversity's flow.

The tricky thing about this position is that it does not crudely establish the superiority of white culture to which it then demands conformity. It insists on irreducible cultural diversity. Nash defines his core as "political and moral values"—government by the people, a government of laws, and "common entitlement as individuals to liberty, equal opportunity, and impartial treatment under the law."[35] This requires *political* unity, which means not just holding particular common values, but the fact of holding common values in itself. These common values rule any conceivable negotiations a person or group would conduct with other persons and groups. New values would not emerge from the negotiations to mediate them, for the mediation would already be in place. Diane Ravitch, to cite another example, endorses criticism of racial regimes and practices as long as they do not threaten the core with one view's excessive autonomy. "Segregation of, or separatism by, any group is not multicultural; Afrocentrism is a sort of intellectual apartheid, and as such is the antithesis of multiculturalism."[36] Multiculturalism properly focuses on "the interaction of diverse peoples," the social condition of cultural mixing. This mixing implicitly takes place on some kind of common ground. Todd Gitlin traces the decline of a progressive national agenda to "the fragmentation of commonality politics."[37] Gates cites Cardinal Newman to envision the desired intensity of union: although society cannot achieve such a state, "the university should promote 'the power of viewing many things at once as one whole, of referring them severally to their true place in the universal system, of understanding their respective value, and determining their mutual dependence.'"[38]

While these writers are reluctant to state the system of positive norms to which different cultures must adhere (even Nash's are largely procedural), they claim that a proper sense of common features will create an orderly foundation. Cultural difference rests on political unity, and does so not through coercion or exclusion so much as through consensus about what the "mutual dependence" will look like. These writers support multi-culturalism while rejecting multi-politics. They are concerned lest diverse cultures express not underlying oneness but separate polities, distinctive political principles, and political autonomy. Some principle of commonality must govern the relation between culture and politics.

No formula can predict the assimilative intensity of any particular vision of such underlying unity, which varies. The assimilative power depends on a structure of feeling about what comes first, about what is most urgent. A remark by Stephen Steinberg suggests the stakes: "If there is an iron law of ethnicity, it is that when ethnic groups are found in a hierarchy of power, wealth, and status, then conflict is inescapable. However, where there is social, economic, and political parity among the constituent groups, ethnic conflict, when it occurs, tends to be at a low level and rarely spills over into violence."[39] Steinberg thinks *parity* is the most important prerequisite to social peace; it is more important than shared values. Nash et al. put shared values ahead of parity, which they leave virtually unmentioned. Assimilation sufficient to produce a cultural or moral core is, for them, the precondition of equitable rules. But for Steinberg and the multiculturalists we will discuss, equity is the precondition of any kind of valuable common ground.

Although the second kind of contemporary pluralism (that of Nash et al.) is an improvement over the first, it retains the three-part assimilationist-pluralist alliance in a more generous form. First, it encourages cultural diversity as long as that does not affect political unity. Second, it grants the legitimacy of group consciousness around racial as well as ethnic difference, but casts a perpetual shadow of a higher unity over such differences. Group life carries the stigma of something rich but incomplete and partial compared to life in common.

Finally, these pluralists generally reject cultural parity. They try not to make a big deal out of this, and offer a substitute for parity—cultural *interaction*. This is fine in itself, but it says nothing about the conditions, equal or unequal or some combination, under which interaction takes place. Do, say, Hopi culture and Anglo-American culture meet and intermingle as though meaningfully equal? Does the long history of political inequality and subordination play *no* role in controlling the cultural outcome? How might the distortions of such inequality be overcome? These pluralists avoid the question. Sometimes they act as though "interaction" takes care of it, sometimes they claim that the issue is epistemologically misguided, sometimes they suggest that the real issue is aesthetic value that is unrelated to "politics," sometimes they critique equality without proposing an alternative. In any case, the issue of parity hangs in midair.

Or so it hangs until the question of parity becomes more obviously political. A crucial example is the moderate pluralists' response to the old issue of nationalist separatism. For Ravitch, Afrocentrics are not entitled even to sit at the negotiation table, and her reason is their alleged separatist agenda. The problem with nationalism for white people has generally been the reverse of separatism: Chicano, Indian, and Black militancy has threatened not to separate and go away but to stay and change society's basic ground rules. The moderate pluralists' hostility to separatism suggests the importance they vest in unity. It also suggests what unity supposedly guarantees: that these ground rules will remain the same. The idea of a core culture rejects separatism by reasserting that these fundamental rules are not open to change. (One of the rules, to offer only one instance, has been that the prevailing forms of due process in university admissions, police procedure, criminal trials, job promotion, and so on, are color-blind, even though critics have charged that these processes are unconsciously pro-white.) The priority of a core to multicentric negotiations stigmatizes those who want to change the core as attacking the structure of civil society. Hence Ravitch's categorical rejection of Afrocentricity. By challenging core Western or white American values, whether well or badly, Afrocentricity seems to challenge white political governance of at least school curricula. She calls Afrocentricity apartheid, apparently imagining the same total loss of political sovereignty that term meant for Black South Africans, this time applied to whites.[40]

We could continue to call the Schlesinger group and the Nash/Ravitch group "pluralists," since they all are. The latter group in particular is responsible for significant cultural and intellectual improvements.[41] But to call all of them pluralists would be to endorse the illusion that "pluralism" has a single, definable meaning. It would also encourage the incorrect view that pluralism consists of a benign balance between unity and multiplicity that can be fair and good to all groups in America. In the face of dissent from some groups, these two kinds of pluralists use unity to control whatever serious autonomy and shifts in power multiplicity might generate. To object to such uses of unity is not to say that all Euro-American norms are bad. It is to say that these forms of pluralism diminish our ability to discuss the harm they may do to others.

These major variants of pluralism are fundamentally assimilationist. Clearer names for the teams will help: let's call Schlesinger's the *cultural supremacists*, and Ravitch's the *cultural unionists*. Their modes are different, but they both mix assimilationism with pluralism and naturalize (a more or less benevolent) white-majority rule. Sure, they're all pluralists, but it would help discussion to get their fundamental companion assumptions up front.

We'd like to turn now to *multiculturalism*, and reserve the word for those who oppose crucial elements of these two variants of pluralism. Multiculturalists, in the strict sense, do this not by rejecting pluralism, as some like to suggest, but by building the alliance missing from the mainstream consensus, the alliance between pluralism and nationalism.

Multiculturalism in Education: The 1970s

A number of trends converge in multicultural educational thought in the early 1970s, and our brief account here can only focus on some common elements without doing justice to the concept's variety.[42]

The word "multicultural" had a fitful beginning in the World War II era, appearing in non-trendsetting situations such as a *New York Herald-Tribune Books* attack on prejudice on 27 July 1941, or, in 1959, a description of Montreal as multicultural (*Oxford English Dictionary*). The word had a far more developed existence in British Commonwealth countries such as Canada and Australia. The Canadian case is particularly interesting, as multiculturalism is one of the ways in which that nation has sought to see itself as comprised of many nations, including the First Nations (indigenous peoples) and a largely separate society, Quebec. A proper survey of these countries unfortunately lies beyond our scope. Nonetheless, the United States' understanding of multiculturalism will remain incomplete until it develops a picture of other international varieties.

In the United States, multiculturalism had arisen most directly from a concern with the experience of schoolchildren. For children of American Indian, Mexican-American, African-American, or Asian-American backgrounds, there is never a single America, in the view of multicultural educators, but always at least two. Such children live in the culture of their home or community, and they go to school in a culture that is sharply distinct. Multicultural theory focuses on children who were not considered white by their schools or society. Their two worlds are more sharply polarized than those of white ethnics like Polish Americans, whose home culture and language are also distinct from the English-speaking Anglo sphere of school. Mexican-American children, for example, are divided from white or Anglo society not so much by "ethnicity" in the traditional sense as by race and color. This means that their community is designated inferior in a way that the Polish or Italian community is not. A number of writers pointed out that African-American and Mexican-American children have almost always been considered "culturally deficient," and this divides their lives.

In this situation, assimilation was generally impossible, since white society regarded children of color as culturally defective as a group (although, of course, unusual individuals would always rise out of difficult circumstances). Or if not impossible, assimilation would be undesirable from the other side, since it would require the wholesale rejection of the home culture that the majority culture regarded as little more than a handicap. Starting from the "bicultural" lives of racialized children, multicultural education theorists distinguished "cultural pluralism" from assimilationism:

> The form of cultural pluralism we wish to describe more fully concentrates on the *bicultural* reality of many Mexican American children living in the United States today. . . . The basic educational issue in our interpretation of cultural democracy concerns the need for providing Mexican American children with the educational experiences necessary to enhance their right to be able to function in *both* cultural worlds, the cultural world of the Mexican American as well as the cultural world of the Anglo-American.[43]

Assimilation to a single national culture is to be replaced by mobility between related but discrete spheres of everyday life. Many Americans lead lives in which their world is at least dual, and multicultural theorists rejected ideals of assimilationism that ignored this ordinary reality. Schooling should not, in their view, take bicultural children and turn them into monocultural Anglicized adults, but should endorse biculturality as a way of life. Multiculturalism in the 1970s endorsed it as an *American* way of life, and called for cultural assimilation to be replaced by cultural democracy. This meant that "an individual can be bicultural and still be loyal to American ideals."[44]

As cultural democracy, 1970s multiculturalism built on a strong version of cultural pluralism. While noting the continual *interdependence* of various cultures, it insisted on each culture's *independence*.[45] "Cultural pluralism is neither the traditionalist's separatism nor the assimilationist's melting pot. It is a composite that recognizes the uniqueness and value of every culture. Cultural pluralism acknowledges that no group lives in isolation, but that, instead, each group influences and is influenced by others."[46] Unlike the supremacist and unionist pluralism discussed earlier, this *multicultural plural-ism* did not attempt a balance between diversity and unity, but eliminated the pole of unity altogether. The single core (interacting with multiple cultures) is replaced by a multiplicity of distinct cultures at the level of everyday life. The Mexican-American child would then no longer be conceived of as moving from her "subculture" into a "common culture" but as moving between partially overlapping and yet distinct cultures. She would be well aware that the latter, "Anglo" culture is dominant, supplying the national language, the law of the land, the structure of economic opportunity, the mainstream office behaviors, and so on. But this Anglo culture would not be seen as the unifying, official culture so much as another and socially more powerful one. The important point was that the Mexican-American child would be conceived as moving between two sides of her bicultural life rather than balancing a particularistic identity with a common culture. Multicultural pluralism replaced a single cultural core with multiple cultural domains.

A second feature distinguishes 1970s multiculturalism. While weaker forms of pluralism regard group identity as a threat to individuality, 1970s multiculturalism saw the two as compatible and complementary. Arturo Pacheco describes "democratic pluralism" as distinguished by "a balance of power between competing and overlapping religious, ethnic, economic, and geographical groupings." It is "a more accurate description of actual democracy in America than is classical liberalism, which bases itself on a notion of individual, rather than group, participatory democracy."[47] Pacheco does not see this as a threat to individualism but as a description of the multicentered political bargaining process. Manuel Ramírez and Alfredo Casañeda clarified Milton Gordon's position on the link between group and individual rights in *Assimilation in American Life* (1964). Gordon writes that "the system of cultural pluralism . . . has frequently been described as 'cultural democracy,' since it posits the right of ethnic groups in a democratic society to maintain their communal identity and their own subcultural values. . . . However, we must also point out that democratic values prescribe free choice not only for groups but also for individuals."[48] Ramírez and Casañeda emphasized the falseness of any choice between remaining ethnic (part of a group) and assimilating (becoming an individual without alliances in a mixed group). When one is not compelled to assimilate one's individuality to a particular "core" culture, one can retain one's own racial or ethnic identity while circulating among other races and ethnicities.

We could say, then, that *the unnecessary choice between individual and group identity is imposed by assimilationism itself.* The wedge between oneself and one's group is driven *only* by the demand that you be more like the dominant culture than you are. If a Mexican-American can interact with Anglo culture without having to resemble that culture wholesale, then she can retain her ethnic/racial identity as Mexican-American while being treated as an individual by both her own and Anglo culture. The bifurcation here is of course awkward and artificial, but that's the problem such talk addresses. Anglo-American and Mexican-American cultures intersect, differ, overlap, and diverge. Multiculturalism in the 1970s often claimed that in such cases, the dual-culture person should not be divided by a false choice between individuality and group life.

Imagining that one can be one's peculiar self and circulate generally, free of assimilationism, multicultural education theorists thus found no educational loss in retaining racial and ethnic identities in all their local particularity. Indeed, they saw this as a gain. Many educators had assumed that particularity breeds intellectual mediocrity. By contrast, the multiculturalists argued that the presence of local culture enhanced "general" knowledge. For example, if a community's adults have remarkable math skills in ordinary instances of calculating the costs of buying different amounts of different foods for their families, but lack formal training in abstract math, then teaching math through these concrete problems could enhance not only learning but the meaning and uses of math. Race consciousness and local life made one smart and mobile, not stuck and limited.

A third feature of 1970s multiculturalism is that multiculturalists were militant in their opposition to cultural supremacism and insisted on some form of cultural equality. They vigorously opposed all forms of the cultural deficiency thesis when applied to non-Anglo cultures. James A. Banks defines the "cultural-difference (or multicultural) hypothesis" as rejecting both cultural deficiency and assimilationism on the grounds that "ethnic minorities have rich and diverse, not deprived, cultures."[49] Other authors invoked Kallen's cultural pluralism in defense of the general equality of different cultures. "Kallen interpreted the term 'equal' as it appears in the Declaration of Independence, and the Preamble and the Amendments to the Constitution, as affirmation of the right to be different."[50] Pacheco defined strong multiculturalism as producing "students who can function in a culturally plural society, one in which there is parity between various cultural groups."[51]

It is at this point that these writers made their most fundamental move. Rather than calling for mutual cultural respect or cultural parity in the abstract, they tied cultural parity to empowerment and the equalization of power relations. Pacheco, for example, founds pluralism on parity in this way:

> More sensitive to the lack of parity in real life, [multiculturalism] attempts, through a variety of structural arrangements in the school, to aggressively support the right of a cultural group to maintain itself, it perceives that parity of power and decision making among groups is crucially important, and it assumes that the school has a critical role to play in bringing cultural pluralism about in the greater society.[52]

Again and again, multicultural educators insisted on a *multidimensional* approach to cultural parity. This approach entailed not only the affirmation of a student's cultural identity and heritage, but required consideration of curriculum, teacher attitudes, racial views, gender relations, school administration, the features of the community, and economics. In their literature review of the fifty-four articles and twenty-two books they consider fully multicultural, Sleeter and Grant summarize the main issues as "institutional racism in society and schools, unequal power relationships among racial groups, and economic stratification and social class."[53] The authors of these articles and books generally regard these issues as indissociable from the more conventional educational domain of curriculum or heritage. Although Sleeter and Grant think the issue of social stratification is often underplayed, they noted that "social stratification, as well as racial oppression, has provided much of the impetus for recognizing the need for multicultural education" in the first place.[54] At every point in this work, the "desire not to have to assimilate culturally" went hand in hand with "the desire to have power and economic resources equal to Whites."[55] Multicultural education, always focusing on benefiting people of color, saw such benefits depending on the combination of equitable cultural interaction with changed social and economic relations. "Cultural equality" or equity entailed genuine political parity and power sharing.

Pluralist Nationalism in the 1960s

We've emphasized the existence of a strong pluralist tradition that sees cultural differences finding their "resolution" in equity rather than assimilationist unity. But this *multicultural* pluralism owes most of its public life and development to the history of nationalist thought among people of color in the United States. Here we are unable to do justice either to criticisms or to the richness and complexity of nationalist thought. As is the case with Afrocentricity, important critiques and even major overhauls of nationalism from within Native American, African-American, or Chicano communities have been drowned out by wholesale white rejection. The latter skips over nationalism's focus on white racist political and cultural views in favor of charging it with all kinds of race-based divisiveness, the suspiciously simple mirror-image of features nationalism attributes to whites. Although some nationalist thought is separatist *and* militantly antipluralist, this usually follows from its regarding pluralism as an instrument of white supremacism.[56] Given our argument thus far, it will be clear that we think this view is often correct, since whites have so often failed—and downright refused—to separate pluralism from Anglo-norm assimilationism. Strong multiculturalism picked up some good portion of its hostility to supremacist and unionist pluralism from the nationalist attack. It was nationalist thought, Black nationalist thought in particular, that by the early 1970s demanded autonomy from white America on the basis sometimes of separatism but also of *equalized* interaction.[57]

We can invoke only a couple of examples, and we pick two icons precisely because they are emblems of nationalism at its supposed climax of militant separatism.[58] Black Panther leader Huey Newton rejected "cultural nationalism, or pork chop nationalism," which he attributed to those "concerned with returning to the old African culture and thereby regaining their identity and freedom."[59] Cultural nationalists turned out for Newton to have two major blindnesses. They overlooked the socialist project of "revolutionary Nationalism," which knows that "we must destroy both racism and capitalism."[60] And they didn't "understand the white revolutionaries because [they] can't see why anyone white would turn on the system. So they think that maybe this is some more hypocrisy being planted by white people."[61] Newton desired separatism as the basis of revolutionary Black solidarity even as he sought cross-racial support from white radicals. As he put it, "we feel as Malcolm X felt that there can be no black-white unity until there first is black unity."[62] Newton's rejection of the cultural nationalist is a rejection of separatism as a final goal. At least in his official statements, separatism was a means to equality among racial groups. Once Black America had power enough to be treated equitably by whites, Black autonomy could survive and vitalize interaction with whites. Once in this condition of egalitarian pluralism, to use a phrase foreign to Newton's vocabulary, Black America not only would better endure white America but would change it. It is pluralism rather than separatism per se that leads to the hoped-for Black influence over white. Newton envisioned not reverse racism but reverse power, not the drawing of essentialist racial lines but the crossing of history's color line with new political equality.

Much 1960s Black nationalist thought—to stick with one of the United States' several nationalist traditions—anticipates the major features of the strong version of pluralism we've noted in 1970s multiculturalism. First, it rejected white-norm assimilationism as racist and oppressive to Black people. Black Power meant insisting on the "ethnic basis of American politics," which had extended beyond white ethnicity to describe U.S. institutions as color-blind and race-neutral. Vivid condemnations of white racism, reintensified in the Black Power period, are exactly that: condemnations of white racism. Quite often, whites had felt that these spilled over into condemnations of white presence or white existence. They did, particularly where assimilationism had enabled whites to suggest that their own perspectives and interests could stand for those of the nation. In these quite common cases, a white presence made the discussion of racial differences and inequities impossible. Black and other nationalisms were calling for a genuine political pluralism to replace white supremacy.

Second, nationalism regarded individualism's rejection of group consciousness as an obstruction of the racial facts of life. Kwame Toure (formerly Stokely Carmichael) and Charles V. Hamilton cite a statement of the National Council of Churches on this point. "America," the council suggests, "has asked its Negro citizens to fight for opportunity as *individuals*, whereas at certain points in our history what we have needed most has been opportunity for the *whole group*, not just selected and approved Negroes. . . . We must not apologize for the existence of this form of group power, for we have been oppressed as a group and not as individuals."[63] Since racialization operates through a Black American's group affiliation, civil rights premised on a color-blind ignorance of that affiliation will always be inadequate. "It is a commentary on the fundamentally racist nature of this society that the concept of group strength for black people must be articulated."[64] Nationalism spreads awareness of the direct transmission between one's group affiliation and one's individual identity. As Wahneema Lubiano more pointedly puts it, "black nationalism has been the articulated consciousness of black Americans' awareness of their place in the state's intentions."[65]

Third, Black Power continually sought cultural and political equality. Toure and Hamilton sharply distinguished between the presence of Black people under white control and equal Black community control. "Black visibility is not Black Power. . . . The power must be that of a community, and emanate from there. . . . The goal of black self-determination and black self-identity—Black Power—is full participation in the decision-making processes affecting the lives of black people."[66] Toure and Hamilton write that the "concept of Black Power rests on a fundamental premise: *Before a group can enter the open society, it must first close ranks.* By this we mean that group solidarity is necessary before a group can operate effectively from a bargaining position of strength in a pluralistic society."[67] Self-rule requires political equality between the races, and on this count Black nationalism is pluralist, and yet pluralist in a way that would indeed revolutionize American society. The revolution would consist of basing peace on justice by putting group autonomy and equity ahead of traditional demands for assimilation to the core that seems to many to be so biased toward white people and their preferences.

In short, Black Power and related movements had developed a historically pivotal conjunction of *pluralism and nationalism* when their public influence began to wane.[68] These movements combined group autonomy and interaction with other groups, but further insisted that the combination rested on a continual striving for intergroup political equality. Rather than moderate pluralism's balance between unity and multiplicity, they envisioned a federation based on equitable negotiation among multiple groups. Such a federation would protect group autonomy and the still-dreaded "group rights." Nationalism in the 1960s amplified the second and third traits we've been considering beyond moderate recuperation. Race consciousness and political equality, given U.S. racial history, went well beyond the loosening of the core that moderate pluralists had imagined. The pluralist-nationalist sense of the minimum requirements of true pluralism incorporates social and cultural *equity* into the obvious *diversity* of racial groups. Nationalist elements have been subject to unceasing attempts at expulsion on the trumped-up charge that they entirely reject the pluralism that, to repeat, they have in fact attempted to make real.

We've been suggesting that a continuity exists between the strong version of cultural pluralism that was born to oppose assimilationism, 1970s multiculturalism, and nationalism. This nationalism includes some completely reconstructive attacks (feminist especially), which we will touch on later. Were this tradition to have prevailed, our point here would be obvious to white racial common sense: the multiculturalism that built on both pluralism and nationalism is the *only* meaningful form of cultural pluralism in existence, for it is the only form that is not a variant of assimilationism.[69]

Multiculturalism in the 1990s

> The primary criterion for a strong version of multiculturalism is that it
> not be reducible to a pluralism structured in dominance.
> Peter Erickson[70]

These days, anything slightly less white than *Dr. Zhivago* can bill itself as multicultural. This sprawling, meaningless usage makes even the narrowest material seem more inclusive and equitable than it actually is. But the history we have outlined should make it relatively easy to pick the real antias-similationist out of the crowd of pretenders. It may also make it easier to see the kind of reconstructive research the concept could sponsor.

In colleges and universities, multiculturalism would have gotten nowhere without the decades-long work of ethnic studies and women's studies departments. In the 1970s, multicultural educators and ethnic studies college faculty tended to work at a distance, and ethnic studies programs, in our unsystematic opinion, continue to keep multiculturalism at arm's length, judging it a treacherous ally, and with many good reasons, some of which are spelled out in the essays collected here. This does not change the fundamental historical fact that mild reforms, such as "diversity" in general education requirements, came only after long years of effort on the part of faculty and students in these small race and gender programs. From the mid-1960s onward, ethnic studies programs demanded the integration of all levels of the university and the curricular inclusion of the histories of people of color in the United States. They also went beyond inclusion per se, calling for structural changes in the university as well as in the methodological foundations of their neighboring, more traditional disciplines. Ethnic studies scholars uncovered the signs of American race relations in social science and humanities research that generated major empirical and interpretive errors about communities of color. Most generally, they produced a powerful version of the three-part alternative to assimilationism-based social research. They established the autonomy of culturally specific knowledges from traditional "core" disciplines. They suggested that community ties and local knowledge improved rather than spoiled research. And they claimed that Anglo-European cultural supremacism or just plain old racism obscured these truths with their traditionalist epistemologies.[71] Ethnic and women's studies are slightly to one side of our subject here, but their contributions have been indispensable to the content and conditions of multiculturalism's appearance in the university.

The recent attacks on multiculturalism sensed that one wing of the multicultural house was not only promoting cultural diversity and tolerance but reviving alternatives to assimilationism as a basis of social peace and justice. The three general aspects of strong pluralism or multiculturalism we've been describing acquired new life and emphasis in the late 1980s.

First, multiculturalism was more hospitable than some variants of nationalism and pluralism to a whole range of perspectives for which assimilation was poison. A concept whose major adversaries had at one time been identified mostly through race and ethnicity now had to take on challenges of gender, sexuality, new panethnicities, and new "nations" like Queer Nation in unpredictable combinations. By 1990, over twenty-five years of work had made visible a whole raft of exceptions to the veiled universalism and group unity on which assimilationist pluralism had relied. The women's movement put gender difference on the table. Gay and lesbian activism and research made heterosexuality seem as much a limitation as an artificial norm. Research on class and economic segmentation continued to produce startling results. Socialist feminism tried to think through the complex interrelations of gender and class. African-American women had been crucial to the formulation of the civil rights and Black Power moments from the beginning, and, like Chicana feminists, became increasingly visible critics of the masculinist politics of nationalism and the usual understanding of racialized communities.[72] Feminists of color placed race at the center of the study of gender; one turning point came in the early 1980s with the publication of two widely noted anthologies, *This Bridge Called My Back: Writings by Radical Women of Color* and *All the Women Are White, All the Blacks Are Men, but Some of Us Are Brave: Black Women's Studies.*[73] And lesbian and gay thinkers injected sexual difference into revised understandings of raced, gendered, or classed communities. The current hue and cry about social fragmentation and special interests testifies to a growing sense of sociocultural complexity even in the more obtuse reaches of the high-velocity media world.

The apparent chaos of multicultural knowledge has been a huge conceptual step forward and even signals a modest success. It promotes new degrees of subtlety in the understanding of social and cultural life. Crossover developments like those listed earlier each transformed an apparently neutral, generalizable feature of the American norm—such as heterosexual marriage—into a particularity, a partiality, a perspective, a potential discriminatory bias. The 1980s backlash against "difference" was a tacit response to the loss of the assimilative power of a presumptive common culture. One could detect a dread of *cultural* coexistence with the different, even when the different ones could still be *economically and politically* subordinated. Something like Rush Limbaugh's panicky ridicule of ever less politicized differences, like vegetarianism, suggests a continual concern that the old normalcies face challenges on a hundred fronts. How else to explain this kind of mournful lament: "Most often, what we believe in is made fun of, lampooned, impugned, and put down. Then, we don't want to feel that way. We want to feel as much a part of the mainstream as anybody else"?[74] Although he is winning nearly all his political battles, Rush rightly feels marginal to a diversity that is becoming an accomplished fact in the realm of culture. There, through "identity" and the rest, he is being made to share.

Second, multiculturalism has strongly endorsed racially based group identities and *antiessentialism* at the same time. Antiessentialism describes the way an identity can have a complex social reality without possessing a fixed essence or substance to distinguish it from others. Various nationalisms, feminisms, and other movements have, to the contrary, been accused of essentialism, of presuming a "core" of Chicanoness or femininity that unites a community around some common, fixed characteristics. Many commentators on identity politics have lived through the abundant political failures of essentialism, but retain the use of *social* identities even as they have long repudiated the dream of sharing essential identities with a passion born of painful experience. Multiculturalism in the 1990s builds on the work of a number of writers and activists who have been devising ways of talking about how identity has social actuality and meaning while being multiple, shifting, indeterminate, and antiessentialist at the same time.[75] So, for example, in their recently published volume on multicultural education, Cameron McCarthy and Warren Crichlow start things off by saying race is both real and changeable:

> Racial difference is the product of human interests, needs, desires, strategies, capacities, forms of organization, and forms of mobilization. And that these dynamic variables which articulate themselves in the form of grounded social constructs such as identity, inequality, and so forth, are subject to change, contradiction, variability, and revision within historically specific and determinate contexts. We maintain that "race" is a social, historical, and variable category.[76]

The lack of a fixed meaning for "race" or for specific uses such as "Chicana" does nothing to diminish the category's social importance and analytic necessity. Quite the contrary: antiessentialism increases and refines it.

A crucial test of antiessentialist race consciousness will continue to revolve around affirmative action. Some have argued that once we understand the multiple and sometimes contradictory and indeterminate sources of racial identity, we can no longer use race as an index of disadvantage. Antiessentialism has been used in this way by conservatives, who have contested any group-based challenge to a meritocratic identity based on pure individual performance. This argument goes hand in hand with the premature claim of the declining significance of race. The backlash against affirmative action programs has spearheaded the charge against race consciousness of any kind, and the success of renewed explanations for the ongoing need for these programs will largely determine the practical utility of the concept of multiculturalism itself.

In fact, antiessentialist understandings of racial identity as multiply determined make it *easier* to show that white-majority institutions are white rather than neutral. They make it easier to show that white attitudes need not necessarily be racist or supremacist to have a racially differentiating effect, to have a racially marked presence. They help demonstrate how cultural identities are woven into legal and economic procedure so that even supposedly neutral process reflects the culture that produced it. They show that "merit" too consists of a set of choices established within a particular social context: particular test skills may be favored over experience with economic adversity, and so on. More nuanced descriptions of racial influence help show the ways that culture racializes the choices that lie behind all its procedures. These choices can be unconscious, as in the case where blanket "neutrality" is declared. They can be conscious, as in affirmative action programs. In a culture habituated to believing in the neutrality of even the 80, 90, or 95 percent white institution, these more nuanced descriptions of actual racial influence can promote more open decisions about racial policy.[77]

Third, the strong version of 1990s multiculturalism has cemented the conjunction of antiassimilationist cultural pluralism with political parity. In 1990, Ted Gordon and Wahneema Lubiano of the University of Texas at Austin rejected those forms of multiculturalism that overlook political equity: "Multiculturalism . . . is understood at its most simplistic to mean exposure to different cultures. Simple exposure, however, is absolutely meaningless without a reconsideration and restructuring of the ways in which knowledge is organized, disseminated, and used to support unequal power relations."[78] A "transformative multiculturalism" rejects the divide between culture and politics, and links genuine cultural inclusion to political power sharing. This involves more than broadening cultural discourse. It means changing the racial composition of the institution in question: "cross-cultural work . . . depends upon the presence of a critical mass of people of color (all levels of the University). . . . multiculturalism demands empowered *people* of color as well as empowered *areas* of knowledge."[79] A real multiculturalism requires political as well as cultural inclusion, requires the sharing of power among relevant groups.[80] Although culture cannot be simply reduced to politics, this multiculturalism argues, cultural diversity within institutions that are still white-dominated lacks redeeming social value.

A lot of valuable research affirmed the indissociability of cultural and social dynamics. Becky W. Thompson and Sangeeta Tyagi begin their edited volume on multicultural education by noting that the "acceptance of new voices and new perspectives goes hand in hand with vigorous and committed efforts at affirmative-action hiring at all levels within educational institutions."[81] In other words, changes in culture are cosmetic without changes in the polity. In the same volume, Chandra Talpade Mohanty writes that a merely "attitudinal engagement with diversity" must be supplemented by the history of inequities that work at the level of racialized groups.[82] Also criticizing a weak multiculturalism that "celebrate[s] diversity without adequately analyzing power differentials among groups positioned by racial categorizations and inequalities," Leslie G. Roman suggests the need for white students and educators to "take effective responsibility and action for 'disinvesting' in racial privilege."[83] Christine E. Sleeter argues that education cannot become truly multicultural "without specifically interrogating the racial identities of a predominantly white teaching force." Further, multiculturalism must regard racism not as an individual "misperception but as a structural arrangement among racial groups."[84]

Strong multicultural notions of education invoke the need to pursue a whole range of goals at the same time. In her comprehensive volume *Affirming Diversity*, Sonia Nieto argues that multiculturalism requires attention to "racism, discrimination, and expectations of students' achievement," to "[s]tructural factors such as school organization and educational policies and practices," *and* to "[c]ultural and other differences such as ethnicity, race, gender, language, and class."[85] Again, multiculturalism is never reducible to a stress on cultural heritage, or to personal identity, or to a more racially balanced school administration, but refers to the dynamic interaction of these features and more. These multiculturalists do not collapse all these terms into one another, but also regard the conceptual isolation of the "cultural," "educational," "scholarly," "political," and so on as falsifying their inevitable interaction.

More general institutional commentary of the multicultural kind has also increasingly insisted on a similar dependence of cultural on economic parity. David A. Hollinger argues that those who criticize multiculturalism as leading to the "Balkanization of America" should focus their complaints not "on the educational and political programs of ethno-racial 'separatists' [but] . . . instead, on the rigidification of the class structure."[86] Mable Haddock and Chiquita Mullins Lee note that "for multiculturalism to become a reality in cultural programming, rather than an empty slogan, there must be a shift in power. Neither arts councils, nor the heads for the Corporation for Public Broadcasting (CPB), PBS, and other corporations are committed to sharing the power to make funding decisions with those outside their immediate purview. Were they to share power equitably with people of color, there would be substantial changes."[87] Politics cannot be seen as something added on to culture here and there as a luxury, a vendetta, a bias. The survival of cultural diversity depends on greatly enhanced political and economic equality.[88]

This multiculturalism draws at the same time on cultural pluralism and the specific kind of nationalism described earlier. In doing so, it has continued to develop a tradition of racial thought that is quite distinct from the assimilationist pluralisms that have sometimes used the same tag of multiculturalism. It takes a *multicentered* national culture as encompassing the intersectionality of race with a range of the identities and forces *in addition to race* that comprise social life. It supports *race consciousness* along with *antiessentialist* notions of identity and social structure, and refines our understanding of the way racial and other dimensions of culture influence even apparently neutral institutions. And it puts *political equity* at the center of any discussion of cultural interaction. The result is not merely criticism of assimilationist wishes on a variety of fronts, though that remains indispensable, but visions of a postassimilationist America. This multiculturalism imagines the necessary transformation of subjectivity itself. It does not seek a hardening of categories. To the contrary, it concentrates on those cultures that are already renegotiating areas of broad overlap from the standpoint of their own independent practices.

A New Starting Point

Racial assimilationism is a pillar of conservative cultural rule in America, and always has been. It preempts full debate on cultural questions and on a range of public policy issues by supporting a majority group making ground rules for everyone before discussion takes place.

By contrast, a basic requirement of power sharing is shared control over definitions of social injury and remedy. This kind of sharing has been mostly impossible.[89] White liberalism has generally consented to the prevailing racial common sense that, after the middle 1960s, race has ceased to be a serious obstacle to the advancement of people of color. This consent has become one of the ground rules. Thus, assimilationism continues to be the preferred solution to the problems of minorities and women. Economic and social control takes a back seat to integration, which has meant ongoing retention of control by the white majority. Liberal consent to assimilationist pluralism has damaged discussions of race, to say nothing of racial progress.

Multiculturalism, in the stronger sense we've described here, has, since the 1970s, not assumed that its primary goal of improving the lives of people of color can be achieved through assimilation. It thus links its promotion of a multiracial terrain to finding alternatives to common culture. It offers a different basis of social interaction and peace than does white norming, which has been hard for its nonwhite subjects to distinguish from the coercions of poverty, exclusion, and second-class citizenship.

Where multiculturalism can combine the best of the pluralist and the nationalist traditions, it offers an alternative to cultural assimilationism. It offers an alternative racial common sense that is complexly figured yet unrelenting about a few starting points. It addresses racism prominently. It respects group autonomy *and* the complicated divisions and differences within and among racially marked groups. It focuses on equity as a primary principle. It is committed to the patience and effort required to let solutions emerge from the process of confrontation and debate. In short, multiculturalism suggests that a new basic structure of intergroup negotiation could replace *e pluribus unum* to good effect.

Multiculturalism is and will remain a type of cultural pluralism. But it promotes norms of its own, alternative ground rules, a different starting point. It offers itself as an alternative jumping-off place. It offers a specific kind of *recognition* as a form of citizenship, in which various parties get to the table in an autonomous and equal state. It does not predict the kind of substantive policy, political and economic alterations, the social *reconstruction,* that could follow. Will multiculturalism promote racial justice? Will it link racial justice to the redistributive project necessary for economic equality? Will it redefine racial justice and economic equality as constitutively feminist and antihomophobic? Will it take its "multi" prefix seriously in grappling with the reality of transracial coalition and conflict? Will it reach for the kind of international perspective no longer readily available in the United States? Will it even lead to the reformation of cultural knowledge that it sometimes promises? No. Not really. Not in itself. But multiculturalism may be viewed as a *precondition* for these different kinds of work. As a form of cultural pluralism, it would be a precondition with a long though obscured tradition in the United States, one with some built-in mass appeal. And it would weaken the assimilationist grip on a multiculturalist ideal that is rapidly being adopted by the state, the corporation, the military, the arts council, the university. Multiculturalism would simply make real cultural pluralism do what it says it means. That in itself would make quite a difference.

Notes

1. Manning Marable, *The Crisis of Color and Democracy: Essays on Race, Class and Power* (Monroe, Maine: Common Courage Press, 1992), 252.

2. Ibid., 252–56.

3. Cornel West, *Race Matters* (New York: Vintage Books, 1994), 19.

4. *The American Heritage Dictionary of the English Language,* ed. William Morris (Boston: Houghton Mifflin, 1980), 1009.

5. Cited in Arthur Schlesinger Jr., *The Disuniting of America* (Knoxville, Tenn.: Whittle Direct Books, 1991), 13. Schlesinger is best known for stressing unity over multiplicity. W. E. B. Du Bois's famous notion of African-American double consciousness in *The Souls of Black Folk* (1903) bears a strong relation to cultural pluralism. Du Bois never uses the term; the term in its white development was often (mis)used against ideas like his, and his own thought moved in a different direction. But note the book's early reference to "the ideal of fostering and developing the traits and talents of the Negro, not in opposition to or contempt for other races, but rather in large conformity to the greater ideals of the American Republic, in order that some day on American soil two world-races may give each to each those characteristics both so sadly lack" (*The Souls of Black Folk,* intro. Henry Louis Gates Jr. [New York: Bantam, 1989], 8). Du Bois simultaneously imagines an interaction between two races that remain separate, and yet veers toward pluralism's perennial assimilationist fascination with American ideals that encompass both.

6. Troy Duster, "The Diversity of California at Berkeley: An Emerging Reformulation of 'Competence' in an Increasingly Multicultural World," in *Beyond a Dream Deferred: Multicultural Education and the Politics of Excellence,* ed. Becky W. Thompson and Sangeeta Tyagi (Minneapolis and London: University of Minnesota Press, 1993), 248.

7. Horace M. Kallen, *Cultural Pluralism and the American Idea: An Essay in Social Philosophy,* with comments by Stanley H. Chapman, Steward G. Cole, Elizabeth F. Flower, Frank P. Graham, R. J. Henle, S. J., Herold C. Hunt, Milton R. Konvitz, Leo Pfeffer, and Goodwin Watson (Philadelphia: University of Pennsylvania Press, 1956), 85.

8. Ibid., 97.

9. Ibid., 82.

10. Ibid., 23. We have omitted Kallen's biologistic continuation, which mixes complicatedly with his culturalism.

11. Ibid.

12. Ibid.

13. Ibid., 98.

14. Ibid.

15. For a brief summary, see Michael Omi and Howard Winant, *Racial Formation in the United States: From the 1960s to the 1990s,* 2d ed. (New York: Routledge, 1994), 15–16. For an account that ties "ethnic pluralism" to the simultaneous assimilation of white ethnics and subor-

dination of African Americans, see Stephen Steinberg, *The Ethnic Myth: Race, Ethnicity, and Class in America,* 2d ed. (Boston: Beacon Press, 1989), 42. Steinberg concludes that "at the same time that the nation pursued a policy aimed at the rapid assimilation of recent arrivals from Europe, it segregated the racial minorities who, by virtue of their much longer history in American society, had already come to share much of the dominant culture."

16. Arthur Levine and Ette Cureton, "The Quiet Revolution: Eleven Facts about Multiculturalism and the Curriculum," *Change* (January–February 1992): 29.

17. Robert Leiken, "O Their America," *Times Literary Supplement* (22 May 1992): 6.

18. Roger Kimball, *Tenured Radicals: How Politics Has Corrupted Our Higher Education* (New York: Harper Perennial, 1990), 193.

19. Schlesinger, *The Disuniting of America,* 6.

20. Ibid., 70, 71. Schlesinger is thinking of immigrants here, but the process is much the same for U.S. citizens who are newcomers to the cultural mainstream.

21. Ibid., 76.

22. Ibid.

23. Ibid., 82.

24. This paragraph is based on a discussion in Avery Gordon and Christopher Newfield, "White Philosophy," *Critical Inquiry* (summer 1994): 753. That essay offers a fuller criticism of pluralist supremacism or liberal racism.

25. For an interesting comparison, see Etienne Balibar's valuable analysis of nonbiological racialist thought in postcolonial France (Etienne Balibar, "Is There a 'Neo-Racism'?" in Balibar and Immanuel Wallerstein, *Race, Nation, Class* [1988; London and New York: Verso, 1991], 17–28). The "neo" should not mislead us into thinking this is a new development, at least in the United States. Kallen, as noted earlier, was already tracing it to antebellum New England culture.

26. Critiques of neutrality in the law were developed by a number of writers in the Critical Legal Studies and Critical Race Studies movements. On color blindness specifically, see Neil Gotanda, "A Critique of 'Our Constitution Is Colorblind': Racial Categories and White Supremacy," *Stanford Law Review* 44 (1991): 1–68. See also Patricia J. Williams, *The Alchemy of Race and Rights* (Cambridge: Harvard University Press, 1991), especially "The Death of the Profane" and "The Obliging Shell"; and Gary Peller, "Race Consciousness," *Duke Law Journal* (1990): 758–847. Peller analyzes the "social compromise" by which "the price of the national commitment to suppress white supremacists would be the rejection of race consciousness among African Americans" (760).

27. Gary B. Nash, "The Great Multicultural Debate," *Contention* 1:3 (spring 1992): 1–28.

28. Schlesinger, *The Disuniting of America,* 71.

29. Nash, "The Great Multicultural Debate," 24.

30. Henry Louis Gates Jr., "Pluralism and Its Discontents," *Contention* 2:1 (fall 1992): 71.

31. For a discussion that seeks to avoid attributing equal value to other cultures while insisting on interaction based on a mutual presumption of (some) value, see Charles Taylor, *Multiculturalism and "The Politics of Recognition,"* ed. Amy Gutmann (Princeton, N.J.: Princeton University Press, 1992), 68. Taylor sees no right to equality but does believe in a right to recognition (as we are formed by being recognized by the other) (36, 64).

32. Nash, "The Great Multicultural Debate," 23.

33. Ibid., 24.

34. Ibid., 25.

35. Ibid.

36. Diane Ravitch, "In the Multicultural Trenches," *Contention* 1:3 (spring 1992): 34.

37. Todd Gitlin, "From University to Difference: Notes on the Fragmentation of the Idea of the Left," *Contention* 2:2 (winter 1993): 22. Gitlin mourns the passing of "the early New Left pol-

itics of universalist aspiration," which were replaced by the "late New Left politics of dispersion and separateness" (32). One could more plausibly argue that universalist aspiration necessarily and justly foundered on the rock of race after 1965, and that "late" New Left politics had to attempt cross-racial connections in the awareness that even the Vietnam War did not provide a universalizing, unifying issue for the Left, much less the Port Huron Statement's 1962 invocation of "human brotherhood" (cited by Gitlin, 30).

38. Gates, "Pluralism and Its Discontents," 74.

39. Steinberg, *The Ethnic Myth*, 170.

40. This says nothing about the virtues of Afrocentric interpretations of historical epochs and peoples. Although white commentary has been little more than one long hatchet job, Black critiques have been more telling. For an excellent analysis of white attacks on nationalism from the position of integration that has influenced our own thinking, see Peller, "Race Consciousness."

41. The value of Nash's position appears clearest when under attack from the Right. The *MacNeil/Lehrer News Hour* devoted a segment to criticisms of his National Standards, voiced in this case by the director of the National Endowment for the Humanities under Ronald Reagan and George Bush, Lynne Cheney. Nash was asked, "When you all were creating this document, you did come under pressure from various groups—women's groups, minority groups—to include politically correct, in their view, views of American history. Is that true? Were you under pressure to change or amend what you were creating?" Nash replied: "I don't know of any politically correct groups. I know of American women. I know of Black Americans and American Indians. I do know that these groups have been absent from most of the textbooks and it is because of the historical amnesia concerning these groups that it is due time to have them restored to their proper place in the making of American history. Ms. Cheney thinks we will disunite America by paying attention to these groups. But we have been disunited, and we're more likely to be united if we take proper and due account of the contributions and the struggles of these forgotten groups." Although we are wary of his ongoing goal of unification (and of national standards), we admire Nash's long-term labor—along with that of his multitude of collaborators on this project—on behalf of greater inclusion in all primary and secondary school curricula.

42. For a valuable survey and taxonomy of multicultural education literature, see Christine E. Sleeter and Carl A. Grant, "An Analysis of Multicultural Education in the United States," in *Facing Racism in Education* (1987), ed. Nitza M. Hidalgo, Caesar L. McDowell, and Emilie V. Siddle (Cambridge: Harvard Educational Review Reprint Series no. 21, 1990), 138–61. The authors use fourteen categories to sort their long bibliography into five types: "Teaching the Culturally Different"; "Human Relations" approaches; "Single Group Studies"; "Multicultural Education"; "Education That Is Multicultural and Social Reconstructionist" (139). We are using the term multiculturalism to cover principally the last three of these categories. In any case, internal differences are smaller than those between the multicultural and other pluralist types we have discussed.

43. Manuel Ramírez III and Alfredo Casañeda, *Cultural Democracy, Bicognitive Development, and Education* (New York: Academic Press, 1974), 28.

44. Ibid., 11.

45. "For example, the statement of the Steering Committee of the National Coalition for Cultural Pluralism defines the concept of cultural pluralism as 'the perspective used by different social groups in their attempt to survive as *independent*, yet *interdependent*, segments of society'" (Arturo Pacheco, "Cultural Pluralism: A Philosophical Analysis," *Journal of Teacher Education* 28:3 [May–June 1977]: 16).

46. The ASCD Multicultural Education Commission, "Encouraging Multicultural Educa-

tion," in *Multicultural Education: Commitments, Issues, and Applications,* ed. Carl A. Grant (Washington, D.C.: Association for Supervision and Curriculum Development, 1977), 3.

47. Pacheco, "Cultural Pluralism," 18.

48. Cited by Ramírez and Casañeda, *Cultural Democracy,* 26. In general, Gordon may stress the priority of group life more than Ramírez and Casañeda concede.

49. James A. Banks, "Multiethnic Education and the Quest for Equality," *Phi Delta Kappan* (April 1983): 584.

50. Ramírez and Casañeda, *Cultural Democracy,* 25.

51. Pacheco, "Cultural Pluralism," 20.

52. Ibid. We have replaced Pacheco's term "cultural diversity" with "multiculturalism" to avoid terminological confusion.

53. Sleeter and Grant, "An Analysis of Multicultural Education," 146.

54. Ibid., 149.

55. Ibid.

56. Even a nationalist anger that trashes cross-racial coalitions criticizes not coalitions per se but the posture of the prospective partner. In a well-known passage, the Chicago office of the Student Nonviolent Coordinating Committee (SNCC) writes, "We have to learn that black is so much better than belonging to the white race with the blood of millions dripping from their hands that it goes far beyond any prejudice or resentment. We must fill ourselves with hate for all white things. This is not vengeance or trying to take the white oppressors' place to become new black oppressors but is a oneness with a worldwide black brotherhood" (Chicago Office of SNCC, "We Want Black Power," leaflet [Chicago: Chicago Office of SNCC, 1967]; reprinted in August Meier et al., eds., *Black Protest Thought in the Twentieth Century,* 2d ed. [Indianapolis and New York: Bobbs-Merrill, 1971], 487). The call for a separate oneness expresses a sense of the impossibility of alliances with a white majority that has such a long history of extreme anti-Black activity.

57. In reverse order, Wahneema Lubiano notes that the message of Black nationalism "has been described variously as either an example of a 'better' world directed at the rest of the actually existing world and/or as a meaning available only within the group" ("Standing in for the State: Black Nationalism and 'Writing' the Black Subject," *Alphabet City* 3 [October 1993]: 20).

58. The case would be somewhat different were we to focus on the American Indian movement, for example, or the Chicano movement, or recent alternations of these traditions. Chela Sandoval, for example, does not contrast assimilationism and separatism with pluralism but with oppositional and then differential consciousness ("U.S. Third World Feminism: The Theory and Method of Oppositional Consciousness in the Postmodern World," *Genders* 10 [spring 1991]: 1–24).

59. *Huey Newton Talks to the Movement* (Chicago: Students for a Democratic Society, 1968; reprinted in Meier et al., eds. *Black Protest Thought*), 495.

60. Ibid., 496.

61. Ibid., 498–99.

62. Ibid., 500–501.

63. National Council of Churches, paid advertisement, *New York Times,* 31 July 1966, cited in Stokely Carmichael and Charles V. Hamilton, *Black Power: The Politics of Liberation in America* (New York: Random House, 1967), 49.

64. Ibid.

65. Lubiano, "Standing in for the State," 20.

66. Carmichael and Hamilton, *Black Power,* 46–47.

67. Ibid., 44.

68. In his afterword to the 1992 reissue of *Black Power,* Hamilton writes, "The call for Black Power in the 1960s was not a call for racial isolation. Yes, it was an honest recognition that for

any group—racial, ethnic, economic—to become a respected, effective player in the American political system, cohesive organization was crucial. . . . When blacks began applying this [common] lesson to themselves they immediately were branded 'separatists' and ill-advised activists who sought to 'go it alone'" (*Black Power* [1967; New York: Vintage-Random House, 1992], 203). This hasty branding continues to control our understanding of nationalist movements that focused on overall political change. (Kwame Toure notes simply that "the book does not advocate Revolution. It preaches reform" [187].)

69. We continue to use "cultural pluralism" in its specific sense. It does not encompass other forms of multiple identities or coalition politics (racial hybridity, women of color, and others). Lubiano uses the concept of Black common sense in "Standing in for the State" (20).

70. Peter Erickson, "What Multiculturalism Means," *Transition* 55 (1992): 113.

71. For a recent survey of some of these long-standing issues, see Johnella E. Butler and John C. Walter, eds., *Transforming the Curriculum: Ethnic Studies and Women's Studies* (Albany: State University of New York Press, 1991); see especially the essays by Butler, Johnetta B. Cole, and R. A. Olguin.

72. A very interesting early account is Angela Davis, *Angela Davis: An Autobiography* (1974; New York: International Publishers, 1988). See also Toni Cade, ed., *The Black Woman: An Anthology* (New York: New American Library, 1970).

73. Cherríe Moraga and Gloria Anzaldúa, eds., *This Bridge Called My Back: Writings by Radical Women of Color* (Watertown, Mass.: Persephone Press, 1981); Gloria T. Hull, Patricia Bell Scott, and Barbara Smith, *All the Women Are White, All the Blacks Are Men, but Some of Us Are Brave: Black Women's Studies* (New York: Feminist Press, 1982). See also Sara Evans, "Black Power—Catalyst for Feminism," in *Personal Politics: The Roots of Women's Liberation in the Civil Rights Movement and the New Left* (New York: Vintage Books, 1979); and Paula Giddings, "The Women's Movement and Black Discontent," in *When and Where I Enter: The Impact of Black Women on Race and Sex in America* (New York: Bantam Books, 1984).

74. Rush Limbaugh, radio broadcast (1992) cited in Thomas Byrne Edsall, "America's Sweetheart," *New York Review of Books,* 6 October 1994: 9.

75. Nearly all of the contributors to this volume have explored in various places the ways a category like "African American" or "lesbian" or "male" can lack an essence while retaining a systematic, determinate set of social effects. For an interesting exception, see Lourdes Portillo's remarks in chapter 12. Other writers trying to think about social determinacy in antiessentialist ways include Gloria Anzaldúa, Homi Bhabha, Ed Cohen, Diana Fuss, Stuart Hall, Donna Haraway, June Jordan, Duncan Kennedy, Ernesto Laclau, Kobena Mercer, Chantal Mouffe, Gayatri C. Spivak, and Patricia J. Williams.

76. Cameron McCarthy and Warren Crichlow, "Introduction: Theories of Identity, Theories of Representation, Theories of Race," in *Race, Identity, and Representation in Education* (New York and London: Routledge, 1993), xv. See also the discussion of the reality of race in quotation marks in Angela Y. Davis's contribution to this volume.

77. For a persuasive description of the white bias in ordinary medical school procedures, see Joel Dreyfuss and Charles Lawrence III, *The Bakke Case: The Politics of Inequality* (New York: Harcourt Brace Jovanovich, 1979), especially "The Best Doctors."

Medical school admissions are a particularly interesting case because their procedures have frequently landed in court. Scientific competence is obviously of critical importance in the successful practice of medicine, and like other such knowledges has been subject to long and elaborate sequences of objective testing. It seems relatively easy to determine whether a person scored an 80 or an 89 on an exam, and to eliminate most racial bias from such a test. The life-and-death aspects of medical practice make the idea of passing on incompetent physicians for ostensibly political reasons particularly abhorrent, even for those who agree that the medical profession should represent the national population as much as it can. It seems preposterous to claim that testing for the maximum possible medical skill is a white idea, for it appears so obviously to be a desire for objective merit that any culture can share.

But the issue in such famous cases as *Bakke v. Regents of the University of California* has generally been *what* exactly constitutes merit and how to adjudicate the different perception of candidates for admission. One could favor mathematical achievement, or commitment to future service in poor or rural areas, or one's goals as a specialist, or "personal qualities" that would positively affect a medical practice. The Association of American Medical Colleges had singled out one of these, formally recommending that "medical schools must admit increased numbers of students from geographical areas, economic backgrounds and ethnic groups that are now inadequately represented" (19). Competence in all relevant areas was required—applicants committed to rural service but incompetent in math would rarely if ever be admitted. But one candidate with a slightly lower math score than another could be preferentially admitted on the basis of some other quality, such as an interest in bioengineering research, or in public health, and so on.

Given the same pool in which qualified applicants outnumber positions, different kinds of admissions committees working with different assumptions will produce very different classes of medical students. A group dominated by faculty seeking the "smartest" class and who equate smartness with test scores will produce a class of MCAT wizards (although these scores only weakly correlate with future performance as medical students or physicians). A committee with some members also concerned with the inferior collective health of African Americans will produce students with good grades and test scores *and* demonstrated interest in and knowledge about these kinds of medical issues. Members who believe that the United States must keep its technological edge in high-cost treatment of the most serious illnesses will favor students with good grades and test scores *and* strong technical interests. These are complex situations, and clearly the racial and ethnic composition of the committee will not be the sole influence, nor will it have a simple, determinate effect. Nonetheless, the institution is not *neutral* on any of these issues. It defines good doctors as having one set of qualities, or another set, depending on what people and interests operate the institution. Speaking with historical patterns in mind, a 95 percent white committee *may* produce a racially diverse class with more interest in general practice in underserved areas than in highly paid specialization. But it is less likely to than a committee comprised itself of people of diverse backgrounds. Although we are all reluctant to resort to stereotyping, it can nonetheless be said that medical schools are not neutral but either more or less "white," that a white medical school will usually produce different kinds of doctors than one less white, and that such differences can be measured.

78. Ted Gordon and Wahneema Lubiano, "The Statement of the Black Faculty Caucus," in *Debating P.C.: The Controversy over Political Correctness on College Campuses*, ed. Paul Berman (New York: Dell-Laurel, 1992), 249–50.

79. Ibid., 252–53.

80. Similarly, Ray Davis, executive director of the Student Coalition against Apartheid and Racism (SCAR), says, "By the mid- to late '80s, students and faculty recognized that universities as a whole were still Eurocentered. We saw that what we needed to do was to change the university, not just add a department. . . . Multiculturalism will be one of *the* issues in the '90s. . . . [It intersects] the same issues of what is equality and who has advantages over whom" (quoted in Sarah Ferguson, "The Campus and Beyond: Postwar Activists State Their Case," *Voice Class Action, Village Voice* [20 August 1991]: 8).

81. Becky W. Thompson and Sangeeta Tyagi, "Introduction," in *Beyond a Dream Deferred*, xiv.

82. Chandra Talpade Mohanty, "On Race and Voice: Challenges for Liberal Education," in *Beyond a Dream Deferred*, 41–65.

83. Leslie G. Roman, "White Is a Color! White Defensiveness, Postmodernism, and Anti-racist Pedagogy," in *Race, Identity, and Representation in Education*, 71, 84.

84. Christine E. Sleeter, "How White Teachers Construct Race," in *Race, Identity, and Representation in Education*, 157.

85. Sonia Nieto, *Affirming Diversity: The Sociopolitical Context of Multicultural Education* (New York: Longman, 1992), xxvi–xxvii.

86. David A. Hollinger, "Postethnic America," *Contention* 2:1 (fall 1992): 90. David Reiff, on the other hand, doubts that multiculturalism is capable of a conjunction of politics, economics, and culture: "For all their writings on power, hegemony, and oppression, the campus multiculturalists seem indifferent to the question of where they fit into the material scheme of things. . . . Are the multiculturalists truly unaware of how closely their treasured catchphrases—'cultural diversity,' 'difference,' the need to 'do away with boundaries'—resemble the stock phrases of the modern corporation: 'product diversification,' 'the global marketplace,' and 'the boundary-less company'?" (David Reiff, "Multiculturalism's Silent Partner: It's the Newly Globalized Consumer Economy, Stupid," *Harper's* [August 1993]: 64).

87. Mable Haddock and Chiquita Mullins Lee, "Whose Multiculturalism?: PBS, the Public and Privilege," *Afterimage* (September 1993): 17.

88. Los Angeles launched a great deal of discussion of the links between meaningful multiculturalism and economic reconstruction. About one year after the Los Angeles revolt was catalyzed by the acquittal of the white LAPD officers who beat Black motorist Rodney King, the city's citizens replaced Black Democratic mayor Tom Bradley with white Republican Richard Riordan. The *LA Weekly*'s Harold Meyerson comments: "The *Times* exit poll showed that the two issues that mattered most to voters were 'Jobs/the economy,' mentioned by 52 percent, and 'Crime/gangs,' mentioned by 37 percent. From the beginning, [liberal candidate Michael] Woo was playing catch-up on crime; the issue on which he could have gone on the offensive was the economy. It wasn't enough simply to attack [conservative businessman Richard] Riordan as the personification of Reaganomics; Woo had to stand for a distinct economics of his own. He might have borrowed government-as-incubator-of-small-business from primary rival Linda Griego, or government-as-catalyst-for-manufacturing from Nick Patsaouras. . . . [Such] proposals would not have assured victory, but Woo could have used any one of them to contrast himself with Riordan. . . . Without them, though, Woo couldn't even provide his union supporters with an argument on his behalf. On election day, white voters from households with union members voted for Riordan, 61 percent to 39 percent. . . . The lesson for liberal L.A., for South-Central and the Eastside, couldn't be clearer: multiculturalism, divorced from economics, can get you a government grant or win you a primary. It is not the path to power, or to change" (Harold Meyerson, "The Word on Woo," *LA Weekly*, 18–24 June 1993: 12).

89. For the earlier numbers, see William Brink and Louis Harris, *Black and White: A Study of U.S. Racial Attitudes Today* (New York: Simon and Schuster, 1967), and Dreyfuss and Lawrence, *The Bakke Case*, 108, 144.

CHAPTER SEVEN

Manichaeism and Multiculturalism

CEDRIC J. ROBINSON

History as a value in itself is a very European phenomenon. Europeans are
the ones who go about investigating the history of other peoples.
Michael Landmann[1]

Since even Dinesh D'Souza, one of the most resolute critics of multiculturalism, acknowledges that one of its appropriate uses would be "as a complement to rather than as a substitute for study of the West,"[2] I believe it is permissible to initiate our interrogation of the multiculturalist polemic with an
exemplary instance of the specular imagining from a Western interior.[3] Put
in another way, we will begin with an event that was indisputably domiciled
in the West, but we will rely on reports from spectators who, though irre-
trievably and materially positioned in Western society, imagine and realize a
joint and mutually ratified peripheralization with the West. (Momentarily, I
shall provide evidence of the existence of such creatures.) But in the stead of
D'Souza's favorite elite antagonists in the academy ("student protestors, faculty advocates, and ideologically sympathetic administrators"),[4] I intend to
summon less privileged informants.

Leonard Smith, now a retired transit policeman, was a barely twenty-
year-old enlisted man when, in April 1945, he stood before the broken gates
of the concentration camp at Dachau. Smitty's presence at Dachau was ac-

counted for by his membership in the all-Black 761st tank battalion of the Third Army, a frontline combat unit in the segregated U.S. Army. That same April, the grotesque scene Smith observed at Dachau was being repeated at Buchenwald, another concentration camp, for the 183rd Combat Engineer Corps, also an all-Black unit. As history has not always recorded, Smitty and his shocked Black comrades were the first American troops to encounter the horrors of the concentration camps. Their reactions are worth noting.

Smitty recalled: "I got angry . . . all of these human skeletons, falling out of the doors, came out. We said, 'Oh my God, what is this?' It made us so angry. I couldn't understand how another human could treat other humans like that."[5] And at Buchenwald, Leon Bass, a twenty-year-old Black corporal, had almost the identical thought: "I just said to myself, my God, what is this? What's happening here? How could people do this to other people?"[6] From another perspective, one of the fifty-three thousand survivors remembered the "black soldiers of the Third Army, tall and strong, crying like babies, carrying the emaciated bodies of the liberated prisoners."[7] At Buchenwald, Elie Wiesel, then a sixteen-year-old prisoner, recalled: "I'll never forget their eyes, the rage, the anger. Their reaction was so profound."[8]

Although it was clear to Smitty and Bass that they were at that moment confronting some sort of moral deficiency that also implicated their own racial experience of American oppression, their anguish was for another. Their anger, and the tears shed by their brothers, resulted from the specular pain of recognition and amazement: this wasteland of broken humanity issuing from the camps was themselves and beyond themselves. It was history, both familiar and exteriorized, which they bore in their arms. Forty years later, a journalist insisted that "none of the young soldiers . . . were prepared for the sights." But Buchenwald, Bass remembered, "made me aware that I was not alone in my suffering" and that "there were a host of other folk out there who for a host of different reasons were being mistreated." The Buchenwald inmates, he said, "reached the ultimate. I saw this and said, 'My God, that could happen to me.'"[9]

Fifty years later, E. G. McConnell, a third witness among the young Black soldiers, peered into the Dachau cremation ovens and pronounced: "This is the ultimate end of slavery. They worked the poor devils to death. Worked them down to the bone. They burned them; they sold the ashes."[10] Bass's and McConnell's reactions to the death camp provide evidence, I submit, for the specular imagining.

What Smitty, McConnell, and Bass and their comrades did not know was that what they had come upon was a reenactment, on a larger, grander scale, of a particular ritual of racial degradation that extended back nearly two hundred years. Londa Schiebinger has recovered the beginnings of this most characteristic manifestation of evil:

> In the 1780s Duke Frederick II of Hessen-Kassel settled a colony of Africans at Wilhelmshohe (near Kassel), high above the Eder river, in order to study their customs and anatomy. Originally intended to house Chinese, the colony was built with pagodas and oriental gardens. Since Chinese were either too expensive or simply not available, the colony was settled with Africans. The medical doctor in charge of the colony, Ernst Baldinger, noted that the Africans settled there did not flourish; most died of tuberculosis or committed suicide. Their bodies were turned over to Germany's leading anatomist: Samuel Thomas von Soemmerring. From his dissections of "several Negro bodies of both sexes" (one woman, one child, and at least two men), along with his earlier observations of them in public baths, Soemmerring prepared his 1784 *Über die körperliche Verschiedenheit des Mohren von Europäer* (Concerning the physical difference between the Moor and the European)—a book that served as a basic text on the African physique until well into the nineteenth century.[11]

In 1945, those young Black troops could not have known, factually, of the existence of this earlier human exhibit and anatomical laboratory. Alternatively, however, I suspect they already comprehended, intuitively and consciously, the profound moral deficit from which it issued: the subordination and perversion of knowledge by its suturing to the interests of power and privilege. Such exercises of prerogative provided the conditions for the emergence of Western racial science. Let me remind you, in Professor Landmann's more genteel imagination, that "Europeans are the ones who go about investigating the history of other peoples."

In the eighteenth century, Europe's most eminent scholars had less need for Landmann's euphemisms for domination: Hegel candidly found nothing worthy of the name of history outside Europe; and Linnaeus and Kant concurred in their own fashion with this appropriation of history by fastening on anatomy as the code for the non-West. With the notable exception of Blumenbach, Europe's scientists found sufficient taxonomic proof of the inferior difference of women, African, and pre-American native males in the simple fact that these assorted creatures lacked beards: "the want," as Richard McCausland reported in 1786 in the *Philosophical Transactions of the Royal Society of London*, "of one very characteristic mark of the [male] sex."[12] As such, Duke Frederick and the doctors Soemmerring and Baldinger joined the illustrious company of Kant, Winckelmann, von Schlegel, Schiller, and a host of others in Germany, of de Buffon, Lamarck,

Fontenelle, and Gobineau in France, and of Tyson, Camper, Knox, Hunt, and Galton in Britain.[13]

And finally, in the mid-eighteenth century (as Donna Haraway has reminded us), Linnaeus, the Swede, had invented the primate order, "the first Order of Nature," by renaming Homo sapiens, monkeys, apes, lemurs, and bats.[14] "Literally and figuratively," Haraway writes, "primate studies were a colonial affair, in which knowledge of the living and dead bodies of monkeys and apes [and now, we must add, African men, women, and children] was part of the system of unequal exchange of extractive colonialism."[15] The imaginary factualities of racism, sexism, and science conspired with colonialism, demonstrating anew that "deeds, as opposed to words, are the parents of facts. That is, human action is at the root of what we can see as a fact, linguistically and historically."[16]

The recovery and exposure of just such deliberate, mean-spirited, and oftentimes consciously self-interested exercises within the history of modernist Western inquiry is one function and one result of multicultural research. The superior instances of multicultural scholarship extend and deepen the emphatic moral revulsion experienced by Smitty, McConnell, Bass, and their brethren at the gates of hell. And in the mirroring images affiliating the casualties of race, ethnicity, class, and gender, multiculturalist inquiry provokes an alternative dialectic of ethics between the desperate particularity of the Same and the anguished universality of the Other. However, it is precisely this desperate particularity that most frequently animates the opposition to multiculturalism.

On this score, consider for a moment William F. Buckley's *God and Man at Yale* (1951), which sought to defend "the Christian and individualist West" from the onslaught of liberalism. Buckley was by no means the first American patrician to lament the appearances of democratic parties in the academy and the falling away of certain privileges of the ruling classes. What distinguished Buckley was his ability to recruit, train, and nurture the polemical skills of his coreligionists in a para-academic domain through such organs as satellite think tanks, the *National Review*, his varied publishing operations, and his nationally televised program, *Firing Line*. Buckley's activities, clearly distinguishable from the more crude fascistic impulses of Robert Welch, Robert Scaife, the Coors family, and others of the John Birch ilk, prepared the ground for Reagan-era right-wing publicists like Edward Shils, Allan Bloom, Dinesh D'Souza, Diane Ravitch, Lynne Cheney, Gertrude Himmelfarb, and the neoconservatives grouped around *Commentary* (Norman Podhoretz, Midge Dichter, Ben Wattenberg, etc.), *Policy Review*, the *New Republic, Academic Questions* (published by the National Association of Scholars), and the American Enterprise Institute.

Thus when Shils's *The Academic Ethic* appeared in 1984, indicting the burdens of "social justice" and "meeting societal needs" and other recent diversions from "the methodological discovery and teaching of truths about important things" within the academy, the terrain was already well tilled.[17] Buckley, Shils, and the more fugitive works of Sidney Hook became the most immediate progenitors to what eventually would become the better-known neoconservative tracts: Allan Bloom's nostalgic *The Closing of the American Mind* and D'Souza's sophomoric *Illiberal Education.*

The thread that sutures these works is the assertion of an imaginary transcendent universal culture—the West—and the near destruction of its cathedral, the academy. As Thomas Short put it in the first issue of *Academic Questions*, what must be emphasized in the academy is "how Western civilization, rather than being racist, sexist, classist, and ethnocentric, is actually the [sole] source of those principles and ideals by which diversity of opinion is sought, diversity of cultures honored, and individuals of all types respected."[18] On the other hand, the proponents of multiculturalism are represented as the barbarians at the wall, laying siege to the cultural canons exhibited and taught in the university of the thirties, forties, fifties, and early sixties, the undergraduate years of neoconservatives' nostalgia.[19] Tactically, what the neoconservatives truly seek to preserve is that conceit which Hayden White has described as "modern Western culture's notions about its own identity, its status as a (or rather *the*) civilization."[20]

The recurring strategy of neoconservatism, according to Joan Wallach Scott, is "to neutralize the space of ideological and cultural nonconformity by discrediting it."[21] In essence, neoconservatives pursue a political agenda that accords with the central premise of the multiculturalist critique "that the production of knowledge is a political enterprise."[22] What concerns neoconservatives, then, is neither culture nor (as Scott and others have put it) "white male privilege." They wish to erase the exposed seam, the nexus between power and regimes of knowledge so forcefully articulated by Michel Foucault.[23] How else can one defend their specious histories of knowledge, which invoke some pristine mythical moment in the life of the American academy? What else might explain the compulsion of Buckley, Shils, Ozick, Bloom, or D'Souza to tortured fantasies of an imaginary edifice they might restore from the predations of "politicization, bureaucratization and government interference"?[24]

To read Dinesh D'Souza, one would never know that Jews were deliberately excluded from university faculties until after WWII, that women were until recently systematically denied appointment at most research universities because of their sex, and that blacks were not admitted as students or hired as faculty at many public and private universities until the 1960s.[25]

And what would Shils make of Yale's involvement in the Office of Strategic Services (oss) and the Central Intelligence Agency; Harvard's sympathies for eugenics; the University of California's involvement in agribusiness; or, in the nineteenth century, the curricular revolution at Dartmouth in the early 1880s; the rejection of history, sociology, economics, and political science by the faculty at the University of Pennsylvania; or Thomas Jefferson's Aristotelian objectives in the founding of the University of Virginia? And these instances were comparatively small potatoes when we recall the Anglican determination of education at Oxford and Cambridge, and Harvard's and Yale's and Oxbridge's intellectual subsidization of race science in the nineteenth century.[26]

Perhaps because the majority of the opponents of multiculturalism have only a tenuous grasp of their own history, they have often resorted to the most blatant restagings of suppression (e.g., enlisting George Bush in the attack on "political correctness"; Education Secretary William Bennett's Platonic pronouncements on American virtue and the Western classics; and National Endowment for the Humanities chair Lynne Cheney's attacks on critical scholarship). And though one might be tempted to invoke McCarthyism, a truer parallel comes from Europe's Middle Ages: the extinguishment of heresy. Unlike McCarthyism, during which the "responsible" classes and their intelligentsia remained in the shadows, feigning embarrassment with the excesses to which popular hysteria drove them, the present crop of suppressionists makes the boldest and most public claims to the pursuit of the true faith: intellectual freedom.[27]

The most telling resemblance between the present neoconservatives and their medieval predecessors, however, is paradox. From Augustine, in the fifth century, to the first Inquisition in the thirteenth century, Christian intellectuals had rigorously attempted the erasure of such heresies as Manichaeism, the dualistic sect that asserted that "Good was everywhere locked in conflict with evil . . . with no morally gray areas in between."[28] Eventually, of course, in the very process of eradicating the dualist heresy, Christianity appropriated Manichaeism and its stark dichotomous worldview. Indeed, Manichaean fantasies of existential opposition became a frequent rhetorical strategy for instantiating social and international interests. As Frantz Fanon discovered within the colonial apparatuses of the Caribbean and Africa, the irrationalist discursive practices of Western racism assumed a Manichaean presence resistant to class politics.[29]

We must recognize, however, that the Manichaeism of the Right opponents of multiculturalism is mirrored in some of the truth claims of liberal multiculturalist discursive practices (for example, "white male privilege") and particularist cultural studies (the essentialist assertions made on behalf of gender, race, and ethnicity). As Lisa Lowe has indicated elsewhere, Minority Discourse is one mode of connection that rehabilitates multiculturalism.[30] S. P. Mohanty has most effectively captured the thrust of Minority Discourse. Mohanty queries:

> How do we negotiate between my history and yours? . . . our various pasts and presents . . . ? It is necessary to assert our dense particularities, our lived and imagined differences; but could we afford to leave untheorized the question of how our differences are intertwined and, indeed, hierarchically organized? Could we, in other words, afford to have *entirely* different histories . . . in entirely heterogeneous and discrete spaces?[31]

Mohanty argues that we cannot afford such forfeiture. And Jon Cruz has nominated Marxism as that theoretical enterprise that best encompasses the significations of our "various pasts and presents." I am less certain that Marxist theory, with all its Victorian positivistic, scientific, messianic, and Eurocentric baggage, is up to the task. And Marx himself would have few regrets or legitimate complaints if we moved on. Like the civilization in which it was conceived, and the architectonic world-system it sought to comprehend, Marxism was in actuality composed of antagonistic differences that fracture the economy and the elegance of a unitary or totalizing theory of history. A very different unifying narrative is required, and most certainly not one that presupposes that difference will and ought to be oxidized by the economies of commodity production.

I suggest that a radical impulse in multiculturalism constitutes both a critique of the absences and an appropriation of the positive contributions of Marxism. We are not the subjects or the subject formations of the capitalist world-system. It is merely one condition of our being. Amilcar Cabral recognized that fact when he insisted that " it is generally within the culture that we find the seed of opposition."[32] Multiculturalism, then, is a site of discursive resistance, an emblem and articulation of the several trajectories of "objective" opposition (religious, nationalist, feminist, etc.) mounted by our peoples in the everyday world.

Notes

1. Michael Landmann, "The Means as an End in Itself: Europe as the Perfection of Mankind," *History of European Ideas* 2:3 (1981): 188.

2. Dinesh D'Souza, "Multiculturalism 101: Great Books of the Non-Western World," *Policy Review* (spring 1991): 22.

3. I owe the notion of the specular subject identity to Abdul JanMohamed. See his "Worldliness-without-World, Homelessness-as-Home: Toward a Definition of the Border Intellectual," unpublished manuscript.

4. D'Souza, "Multiculturalism 101," 24.

5. Quoted in Susan King, "A Liberating 'Experience,'" *Los Angeles Times: TV Times*, 8–14 November 1992: 5. In 1985, the *New York Times* substituted Russian troops for the Black American troops who liberated the camps.

6. Quoted in William Stevens, "For Survivors and Liberators, a Commemoration," *New York Times*, 14 April 1985: 28.

7. *New York Times*, 8 November 1992, section 2: 30.

8. Quoted in Stevens, "For Survivors and Liberators," 28.

9. Ibid. At Bergen-Belsen, one survivor, Sigmund Strochlitz, remembered the British liberators as "young soldiers with boyish faces. They seemed confused at the sight of us, their eyes wandering in disbelief. They didn't know what to do."

10. *Fighting on Two Fronts in World War Two*, a documentary film by William Miles and Nina Rosenblum, aired on PBS-TV, 11 November 1992.

11. Londa Schiebinger, "The Anatomy of Difference: Race and Sex in Eighteenth-Century Science," *Eighteenth-Century Studies* 23:4 (summer 1990): 387.

12. Ibid., 391ff.

13. George Mosse, *Toward the Final Solution: A History of European Racism* (London: J. M. Dent and Sons, 1978).

14. Donna Haraway, *Primate Visions* (New York: Routledge, 1989), 9.

15. Ibid., 19.

16. Ibid., 3.

17. Quoted in John Thelin, "The Curriculum Crusades and the Conservative Backlash," *Change* (January–February 1992): 18.

18. Quoted in Edward Jayne, "Academic Jeremiad: The Neoconservative View of American Higher Education," *Change* (May–June 1991): 39.

19. For two instances of neoconservative undergraduate nostalgia, see the quote from Edward Shils in Thelin, "The Curriculum Crusades," 20; and Cynthia Ozick's memories in "A Critic at Large: T. S. Eliot at 101," *New Yorker*, 20 November 1989 (treated in Bruce Robbins, "Othering the Academy: Professionalism and Multiculturalism," *Social Research* 58:2 [summer 1991]: 360).

20. Hayden White, "Between Science and Symbol," *Times Literary Supplement*, 31 January 1986: 109.

21. Joan Wallach Scott, "The Campaign against Political Correctness: What's Really at Stake?" *Change* (November–December 1991): 30.

22. Ibid.

23. Michel Foucault, *Power/Knowledge* (New York: Pantheon Books, 1980).

24. Thelin writes: "For example, Shils' criticism of the external connections of the modern university overlooks the 'Wisconsin Plan' of the early 1900s, whereby campus and capitol in Madison meant that state university faculty often were intended to contribute to policy discussions; at the federal level, New Deal involvement of professors as experts in the 1930s set a precedent that has been followed for well over half a century. The presence of sponsored research in the evolution of such institutions as The California Institute of Technology in the 1920s indi-

cated that the role of professor did not preclude involvement in research and analysis of contemporary public affairs and national projects" ("The Curriculum Crusades," 18).

25. Scott, "The Campaign against Political Correctness," 32.

26. For the histories of the American academy's complicity in race science, secret government, and the suppression of intellectuals, see, respectively, John Trumpbour, ed., *How Harvard Rules* (Boston: South End Press, 1989); Robin Winks, *Cloak and Gown* (New York: William Morrow, 1987); and Ellen Schrecker, *No Ivory Tower* (New York: Oxford University Press, 1988).

27. For McCarthyism's anti-intellectualism, see Richard Hofstadter's *Anti-Intellectualism in American Life* (New York: Alfred A. Knopf, 1965).

28. Frederick H. Russell, "'Only Something Good Can Be Evil': The Genesis of Augustine's Secular Ambivalence," *Theological Studies* 51:4 (December 1990): 699.

29. See Cedric J. Robinson, "Fanon and the West: Imperialism in the Native Imagination," *Africa and the World* 1:1 (October 1987): 33.

30. Cf. Abdul JanMohamed and David Lloyd, "Toward a Theory of Minority Discourse," *Cultural Critique* 6 (spring 1987): 5–12.

31. Quoted in Scott, "The Campaign against Political Correctness," 39.

32. Amilcar Cabral, "National Liberation and Culture" in *Return to the Source* (New York: Monthly Review Press, 1973), 43.

PART II

Rethinking the Political Subject

CHAPTER EIGHT

Conjugating Subjects
in the Age of Multiculturalism

NORMA ALARCÓN

This essay is necessarily layered as I attempt to write and connect circuits of signification arising in specific historical locations, while also attempting to bring into view their relationality through processes of appropriation, translation, and recodification. Terms such as subject(ivity), *différance*/difference, identity, experience, history, resistance, negritude, and *mestizaje* are implicated in such processes. These, however, will be threaded through the term *essential(ism)* to bring into relief the politics of "identity" on the one hand, and the cultural politics of "difference" on the other, as well as the consideration of the complex possibilities of "identity-in-difference" as a privileged nexus of analysis. Moreover, following, implicitly or explicitly, the diverse uses or charge of the vexed term *essentialism* may aid the reader to weave the layered text. (May my "instructions" be simpler to follow than those for assembling a bicycle.)

In the preface to her book *Between Past and Future: Eight Exercises in Political Thought*, Hannah Arendt meditates on the "lost treasure" of the generation that came of age during and after World War II. That "lost treasure," I suggest to you, is the loss of a *grand récit*, or a coherent metanarrative, or exhausted versions of some metaphysics. (As an aside, conquest, displacement, migration, and colonization have had similar effects for non-Europeans. Thus, it may be argued that that global war had the effect of putting in question both in the "center" and the "periphery" the value of modernity, reason, and enlightenment; that is, highlighting their dark sides. Moreover, the unique historical role of the United States in this potential binarization gives its entry into the debates of modernity and postmodernity peculiar twists.)

Arendt points out that the loss is beset by a "namelessness." It is an unwilled situation. It was without testament. It had no story. She resolves the metaphors by suggesting that the "lost treasure" be named "tradition— which selects and names, which hands down and preserves, which indicates where the treasures are and what their worth is." However, because there no longer seems to be a "willed continuity in time and hence, humanly speaking neither past nor future," she asserts that we face a situation totally unforeseen by any tradition, because no "testament had willed it for the future."[1]

Through that moment of virtually total social and political breakdown, Arendt suggests, there set in a recognition of the existential experience of the rupture between "thought and reality"; that is, "thought and reality [had] parted company."[2] Arendt locates the moment of recognition in the aftermath of World War II, "when it began to dawn upon modern man that he had come to live in a world in which his mind and his tradition of thought were not even capable of asking adequate, meaningful questions, let alone of giving answers to its own perplexities."[3] In a sense, that West European experience, which promotes the growth of existentialism with its inversion of the "essence-existence" binary (Jean-Paul Sartre, *Search for a Method* [1968]), and which is followed by poststructuralism, attempts to interrogate and contest through these theoretical trends the assertion that "Modern[ist] philosophy began with a loss of the world . . . [indeed] the autonomous bourgeois subject . . . began with the withdrawal from the world."[4]

The most recent challenges to that subject have emerged with a larger degree of convergences than we have recognized. Although Arendt was writing in the 1950s, that same decade promotes the proliferation of the "new" social movements on a global scale and their concomitant "politics of identity-in-difference." Thus, for example, even as Arendt is rewriting the epistemological politics of Western philosophy, Simone de Beauvoir is rewriting the ontological and epistemological sexual politics in *The Second Sex*.[5] Moreover, in the United States, even as Jacques Derrida was addressing the French Philosophical Society in January 1968 with his groundbreaking theorization of *différance*, people of Mexican descent, under the recodified name Chicano, signaling *différance*, were mobilizing in Los Angeles for the school walkouts of March 1968.[6] In brief, with broad strokes I am attempting to convey the convergence of discourses of identity-in-difference as linked to the "essence-experience" binary that it has taken so long to recognize as the patriarchal "West" engages in resistances of its own.

The potential of the discourse of identity-in-difference and its nuances was derailed by the oversimplified hegemonization of a universalized concept of woman aided and abetted by the media, for example.[7] The hegemonization of feminism as woman brought on an attack by a patriarchal media commodification of feminism on the assumption that feminism entailed a strictly recodified appropriation of the autonomous, self-determining, bourgeois, unified subject presumed to be male-owned, as if that kind of subject was essential to maleness—that is, if women claimed that facet of the subject as well, what was man to do? In other words, feminism was read by the Reaganomic media as a mimetic inversion of an essential aspect of maleness, which produced anxiety. These processes of identification and counteridentification between unified man and unified woman barely permitted the articulations (in both senses of the word—enunciation and linkage) of a politics of identity-in-difference by "women of color" to be heard in the United States. Historically, racialized women were not heard until postmodernism in the 1980s invaded the hegemonic 1970s liberal agenda of feminism. Poststructuralist theory made it possible to mis(manage) a variety of other feminist discourses (i.e., socialist, radical, Marxist, "of color," and so on).[8]

By working through the "identity-in-difference" paradox, many racialized women theorists have implicitly worked in the interstice/interface of (existentialist) "identity politics" and "postmodernism" without a clear-cut postmodern agenda. Neither Audre Lorde's nor Chela Sandoval's notion of difference/differential consciously subsumes a Derridean theorization—though resonance cannot be denied and must be explored—so much as represents a process of "determinate negation," a nay-saying of the variety of the "not yet," that's not it. The drive behind the "not yet/that's not it" position in Sandoval's work is termed "differential consciousness," in Lorde's work, "difference," and in Derrida's work, *différance*. Yet each invokes dissimilarly located circuits of signification codified by the context of the site of emergence, which nevertheless does not obviate their agreement on the "not yet," which points toward a future. The difficulties of articulating these sites across languages, cultures, races, genders, and social positions are painfully hard but yield a space for debate beyond "ethnocentrisms" without denying them.

Arendt herself, in an effort to theorize the critical interstitial intervention

of the existential and historical subject who has lost the testamental "treasure," turns to Kafka to provide her with the poetics for a theorization of the
gap. It is there, in the interstice, that Arendt thinks the simultaneity of time-
and-space, thought-and-event will henceforth take place. Kafka's valuable
parable is as follows:

> She has two antagonists: the first presses her from behind, from the origin.
> The second blocks the road ahead. She gives battle to both. To be sure, the
> first supports her in her fight with the second, for it wants to push her for-
> ward, and in the same way the second supports her in her fight with the first,
> since it drives her back. But it is only theoretically so. For it is not only the
> two antagonists who are there, but she herself as well, and who really knows
> her intentions? Her dream, though, is that some time in an unguarded
> moment—and this would require a night darker than any night has ever
> been yet—she will jump out of the fighting line and be promoted, on
> account of her experience in fighting, to the position of umpire over her
> antagonists in their fight with each other.[9]

Arendt translates Kafka's forces into past and future. The fact that there is
a fight at all is due to the presence of the (wo)man. Her insertion, her inscription, breaks up the motion of the forces, their linearity. This causes the
forces to deflect, however lightly, from their original direction. The gap
where she stands is an interstice or interval.[10] It is a time-space from which
she can simultaneously survey what is most her own and that "which has
come into being" through her "self-inserting appearance." Arendt falters, as
does every theorist including Derrida, as to what precisely drives one to that
differential self-insertion through which "a double gesture, a double science,
a double writing, practice an *overturning* of the classical opposition *and* a
general displacement of the system."[11] (Psychoanalysis and its theory of the
unconscious provide for some a venue for understanding such impulses
within the subject; for others it is the experience of "otherization" *between*
subjects.) However, anyone outside of contexts that entail "classical oppositions" proper to the West's systematizing reasoning processes is likely to
practice more than "double" gestures and writings. Thus Gloria Anzaldúa,
through the textual production, self-insertion, and speaking position of a
"mestiza consciousness," disrupts the possibility of such tidiness.[12] A different tactic with similar effects is that of Luce Irigaray, who disrupts the tidiness of deconstruction's use of the feminine by introducing the contingent
woman outside of metaphysical circuits of representation and meaning.[13]
She is the one who engages the essentialization of Woman and renegotiates
symbolization.

Both Anzaldúa and Irigaray have been suspected of essentializing: the first on the basis of race, that is, *mestizaje,* and the second on the basis of the female body. The charges against Anzaldúa are made at conferences, or muttered in classrooms and academic hallways, while those against Irigaray are subject to extensive debates with a healthy bibliography.[14] (In the United States, the debate on race and [anti]essentialism has been largely left to African-American theorists and Diana Fuss, while the debate with respect to Chicanas and Latin Americans and other groups is largely obscured as the discourses of race continue to binarize into black and white.)

Taking up the question of essentialism and race from another angle, Jean-Luc Nancy resists the possibility of turning *mestizaje* into "a substance, an object, an identity . . . that could be grasped and 'processed.'" He deplores the notion that one could be a mestiza or a mestizo. "Everything," he continues, "everyone—male, female—who alters me, subjects me to *mestizaje.* This has nothing to do with mixed blood or mixed cultures. Even the process of 'mixing' in general, long celebrated by a certain theoretical literary and artistic tradition—even this kind of 'mixing' must remain suspect: it should not be turned into a new substance, a new identity."[15]

Even as he wants to valorize the notion of *mestizaje,* indeed claim the term mestizo for himself, he cautions against "biologisms," or even cultural mixing, and cautions against ultimate *meaning* by having us place ourselves "on the border, on the very border of *meaning.*"[16] To be pinned down by meaning and intentionality, to mean, is to essentialize. The pursuit of identity as a quest for meaning closes off possibility. This quest for meaning can also appear, in postmodernist terms, as the drive to privilege our constructedness through the deconstruction of our essential(izing) quest for identity meaning. Nancy speaks of the constructed subject who is traversed by the world and by others in such ways that he is never pure. The subject is unbounded and open to the other through *mestizaje,* "[s/he who] alters me, subjects me to *mestizaje.*"[17] Significance cannot come to rest, cannot stop; intersubjectivity as well as interaction with the world is always at play. However, we are indeed in the face of a paradox/contradiction. For Nancy does not want us to mistake his meaning of the term. In wanting to set it free and make it open to the future in specific ways, we are cautioned that this does not mean "mixed blood," or "mixed cultures," one of the modes in which Anzaldúa, for example, employs the term. With that prohibition he closes up the time and space of *mestizaje;* it is now under control, yet of course open to the future "toward infinity." Thus is Nancy subjected to the politics of his own location, "a twentieth-century Frenchman, . . . of Spanish and Viking, of

[handwritten marginal note:] —todo es mestizaje

Celt and Roman." What I mean to say is that the politics of his own location, his own time and space, leads him to appropriate and recodify the notion such that now it refers to the specificity of his own history, the "melting pot" that is France. Although he too is a mestizo, it is a kind open to the drift of the future, "on the border, on the very border of *meaning*." Indeed, one may view Anzaldúa's work as doubly located on the "border of meaning"—that is, the U.S.-Mexican geopolitical border as juridical sociopolitical division, which simultaneously opens up the past and the future as unfolding "borders of meaning" wherein Kafka's (wo)man struggles; insofar as there is meaning, it emanates from the prohibition itself. The historical discussion of "mixed blood" in the Americas, including its juridical normalizations, further problematizes Nancy's prohibition since it might silence the legal history of the racialization of the pre- and post-Columbian subject, of (post)slavery African Americans, and of the migratory/diasporic travails of others such as Chicanos.

Another example of a different kind of prohibition, yet with similar silencing effects, appears in Frantz Fanon's rejection of Jean-Paul Sartre's translation of negritude into class on the grounds that the former is too particularistic/concrete and the latter abstract and universal, whereas Fanon suggests that the former is a "psychobiological syncretism," a methodical construction based on experience.[18] Fanon cites Sartre saying that negritude

> "appears as the minor term of a dialectical progression: The theoretical and practical assertion of the supremacy of the white man is its thesis; the position of negritude as an antithetical value is the moment of negativity." . . . Proof was presented that my effort was only a term in the dialectic. . . . I defined myself as an absolute intensity of beginning. So I took up my negritude, and with tears in my eyes I put its machinery together again. What had been broken to pieces was rebuilt, reconstructed by the intuitive lianas of my hands.[19]

The very inflected force of the selected theoretical frameworks from a universalizing center expels the narratives and the textualization of difference and resistance.

It may be true that the expulsion itself produces a resistance; that is, resistance becomes the site of the emergence of meaning itself and its concomitant practices should there be no other resistance to deflect the projected course of meaning. But in Sartre, as Fanon reads him, the coexistence of prohibitions and resistances forecloses conditions of possibility for the renegotiation of relations and structures. The very emergences of syncretic new subjects, recodified on their own terms and rehistoricized anew, are dismissed without taking up the task of piercing beneath, uncovering the structure, relations and possibilities that present themselves as the conditions of the possibility of the [new subject's] appearing as it does. The maneuver to avoid the probing is done through a reobjectification of the "new subject," a reification or a denial of the historical meaning posited by the differential signifier. As a result the difference is not fully engaged as a resistance to the monologizing demands of the West. The desire to translate as totalizing metaphorical substitution without acknowledging the "identity-in-difference," so that one's own system of signification is not disrupted through a historical concept whose site of emergence is implicated in our own history, may be viewed as a desire to dominate, constrain, and contain. Sartre's desire reflects the "center"'s own resistance to negotiating meaning and structure.

Sartre allows the possibility that racial difference may be ontologized in the process of exploring *mestizaje* or negritude as "psychobiological syncretism" to lead to a prohibition rather than a careful evaluation of how the drive to decolonize, to free up the subject from subjection, has embattled her inscription as represented by Kafka's allegorical parable. If to "ontologize difference" in the pursuit of identity and meaning as modes of resistance to domination entails essentializing by relying on the concept of an authentic core that remains hidden to one's consciousness and that requires the elimination of all that is considered foreign or not true to the self, then neither Anzaldúa nor Fanon are essentialists at all. Both are quite clear that the pursuit of identity through "psychobiological syncretism" is one engaged through the racial difference imputed to them as a stigma that is now revalorized through reconstruction in historical terms.

Where does the terror of the "ontologization of difference" come from if not from the possibility that the result will continue to be inequality in the face of a liberal legal subject that has been naturalized on masculine terms? This particular fear is more pronounced in feminist theory than in anti-essentialist theories of race because, as I stated earlier, the latter is dominated by men who do not bother to remark gender. The possibilities that the combination of gender with race may transform our mode of speaking about the constructedness of the subject from both the outside *and* the inside are virtually unexplored by men.

One sign of this is that Derrida's considerations on the two interpretations of interpretation have not been explored as simultaneous *and* irreconcilable in conjunction with the "obscure economies" that emerge in instances such as Kafka's parable.[20] Derrida describes these "two interpretations of interpretation": "The one seeks to decipher, dreams of deciphering a truth or an origin which escapes play and the order of the sign, and which lives the necessity of interpretation as an exile. The other, which is no longer turned toward the origin, affirms play and tries to pass beyond man and humanism."[21] Further, it is not a question of choosing one or the other since both are irreducible and to choose is to trivialize. Thus, Derrida continues, "we must conceive of the common ground, and the *différance* of this irreducible difference."[22] The fact that the resistant texts of minoritized populations in the United States are often read as interpretation number one and charged with essentializing, as is the case in Fuss's treatment of African-American women critics and the debate on Irigaray, is a misreading in light of the theorists' own resistance to conjugating both interpretations of interpretation and its significance for the present. It is often the case as well that no one claims an "immutable origin"; however, the anxiety of pursuing the "*différance* of this irreducible difference" continues to surface as a charge of essentialism on the one hand, and a fear of losing ground on the equality battlefront, given patriarchal resistance to equality via a naturalized liberal subject whose criteria we all must be, on the other; that is, while identity now labors under a charge of essentialism, difference is now checked by the charge of inequality. The double bind of *différance* emerges in the struggle between the old-age metaphysics of *being* and the liberally inspired politics of *becoming*—dare I say the past and the future?

Fuss struggles with this double bind, justifying "the stronger lesbian endorsement of identity and identity politics" on the basis that it may indicate that "lesbians inhabit a more precarious and less secure subject position than gay men."[23] Interestingly, she argues for the progressiveness (i.e., antiessentialism) of lesbian scholarship by arguing via Heidegger for the metaphysical unity of identity as a fictional coherence that "theories of 'multiple identities' fail to challenge effectively." The unity of identity even as fictional coherence can be maintained and thereby make "identity politics" theoretically acceptable if one does away with the claim of "multiple identities"; that is, *différance* must be relocated to the "space *within* identity" and withdrawn from the "spaces *between* identities."[24] A theory of the fictional unity of identity via the Freudian-Lacanian unconscious is selected by Fuss, in my view, in order to salvage, through complementariness, the autonomous, self-determining, liberal bourgeois subject that is important to the kind of struggle made necessary by currently hegemonic views of juridical equality.[25] In the process, however, she discards "the spaces *between* identities," which are paramount to cross-cultural exploration and analysis of "women of color." Thus, one of the major questions that arises in these theoretical debates is, What is behind the antiessentialist position? Certainly it is one that too readily assumes that the other is, of course, being essentialist. What are the stakes in such oppositional arguments wherein one is either implicated in Derrida's interpretation number one or interpretation number two, but not, shall we say, engaged in a struggle such as that of Kafka's (wo)man?

In Anzaldúa's terms, "mestiza consciousness" reveals a "tolerance for contradictions," paradox, and ambiguity because the term "mestiza" projects a confluence of conflicting subject positions that keep "breaking down the unitary aspect of each new paradigm."[26] M. Y. Mudimbe designates an "intermediate space between the so-called . . . tradition and the projected modernity of colonialism." It is apparently an urbanized space in which "vestiges of the past, especially the survival of structures that are still living realities (tribal ties, for example), often continue to hide the new structures (ties based on class or on groups defined by their position in the capitalist system)"; at any rate, this intermediary space "could be viewed as the major signifier of underdevelopment. It reveals the strong tension between a modernity that often is an illusion of development, and a tradition that sometimes reflects a poor image of a mythical past."[27] These in-between/interstitial zones of instability present us with paradigms of "obscure economies." In these zones theoretical frameworks are both affirmed and resisted, especially when experiential and historical meanings are erased and differences go unengaged, their irreducibility unnamed despite the risk of misnaming.

In resonance with Anzaldúa, Chela Sandoval claims that

> U.S. Third World feminism represents a central locus of possibility, an insurgent movement which shatters the construction of any one of the collective ideologies as the single most correct site where truth can be represented. . . . What U.S. Third World feminism demands is a new subjectivity, a political revision that denies any one ideology as the final answer, while instead positing a *tactical subjectivity* with the capacity to recenter depending upon the kinds of oppression to be confronted. This is what the shift from hegemonic oppositional theory and practice to a U.S. third world theory and method of oppositional consciousness requires.[28]

Sandoval calls attention to the many "women of color" who have pointed the way toward the development of a "new subject of history" and as such a "new political subject." Aída Hurtado has claimed that "women of color" develop political skills "like urban guerrillas trained through everyday battle with the state apparatus."[29] For Cherríe Moraga, feminist "guerrilla warfare" is a way of life. "Our strategy is how we cope" on an everyday basis, "how we measure and weigh what is to be said and when, what is to be done and how, and to whom . . . daily deciding/risking who it is we can call an ally, call a friend."[30]

Citing Audre Lorde's remarks at a 1979 conference commemorating the thirtieth anniversary of the publication of *The Second Sex,* Sandoval points to the fact that "ideological differences" must be seen as "a fund of necessary polarities between which our creativities spark like a dialectic. Only within that interdependency" of historical and ideologically positioned differences "can the power to seek new ways of being in the world generate . . . the courage and sustenance to act where there are no charters."[31] In a sense, if, as Moraga also claimed, feminists of color are "women without a line," coalescing with Sandoval, then the "new subject of history" is the one who struggles "to insure our survival," who is always "challenging women to go further," who in my view engages a politics of the "not yet," in the interstice between past and future.[32] As Sandoval herself states, the "politics of the not yet" waged by U.S. Third World feminists is that of "differential consciousness" that posits no "ultimate answers, no terminal utopia . . . no predictable final outcomes. . . . Entrance into this new order requires an emotional commitment within which one experiences the violent shattering of the unitary sense of self, as the skill which allows a mobile identity to form. . . . Citizenship in this political realm is comprised of strategy and risk."[33]

Who is this "new subject of history" whose "identity-in-difference" politics was so dramatically documented in *This Bridge Called My Back* and given form in the context of second-wave, that is, contemporary, feminism, whose existential writings foreshadowed, *avant la lettre,* the poststructuralist subject, yet emerged as a paradoxical, contradictory subject whose own pursuit of "identity politics" was fissured by every other sentence through an affirmation of difference that questioned every category of import to the formation of a new society? Categories such as nation, class, race, gender, sexuality, and ethnicity were intermittently questioned and disrupted. In brief, her very constitution as a "speaking subject" called attention to contradiction and difference as her constitutive ground through discursive political and intersubjective practices. When Sandoval publishes her essay ten years later, she calls it "differential consciousness." She gives it a name that at its core signals a situated (located in the interval/gap/interstice/time-space) subject whose practice "cannot be thought *together.*"[34] It cannot be thought simultaneously because the reinscription is thought out from the site of displacement, which is subject to misnaming, misrecognition, misalliance, as

well as hitting the mark. It cannot be thought together because it aims to situate that which has no place and through naming may fall short of the
mark. The name may never be quite "it" because names are "relatively unitary . . . structures" whose oppositional status one may not intend, yet may
take over. When Sandoval claims that the differential consciousness that
calls for entering the "between and amongst" demands a mode of consciousness once relegated to the province of intuition and psychic phenomena, but
which now must be recognized as a specific practice, she is in effect moving
us toward and/or finding the relationality between the inside, as affirmed by
Fuss (per the discussion earlier), and the outside as the cross-cultural, intersubjective site; that is, she poses the challenge of resistance to oppositional
hegemonies through a *différance* that works inside and outside on multiple
planes—a factor that works itself out through a "speaking subject" conscious that she can be "constituted by discourse and yet not be completely
determined by it." Benhabib asks, "What psychic, intellectual or other
sources of creativity and resistance must we attribute to subjects for such
[agential variation to discursive subject determination] to be possible?"[35]
Hannah Arendt called it "spirit," others call it "aesthetics," yet others have
called it a "project," a "sparking dialectic." Anzaldúa calls it the "Shadow
Beast." All grope for the impulse; as stated earlier, some have settled for the
"unconscious"—a metaphor for the drives and impulses toward structural
and symbolic change in the name of feminism.

The critical desire to undercut subject determination through structures
and discourses, in my view, presupposes a subject-in-process who constructs *provisional* identities, or Sandoval's *tactical subjectivity*, which sub-
sume a network of signifying practices and structural experiences imbri-
cated in the historical *and* imaginary shifting national borders of Mexico
and the United States for Chicanas, for example. (Other "borders" that mediate [im]migration might be invoked.) A subject-insertion into such a geographical economy and politics may presuppose not only specific historical
sociosymbolic texts but a situated contemporaneous horizon of meanings
and intentions that swerve away from those produced and enunciated by
Euro-Americans and Europeans, especially when the latter produce structures and discourses of containment that resist change. Identity formations
through differentially theorized experience and history—in this instance,
through the term Chicana, thus signaling a historically raced/gendered/
classed position forged through the interstices of two nation-states—propose
a subject-in-process, desirous of self-determination yet "traversed through
and through by the world and by others. . . . It is the active and lucid agency

that constantly reorganizes its contents, through the help of these same contents, that produces by means of a material and in relation to needs and ideas, all of which are themselves mixtures of what it has already found there before it and what it has produced itself."[36] Through the speaking critical subject-in-process, cultural production reintroduces what was there before in new and dynamic combinatory transculturations. A bi- or multiethnicized, raced, and gendered subject-in-process may be called upon to take up diverse subject positions that cannot be unified without double binds and contradictions. Indeed, what binds the subject positions together may be precisely the difference from the perceived hegemony and the identity with a specific autohistory. The paradoxes and contradictions between subject positions move the subject to recognize, reorganize, reconstruct, and exploit difference through political resistance and cultural productions in order to reflect the subject-in-process. It is not a matter of doing away with the discourse of the other "because the other is in each case present in the activity that eliminates [it]."[37] The traces of a process of elimination may construct the subject as much as the efforts to incorporate. A critical subject-in-process who reorganizes "contents" upon the demands of the contingent moment and context may discover that it is in the inaugural transitional moment from being traversed to reconfiguration that the political intention as well as the combinatory transculturating takes place. Through such time-spaces one can discover diverse cultural narrative formations, translations, appropriations, and recodifications, which generate texts that are "hybrid" or "syncretic" and, far from wanting to remain at rest in that taxonomy, make a bid for new discourse formations bringing into view new subjects-in-process. In Gloria Anzaldúa's terms, these are the "borderlands" through which the "theory circuits" of geopolitics and critical allegories find resonance but the zones of figurations and conceptualizations remain non-equivalent; that is, the very contingent currents through which the geopolitical subject-in-process is dislocated and forced into (im)migration will retain an irreducible difference that refuses to correspond neatly to the subject's account of herself and the theory we produce to account for her appearance.

As transnational geopolitics with a concomitant production of "new" subjects of history come into contact with theoretical and critical allegories of the liberal political subject, the "new citizen subject," in Chela Sandoval's terms (see earlier discussion), and the "cultural politics of difference, or identity-in-difference," are subsumed under "multiculturalism." However, as

I will argue, "multiculturalism" and the "cultural politics of difference" are neither equivalent nor homologous. The term "multiculturalism" appears to be a quick metaphoric fix signaling inclusion that both comprehends the commodifications of difference and refuses to hear the implications for the production of knowledge and the material grounds that give rise to revised social and political histories as well as the "cultural politics of difference"; that is, "multiculturalism" serves a functional end in the political economy of culture that fails to grasp the substantive claims generated through what Cornel West has named "the new cultural politics of difference." Yet, "multiculturalism" has, in our time, become the discourse of choice for a multiplicity of national and transnational agendas to name the traffic in goods and peoples, the referential subjects of this complex discursive economy. Like most ideological formations, "multiculturalism" harnesses and distorts the production of the interpellated.[38]

Etienne Balibar suggests that the current multiculturalism has become a lightning rod that produces a neoracism. It is, after all, the "unmeltables" who are the metaphoric subjects, daily in the media, of multiculturalism's discourse. The currently renewed, "genetic"-based attack on African Americans' "measured" IQ levels suggests that, at the end of the twentieth century, the so-called nineteenth-century racist biologism converges with the end-of-the-twentieth-century culturalism to bespeak the racialized panic of our "liberal" society and the age-old questions of administering heterogeneity. As the media "educates" the public, both IQs and multiculturalism are raced, permitting "liberal" discourse to assume a mediating position in the face of right-wing attacks on "unmeltables." How, one might ask, is that position articulated, and is it possible to make productive critical interventions in the contemporary discourse of multiculturalism as mediated by politically liberal critiques, or is it the kind of octopus that ensnares one in its multiple tentacles? Jürgen Habermas, I think, does a creditable job of outlining the potential multicultural tentacles—feminism, ethnic minorities, nationalism, Eurocentrism as Western cultural hegemony, philosophical discourses, the question of rights and political correctness—especially as these are embroiled in producing discourses that also narrate the "cultural politics of difference."[39] However, the point of my analysis at this juncture is to do a preliminary mapping of how liberal academic thinkers mediate the "cultural politics of difference" and have it end up recodified as "multiculturalism." In brief, the question might well be, What is the ground for the formation of a critical and political culture that is not equivalent to a recodification as "multiculturalism?"[40]

Even an eminent intellectual such as Arthur Schlesinger Jr., for example, is reduced to incoherent, murky thinking when faced with multiculturalism and its implications for the location from which he reads it. He fears a dismantling of "his" institutions. Insofar as he reads Afrocentrism as the total negation of what he thinks he stands for, clear thinking collapses and his text, *The Disuniting of America*, becomes the occasion for hysteria and paranoia. The hysteria enters in when he deploys unremarked contradictory arguments in a surreal stream-of-consciousness fashion, and the paranoia when he sees the nation-state crumbling before him as a result of the "cultural politics of difference" or of "multiculturalism," as school boards have recoded it.[41] The recoding in itself is a disservice to a complex cultural and political questioning that at a minimum goes back to the constitution of the nation-state, leading up to and unfolding from the Constitution itself. In this context, "multiculturalism" becomes a wimpy kind of name that returns one to the notion of cultural contribution to the making of the nation, which permits a kind of blindness in which "American" culture becomes fused with the "political contract" and the rest is pasted on such that most nonwhites will remain not-American, but "raced ethnics" in perpetuity. There is, however, the possibility of seeing "American" culture as the consistent failure to make good on its ideal horizon of meanings and on the institutional interpretation of the political contract. "We the people" can be analyzed along its historical trajectory as in effect meaning some and not others, hence the desire for a strong revisionist historical and social map that is tied to a reconstructionist project. On the other hand, when "the cultural politics of difference" are practiced as a strictly oppositional formation of a minoritized "we the people" held up to a capitalized "We the People," another kind of boundary is constructed, which in effect converges as well with some liberal understandings of multiculturalism as celebratory heterogeneous representations. These responses, in my view, are symptomatic of deep dialogic complicity in the formation of all "American" subjects, though some are constantly on trial as to their "Americanness." To see one's self-representation textualized is not to come to terms with its dialogic construction and contestation. Grasping the dialogic constructions, however, creates passages that undermine, for example, Stuart Hall's observation that "far from collapsing the complex questions of cultural identity and issues of social and political rights, what we need is *greater distance between them* [sic]. We need to be able to insist that rights of citizenship and the incommensurability of cultural difference are respected and the *one is not made a condition of the other* [sic]."[42] How can we simultaneously deal with the contemporary desire to renegotiate the "political contract," maintaining distant equilibrium between equal citizenship rights and cultural difference, when faced with a history where "rights of citizenship" have been conditioned by identitarian sameness with the contingently historical bourgeois liberal subject and not in conjunction with difference—that is, race, gender, sexuality, and social position—but its expulsion? At this juncture the traffic between cultural and political practices is heightened and highly dependent on whether one is or is not viewed as a social equal and on asking what is producing social and political inequality. Moreover, if indeed the construction of differences has been historically produced in a dialogical manner between discrete sets of social relations, one must question, as I have earlier, the boundaries that such an analytic and interpretative nexus produces and that make it impossible to grasp articulations across the "cultural politics of difference or identity-in-difference." The fact that the latter often appears virtually impossible, indeed, does tend to make it homologous to "multiculturalism."[43]

Consequently, and in fairness to Stuart Hall, I would argue that although there may be a distinction to be made with respect to the "incommensurability of cultural difference" and "rights of citizenship," the struggle of the "cultural politics of difference" is precisely about the "distance between them" and how the distanced is functioned. What is involved in the "distance between them" that we take, or what is at stake in making or not making one "a condition of the other"? Such "distance" should be functioned in more as an analytical pause for critique and productive resolutions than as unquestioned separation of spheres of interest. It would be more productive, then, to ask with Cornel West, what the political consequences are of (strategic) cultural identity-in-difference formations as an effect of previous overdeterminations of culturally raced identities. As distinct from liberalized "multiculturalist" discourses, the "cultural politics of difference" "acknowledge[s] the uphill struggle of fundamentally transforming highly objectified, rationalized and commodified societies and cultures in the name of individuality and democracy."[44] In effect the raced-ethnic overdeterminations have taken place a priori in the Americas, certainly in the United States, "in the name of individuality and democracy," as tied to economistic opportunity and desire.

Multiculturalism is only the latest discourse on the "table" to rehearse once again the discursive positional traps that emerge from deep-seated structural inequalities, which, moreover, have been sedimented over hundreds of years. Because "multiculturalism" in the United States is often perceived through the ongoing ethnic genocide and fighting in Eastern Europe, it gives rise in the United States to paranoia, on the one hand, which only seems to have the effect of triggering more racism, on the other, especially in light of a much-publicized economic decline and restructuration.[45] Thus, "multiculturalism," a name never advanced in the first place by U.S. activists and intellectuals of the "cultural politics of difference," has moved from revising the K-12 curriculum to focusing on the academy, and is served up as rethinking the foundational epistemology, but not practice, of liberalism. As demonstrated in the recently reissued meditation on "the politics of recognition" by Charles Taylor in a collection sold as *Multiculturalism and the Politics of Recognition*, liberalism is not the same for the Canadian thinker as it is for Jürgen Habermas, a German one. (The question, What are the historical and political conditions that make the difference possible? is beyond the scope of this essay; certainly, however, the geographic position of each exerts pressure on his thinking. In short, the Americas are not Europe.) While, on the one hand, Taylor appears as a benign patriarch for whom boundaries may be blurred, questioned, or reasserted periodically, and who even invokes, though he doesn't account for, a dialogic subject/group formation, Habermas, on the other, wants to draw boundaries everywhere and exercise a strong control over their porosity and permeability. "Constitutional patriotism" and "procedural consensus" are the twin pillars for the hard-and-fast universalism Habermas proposes.[46]

Charles Taylor provides philosophical merit to the discourse of multiculturalism with his meditative and critical essay "The Politics of Recognition," which has been translated into Italian, French, and German. In a sense this signals the modes through which some European and Euro-American thinkers understand what I've been calling with Cornel West "the cultural politics of difference." To codify the latter as "multiculturalism" is tantamount to an effort to displace "the cultural politics of difference" embraced by many intellectuals in the United States and to rethink them through an invocation of liberal epistemological foundations. At the core of this rethinking is the question of individual rights and citizenship as a unit.

Taylor's invocation of liberal epistemological foundations has the virtue of sincerely trying to explore the contradictions that "the cultural politics of difference" (or, as he entitles them, "the politics of recognition") has uncovered in the liberal political agenda. Taylor perceives two modes of politics: (1) the politics of difference "as an individual and also as a culture"; and (2) the claim to cultural equal worth.[47] He admits that the liberal principle of blindness to difference has not been successful in its application and that perhaps "the very idea of such a liberalism may be a kind of pragmatic contradiction, a particularism [of liberal thought] masquerading as the universal."[48] Moreover, he cannot imagine a "common project" that is compatible with differentiation, but he would like to. As a result, he wonders if there is not middle ground wherein there is a "willingness to be open to comparative cultural study of the kind that must displace our horizons in the resulting fusions."[49] Borrowing from H. G. Gadamer, he hits upon the possibility of a coming "fusion of horizons" that "operates through our developing new vocabularies of comparison, by means of which we can articulate these contrasts."[50] The gesture to dialogism and conversation is not given up by Taylor even though "equal worth" cannot be demanded as a right. Such "equal worth" can only be accomplished or established through conjunctural conversations, otherwise they polarize into demands of cultural "equal worth" and "self-immurement within ethnocentric standards."[51] Stated from this angle, there is a strong desire on Taylor's part to understand the "cultural politics of difference" and the flaws it uncovers in the liberal political and aesthetic project. He questions procedural liberalism and finds it inhospitable because it continues to pretend a blindness to differences and "pretends to offer a neutral ground in which people of all cultures can meet or coexist."[52]

In appropriating G. H. Gadamer's notion of "fusion of horizons," Taylor is actually proposing, though not specifying, different "reading" practices. Gadamer's project is to outline the reading practices appropriate to the "hermeneutic experience" wherein the "conversation" takes place between the critical reader and the literary object. It is a practice that, in his view, may account for but surpasses historicism, such that the aesthetic is the teleological site for the "fusion of horizons" between reader and text.[53] Taylor swerves from this ethnocentric project to insist on conversation between diverse ethnocultural critical readers and claimed texts. From this point of view, "equal [cultural] worth" is deferred through the conversation and the criterion of worth is as yet undetermined. Gadamer's ethnocentric project is undergirded by an insulated diachronism that insists, as Habermas notes in another context, on "the ontological priority of linguistic tradition before all possible critique."[54] Taylor's repositioning of "fusion of horizons" as the outcome to be achieved through conjunctural conversations between critical readers of different cultural formations disrupts and displaces Gadamer's map of the "hermeneutic experience." In fact, it opens it up to the possibility of a nonethnocentric critical discourse.

Given the desire for dialogism, Taylor's good intentions are too slippery for his interlocutors. His implicit understanding that there's more here than a "politics of recognition," which is only a first step for the conversation to take place, leads to a concomitant reciprocity of I's and We's that become polylogical given their formations in the context of nation making, which, no matter how veiled, is understood in the context of Canada, as I then understand it in the context of the United States; that is, a history hovers throughout the discussion. His interlocutors, however, panic over the emphasis given to collective groups' goals, which perhaps undermines the attachment to individual rights and individual freedom and the construction of citizenship on these grounds rather than collective goals. (See, for example, the comments by Steven Rockefeller and Michael Walzer in the volume.) The possibility of conversations that may give rise to uncontrolled "fused horizons" is a source of panic to them. And perhaps no one in the volume speaks to it more forcefully than Jürgen Habermas, while Rockefeller and Walzer retreat to notions of "universal identity as human beings," completely divorced of the nation-form that confers identities, whether they be a "matter of citizenship, gender, race, or ethnic origin."[55] The more sophisticated Habermas understands that the question of the nation-form cannot be obliterated. The nation-form cannot eschew its relationality to its subjects. Given this, then, one has to return to that which is fundamental for the nation, its legal system and its conferring of basic rights, which are individual and in contradiction to collective rights. The latter may be protected as cultural lifeworlds, but subject to the political culture of the nation-form, "the ethical integration of groups and subcultures with their collective identities must be uncoupled from the abstract political integration that includes all citizens equally."[56] What is that "abstract political integration"? Isn't that often made substantive and hence not abstract through the narrative of the nation-form, which continually strategizes to include or exclude citizenship and aestheticized "hermeneutic experience"? What does it mean to have "constitutional principles" interpreted or thoroughly distanced "from the perspective of the nation's historical experience" when the narrative of that very national experience is in question, as is the case in Canada, the United States, and the Americas?

Taylor sees the "common political culture" as something to be achieved, while Habermas takes it to be in place, resting on the constitutional rights and principles "form the fixed point of reference of any constitutional patriotism that situates the system of rights within the historical context of a legal community."[57] We get closer to Habermas's desire here, since it would appear that it is not so much the "nation's historical experience" in general and the formation of its subjects, as it is the "historical context of a legal community" that should prevail. I take this to suggest that it is the "historical legal community" that will have priority over any other notion or version of history. This is confirmed by the assertion that "in complex societies the citizenry as a whole can no longer be held together by a substantive consensus on values but only a consensus on the procedures for the legitimate enactment of laws and the legitimate exercise of power."[58] A strong proceduralism is the glue that will hold society together, not conversations over time that seek "fusion of horizons" as utopic possibility. In the age of poststructuralist thought, the question of universality will now reside in the rationality of the legal community.

In a sense, Habermas faults Taylor for too much philosophical thinking and not enough legalistic politics. At stake in the latter is the strong preservation of individual rights and freedom as the hallmark of citizenship. The swipes at poststructuralist thought that are taken by most in the book are conditioned by its deconstruction of the transcendental and sovereign subject on which "enlightened" modernity has depended for the maintenance of its self-contradictory empowered legitimacy and which subsequently makes it necessary to speak of two levels of integration, those that aspire to "our" political culture and those that remain in a "subpolitical level," that is, "ethnics" or, as Habermas refers to these, "lifeworlds" as a reconfiguration of pluralism now coded as multiculturalism. Consequently, the latter are misrecognized as culturally bounded in discrete forms and may claim the right to participate in the "political culture" by discarding "difference." What difference is at this level of discourse, I presume, is adjudicated by the modern liberal subject of the contingently prevailing political culture-in-law. What is citizenship continues to be on trial and, I suppose, will be juridically administered by the self-legitimated "political culture." While Taylor emphasizes the cultural discussion and postpones the political outcome, Habermas emphasizes the political legal culture and contains rather than postpones the cultural outcome. The former is portrayed as too philosophical and involved in questions of intersubjectivity; the latter ultimately and implicitly discards the intersubjective dimension except in a discussion of feminism, a version that appears to be already and conveniently homogenized by Habermas into his liberalism—a curious exception, to say the least, yet a minimalist gesture to the epistemological problems that feminism has raised so successfully.[59] That gesture remains too isolated from the a prioris of legal history and its production of the "political culture" already in place. On the other hand, the "cultural politics of difference" is already embroiled in claims of the historical experience of the nation-making form, which is also a political culture whose adjudications have indeed been intersubjective throughout.[60]

The clarity of thought in Habermas should not be underestimated, especially its apparent administrative resolutions in "the historical context of a legal community." It interpellates a historically constructed Anglo-America and those who have been able to seek protection and entitlement through that proceduralism. Insofar as the theorists and practitioners of the "cultural politics of difference," each in turn and formed around their historical constitutedness, have engaged in a dialogism with the proceduralist "center," we have not been able to produce a notion of the coalitional subject. White paranoia and panic have reached extreme proportions in California, as reflected in the negative adjudication of Rodney King's rights[61] and those of (im)migrants via the passage of Proposition 187 and of the upcoming (irony not intended) California *Civil Rights* Initiative.

Notes

1. Hannah Arendt, *Between Past and Future: Eight Exercises in Political Thought* (New York: Penguin Books, 1978), 6.

2. Ibid.

3. Ibid., 9.

4. Seyla Benhabib, *Situating the Self: Gender, Community and Postmodernism in Contemporary Ethics* (New York: Routledge, 1992), 205–7.

5. Simone de Beauvoir, *The Second Sex*, trans. H. M. Parshley (New York: Vintage Books, 1974).

6. Carlos Múñoz, *Youth, Identity, Power: The Chicano Movement* (London: Verso, 1989).

7. See Susan Faludi, *Backlash: The Undeclared War against American Women* (New York: Crown Publishers, 1991).

8. See Alison M. Jaggar, *Feminist Politics and Human Nature* (Totowa, N.J.: Rowan and Allanheld, 1983).

9. Cited in Arendt, *Between Past and Future*, 7.

10. Jacques Derrida, *Margins of Philosophy*, trans. Alan Bass (Chicago: University of Chicago Press, 1982).

11. Ibid., 329.

12. Gloria Anzaldúa, *Borderlands/La Frontera: The New Mestiza* (San Francisco: Spinsters/Aunt Lute, 1987).

13. Luce Irigaray, *Speculum of the Other Woman*, trans. Gillian C. Gill (Ithaca, N.Y.: Cornell University Press, 1985). For commentary on deconstruction's use of the feminine, see Rosi Braidotti, *Patterns of Dissonance: A Study of Women in Contemporary Philosophy*, trans. Elizabeth Guil (New York: Routledge, 1991); and Gayatri C. Spivak, "Displacement and the Discourse of Woman," *Displacement: Derrida and After*, ed. Mark Krupnick (Bloomington: Indiana University Press, 1983), 169–96.

14. See, for example, Judith Butler, *Gender Trouble: Feminism and the Subversion of Identity* (New York: Routledge, 1990); Nancy Fraser and Sandra Lee Bartky, *Revaluing French Feminism: Critical Essays on Difference, Agency & Culture* (Bloomington: Indiana University Press, 1992); and Toril Moi, *Sexual/Textual Politics* (London: Methuen, 1985).

15. Jean-Luc Nancy, "Cut Throat Son," *An Other Tongue*, ed. Alfred Ortega (Durham, N.C.: Duke University Press, 1994).

16. Ibid., 123.

17. Ibid.

18. Frantz Fanon, "The Fact of Blackness," in *Anatomy of Racism*, ed. David Theo Goldberg (Minneapolis: University of Minnesota Press, 1990), 120.

19. Ibid., 120, 124.

20. Jacques Derrida, *Writing and Difference*, trans. Alan Bass (Chicago: University of Chicago Press, 1978), 293.

21. Ibid., 292.

22. Ibid., 293.

23. Diana Fuss, *Essentially Speaking: Feminism, Nature and Difference* (New York: Routledge, 1989), 98.

24. Ibid., 103.

25. See Kimberlé Crenshaw, "Demarginalizing the Intersection of Race and Gender in Antidiscrimination Law, Feminist Theory, and Antiracist Politics," *Chicago Legal Forum* (1989).

26. Anzaldúa, *Borderlands/La Frontera*, 79–80.

27. M. Y. Mudimbe, *The Invention of Africa* (Bloomington: Indiana University Press, 1988), 5.

28. Chela Sandoval, "U.S. Third World Feminism: The Theory and Method of Oppositional Consciousness in the Postmodern World," *Genders* 10 (spring 1991): 14.

29. Aída Hurtado, cited in ibid., 14–15.

30. Cherríe Moraga and Gloria Anzaldúa, *This Bridge Called My Back: Writings by Radical Women of Color* (Watertown, Mass.: Persephone Press, 1981), xix.

31. Sandoval, "U.S. Third World Feminism," 15.

32. Moraga and Anzaldúa, *This Bridge Called My Back*, 127.

33. Sandoval, "U.S. Third World Feminism," 23.

34. Derrida, *Margins of Philosophy*, 19.

35. Benhabib, *Situating the Self*, 218.

36. Cornelius Castoriadis, *The Imaginary Institution of Society*, trans. Kathleen Blamey (Cambridge: MIT Press, 1987), 102–3.

37. Ibid., 106.

38. I use the term "transnational" as a mediating analytical category that enables a nexus for critical intervention across and between nation-states and opens up a ground for the critique of the representations, practices, and discourses that emerge in the conjunctural constitutiveness of historical subjects. This approach would beg the question of how one can generate a postnationalist critical discourse. For further discussions of transnational critique see Frederick Buell, *National Culture and the New Global System* (Baltimore: Johns Hopkins University Press, 1994). For further discussion of "The New Cultural Politics of Difference," see Cornel West, *Keeping Faith: Philosophy and Race in America* (New York: Routledge, 1993), 3–32.

39. Etienne Balibar, "Is There a 'Neo-racism'?" in Etienne Balibar and Immanuel Wallerstein, *Race, Nation, Class: Ambiguous Identities* (London: Verso, 1991), 17–28; and Richard J. Herrnstein and Charles Murray, *The Bell Curve: Intelligence and Class Structure in American Life* (New York: Free Press, 1994).

40. Charles Taylor et al., *Multiculturalism and the Politics of Recognition* (Princeton, N.J.: Princeton University Press, 1994), 116–22. David Palumbo-Liu is congnizant of the fact that once a discourse such as multiculturalism makes a bid for hegemonic mediation of identity-in-difference, perhaps the best that minoritized intellectuals can do is to turn our critical mapping lens through it as well. Consequently, he calls for a critical multiculturalism. As he notes, ideologically, multiculturalism becomes a recodification of pluralism for the era of trans-

nationalisms and globalisms. See his edited anthology, *The Ethnic Canon: Histories, Institutions, and Interventions* (Minneapolis: University of Minnesota Press, 1995), 1–27.

41. See Michael Bérubé, "Disuniting America Again," in *Public Access: Literary Theory and American Cultural Politics* (London: Verso, 1994), 225–42.

42. Stuart Hall and Martin Jacques, eds., *New Times: The Changing Face of Politics in the 1990s* (London: Verso, 1990), 35.

43. Carl Gutiérrez-Jones makes a solid argument for the interfacing juncture of aesthetics and legal culture in *Rethinking the Borderlands: Between Chicano Culture and Legal Discourse* (Berkeley: University of California Press, 1995).

44. West, *Keeping Faith,* 30.

45. See Michael A. Bernstein and David E. Adler, eds., *Understanding American Economic Decline* (Cambridge: Cambridge University Press, 1994).

46. Taylor et al., *Multiculturalism and the Politics of Recognition,* 135.

47. Ibid., 42–43.

48. Ibid., 44.

49. Ibid., 68.

50. Ibid., 67.

51. Ibid., 68, 72.

52. Ibid., 62.

53. H. G. Gadamer, "The Hermeneutical Experience," in Joseph Margolis, ed., *Philosophy Looks at the Arts: Contemporary Readings in Aesthetics,* 3d. ed. (Philadelphia: Temple University Press, 1987), 501.

54. Cited in Christopher Norris, *Contest of Faculties: Philosophy and Theory after Deconstruction* (London: Methuen, 1985), 26.

55. Taylor et al., *Multiculturalism and the Politics of Recognition,* 88.

56. Ibid., 133–34.

57. Ibid., 134.

58. Ibid., 135.

59. Ibid., 115–17.

60. See Priscilla Wald, "Terms of Assimilation: Legislating Subjectivity in the Emerging Nation," in Amy Kaplan and Donald E. Pease, eds., *Cultures of United States Imperialism* (Durham, N.C.: Duke University Press, 1993), 59–84.

61. See Robert Gooding-Williams, ed., *Reading Rodney King, Reading Urban Uprising* (New York: Routledge, 1993).

CHAPTER NINE

Injury, Identity, Politics

WENDY BROWN

Taking enormous pleasure in the paradox, Stuart Hall tells this story of the postwar, postcolonial "breakup" of English identity:

> In the very moment when finally Britain convinced itself it had to decolo-
> nize, it had to get rid of them, we all came back home. As they hauled down
> the flag [in the colonies], we got on the banana boat and sailed right into
> London. . . . [T]hey had ruled the world for 300 years and, at last, when they
> had made up their minds to climb out of the role, at least the others ought to
> have stayed out there in the rim, behaved themselves, gone somewhere else,
> or found some other client state. But no, they had always said that this [Lon-
> don] was really home, the streets were paved with gold, and bloody hell, we
> just came to check out whether that was so or not.[1]

In Hall's mischievous account, the restructuring of collective identity and political practices required by postcoloniality did not remain in the hinterlands but literally, restively, came home to roost. The historical "others" of colonial identity cast free in their own waters sailed in to implode the center of the postcolonial metropoles, came to trouble the last vestiges of centered European identity with its economic and political predicates. They came to make havoc in the master's house after the master relinquished his military-political but not his cultural and metaphysical holdings as *the* metonymy of man.

Hall's narrative of the palace invasion by the newly released subjects might also be pressed into service as metaphor for another historical paradox of late twentieth-century collective and individual identity formation: in the very moment when modern liberal states fully realize their secularism (as Marx put it in "On the Jewish Question"), just as the mantle of abstract personhood is formally tendered to a whole panoply of those historically excluded from it by humanism's privileging of a single race, gender, and organization of sexuality, the marginalized reject the rubric of humanist inclusion and turn, at least in part, against its very premises. Refusing to be neutralized, to render the differences inconsequential, to be depoliticized as "lifestyles," "diversity," or "persons like any other," we have lately reformulated our historical exclusion as a matter of historically produced and politically rich *alterity*. Insisting that we are not merely positioned but fabricated by this history, we have at the same time insisted that our very production as marginal, deviant, or subhuman is itself constitutive of the centrality and legitimacy of the center, is itself what paves the center's streets with semiotic, political, and psychic gold. Just when polite liberal (not to mention, correct leftist) discourse ceased speaking of us as queers, colored girls, or natives, we began speaking of ourselves this way. Refusing the invitation to absorption, we insisted instead upon politicizing and working into cultural critique the very constructions that a liberalism increasingly exposed in its tacit operations of racial, sexual, and gender privilege was seeking to bring to a formal close.

These paradoxes of late-modern liberalism and colonialism, of course, are not a matter of simple historical accident—indeed, they are both incomplete and mutually constitutive to a degree that belies the orderly chronological scheme Hall and I have imposed on them in order to render them pleasurable ironies. Moreover, the ironies do not come to an end with the Jamaican postcolonials sailing into London, nor with the historically subordinated constructing an oppositional political culture and critique out of their exclusion from the family of Man. Even as the margins assert themselves as margins, the denaturalizing assault they perform on coherent collective identity in the center turns back on them to trouble their own. Even as it is being articulated, circulated, and lately institutionalized in a host of legal, political, and cultural practices, identity is unraveling—metaphysically, culturally, geopolitically, and historically—as rapidly as it is being produced. The same vacillation can be seen in the naturalistic legitimating narratives of collective identity as nationalism. Imploded within by the insurrectionary knowledges and political claims of historically subordinated cultures, and assaulted from without by the spectacular hybridities and supranational articulations of late twentieth-century global capitalism as well as crises of global ecology, nation formation, loosened from what retrospectively appears as a historically fleeting attachment to states, is today fervently being asserted in politico-cultural claims ranging from Islamic to deaf, indigenous to Gypsy, Serbian to queer.

Despite certain convergences, articulations, and parallels between such culturally disparate political formations in the late twentieth century, this essay does not consider the problematic of politicized identity on a global scale. Rather, as an argument for substantial historical and geopolitical specificity in an exploration of the problematic of political identity, this essay examines selected contradictory operations of politicized identity *within* late-modern democracy, considering politicized identity as both a production *and* a contestation of the political terms of liberalism, disciplinary-bureaucratic regimes, certain forces of global capitalism, and the demographic flows of postcoloniality, which together might be taken as constitutive of the contemporary North American political condition. In recent years, enough stalemated argument has transpired about the virtues and vices of something named identity politics to suggest the limited usefulness of a discussion of identity either in terms of the timeless metaphysical or linguistic elements of its constitution or in terms of the ethical-political rubric of good and evil. Beginning instead with the premise that the proliferation and politicization of identities in the United States is not a moral or even a political choice but a complex historical production, a more useful contribution from scholars might consist of elucidating something of the nature of this production, in order to locate within it both the openings and the perils for a radically democratic or counterhegemonic political project.

Many have lately asked how, given the totalizing, regulatory, and "othering" operations of identity in/as language, identity can avoid reiterating such investments in its ostensibly emancipatory mode.[2] I want to ask a similar question but in a historically specific cultural-political register, not because the linguistic frame is unimportant but because it is insufficient for discerning the character of politicized identity's problematic investments. Thus, my focus here will be on selected contradictory operations of politicized identity *within* late-modern democracy, considering politicized identity as both a production *and* a contestation of the political terms of liberalism, disciplinary-bureaucratic regimes, certain forces of global capitalism, and the demographic flows of postcoloniality, which together might be taken as constitutive of the contemporary North American political condition. The specific questions framing the work of this paper are these: First, given the subjectivizing conditions of identity production in a late-modern capitalist, liberal, and disciplinary-bureaucratic social order, how can reiteration of these production conditions be averted in identity's purportedly emancipatory project? In the specific context of contemporary liberal and disciplinary-bureaucratic discourse, what kind of political recognition can identity-based claims seek—and what kind can they be counted on to want—that will not resubordinate the subject that is itself historically subjugated through identity, through categories such as race or gender that emerged and circulated as terms of power to enact subordination? The question here is not *whether* denaturalizing political strategies subvert the subjugating force of naturalized identity formation, but *what kind* of politicization, produced out of and inserted into *what kind* of political context, might perform such subversion. Second, given the averred interest of politicized identity in achieving emancipatory political recognition in a posthumanist discourse, what are the logics of pain in the subject formation processes of late-modern society that might contain or subvert this aim? What are the particular constituents—specific to our time yet roughly generic for a diverse spectrum of identities—of identity's desire for recognition that seem as often to breed a politics of recrimination and rancor, of culturally dispersed paralysis and suffering, a tendency to reproach power rather than aspire to it, to disdain freedom rather than practice it? In short, where do the historically and culturally specific elements of politicized identity's investments in itself, and especially in its own history of suffering, come into conflict with the need to give up these investments in the pursuit of an emancipatory democratic project?

I approach these questions by offering first a highly selective account of the discursive historical context of identity politics' emergence in the United States and then elaborating, through reconsideration of Nietzsche's genealogy of the logics of *ressentiment*, the wounded character of politicized identity's desire within this context. This is not an essay about the general worth or accomplishments of the oppositional political formation called "identity politics." It is, rather, an exploration of the ways in which certain aspects of the specific genealogy of politicized identity are carried in the structure and temperament of its political demands, ways in which some of the emancipatory aims of politicized identity are subverted not only by the constraints of the political discourses in which its operations transpire, but by its own wounded attachments.

The tension between particularistic "I's" and a universal "we" in liberalism is sustainable as long as the constituent terms of the "I" remain unpoliticized— as long as the "I" itself remains unpoliticized on one hand, and the state (as the expression of the ideal of political universality) remains unpoliticized on the other. In other words, the latent conflict in liberalism between universal representation and individualism remains latent, remains unpoliticized, as long as stratifying powers in civil society remain naturalized, as long as the "I" remains politically unarticulated, as long as it is willing to have its free-dom represented abstractly, in effect, to subordinate its "I-ness" to the ab-stract "we" represented by the universal community of the state. This subor-dination is achieved either by the "I" abstracting from itself in its political representation, thus trivializing its "difference" so as to remain part of the "we" (as in homosexuals who are "just like everyone else except for who we sleep with"), or by the "I" accepting its construction as a supplement, com-plement, or partial outsider to the "we" (as in the history of women being "concluded by their husbands," to use Blackstone's phrase, or homosexuals who are just "different," or Jews whose communal affiliations lie partly or wholly outside their national identity). The history of liberalism's manage-ment of its inherited and constructed "others" could be read as a history of variations on and vacillations between these two strategies.

The abstract character of liberal political membership and the ideologi-cally naturalized character of liberal individualism together work against politicized identity formation.[3] A formulation of the political state and of citizenship that, as Marx put it in "On the Jewish Question," abstracts from the substantive conditions of our lives, works to prevent recognition or ar-ticulation of differences *as* political—as effects of power—in their very con-struction and organization; they are at most the stuff of divergent political or economic *interests*.[4] Equally important, to the extent that political mem-bership in the liberal state involves abstracting from one's social being, it involves abstracting not only from the contingent productions of one's life circumstances but from the *identificatory* processes constitutive of one's so-cial construction and position. We are invited to seek equal deference— equal blindness—but not equalizing *recognition* from the state, liberalism's universal moment.[5] Indeed, as Marx discerned in his critique of Hegel, the universality of the state is ideologically achieved by turning away from and thus depoliticizing, yet at the same time *presupposing*, our collective particulars, not by embracing them, let alone emancipating us from them.[6] In short, "the political" in liberalism is precisely not a domain for social identification: expected to recognize our political selves in the state, we are not led to expect deep recognition there.

While this détente between universal and particular within liberalism is potted with volatile conceits from the outset, it is rather thoroughly unraveled by two features of late-modernity, spurred by developments in liberalism's companion powers: capitalism and disciplinarity. On one side, the state loses even its guise of universality as it becomes ever more transparently invested in particular economic interests, political ends, and social formations—as it transmogrifies from a relatively minimalist, "night watchman" state to a heavily bureaucratized, managerial, fiscally enormous and highly interventionist welfare-warfare state, a transmogrification occasioned by the combined imperatives of capital and the autoproliferating characteristics of bureaucracy.[7] On the other side, the liberal subject is increasingly disinterred from substantive nation-state identification, not only by the individuating effects of liberal discourse itself but through the social effects of late twentieth-century economic and political life: deterritorializing demographic flows; the disintegration from within and invasion from without of family and community as (relatively) autonomous sites of social production and identification; consumer capitalism's marketing discourse in which individual (and subindividual) desires are produced, commodified, and mobilized as identities; and disciplinary productions of a fantastic array of behavior-based identities ranging from recovering alcoholic professionals to unrepentant crack mothers. These disciplinary productions work to conjure and regulate subjects through classificatory schemes, naming and normalizing social behaviors as social positions. Operating through what Foucault calls "an anatomy of detail," "disciplinary power" produces social identities (available for politicization because they are deployed for purposes of political regulation) that crosscut juridical identities based on abstract right. Thus, for example, the welfare state's production of welfare subjects—themselves subdivided through the socially regulated categories of motherhood, disability, race, age, and so forth—potentially produces political identity through these categories, produces identities *as* these categories.

In this story, the always imminent but increasingly politically manifest failure of liberal universalism to be universal—the transparent fiction of state universality—combines with the increasing individuation of social subjects through capitalist disinternments and disciplinary productions. Together, they breed the emergence of politicized identity rooted in disciplinary productions but oriented by liberal discourse toward protest against exclusion from a discursive formation of universal justice. This production, however, is not linear or even, but highly contradictory: while the terms of liberalism are part of the ground of production of a politicized identity that reiterates yet exceeds these terms, liberal discourse itself also continuously recolonizes political identity *as* political interest—a conversion that recasts politicized identity's substantive and often deconstructive cultural claims and critiques as generic claims of particularism endemic to universalist political culture. Similarly, disciplinary power manages liberalism's production of politicized subjectivity by neutralizing (re-depoliticizing) identity through normalizing practices. As liberal discourse converts political identity into essentialized private interest, disciplinary power converts interest into normativized social identity manageable by regulatory regimes. Thus, disciplinary power politically neutralizes entitlement claims generated by liberal individuation, while liberalism politically neutralizes rights claims generated by disciplinary identities.

Contemporary politicized identity contests the terms of liberal discourse insofar as it challenges liberalism's universal "we" as a strategic fiction of historically hegemonic groups and asserts liberalism's "I" as social—both relational and constructed by power—rather than contingent, private, or autarkic. Yet it reiterates the terms of liberal discourse insofar as it posits a sovereign and unified "I" that is disenfranchised by an exclusive "we." Indeed, politicized identity emerges and obtains its unifying coherence through the politicization of *exclusion* from an ostensible universal, as a protest against exclusion, a protest premised on the fiction of an inclusive/universal community, a protest that reinstalls the humanist ideal insofar as it premises itself upon exclusion from it. Put the other way around, insofar as they are premised on exclusion from a universal ideal, politicized identities require that ideal, as well as their exclusion from it, for their own perpetuity as identities.[8]

Politicized identity is also potentially reiterative of regulatory, disciplinary society in its configuration of a disciplinary subject. It is both produced by and potentially accelerates the production of that aspect of disciplinary society that "ceaselessly characterizes, classifies, and specializes," which works through "surveillance, continuous registration, perpetual assessment, and classification," through a social machinery "that is both immense and minute."[9] A recent example from the world of local politics makes clear politicized identity's imbrication in disciplinary power, as well as the way in which, as Foucault reminds us, disciplinary power "infiltrates" rather than replaces liberal juridical modalities.[10] Recently the city council of my town reviewed an ordinance, devised and promulgated by a broad coalition of identity-based political groups, which aimed to ban discrimination in employment, housing, and public accommodations on the basis of "sexual orientation, transsexuality, age, height, weight, personal appearance, physical characteristics, race, color, creed, religion, national origin, ancestry, disability, marital status, sex or gender."[11] Here is a perfect instance of the universal juridical ideal of liberalism and the normalizing principle of disciplinary regimes conjoined and taken up within the discourse of politicized identity. This ordinance—variously called the "purple hair ordinance" or the "ugly ordinance" by state and national news media—aims to count every difference as no difference, as part of the seamless whole, but also to count every potentially subversive rejection of culturally enforced norms as themselves normal, as normalizable, and as normativizable through law. Indeed, through the definitional, procedural, and remedies sections of this ordinance (e.g., "sexual orientation shall mean known or assumed homosexuality, heterosexuality, or bisexuality") persons are reduced to observable social attributes and practices; these are defined empirically, positivistically, as if their existence were intrinsic and factual, rather than the effect of discursive and institutional power; and these positivist definitions of persons as their attributes and practices are written into law, ensuring that persons describable according to them will now become regulated through them. Bentham couldn't have done it better. Indeed, here is a perfect instance of how the language of recognition becomes the language of unfreedom, how articulation in language, in the context of liberal and disciplinary discourse, becomes a vehicle of subordination through individualization, normalization, and regulation, even as it strives to produce visibility and acceptance. Here, also, is a perfect instance of the way in which differences that are the effects of social power are neutralized through their articulation as attributes and their circulation through liberal administrative discourse. What do we make of a document that renders as juridical equivalents the denial of employment or housing to an African American, an obese man, and a white middle-class youth festooned with tatoos and fuschia hair?

What I want to consider, though, is why this strikingly unemancipatory political project emerges from a potentially more radical critique of liberal juridical and disciplinary modalities of power. This ordinance, I want to suggest, is not simply misguided in its complicity with the rationalizing and disciplinary elements of late-modern culture; it is not simply naive with regard to the regulatory apparatus within which it operates. Rather, it is symptomatic of a feature of politicized identity's *desire* within liberal-bureaucratic regimes, its foreclosure of its own freedom, its impulse to inscribe in the law and in other political registers its historical and present pain rather than conjure an imagined future of power to make itself. To see what this symptom is a symptom of, we need to return once more to a schematic consideration of liberalism, this time in order to read it through Nietzsche's account of the complex logics of *ressentiment.*

Liberalism contains from its inception a generalized incitement to what Nietzsche terms *ressentiment,* the moralizing revenge of the powerless, "the triumph of the weak as weak."[12] This incitement to *ressentiment* inheres in a constitutive paradox of liberalism between individual liberty and social egalitarianism, a paradox that produces failure-turned-to-recrimination by the subordinated, and guilt-turned-to-resentment by the "successful." However, it is not only the tension between freedom and equality, but also the prior presumption of the self-reliant and self-made capacities of liberal subjects, conjoined with their unavowed dependence on and construction by a variety of social relations and forces, that makes *all* liberal subjects, and not only markedly disenfranchised ones, vulnerable to *ressentiment.* It is their situatedness within power, their production by power, and liberal discourse's denial of this situatedness and production that cast the liberal subject into failure, the failure to make itself in the context of a discourse in which its self-making is assumed, indeed, is its assumed nature. This failure, which Nietzsche calls suffering, must either find a reason within itself (which redoubles the failure) or a site of external blame upon which to avenge its hurt and redistribute its pain. Here is Nietzsche's account of this moment in the production of *ressentiment:*

> For every sufferer instinctively seeks a cause for his suffering, more exactly, an agent; still more specifically a *guilty* agent who is susceptible to suffering—in short, some living thing upon which he can on some pretext or other, vent his affects, actually or in effigy.... This ... constitutes the actual physiological cause of *ressentiment,* vengefulness, and the like: a desire to deaden pain by means of affects ... to deaden, by means of a more violent emotion of any kind, a tormenting, secret pain that is becoming unendurable, and to drive it out of consciousness at least for the moment: for that one requires an affect, as savage an affect as possible, and, in order to excite that, any pretext at all.[13]

Ressentiment in this context is a triple achievement: it produces an affect (rage, righteousness) that overwhelms the hurt; it produces a culprit responsible for the hurt; and it produces a site of revenge to displace the hurt (a place to inflict hurt as the sufferer has been hurt). Together these operations both ameliorate (in Nietzsche's terms, "anaesthetize") and externalize what is otherwise "unendurable."

Now, what I want to suggest is that in a culture already streaked with the pathos of *ressentiment* for these reasons, there are several characteristics of late-modern postindustrial societies that accelerate and expand the conditions of its production. My listing will necessarily be highly schematic: First, the phenomenon William Connolly names "increased global contingency" combines with the expanding pervasiveness and complexity of domination by capital and bureaucratic state and social networks to create an unparalleled individual powerlessness over the fate and direction of one's own life, intensifying the experiences of impotence, dependence, and gratitude inherent in liberal capitalist orders and constitutive of *ressentiment*.[14] Second, the steady desacralization of all regions of life—what Weber called disenchantment, what Nietzsche called the death of god—would seem to add yet another reversal to Nietzsche's genealogy of *ressentiment* as perpetually available to "alternation of direction." In Nietzsche's account, the ascetic priest deployed notions of "guilt, sin, sinfulness, depravity and damnation" to "direct the ressentiment of the less severely afflicted sternly back upon themselves . . . and in this way [exploited] the bad instincts of all sufferers for the purpose of self-discipline, self-surveillance, and self-overcoming."[15] However, the desacralizing tendencies of late modernity undermine the efficacy of this deployment and turn suffering's need for exculpation back toward a site of external agency.[16] Third, the increased fragmentation, if not disintegration, of all forms of association until recently not organized by the commodities market—communities, churches, families—and the ubiquitousness of the classificatory, individuating schemes of disciplinary society combine to produce an utterly *unrelieved* individual, one without insulation from the inevitable failure entailed in liberalism's individualistic construction. In short, the characteristics of late-modern secular society, in which individuals are buffeted and controlled by global configurations of disciplinary and capitalist power of extraordinary proportions and are at the same time nakedly individuated, stripped of reprieve from relentless exposure and accountability for themselves, together add up to an incitement to *ressentiment* that might have stunned even the finest philosopher of its occasions and logics. Starkly accountable yet dramatically impotent, the late-modern liberal subject quite literally seethes with *ressentiment*.

Enter politicized identity, now conceivable in part as both product of and "reaction" to this condition, where "reaction" acquires the meaning Nietzsche ascribed to it, namely, an effect of domination that reiterates impotence, or, a substitute for action, for power, for self-affirmation that reinscribes incapacity, powerlessness, and rejection. For Nietzsche, *ressentiment* itself is rooted in "reaction"—the substitution of reasons, norms, and ethics for deeds—and suggests that not only moral systems but identities themselves take their bearings in this reaction. As Tracy Strong reads this element of Nietzsche's thought:

> Identity . . . does not consist of an active component, but is reaction to something outside; action in itself, with its inevitable self-assertive qualities, must then become something evil, since it is identified with that against which one is reacting. The will to power of slave morality must constantly reassert that which gives definition to the slave: the pain he suffers by being in the world. Hence any attempt to escape that pain will merely result in the reaffirmation of painful structures.[17]

If *ressentiment*'s "cause" is suffering, its "creative deed" is the reworking of this pain into a negative form of action, the "imaginary revenge" of what Nietzsche terms "natures denied the true reaction, that of deeds."[18] This revenge is achieved through the imposition of suffering "on whatever does not feel wrath and displeasure as he does"[19] (accomplished especially through the production of guilt), through the establishment of suffering as the measure of social virtue, and through casting strength and good fortune ("privilege," as we say today) as self-recriminating, as its own indictment in a culture of suffering: "it is disgraceful to be fortunate, there is too much misery."[20]

But in its attempt to displace its suffering, identity structured by *ressentiment* at the same time becomes invested in its own subjection. This investment lies not only in its discovery of a site of blame for its hurt will, not only in its acquisition of recognition through its history of subjection (a recognition predicated on injury, now righteously revalued), but also in the satisfactions of revenge that ceaselessly reenact even as they redistribute the injuries of marginalization and subordination in a liberal discursive order that alternately denies the very possibility of these things or blames those who experience them for their own condition. Identity politics structured by *ressentiment* reverses without subverting this blaming structure: it does not subject to critique the sovereign subject of accountability that liberal individualism presupposes, nor the economy of inclusion and exclusion that liberal universalism establishes. Thus, politicized identity that presents itself as a self-affirmation now appears as the opposite, as predicated on and requiring its sustained rejection by a "hostile external world."[21]

Insofar as what Nietzsche calls slave morality produces identity in reaction to power, insofar as identity rooted in this reaction achieves its moral superiority by reproaching power and action themselves as evil, identity structured by this ethos becomes deeply invested in its own impotence, even while it seeks to assuage the pain of its powerlessness through its vengeful moralizing, through its wide distribution of suffering, through its reproach of power as such. Politicized identity, premised on exclusion and fueled by the humiliation and suffering imposed by its historically structured impotence in the context of a discourse of sovereign individuals, is as likely to seek generalized political paralysis, to feast on generalized political impotence, as it is to seek its own or collective liberation through empowerment. Indeed, it is more likely to punish and reproach—"punishment is what revenge calls itself; with a hypocritical lie it creates a good conscience for itself"—than to find venues of self-affirming action.[22]

But contemporary politicized identity's desire is not only shaped by the extent to which the sovereign will of the liberal subject, articulated ever more nakedly by disciplinary individuation and capitalist disinternments, is dominated by late twentieth-century configurations of political and economic powers. It is shaped as well by the contemporary problematic of history itself, by the late-modern rupture of history as a narrative, history as ended because it has lost its end, a rupture that paradoxically produces an immeasurable heaviness to history. As the grim experience of reading *Discipline and Punish* makes clear, there is a sense in which the gravitational force of history is multiplied at precisely the moment that history's narrative coherence and objectivist foundation are refuted. As the problematic of power in history is resituated from subject positioning to subject construction, as power is seen to operate spatially, infiltrationally, "microphysically" rather than only temporally—permeating every heretofore designated "interior" *space* in social lives and individuals—as the erosion of historical metanarratives takes with them both laws of history and the futurity such laws purported to assure, as the presumed continuity of history is replaced with a sense of its violent, contingent, and ubiquitous *force*, history becomes that which has weight but no trajectory, mass but no coherence, force but no direction; it is war without ends or end. Thus, the extent to which "dead generations weigh like a nightmare on the brains of the living" is today unparalleled even as history itself disintegrates as a coherent category or practice. We know ourselves to be saturated by history, we feel the extraordinary force of its determinations; we are also steeped in a discourse of its insignificance, and above all, we know that history will no longer (always already did not) act as our redeemer.

I raise the question of history because, in thinking about late-modern politicized identity's structuring by *ressentiment*, I have thus far focused on its foundation in the sufferings of a subordinated sovereign subject. But Nietzsche's account of the logic of *ressentiment* is also tethered to that feature of the will which is stricken by history, which rails against time itself, which cannot "will backwards," which cannot exert its power over the past—either as a specific set of events or as time itself:

> Willing liberates but what is it that puts even the liberator himself in fetters? "It was"—that is the name of the will's gnashing of teeth and most secret melancholy. Powerless against what has been done, he is an angry spectator of all that is past. . . . He cannot break time and time's covetousness, that is the will's loneliest melancholy.[23]

Although Nietzsche appears here to be speaking of the will as such, Zarathustra's own relationship to the will as a "redeemer of history" makes clear that this "angry spectatorship" can with great difficulty be reworked as a perverse kind of mastery, a mastery that triumphs over the past by reducing its power, by remaking the present against the terms of the past—in short, by a project of self-transformation that arrays itself against its own genealogical consciousness. In contrast with the human ruin he sees everywhere around him—"fragments and limbs and dreadful accidents"—it is Zarathustra's own capacity to discern and to make a future that spares him from a rancorous sensibility, from crushing disappointment in the liberatory promise of his will:

> The now and the past on earth—alas, my friends, that is what *I* find most unendurable; and I should not know how to live if I were not also a seer of that which must come. A seer, a willer, a creator, a future himself and a bridge to the future—and alas, also as it were, a cripple at this bridge: all this is Zarathustra.[24]

Nietzsche here discerns both the necessity and the near impossibility—the extraordinary and fragile achievement—of formulating oneself as a creator of the future and a bridge to the future in order to appease the otherwise inevitable rancor of the will against time, in order to redeem the past by lifting the weight of it, by reducing the scope of its determinations. "And how could I bear to be a man if man were not also a creator and guesser of riddles and redeemer of accidents?"[25]

Of course, Zarathustra's exceptionality in what he is willing to confront and bear, in his capacities to overcome in order to create, is Nietzsche's device for revealing us to ourselves. The ordinary will, steeped in the economy of slave morality, devises means "to get rid of his melancholy and to mock his dungeon," means that reiterate the cause of the melancholy, that continually reinfect the narcissistic wound to its capaciousness inflicted by the past. "Alas," says Nietzsche, "every prisoner becomes a fool; and the imprisoned will redeems himself foolishly."[26] From this foolish redemption—foolish because it does not resolve the will's rancor but only makes a world in its image—is born the wrath of revenge:

> "that which was" is the name of the stone [the will] cannot move. And so he moves stones out of wrath and displeasure, and he wreaks revenge on whatever does not feel wrath and displeasure as he does. Thus the will, the liberator, took to hurting; and on all who can suffer he wreaks revenge for his inability to go backwards. This . . . is what *revenge* is: the will's ill will against time and its "it was."[27]

Revenge as a "reaction," a substitute for the capacity to act, produces identity as both bound to the history that produced it and as a reproach to the present that embodies that history. The will that "took to hurting" in its own impotence against its past becomes (in the form of an identity whose very existence is due to heightened consciousness of the immovability of its "it was," its history of subordination) a will that makes not only a psychological but a political practice of revenge, a practice that reiterates the existence of an identity whose present past is one of insistently unredeemable injury. This past cannot be redeemed *unless* the identity ceases to be invested in it, and it cannot cease to be invested in it without giving up its identity as such, thus giving up its economy of avenging and at the same time perpetuating its hurt—"when he then stills the pain of the wound, he at the same time reinfects the wound."[28]

In its emergence as a protest against marginalization or subordination, politicized identity thus becomes attached to its own exclusion both because it is premised on this exclusion for its very existence as identity, and because the formation of identity at the site of exclusion, as exclusion, augments or "alters the direction of the suffering" entailed in subordination or marginalization by finding a site of blame for it. But in so doing, it installs its pain over its unredeemed history in the very foundation of its political claim, in its demand for recognition as identity. In locating a site of blame for its powerlessness over its past—a past of injury, a past as a hurt will—and locating a "reason" for the "unendurable pain" of social powerlessness in the present, it converts this reasoning into an ethicizing politics, a politics of recrimination that seeks to avenge the hurt even while it reaffirms it, discursively codifies it.

Politicized identity thus enunciates itself, makes claims for itself, only by entrenching, restating, dramatizing, and inscribing its pain in politics and can hold out no future—for itself or others—that triumphs over this pain. The loss of historical direction, and with it the loss of futurity characteristic of the late-modern age, is thus homologically refigured in the structure of desire of the dominant political expression of the age—identity politics. In the same way, the generalized political impotence produced by the ubiquitous yet discontinuous networks of late-modern political and economic power is reiterated in the investments of late-modern democracy's primary oppositional political formations.

What might be entailed in transforming these investments in an effort to fashion a more radically democratic and emancipatory political culture? One avenue of exploration may lie in Nietzsche's counsel on the virtues of "forgetting," for if identity structured in part by *ressentiment* resubjugates itself through its investment in its own pain, through its refusal to make itself in the present, memory is the house of this activity and this refusal. Yet erased histories and historical invisibility are themselves such integral elements of the pain inscribed in most subjugated identities that the counsel of forgetting, at least in its unreconstructed Nietzschean form, seems inappropriate if not cruel.[29] Indeed, it is more likely that we have reached a pass where we ought to part with Nietzsche, whose skills as diagnostician usually reach the limits of their political efficacy in his privileging of individual character and capacity over the transformative possibilities of collective political invention, in his remove from the refigurative possibilities of political conversation or transformative cultural practices. For if I am right about the problematic of pain installed at the heart of many contemporary contradictory demands for political recognition, all that such pain may long for more than revenge is the chance to be heard into a certain reprieve, recognized into self-overcoming, incited into possibilities for triumphing over, and hence losing, itself.

Our challenge, then, would be to configure a radically democratic political culture that can sustain such a project in its midst without being overtaken by it, and without abetting the steady slide of political into therapeutic discourse, even as we acknowledge the elements of suffering and healing we might be negotiating. What if it were possible to incite a slight shift in the character of political expression and political claims common to much politicized identity? What if we sought to supplant the language of "being"—with its defensive closure on identity, its insistence on the fixity of position, its equation of social with moral positioning—with the language of "wanting"? What if we were to rehabilitate the memory of desire within identificatory processes, the moment in desire—either "to have" or "to be"—prior to its wounding?[30] What if "wanting to be" or "wanting to have" were taken up as modes of political speech that could destabilize the formulation of identity as fixed position, as entrenchment by history, and as having necessary moral entailments, even as they affirm "position" and "history" as that which makes the speaking subject intelligible and locatable, as that which contributes to a hermeneutics for adjudicating desires?

If every "I am" is something of a resolution of desire into fixed and sovereign identity, then this project might involve not only learning to speak but to *read* "I am" this way, as in motion, as temporal, as not-I, as deconstructible according to a genealogy of want rather than as fixed interests or experiences.[31] The subject understood as an effect of an (ongoing) genealogy of desire, including the social processes constitutive of, fulfilling, or frustrating desire, is in this way revealed as neither sovereign nor conclusive even as it is affirmed as an "I." Might such a deconstruction, paradoxically, be that which reopens a desire for futurity where Nietzsche saw it inevitably foreclosed by the logics of rancor and *ressentiment*?

Such a slight shift in the character of the political discourse of identity eschews the kinds of ahistorical or utopian turns against identity politics made by a nostalgic and broken humanist left as well as the reactionary and disingenuous assaults on politicized identity tendered by the right. Rather than opposing or seeking to transcend identity investments, the replacement—even the admixture—of the language of "being" with "wanting" would seek to exploit politically a recovery of the more expansive moments in the genealogy of identity formation, a recovery of the moment prior to its own foreclosure against its want, prior to the point at which its sovereign subjectivity is established through such foreclosure and through eternal repetition of its pain. How might democratic discourse itself be invigorated by such a shift from ontological claims to these kinds of more expressly political ones, claims that, rather than dispensing blame for an unlivable present, inhabit the necessarily agonistic theater of discursively forging an alternative future?

Notes

1. Stuart Hall, "The Local and the Global," in *Culture, Globalization, and the World System: Contemporary Conditions for the Representation of Identity,* ed. Anthony King (Albany: State University of New York Press, 1989), 24.

2. "An identity is established in relation to a series of differences that have become socially recognized. These differences are essential to its being. If they did not coexist as differences, it

would not exist in its distinctness and solidity. . . . Identity requires difference in order to be, and it converts difference into otherness in order to secure its own self-certainty" (William Connolly, *Identity/Difference: Democratic Negotiations of Political Paradox* [Ithaca, N.Y.: Cornell University Press, 1991], 64). I cite from Connolly rather than the more obvious Derrida because Connolly is exemplary of the effort *within* political theory to think about the political problem of identity working heuristically with its linguistic operation. I cite from Connolly as well because the present essay is in some ways an extension of a conversation begun at a 1991 American Political Science Association roundtable discussion of his book. In that discussion, noting that Connolly identified late modernity as producing certain problems for identity but did not historicize politicized identity itself, I called for such a historicization. To the degree that the present essay is my own partial response to that call, it—as the footnotes make clear—is indebted to Connolly's book and that public occasion of its discussion. A short list of others who have struggled to take politicized identity through and past the problem of political exclusion and political closure might include Stuart Hall, Trinh T. Minh-ha, Homi Bhabha, Paul Gilroy, Aiwah Ong, Judith Butler, Gayatri Spivak, and Anne Norton.

3. John Locke's *Letter on Toleration* (1689) signals this development in intellectual history. The three-hundred-year process of eliminating first the property qualification and then race and gender qualifications in European and North American constitutional states heralds its formal political achievement.

4. Karl Marx, "On the Jewish Question," in *The Marx-Engels Reader*, 2d ed., ed. R. Tucker (New York: W. W. Norton, 1974), 34.

5. John Locke, *Letter on Toleration*; John Stuart Mill, *On Liberty*; George Kateb, "Democratic Individuality and the Claims of Politics," *Political Theory* 12:3 (August 1984).

6. In "On the Jewish Question," Marx argues: "Far from abolishing these *effective* differences [in civil society, the state] exists only so far as they are presupposed; it is conscious of being a political state and it manifests its universality only in *opposition* to these elements" (*The Marx-Engels Reader*, 33). See also Marx's *Critique of Hegel's Philosophy of Right*, ed. J. O'Malley (Cambridge: Cambridge University Press, 1970), 91, 116.

7. Jürgen Habermas's *Legitimation Crisis*, trans. T. McCarthy (Boston: Beacon Press, 1975), and James O'Connor's *Fiscal Crisis of the State* (New York: St. Martin's Press, 1973) remain two of the most compelling narratives of this development. Also informing this claim are Max Weber's discussion of bureaucracy and rationalization in *Economy and Society*, and Sheldon Wolin's discussion of the "megastate" in *The Presence of the Past*, as well as the researches of Claus Offe, Bob Jessop, and Fred Block.

8. As Connolly argues, politicized identity also reiterates the structure of liberalism in its configuration of a sovereign, unified, accountable individual. Connolly urges, although it is not clear what would motivate identity's transformed orientation, a different configuration of identity—one that understands itself as contingent, relational, contestatory, and social. See Connolly, *Identity/Difference*, especially pp. 171–84.

9. Michel Foucault, *Discipline and Punish*, trans. A. Sheridan (New York: Vintage Books, 1979), 209, 212.

10. Ibid., 206.

11. From a draft of "An Ordinance of the City of Santa Cruz Adding Chapter 9.83 to the Santa Cruz Municipal Code Pertaining to the Prohibition of Discrimination" (1991).

12. A number of political theorists have advanced this argument. For a cogent account, see Connolly, *Identity/Difference*, 21–27.

13. Friedrich Nietzsche, *On the Genealogy of Morals*, trans. W. Kaufmann and P. J. Hollingdale (New York: Random House, 1967), 127.

14. Connolly, *Identity/Difference*, 24–26.

15. Ibid., 128.

16. A striking example of this is the way that contemporary natural disasters, such as the 1989 earthquake in California or the 1992 hurricanes in Florida and Hawaii, produce popular and media discourse about relevant state and federal agencies (e.g., the Federal Emergency Management Agency [FEMA]) that come close to displacing onto the agencies themselves responsibility for the suffering of the victims.

17. Tracy Strong, *Friedrich Nietzsche and the Politics of Transfiguration*, expanded edition (Berkeley: University of California, 1988), 242.

18. Nietzsche, *Genealogy of Morals*, 36.

19. Friedrich Nietzsche, *Thus Spoke Zarathustra*, in *The Portable Nietzsche*, ed. W. Kaufmann (New York: Penguin Books, 1954), 252.

20. Nietzsche, *Genealogy of Morals*, 124.

21. Ibid., 34.

22. Nietzsche, *Thus Spoke Zarathustra*, 252.

23. Ibid., 251.

24. Ibid., 250–51.

25. Ibid., 251.

26. Ibid.

27. Ibid., 252.

28. Nietzsche, *Genealogy of Morals*, 126. In words that could easily characterize the rancorous quality of many contemporary institutions and gatherings—academic, political, cultural—in which politicized identity is strongly and permissibly at play, Nietzsche offers an elaborate account of this replacement of pain with a "more violent emotion," which is the stock-in-trade of "the suffering": "The suffering are one and all dreadfully eager and inventive in discovering occasions for painful affects; they enjoy being mistrustful and dwelling on nasty deeds and imaginary slights; they scour the entrails of their past and present for obscure and questionable occurrences that offer them the opportunity to revel in tormenting suspicions and to intoxicate themselves with the poison of their own malice: they tear open their oldest wounds, they bleed from long-healed scars, they make evildoers out of their friends, wives, children, and whoever else stands closest to them. 'I suffer: someone must be to blame for it'—thus thinks every sickly sheep" (127).

29. This point has been made by many, but for a recent, quite powerful phenomenological exploration of the relationship between historical erasure and lived identity, see Patricia Williams, *The Alchemy of Race and Rights* (Cambridge: Harvard University Press, 1991).

30. Jesse Jackson's 1988 "Keep hope alive" presidential campaign strikes me as having sought to configure the relationship between injury, identity, and desire in just this way and to have succeeded in forging a "rainbow coalition" *because* of the idiom of futurity it employed—want, hope, desires, dreams—among those whose modality during the 1980s had often been rancorous.

31. In Trinh T. Minh-ha's formulation, "to seek is to lose, for seeking presupposes a separation between the seeker and the sought, the continuing me and the changes it undergoes" ("Not You/Like You: Post-Colonial Women and the Interlocking Questions of Identity and Difference," *Inscriptions* 3–4 [1988]: 72).

CHAPTER TEN

Multiculturalism as Political Strategy

CYNTHIA HAMILTON

The intellectual discourse on multiculturalism has focused on the nature of representations of history, culture, and society. Although the objective is one of a general rejection of approaches that present homogeneous and monolithic interpretations, what has been undertaken is no less a task than resisting the commodification of culture projected by the image-making industries of film, TV, and advertising. However, what multicultural writers offer as alternative vision often comes in a particularized form, one that relies on individualized rather than group representations.

Focusing on the conceptual character and challenge of "multiculturalism" has obscured its important political (and policy) function. Universities, governments, corporations all have policies governing multiculturalism in hiring, curriculum, and so on. Can we assume that the objectives of scholars and those of institutions diverge? It might be useful for us to begin to consider the ways in which multiculturalism has been used as an institutional practice to obscure and thereby help preserve existing relations of domination and power. Used this way, multiculturalism redirects—even refashions—social conflict regarding racial inequality. Without discounting the political work and objectives of civil rights reformers, Kristin Bumiller, in her book *The Civil Rights Society,* explores the role of law in shaping/reshaping social conflict. In her discussion of the results of the constitutional revolution that laid the basis for antidiscriminatory law in the post-Civil War period, she acknowledges that "The 'Negro question' became part of a strategy for enlarging the base of federal control."[1] She concludes that antidiscrimination ideology and protective legislation may perpetuate patterns of behavior that maintain discriminatory practice. "Instead of providing a tool to lessen inequality, legal mechanisms, which create the legal identity of the discrimination victim, maintain divisions between the powerful and powerless by means that are obscured by the ideology of equal protection."[2] Similarly, the current use of multiculturalism obscures the historical and ideological role of race. By treating race and ethnicity interchangeably, we lose sight of the historic use of race and ethnicity as a cover for relations of economic domination. In fact, some might argue, little has changed since the turn of the century when industrialists like Henry Ford used race as a mechanism of control and domination by employing Blacks on the assembly line as a way of reminding white workers that he alone would control relations on the job. A similar objective is expressed by Thornton Bradshaw, the late chairman of the board of Atlantic Richfield Company, in explaining his reasons for relocation of the company headquarters from New York to Los Angeles:

> The United States for a long time consisted of fairly rigid groups characterized by the farmer, the small businessman, the New York intellectual, the Jews, the Hamtramack Polish. They were expected to act as groups. That has changed. The West is now the place where history is being made. It's due largely to radio and television. We're developing a common culture. We are no longer these groups bound together. We are individuals. . . . This kind of breaking out, that's what California and the West represent.[3]

The objective, for both Ford and Bradshaw, was to move away from any basis for group identification and toward individualized notions to prevent the formation of distinct cultural group formations by maintaining flux and instability. The workplace of the early twentieth century became the arena in which culture in America was shaped and reshaped. It was and remains the stage on which "differences" are erased or elaborated. When is "multiculturalism" a tool for change? How has it been used to manipulate change in the interest of existing relations of domination? A review of the history of culture in the workplace may help to provide answers.

Culture has always been a process. For immigrants newly arrived in the United States, the culture of their past had to prove useful in their struggle to adjust to urban life and factory work or be discarded. Therefore, ethnic cultures would succumb to the homogenization process that substituted

"Americanization." Only in times of distress do we see elements of ethnic culture being called up as a defense or a tool to fight back. For Black Americans, culture was linked to a material base, to community formations; culture was an essential tool of resistance because it defined the terms of solidarity. In the twentieth century, in urban communities, culture provided a balance for Blacks living with the self-effacement of Jim Crow; culture was an essential counterpoint to the dominant society's debasement and insults, which denied Blacks any social or human worth.

Work and the New "Culture"

In his essay "Racism & Culture," Frantz Fanon describes what he calls the doctrine of "cultural hierarchy."[4] Racism that is phenotypically determined, he says, is transformed into cultural racism in which certain forms of existing, not individual men, become the object of racism. He also says that racism "vitiates American culture."[5] Therefore we get a complete distortion of the many cultures present in the society. By looking at the role of culture in the workplace, we are able to see how this cultural hierarchy is established and how the ruling class achieves a harmony of economic relations and ideology.

Resistance was a natural by-product of culture for those lowest on the economic scale. For many new immigrants to the cities, which included many Black American migrants from the South, their cultures were a result of nonindustrial settings and thereby gave legitimacy to alternative work styles and values. Therefore a "work ethic" had to be imposed. To accomplish this, employers fashioned an environment that gave the appearance of recognizing ethnic cultures. The workplace forged its own culture from a synthesis of stereotypes about ethnic cultures.

The "middle-class, white" ideal is therefore a fiction created in opposition to the multitude of ethnic fictions that dominated the late nineteenth century. For example, a review of the characteristics attributed to immigrant groups reflects a "pecking order" that could be identified in industry and was reproduced in housing and social relations and later marked occupational mobility. Of Germans it was said that "they are a stable group, property/home owners who send their children to school; thrifty, frugal, industrious, and productive."[6] Germans easily assimilated into local culture and politics and were for the most part committed to Bourbon Democracy or stalwart Republicanism. Most belonged to the Lutheran church, but the few Catholics among them dominated the Roman church hierarchy. Poles, on the other hand, were described as "ignorant newcomers; generally considered thrifty and industrious, somewhat less stable than the Germans in times of unemployment, given to quarreling and pilfering."[7] Italians, almost from the beginning, were categorized as itinerant laborers, moving with the seasons in search of work with railroad construction gangs or on the levees of New Orleans. They were described as "untidy in their habits but not destructive; ignorant of English and American methods and technology; suited only for common labor; they were prone to quarreling among themselves and resorted to violence; there was a natural disposition to laziness and they drank too much."[8] Hungarians did not fare much better. Although they were considered industrious and honest, it was said that "Hungarians chose to live in wretched housing. Their habits of cleanliness, regardless of the environment or their personal means, left much to be desired. According to one investigator, they were just too interested in saving as much of their earnings as possible so that they could take their savings back to Hungary."[9] Lastly, the Greeks were said to be even more unstable than Italians and too volatile to accept industrial discipline.[10]

Thus we find that particular ethnic groups were the "favorites" in certain industries. The knitting industry relied heavily on German and Polish girls because "They appeared to have a particular aptitude to the work."[11] Employers in the ice business preferred Poles and Swedes. Railroad bosses preferred "hoboes . . . they can do four or five times the work a gang of Greeks or Bulgarians can do." Korman found that Pabst Brewing Company staffed most of its departments with Germans and hired non-Germans, usually Polish girls, only for the most unskilled tasks in the bottling department. An Italian straw boss in the chipping room of the foundry at International Harvester made sure his department was completely Italian, while a Scottish-born foreman who had worked for about fifty years in International Harvester's foundry believed Poles made the best workers in the department, even better than his own countrymen. All of these examples are from Milwaukee and reflect the composition of the city and the amount of time each group had spent in the area. The patterns, however, were repeated in city after city throughout the United States. Responses to work obviously varied with the circumstances of each group; however, industrialists used these responses to work as a way of generalizing cultures; they explained discontent and conflict in terms of pathological tendencies or innate inadequacies of the groups themselves.

The intentions of immigrants on arrival in the United States certainly would affect their approach to work. Those who saw their stay as temporary would respond quite differently than those who intended to make their homes permanently in new lands. On a mass scale this is quite apparent. As immigrants began to see themselves in a new light and view their status differently in America, the behavior they exhibited changed. They became more concerned with the permanent benefits of work and thus forced employers to change both their attitudes and the work conditions.

The need to inculcate the new work ethic was essential in the United States for the development of capitalist productive relations. Therefore, cultural habits and attitudes (good and bad) were incorporated or transformed by industrialists in an effort to maintain control.

Culture is not a static set or pattern of social relations, beliefs, and attitudes. This becomes clear in looking at the experience of millions of immigrants newly arrived in the United States. In their struggle to adjust to urban life and factory work, the baggage of the past had to prove useful or be discarded. Some immigrants came to the United States with factory experience; others were in fact transplanted urbanites. When these two conditions existed, the newcomer found him/herself at an advantage. But for all immigrants the very process of being transplanted into a new environment without the security of tradition and of that which is familiar and necessary for self-development meant that culture would take on new dimensions and meaning.

The struggle for survival among immigrants was plagued by prejudice. Each successive wave of immigrants was confronted by a form of institutional racism. The Irish, Catholics, Chinese, Italians each faced the contradiction of, on the one hand, needing to preserve their communities—rooted in common language, descent, and custom—and, on the other, feeling the pressure to deny these ties and be accepted as "Americans." Work became the central focus of all political, social, cultural, and economic concerns. It was no longer just a means to other ends. Work had meaning in the new industrial society, in and for itself. It determined what men were, could be, or hoped to be. Therefore, cultural habits and social relations could no longer simply be taken for granted. All traditions had to pass the test of function in a new environment. Social norms had to prove their usefulness in the work arena. For example, company housing and even home ownership did not meet with immediate success with all immigrants. Many preferred the boarding system, not only because of the lack of expense, but also because it provided social relief. For men, many of whom were in the United States without family, it was a surrogate structure. Still others, of course, were simply trapped by the nexus of poverty, which landlords made worse by allowing overcrowded housing to disintegrate on top of its inhabitants.

Culture posed the most serious threat to management dominance. In response, industry had to find ways of involving itself in the personal lives of workers and did so by implementing everything from punitive measures to prevent worker cooperation to wage incentives, welfare programs (like housing and social engineering), and language training.

In many instances, industries were able to reinforce negative work patterns for their own ends as well. For example, steel and railroad industries found themselves, in the period before industrial organization, paradoxically encouraging irregular and undisciplined behavior *off* the job; their workers—men—lived in company boarding arrangements where they had to look outside for food, amusement, and the small comforts of home. These men were completely rootless, with the factory as their only common frame of reference. Without community, wife, or family, they were easy sources of scab and low-wage labor.

On the job, however, industries found undisciplined behavior disruptive. Iron manufacturers resorted to fines for drinking, but could never resolve the problem of absenteeism. They also found it necessary to institutionalize many traditional customs to encourage and ensure good work. Festivals and parades could not be prevented, so they were incorporated by industry and used to celebrate the completion of a product or the construction of a new facility, or to commemorate management. Industries simply made themselves the center of traditional rituals.

The rituals of the "Goose Egg" (heavy drinking) and "Blue Monday" (traditionally practiced by skilled workers and artisans as a day off for sharpening tools) plagued industry most. And in some cases the only solution was new technology and improved machinery, which would make these men expendable. We see here a clear connection between technological advance and the owners' desire for control in industry.

The destruction of the cultural autonomy of ethnic groups was thus achieved indirectly and directly through the work process. Ethnic communities facilitated cultural contact outside the workplace, but inside a new culture of work was being constructed. Over time this has become the standard for behavior and values. As ethnic communities disappear, there is no alternative.

Classless Culture

Contemporary race relations and the most recent expression of racial backlash can only be understood as a reaction, not simply of prejudice and institutional racism but also as a consequence of the increasing state of anomie within society (particularly among whites). As European Americans have lost their ethnic identification and culture, little of substance has been substituted. Racism and white supremacist expressions therefore have come to play a dual function in American society: racism obscures class distinctions and similarities and at the same time provides a source of cultural belonging for Europeans whose culture has been lost.

Analysts have overlooked the work process in discussions of culture and therefore often misapply the ideas of cultural pluralism, which presumably lead to an image of an amalgamation of cultures, the "melting pot" thesis. Far from a mixture of cultures, what has emerged as "American" culture is a set of values and behavior ironically devoid of any references to working-class, ethnic immigrant, or non-Western European influences. What was produced in the United States was a culture of assimilation, which required immigrants to release all of their unique references and transcend their class orientation. To be American, one had to strive to be nonethnic and non-working-class. This process obscured relations of power and the promotion of a new "synthetic" culture that helped to eradicate all references to working-class resistance. This process dramatically transformed culture as a vital adaptive mechanism for all groups.

Social-science views about ethnicity in the United States have been integrated into ideas about mobility to avoid discussion of the organization of power in society. Popular interpretations present the view that immigrants arrived in America with nothing and that they were able to improve their status economically and politically. Two important corollaries to this idea of ethnic immigrant mobility are (1) the idea that groups prospered as whole units rather than as individuals and (2) the idea that one's ethnic identification was and is a function of choice, and one may freely associate rather than be "labeled." The emphasis on mobility and free association has been used repeatedly to deny the existence of institutional racism and class stratification.

Social scientists do concede that these ideas about mobility and free association are a bit optimistic but have not changed their analysis of the ethnic, immigrant experience in America. Therefore, it is important to assess the function of ethnicity and, by extension, race. What we find is that (1) ethnicity was a variable used by employers in an effort to prevent trade unionism; (2) ethnic groups have not been allowed to prosper or survive as whole units but rather as individuals; and (3) ethnic group identity today is a reaction to the social movements of the 1960s and the lack of common sources of identity within the population (for example, job, class, community are no longer sources of identity because they are so impermanent).

Work was the source of a new identity and culture for immigrants early in this century. Black Americans were not part of that homogenization process until after 1965, and then it was to counter the cultural and political movement of the time. But as Blacks were welcomed to the work culture, it was losing its hold on white Americans.

The disappearance of sources of identity was recorded in the reports prepared for the nation's Bicentennial celebration. In the Working Papers of the Rockefeller Foundation, Michael Novak wrote:

> Almost everywhere, people see in their own cultural history . . . a new defense against certain evils of modern life and a reliable resource for some of the humanistic values that have always given life its savor. Too little stands between the solitary individual and the bureaucratic power of the large modern state; intermediate social bonds have been weakening—family, kinship, group loyalties, churches, neighborhoods, regions.[12]

However, even though the report suggests a yearning for a cultural past, it views ethnic group identification as merely a consequence of choice for individuals. The report laments that non-Europeans in the United States (African Americans, Native Americans, and Chicanos) "resorted to militancy" and social movements to express racial identification. Throughout, the report underscores the idea that "ethnicity . . . is a phenomenon to be studied in individuals rather than in groups."[13] The report proposes a method for the standardization of ethnic identification using education as a tool for controlling expressions among "all hyphenated Americans." The Rockefeller report is another testimony to the need to constantly present alternatives to working-class resistance. It treats race and ethnicity as the same. However, there can be little disagreement that those whose appearance physically distinguished them (and who were subject to slavery) have experienced the greatest alienation and exclusion in society. By treating race and ethnicity as synonyms, the report (as well as other such studies) helps justify the vilification of African Americans who have failed the test of assimilation.

Conclusion

Despite the prevalence of the language of diversity and multiculturalism, we find a society still unable to confront race and racism, a society unable and unwilling to recognize structures of domination, and therefore increasingly unable to conceptualize social change. According to Hazel Carby, "Theories of difference and diversity in practice leave us fragmented and divided but equal in an inability to conceive of radical social change."[14]

The philosophy and practice of pragmatism have made it legitimate to transform all discourse into tools for maintaining the status quo (and thereby the interests of the few). This is particularly apparent when we consider legislation resulting from confrontations challenging the status quo. Since 1964 we have seen Republicans and Democrats use such policies (Civil Rights Act, Voting Rights Act, Community Development Act, Affirmative Action, etc.) to build constituencies (and channel public dollars into private hands), often at the expense of serious social needs. Academics provide the perfect cover by continually steering our concerns away from material conditions and emphasizing the individual.

The review of the historical use of ethnicity confirms its political function in the United States. Mobility required a loss or relinquishing of ethnic group identification and its replacement by the philosophy of individualism. This helps to explain the contemporary reaction or racial backlash. When Blacks, for example, call for group access and opportunity for mobility, the reaction in the general population takes the form of renewed group, and thereby racial, identification. The political campaigns of George Wallace, Richard Nixon, Ronald Reagan, and even George Bush, were all symptomatic of this reaction. The tenor of the campaigns was that of a return to "tradition," a cultural reaction to the "outsiders" who represent a threat to the homogeneity of society. But the reaction really results from resentment by those who have been convinced to give up group identification and rights and have gained little in return. When other groups remain cohesive (by choice or default) they (whites) fear the groups' potential power and are confronted with the realization of what they themselves have given up. The new group identification is seen as a threat to individualism, and in some ways this reaction is accurate. Any precedence in the United States for the protection of a class or group of persons would automatically expose the vulnerability of acting alone and thereby discredit individualism.

The dismantling of all of the sources of identity and working-class culture under capitalism left only one arena for collective thought and action, the workplace. Left alone, work could have produced a group consciousness, and for that reason we understand why so much attention was focused on the work environment and work behavior. The revival of ethnicity in the United States, viewed in this light, is no more than an expression of alienation experienced by workers who have no source of identification in the face of the decline of neighborhoods and the transformation of work.

Ethnicity within this context has come to replace occupational identity. Unlike their immigrant ancestors, Americans see no intrinsic value in being identified as workers. Ethnicity is therefore donned as a costume at appropriate times of the year in an effort to create a sense of unity and belonging, a response to alienation.

The height of workers' class consciousness was, of course, 1932–45. The post-World War II era has been important because changes in the domestic political economy have undermined worker consciousness and solidarity. Industry led the way by physically relocating outside of urban industrial cities. The movement of industry to suburbs and the corresponding housing patterns were aided by government subsidy. All new industrial construction financed by government for the war effort, for example, was in plants outside established urban areas. After the war, this relocation escalated. Workers, of course, followed industry, and this was made possible by government legislation that made financing for homes available to the average worker and to returning veterans. As America experienced this new stage of the American Dream—home ownership—the process of developing political consciousness was reversed. Collectivism in the workplace was replaced by individualism in everyday life. Suburban life simply did not lend itself to the shared experiences of urban life. As the workplace was separated physically from the community, workers' lives became even more privatized and group identification became more difficult. Ironically, this loss of group identification now stands as an impediment to the expression of the very individualism Americans value. According to Émile Durkheim, anomie develops when the prerequisites for individuality are absent; these prerequisites are relations between people. In destroying group networks, the United States has placed its own future at risk.

Notes

1. Kristin Bumiller, *The Civil Rights Society* (Baltimore: Johns Hopkins University Press, 1988), 43.

2. Ibid., 2.

3. Joel Kotkin and Paul Grabowicz, *California Inc.* (New York: Rawson, Wade, 1982), 107.

4. Frantz Fanon, "Racism & Culture," in *Toward the African Revolution* (New York: Grove Press, 1967), 31.

5. Ibid., 36.

6. Gerd Korman, *Industrialization, Immigrants, and Americanization: The View from Milwaukee* (Madison: State Historical Society of Wisconsin, 1967), 42.

7. Ibid., 44.

8. Ibid., 45.

9. Ibid.

10. Ibid., 45–46.

11. Ibid., 65.

12. Michael Novak, "On Cultural Ecology: The United States as Nervous System of the Planet's Cultures," in *Working Papers, a Guide to Ethnic Studies Programs in American Colleges, Universities and Schools* (New York: Rockefeller Foundation, 1975), vi.

13. Ibid.

14. Hazel Carby, "The Politics of Difference," *Ms.* (September–October 1990): 85.

CHAPTER ELEVEN

Racialization in the Post-Civil Rights Era

MICHAEL OMI

In May 1991, there were two senior proms at the Brother Rice High School, a Catholic college preparatory academy in Chicago—an official one that was virtually all white, and, for the first time, an alternative all-black one (Wilkerson 1991).

Popular music, in this instance, provided the rallying point for racial consciousness and self-segregation. The trouble began when a white prom committee announced that the playlist for the music to be featured at the prom would be based on the input of each member of the senior class. Each student would list his/her three favorite songs, and the top vote-getters would be played. While this procedure was ostensibly democratic, African-American students (who comprised 12 percent of the school) complained that their preferences would be effectively shut out in a system of majority rule—songs by Marvin Gaye would be overwhelmed by those of Bon Jovi.

But parity was not the only issue. One African-American senior noted that even if they got half the requests, folks would still be unhappy since "we would have sat down during their songs and they would have sat down during ours." So the African-American students organized their own prom against the wishes of school administrators, who disavowed the prom and barred the use of the Brother Rice name. The principal of the school, Brother Michael Segvich, said: "There is only one prom this year at Brother

Rice. [The black prom] is something we don't want. I think it has to do with racism."

Ah yes, but racism on whose part? The controversy over two proms raises a host of questions regarding fairness and representation, the relationship of majority and minority cultures, and, as Aretha Franklin has so eloquently put it, "Who's zoomin' who?" In essence, these are issues that debate the very meaning of racial integration and equality in American life.

Although educational institutions have been formally integrated for decades, we are nonetheless witnessing a growing *balkanization*—a pattern of separation, segregation, and assertion of "difference"—among students of different racial backgrounds, and a parallel increase in racial conflict and tension. Such problems are by no means confined to the schools. Workplaces, neighborhoods, the media, and political parties are equally the sites of conflicts and dilemmas regarding their racial organization and makeup.

Despite legal guarantees of formal equality and access, race continues to be a fundamental organizing principle of individual identity and collective action. I would argue that, far from declining in significance (as William Julius Wilson [1978] would have us believe), the racial dimensions of political and social life have expanded in the post-civil rights era.

Racialization

In my work with Howard Winant (1986), we employ the term *racialization* to signify the extension of racial meaning to a previously racially unclassified relationship, social practice, or group. A historical example is the consolidation of the racial category of *black* in the United States from Africans whose specific identity had been Ibo, Yoruba, or Bakaongo, among other West African tribal identities. Parallel to this was, as Winthrop Jordan ([1968] 1977) observes, the emergence of *white* as a term of self-identity evolving from earlier conceptions of *Christian, English,* and *free.*

In what follows, I extend this notion to account for the complexity of race in the current period. In the post-civil rights era, new forms and expressions of racialization have developed. These include the emergence and consolidation of new racial categories; the phenomenon of groups confronting previously unexamined questions regarding their racial identity and status; and the increasing interpretation of seemingly "nonracial" issues through a framework of racial meanings. To illustrate these developments, I briefly discuss the development of new racial subjects as a result of panethnic consciousness; the emerging crisis of white identity; and the overall racialization of politics.

Panethnicity and the Development of New Racial Subjects

The post-civil rights period has witnessed the rise of *panethnicity* as a phenomenon of racialization. Groups that were previously self-defined in terms of specific ethnic background, and that were marginalized by the seemingly more central dynamic of black/white relations, began to confront their own racial identity and status in a political environment of heightened racial consciousness and mobilization.

Prior to the late 1960s, for example, there were no "Asian Americans." In the wake of the civil rights movement, distinct Asian ethnic groups, primarily Chinese, Japanese, Filipino, and Korean Americans, began to frame and assert their "common identity" as Asian Americans.

The *racialization* of Asian Americans involved the muting of profound cultural and linguistic differences, and of significant historical antagonisms, that existed among the distinct nationalities and ethnic groups of Asian origin. In spite of diversity and difference, Asian-American activists found the political label a crucial rallying point for raising political consciousness about the problems in Asian ethnic communities and in asserting demands on state institutions.

David Lopez and Yen Espiritu (1990) have explored this process and define panethnicity as "the development of bridging organizations and solidarities among subgroups of ethnic collectivities that are often seen as homogeneous by outsiders." While noting that panethnicity is shaped by an ensemble of cultural and structural factors, Lopez and Espiritu conclude that a specific concept of race is fundamental to the construction of panethnicity: "Those . . . groups that, from an outsider's point of view, are most racially homogeneous are also the groups with the greatest panethnic development" (219-20).

I view the rise of panethnicity as a process of racialization that is driven by a dynamic relationship between the specific group being racialized and the state. The elites representing such groups find it advantageous to make political demands by using the numbers and resources panethnic formations can mobilize. The state, in turn, can more easily manage claims by recognizing and responding to large blocs as opposed to dealing with the specific claims of a plethora of ethnically defined interest groups. Within this context, conflicts often occur over the precise definition of various racially

defined groups, and their adequate representation in census counts, reap-
portionment debates, and minority aid.

Panethnic consciousness is unstable and susceptible to strategic manipulation. Recently, in San Francisco, Chinese-American architects and engineers protested the inclusion of Asian Indians under the city's minority
business enterprise law (Chung 1991). Citing a Supreme Court ruling that
requires cities to narrowly define which groups had suffered discrimination
to justify specific affirmative action programs, Chinese Americans contended that Asian Indians should not be considered "Asian." At stake were
obvious economic benefits accruing to designated "minority" businesses.

What this demonstrates is that panethnic consciousness and organization are, to a large extent, contextually and strategically determined. At times
it is advantageous to be in a panethnic bloc, and at times it is desirable to
mobilize along particular ethnic lines. A dynamic of inclusion and exclusion
pervades the politics of panethnicity as racial and ethnic definitions and
boundaries are drawn and contested.

The Emerging Crisis of White Identity

The 1990 United States Census revealed that the racial composition of the
nation changed more dramatically over the past decade than at any time this
century (Barringer 1991). Today, nearly one in every four Americans is of
African, Asian, Latino, or Native American ancestry. The stunning increase
in what used to be thought of as "minority" populations in the United States
renders much of the very language of race relations obsolete and incongru-
ous. For example, by 2003, white Americans are expected to make up less than
50 percent of the state of California. And the demographics of the workplace
and the campus are changing faster than those of the general population.

The prospect that whites may not constitute a clear majority or exercise
unquestioned racial domination in particular institutional settings has led
to a *crisis of white identity*. In this respect, whites have been racialized in the
post-civil rights era.

By the early 1970s, a backlash could be discerned against the institutionalization of civil rights reforms and the political realignments set in motion in
the 1960s. There was a growing popular disenchantment with the civil rights
vision—particularly the perceived shift in emphasis from individual opportunity to group preferential treatment. As one respondent noted in Stanley
Greenberg's *Report on Democratic Defection* (1985), the "average American
white guy" gets a "raw deal" from the government because, "blacks get ad-

vantages, Hispanics get advantages, Orientals get advantages. Everybody but the white male race gets advantages now" (70).

The idea that white racial identification could be a handicap seems historically unprecedented. For the most part, prior to the civil rights challenge, white identity, whiteness, was "transparent," its meaning unproblematic. In the wake of the civil rights challenge, however, it became necessary to reevaluate the meaning of whiteness.

In this reconceptualization of whiteness, traditional articulations of ethnicity have proven inadequate. Recent research by Mary Waters (1990) and Richard Alba (1990) suggests that most whites do not experience their ethnicity as a definitive aspect of their social identity. The specifically ethnic components of white identity are fast receding with each generation's distance from the old country. Most are unable to speak the language of their immigrant forebears, uncommitted to ethnic endogamy, and unaware of their ancestors' traditions (if in fact they can still identify who their ancestors are). Waters suggests that whites perceive their ethnicity dimly and irregularly, picking and choosing among its varied strands to exercise an "ethnic option."

The "twilight of white ethnicity" in a racially defined, and increasingly polarized, environment means that white racial identity will grow in salience. The racialization process for whites is very evident on many university campuses as white students encounter a heightened awareness of race that calls their own identity into question. In a recent study on racial diversity (Institute for the Study of Social Change 1991) conducted at the University of California at Berkeley, white students expressed the problematic nature of their racial identity:

(Student 1): Many whites don't feel like they have an ethnic identity at all and I pretty much feel that way too. It's not something that bothers me tremendously but I think that maybe I could be missing something that other people have, that I am not experiencing.

(Student 2): Being white means that you're less likely to get financial aid. . . . It means that there are all sorts of tutoring groups and special programs that you can't get into, because you're not a minority.

(Student 3): If you want to go with the stereotypes, Asians are the smart people, the Blacks are great athletes, what is white? We're just here. We're the oppressors of the nation. (37)

Here we see many of the themes and dilemmas of white identity in the post-civil rights period: the "absence" of a clear culture and identity, the "disadvantages" of being white with respect to the distribution of resources, and the stigma of being perceived as the "oppressors of the nation."

Increasingly, whites are seeing themselves as a new panethnic group—Euro-Americans. Dale Warner, secretary of the European American Study Group in San Jose, states that European Americans who do not start speaking out as European Americans "are not engaged in the public discourse of our times." He goes on: "We've left our chair at the multicultural table empty, and the multicultural table is where the debate is, where the deals are being made—about voting rights, immigrant services, immigration laws, redistricting, health policy. More and more, it's now being built around ethnicity" (quoted in Ness 1992).

I would disagree with the last statement and contend that the issue is race. Nonetheless, the sentiments remain clear. Whites are concerned that their interests as *whites* are not being articulated, advanced, and addressed.

In the post-civil rights era, whites have not been immune to the process of racialization and have had to consider the racial implications of an order that now formally disavows "white skin privilege." The changing demographic scene, global economic competition, and America's overall fall from grace have provoked a profound crisis of white identity. What direction this takes politically—the White Aryan Resistance or opposition to "politically correct" multicultural education—remains to be seen.

The Racialization of Politics

The civil rights movement challenged the racial understandings and practices of the times and ushered in a period of desegregation efforts, "equal opportunity" mandates, and other state reforms. Despite these tremendous accomplishments, the patterns of institutional discrimination have proven to be quite entrenched, and the precise meaning and legal status, if any, race should have in various institutional settings remains undefined. The repressive racial order of legally sanctioned segregation has been overthrown, but no clear and consensual racial order has been consolidated in its place.

One paradoxical result of all this is that, far from decreasing, the significance of race in American life has expanded and the racial dimensions of politics and culture have proliferated. As we have seen, new racial identities and meanings continue to be created as a result of panethnic linkages. And as the "complexion" of American society changes, in a climate of "affirmative" racial policy, whites too are experiencing the contradictions and conflicts of racial identification.

The absence of a clear post-civil rights understanding of race has meant that issues of racial equality and racial identity have been vulnerable to *rearticulation* from political projects on the right. These have ranged from what Ronald Walters (1987) calls "white racial nationalism" to neoconservative critiques of affirmative action and other supposedly "color-conscious" remedies.

Political issues have been increasingly interpreted through a framework of racial meanings. Jesse Helms's come-from-behind Senate campaign in 1990, the late Lee Atwater's "Willie Horton" ad campaign for President Bush, and David Duke's surprising show of support in various Louisiana bids are all eloquent testimony to the fact that the race card can be played effectively and does win elections. Racially "coded" and racially explicit appeals have come to dominate electoral contests and hence there has been an increasing racialization of politics.

Much of this has taken the form of a concerted backlash against the perceived social impact of an increasingly diverse population. David Duke, declaring his candidacy in December 1991, argued that immigration should be a major issue in the presidential election. The time had come, he stated, to severely limit immigration into our society: "What's happening is, we are unraveling. We're losing our way. This country is overwhelmingly European descent. It's overwhelmingly Christian. And if we lose our underpinning, I think we're going to lose the foundations of America" (quoted in Toner 1991).

Other political initiatives are indicative of an overall intolerance toward diversity. In the summer of 1992, U.S. English began a $1.6 million campaign against congressional representatives who oppose a House bill declaring English the official U.S. language. Norman Shumway, the organization's chairman and a former Republican Congressman from California, says, "There are people coming to this country who feel they don't have to learn English, and we think that's a threat" (quoted in Levy 1992).

While the civil disorders in South Central Los Angeles momentarily led to a reconsideration of liberal social policy, a hard line quickly gained ground. Pat Buchanan, in his speech to the 1992 Republican convention, argued that Republicans need to shift their campaign from the Cold War to the cultural war for the soul of America: "As America's imperial troops guard frontiers all over the world, our own frontiers are open, and the barbarian is inside the gates. And you do not deal with the Vandals and Visigoths who are pillaging your cities by expanding the Head Start and food stamp programs" (quoted in Wills 1992).

The overall racialization of politics projects a grim vision of the future in which multiracial and multicultural diversity is openly resisted and legislated against, instead of celebrated.

Toward a New Politics?

Any progressive political project will have to address the racialization of politics and seek to challenge and deconstruct the racial meanings attached to, or embedded in, a range of issues, from immigration to foreign trade imbalances.

In the post-civil rights era, such a progressive racial politics needs to reassess the adequacy of the original civil rights vision to deal with contemporary patterns of inequality. This would include an examination of the impact of class and class relations within and between racially defined groups and of their meaning for race-specific remedies. Such a politics also needs to rethink minority demands in such a way as to avoid a zero-sum game. Group-specific demands need to be articulated in universal terms and an attempt must be made to mobilize and consolidate a majoritarian political bloc.

This does not mean submerging the issue of race, however, nor viewing hints of race consciousness as racism. The prevailing tendency to racialize American politics needs to be challenged directly. As we head into the Clinton years, let us remember that a strategy of economic growth that ignores the specificity and relative independence of racial problems will not solve those problems, nor make them go away.

References

Alba, Richard D. 1990. *Ethnic Identity: The Transformation of White America.* New Haven: Yale University Press.

Barringer, Felicity. 1991. "Census Shows Profound Change in Racial Makeup of the Nation." *New York Times* (11 March).

Chung, L. A. 1991. "S.F. Includes Asian Indians in Minority Law." *San Francisco Chronicle* (25 June).

Greenberg, Stanley B. 1985. *Report on Democratic Defection.* Unpublished report prepared for the Michigan House Democratic Campaign Committee.

Institute for the Study of Social Change. 1991. *The Diversity Project: The Final Report.* University of California, Berkeley (November).

Jordan, Winthrop. [1968] 1977. *White over Black: American Attitudes toward the Negro, 1550–1812.* New York: W. W. Norton.

Levy, Dan. 1992. "U.S. English Goes National with Campaign." *San Francisco Chronicle* (9 July).

Lopez, David and Yen Espiritu. 1990. "Panethnicity in the United States: A Theoretical Framework." *Ethnic and Racial Studies* 13: 198–224.

Ness, Carol. 1992. "Eurocentrism Gains a Voice." *San Francisco Examiner* (2 February).

Omi, Michael, and Howard Winant. 1986. *Racial Formation in the United States: From the 1960s to the 1980s.* New York and London: Routledge.

Toner, Robin. 1991. "Duke Takes His Anger into 1992 Race." *New York Times* (5 December).

Walters, Ronald V. 1987. "White Racial Nationalism in the United States." *Without Prejudice* 1: 7–29.

Waters, Mary C. 1990. *Ethnic Options: Choosing Identities in America.* Berkeley and Los Angeles: University of California Press.

Wilkerson, Isabel. 1991. "Separate Senior Proms Reveal an Unspanned Racial Divide." *New York Times* (5 May).

Wills, Garry. 1992. "The Born-Again Republicans." *New York Review of Books* (24 September).

Wilson, William Julius. 1978. *The Declining Significance of Race: Blacks and Changing American Institutions.* Chicago: University of Chicago Press.

CHAPTER TWELVE

Screening Resistance

LOURDES PORTILLO AND ROSA LINDA FREGOSO

ROSA LINDA FREGOSO: I first met Lourdes Portillo in Santa Barbara in 1987 when I had the honor of introducing her at the premiere of her film *Las Madres de la Plaza de Mayo.* Since then, I have had the occasion to write about her work and to undertake readings of two of her films, *Después del Terremoto* (After the earthquake) (1979) and *La Ofrenda* (The offering) (1990).[1] In my estimation, these two films enact what Chela Sandoval terms "differential consciousness."[2] More properly, they inscribe the tactical subjectivity deployed by U.S. Third World feminists since the 1960s. During the decade of the 1970s, feminist film criticism tended to view cinematic practices in terms of a series of binary oppositions: commercial versus independent, mainstream versus oppositional, documentary versus experimental, or narrative-driven versus avantgarde, nonnarrative cinema. Lourdes Portillo's films resist such rigid binary constructions of cinematic practices. Her films are all narrativedriven; however, they are not straightforwardly didactic; a genuine mix of complexity, self-reflexivity, and a concern for the aesthetics of reception characterize them. Indeed, I have learned from viewing and reviewing Lourdes Portillo's films that each viewing unlocks a different textual door because her films enact the multiple articulations of race, class, and gender. Cultural conflict drives most of Portillo's projects, yet I would argue that she orchestrates an aesthetics of reception and an aesthetics of subtlety that make for polyvocal, multivalent, cultural forms. These cultural forms inscribe Third World feminists as their foremost spectators. Portillo's films are not, however, just about Third World, or, subaltern subjects, but are about subjectivities; her films position spectators on multiple sides and in various locales of conflict and engagement.[3]

RLF: Let's begin with how you got started as a filmmaker in the Bay Area.

LOURDES PORTILLO: Well, it's a very long story. We don't have enough time to hear it and I don't have the patience to retell it after I've lived it. . . . I was always interested in film. I began working in film in Los Angeles as a camera assistant for an educational film company. At that time, I was studying political science and I realized that it was film that I could do best. There are moments in one's life when you find out that there are some things that you can't do—I couldn't type, well, not very fast—and there are other things that feel very natural to do. I realized I could work in a crew with a group of people. And I liked creating an alternate kind of reality. I stopped making films for a while when I got married and had children because I didn't have time to do the work. Instead, I studied film. Later, when I moved to San Francisco, I worked with a collective there called Cine Manifest, which was a group of Marxist filmmakers. I was getting two different kinds of education: a political education and a free associative filmic education. That's how I began working in film.

RLF: You've done commissioned work, but you've stayed pretty much in the independent circuit. Tell us why you made that decision.

LP: Coming from San Francisco and having children made me realize that I couldn't move to Los Angeles and try to make it in Hollywood. It was the 1970s and if I went to the offices of the funders, or to whomever was in charge, I'd probably look like their maid and they wouldn't trust me with a million dollars. So I decided I would make independent film in San Francisco where there was a lot of opportunity for me to grow and to make films. I think that's the real reason. The other reason I realized later as I made more films: I didn't want to compromise as much as one needs to compromise. It was a very big luxury to remain independent.

RLF: Can you elaborate a little bit more about the compromises?

LP: After having worked in television, I realized that your voice is so manipulated to fit into the format they're used to that it is very deadening. I imagined that television was just like a small version of what Hollywood might be.

Después del Terremoto

RLF: Let's talk about your first film, *Después del Terremoto* (1979), which is about a Nicaraguan woman who migrates to San Francisco after the Nicaraguan earthquake of 1976. You've mentioned to me that it is indicative of filmmaking at a particular historical moment. Could you give us some background on why you decided to do a film about a Nicaraguan woman in San Francisco and her desire to purchase a television set?

LP: *Después del Terremoto* was made at the beginning of the Nicaraguan insurrection. I was involved with people living in San Francisco who were involved in the insurrection, one of whom is my friend and collaborator Nina Serrano. We talked to the Sandinistas and told them that we wanted to make a film about what was happening *here*, not in Nicaragua, because it was very dangerous to go to Nicaragua at that time. They said, "Perfect. Do it. We support you." So we proceeded to get funding, including from the American Film Institute, on the basis of a script that Nina and I wrote. It was a script for a narrative film. If you remember, in the late 1970s, most political film, although there were some exceptions, were documentaries and we were proposing a narrative film. We came back to the Sandinistas and said, "Well, we got funded and this is the film we're going to make," and we showed them the script. They said, "Oh, sorry. We can't support you any longer. This is crazy. You have to do something that really expresses what we need expressed." And so that was a parting of the ways.

RLF: You did a docudrama. What made you decide against the documentary format?

LP: It was a practical decision. It was very impractical for us to go to Nicaragua then.

RLF: But, you could have made a documentary about the immigrants' experiences or about the struggle of Sandinistas in exile. Instead, you made more of a fictional docudrama, a scripted narrative film, where you investigate sexual freedom and the freedom to consume within the context of North and Central American politics.

LP: We had a story in mind, so it was harder to find the subjects than just to recreate the story. That's how we came to that decision.

RLF: There's a climactic scene in *Después del Terremoto* I'd like to ask you about. The younger and older women have been preparing for the birthday celebration of the matriarchal elderly Latina. Different genders, generations, and ideological positions are depicted. People are dancing, eating, and celebrating. The scene culminates when Roberto, the protagonist Irene's boyfriend, who has just returned from Nicaragua, is asked to show his slides of the aftermath of the earthquake. In the first series of slides, Roberto provides general information about the earthquake, its effects on people, the casualties, the devastation of homes and schools, and so on. Roberto's tone and demeanor change from a neutral account of the events to a more political analysis of the corruption of the dictator Somoza and the repression of political activists. As we learn, Roberto was imprisoned for stealing food from the government and giving it to the poor. As Roberto voices condemnation of U.S. support for the dictatorship, one of the tamale-making *tías* intervenes. As she stands up before Roberto, the slide show is transposed from the makeshift screen to her white apron, projecting images of Nicaragua onto her body. She says, "Stop this slide show. I don't want to hear anymore." I call this scene the moment of implosion; it's where all the narrative strands come together. But, interestingly, it reveals the kinds of contradictions or divisions that are always part of political communities. Is that what you intended?

LP: Sure. We wanted to give the situation a human depth, to actually contextualize it the way it really was. We wanted to show that there are political concerns, there are contradictions, and there are oppositions. It wasn't just one-way, you know.

RLF: Like Roberto, who's just come from Nicaragua? He has a specific kind of revolutionary discourse, and he's young. You create a situation in which the women are much older. They have had to survive here and are a little more fearful than he: they know the realities. Why did you choose to focus on an older woman to convey these dynamics of the political community?

LP: I think the women in the film represent the women of that time. They were very aware of what happened during the Somoza regime and that's the reason why they were in the United States. Youth is always

Scene from *Después del Terremoto*

much more idealistic and stronger in a certain way, but blinder too. We felt that the older women have traditionally filled that role of consciousness-raising in the community, so we were just representing that.

RLF: Do you believe that is why the Sandinistas didn't want you to do the film the way you proposed?

LP: I think that the Sandinistas had an objective in mind. I don't think that was a bad thing; they might not have won the war without such single-mindedness. In a sense, and I don't mean a negative sense, we were a bit frivolous. At the same time, we were trying to do something that was meaningful beyond the single objective of winning the war and then discarding the film. One of the things that I find so interesting and important about the film is that gender is at the center of cultural conflict.

Las Madres de la Plaza de Mayo

RLF: Lourdes Portillo is best known for her documentary film, *Las Madres de la Plaza de Mayo*, about the mothers of the disappeared in Argentina. The film received twenty international and national awards.

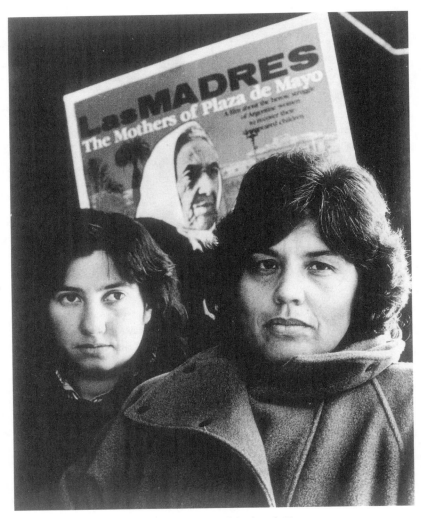

Scene from *Las Madres de la Plaza de Mayo*

Meanwhile, General Rivera had suspended all civil rights. At bus stops, at work and in cafés. People were taken away. Disappeared . . .

LP: The story of the mothers is so poignant and painful that the film sort of made itself in many ways. I mean, there was nothing to do but to record what happened and that was sufficient.

RLF: How was it received in Argentina?

LP: They loved it. They loved the film because we brought it to the Cultural Center in San Martín to screen after the dictatorship had fallen. There was a line nine blocks long to see the film. They wanted to see the truth. They hadn't been told the truth for a long time and this was the first exposure that they had to it. They had never seen on the screen a representation about the disappeared and the struggle of the mothers.

Mirrors of the Heart

RLF: Let's turn now to a commissioned work about identity in Latin America, *Mirrors of the Heart* (1992). Could you share your thoughts with us about this film?

LP: I wanted to make a film about identity from my experience as a Mexican. I was born in Mexico. The Indians in Bolivia had a similar experience and it was their experience I wanted to translate to the screen. The film is about ethnic identity, how the indigenous people of the Americas have defined themselves and how the colonizers define them. It is about the conflict around those two definitions. This film was an Annenberg project, which involved ten, fifteen—I don't remember exactly—academics who were to tell me whether I was correct or not about what I was perceiving, or if it fit within their theories of what identity was. I had a lot of problems with them. This is my vengeance now.

RLF: What did the academics tell you identity was?

LP: They insulted me. They called me an essentialist, which I took as a compliment. In one important scene, we hear Raul Julia reading a stilted narration that I fought over for months and months and never really won. I would win two words and they would win thirty, and it went on like that forever. Does this man choose to have his hair curled because he wants to be up-to-date, or because he wants to seem less indigenous? From my research and from who this man was, he didn't want to be indigenous. He wanted to fit into the urban setting of La Paz. He had come from the country and to be an Indian in La Paz is not a nice thing. Anything one can do to hide that, he will do. He did look better with a perm, though.

RLF: Can you say more about shifting identities?

LP: Yes. One particular scholar from Princeton—I won't name any names, but someday you may find out who she is—had this theory, a

Scene from *Mirrors of the Heart*

theory I think a lot of you also share. This theory says that identity is fluid. From my experience, I don't believe that identity is fluid. Perhaps over a series of generations you can change aspects of yourself or aspects of your children will change; maybe your children will be whiter, or maybe they will look indigenous. But when an indigenous person moves from the country to an urban setting, he is undoubtedly indigenous. The Criollos, or descendants of the Spaniards, will never mistake him for anything other than an indigenous person. The theory implies that if you come to the city, get a perm and a job in which you do somewhat well, and call yourself a Cholo, a mestizo, or a mixed-blood person, then you've changed your identity. In fact, in the eyes of the people around you, your identity has *not* changed. And this was the argument that went back and forth between myself and this particular scholar. She had curly blond hair, in case you ever recognize her, and she said that during the 1970s she had an Afro. I was appalled. I just gave up. I said, "No, I can't do this anymore. I'm going to quit. I don't care." She had an Afro. You know, she's crazy.

RLF: A point to emphasize is that some people, because of their skin color, have the privilege of being able to slip and slide in categories whereas other people do not have that ability.

LP: Exactly.

RLF: A Black man walks into a ritzy store in San Francisco and the electronic cameras go on just because no matter how well-dressed he may be, he still wears his race on his body.

LP: I also think that it's easier for a white person to *feel* like he or she can be indigenous, as in the film *Dances with Wolves*, you know? But an Indian can't be white. That was the argument in very simplistic terms. I am kind of a simple person. No, I mean I like to simplify things. That's why they call me an essentialist.

The Trial of Christopher Columbus

RLF: Lourdes's newest film is called *The Trial of Christopher Columbus* (1992) and stars the Chicano comedy troupe Culture Clash. History has found Columbus innocent, but Portillo has not in this film. Why did you choose comedy for this film?

LP: That is the medium I'm using to try to synthesize my political thinking and my emotional state to bring you some sort of spectacle all at the same time. I thought a mixture of political satire, humor, and experimentation with video would bring something new to the argument. I like to laugh. I really think it makes me feel good. You know, after I laugh I feel better. Maybe I won't get a heart attack after all.

Scene from *The Trial of Christopher Columbus*

List of Completed Works by Lourdes Portillo

The Trial of Christopher Columbus (1992)
An 18-minute video. A political satire with Culture Clash, the comedy trio. Verbal satire, physical comedy, and state-of-the-art video techniques are used to dramatize a faux-trial of Columbus in a present-day courtroom.

Mirrors of the Heart (1992)
A one-hour documentary for WGBH in Boston for *The Americas,* a ten-part series on Latin America broadcast in 1993. *Mirrors of the Heart* explores the notions of ethnic identity, and was filmed on the island of Hispaniola and in the highlands of Bolivia.

"The Aztec Myth of Creation" (1991)
A screenplay for an animated feature for animator Patricia Amlyn. Funded by the National Endowment for the Humanities. It is presently in production.

Vida (1990)
A short narrative film for AIDSFILMS that depicts the struggle of a young Latina woman in New York coming to terms with the dangers of AIDS. Recipient of a Gold Award at the International Film and TV Festival in New York City, a Golden Eagle, and a Silver Apple at the National Educational Film Festival. Vida received an honorable mention at the San Antonio Film Festival.

La Ofrenda (1990)
A lyrical, 16mm documentary film that portrays the attitudes that Chicanos and Mexicans have toward death. The film has received several awards, including a Blue Ribbon from the American Film and Video Association, as well as honors from the Independent Documentary Association and the Latino Film Festival in San Antonio, Texas.

Las Madres de la Plaza de Mayo (1986)
A one-hour documentary depicting the story of the mothers of the disappeared in Argentina. The mothers forced the military regime into an accounting for their disappeared ones. Recipient of twenty national and international awards, including a 1986 Oscar nomination for Best Documentary and an Emmy nomination.

"Chola" (1982)
Original screenplay, commissioned by American Playhouse, about a teenage Salvadoran refugee in San Francisco, an orphaned girl who has come to live with her grandmother in the United States.

Después del Terremoto (1979)

A 16mm, half-hour narrative about a Nicaraguan maid trying to adapt to America and her dilemma over her impending marriage to a Nicaraguan revolutionary. Recipient of awards in Poland and Cuba.

All films distributed by Xochil Films, 918 Esmeralda, San Francisco, CA 94110.

Notes

1. See Rosa Linda Fregoso, "*Nepantla* in Gendered Subjectivity," in *The Bronze Screen* (Minneapolis: University of Minnesota Press, 1993).

2. Chela Sandoval, "U.S. Third World Feminism: The Theory and Method of Oppositional Consciousness in the Postmodern World," *Genders* 10 (spring 1991).

3. I occupy a particularly complicated role as spectator and critic. I have established a friendship with Lourdes Portillo and I was very ambivalent about that friendship because I had to resolve how to separate my critical work from my subjective enthusiasm and admiration for her as a mother (she has been a single mother of three sons; I was a single parent at a very young age). I had to separate this personal human feeling and connection I have with Lourdes from a much more objective assessment of her work. As much as I realize the impossibility of separating the subjective from the objective, it has nevertheless been a problem I have taken very seriously. Those of us who do literary criticism can certainly agree that it is much less conflicting to offer a negative critique of a text written by an author long dead than by one who is living. A nineteenth-century author can be criticized without the danger of retribution. The author won't not talk to you, and she or he won't respond to negative reviews of your book or deny permission for citations. I have always been suspicious of the kind of compromises inherent in befriending one's object of analysis. For example, I had some problems with a scene in Lourdes's film *La Ofrenda* about a cross-dresser. I felt I had to write about its contradictions, but I also felt that I had to talk to Lourdes about it and tell her I was going to do this. My hunch was that she would tell me that I had it all wrong and that I didn't understand what she was trying to do. When I told her how disturbed I was about the scene, she blew me away with her response. She said, "That's fine. Write about its problems and contradictions. I don't have any problem with being contradictory. Rosa Linda, I don't claim to be politically correct."

PART III

Reading Multicultural Narratives

CHAPTER THIRTEEN

Language and Other Lethal Weapons

Cultural Politics and the Rites of Children as Translators of Culture

ANTONIA I. CASTAÑEDA

Age 7: El doctor[1]

"Dile que no puedo respirar—que se me atora el aire. Dile..." How do I say "atora"?

"Tell your mother that she has to stop and place this hose in her mouth and press this pump or else she will suffocate."

"¿Qué dice? ¿Qué dice?"

He is sitting behind this big desk, and my mother is sitting beside me and holding onto my hand very tightly.

I ... what does suffocate mean? How do I translate this? I don't have the words.

"¿Qué dice? ¿Qué dice?"

"I ... uh ... Dice que... uh ... Dice que si no haces lo que te dice te mueres."

"Dile que cuando me acuesto por la noche que no puedo resollar." "Resollar," what does that mean?

Her gasps came out quickly and sounded so awful: a croaking sound that seemed to hurt from deep inside her throat. I sit in front of the big desk remembering, hearing her sounds, and feel again the terror of last night and every time I heard her and could not help. I do not have the words to help her. She will die. And all I could do was sit there and hold her hand and listen to her gasp and gasp for air—for breath that would not reach her, her eyes popping out—and watch her die. She called me her *lengua*, her *voz*. If she dies, it will be my fault.

I tell the doctor she cannot breathe and will die. And he says something I cannot understand about asthmatics and how there is little he can do except give her this pump and that I should be sure to tell her not to panic.

Panic. What does that word mean? How do I say panic?

How does a seven-year-old girl, not yet in the second grade, translate the life and death words "atora," "suffocate," "resollar," "panic"? How does she explain and interpret words she does not know in either language, while knowing at the same time that her mother's life sits on her tongue and on what she does with the words given her? Where in her seven-year-old knowledge does she find the meaning of words that hold the life or death of the mother who calls her "mi lengua"—her tongue—the fleshy, movable organ attached to the floor of the mouth with which words are made? What cultural rites are these in which children become adults long before puberty?

Age 8: La cuenta

"Dile que no le podemos pagar toda la cuenta porque ha llovido mucho y no hemos podido pizcar. Pero que aquí están estos centavitos y luego luego se la pagamos tan pronto que trabajemos... y que queremos llevar una poca comida hoy—que si nos extiende el crédito un poquito. Andale, dile."

He looks at me from behind his counter and says, "What? What'd she say?"

"My mother said we can't pay all the bill today—because of the rain we have not been able to work—and we will pay the rest real soon, as soon as we work . . . and can we have a little more food on credit?"

He looks at me, then he looks at her, and we stand there in front of him. He starts to say something I cannot hear.

"¿Qué dice? ¿Qué dice?" my mother asks. "Andale, dile que sí le pagamos—nomás que ahorita no hay trabajo."

I start to speak to him again. I look up to talk to him, and he stares down at me, and the look I see in his eyes tells me that he does not believe we will pay our bill. I have seen that same look on people's faces in town when we all get out of the back of the truck by the city park, and me and my friends walk down the street—in Toppenish—the people just stare at us and glare at us with eyes that tell us we do not belong there. It is the same look the man at the restaurant gave us—at that place where we stopped on our way from Texas—when he wouldn't sell us milk for the baby's bottle.

"¿Qué dice? ¿Qué dice?" my mother asked.

"Nada mamá. No dice nada. Mejor vámonos. No nos van a dar más crédito."

What cultural issues are at stake for child translators? How do they interpret for themselves the cultures they must translate for others? What are the politics they confront each time they translate cultures? How do they negotiate their culture of origin, which cannot protect them and in which the roles of parent and child are inverted as children become the tongues, the lifeline, the public voice of parents, family, and sometimes communities? How do they negotiate the culture they must translate for their parents—the culture that assaults and violates them, their families, and their communities with its assumptions and attitudes about them as well as with its language and other lethal weapons?

Age 15: El rifle

"Ay tocan a la puerta. Trae rifle. Ha de ser uno de esos gringos que cazan faisanes. Anda ver qué quiere."

I open the door to a man with a hunting rifle.

"Does Raaool Valhenzoola live here? Is he here? I want to talk to him."

"¿Qué dice? ¿Qué dice? ¿A quién busca? ¿Busca a Raúl?"

"Si mamá, busca a Raúl. Quédate adentro. No, my brother's not home. He's working."

"Well, you tell your brother that I came here to order him to stay away from my daughter. You tell him I catch him anywhere near Janice, or even lookin' at her, he'll be sorry. You tell him I have friends, and they know who he is. You tell 'im, girlie, you tell 'im."

I look past him, past the lingering swirls of dust his truck tires had stirred up on the dirt road, and know what the people in the camp meant when they told us stories about the Texas Rangers.

"¿Qué dice? ¿Qué dice? ¿Qué quiere con Raúl?" my mother cries from somewhere behind me.

I tell him to put the rifle down because he is scaring my mother and to please leave. I step back inside the house and close the door. What can I tell her that she doesn't already know?

Who are these children who speak in tongues and live in fire? What happens to them as they move through the educational system—the system of which most of us are products, the system to which we send our children, the system that employs us, the system that does violence to our mental integration, and the system that historically has also done violence to our physical selves precisely because we spoke languages other than English?[2] Although many Chicano/Latino children are pushed out of the public educational system in places like Texas and California, they and all children in the United States are steeped in lessons about rugged individualism, democracy, "American" nationalism, equality, justice, merit, and fair play. What do children of color, children of farmworker families, and other working-class children, whose daily experiences belie the national myths, understand and know about these myths?

If we are to decolonize national myths, we must understand how different people have lived the American myths: the historical myths about inventing America that refer to invasion as discovery (as Angela Davis noted during her keynote address at the Translating Cultures conference held in Santa Barbara in 1992) and the ideological myths that sustain U.S. imperialism, genocide, racialism, and economic exploitation and have done so since the founding of this nation.[3] These myths, and the attitudes and the violence they foster, are intrinsic to the political, economic, social, and cultural values of the United States and are the toxic particles that we ingest with every breath.

These myths include the notion that the United States, symbolized by "The West," is a classless, casteless society where equality and justice for all reign supreme, where merit and hard work are rewarded, and where education—which is free and available to all children—is the key to success. Certainly children are vitally aware of the popular heroes and heroines of the western frontier, including every white-hatted cowboy who ever rode a horse across the vast expanses of the silver screen, dispensing evenhanded justice with his faithful but rather dumb—sometimes ethnic—sidekick and greeted by a blonde beauty at the end of the dusty trail.

Those of us living in California know firsthand how deeply rooted and pervasive are the national myths surrounding the "frontier" and "The American West." Not only is California the most romanticized, mythologized, and distorted of the western states, but the West and how the West was spun, who spun it, how it is now being spun, and who is authorized to spin it, are among the most highly contested issues in the ideological—euphemistically called cultural—wars now being waged on battlefields across the nation: newspapers, popular magazines, academic journals, conferences, public school textbooks, the National Museum of American Art, and the National Museum of American History.[4]

These wars are about national myths, about ideology and who controls it. They are about "The West as America"—to use the title of the bitterly contested exhibit at the National Museum of American Art, site of one of the most acrimonious battles waged during the cultural wars of 1991.[5]

What is the relationship between those myths and the politics of translating cultures? What rites of passage are these that require children to conceive the significance of, construe, and interpret entire cultural universes for adults, universes that include every possible human experience: a nation's mythology and ideology, a sibling's arrest, pregnancy and pre- and postnatal care, an argument with a boss who refuses to pay the wages he agreed to pay? What rites are these in which childhood's boundaries are transgressed each time a child is required to translate—and thus mediate, negotiate, and broker—adult realities across cultures?

These questions are guiding my current research on a social history of Tejana farmworkers. How did Tejana farmworkers and their families who migrated between Texas and the state of Washington live this nation's national myths? Based on interviews with women who lived in five labor camps in different parts of Washington State, this work examines the lives of Tejanas who came of age during the two decades after the Second World War, from about 1945 to 1965.

These were the decades of the Bracero Program, which recruited more than 4.5 million Mexican men to work in agriculture and industry in the western/southwestern United States, and of Operation Wetback, which in 1954 alone deported a million "aliens."[6] These were the decades of aggressive anti-immigrant sentiments, expressed in national efforts such as the McCarran-Walter Act, which aimed to tighten immigration laws and to intensify the screening and deporting of "aliens."

The calls for immigrant labor coincided with the economic booms that began with the First World War and accompanied all major wars in this century. Anti-immigrant laws and waves of deportations were symptoms of the economic downturns that inevitably followed. The first laws restricting immigration were enacted in 1922, after the end of the First World War. In 1930-33, during the Great Depression, three hundred thousand Mexicans and Mexican Americans were forcibly "repatriated" to Mexico; in 1953-54, Operation Wetback deported more than twice the number of Mexicans contracted under the Bracero Program during the same period.[7]

These were the decades in which New Deal spending and subsidies to

agriculture—including the building of monumental dams—provided agribusiness with cheap water for irrigation and electric power.[8] Irrigation transformed arid western wastelands into verdant, fertile agricultural valleys with
undulating fields of row crops, fruit orchards, and hop yards endlessly
stretching out under liquid blue skies. Twentieth-century agricultural corporations required massive armies of seasonal, mobile manual labor, which
they obtained not only through the public recruitment of braceros from
Mexico but also through the private recruitment of Mexicano/Chicano families, especially from isolated rural communities of South Texas where
racism, segregated schools, the hated *rinches*, and "no Mexicans or dogs allowed" signs at the front doors of restaurants were the norm.

During these decades, entire Tejano families, both nuclear and extended,
began an annual migrant work cycle from Texas, to Arizona, to California, to
Washington, to Oregon, to Idaho, and back to Texas. The children of these
South Texas communities, where earlier generations of native-born children
had often been refused even rudimentary education in English because the
town had "no school for Mexicans," were the girls and boys who scrambled
onto the beds of tarp-covered flatbed trucks to migrate to *las piscas*, to live in
labor camps, and to labor alongside their parents, older siblings, and other
relatives in the row, field, and orchard crops of the Yakima, Skagit, and Wenatchee valleys. Some of these families settled out early on and, in the late
1940s and early 1950s, began to form the nucleus of Chicano communities in
the Pacific Northwest.

Most of the families lived in labor camps—some of which had communal showers, outside toilets, and communal laundries that consisted of large
steel tubs with built-in washboards; others had neither showers nor laundries. Located at the end of long dusty roads or set far beyond groves of trees
that hid the ramshackle structures from view, the labor camps were not visible from the highway. Thus the camps, and their inhabitants, were rendered
invisible to the local citizenry. Ostensibly, migrant farmworkers did not
exist.

What existed instead were inflammatory newspaper headlines, which
decried the threat "illegal Mexican aliens" posed to local resources, and
McCarthyism and anticommunist hysteria, which denounced as subversive
and/or homosexual anyone even remotely suspected of harboring radical
political sympathies and posing an internal threat to national security. Historically defined as racial, sexual, and political threats, people of color were
now at even greater risk. What also existed were Hollywood's countless renditions of the West as America, which Chicano, Amerindian, Black, and

Anglo children could see on Saturday afternoons at the segregated Liberty Theater in Toppenish, Washington—the heart of the Yakima Indian Reservation. Above all, what existed were the myths.

Thus, for people of Mexican descent, whose historical communities had existed under a state of siege since the end of the U.S. war with Mexico in 1848, the repressive politics, policies, and culture of the 1950s were a postwar manifestation of historical patterns of repression, now further justified by nativist as well as racist arguments that Mexicans were foreigners. For the migrant farmworker families of the Tejanas interviewed for this study, the "keep America pure" ideology, the economic and political policy of containment, and the cultural and political repression of the 1950s conveyed the clear message that people of Mexican descent were un-American, subversive, and unwelcome.

During these decades, the women whose stories begin and end this chapter translated for their families and their communities. During the decade of the 1950s, in particular, Cold War politics and the gender, racial, class, and sexual politics of containment further converted these women of color—and, in fact, all people of color—into "the enemy within."

As children, the women I interviewed translated for parents, family, and community, and the question of how they experienced the national myths is a critical political, and thus cultural, question. Their oral histories reveal that the act of translation is informed by unequal power relationships. Translation usually occurs under conditions of conflict and stress. It is frequently traumatic, and the trauma is long-lasting. Children are often at the center of the process of translation, and they experience that trauma more strongly than adults. What, then, do we make of children translating cultures? How do we assess, analyze, theorize, and interpret this experience, which in most cases continues into their own adulthood and generally until their parents' death?

The current body of knowledge and literature on translation privileges the written word. It largely focuses on the translation of written texts, principally all genres of literature, or seeks to teach businesses how to train workers to be translators and thus to digest "unassimilated diversity," to quote Angela Davis again. It yields little of value for examining and understanding the experience of child translators.

Recently, social-science scholars and practitioners—particularly linguists, psychologists, anthropologists, and social workers—have begun to examine and debate issues pertinent to children as translators.[9] Generally, however, these scholars have cast the experience as a recent phenomenon specific to immigrant children and their families. They have centered the debate on the psychological or linguistic "costs and benefits" to the individual child.

One side argues that translating for parents and family is harmful to the child's psychological development and that, because children play an adult role while they are translating, they may grow up too quickly and resent or lose respect for their parents.[10] This perspective is exemplified by Richard Rodriguez's undernourished *Hunger of Memory: The Education of Richard Rodriguez* (1981).[11] Rodriguez accepted and internalized the tenets of a racist, classist society that deemed everything about him—the color of his skin, his language, his physiognomy, and his working-class origins—wrong, unacceptable, and un-American. He internalized these notions and relinquished his Mexican self, choosing education over family, erudite English over Spanish, a "public" Euro-American life over a "private" Mexican one. In rejecting his Mexican self, Rodriguez has, in fact, been accepted by Euro-America and has become the darling of certain segments of the white intelligentsia.

The other side of the debate argues that translating can help children develop language skills and understand American institutions. In 1991, Lowry Hemphill, a specialist in language development at Harvard University, stated that translating is not necessarily something that should be discouraged, since it is "part and parcel of the whole experience of being an immigrant child. People do what they have to do to get by."[12] Ernesto Galarza, whose autobiographical *Barrio Boy: The Story of a Boy's Acculturation* (1971) reveals translating as empowering, learned very early—in a remote, mountainous village in Mexico and in a multiethnic, working-class barrio in Sacramento—to see himself in relation to his family, his community, and his class and to understand and interpret the world in terms of power relationships and class differences.[13] Galarza embraced the experience of translating and transformed it into a powerful tool with which to give public voice to the struggle for the rights of industrial workers, including farmworkers, throughout the world. Within that framework, translating was a powerful, positive, and valuable skill to be used and shared with others.

Most scholars ignore, however, the global history of imperialism in general and the history of U.S. imperialism in particular. In so doing, they reify one of the pivotal national myths that still undergirds U.S. imperialist ideology: the myth that the American continents were largely unpopulated, or only partially inhabited, when Europeans landed on these shores. For California and the West, this reaffirms the myth of the "bloodless conquest" and ignores demographic studies of the last two decades that debunk this myth, provide new data confirming high population density, particularly in Mexico and California, and describe the genocide and demographic holocaust wrought upon native peoples by European conquest and colonization. The myth of unpopulated continents has not only served to rationalize genocide of Amerindians but has also enabled scholars to ignore the fact that Europeans had to communicate with the people living here. Europeans did not initially speak indigenous languages; somebody had to translate, and that somebody was often a child.

Thus, the issue of translating cultures, and specifically the experience of children as translators, is a historical as much as a contemporary issue and experience. It is by no means solely or even principally an immigrant experience, at least not historically. Beginning with Malintzín, or La Malinche, as she is also known—a fourteen-year-old girl who was given, with nineteen other young women, by the Chontal Maya of the Tabasco coast to the Spaniards in 1519 and became translator, lover, and tactical adviser to Hernán Cortés—the experience of translating cultures has been lived by native-born children and adolescents, including Tejana farmworkers.[14]

Throughout the Spanish-Mexican periods, both Amerindian and mestizo children and adolescents captured in war, raids, and slaving expeditions in the northern frontier of Mexico could find themselves translating cultures, as in the case of boys and young men who worked for the military as scouts, horse-breakers, or herders, and in that of young servant girls who worked in the homes of soldiers and settlers. Indian children, in particular, were often captured, traded, or sold into slavery by Spanish-Mexican military forces and, after the Euro-American conquest, by settlers and paramilitary groups.[15]

On another level, but also in terms of culture, children were at the center of the strategies employed by Spanish-Mexicans as well as Euro-Americans to detribalize native peoples. Catholic missionaries and the Euro-American educational system went to great lengths to "denaturalize or deculturalize" native peoples through their children: in missions, in the case of the Jesuits and the Franciscans, and in Indian boarding schools, in the case of Euro-American educators.[16] This is fundamentally what the contemporary English-only movement is all about. Historically, the effort was to subvert the authority of the parents and the community by inverting the parent-child relationship and making the child the authority in certain realms, including the ability to communicate with whoever represented the ruling colonial authority or power.

Although Malintzín's narrative relating her experience is not available, we know that her acts of translation, as well as her sexuality, earned her the opprobrium of a Euro-centered, patriarchal Mexicano/Chicano history and culture, which portrays her—the symbolic mother of the mestizo peoples—as a traitor and a whore. In the past decade and a half, however, Native American and Chicana writers and scholars have reinterpreted the documentary record and inverted the spurious sexualized and racialized image of Malintzín, claiming this Indian woman as our own, even as lesbian.[17]

Reinterpretations of Malintzín by Chicana and Native American scholars Adelaida del Castillo, Norma Alarcón, and Inés Hernández center on issues of subjectivities, translation, and agency. Del Castillo interprets Malintzín as a gifted linguist, a young woman who made well-considered choices based on her realities and those of her people. Alarcón examines La Malinche as a paradigmatic figure of Chicana feminism. Hernández draws upon the syncretic ceremonial dance tradition of the Concheros of "la Gran Tenochtitlán, in which La Malinche is the path-opener—the front(line)—the vanguard," to discuss how in the contemporary period we can choose to be Malinches in a political, social, and intellectual context.[18]

The Malinches of today, she states, are "all of the women who have accepted their role as 'tongues' and demanded that their voices be heard."[19] Including especially Rigoberta Menchú, who learned Spanish—the language of the oppressor—and made it her own, just as she learned and used the Bible as an organizing text and tool in her community; these women join their voices and their skills in the global struggle to end exploitation and oppression in all their forms.

With these very few exceptions, and linguist Frances Karttunen's most recent work, *Between Worlds: Interpreters, Guides, and Survivors* (1994), which discusses the young translators Malintzín and Sacajawea within a global context and experience, scholars have yet to focus on the spoken word and the act of oral translation across unequal relations of power based on age, gender, race, class, and culture. Centering gender and the experience that women have had as child translators and examining the pressures, conflicts, and contradictions that arise when they must translate in a context of unequal power raises critical epistemological and theoretical questions for feminism, and for feminist scholars seeking to theorize history, politics, and culture.

What did a Tejanita of seven summers know and interpret as she broke through multilayered power differentials to translate for a mother facing racist male creditors, doctors, police, or school authorities? What did a teenage Mexican girl of fifteen understand about sexuality, race, and violence when she had to translate her family's needs to a store owner who made sexual overtures to her every time she came into the store in the same town where a white man with a hunting rifle came to threaten her brother away from his daughter. How did these young Tejanas negotiate translating across two patriarchal cultures during the 1950s—their own, which sexualized them, and another, which sexualized and racialized them while disparaging their class origins? How did working-class Mexican girls live and interpret the cultural politics of the Cold War, of which one central ideological tenet, feminist scholars have concluded, was a domestic revival that centered the family, prescribed traditional gender roles, and prized marital stability.[20]

How did these girls and young women assimilate, accept, and/or resist this experience? What did they change, and how were they changed by the act of translating cultures across space, time, and circumstance? Although still in its very early stages, this study of Tejana farmworkers reveals that the act of translating, and the corollary rites that working-class womanchild translators passed through, challenge current feminist theories about consciousness, identity, choice, power, and the politics of culture.

Age 10: La escuela

"Dile que venimos con Doña Chelo para averiguar por qué espulsaron a Mariquita."

"Sí, y dile que…"

The door opens, and the principal comes out, asking, "Who is Mrs. Rodríguez?"

I touch Doña Chelo's arm. She looks at me and steps forward with her hand outstretched.

"We can't have all these Mexican kids disrupting our school."

"¿Qué dice? ¿Qué dice?" Doña Chelo asks.

"If this is Marrría Rodríguez's mother, tell her that her daughter bit the school nurse, and we had to expel her."

"Dile que Mariquita no tiene piojos. Que soy muy limpia—cada noche caliento tinas de agua y baño a todos mis muchachos y los mando muy limpiesitos a la escuela. Y a Mariquita le hago sus trenzas cada mañana. Por qué le echaron todo ese polvo tan apestoso? Dile que la asustaron y la humillaron."

"Doña Chelo says her family is very clean. She heats water every night for baths and sends her children to school clean every day. She braids Mariquita's hair every morning. Why did you pour that ugly powder on her? You scared Mariquita and hurt her."

"Tell her that we do this every year in March when all you kids from the camps start coming in. Tell her that the lice powder is not harmful and that the school nurse tries not to get it in their eyes or mouth. There was no reason for Marrría to cry and scream like she did. And then when the nurse tried to hold her down, she screamed even louder and bit and kicked and hit our poor nurse. Tell her she should send her children to school clean and neat. And she should teach her children to behave, to respect school authorities."

"¿Qué dice? ¿Qué dice? ¿Cuándo puede regresar Mariquita a sus clases? ¿Cómo puede aprender si me la expulsan? Yo no quiero que se queden burros como nosotros, que no nos admitían a las escuelas en Tejas. Dile, Nenita. Dile."

"Les estoy diciendo, Doña Chelo. Les estoy diciendo."

Notes

I thank the Tejanas from El Golding, El Six, Crewport, y los otros campos de labor del valle de Yakima. Their translating stories are the heart of this paper. I thank Arturo Madrid, Alicia Gaspar de Alba, and Deena González for reading and commenting on this essay. I thank Elizabeth Forsyth for editorial assistance.

1. The four translation stories in this paper derive from a larger study of Tejana farmworkers based, in part, on oral histories. These stories are composites of translation stories related by the Tejanas I interviewed and my own childhood experiences of translating.

2. Guadalupe San Miguel, *"Let All of Them Take Heed": Mexican Americans and the Campaign for Educational Equality in Texas, 1910–1981* (Austin: University of Texas Press, 1987); Charles M. Wollenberg, *All Deliberate Speed: Segregation and Exclusion in California Schools, 1855–1975* (Berkeley, Los Angeles, and London: University of California Press, 1978).

3. Angela Y. Davis, keynote address at the conference "Translating Cultures: The Future of Multiculturalism?" University of California, Santa Barbara, 11–14 November 1992.

4. For articles in newspapers and popular journals, see Kay Larson, "How the West Was Done," *New York*, 17 June 1991; Miriam Horn, "How the West Was Really Won," *U.S. News & World Report*, 21 May 1990: 56–65; Kim Masters, "Two Senators Charge Smithsonian with Leaning Left," *Houston Chronicle*, 16 May 1991: 17A; Robert Hughes, "How the West Was Spun," *Time*, 13 May 1991: 79–80; Eric Foner and Jon Wiener, "Fighting for the West," *Nation*, 29 July–5 August 1991: 163–66; Richard Bernstein, "Unsettling the Old West," *New York Times Magazine*, 18 March 1990: 34, 57–59. The scholarly literature on the subject is vast. For recent scholarship, see Susan Lee Johnson, "'A Memory Sweet to Soldiers': The Significance of Gender in the History of the American West," and David Gutiérrez, "Significant to Whom? Mexican Americans and the History of the American West," *Western Historical Quarterly* (November 1993): 495–517 and 519–39,

respectively; Antonia I. Castañeda, "Women of Color and the Rewriting of Western History: The Politics, Discourse, and Decolonization of History," *Pacific Historical Review* (November 1992): 501–33; Brian Dippie, "The Winning of the West Reconsidered," *Wilson Quarterly* (summer 1990).

5. For the publication from this exhibit, see William H. Truettner, ed., *The West as America: Reinterpreting Images of the Frontier, 1820–1920* (Washington and London: Smithsonian Institution Press, 1991).

6. For an overview of twentieth-century Chicano history, upon which this section is based, see Rodolfo Acuña, *Occupied America: A History of Chicanos*, 3d ed. (New York: Harper and Row, 1988). For discussion specific to the Bracero Program, see Erasmo Gamboa, *Mexican Labor and World War II: Braceros in the Pacific Northwest, 1942–1947* (Austin: University of Texas Press, 1990), and Ernesto Galarza, *Merchants of Labor: The Mexican Bracero Story* (Santa Barbara, Calif.: McNally and Loftin, 1964).

7. Abraham Hoffman, *Unwanted Mexican Americans in the Great Depression* (Tucson: University of Arizona Press, 1974).

8. Michael P. Malone and Richard W. Etulain, *The American West: A Twentieth Century History* (Lincoln and London: University of Nebraska Press, 1989).

9. For an important discussion of the politics of linguistic domination, and its centrality to the politics and policies of Spanish colonialism in Mexico, see Jorge Klor de Alva, "Language, Politics, and Translation: Colonial Discourse and Classic Nahuatl in New Spain," in *The Art of Translation: Voices from the Field*, ed. Rosanna Warren (Boston: Northeastern University Press, 1989), 143–62.

10. Zita Arocha, "Like Most Children of Immigrants, I Suffer from a Split Psyche," *Los Angeles Times*, 27 October 1991; Lowry Hemphill, "For Immigrants' Children, an Adult Role," *New York Times*, 15 August 1991.

11. Richard Rodriguez, *Hunger of Memory: The Education of Richard Rodriguez* (Boston: David R. Godine, 1981). Omission of the accent in "Rodriguez" is consistent with the way the author of *Hunger of Memory* spells his family name.

12. Lowry Hemphill, "For Immigrants' Children, an Adult Role," *New York Times*, 15 August 1991.

13. Ernesto Galarza, *Barrio Boy: The Story of a Boy's Acculturation* (Notre Dame and London: University of Notre Dame Press, 1971).

14. Frances Karttunen, *Between Worlds: Interpreters, Guides, and Survivors* (New Brunswick, N.J.: Rutgers University Press, 1994); Inés Hernández, "An Open Letter to Chicanas," in *Without Discovery: A Native Response to Columbus*, ed. Ray González (Seattle: Broken Moon Press, 1992), 153–66; Norma Alarcón, "Traddutora, Traditora: A Paradigmatic Figure of Chicana Feminism," *Cultural Critique* (1990): 57–87; Norma Alarcón, "Chicana Feminism: In the Tracks of 'The' Native Woman," *Cultural Studies* 4 (October 1990): 248–55; Adelaida del Castillo, "Malintzín Tenépal: A Preliminary Look into a New Perspective," in *Essays on La Mujer*, ed. Rosaura Sánchez and Rosa Martínez Cruz (Los Angeles: Chicano Studies Center Publications, 1977), 124–49.

15. L. R. Bailey, *Indian Slave Trade in the Southwest: A Study of Slave-taking and the Traffic in Indian Captives* (Los Angeles: Westernlore Press, 1966). For a collection of captivity narratives, all related from a non-Indian perspective, see the Largland Library of *Narratives of North American Indian Captivities* (New York and London: Garland Publishing, 1976), 311 titles in 111 volumes.

16. For discussion about Jesuit and Franciscan strategies of using children to invert the lines of authority among native peoples, see Karen Anderson, *Chain Her by One Foot: The Subjugation of Native Women in Seventeenth-Century New France* (New York and London: Routledge, 1991), 159–61; Ramón Gutiérrez, *When Jesus Came, the Cornmothers Went Away: Marriage, Sex-

uality and Power in New Mexico, 1500–1846 (Stanford, Calif.: Stanford University Press, 1991), 74–76.

17. See note 14.

18. Hernández, "An Open Letter to Chicanas," 159.

19. Ibid.

20. Elaine Tyler May, *Homeward Bound: American Families in the Cold War Era* (New York: Basic Books, 1988).

CHAPTER FOURTEEN

The Spanish Colón-ialista Narrative

Their Prospectus for Us in 1992[1]

ANGIE CHABRAM-DERNERSESIAN

As a Chicana Riqueña subject residing in California's semirural Yolo County, I was drawn into the 1492–1992 connection by the particular forms of media knowledge that interpellated Us in culturally specific ways that I could not ignore. After all, I was entrusted to teach Chicana/o culture and its roots. I had labored long and hard with many others on behalf of Chicana/o speakers of Spanish and for a more equitable representation of Chicana/o literature within an overarching "Spanish" curriculum. Like many of my contemporaries, whose situated bodies are crisscrossed by competing transnational interests and histories of colonialism, I reviewed the five-hundred-year celebration with an eye toward understanding the crucial matter of how it framed the cultural and ethnic problematics generally associated with multiculturalism. Following the notion that "identities concern the ways in which we are positioned and in turn position ourselves within the narratives of the past,"[2] I responded to this initial concern with this essay, which proposes a critical examination of a hegemonic construction of national identity: the Colón-ialista narrative and its prospectus for Us in 1992.

This unconventional term, Colón-ialista, was inspired by a Chicana/o art exhibit protesting the celebration of the Quincentenary.[3] As I understand it, this term deliberately breaks with the rhythms of the Spanish word *colonialista* by inscribing a hyphen, which initiates a stop, calling attention to the gender-specific construction of national identity through the naming of a particular masculine subject. Graphing Colón this way enables Us to visualize someone else's body at the center of national identity. At the same time, the hyphen links his particular historical identity to a colonial system and a form of discursive power inscribed in the Spanish language. Thus Colón surfaces as the original colonizer, as visualized in the root of the term, *colón-ialista*, which describes the colonizing *action* by naming within its borders the colonizing *agent*. With this semantic construction it could be said that the Colón-ialista narrative carries forward this function through its recentering of Colón and colonial interests as they are inherited from the colonial system and as they are refurbished, retold, and reenacted under present conditions within the capitalist system and its global representations. Thus the Colón-ialista narrative offers the "authoritative" rendition of a nation's or a continent's "founding" identity narrative; it is the narrative that communicates a "selective tradition" propagated by dominant cultures.[4] Insofar as this narrative counts with the cultural and economic capital of various nation-states and its reenactment is normalized to the point of being a fundamental part of the national patrimony, at times occupying a sacred space, this is by far a supernarrative.

In daily life this Colón-ialista narrative is inextricably linked to officially sanctioned "prepackaged events" and "commemorations" that "contribute to the continuous mythmaking process" of the nation as it is reconstituted with the foregrounding of particular temporal sequences of a hundred years. These sequential commemorations, which reenact the Colon-ialista narrative, are supposed to "adorn the past with certainty," so that the proof of the happening is in the cyclical inevitability of its celebration.[5] Within these commemorative narratives, geographical, political, linguistic, cultural, and ethnic genealogies and boundaries are drawn around Colón, his exploits, and the requisites of shifting Euro-American centers, abroad and at home.

The particular Colón narrative I have selected for analysis is probably not the one generally experienced in the local electronic or print media or on cable's much-watched CNN. I am referring to that revision of 1492 that unfolded in the *Spanish*-language print media in the United States and Spain around 12 October 1992. My focus is deliberate: this is a circuit that is generally overlooked as a productive ground for ideological and political analysis of narrativized identities and the political positions that map out and construct local knowledge about ourselves, the world, and our relationships to one another. This lack of attention has worked to the detriment of critical cultural studies because the analysis of this medium promises to yield a greater understanding of the competing transnational identities that configure Chicanas/os. The critical analysis of this medium also has the potential to problematize the view that cultural productions that speak in partially incorporated, transnational, or alternative "linguistic" realms are somehow outside of the dominant culture's menacing grip. To the contrary, this paper will speak to the existence of multiple effects of various dominant identities that seek to make a home for Us through the narrative rehearsed on Columbus Day. The subhead of this next section ("The Quincentenary Has Put Spain in Her Place") evokes a number of issues surrounding the politics of representation associated with multiculturalism and the translation of cultures across national communities and state-sanctioned borders.

Rather than framing these issues around the counter-Colón-ialista narrative of 1992 and its oppositional identities, I center my discussion around the ways in which the Colón-ialista narrative purposefully enlists subjugated identities "over here" through an international "*His*panic" register that intersects predominant multicultural paradigms in the United States. These paradigms frequently revisit cultural pluralism and the melting-pot theories of national culture, and they footnote inequalities (race, class, and gender) as well as the underrepresented social groups that are foregrounded within their critical epistemologies. Not surprisingly, these epistemologies are themselves displaced as the self-proclaimed authors of this multiprolonged and seemingly limitless multicultural framework supplant critical genealogies, racial memories, social hierarchies, and situated knowledges with an ideal essentialist Americana/o subject. This subject is alleged to be amenable to all of Us but is not supposed to be recognized by any of Us in particular.

Thus the demise of the political subject of Chicana/o Studies, African-American Studies, American Studies, Asian-American Studies, Feminist Studies, Native American Studies, and studies of the subaltern is contemplated through its dilution and utter fragmentation into an unrecognizable and equally foreign mixture of traditions and practices. Here transparent social beings are refashioned into an ideal national unity, purported to be universal. In a maneuver typical of those neoconservatives who would oppose the most watered-down forms of multiculturalism as un-American, such a construct is often linked to the preservation of a fabric of U.S. society that is allegedly being threatened by those who might unravel it. How? By openly naming and configuring social privilege and difference and the *distances* that these elements necessarily produce in the lives of human subjects today and in the way they live out and define culture.

The markedly nationalistic movement that has triggered these contradictory processes of fragmentation and reunification within multiculturalism can be seen as offering a reaction to the growth of international and ethnic communities in the United States and the nation's unequivocal and widespread participation in a global economy. In an attempt to ward off the ill effects of these nationalist constructions and, at the same time, incorporate these international dynamics, some cultural practitioners have abandoned multiculturalism because of its insular translation of national culture. Others have sought to reclaim multiculturalism as a viable, although contested, territory by restoring its political ground, communities, intellectual traditions, and potential global dimensions across particular social, cultural, and political linkages. Notwithstanding this response, multiculturalism continues to be constructed primarily as a national phenomenon; thus little attention is paid to the existence of competing forms that originate outside of this now fully transnational context.

The Columbus Day narrative provides an avenue for initiating this kind of inquiry, first because it provoked a host of muticultural readings and/or interpretations in the United States, and second because it furnished a connection with Spanish/European variants of "multiculturalism" that compete with these national readings and offer significant divergences as well. By placing my emphasis here, I seek to call attention to the various fronts on which an effective counter-Colón-ialista narrative can be launched.

"El Quinto Centenario ha puesto a España en su lugar"
(The Quincentenary Has Put Spain in Her Place)—Luis Yáñez

In his essay "Good Day Columbus" Michel-Rolph Trouillot describes the naming of "the fact" of 12 October 1492 as a "narrative of power disguised as innocence."[6] A number of newspaper articles appearing in Madrid's *El País* very deliberately offer a "predominant Spanish rendition" of 1492–1992 as a way of fostering a balanced account of the Columbus debate and appear to confirm this assessment. However, in and of itself this assessment runs the risk of contributing to the idea of timeless, universal narratives of power that don't bear the imprint of change or register the traces of their context.[7] If it is true, as John Fiske has proposed, that ideology is "engaged in a constant struggle not to just extend its power, but to hold onto the territory it has already colonized,"[8] then it follows that the narratives that frame them are subject to substantial revision as well. Many of the Spanish-language articles commemorating Columbus Day bear this out. They offer a number of twists in the Colón-ialista narrative that newly interpellate not only Spanish and Latin American but also Chicana/o and indigenous subjects.

To start with, much of the official discourse on 1492 that is intended for popular consumption consciously seeks to distance itself from the old-style colonial discourse normally associated with the Golden Age of Spanish politics: the Empire. In its revised forms, the Colón-ialista narrative tempers its patriotic fervor, mediates its Spanish nationalism with a Euro-Latin American representation, and aggressively seeks to "modernize" itself in the contemporary world order by ridding itself of anachronistic expressions and historic recriminations. This is a Colón narrative that reinvents the legacy of 1492 by minimizing references to the "facts" of the Conquest and its aftermath and seeks to reconcile political opposites by appealing to a new Euro-American unity: *La Hispanidad*/Hispanism or Hispanics.[9] Finally, this Colón has abandoned the Yankee colonizer and his political exploits in Wounded Knee and Aztlán while seeking less accountability for the Spanish colonizer for his exploits elsewhere.

Within this recasting of the Columbus narrative, events of the past are often blurred or confounded with those of the present. That this is the case is not surprising since those who defend the colonial Spanish positionality as the dominant one also consciously seek to distance readers from the historical realities of 1492, and the benefits and/or atrocities they may have engendered for contending groups. At the same time, these realities are translated, often refashioned within cryptic historical reconstructions that are so preposterous—so far from general understandings of the nature of these events—that they often reveal themselves to be outright distortions of history, although this is not the intended effect.[10]

I have pieced together some of the dominant strands of the public discourse around the commemorations of 1492 in order to examine some of its constitutive elements, although it is important to note that not all Colón narratives propose to arrive at his identity in this way. An example can be found in Félix Monteira's interview with Luis Yáñez, the president of the Society for the Celebration of the Quincentenary. At one point in the interview, Yáñez emphatically claims that the "commemoration in Spain isn't a celebration of victory which only seeks to increase her past glory"; at another, he assures his reading public that "the Quincentenary has served to put Spain in her place."[11] Thus, he bolsters the claim made by other newspaper editorials that the Quincentenary has offered the nation "capitalidad cultural europea," roughly, a form of European cultural capital. Following this line of thinking, the editorial, "Octubre del 92," featured by Jesús de

Polanco and company of *El País,* proposes that "five hundred years after the conquest, the day of Hispanism isn't vindicating a model of Conquest or colonization, but rather the importance of *some* exposides that presupposed the *most* important external projection of Spaniards."[12] The editorial proposes that without these transcendental events (which we all recognize despite their erasure), "contemporary history would not be intelligible" and "an important *fact of civilization* would be erased." Thus, the significance of the Conquest and the Quincentenary is magnified to encompass an unprecedented scale and an unwarranted value in singularly forging the political and cultural entity that we recognize as *América*. At the same time, Polanco et al. seek to detach themselves and their readers from the social, political, and cultural process that such a "spectacular external projection" necessarily entailed. Interestingly enough, this logic echoed that of the pope, who kept insisting that his visit to the New World around 12 October 1992 wasn't a commemoration of the Conquest, but a celebration of Christianity, as if the two weren't historically linked.[13]

These reflections not only demonstrate the flawed and contradictory logic that frames the Spanish Eurocentric Colón narratives; they also register the impact of the context of 1992, thus bringing home the reality that even neocolonial discourses require adjustments of the original colonizing mission if they are to close the circuit of consumption with revised Colón identity, or if they are to compete with other Eurocentric interpretations, perceived to be more generous in their constructions. In the case of Spain, this proves to be particularly relevant, since the Spanish public, the target for such a narrative revival, proved to be somewhat divided by a recent poll, with at least 38 percent accepting the Spanish history of colonization *while admitting to errors,* 33 percent claiming pride in the epoch, 9 percent claiming that Columbus Day shouldn't be celebrated, and at least 5 percent claiming, "I'm embarrassed about that part of my history because the Conquest was, after all, a genocide."[14]

Other contextual pressures can also be seen as impinging on the revision of the Colón-ialista narrative, including the undeniable political and cultural significance of the fact of American independence from Spanish colonial rule and the increased transnational visibility of the indigenous resistance movements throughout the Americas and Europe. Significantly, the resistance to Colón incorporated Spanish protests in Barcelona and Toledo and a youth protest in Sevilla that sidestepped official attempts to purge the nation of the guilt of Conquest by openly seeking the *perdón* (forgiveness) of *América* (the continental Americas).[15] From the patrons of local Spanish bars who sported T-shirts reading "No al/to 92" to the young Chicana/o activists in Aztlán who wore *camisetas*[16] with Malaquías Montoya's graphic rendition of a virus-ridden Columbus flanked by the phrase "Chále con Colón" (The heck with Colón), these sectors have not only interrupted the terms of the old-style Spanish colonial discourse, they have also generated a contentious dialogue that carries over into the neocolonial revisions that commemorated 1492 in 1992.

Just as local conservatives have emerged to counteract the progressive agenda associated with Ethnic and Women's Studies in the United States, the proponents of the Colón-ialista narrative in Spanish newspapers actively seek to contest those oppositional framings of *indigenistas*/indigenous peoples that countered "discovery" with "*genocidio*/genocide," "*encuentro*/encounter" with "*colisión*/collision" or "*encontronazo*/crash," and "*España*/Spain" with "*América*." The anti-Colón movement has left a lasting imprint on the popular imagination that even the proponents of Colón cannot ignore: the idea that even in 1992, 1492 is a wound that continues to bleed.[17]

As we shall see, this Spanish revision of the national identity also responds to new social and political objectives, not the least of which is Spain's current efforts to rearticulate her relationship to Europe, Latin America, and the world economy. The Quincentenary and its Colón narrative were, after all, political, state-sanctioned events, and as such they incorporated not only ideological, but also material and institutional, practices. As Javier Solana notes in his editorial "V Centenario, Proyecto Cumplido" (The Quincentenary, the completed project): "In our country, the commemoration of the Quincentenary has been fundamentally a political project, a project of the state.... Of the state not only the central administration, but ... an infinite number of private associations and public ones have participated."[18]

Yáñez's account of the significance of 1492–1992 goes far beyond this particular rendition, for it constructs the Quincentenary and its related programs (the Expo and the Olympic Games) as symbolic re-creations of a Spanish imperial enterprise.When asked whether he took offense at the fact that the Quincentenary was often reduced to the Expo and the Olympics, the president of the committee went a step further and fully embellished the Quincentenary program with the language and characteristics of the Columbus voyage and the Conquest, extending as well the field of its projected influence: "No, because I conceive of the Quincentenary as an arch that includes *many* things. ... The Olympic Games are secured in 1986 because in 1992 the Quincentenary was being celebrated. And, let's not say anything about the Expo; that is a part of the Quincentenary program. They have been *the flagships*, spectacular projection toward the outside."[19] With this description Yáñez recovers the militaristic interpretation that was played down in Polanco's initial revision of the events commemorating 1492, repeating in this instance the idea that the Conquest was "a spectacular projection." Thus traces of the old-style colonial narrative are reenlisted at the symbolic-imaginary level, this time through a contemporary Spanish register and cultural practice: the Expo. At the same time, the convergence, 1492-1992, seems to offer the possibility for an unprecedented Spanish basking in glory, despite declarations to the contrary, for Yáñez elaborates: "The Quincentenary has put Spain in her place. . . . 1992 can be summarized with a slogan that has been created abroad and used from Japan to the United States: 'The Year of Spain.' The triumph of this strategy . . ."[20]

It is here where the essence of this Colón-ialista narrative is captured: this is a narrative that recenters an imperial Spain while displacing *América*, that speaks itself while pretending to represent a largely unspoken *América*.[21] This is a narrative that envelopes history—that history that hurts Us—within a sanitary colonial mythology that has edited out the realities of the violence of the Conquest and the forms of domination that such an enterprise necessarily entailed. This is a narrative that very deliberately constructs itself as being "measured," as leaving behind the contentious discursive positions of the "sí's/yeses and the noes" and their passion of remembrances, while at the same time taking solace in the brutality of other (especially Anglo-American) conquests.

Finally, this is a narrative that offers a conservative counterdiscourse to resistance, while at the same time carefully privileging its positionality within its founding account to the exclusion of the other narratives protesting against Colón that unfolded on the streets, in the newspapers, and on television. I am referring to counterdiscourses and countercelebrations that were foregrounded in Spanish-language newspapers such as *La Opinión* in articles such as "Marchas, festejos y contrafestejos caracterizan el 'Día de la Raza' en los países latinoamericanos." For example, the following events, documenting resistance in the Americas, were covered in *La Opinión*:[22]

> Mexico City: Amid screams of "Christopher Columbus to the firing line" and throwing eggs, paint, and rocks at the monument of the conqueror . . . hundreds of *indígenas* danced and protested, singing . . . "Thief, we don't want you in the pantheon."

> Guatemala: The natives of this Central American country marched through the center of the capital to commemorate five hundred years of "Indigenous,

Black, and Popular Resistance," and at the end of the march they gave the government a memorial claiming recognition of their identity and rights. . . . The guerrilla leadership of the URNG (Unidad Revolucionaria Nacional Guatemalteca) publishes a declaration . . . commemorating the five hundred years of resistance and struggles of the indigenous peoples of Latin America against "the Conquest, colonization, and oppression."

Panama: Indigenous peoples marched in front of the Spanish embassy, where they danced and demonstrated their anger over the celebration.

El Salvador: A group of Salvadoran aborigines throws red paint on the statues of Colón and Queen Isabella that grace the entrance to the National Palace.

Costa Rica: A peaceful demonstration, including the leaders of twenty-one indigenous groups, took place on the streets of Costa Rica. The protest changed in mood when another angry group burned the flags of the United States and Spain.

Ecuador: Five hundred years of popular and indigenous resistance is celebrated.

Colombia: Groups of Indians from different regions of Colombia gathered today to protest the celebration of the five hundred years of the arrival of Columbus in America. The Indians were in agreement that the cultural rupture between the two worlds was still present. In Popayán, more than ten thousand Indians and farmworkers (mostly Guanbinos) marched silently and blindfolded in protest against the celebration of the "discovery" of America.

Paraguay: Seventeen indigenous tribes refuse to celebrate the Quincentenary while the president, Andrés Rodríguez, declares the occasion a free day . . .

Bolivia: In La Paz, between twenty-five thousand and thirty thousand persons of different ethnicities, most of whom were Indian and who had arrived from the Aymara communities, gathered in a protest against colonization.

Argentina: Representatives of indigenous movements end the four-day hunger strike they were waging in front of the house of the government in the context of a protest against the genocide of the Conquest.

Chile: Indigenous protesters briefly took over various university buildings while leftists exploded a bomb in front of the Spanish embassy.

Santo Domingo: Protests are held throughout the country against a state-funded monument of Columbus that cost twenty-five million dollars.

Aztlán: Students at UCLA offer a countercelebration in honor of the dead in the brutal Conquest.

The narrative of Colón-ialismo is presenced through omissions of such resistance. This narrative does not fashion itself from the force of arrows, horses, or crosses, but through the power of discourse itself, through the creation of a selective tradition within electronic media and cultural *histories*, and through the highly sophisticated mediums of government politics, public relations campaigns, and economic enterprises as they activate the desire for empire. This particular rendition of the Quincentenary as the "colonial enterprise" alerts us to the ethnocentric dimensions of this commemoration that had been shadowed under a diplomatic outreach directed at the Latin American republics.[23] This dimension also serves to explain the reasons for the distancing from Old World politics. The positioning of Spain within a new world order, alongside the United States and Japan, is itself intended to be a sign of her desired prominence in the contemporary period. This re-creation of the Quincentenary thus returns a position lost to her through independence and subordination to other Euro-American centers, permitting her to relive her imperial legacy without the nagging memory of past or present complications.

An understanding of the re-creation of this brand of Spanish hegemony is not complete without referring to the cultural, ethnic, and linguistic configurations that play into the equation, for if the United States and Japan are linked to the economic program of the future where Spain is more than just a marginal contender, Spain's imperial influence is affirmed in the present at the sociocultural level through a reconfiguration of her relations with the Spanish-speaking inhabitants of the Americas. This configuration draws its inspiration from a colonial past but reaffirms its legacy in the historic present. Spain might be short on hard capital, she may have been displaced as an imperial power, but, as the proponents of the Colón narrative explicate, she is rich in culture and language. The extent of her power and influence in Latin America is confirmed at this level by a series of claims regarding the extensive domain of the Spanish language; the failure of indigenous dialects and American republics to marshal up an independent "national" expression; the enduring presence of Spanish colonial institutions in the Americas and the existence of a Spanish stock through the ethnic identity of *mestizaje*. For all practical purposes, the Spanish and American republics are characterized through the *same* language, culture, and religion—the ones intentionally associated with an original colonizing culture.

These perspectives are well illustrated in the "Octubre del 92" *El País* newspaper article, where the editorial group argues that a "common" language is the legacy Spain has left to Latin Americans and that it is *this* language that permits Latin Americans to project themselves as political, cultural, and economic entities and to participate in a joint "unfolding of civilization" with Spain. Nicolás Sánchez-Albornoz also commemorates the Quincentenary through a politically charged construction of the Spanish language. He charts five hundred years of a continual linguistic expansion that began with the Conquest and continues to the present day and credits this legacy with guaranteeing the "supremacy" of the Spanish language.

Like others, he minimizes the role of the actual Spanish Conquest in unleashing this much-celebrated expansion—he even attributes it to Latin Americans (particularly the dominant classes: the creoles) who seized the colonial impetus. However, to the degree that he appeals to a long-standing, uninterrupted linguistic legacy that coincides with the five hundred-year commemoration, and to the degree that he links this legacy to the acts of those colonizers who purportedly generated its growth from 1500 to 1650 by regrouping into insular nuclei in order to preserve the language intact, his rendition also generates the notion of an original linguistic capital that is unmistakenly Spanish. Only by undervaluing the regional and national variations of Spanish and the force of indigenous languages and by isolating those demographic, political, and communicative necessities associated exclusively with the Spanish language can he chart the "dominion of the Spanish language."[24]

From a quite different perspective, Miguel Oviedo attempts to furnish a more balanced account of the Conquest, exploring its violence toward the indigenous peoples and recording Spanish opposition to its unfolding.[25] However, like many of his contemporaries who support the five hundred-year commemoration, Oviedo adheres to the idea that the Conquest rendered a productive legacy with the by-product of cultural *mestizaje*: the fusion of two cultures into one. As he describes it, this was a "fusion," not an "exclusion," and from this fusion a new culture emerged that was different from the original cultures but shared their roots.[26] It is to Oviedo's credit that he recognizes that *América* is a multicultural and multiethnic construct, that he creates a distance from those who view this fusion as part of an original colonizing design. However, his notion of *mestizaje* is also a flawed and totalizing concept.[27]

Oviedo's assessment of what the Conquest actually left behind after five hundred years confirms the problematic nature of this equitable fusion, for, as he sees it, what's left behind after all is done is a "society that, with its own variations, is a new variation of *Occidental* culture, an inheritor of a vast spiritual and intellectual legacy."[28] Above all, what is left behind, once Occidental culture has become the new centralizing space, is the Spanish language—"the language in which we Spanish Americans can communicate among ourselves and across the Atlantic." Here, from within this Eurocentric lens, *mestizaje does* exclude peoples and cultures,[29] and for Oviedo the Spanish language is capable of becoming a powerful instrument of

> expression, the key to our (their)[30] universal vocation, and the promise that one day, understanding one another, we (they/Hispanics) will never commit the error of the first Spanish *discoverer* who, upon seeing in front of him a naked human being, who was *incapable of reading* and *ignorant of God,* thought he was a monster. That is to say, an aberration of nature, an enemy, a war booty, instead of seeing him for what he was: *his* likeness. [31]

This projected mimesis sins by virtue of its lack of cognizance of the dynamic interplay between similarity and difference that occurs in the relations between fully contested ethnic identities. This description also threatens to reinscribe the civilization/barbarism opposition, so long ago discarded for its racist overtones and stereotyping, by failing to fully interrogate the founding presumptions of the conqueror—not the discoverer—toward the Indian, and by failing to ask: Who was ignorant? Who was incapable of reading or writing another's culture? And: Why should *Spanish* (this code of Spanish) be the key to our/*their* vocation and expression? In addition, in 1992 Oviedo cannot imagine an indigenous viewpoint that is centered in a positionality or a linguistic framework substantially different from the one inherited from the conqueror. He fails to comprehend how this particular rendition of the Spanish language, which is so crucial for those who seek to rescue the Quincentenary from all of its evils in an effort to salvage a productive colonial legacy, promotes not only alliances but also *ruptures* between peoples, how those who do not privilege Spanish in this way are left out of the orbit of transnational communication and a place in the world's representational landscape.

Other problems loom ahead in the literature overtly celebrating the Quincentenary. This linguistic transatlantic network featuring Spanish dominance is often encircled with its own cultural space with the notion of *La Hispanidad,* historically, a euphemism for Spanish-centered. Here the various Spanish, Latin American, and Chicana/o traditions are held to celebrate these inherited "common" cultural and ethnic traditions. At the political level, this global essentialism acts to legitimate Spanish power and to cancel out the growing force of competitive American identities that propose radical deviations from this model, such as the *indigenista* and popular resistance movements, and/or Chicana/o countercelebrations. Rather than functioning as independent ethnic, political, and cultural entities, these elements become symbolic extensions of Spain's old cultural and political empire as it is recoded and refashioned through the political imaginary and the Spanish language of "Sí al/Yes to 1992."

Once again the irony is that this is set forth as an entirely *new* multicultural vision. This vision is problematic, not only because it distorts history in the service of revised but nevertheless visible old-style colonial interests, but because its code for doing so has changed. This code has become more contemporary, more familiar—more "American." In short, it has come home to newly invade our *casa*/house and to reformulate the terms of political and ethnic relations over here.[32] For Chicanas/os this twist is particularly challenging since debates on multiculturalism have generally functioned with reference to contestations of an Anglo-American center and a more recent construction of political domination and whiteness. The framing of multiculturalism within the confines of the five hundred-year commemoration involves another locus of contestation, another source of ethnic and political conflict, one that potentially reinscribes hierarchies from centuries past, renewing them through a centralizing imperial channel: in this case the Spanish press, as it echoes, reappropriates, and redefines the language of contemporary social relations.

This "colonial multiculturalism" is jarring, for it is not only a reinvention of the melting pot that proposed to fuse Chicanas/os into a dominant Anglo/European Center. This construction also nourishes homogeneous visions of Spanish culture, purist notions of the Spanish language, and a complete denial of cultural, ethnic, and racial differences among the different mestizo and indigenous populations associated with what we know as *América*, before as well as after the Conquest.[33] For Chicanas/os, as well as for other groups that are constructed under this seemingly pluralistic notion of His*panidad* (Colón's), this construction is very problematic. This multicultural border is intersected by another fence/*frontera*/border that also obfuscates the realities of oppression, unequal access to discourse, and the power of dominant regimes of representation to make us experience ourselves as "other/Colóns."

To put it bluntly, Chicanas/os are simultaneously countering the Colón-ialista narratives of two empires: one presumed dead (the Spanish empire) and one known to be alive (the dominant culture here). Although unequal in strength and influence in the contemporary world, they have nonetheless configured Us according to their cultural, political, and social designs and significant capital and ideological investments, but not without resistance.

500 Years of Resistance

Contrary to what is frequently posited in studies of culture—the idea that "transnational" identities are essentially "progressive," "productively" hybrid, and "free" to relocate though mental or physical migrations without border patrols (within the academy, in the streets, or on the border)—I would argue that this particular transnational identity is regressive. It has indeed placed Us within a series of multiethnnic constructions that purposefully stop right where our emergent and oppositional agencies begin. Thus this transnational formation of American identities is unable to offer an alternate avenue of representation, shadowed as it is by the towering frames of the Hispanic or Anglo Columbus.[34] The best it can do is offer bicultural/transcultural options of self-effacement. Cognizant of the double-forked tongue of the neocolonial discourse, many Chicanas/os have resisted these European and North American constructions, identifying the Colón narrative for what it is: a recentering project, an enterprise/*empresa* that places Spain back in its desired place: at the front of the flagship of a new European/American configuration.

Interestingly enough, in the period of its gestation, her promoters have captured a new cultural and linguistic marketplace in the Americas, through which another Spanish hegemony is being mapped out through a renewed European presence. Ironically, this construct is inclusive of Chicanas/os in an essentialist and colonizing way. But this characterization does not suffice if we are to understand the predicament of our double positioning. Although miles apart in terms of their geographic and political configurations, the dominant constructions of the Colón-ialista narrative share a similar characteristic: they commonly polarize their constructions and frequently conceal their partnership and complicity.

I am referring to the way in which the Yankee Columbus and the Spanish Colón work together to produce a type of master narrative of the colonial order: past and present, here and there. In both versions, the Columbus controversy tends to overlook the continued effects of the "imperial" presences in our daily lives and their mediating institutional effects on our own fractured self-representations. For these linkages to be made between the commemorative holiday and every day, for these effects to be visible, it is necessary to go beyond particular celebrations of the Quincentenary and the supernarrative surrounding Colón, to see how these representations are sustained in yearly cultural, educational, and political programs that do not necessarily subscribe to his particular identity directly but that nourish this type of construction of the national identity.

This type of connection was symbolically rendered by a group of students at the University of California, Davis. Four years ago they dramatically encountered these imperial presences as they protested against a Spanish-Castilian-centered curriculum and against cultural disrespect through newspaper campaigns against the Department of Spanish, marches through that academic unit, complaints to the Department of Civil Rights, and finally a hunger strike. Although they did not frame their opposition in terms of a protest against Colón per se, they nonetheless appealed to his afore-mentioned effect: *colonialismo*/colonialism. Ironically, it was the extensive dominion of that language, hailed by Spanish editorials covering the Quincentenary debate as one of Spain's most laudable accomplishments and a unifying force, that was under dispute here. Through their protest the students interrogated the supremacy of Spanish and revealed a transnational institutional complicity, thereby linking educational practices and a Eurocentric view of culture to the kind of cultural logic delivered by Sánchez-Albornoz and Oviedo.[35]

The *Davis Enterprise* described one of the early chapters of this ongoing protest movement in an article by Elisabeth Sherwin: "About 100 Chicano Latino students carried signs and marched at UCD on Jan. 29 to bring attention to their problems. They charged the Spanish department with treating Mexican and Chicano students as second-class citizens, scorned for speaking Street Spanish instead of the more academically acceptable Castilian Spanish."[36] As Sherwin explains, the UCD task force "found that the complaints of many Chicano/Latino students were valid, including the students' perception of an unjustified attitude held by some faculty, teaching assistants, lecturers and students that Castilian Spanish, as opposed to Mexican Spanish, is the preferred regional variety."[37] In reality, the complaints spanned a much broader terrain because "the emphasis of foreign language departments on classic literature and the use of the standard forms of language to the exclusion of contemporary forms of ethnic literature and dialectical varieties used by ethnolinguistic minority groups" were "clearly viewed by . . . students as an attempt to invalidate their language and culture, and to reject their very ethnic identity."[38] Like those who would later counter Colón, these students often complained that access to their national cultural and linguistic traditions, to the images, histories, and tongues of people with an indigenous claim to the language and a local culture, was being subverted by predominant academic constructions of Spanish that reenacted a colonial linkage to Spain and communicated a profound disregard for these native cultures.

Upon breaking with the oppressive silence that marked the Chicano/a experience with Spanish and claiming their right to their cultural and linguistic terrain, these Chicana/o speakers exposed the vestiges of a colonial system in the very heart of a national educational system that long ago rid itself of England's colonizing grip. Those on the receiving end of exclusion could have predicted this revelation: the Chicana/o movement had primed Chicanos and Chicanas for this type of contention, with its displacement of the imperial Spaniard from the center of the *mestizaje* image, its diffusion of poems that addressed cultural and linguistic displacements with verses such as "España chingó in Spanish" (Spain screwed us in Spanish),[39] and its recovery of poems that subverted the lingocentrism of standard Spanish and English by crossing their borders illegally.

Suffice it to say that this protest produced quite a lot of consternation within the greater reading public, which was amazed to find yet another crisis of Western civilization brewing in Davis, in *Spanish* classes, within a university known for its agricultural programs. Unbeknownst to many, this protest signaled a rejection of the (peninsular) Spanish-only movement that had put Spain in her place institutionally across these United States in a wide array of programs that *claimed* to represent the Spanish-speaking traditions and diverse cultural identities of the Americas. Long before the unfortunate birth of the PC narrative in English, long before the lamentable de-Americanization of Ethnic Studies by nineties-style Rush Limbaugh-type conservatives, the Spanish-only principle had censored Us through its policing of the Spanish language, its containment of Chicana/o, Mexicana/o, Latina/o cultures, and its all too effective management of the institutional space we call Spanish—a space that renarrativizes alternative histories, traditions, and cultures by inserting our emergent identities into their canonical narratives, where these Chicana/o identities are either marginalized or made to appear incompetent against an unfair standard of *their* past, a past commemorated by the very force of its legitimacy and repetition in U.S. academies.[40] This space regulated and continues to regulate how Spanish should be spoken and whose Spanish *lengua*/language merits canonization. This space determines who is a partner or an outlaw in intellectual discourse. This space foregrounds an ethnicity, a body, a subject that is not figured as our own but that is nonetheless represented as such by most U.S. educational institutions.

However, the student protest, which was covered in newspapers from San Juan to New Delhi, from San Francisco to New York, countered the dominant Spanish placement in U.S. culture with the responses: "Spanish is *our* language too, and if you don't like it, the hell with you" and "Aquí estamos y no nos vamos/We are here and we're not going anywhere." The Spanish crisis was instructive for others as well, who became attuned to the power-knowledge connection in Spanish through protest chants such as "Equal Rights, Equal Space, Don't Throw Racism in Our Face." They cut through the imperial Spanish register, which promotes not only Colón but also a traditional Spanish canon, coding their transnational resistance and language in terms taken from the civil rights movement over here.

Just as Columbus Day could never be their day from this critical oppositional space, Spanish could never be a neutral zone where tourists prepared for travel to a native land of enchantment, a grammar detached from its producers and their interests, a homogeneous space where stylistics obfuscated the relations of power and dominance and where Castilian dominated *pachuca/o caló* or Chicano/Mexicano Spanish without resistance. Four years before Sánchez-Albornoz would commemorate the Quincentenary by projecting his image of linguistic democracy in America as a type of productive "Hispanic" legacy of the Conquest to be celebrated in 1992, these Chicanas/os had proven him wrong through this protest, which signaled the existence of unequal access to one's own voice and culture in the *Américas*.[41] They would prove him wrong again, along with other indigenous resisters who, on 12 October 1992, wrote "No Colón" in various indigenous languages, disputing the widespread claims of a univocal form of expression defended by the proponents of the Colón-ialista narrative.

What worked against consent to the Colón-ialista narrative at the university in January of 1990 and in the nation's streets in October 1992 was the resisters' exposing of the discrepancy between this dominant Spanish ideology and their social experience and location. This provided the "keywords" with which to unravel the master's narrative, allowing other kinds of readings as well.[42] This kind of critical literacy can be fortified through an examination of how their experiences are implicated in the changing vectors of power that grace transnational relations between global cultures in the nineties. Thus it becomes possible to see the connection between this type of media knowledge and the one we experienced in English, which centered Colón within a Hollywood pantheon of loved movie stars and placed him at the center of national identity through parades, televisual encounters, and the government's blessings.

Television accounts of the controversy often read like a replay of the Conquest, with their images of the voyage to *América*, the pope's journey to

Santo Domingo, Colón's boatlike resting place lighting up the profile of a cross that bordered the shacks of *la gente*/the poor people, the forces of resistance: the modern *indigenista* resisters in San Francisco and Santo Domingo, the combat with the police (the modern conquistadores?). The shifting camera angles take us from here to there (Santo Domingo) and back again.

Thus the spectacle of the Conquest was replayed on 12 October 1992 through a reinscription of fully contested identities within an electronic dramatization of "the original journey." Their political and ideological distances were not blurred with voiced-over news broadcasts, print-media interpretations, and news specials that proposed a multicultural solution that both interpretations were valid and that a "neutral" balance was being furnished by simply telling *both* sides of the story. Instead, televisual images revealed a show of contested might: police on horseback, a display of national legitimacy, what some might call a "mini" *encontronazo*/crash, *conquista*/conquest on the streets of San Francisco that sealed the desired national identity and an Anglo/Hispanic romance with conquest. At the same time, the voices of the protesters seeking recognition of the land, an alternative tradition, and urging the pope to "go home" would not be silenced in this fully engaged struggle over the right to representation within the nation's founding identity narrative.

Whether in English or in Spanish, the state-generated Colón-ialista narrative seeks to redomesticate and silence those who do not call themselves Colón, those who do not call him their *papá*/father, and those who dare call themselves someone else. The Colón narrative locates us in discursive locations that are not ours, that are not home although they are reproduced here, and that seek to evict us from a truly egalitarian multicultural *encuentro*/encounter. It behooves us to define our positionalities with respect to the Colón narrative. Otherwise we might end up dreaming someone else's *sueño americano*/American dream, more appropriately, someone else's American nightmare. José Montoya, a movement poet, referred to this as "the Yankee nightmare"/"la pesadilla yanqui," and the students who protested against hispanization at UC Davis referred to this as "the Spanish nightmare/"la pesadilla española."

This definition also entails recognizing the silencing of the other gender in the gendered constructions of Colón, 1492–1992, and *his América*. The Colón-ialista narrative provides an unprecedented space for this type of examination, for it is *he* who is the essential subject of not one, but five centuries. As the emblematic figure of Old World and New World masculinity, *he* has had the task of embodying and configuring U.S. national identity, something that is unheard of for other underrepresented males who find themselves at the margin/*al margen* of this type of "unequal opportunity." For those of us who call ourselves Chicanas, those who choose to narrate her-story, the *mujer*/woman's story, the Colón-ialista narrative, which inscribes *his* body as the space for national identification, offers even greater levels of violence. Perhaps that is why it is *our* bodies (the young woman assassin who takes charge and kills Colón in the film *The Trial of Christopher Columbus*, for instance)[43] that so often light the match that fuels the flame of resistance to *His*panism—the construction of *his día*/day, *his lengua* (tongue/language), *his* subject, and *his* body/*cuerpo*.

Notes

1. I dedicate this essay to all of those students who valiantly stood up and fought for the rights of Chicana/o Latina/o speakers of Spanish and for equal representation of Chicana/o literature within the Spanish curriculum at the University of California, Davis. I would also like to acknowledge my friend and brother Richard, my compañero Zaré Juan, and my dear colegas Vicki, Mike, and María for their powerful support and wonderful humor during this protracted struggle, which taught me more about the politics of location than I could ever have learned from textual renditions of cultural theories and subjects. Coverage of this struggle spanned several issues of the student newspaper at UC Davis, The *Third World Forum*, from 1990 to 1992.

2. I have taken this idea from Stuart Hall, "Cultural Identity and Cinematic Representation," *Frame Works* 36 (1989): 70.

3. Counter Colón-ialismo is an exhibit that addresses the "Quincentenary of America, the 500 year anniversary of Columbus' (Colón's) discovery of America," according to the brochure announcing the events featured therein. The exhibit was curated by Patricio Chávez, Liz Lerma, and Sylvia Orosco. In the book *Counter Colón-ialismo* (San Diego: Centro Cultural de la Raza, 1991), the curatorial staff elaborates: "The word 'Colón' is also the root of colonialism, colony, colonial, colonist, and colonize. The word colonialism refers to the policy of one nation which seeks to control and dominate the peoples and resources of another nation. Thus the play on words. And the word 'counter' describes our perspective or approach to the concept of colonization or colonialismo" (1).

4. Raymond Williams coined the term "selective tradition" in *Problems in Materialism and Culture* (London: Verso, 1980), 39.

5. For an excellent rendition of this topic, see Michel-Rolph Trouillot, "Good Day Columbus: Silences, Power and Public History (1492–1892)," *Public Culture* 3:1 (fall 1990): 4–20.

6. Ibid., 3.

7. I do not mean to suggest that Trouillot effects this type of strategy in his essay, but rather I caution against the mechanistic application of his arguments in 1992 without the necessary qualifications.

8. John Fiske, "British Cultural Studies and Television," in *Channels of Discourse*, ed. Robert C. Allen (Chapel Hill: University of North Carolina Press, 1987), 260.

9. Although *Hispanidad* is normally associated with the Spanish-speaking American republics and the different groups residing in these countries, this identity is also related to the term "Hispanic." As Jack Forbes explains, the concept of Hispanic means "Spanish" or "Spanish-derived." He later elaborates: "The use of Hispanic or Spanish-origin categories achieves the end of continuing to empower white Spanish-speaking elites at the expense of people of mes-

tizo, Indian, and African origin and of masking the hierarchical, color-ranked class structure and racial ethnic diversity within the Spanish-speaking and Latin American origin populations." See Jack Forbes, "The Hispanic Spin," *Latin American Perspectives* 19:4 (1992): 59–78; 65.

10. As I point out later, the Conquest becomes a contemporary sign for civilization: multiculturalism and a kind of ideal laboratory for the successful diffusion of the Spanish language.

11. These quotes referring to the interview are taken from the Félix Monteira's "Entrevista con Luis Yáñez," *El País*, 12 October 1992: 14. These and all other quotes from Spanish-language newspapers are my translations of the original versions.

12. This line of thinking appears in an editorial piece, "Octubre del 92," following a list of editors, headed by Jesús de Polanco, which reads: "La celebración del V Centenario, del que la Expo ha sido el buque insignia, constituiría un fiasco si no siriviera para reforzar los elementos integradores, a uno y otro lado del Atlántico, de la *aventura* del Descubrimiento, El Día de la Humanidad… A cinco siglos de distancia, no es el modelo de conquista ni de colonización lo que se reinvindica, sino la significación histórica de unos episodios que supusieron el más importante esfuerzo de proyección exterior de los españoles y sin los que sería ininteligible la historia moderna" (*El País*, 12 October 1992: 10). In the typical doublespeak of this narrative, Polanco goes on to state that to celebrate the five hundred years is to celebrate the unfolding of a "project of *civilization* that is shared beween Spain and the Latin American countries." Like many of his contemporaries, he describes the events surrounding 1492-1992 as an adventure story, as a national holiday, reminiscent of our fourth of July.

13. Fernando Orgámbides reported in *El País* that several popular organizations protested the visit of the pope to Santo Domingo, asking him to condem the extermination of Indians that took place during and after the Conquest. As the article reads, the pope avoided the controversy, which mushroomed into a series of street protests, by stating that his mission was "to give thanks to God for these five hundred years of evangelization" and for the "message of salvation to this continent" ("El papa evita la polémica sobre el V Centenario," *El País*, 13 October 1992: 14).

14. "El Rey reclama en Sevilla una mayor integración con Iberoamérica," *El País*, 12 October 1992: 15.

15. For an account of this see "Cuarenta arrestados en Barcelona tras los actos del Doce de Octubre," *El País*, 13 October 1992: 19. According to these reports, those who favored and disputed the five hundred-year celebration clashed in Barcelona. In Sevilla, Spanish youths protested in front of the Expo exhibit, while in Tlavera de la Reina, the committee in solidarity with Latin America dedicated a mural with the words: "500 years of Indigenous and Popular Resistance."

16. The Mexican-Chicana/o word for T-shirt.

17. This description was inspired by José Miguel Oviedo, who characterized the Conquest as "una herida abierta de la cual sigue manando sangre." See "La Conquista, 500 años después," *El País*, 13 October 1992: 18.

18. Javier Solana, "V Centenario, un proyecto cumplido," *El País,* 12 October 1992: 16.

19. Monteira, "Entrevista con Luis Yáñez." The "Octubre del 92" editorial, from the same issue, also incorporates the idea of the Quincentenary as flagship.

20. Ibid.

21. I am influenced here by Stuart Hall's reading of Africa in his essay "Cultural Identity and Cinematic Representation."

22. These translated summaries are taken from "Marchas, festejos y contrafestejos caracterizan el 'Día de la Raza' en los países latinoamericanos," *La Opinión*, 13 October 1992: 7A; "Confusión y controversia por Colón," *La Opinión,* 12 October 1992: 10A; and Robert Lindo, "Contracelebración en la UCLA, entre danzas y cánticos," *La Opinión*, 13 October 1992: 1A.

23. The Colectivo Quijano offered a critique of this type of altruism in its editorial "América

Latina y nosotros" (*El País*, 12 October 1992: 12), where it proposes that the Spanish public abandon and reject a pejorative attitude toward Latin Americans, who are often referred to as "sudacas" and are marginalized and disempowered in Spain today.

24. Nicolás Sánchez-Albornoz summarizes the prevailing sentiment in his editorial "500 años" (*La Opinión*, 12 October 1992: 11), where he emphasizes the perdurability of the Spanish language, noting that it has not lost its prestige in the world with political decline (the independence of the Spanish-speaking Americans, Indians, etc.) but rather fortified itself, leaving behind the indigenous languages. What would Sánchez-Albornoz make of the mushrooming of indigenous dialects through Mexico into the United States that now promises a mixture with Chicana/o Spanish and caló (a youth argot popularized by *pachuchos* and a dialect of Chicana/o Spanish)? This decline of indigenous languages is disputed in another editorial entitled "1492–1992" (*La Opinión*, 12 October 1992), where Ignacio Lozano Jr. and his editorial group suggest that "Cinco siglos de opresión no han logrado, sin embargo, aniquilar a estos pueblos aborígenes. Su reclamo de una identidad propia e inconfundible se hace sentir hoy más que nunca" (11A).

25. Oviedo, "La Conquista, 500 años después."

26. Oviedo appears to be suggesting that multiculturalism did not exist prior to the Conquest, that the Indians were culturally and linguistically the same.

27. Suffice it to say that this notion has been disputed by those *indigenistas* who neither consider themselves to be fused nor to be participants in mestizo cultures or ethnicities.

28. Oviedo, "La Conquista, 500 años después"; italics mine.

29. We can only presume that strands of Native American and indigenous cultures are expressed at the periphery of this construct, although they are not named.

30. I draw these parenthetical comments in order to distinguish between the Colón-ialista narrative that is being reinscribed in this editorial and the plurality of Us's who resist incorporation into such a narrative and its colonial subjectivity in 1992. Italics are mine—they indicate an unfortunate complicity with the old-style colonial discourse.

31. Oviedo, "La Conquista, 500 años después."

32. See, for example, the editorial "500 años," where Sánchez-Albornoz uses Latin American and Caribbean immigration into the United States and its diversifying effect as proof of the widespread dominion and supremacy of the Spanish language as a by-product of the legacy of 1492. Suffice it to say that for Sánchez-Albornoz, this type of construction is not contested by Chicanas/os and other indigenous peoples.

33. This type of national construction has been under attack for years within Spain itself by a number of subordinated groups protesting linguistic, cultural, and political discrimination, with the Basques being the most militant in their opposition to Spanish hegemony. Unfortunately, traditional Spanish language departments, which reinscribe a fictive Spanish center that neutralizes contestation by marginalized cultures in Spain, have worked against the formation of strategic alliances across the Atlantic between subaltern groups on both sides.

34. For an account of the changing image of Columbus, see Trouillot's "Good Day Columbus."

35. It would be important to review this type of linguistic contestation from transnational perspectives, including a comparative analysis of how this resistance is constructed across the national borders of Spain and the American republics and into the United States.

36. Elisabeth Sherwin, "Change Advised in the Spanish Curriculum," *Davis Enterprise*, 15 March 1990: 1.

37. Ibid.

38. Lorena Natt, "U.S. Probes Alleged UCD Hispanic Bias," *Sacramento Bee*, 14 March 1990: 2. The Federal Office of Civil Rights launched its own investigation into allegations of discrimination against Chicana/o Latina/o students. The investigation took into account incidents of

screening by skin color of students who protested against being unfairly singled out in Spanish classes, according to the Trueba Report. Other newspaper reports, including those provided by the student newspaper *Third World Forum*, also included student discontent over being arbitrarily sent to *special* "native speaker classes" because of their Chicano/Mexican/Latin American dialects.

39. Louie the Foot, "Cortés Nos Chingó in a Big Way the Huey," *Festival Flor y Canto*, vols. 4 and 5 (Albuquerque, N.M.: Pajarito Publications, 1980): 95.

40. It is precisely because of the association of the name of the language—Spanish—with the name of the colonizing, ethnic group associated with the Conquest that many Chicanas/os are beginning to rethink the naming of their linguistic expression. In order to avoid these linkages between one's voice and the inscription of a colonial subject, Chicanas/os are exploring ways of engaging the multiplicity of their *lenguas*/languages in order to avoid the narrow nationalistic denominations associated with singular renditions that compartmentalize their hybrid voices.

41. Sánchez-Albornoz argues against those whom he views as proposing that Spanish has degenerated into national languages. He argues: "Los lingüistas conocen, en cambio la existencia de una koiné en la que participan en igualdad de derechos todos los usarios de español." His entire essay is aimed at reinforcing the idea of a linguistic system in which satellite and metropolis enjoy the same linguistic capital regardless of historical circumstances.

42. I have borrowed the term "keywords" from Raymond Williams, *Keywords* (New York: Oxford University Press, 1983).

43. This film was produced by Lourdes Portillo and stars Xochtil Peralta, a Chicana actress, as the successful Colón resister.

References

Chávez, Patricio, Liz Lerma, and Sylvia Orosco. *Counter Colón-ialismo*. San Diego: Centro Cultural de la Raza, 1991.
Colectivo Quijano. "América Latina y nosotros." *El País,* 12 October 1992.
"Confusión y controversia por Colón." *La Opinión,* 12 October 1992.
"Cuarenta arrestados en Barcelona tras los actos del Doce de Octubre." *El País,* 13 October 1992.
"El Rey reclama en Sevilla una mayor integración con Iberoamérica." *El País,* 12 October 1992.
Fiske, John. "British Cultural Studies and Television." In *Channels of Discourse,* ed. Robert C. Allen. Chapel Hill: University of North Carolina Press, 1987. 254–90.
Forbes, Jack. "The Hispanic Spin." *Latin American Perspectives* 19:4 (fall 1992): 59–78.
Hall, Stuart. "Cultural Identity and Cinematic Representation." *Frame Works* 36 (1989): 68–81.
Lindo, Robert. "Contracelebración en UCLA, entre danzas y cánticos." *La Opinión,* 13 October 1992.
Louie the Foot. "Cortés Nos Chingó in a Big Way the Huey." *Festival Flor y Canto*, vols. 4 and 5. Albuquerque, N.M.: Pajarito Publications, 1980.
Lozano, Ignacio, Jr., et al. "1492–1992." *La Opinión,* 11 October 1992.
"Marchas, festejos y contrafestejos caracterizan el 'Día de la Raza' en los países latinoamericanos." *La Opinión,* 13 October 1992.
Monteira, Félix. "Entrevista con Luis Yáñez." *El País,* 12 October 1992.
Natt, Lorena. "U.S. Probes Alleged UCD Hispanic Bias." *Sacramento Bee,* 14 March 1992.
Orgámbides, Fernando. "El papa evita la polémica sobre el V Centenario." *El País,* 13 October 1992.
Oviedo, José Miguel. "La Conquista, 500 años después." *El País,* 13 October 1992.
Polanco, Jesús, et al. "Octubre del 92." *El País,* 12 October 1992.
Sánchez-Albornoz, Nicolás. "500 años." *La Opinión,* 12 October 1992.

Sherwin, Elisabeth. "Change Advised in the Spanish Curriculum." *Davis Enterprise*, 15 March 1990.

Solana, Javier. "V Centenario, un proyecto cumplido." *El País,* 12 October 1992.

Trouillot, Michel-Rolph. "Good Day Columbus: Silences, Power and Public History (1492–1892)." *Public Culture* 3:1 (fall 1990): 1-24.

Williams, Raymond. *Keywords.* New York: Oxford University Press, 1983.

———. *Problems in Materialism and Culture.* London: Verso, 1980.

CHAPTER FIFTEEN

Multiculturalism and Racial Stratification

NEIL GOTANDA

Overlooked by much of the national media in its coverage of the 1992 Los Angeles civil disturbances was the case of *People v. Soon Ja Du.*[1] The trial of Du Soon Ja[2] for the grocery-store shooting of fifteen-year-old Latasha Harlins has helped to define subsequent relations between Asian Americans and African Americans.

Crucial to understanding the role of the courts in this incident is the statement of the judge that accompanied her pronouncement of sentence. Instead of their stated goal of reducing tensions, I will argue that the judge's culturally coded comments show how institutions like the judicial system may manage "minority-minority" conflict.

Du Soon Ja, a fifty-one-year-old Korean immigrant mother and store owner, shot and killed a fifteen-year-old African-American girl in a dispute and fight over a bottle of orange juice. Coming after a national series of incidents involving Korean grocers in African-American neighborhoods, the case was followed closely in the press.

After a tense jury trial marked by demonstrations and courtroom outbursts, Du was convicted of voluntary manslaughter. Attention then focused on the sentence of newly appointed Los Angeles Superior Court Judge Joyce A. Karlin. Karlin was widely expected to sentence Du to prison time, with most speculation centering on the length of the sentence. However, instead of a prison sentence, Karlin sentenced Du to probation with prison time suspended, a small fine, and a requirement of community service.[3] Judge Karlin immediately became a center of controversy because the sentence was regarded as far too lenient. Many critics accused her of being at best insensitive, and at worst racist.[4] The Los Angeles County district attorney appealed the sentence, but the California Court of Appeal affirmed the decision.[5]

The statement explaining a sentence is referred to as a sentencing colloquy. I will use Karlin's short sentencing colloquy (reproduced at the end of this essay) as a text—interpreting her language to illustrate the hidden assumptions and implications in her statement and sentence.

Recognition and use of the idea of culture are sometimes offered as a positive alternative to the reenshrinement of racial subordination that comes with the repetition of traditional racial usages. The colloquy reveals how multicultural techniques can function to maintain the centerpiece of the old racial order—White privilege. As the racial, ethnic, and cultural complexities of Los Angeles continue to develop, this case illuminates some of the ongoing rearrangements of race, culture, subordination, and power.

Karlin's Multiculturalism

Karlin makes extensive use of particular culturally specific characterizations. The defendant Du is portrayed as a good mother and wife, as a hardworking shopkeeper, as an innocent victim of circumstance acting in self-defense. The real victim, Latasha Harlins, is presented as a criminal shoplifter, as aggressive and violent, as associated with gangs. These portrayals are woven together from fact and speculation and extend existing racial stereotypes.

Judge Karlin structures the sentencing colloquy in a way that illustrates her adherence to the color-blind technique. Karlin specifically recognizes the African-American and Korean communities in the opening and closing paragraphs of the colloquy (¶ 1–2, 41).[6] In her actual sentencing comments, however, Karlin makes no explicit reference to Koreans or African Americans.

Thus, the judge does not make specific reference to Black, African-American, Korean, or Asian in the main body of the colloquy. Instead, it is the use of the cultural characteristics themselves that emphasizes and circumscribes the contrasting groups—Korean and African-American. Links to Koreans and African Americans are made in prefatory and concluding comments. The crucial racial connections lie in the background understanding that these individuals are representatives of communities in conflict.

The use of cultural markers and the avoidance of the Korean and African-

American labels are of particular importance in the legal context. Avoidance of racial or ethnic labels is supportive of the doctrine of constitutional color blindness. Under that ideology, any consideration of race in governmental decision making is either questionable or unconstitutional.[7]

Karlin's use of multicultural markers goes beyond the traditional legal prescription for color blindness. Instead of a judicial fiat that race shall not be taken into consideration in her deliberations, Karlin uses the various cultural attributes and stereotypes as a multicultural alternative to race. Her implicit adoption of these cultural markers as a substitute for race validates the significance of the cultural stereotypes she employs.

The specific content of these stereotypes and cultural attributes is also of significance. Within the boundaries of the cultural markers that substitute for race and ethnicity, Karlin utilizes attributes that differ from traditional Black-White racial subordination. Instead of a model that emphasizes the subordinate position of *all* racial and ethnic minorities, Karlin creates a tiered, hierarchical structure *between* minorities. The cultural attributes of defendant Du are favorable, and portray a sympathetic, Korean "model minority." Placed in opposition is the more familiar cruel stereotype of African American as criminal and gang member.

The difference in this context is that the African-American minority is not judged against the majority society. Rather, the African-American minority is measured against and therefore "monitored" by the Korean minority. The Korean "model minority" is thus the measure of the African-American "monitored minority."

Implicit also is the idea that "monitored" and "model" racial minorities are subordinate to an "invisible majority." That invisible majority is, I believe, the White majority and its position of White racial privilege.

Judge Karlin's Sentencing Colloquy

In this section, my examination of the text of Judge Karlin's colloquy shows how Karlin sympathizes with Du and presents the victim Latasha Harlins in a harsh and unfavorable light. These contrasting portrayals are presented by associating Du and Harlins with various culturally based racial stereotypes.

The individualized racial characterizations of Du coincide with and reproduce the image and structure of Koreans and Asian Americans as a "model minority." Karlin emphasizes Du's "model minority" status by portraying her as an "innocent shopkeeper." Karlin does not articulate, but understands, and expects others to understand, that Du is a Korean shopkeeper. Du Soon Ja is a representative successful shopkeeper and, by implication, the Korean community is a successful "model minority."

Latasha Harlins is portrayed as a criminal and associated with gangs and gang violence. Judge Karlin emphasizes the "monitored minority" aspect of Harlins by improperly balancing Du against Harlins. In the traditional approach to sentencing, valuation of the "worth" of the victim is only one among many considerations. Judge Karlin, however, makes constant comparisons between the two throughout the colloquy. This use of Du as the "model" against which the victim Harlins is measured emphasizes the monitoring dimension to Karlin's social hierarchy.

Karlin describes Du as a fifty-one-year-old woman who is a victim of circumstances (¶ 29), including gang terror (¶ 29, 33), and a gun altered by unknown thieves (¶ 29). Further, Du was present on the day of the killing only because of her maternal loyalty to her son (¶ 33–34), to shield her son from the repeated robberies (¶ 33) and "to save him one day of fear" (¶ 34). And Karlin is generally sympathetic to the hardships faced by innocent shopkeepers who are under frequent attack (¶ 24–36).

Judge Karlin portrays defendant Du as an innocent victim. In the colloquy, Du is a hard worker and has no criminal record (¶ 19). Gangs terrorize Du's family while they operate the store (¶ 29–33). The actual killing was the result of the assault by Harlins upon Du (¶ 38) and the modification of the revolver by unknown thieves who had rendered the revolver "defective" (¶ 29, 32).[8]

Harlins is described as having likely committed a criminal assault upon Du (¶ 26–29) after an act of shoplifting (¶ 25). Harlins is an example of shoplifters who attack shopkeepers after being caught in the act (¶ 24–26). Further, Karlin associates Harlins with gang theft and terror (¶ 33); Harlins is the person who caused Du to commit a criminal act when Du had previously led a crime-free life (¶ 38).

Judge Karlin also stereotypes Harlins through continued references to gangs and gang terror. These references to gangs are not an allegation that Harlins was herself a gang member. Judge Karlin connects "gangness" with African Americans, ignoring the widespread presence of gangs comprised largely of Asians. Karlin emphasizes her appreciation of "gangness" by using the word "terror" three times in her colloquy: "victimized and terrorized by gang members" (¶ 29); "the very real terror experienced by the Du family" (¶ 33); "repeated robberies and terrorism in the same store" (¶ 33).

Judge Karlin's omission of any humanizing information about Harlins works to demonize her. Karlin might have done well to note a number of facts related by the court of appeal about Latasha Harlins:

> The probation report also reveals that Latasha had suffered many painful experiences during her life, including the violent death of her mother. Latasha lived with her extended family (her grandmother, younger brother and sister, aunt, uncle and niece) in what the probation officer described as "a clean, attractively furnished three-bedroom apartment" in South Central Los Angeles. Latasha had been an honor student at Bret Harte Junior High School, from which she had graduated the previous spring. Although she was making only average grades in high school, she had promised that she would bring her grades up to her former standard. Latasha was involved in activities at a youth center as an assistant cheerleader, member of the drill team and a summer junior camp counselor. She was a good athlete and an active church member.[9]

Another significant dimension of Karlin's "humanizing" of Du and "demonizing" of Harlins occurs in the question of *punishment*. Karlin omits any direct consideration of punishment. Instead, Karlin *balances* Harlins against Du, African American against Asian American.[10]

First, Karlin balances Du against Harlins by noting that in determining whether probation is appropriate, she must determine "the *vulnerability of the victim*" (¶ 23). Although the issue of vulnerability is in theory applicable only to the *victim*, Karlin proceeds to apply it to both Harlins *and* Du. Because Harlins "used her fists as weapons," Karlin declares that she was not vulnerable. Karlin does not mention the fact that Du shot Harlins in the *back* of the head, which demonstrates that Harlins was "vulnerable" to an attack by Du. Karlin follows this with a non sequitur implying that Harlins was not vulnerable because she was an accused shoplifter and therefore had not been justified in her assault upon Du (¶ 24–25). In contrast, Karlin describes Du's situation sympathetically: shopkeepers like Du seem unable even to accuse customers of shoplifting without fear of being assaulted.

Second, Karlin states that under the statute she is to consider "criminal sophistication" in deciding the propriety of probation. Although the consideration is meant to apply to the criminal sophistication of the *defendant*, Karlin ultimately balances Harlins's criminality against Du's criminal sophistication against the victim's alleged criminality (¶ 27). Karlin describes Du as lacking "any degree of criminal sophistication in her offense," as a woman "who would not be here today" but for "unusual circumstances" (¶ 28–29). Judge Karlin believes that Harlins, on the other hand, would have had charges filed against her had she "not been shot" and had the "incident which preceded the shooting been reported" (¶ 26).

Karlin further reinforces her social hierarchy through the use of gendered images of Du and Harlins. Du is portrayed as a good wife—loyally working in the family store. She is even more dramatically portrayed as a good mother—volunteering to work in the store to protect her son. Karlin also focuses attention on Du Soon Ja's status as spouse and wife by never directly mentioning Du's husband. There are references to Du's family and her son, but her husband is omitted. The context for these images is the traditional stereotype of the family as a strength of Asian cultures.

By contrast, any of the available positive gendered images of Harlins as dutiful daughter, church member, and student are ignored and she is portrayed as a criminal. This contrast between Du and Harlins reinforces the social hierarchy through the greater social distance from Judge Karlin—a female lawgiver.

The Model Minority

In this section, I argue that Karlin's racial characterizations of Du and Harlins are more than a by-product of Judge Karlin's personal sympathy or antipathy toward the two individuals. Karlin's racial stereotypes involve a racial map that includes more than just Du and Harlins as representative of Asian American and African American. By differentially distancing herself from Du and Harlins, she is producing a three-tier racial hierarchy that reinforces an existing set of stereotyped images.

The change from older stereotypes to the "model minority" can be seen by describing some of the older images that evolved in the early twentieth century and that have been only partly superseded today. At least one author has speculated on the connection between Edward Said's development of the complex construction of Oriental "otherness" to Europe and the West.[11] John Kuo Wei Tchen argues that British authors Sax Rohmer, creator of Fu Manchu in 1911, and Thomas Burke, author of "Limehouse Nights," set in the opium dens and shabby corners of London's small Chinese quarter, were themselves Orientalists, engaged in constructing racialized images of Chinese that would define American and British identity.[12]

As examples of demeaning stereotypes, Tchen points to Rohmer's Fu Manchu as embodying "evil incarnate," to caricatures of Chinese laundrymen who appeared as comic relief in early films, and to Sessue Hayakawa as an enslaving Japanese antique dealer in Cecil B. DeMille's 1915 film *The Cheat*. The images are not, however, uniform in their attitudes. Tchen examines D. W. Griffith's 1919 film *Broken Blossoms* and finds that Griffith "es-

chews the standard stereotype of the 'heathen Chinee' already well established in the previous century, and adapts the alternative image of the hardworking, good-for-the-West 'John Chinaman.'"[13]

A much more unrelentingly harsh set of images is seen in John Dower's
examination of the mutually hostile propaganda campaigns of Japan and
the United States throughout World War II, *War without Mercy*. During
the war, "yellow hordes" of Japanese were portrayed as apes, monkeys, and
insects.

These images constituted the collective set of stereotypes and constructed identities of Asian Americans, accumulated over a century of U.S.
Asian immigration. The transformation of the Asian American from the
"heathen Chinee" and the "yellow horde" into a "model minority" has been
dramatic and rapid.

The sharp change began in the mid-1960s with the appearance of several
articles in major national news media commenting favorably on the success
of the Asian Americans, at that time mostly second- and third-generation
Japanese and Chinese Americans.[14] Especially noteworthy was a 1966 *New
York Times Magazine* article entitled "Success Story: Japanese American
Style."[15] Those early articles, however, emphasized overcoming adversity,
rather than focusing on their economic success.

In the past decade the stereotype has shifted to emphasize economic
success based on an extremely aggressive work ethic and strong family
cohesion. Lisa Lowe has described the model-minority myth as including
the image of Asians as "aggressively driven overachievers" who "assimilate
well."[16] This version of the "model minority" places Asian Americans in a
reasonably well-to-do class position vis-à-vis other minorities, especially
African Americans.

In the modern context, the image of the Korean grocery-store owner has
become the dominant media image of an Asian American.[17] Sales transactions between Korean grocers and African-American patrons are now exemplary of all social interaction between Asians and African Americans, and
the actions of Korean grocers are exemplary of all Asian-American cultures.

The racial stratification provided by the "model minority" thus provides
Judge Karlin with an ideological framework both to distance herself from
Latasha Harlins individually and to absolve non-Blacks generally, especially
those in the highest tier of the three-tiered system of the "model minority,"
of any social responsibility for the effects of racial subordination on African
Americans.

Conclusion

In conclusion, I offer some questions and suggestions for further exploration. One group of questions concerns the use of cultural forms to create ideological constructions like the "model minority." Another surrounds the difficulty of a racial analysis of Asian Americans and the troubling implications for political coalition.

Karlin's colloquy both reflects the myth of the "model minority" and advances it by providing greater specificity. Karlin ascribes to a Korean grocer a certain class privilege (shopkeeper status), higher social status (strong family), and high moral worth (law-abiding). These are balanced against the demonized Latasha Harlins, who lacks them. The result is that Korean Americans—and, by implication, Asian Americans—are defined by this short list and the resulting narrow stereotype. Omitted is any sense of personal or social history, community or real family life, religion or spirituality, all of which would be part of any historically textured description of Asian Americans.

This entire effort took place in the midst of a now familiar media circus, with full broadcast and print-media coverage. Karlin's efforts were therefore not limited to the courtroom or even to traditional legal texts, but became part of our everyday popular cultural discourse.

Work on the slippery terrain of popular culture and mass media is always difficult. Hampering efforts have been the near-total absence of academic and popular studies of the representation of Asian Americans.[18] Presenting the varied and broad range of experiences encompassed by persons of Asian ancestry in America while combating both model-minority and yellow-peril stereotyping will require a depth of understanding and analysis that is only now emerging.

Perhaps even more difficult is the question of the depth of reality behind the "model minority." If one accepts that there really is a privileging of Asian Americans and that the "model minority" is not simply a fabricated illusion, then an examination of the racial status of Asian Americans in a multiracial model becomes intensely complex.

If one takes the position that "Asians have problems, just like African Americans," then one is implicitly using an analytical framework that says the racial status of Asian Americans is identical to that of African Americans—both are subordinated by Whites. This two-category (White/non-White) framework suggests that the only "real" differences between Asian

Americans and African Americans are minor variations in culture and economic achievement.

If, however, Asian Americans are coming to occupy a class position between Whites and African Americans, then a different analysis is needed. A further exploration of Asian-American as an intermediate racial category would examine whether or not social and economic privileges attach to those persons classified as Asian-American. For example, in economic relations, research could determine whether real property values declined when an Asian American integrated a formerly all-White neighborhood. One could compare whether the decline in values, and any associated racial "tipping," was more severe for African Americans than Asian Americans. An analysis of social attitudes might also reveal a differential between African Americans and Asian Americans around such issues as crime and morality. Similar studies could be carried out in other areas such as income, job discrimination, and portrayals in popular culture.

Recognizing that there is some truth in the "myth of the model minority" seems to me a better starting point for examining whether there is an emerging Asian-American racial category. The difficulty comes in attempting to situate this racial category without succumbing to the "model minority" stereotype. On the one hand, if a real class privilege is emerging for Asian Americans, then long term political coalitions cannot turn on simple calls for recognizing a common history of racial oppression by a White majority. Instead, one must explore more carefully the deeply intertwined issues of class and group privilege to explore where one can find both short- and long-term common interests.

What should not be forgotten amidst these complexities, however, is that interracial and interethnic conflict cannot be divorced from the broader American historical context of racial subordination. One of the historical axes of social subordination in America has been White privileging over African Americans. Even as the possibilities of racial stratification and the embedded ideological constructions of Orientalism are examined, awareness of the continuation of that basic axis of power and privilege must continue.

Sentencing Colloquy

Los Angeles Daily Journal, 22 November 1991: 7: a transcript of remarks by Los Angeles Superior Court Judge Joyce A. Karlin in the sentencing of Soon Ja Du.

[¶ 1] One thing I think both sides will agree on is that nothing I can do, nothing the judicial system can do, nothing will lessen the loss suffered by Latasha Harlins' family and friends. But the parties involved in this case and anyone truly interested in what caused this case can make sure that something positive comes out of this tragedy by having Latasha Harlins' death mark a beginning rather than an end—a beginning of a greater understanding and acceptance between two groups, some of whose members have until now demonstrated intolerance and bigotry toward one another.

[¶ 2] Latasha's death should be a catalyst to force members of the African American and Korean communities to confront an intolerable situation by creating constructive solutions. Through that process, a greater understanding and acceptance will hopefully result so that similar tragedies will not be repeated.

[¶ 3] Statements by the district attorney, (which) suggest that imposing less than the maximum sentence will send a message that a black child's life is not worthy of protection, (are) dangerous rhetoric, which serves no purpose other than to pour gasoline on a fire.

[¶ 4] This is not a time for revenge, and my job is not to exact revenge for those who demand it.

[¶ 5] There are those in this community who have publicly demanded in the name of justice that the maximum sentence be imposed in this case.

[¶ 6] But it is my opinion that justice is never served when public opinion, prejudice, revenge or unwarranted sympathy are considered by a sentencing court in resolving a case.

[¶ 7] In imposing sentence I must first consider the objectives of sentencing a defendant:

1) To protect society.
2) To punish the defendant for committing a crime.
3) To encourage the defendant to lead a law-abiding life.
4) To deter others.
5) To isolate the defendant so she can't commit other crimes.
6) To secure restitution for the victim.
7) To seek uniformity in sentencing.

[¶ 8] The question becomes, are any of these sentencing objectives achieved by Mrs. Du being remanded to state prison?

[¶ 9] Let us start with the last objective first: uniformity in sentencing. According to statistics gathered for the Superior Courts of California, sentences imposed on defendants convicted of voluntary manslaughter last year ranged from probation with no jail time to incarceration in state prison for several years.

[¶ 10] Because of the unique nature of each crime of voluntary manslaughter, and by that I mean the uniquely different factual situations resulting in that crime, uniformity in sentencing is virtually impossible to achieve.

[¶ 11] Which, then, of the other sentencing objectives lead to the conclusion that state prison is warranted?

[¶ 12] Does society need Mrs. Du to be incarcerated in order to be protected? I think not.

[¶ 13] Is state prison needed in order to encourage the defendant to lead a law-abiding life or isolate her so she cannot commit other crimes? I think not.

[¶ 14] Is state prison needed to punish Mrs. Du? Perhaps.

[¶ 15] There is, in this case, a presumption against probation because a firearm was used.

[¶ 16] In order to overcome that presumption, the court must find this to be an unusual case, as that term is defined by law.

[¶ 17] There are three reasons that I find this is an unusual case:

[¶ 18] First, the basis for the presumption against probation is technically present. But it doesn't really apply. The statute is aimed at criminals who arm themselves when they go out and commit other crimes. It is not aimed at shopkeepers who lawfully possess firearms for their own protection.

[¶ 19] Second, the defendant has no recent record, in fact, no record at any time of committing similar crimes or crimes of violence.

[¶ 20] Third, the defendant participated in the crime under circumstances of great provocation, coercion and duress. Therefore, this is, in my opinion, an unusual case that overcomes the statutory presumption against probation.

[¶ 21] Should the defendant be placed on probation?

[¶ 22] One of the questions a sentencing court is required to ask in answering that question is "whether the crime was committed because of unusual circumstances, such as great provocation." I find that it was.

[¶ 23] I must also determine the vulnerability of the victim in deciding whether probation is appropriate. Although Latasha Harlins was not armed with a weapon at the time of her death, she had used her fists as weapons just seconds before she was shot.

[¶ 24] The district attorney argues that Latasha was justified in her assault on Mrs. Du. Our courts are filled with cases which suggest otherwise.

[¶ 25] Our courts are filled with defendants who are charged with assault resulting in great bodily injury as a result of attacks on shopkeepers, including shopkeepers who have accused them of shoplifting.

[¶ 26] Had Latasha Harlins not been shot and had the incident which preceded the shooting been reported, it is my opinion that the district attorney would have relied on the videotape and Mrs. Du's testimony to make a determination whether to file charges against Latasha.

[¶ 27] Other questions I am required to address in determining whether probation is appropriate are "whether the carrying out of the crime suggested criminal sophistication and whether the defendant will be a danger to others if she is not imprisoned."

[¶ 28] Having observed Mrs. Du on videotape at the time the crime was committed and having observed Mrs. Du during this trial, I cannot conclude that there was any degree of criminal sophistication in her offense. Nor can I conclude that she is a danger to others if she is not incarcerated.

[¶ 29] Mrs. Du is a (51)-year-old woman with no criminal history and no history of violence. But for the unusual circumstances in this case, including the Du family's history of being victimized and terrorized by gang members, Mrs. Du would not be here today. Nor do I believe Mrs. Du would be here today if the gun she grabbed for protection had not been altered. This was a gun that had been stolen from the Du family and returned to them shortly before the shooting.

[¶ 30] The court has been presented with no evidence, and I have no reason to believe that Mrs. Du knew that the gun had been altered in such a way as to—in effect—make it an automatic weapon with a hairpin trigger.

[¶ 31] Ordinarily a .38 revolver is one of the safest guns in the world. It cannot go off accidentally. And a woman Mrs. Du's size would have to decide consciously to pull the trigger and to exert considerable strength to do so.

[¶ 32] But that was not true of the gun used to shoot Latasha Harlins. I have serious questions in my mind whether this crime would have been committed at all but for a defective gun.

[¶ 33] The district attorney would have this court ignore the very real terror experienced by the Du family before the shooting, and the fear Mrs. Du experienced as she worked by herself the day of the shooting. But there are things I cannot ignore. And I cannot ignore the reason Mrs. Du was working at the store that day. She went to work that Saturday to save her son from having to work. Mrs. Du's son had begged his parents to close the store. He was afraid because he had been the victim of repeated robberies and terrorism in that same store.

[¶ 34] On the day of the shooting Mrs. Du volunteered to cover for her son to save him one day of fear.

[¶ 35] Did Mrs. Du react inappropriately to Latasha? Absolutely.

[¶ 36] Was Mrs. Du's over-reaction understandable? I think so.

[¶ 37] If probation is not appropriate, and state prison time is warranted, then a short prison term would be an injustice. If Mrs. Du should be sent to prison because she is a danger to others or is likely to re-offend, then I could not justify imposing a short prison term.

[¶ 38] But it is my opinion that Mrs. Du is not a danger to the community and it is my opinion that she will not re-offend. She led a crime free life until Latasha Harlins walked into her store and there is no reason to believe that this is the beginning of a life of crime for Mrs. Du. But if I am wrong, Mrs. Du will face severe consequences.

[¶ 39] For all of these reasons it is hereby adjudged that: on her conviction for voluntary manslaughter, Mrs. Du is sentenced to the midterm of 6 years in state prison. On the personal use of a firearm enhancement, the defendant is sentenced to the midterm of 4 years, to run consecutive to the 6 years for a total of 10 years. Execution of this sentence is suspended.

[¶ 40] Mrs. Du is placed on formal probation for five years on the following terms and conditions:

[¶ 41] Mrs. Du is to perform 400 hours of community service. I strongly recommend that for the maximum impact on Mrs. Du and for the community, this service should be in connection with efforts to various groups to unite the Korean and African American communities.

[¶ 42] Mrs. Du is to pay $500 to the restitution fine [*sic*] and pay full restitution to the victim's immediate family for all out of court expenses for Latasha Harlins' funeral and any medical expenses related to Latasha Harlins' death.

[¶ 43] Mrs. Du is to obey all laws and orders of the probation department and the court.

[¶ 44] If I am wrong about Mrs. Du and she re-offends, then she will go to state prison for 10 years.

Notes

1. Superior Court of Los Angeles County, no. BA037738; *People v. Superior Court (Du)* 5 Cal.App. 4th 822 (1992).

2. The titles of the superior court case and the reported opinion use "Soon Ja Du" and place Du's surname last. In referring to defendant Du in this article, I will follow standard Korean usage in my placement of the family surname.

3. Appeal, at p. 829.

4. See, for example, "Blacks Voice Outrage over Sentence in Girl's Death; Reaction: Some

Fear That Fragile Truce between Korean Merchants and African-Americans Could Be in Danger," *Los Angeles Times*, 17 November 1991: 1; "Blacks Seek to Channel Anger over Sentence," *Los Angeles Times*, 17 November 1991: 1.

5. Largely fueled by sentiment against her sentence in *People v. Soon Ja Du*, three challengers opposed Karlin in her confirmation election. A majority of voters, however, reelected her to a full judicial term. She is not currently assigned to try cases in the criminal division of the Los Angeles Superior Court.

6. References to the sentencing colloquy are by paragraph and are not footnoted.

7. See generally, my discussion in "A Critique of 'Our Constitution Is Colorblind,'" *Stanford Law Review* 44 (1991): 1.

8. Judge Karlin does not mention the choice by Du and her family to operate a store in a racially particularized neighborhood. The appeals court noted that the Du family sold one business and chose to purchase this business in a "bad neighborhood" (Appeal, at p. 828). Had Karlin recognized a "consenting shopkeeper" instead of an "innocent shopkeeper," Karlin could then have allowed an inference that Du understood some of the dangers of operating a small business in a poor neighborhood. Du's use of the revolver would take on a more calculated character. Instead of Du as the innocent victim of a "defective" revolver, her use of the revolver was part of the difficult and sometimes harsh environment in which the Du family had chosen to work. I am not suggesting that self-defense, including armed self-defense, is inappropriate. At issue here is Judge Karlin's understanding of the context for the use of firearms and how Karlin has characterized Du Soon Ja's use of the weapon as completely without fault.

9. Appeal, 829 n. 7.

10. This "measurement" of Du is an aspect of a judge's traditional sentencing function.

11. Edward W, Said, *Orientalism* (New York: Random House, 1978).

12. John Kuo Wei Tchen, "Modernizing White Patriarchy: Re-Viewing D. W. Griffith's *Broken Blossoms*," in *Moving the Image: Independent Asian Pacific American Media Arts*, ed. Russell Leong (Los Angeles: UCLA Asian American Studies Center and Visual Communications, 1991), 133. See also John W. Dower, *War without Mercy: Race and Power in the Pacific War* (New York: Pantheon, 1986), 147–80; Dennis M. Ogawa, *From Japs to Japanese: An Evolution of Japanese-American Stereotypes* (Berkeley: McCutchan Publishing, 1971). More traditional treatments are found in Stuart Creighton Miller, *The Unwelcome Immigrant: The American Image of the Chinese, 1785–1882* (Berkeley: University of California Press, 1969), and Stuart Creighton Miller, *"Benevolent Assimilation": The American Conquest of the Philippines, 1899–1903* (New Haven: Yale University Press, 1982).

13. Tchen, "Modernizing White Patriarchy," 136–37.

14. Bob Suzuki, "Education and the Socialization of Asian Americans: A Revisionist Analysis of the 'Model Minority' Thesis," *Amerasia Journal* 23 (1977): 4.

15. William Petersen, "Success Story: Japanese American Style," *New York Times Magazine*, 9 January 1966: vi–20. Similar articles included Julian Makaroff, "America's Other Racial Minority: Japanese Americans," *Contemporary Review* 210 (1967): 310–14; Barbara Varon, "The Japanese Americans: Comparative Occupational Status, 1960 and 1950–," *Demography* 4 (1967): 809–19. A recent article that discussed the model minority is Don T. Nakanishi, "Surviving Democracy's 'Mistake': Japanese Americans and the Enduring Legacy of Executive Order 9066," *Amerasia Journal* 19 (1993): 7–35.

16. Lisa Lowe, "Heterogeneity, Hybridity, Multiplicity: Marking Asian American Differences," *Diaspora* 1:1 (spring 1991): 24–44.

17. More recently, the *Los Angeles Times* presented a photo essay with accompanying text about Korean grocers and African-American patrons: photographs by Chang W. Lee, article by John W. Lee, "Counter Culture: In Los Angeles, Korean-American Stores Are Sometimes the

Flash Point of Racial Animosity—But They Are Also the Proving Ground for Tolerance" (*Los Angeles Times Magazine,* 17 October 1993: 20–21).

18. I am aware of only two book-length treatments of Asians in popular culture: James S. Moy, *Marginal Sights: Staging the Chinese in America* (Iowa City: University of Iowa Press, 1993), and Darrell Y. Hamamoto, *Monitored Peril: Asian Americans and the Politics of TV Representation* (Minneapolis: University of Minnesota Press, 1994).

CHAPTER SIXTEEN

The Erotic Zone

Sexual Transgression on the U.S.-Mexican Border

RAMÓN GUTIÉRREZ

The images middle-class San Diegans have of Mexicans in general are often shaped by the immediate impressions and images they form of Tijuana. Like the Tijuanenses, who have deep kinship, social, and economic ties to San Diego and to southern California, San Diegans have deep-rooted and long-standing ties to Tijuana. Indeed, since the end of the nineteenth century, Tijuana's growth as a city, in large part, has depended more on prominent capitalists in San Diego than on those farther south in central Mexico. Tijuana's businesses were created with American technology to meet consumption demands located in San Diego and Los Angeles. The Santa Fe Railroad link, which by 1890 connected Los Angeles, San Diego, and Tijuana, is but one early example of this. The telephone wires and electric lines, which by 1914 tied Tijuana to an American economic infrastructure based in San Diego, is another.[1]

The line that marks the boundary between Mexico and the United States is a border that both binds and separates two spaces, two national territories that once were one, and two peoples of numerous classes and multiple ethnicities that are now quite impossible to pull apart. Thousands of Tijuanenses cross into the United States every day to work, to study, and to pass their leisure time shopping in fancy shops in La Jolla, strolling through Balboa Park, or stashing away their millions in San Diego's banks. Commerce and capital move ever more frenetically in the opposite direction as well. Billions of U.S. dollars flow into the *maquiladoras* just across the border. Millions of American tourists visit Tijuana yearly in search of inexpensive leather goods and black velvet paintings of Jesus Christ, Michael Jackson, and Che Guevara. Many San Diego boys count the days until they reach manhood with dreams of Tijuana's bestial sex acts, its drinking and debaucheries, which good Protestant mothers constantly caution their sons will only lead to hell, furry palms, and dissipation.

Educated middle-class San Diegans who understand the social and economic dynamics of the cultural space they inhabit, or whose daily lives are profoundly touched by Mexicans, know that Mexico's human geography is a complex and multifaceted universe never easy to describe in one breath or image. But for the majority of San Diegans, the less educated and more ignorant ones, Mexico and Mexicans are more a concept than a tangible reality. Caricatures, stereotypes, and images, born of ignorance, fed by fantasy, shaped and distorted by the media, and explained by folk aphorisms, are the currency of popular discourse. Whatever the genesis of these perceptions, distorted as they are, they shape the way middle-class Americans refract reflections of themselves onto the "illegal aliens," those nonhuman creatures from another world called Mexico, who constantly threaten to invade sovereign United States space and destroy the essence of American life.

My task here is to explore the way middle-class San Diegans express their fears, the way they construct "illegal aliens," imaginary Mexican enemies at their borders. Let me proceed with my most complex point regarding how Americans shape and organize their symbols of national identification, and conversely, how they shape national others, citizens of other nation-states.

David Schneider, the respected cultural anthropologist, in his book, *American Kinship*, argues that the symbol of "conjugal sexual intercourse" was the key symbol that shaped how middle-class white Americans understood kinship, or that complex set of human relationships that structures how individuals are related to each other:

> Sexual intercourse as an act of procreation creates the blood relationship of parent and child and makes genitor and genetrix out of husband and wife. But it is an act which is exclusive to and distinctive of the husband-wife relationship: sexual intercourse is legitimate and proper only between husband and wife and each has the exclusive right to the sexual activity of the other. . . . Sexual intercourse between persons who are not married is fornication and improper; between persons who are married but not to each other is adultery and wrong; between blood relatives is incest and prohibited; be-

tween persons of the same sex is homosexuality and wrong; with animals is sodomy and prohibited; with one's self is masturbation and wrong; and with parts of the body other than the genitalia themselves is wrong. All of these are defined as "unnatural sex acts" and are morally, and in some cases, legally, wrong in American culture.[2]

The products of sexual intercourse, children born of shared blood and substance, are related to their parents naturally, or by the natural order of things. Father, mother, brother, sister, uncle, aunt, grandfather, and grandmother are related by blood, through acts that originate in intercourse and by a process that is deemed to be natural. People are also related through marriage and marriage is an institution rooted in law and custom. A husband and wife are related and duty-bound to each other through human laws. They are husband and wife, and their parents are in-laws (father-in-law, sister-in-law, son-in-law, etc.).

Middle-class white Americans organize their kin relationships around two orders: the order of nature, which is human and biological, and the order of law, which is based on the rule of reason. These two basic elements—nature and law—on which American notions of relatedness rest, are the basic oppositions through which spatial, political, philosophical, and zoological categories are often constructed and understood. One only has to take for an example how the United States of America defines citizenship and nationality to see this point. Americans are either born into the nation (the order of nature) or they enter it through a legal process (the order of law) and become citizens through a process we call "naturalization." Three types of citizens are possible in the United States: (1) those who are born American but are naturalized citizens of another country, (2) those who are born elsewhere but "naturalized" as Americans (quite frequently by marrying an American citizen), and (3) those who are American by birth and law.[3] Nature and law thus create citizens.

The nature/law code that derives from the domain of kinship creates other basic dichotomies, which are anchored to the symbol of conjugal sexual intercourse and are used to differentiate us/them, insider/outsider, male/female, law-abiding/criminal, human/animal, clean/dirty.

To form a mental picture of how American middle-class stereotypes of Mexico and Mexicans are logically constructed, we can begin at the spatial level, examining how Tijuana first developed as an escape valve for the sexually repressed and regulated American Protestant social body of San Diego. In this case, the international boundary between Mexico and the United States has long been imagined as a border that separates a pure from an impure body, a virtuous body from a sinful one, a monogamous conjugal body regulated by the law of marriage from a criminal body given to fornication, adultery, prostitution, bestiality, and sodomy.

Indeed, Tijuana really came into its own as a city in the 1920s primarily as a haven for American illegal activities. When Prohibition, the outlawing of the production and consumption of alcoholic beverages, was instituted in the United States in 1920, San Diegans rushed across the border to Tijuana to construct their gin mills and their saloons. Soon there were brothels, gambling houses, and all those pleasures and pains prohibited in respectable California society. San Diego newspapers frequently lambasted these activities. "Tia Juana Is a Disgrace to Mexico, a Menace to America," the *Los Angeles Examiner* announced in its headline, continuing that "Tia Juana is a plague spot and ought to be eradicated."[4] Although cries of shock and revulsion similar to these filled the pages of local tabloids, historian Vincent Z. C. de Baca argues that until the early 1940s, much of Tijuana's vice activity was owned and operated by American citizens who lived in Los Angeles and San Diego.[5] Prohibition was eventually abolished in 1935, but by that date the caricature of Tijuana as a den of vice and decadence—as a place of unruly and transgressive bodies—had been firmly fixed in the American psyche.

Shaping the images Americans have of the "other," of the Mexican that inhabits the deepest recesses of fantasy, are a series of concrete events that constantly crystallize the fear that seems to characterize sociocultural relations between San Diegans and Tijuanenses. Whether it be in the 1920s, the 1950s, or the 1990s, the Mexican rapist figures prominently in those fears. One can begin as early as 1926, with the famous Peteet case, to see how the fear and fantasy of rape constantly repeat themselves. The events of this case started on Saturday, 31 January 1926, when Thomas and Carrie Peteet and their two daughters, Clyde and Audrey, checked into Tijuana's San Diego Hotel. The family had crossed into Mexico for five days of vacation. A little gambling and a little drinking was all they had in mind. And, according to local witnesses, they did plenty of that. On Wednesday evening, 3 February, Thomas Peteet and his daughters entered the Oakland Bar, and before long Peteet, apparently drugged, passed out. His daughters met a similar fate, and in that state were abducted and raped. Mr. Peteet came to later that night, discovered by his wife in the street outside the Oakland Bar. The ordeal the girls had suffered was known the next day. Deeply humiliated and shamed when they returned home, the family committed suicide together. The case became a cause célèbre in San Diego. What sorts of outrages were being perpetrated on Americans across the border? Civic, religious, and temperance groups demanded a closed border. "Remove the menace of Tijuana and keep San Diego County a clean, safe, law-abiding community," the San Diego Law Enforcement League constantly proclaimed.[6] Eventually the furor died down, but before it did, this celebrated rape case had created an image of Tijuana and the Mexicans living there as brutes governed by lust and given to crime.[7]

Since the famous Peteet case, the shape of reporting on Tijuana has not changed very much. What is noted in stories are the unregulated sexual activities of American youth. The crimes they commit in Tijuana are rarely noticed; what is done to them makes the evening news.[8] As a headline in a recent story in the *Orange County Register* noted: "Tijuana's wild nights of partying lure teens south, where beatings, robbery and death sometimes await."[9] The story chronicles how young American boys and girls escape the natural-law authority of parents over children with trips to Tijuana where minors are served alcohol, indulge their sexual desires and fantasies, and create a disorder that is never permitted at home. At home, they would be breaking the law. The law codes that order and regulate the body and kinship in American thought stem from the symbol of conjugal marital intercourse. In Tijuana, American boys and girls desecrate marriage by soliciting prostitutes or by becoming the victims of rape. In American middle-class minds, Tijuana is a marginal area that lies beyond the border of the American body politic governed by nature and law. Mexico is a place where vice thrives. There, gambling, liquor, drugs, prostitution, and unnatural sexual activities flourish. And these activities constantly threaten to spill across the border to corrupt the American body politic.

If we cross the border into San Diego County to explore how middle-class San Diegans speak about and imagine the Mexican workers who actually cross the border to cook their meals, to clean their streets, to nurse their babies and to build their homes, we find again a related set of stereotypes best understood by looking at the ways in which nature and law create the moral community of kinship.

The dominant rhetoric concerning Mexican workers in the San Diego area has been marked by two major depictions. First, Mexican workers are "illegal aliens" and thus a menace to public safety. They break the law. They engage in illegal acts, such as seeking work. In times of economic difficulty, they take away jobs that are meant for Americans, and thus are the reason for economic hardship. This argument is well known, and so are its fallacious assumptions, but it nonetheless gets reinforced continually because the Immigration and Naturalization Service, seeking illegals, frequently stages raids at factories and fields. The second depiction of Mexican workers is that they are physically dangerous because they are rapists, the source of drugs and diseases such as AIDS, and a menace to public health because they live in squalor and unsanitary conditions.

Regarding Mexican illegality, consider the 1989 survey sent to voters in San Diego by the American Immigration Control Foundation. The Foundation asked recipients of the survey for their opinions on "America's illegal alien crisis," informed them of what it considered the facts on "illegal aliens," and solicited their dollars. Full of xenophobic rhetoric, the leaflet posed a variety of questions. Question 3 asked: "Which of the problems associated with illegal aliens are the most personally disturbing to you?" The options, to name but the most inflammatory, were: "bilingual public education, bring in diseases like AIDS, loss of jobs for American citizens, drug trafficking and crime." The opening statement of the cover letter that accompanied the poll, stated:

> My forefathers and yours entered America legally. They understood through hard work, obeying the law and contributing to the nation's good, they would EARN the right of citizenship in this great land of opportunity. But what we're dealing with today is quite different. Statistics show our borders have become a floodgate for millions . . . who think little of breaking our laws and living off taxpayers like you and me.[10]

The "illegal alien" as a physically dangerous rapist is a stereotype that has a long history in U.S.-Mexican relations that goes back to the 1926 Peteet case. But more recently, paranoid fantasies about Mexican rapists have reemerged in American public discourse. In September 1986, hysteria over school-aged children who attended the Kelly School in Carlsbad, California, in the northern part of San Diego County, exploded as a result of two incidents. The first involved several migrant workers and a fifteen-year-old girl near the Kelly School. Apparently the girl was walking near the school when three Mexican migrants started to approach her from the front, and three more from behind. An acquaintance of the girl saw the men approaching her and immediately called out to the girl, thus avoiding a "bad situation." Community concern had already been fanned by a newspaper story in the 19 September 1986 issue of the *San Diego Union*. "Aliens Said Preying on School Kids," the headline read. The story quoted Border Patrol Assistant Chief Gene Smithburg reporting that "A new type of crime is being perpetrated by undocumented aliens, extorting lunch money from schoolchildren . . . it's really too bad that something like this happens. The kids are really intimidated." A public outcry was quickly heard and it led to a "roundup" conducted on horseback, helicopter, and all-terrain vehicles. Some three thousand "illegal aliens" were apprehended and returned to Mexico. The idea of adult single men, dark-skinned men, who congregated near innocent children, was more than parents could take. As one resident said, "We hit a nerve that runs through San Diego County."[11]

One sees another permutation of the fear of the Mexican rapist in the "Light Up the Border" campaign that was started in San Diego in 1989 by Muriel Watson, a middle-class white widow of a former U.S. border patrol agent. The main activity of "Light Up the Border" was to get citizens to drive in their cars to Dairy Mart Road, just off Highway 5, about one mile north of the Tijuana–San Diego border, and, at sunset, to turn on the headlights of their cars toward the border. The campaign was a huge success, counting over five hundred cars and some 2,500 participants. These individuals came to "Light Up the Border," says Watson, because "they just share my concern, they all had [newspaper] clippings: 'Oh, look at this, this 16-year-old girl was raped and her throat was slit and they rescued her just in time.' . . . So this was what motivated me . . . pure and simple."[12] Using body metaphors to describe her goals, Watson explained, "The light . . . was just meant to light up this area. . . . This is a main artery, this is a very tender spot."[13]

Many sensationalistic things have been written and reported about "Light Up the Border." This probably is due to the fact that the movement is composed of many desperate elements, among them neo-Nazis and skinheads who are motivated by racist and xenophobic ideas. But, in the mind of Muriel Watson, the movement's founder, her actions are born of a concern for the "aliens." She wants to protect the "aliens" from border rapists. Her intentions are totally altruistic. She and her followers, Watson says, are "good Americans" motivated only by the desire to uphold law and order. Certain physical things had to take place, and one of them was the message to the alien: "Look, you're crossing the border and it is against the law.[14] "Light Up the Border," says Watson, was started to create

> a certain modicum of control. It's just like your own yard in your own house. If you have a fence up, then you keep kids from running across your lawn. . . .
> If you see somebody coming on, you're more aware of it and you're able to better control the flow of whatever goes across your own property. . . . I still ask the question: 'Why are they coming the way they are?' and that has to be resolved. And there's no reason that between two reasonably civilized nations, that the border can't be respected.[15]

The idea that the nation's front yard is being littered with the refuse of rapists, robbers, and petty criminals has been expressed in much of the literature describing the tensions in the northern townships of San Diego County. Here, one of the constant complaints of Americans is that the "aliens" congregate at shopping centers and local business establishments, waiting for work. Gloria Carranza, Transient Issues Coordinator for the City of Encinitas, summed up this fear well:

> The businesses were complaining that the large number of migrants was actually a negative impact to them because they were walking through the establishments or "hanging out" in the morning, looking for employment. In the afternoon they were hanging out, they would be drinking . . . just the intimidation factor of large groups of Hispanic males was an intimidation . . . [it was] a public safety issue.[16]

The composition of the Mexican workforce in Encinitas was large, single, and male—men who did not duplicate the American ideal of compulsory heterosexuality. Nina LeShan, a social worker, described this population and the root of the problem well when she said: "Most of the time, men come up here, and without their family or without any women."[17]

The image of the disease-infested Mexican is often juxtaposed and incorporated in public-safety arguments. In San Diego County the stereotype of the disease-spreading Mexican has become particularly potent primarily because the large-scale development of middle- and upper-class housing has suddenly put the residents of these new tracts in face-to-face contact with the cardboard and plastic shantytowns Mexican workers have constructed as their own shelters. These workers' camps have long existed, but went unnoticed when the area was still predominately rural. There they lived in the most rudimentary and rustic of conditions, without toilets, without running water, without heat or electricity. Then housing starts began. And as the number of Mexican workers arriving to build these fancy houses increased, so too the friction, fueled by the belief that the area was being overrun and that the encampments were a health menace to Americans. The city of Encinitas took the most strident measures against these "illegals." Using force, it proceeded "to clean them [the camps] up," stationing guards to assure that such squatter communities did not develop again. It is significant that the city of Encinitas wanted "to clean up" the camps, for, as Nina LeShan, a social worker and midwife to the Mexican migrants in the area stated, the Mexican were seen "as filth."[18]

In the public and official discourse of the city of Encinitas and its residents, the distinction between "us" and "them," between Americans and Mexicans, between citizens and "aliens," between persons who obey the law and those who are criminals, has been cast as "cleanliness" versus "dirt," as a distinction between healthy bodies and those infested with disease. "Dirtiness" represents the physical threat to the ideal order, to the orderly functioning of society.

Mary Douglas, the cultural anthropologist, in her book *Purity and Danger*, writes that symbolic schemes preoccupied with disease, hygiene, and dirt are often implicit comments about the ideal order of society. Douglas notes:

> If we can abstract pathogenicity and hygiene from our notions of dirt, we are left with the old definition of dirt as matter out of place. . . . It implies two conditions: a set of ordered relations and a contravention of that order. Dirt, then, is never a unique, isolated event. Where there is dirt, there is a system. Dirt is the by-product of a systematic ordering and classification of matter, in so far as ordering involves rejecting inappropriate elements.[19]

What I have been arguing is that in the dominant Anglo-American middle-class culture of the United States, the symbol of marital sexual intercourse is the fundamental foundation on which the moral community rooted in nature and law rests. This is a moral community that grants citizenship principally to those persons who mirror its body order, and resists penetration and excludes those who do not—"illegal aliens," rapists, dirt, and so on. Cultural historian Sander Gilman has noted that coitus creates in all of us a sense of abandonment, an abandonment of the highly ordered and controlled world. Such moments represent the potential loss of control, not only of self, but of our private and public worlds. "Such disorder cannot be contained within the self. It must be expelled into the world. The projection of such disorder, a disorder exemplified by the sexual, . . . [often] take[s] the form of the thought-collective's fantasies about the Other, whether the 'sexual' or the 'racial' Other."[20]

In Mexico, the process of nation building began when single Spanish males raped Indian women. The result was cultural, social, and biological *mestizaje*, the heritage of race mixture that remains the dominant conquest legacy for Mexicans. In the United States, the nation was founded atop Puritan and Calvinist foundations, based on a strict morality and beliefs about what was natural and unnatural, who were and who were not kin by blood and marriage. That legacy of nature and law, which is at the very core of American middle-class kinship ideas, explains how Americans project their hysterias and anxieties and thereby symbolically construct Mexicans.

Notes

1. Vincent Z. C. de Baca, "Moral Renovation of the Californias: Tijuana's Political and Economic Role in American-Mexican Relations, 1920–1935" (Ph.D. diss., University of California, San Diego, 1991), 1–4.

2. David Schneider, *American Kinship: A Cultural Account* (Chicago: University of Chicago Press, 1980), 38.

3. David M. Schneider, "Kinship, Nationality, and Religion in American Culture: Toward a Definition of Kinship," in *Symbolic Anthropology: A Reader in the Study of Symbols and Meanings,* ed. Janet L. Dolgin, David S. Kemnitzer, and David Schneider (New York: Columbia University Press, 1977), 67–68.

4. "Tia Juana Is a Disgrace to Mexico, a Menace to America," *Los Angeles Examiner,* 11 February 1926; quoted in de Baca, "Moral Renovation of the Californias," 12–13.

5. De Baca, "Moral Renovation of the Californias," 10.

6. Quoted in ibid., 8.

7. Ibid., 13–16.

8. See, for example, "Mexican Accuses U.S. of Disinformation Campaign," *San Diego Union,* 21 November 1986; "Pressure, Payoffs Curb Mexican Press," *Los Angeles Times,* 4 March 1987; "Views Differ over Coverage by U.S. Press of Mexico," *San Diego Union,* 11 October 1986.

9. *Orange County Register,* 1 December 1991: K1.

10. Quoted in Isabelle Fauconnier, "Perceptions of and Reactions to Undocumented Workers in San Diego" (senior thesis, University of California, San Diego, 1991), 5.

11. Daniel Wolf, *Undocumented Aliens and Crime: The Case of San Diego* (La Jolla, Calif.: Center for U.S.-Mexican Studies, 1988), 21.

12. Muriel Watson interview, transcript in Fauconnier, "Perceptions," 92.

13. Ibid., 91.

14. Ibid., 42.

15. Ibid., 48, 88.

16. Gloria Carranza interview, transcript in ibid., 53–54.

17. Nina LeShan interview, transcript in ibid., 70.

18. Ibid., 74.

19. Mary Douglas, *Purity and Danger: An Analysis of the Conceptions of Pollution and Taboo* (London: Praeger, 1966), 35.

20. Sander L. Gilman, *Sexuality: An Illustrated History, Representing the Sexual in Medicine and Culture from the Middle Ages to the Age of AIDS* (New York: John Wiley and Sons, 1989), 3.

CHAPTER SEVENTEEN

Site-seeing through Asian America

On the Making of Fortune Cookies

RENEE TAJIMA

I should have seen it coming the day I picked up the *Wall Street Journal* and read that one of the leading Communist Party formations on the Asian-American left was planning a hostile takeover of Shearson Lehman-American Express.

As the 1980s rolled into the 1990s, the changes were already in motion. Chinatown storefronts were now Vietnamese, Burmese, Malay. College admission struggles were being waged around the overrepresentation of Asian Americans, rather than their underrepresentation, as when I was a college student during the 1970s. A new generation of youthful gangsters surfaced in places like New Orleans and Iowa City, while Japanese companies became major players in Hollywood. In Brooklyn, the Red Apple grocery boycott gave national visibility to a decade of escalating tension between Asian immigrants and African Americans. The established Asian-American left—dominated by Chinese and Japanese Americans who had come of age during the Third World mobilizations of another era—were caught off guard. And they would remain ambivalent about their role in succeeding crises of interethnic strife.

It was becoming impossible to get a handle on who the Asian American was, or who we were as a collective. Prior to the 1980s the Asian American was fairly simple to define. We were predominantly Chinese, Filipino, and Japanese; the majority of us were American-born and English-speaking. We shared a common history of labor immigration and racial discrimination, and this history was the crux of our political identity—as Asian Americans and as an aggrieved racial minority. At a time when the struggle for equality was focused on legal protections, the construction of this common identity was the political currency upon which gains in equality were achieved. But demographics ultimately catapulted Asian Americans into the post-civil rights era. The Asian-American population quadrupled during the 1970s and 1980s, and the growth was characterized by a diversity in nationality, language, religion, culture, and class, the likes of which we had never seen before. As we entered the 1990s, the rules of the game had changed irrevocably.

At about this time, I found myself in Los Angeles at a state-of-Asian-America conference sponsored by the Asia Society. The fact of the tony Asia Society's involvement was bewildering enough. Then there were the scores of veteran activists wandering about the Biltmore Hotel like rebels with a caseload, not a cause. Former Marxist-Leninists had become city commissioners, corporate responsibility flaks, public television producers, and party officials. Democratic Party officials. We were The Suits now—still dominating the conference sessions with rhetoric from the 1970s, while new immigrants who represented the voice of the second millennium waited on the sidelines. A *Los Angeles Times* reporter asked me to define the common denominator linking all these disparate Asian nationalities. All I could think of is we all eat rice.

I decided to make a film about this new Asian America, and it turned out to be a road documentary called *Fortune Cookies: In Search of Asian America* (working title).

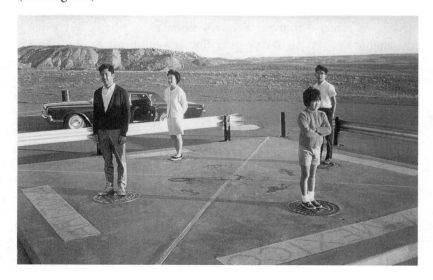

My life on the road began more than thirty years ago in a fire-engine-red Ford Fairlane in which I could stand to my fullest height and spy on America, traveling by like one long, manic theme park on wheels. The World's Fair. The Weeki Wachi mermaid show at Bucaneer Bay. Abe Lincoln's cabin. Tony the Tiger cereal samples, free for the asking at the Kellogg's factory in Battle Creek. The Four Corners. Devil's Peak at dusk.

The fact that the car was this bright, blazing color was an event in itself, because in all other matters, bland was our family motto. Our first real home was a ranch-style split-level on a tract of identical beige split-levels. We shopped the Sears catalog. We were Presbyterians, for god's sake, and I knew from the moment I could comprehend such things as fate and destiny that mine was sealed. I would be an average Jane floating along with the tide. Put it this way: no one has ever been moved to daredevil feats, to wail the blues, or to plumb the soul in psychoanalysis because they need to come to grips with growing up *Presbyterian*.

We were dull by design. My mother Marie had grown up on Los Angeles's Skid Row and spent her teenage years in the Heart Mountain, Wyoming, Relocation Center. Heart Mountain, the camp that ruptured the dignity of my mother and my uncles. And that my grandfather—who worked sixteen hours a day as a custodian at Bullocks and as a houseboy for rich people— regarded as a blessed event. An extended, all-expense paid vacation. Grandpa, who was mightily disappointed when Japan lost the war, and who later developed an intense fascination for women's professional Roller Derby competition. Grandpa had a dark side.

My father, named for Calvin Coolidge, was a high-school linebacker who once played in the state finals at the Coliseum, and the son of a preacher. A Presbyterian preacher, naturally, who counseled the Japanese community to go quietly to the camps. My father went into the Army. As fate would have it, his entire unit was felled by chicken pox and spent the remainder of the war quarantined at Fort Meade. Two months after V-day, my father finally made it to Germany, where he got to meet Ingrid Bergman. He has pictures.

Like most Nisei, once my parents returned to civilian life after the war, they weren't about to do anything to draw attention to themselves. And so the split-level and split identities. We became a family of Oriental Blandings, American Japanese.

Sacramento

The first thing I do before setting off to shoot *Fortune Cookies* is go to meet the actor Victor Wong. I plan to shoot a documentary film about Asian-American identity that is narrated by a fictionalized central character. I need a lead. I loved Victor in *Chan Is Missing*, so I go off to Sacramento to see him. I discover life is stranger than fiction.

Victor is the son of the late Sir King Wong, San Francisco's "Mayor of Chinatown," a prominent businessman, and the veritable crown prince of the prewar MSG business. Photo credit: Quynh Thai

Victor was a rebel. As a teenager he was born again and preached fire and brimstone on Grant Avenue, much to the chagrin of his strict Confucianist father. Worse yet, he went to art school. That was followed by four marriages, to one black woman and three white women. Not one of them a Chinese. He was every Chinese parent's nightmare.

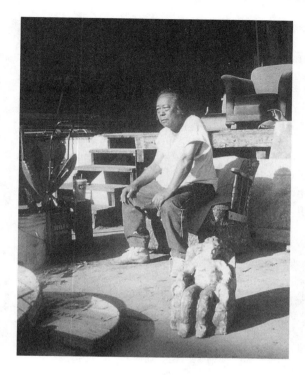

"You put yourself into limbo because you reject one whole thing, which is the Chinese tradition. You have nothing to replace it with. It puts you into a terrible vacuum."
Photo credit: Renee Tajima

Victor is the same age as my own father, but they couldn't have lived more different lives. My father dared to buy a red sedan in a rare moment of devil-may-care, but he was a cautious driver all the way. Victor ran with Jack Kerouac and the Beats, lived dangerously, and once trekked all the way across country just to try out the chilis of various states. He knew he was breaking his father's heart, but Victor couldn't help himself. Although he savored tradition, he found it toxic in large doses. And besides, Victor was born in the same year Babe Ruth hit his sixtieth home run. He married Olive Thurman, the daughter of a famed black theologian, in the year of *Brown v. Topeka Board of Education*. He was a denizen of North Beach, a Chinese Beat, an American in Chinatown. Victor Wong was already having an Asian-American identity crisis in the days when the rest of us were still calling ourselves Orientals.

New York

My casting trip to Sacramento turns into a pilgrimage, with Victor Wong a road guru urging me on my search for Asian America. I do away with any notion of a fictionalized character. No amount of make-believe would match Victor's real-life story anyway. Inspired by Victor, I decide instead, right then and there, that I will drive the same highways I traveled as a child to see for myself how much we've changed. I begin my journey in New York City.

From all outward appearances, Chang Y. Choi is just another small-time businessman who makes fortune cookies in New York's Chinatown. Look beneath the surface, and his Chrystie Street factory is a web of complex economic relationships and social histories that signifies what Asian America has become.

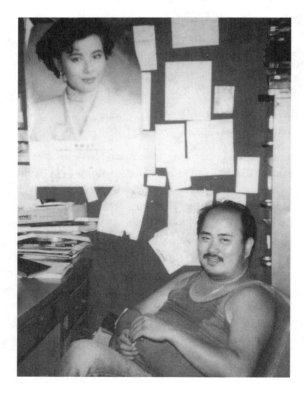

Choi's Golden Star factory manufactures fortune cookies, a confection originated in America but generally served as an after-dinner treat at Chinese restaurants.
Photo credit: Quynh Thai

Mr. Choi says he wants to retire by the time he's forty. "I want to make money five year and retire. OK? I young I can have energy now, I can work, okay? I don't want a . . . Like a forty, fifty, or too old I can't do anything, right? So, I want a keep up about five year, that's it." It could be said that Choi is driven by a Confucian work ethic—and that is the key to success for Asian immigrants like him. But retire by forty? That doesn't come from Confucius. What is it, in the tangled cultural lineage of Choi's many lives from Vietnam to Hong Kong to New York that is the source of his ambition? The Calvinist work ethic imported via Christian missionaries? An innate entrepreneurialism inherent to Chinese diaspora survival? Greed?

And what is the source of my own addiction to Publisher's Clearinghouse and *Reader's Digest* sweepstakes contests? I've even taken to ordering the subscriptions offered, to save me the humiliation of returning my entry under cover of the wretched "No" sticker pasted on the front of the return envelope. My reply is "Yes." Yes, I will take one year of *People* at the low introductory rate of $9.97 in just four easy payments. Yes, I want a shot at millions, at the chance of greeting Ed McMahon and the Prize Patrol at my door, bearing a ticket to independent wealth.

I agonized for years while living in New York because I knew in my heart that they probably toss out all of the Manhattan entries anyway. Winners usually live in places like Indiana, in a single-family residence with a name like Miller festooned on a mailbox hand-painted with roosters and vines, the ample Mrs. Miller shrieking with surprise, wiping away tears of delight on her apron. I couldn't picture the Prize Patrol caravan double-parked on 38th Street to see me, as I peered through a crack in the door behind three dead bolts. "Who's there, *Ed McMahon*? Right. Slip your I.D. under the door."

There are certain prizes in American life that will always be off-limits. Asians need not enter. Nevertheless, something leads me to the mailbox each year, armed with my entry and hopes. Is it the stubborn persistence of the American Dream, ingrained in the immigrant psyche? An Oriental penchant for gambling? Greed? And why, after such industry and hard work, did our Mr. Choi choose to take the ultimate risk? One year after filming in Chinatown, I was to discover that the life of this model immigrant had taken a sordid turn—one that I never would have imagined. But that's for the movie.

It was Wood Moy, not Victor Wong, by the way, who actually played the lead in *Chan Is Missing*. He just looks like Victor, so I must have gotten them confused. Somewhere along the road I realize my error. But nothing is as you remember it anyway, and part of the glory of a road trip is allowing the accidents of fate to propel you along.

New Orleans

Our family travels when I was a child rarely took us south. It was too confusing. Which toilets do we use, the ones for "Whites" or for the "Coloreds"? My mother always told us to use the cleaner one, but that solution never satisfied. Even in childhood I realized there was no place for us in the larger drama of American life. The South only magnified our irrelevance.

I drive to New Orleans in hopes of meeting Harry Lee, the "Chinese Cajun Sheriff" of Jefferson Parish. Sheriff Lee is the highest-ranking Asian-American law-enforcement officer in the nation. He is also the brother of China Lee, the first ever Asian-American *Playboy* centerfold, circa 1964. At over three hundred pounds, Lee is the quintessential good ol' boy and a force in local politics. No one calls Harry Lee irrelevant. He virtually declared war on the *Times-Picayune* when they reported, one Christmas season, that Lee had ordered his deputies to arrest any blacks they spotted driving through the parish at night. Harry certainly knew which side of the latrine to stake his interests on.

I do get to meet the ubiquitous sheriff, however briefly, and he loads me up with Harry Lee souvenir drinking cups and Harry Lee Mardi Gras coins. Unfortunately, he is out on a quail-hunting trip by the time I'm ready to film and I'm left with these long unanswered questions. How have Asians accommodated themselves to the racial climate of the region? What shape does Asian-American identity take far from the diaspora centers on the East and West coasts?

My luck turns when I run across a local scholar named Marina Espina, who has unearthed the history of the first Asian immigrants to America. I'm taken aback when she tells me they were actually Filipinos who settled in Louisiana as early as 1756. They were sailors who had been indentured by the Spaniards and forced to work the galleon trade from Manila to Acapulco. Weary of the brutal conditions on board, they jumped ship in the Louisiana bayou and formed a colony, named Manila Village, on Barataria Bay. *The young generation, they all know. They grew up knowin' they part Filipino. Well because, we heard it. We heard it so they can hear it. When they're grandparents they can tell it to their children. And we have it all written down. All kinds of stories. . . . Well, if we don't know where we come from how do we know where we going?*

The Burtanog sisters are from the oldest Filipino family around New Orleans. They go back eight generations and know just about everyone and everything around here.
Photo credit: Quynh Thai

In the popular imagination, a gathering of Asian-American women typically surrounds a pot of tea or a mah-jongg game. The worlds of literature and cinema prefer Asian-American stories when they are, in reality, stories of Asia, and the tellers only once-removed by migration or birth. It is as if the hugeness of the Asian drama alone can make our lives here in America matter. War, exotica, the sweep of history, the tremors of grand conflicts as cultures are renegotiated. But what of the rest of us, who claim four, five, even eight generations in America, as the Burtanogs do? There are no mah-jongg games and trans-Pacific memories here in the Burtanog household. The defining cultural equation is Five-card Stud and a six-pack of Bud (Lite). The talk is ex-husbands, voodoo curses, and the complicated racial design of New Orleans society.

Sister Mae was the queen
of the Caballeros de
Dimas-Alang Mardi Gras
carnival ball in 1946, the
last year that a Filipino
float would win the
coveted Grand Prize
from the Elks Krewe of
Orleanians.
Photo credit:
Quynh Thai

In the Jim Crow South, Filipinos were considered white by dint of their
Spanish ancestry. They could intermarry, attend school with, and get buried
next to, below, or on top of the more conventionally white citizenry. Audrey
says her brother Walter use to play with another boy on the block named
Willy. But as soon as Walter turned eighteen, Willy, being black, had to start
calling his friend Mr. Walter. Of course the South is no more a nucleus of
racial enmity than the North. Benita Burtanog points out that her Filipino
cousins in California could not marry Caucasians because of antimiscegenation laws that classified Filipinos as Mongolians. It is a testament to
America's perpetual ambivalence toward Asian Americans that miscegenation laws, and attitudes, differ so wildly region by region and state by state.

Of course, nothing is more labyrinthine than Asian Americans' own rules and rankings for proper marriages. Ask a random sampling of Asian parents for their own mating formulas and you will hear any combination of the following: Parent A: "It's OK to marry Japanese or Filipino, but no Korean. Then comes white, then Vietnamese, then Puerto Rican. No black." Parent B: "Korean, Chinese, Indian for my son. Don't care about my daughter as long as he's not white." Parent C: "Chinese OK, then white, then Korean. No Japanese, no Mexican, no black." Parent D: "White or Oriental, I don't care which. Hispanic and Indian people maybe. No black." Parent E: "Must be northern Chinese. Period."

The common denominator is often: African Americans need not apply. When Victor Wong married his first wife, Olive, in 1954, the triumph of *Brown v. Topeka* had no discernible impact on his father, Sir King. Wong Sr. called Olive to an interview, and warned her that the Chinese do not intermarry, that the children would be funny looking. There is a painful irony to Asian bigotry, as we owe so much to the black movement. Antimiscegenation laws that persecuted Asians were struck down when a black woman and her white husband, aptly named the Lovings, went all the way to the Supreme Court to validate their marriage. A whole slew of legal guarantees for Asian Americans were born out of African-American struggles for equality. Voting rights, fair housing, desegregation of schools, affirmative action set-asides, civil rights protections. Even the right to be here.

A legal scholar named John Hayakawa Torok sends me a file of citations on the 1965 immigration reform act. Congress struck down race-based quotas in the so-called Asia-Pacific Triangle, and the Asian-American population multiplied sevenfold within the span of a single generation.

The Immigration and Nationality (McCarran-Walter) Act of 1952, as Amended to 1965

By MARION T. BENNETT

—for compassionate reasons. For other thousands of aliens here illegally, he adjusted their status to that of lawful immigrants. Other thousands were permitted to come in "under parole." Further, the 1952 Act contained a basic inconsistency in that it had such huge loopholes for nonquota immigrants that for the next thirteen years two out of every three immigrants would be classed as nonquota and entered without numerical restriction. This immediately threw the national-origins plan out of balance. It permitted the creation of such large voting blocs from other than the favored area of northern and western Europe that they soon politically controlled major urban centers in the United States, a good many electoral votes, and Congressional districts. By 1965 the political atmosphere would change completely, and in an era of expanding civil rights for minorities, our pluralistic and egalitarian-bent society would reject, through Congress by public law, the concept that white, Anglo-Saxon, western European culture need remain the cornerstone of a truly viable democratic society or was worthy of preservation

though none denied it the nation's debt and honor.[9]

LEGISLATION, 1953–1964

The successful legislative strategy of antirestrictionists in the years 1953–1964, inclusive, is reflected in the fact that in this short period Congress enacted thirty-two public laws, the overall effect of which was to widen the loopholes in the national-origins system to such an extent that it was effectively nullified, although not repealed until 1965. Almost half a million immigrants were permitted to come in as special exceptions to the national-origins formula in these years. They were admitted largely as nonquota immigrants from outside the areas of northern and western Europe, which were given approximately 80 per cent of the quotas under the 1952 Act. The total of exceptions was substantially augmented by administrative waivers of exclusion, adjustment of status, and suspension of deportation. The refugee-parole provisions of the McCarran-Walter Act were also used extensively. Congress, in addition, enacted 4,273 private bills on behalf of individual immigrants, per-

Marion T. Bennett, A.B., LL.B., Washington, D.C., is Chief Commissioner of the United States Court of Claims; a former Member of Congress from Missouri (1943–1949); a Colonel in the Air Force Ready Reserve; author of American Immigration Policies: A History (1963) and of articles on legal subjects in various journals; and consultant to authors of the Immigration and Nationality Act of 1952 and the Judiciary Committees of Congress.

VOLUME 367   SEPTEMBER 1966

THE ANNALS

of The American Academy *of* Political *and* Social Science

THORSTEN SELLIN, *Editor*

RICHARD D. LAMBERT, *Associate Editor*

THE NEW IMMIGRATION

Special Editor of this Volume
EDWARD P. HUTCHINSON

Professor of Sociology
University of Pennsylvania

PHILADELPHIA
1966

Arkansas and Mississippi

Hattiesburg, Mississippi, is a direct shot up Interstate 59 from New Orleans. I go there to meet Bill and Yuri "Mary" Kochiyama, the legendary Japanese-American activists from New York City. The trip is a second honeymoon for the Kochiyamas. They first met here some fifty years ago, when Bill was in basic training with the 442d battalion at Camp Shelby. Yuri at the time was interned at the Jerome, Arkansas, relocation camp just across the Mississippi River. Theirs was the kind of love affair memorialized in music of the era: "I'll be seeing you in all the old familiar places that this heart of mine embraces, all day through . . ." Bill, a young soldier fighting against fascism in Europe, and Yuri a USO volunteer anxious for his safe return. Unlike other wartime couples though, the bride waited behind barbed wire.

The conventional wisdom is that the Nisei never spoke of the internment camps. Not so the Kochiyamas, or my own family. When I was a child, the camps were a constant source of family stories, even vehicles for value lessons of the "when-I-was-young-we-had-to-live-in-barracks" variety. In one of our more rambunctious years as children, my parents tried to prove their point by driving us to the site of the Heart Mountain Relocation Center—a desperately barren place, even in summer. The camp experience has always been ingrained in our family lexicon. To this day, whenever I meet another Japanese American, I ask by way of introduction, "What camp was your family in?" It is a way of breaking the ice and establishing connections. In my lifetime, I have rarely met another Japanese American with whom I did not have some link, via the camps, family, friends of friends, or our family homestead in Japan.

I first met Yuri Kochiyama when I was a student at Harvard-Radcliffe and she was a featured speaker during our annual Malcolm X Weekend. In those days, Asian-American, Latino, and African-American student organizations regularly collaborated on progressive activities. As a veteran of antiracist and human rights struggles and a contemporary of Malcolm X, Yuri was an obvious choice to deliver the keynote. I had produced a three-screen slide show commemorating Third World solidarity for the event, and Yuri, as is her custom, invited me, a complete stranger, to visit her home the next time I was in New York. A few months later, I was on her doorstep—one of thousands of students she and Bill have fed, housed, matched up with prospective romances, and inspired.

Naturally, one of Yuri's first questions was, "Where were your parents in camp?" When I told her my mother Marie (née Ujiiye) was first detained at

Santa Anita Park, the racetrack-turned-detention center in Arcadia, California, a light went on in Yuri's mind and she withdrew to her ubiquitous backroom to fetch a file. Now Yuri is a figure bigger than life because of her great conviction and the boundless energy with which she has battled for equality during four plus decades. But what makes her memorable is her warmth and numerous eccentricities. My sister remembers joining her to watch a National Geographic special on the ant world. When the red ants started subjugating the white ants, Yuri was beside herself with indignation. Then there is the extensive teddy bear collection to which she is intensely devoted—much of which was given to her by luminaries in the arts, letters, and the left.

Yuri remembers virtually everything, and records the rest. She prodigiously notes every name, address, and memorable quality of the legions of people she meets, then takes a snapshot. During the war, she hand-wrote the lyrics to all her favorite romantic ballads—"Stardust," "Mood Indigo," "Rhapsody in Blue." So when I mentioned my mother's name, Marie Ujiiye detainee at Santa Anita Park, Yuri was able to find her listed in a battered diary from 1942. As it turns out, Yuri was my mother's Sunday School teacher and leader of the Crusaders, a group of teenage girls who wrote letters to the Japanese-American GIs stationed overseas.

When Bill was stationed overseas, Yuri wrote him three letters a day.
Photo credit: Quynh Thai

It's not an easy time for Bill and Yuri. They have just lost their daughter Aichi, who was hit by a taxi in midtown Manhattan. They have already buried one child, their eldest son, Billy. I drive the Kochiyamas west across the state to Rosedale, a small town on the Mississippi Delta where Billy lived during the Freedom Summer of 1965. It is fitting that Billy came back here to do civil rights work. Mississippi, during the Jim Crow years of World War II, was a large influence on his parents' passion for equality.

We take a tour through the old training grounds at Camp Shelby with Herb Sasaki, a 442d battalion veteran and retired officer here. "I've told Yuri many times, I wonder why I survived because I was just a plain rifleman, infantry. And all my buddies were wounded or killed and I was one of the very few remaining ones." Bill recalls the shock of racism for Nisei soldiers when they arrived as fresh recruits. African-American GIs, even in full uniform, couldn't get a ride on the Hattiesburg city bus. One day, a group of 100th battalion boys from Hawaii got fed up with the practice. They literally picked the driver up off his seat and threw him off the bus, invited all the black GIs on board, and took over the wheel themselves. The Hawaii Nisei were known for such antics—they hadn't come to Hattiesburg weighted down with the same baggage of racial intimidation as the mainland "Katonks." Herb doesn't remember the antics as fondly as Bill: "Well, we had to stay on the white side. You had to make up your mind. The reason why they had the problems during the war years is because the Hawaiians wouldn't comply with that. They said 'Nobody is going to tell us who we can associate with,' so they did as they pleased."

It turns out the Davises, the family Billy stayed with in Rosedale, still live across the street from city hall. We knock on their door and crowd inside the tiny, veneer-paneled living room, where as many as twenty young activists lived during that Freedom Summer. The Davises all remember Billy, and show us the big Barco-lounger that was his favorite chair. They had no idea he had died.

Bill swaps old war stories with a new generation of soldiers at Camp Shelby.
Photo credit: Quynh Thai

James Ernest Ellington's family owns the land where the War Relocation Authority built the Jerome internment camp. He always thought the camps were an injustice, and so he makes it a point to greet all the Nisei who pass through for one last look at the site.
Photo credit: Quynh Thai

When we travel as children, everything is new. I remember the American landscape as being full of places I never knew before, and places I might conquer someday in my future. But older travelers, like the Kochiyamas, or Victor and the Burtanog sisters, are drawn to the venues of their past, inhabited by the ghosts of people long dead. As a filmmaker, I regularly ask people to reveal their deepest pain, the tragedy of their lives. But in Rosedale, I can't bring myself to ask Bill and Yuri to talk about Billy. On our drive back to Hattiesburg, I remember the day my parents came to New York and invited the Kochiyamas out for a reunion dinner. We ran into another old friend from the camp days, the minister of our family's church and his wife. Each couple had endured the war together. But it strikes me that the strongest bond between them was that each had buried a son. Our minister's son, and Billy, to suicide. My brother Bobby at the wrong end of a drugged-out hit-and-run driver. With all the people I meet during my travels, there is a constant interplay of the particulars of race and history and the universality of death, love, family, dreams that determines the shape of their lives. As if, in striving to assert our singular identity, what we want people to know is that we grieve too.

Before we leave the site of the relocation camp at Jerome. Mr. Ellington has one last story to tell of the incarcerated Japanese. "Lookee here," he says, "when the War Department come and bringing those messages here about the dead, they cry just like the white people. They lost many a son, and a husband."

Chicago

I was a Cubs fan long before I ever considered myself Asian-American.

I was born before the immigration reforms of 1965, a time when Cubbies undoubtedly did outnumber Asian Americans. Our first home in Chicago was a second floor apartment on Roscoe Street in the northside, a fly ball's distance away from Wrigley Field. Those were the glory days of Ernie Banks, voted Most Valuable Player even when his team was in last place. We children were all die-hard loyalists in the footsteps of my father, a man who has waited patiently over a span of forty-five summers for the Cubs to take a pennant. There is something poignant about being a Cubs fan, which prepared me well for being Asian-American. Always waiting, hopelessly, for your ship to come in.

About the time we were moving to our new split-level in the suburbs, Victor Wong was heading for Chicago to perform with the improvisation troupe, Second City Theater. Second City is famous for its comedic alumni like Joan Rivers and *Saturday Night Live* regular John Belushi and company. Victor came on board in 1961, its early days, and he has been one of the only Asian-American members since then. If there is a group that has never been ready, or rather acceptable, in prime time, I suppose we Asian Americans are it. Victor's memories of Second City are not happy ones. "They didn't know what to do with a Chinese character," he says. I'm told by a cast member from those days that when a skit was doing poorly with the audience, the other actors use to hang Victor upside down by his ankles. Not a proud moment for a man whose acting debut was in a Lyon Phelps play directed by his first wife, and who named his son after Anton Chekov.

My first stop in Chicago is the northside—old haunts of Wrigley Field, our old apartment, and finally, Second City. I find Victor's name on the wall of fame in the theater, lonely among all the others both famous and obscure. Then I bring the crew to Roscoe Street to film a shot of my first home. It is far different from what I remember. The red brick facade and concrete steps of our old home movies seem to have been altered unrecognizably by time, reminding me that you can never go home again. As I meditate about the day later in my motel room, my mother calls me to tell me that she's given me the wrong address on Roscoe Street. They say you can't go home again, but if you want to try, make sure you get the right address.

On my way north from Chicago, I stop in the town of Barrington to pay a visit to my Uncle Bill and Aunt Barbara, who have two of everything. Two power mowers, two turkeys on Thanksgiving Day, two VCRs and two TVs stacked one on top of the other in the family room, two sons, two daughters, two freezers, and so on. Some years back my Aunt Barbara converted to Mormonism and it's no wonder. Mormons customarily keep a one-year supply of basic essentials in preparation for Armaggedon, and it was an easy adjustment for my Barbara to upgrade to keeping two dozen of everything.

Barrington is a sheltered, affluent Chicago suburb—the type in which John Hughes typically sets his comedies. As we drive into my aunt and uncle's property, I can see a Christmas tree sparkling through the front window and my aunt peeking through the door. It reminds me of the time twenty-some years ago when my four cousins gathered behind that same window in fright as two slovenly, bushy-haired strangers pounded on the front door. Memories of Charles Manson and the Tate-La Bianca murders were still fresh, and owners of sprawling, self-contained homes in places like Barrington were thinking twice about security in isolation. With this in mind, my cousins were about to call the police when they realized the stranger was actually my brother Mark and his friend Dave. Mark and Dave were on their way from college in Northfield, Minnesota, to an antiwar rally in Chicago and stopped by for a home-cooked meal.

What a difference a war makes.

I don't know why we took such divergent turns from our Chicago cousins. It is typical of Asians of my generation for some to have rebelled, and others to have blended in. My cousins went on to become, respectively, a dentist, a CPA, a registered nurse, and a salesman of scientific measuring instruments. Our own record of adult pursuits includes my sister Marsha, who spent twelve years in college analyzing miniature Indian mogul paintings, and my brother Bobby, who once ran off to a Moonie camp but was kicked out because the Moonies thought he was nuts.

It could have been our move to California in 1966 that set us off on a different course. We left behind a homogenized Mount Prospect, once home to one of the Grand Dragons of the Ku Klux Klan, for Altadena, an integrated southern California community and home at one time or another to, among others, Sirhan Sirhan, David Lee Roth, and Rodney King. Mark and Marsha went off to college in time for the Summer of Love, and there was no turning back for any of us to our Mount Prospect days, or ways. The social revolution wasn't easy on my parents, and especially my father, a lifelong Republican. From 1968 to 1973 or so, roughly the period between Martin Luther

King's assassination and the Paris Peace Talks, my parents stopped taking pictures of us, with the exception of a single snapshot every Christmas. I don't know if it was the hair, the beards, or the general aura of disdain we wore on our faces.

About the only time I was nearly slapped by an aunt was during these years. By the age of fourteen, I had read *The Wretched of the Earth* and *The Autobiography of Malcolm X*, and formed an unbendable ideology of class and race oppression, which gave me no compunction at smirking at my elders' chosen lifestyles, what I perceived as their misguided patriotism, their failure to engage in armed struggle against the internment camps, and other such perceived crimes. Now, my mother and most of my aunts had done domestic work as young women. Those lucky enough to get jobs with wealthy families learned how to entertain and decorate their own homes from the ladies they worked for. They were proud of the lives they had made for themselves, especially this one particular aunt. What set her off might have been a snide remark about the bourgeois aspirations of the Nisei, second-generation Japanese Americans, or some tirade on the general malaise of capitalism. But my aunt could no longer stomach my attack on the lives the Nisei generation had so painfully reconstructed after the Depression and after the camps.

As I write this today, now the same age as my aunt was then, I am, of course, repentant. After all, my sweepstakes and lottery endeavors signify nothing less than my own dreams of a nice home, money for car payments, good colleges for the kids. In those days I use to flinch at that adage, "You'll get more conservative as you get older." I am now forced to admit there is truth in it. But I have also witnessed the political evolution of the Nisei, including my parents and aunts and uncles, in their own right. The redress and reparations movement of the 1980s was a milestone. All of my Nisei relations participated in some way, with a defiance I had never seen before. Through the testimony delivered to the Commission on Wartime Relocation and Internment Camps, we Sansei came to appreciate the context of the times, and the depth of the personal nightmare our parents faced. And during the mobilization for redress and reparations, I believe the Nisei came to rely on the activism and organizing skills their children had developed in the antiwar movement and campus struggles.

Victor Wong has told me in his interview that he never felt he could be a Chinese American, a part of America, until the civil rights movement. The political mobilizations for racial equality and construction of Asian-American identity during the 1960s and 1970s were a turning point for our participation in the public life of the nation. When Alexis de Tocqueville traveled nineteenth-century America, he observed the citizenry's penchant for forming like-minded associations—the organizing units for enacting democracy. He could have added any number of Asian-American mass organizations, labor groups, cultural clubs, and the like, to his list of teetotalers and yeoman's guilds. I don't think there is an Asian American who lived during that period of change who has not been touched by the stunning advances in education, housing, jobs, creative expression, and all sectors of public life.

But there has always been a strain of elitism in the movement, which was encapsulated in my aunt's exasperation with her highfalutin nieces and nephews. Still today, when we, as largely college-educated artists, activists, and scholars, gather to articulate hopes and aspirations of Asian Americans, it is often in a language most Asian Americans would not understand. Nor should they bother to. And there is the estrangement from new immigrants. Just as Asian-American activists were starting to solidify our own ideologies during the 1980s, we were confronted with the arrival of new immigrants and refugees. Among them were virulent anticommunists who associated Marxism and Mao with the Khmer Rouge and the Cultural Revolution. There were refugees who took no particular stock in the notion of Third World solidarity, and were just as likely to regard their black and brown neighbors as antagonists, not brothers and sisters in struggle. There were immigrants who clung tenaciously to the myth of the American Dream— one that we had already rejected in theory, if not entirely in practice. More annoying yet, some went on to achieve that dream, building successful businesses, sending their children to prestigious schools, and supplying real-life material for Model Minority stories in the mainstream press. These new Asian Americans did not fit our vision of an enlightened constituency. Perhaps that is why we found ourselves perplexed by the turn of events of the 1990s.

The Heartland

I can never figure out how Asian immigrants end up in the places where they end up. I recently met two Sikh brothers—at a Passover, naturally—whose parents first settled in a small town in Oklahoma, then relocated to my husband's hometown in the Rio Grande valley of Texas. I've had friends from glamorous cities like Tokyo and Hong Kong who traveled thousands of miles to attend a junior college somewhere in Iowa. How did they even find out about these schools?

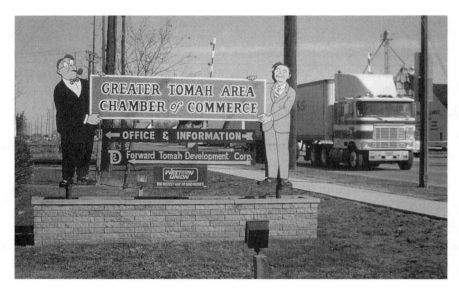

On the road in Wisconsin.
Photo credit: Quynh Thai

Volunteers at the Sheboygan Historical Society.
Photo credit: Quynh Thai

In Sheboygan, Wisconsin, on the shores of Lake Michigan, I meet Charlie Ma, a local restaurateur who came here from Hong Kong as a young man to do just that, study, then work at the local technical college. When he arrived in 1970, he was about the only Chinese in town, but quickly endeared himself by joining the Lion's Club, ringing bells for the Salvation Army during Christmastime, and teaching Chinese cooking classes. "Ma" in Chinese means "horse," so his English name actually translates to Charlie Horse. Mr. Ma's place serves northern Chinese fare cooked by Hmong workers, a decent selection of Rhinelander wines, and offers karaoke singing on a stage next to the main dining room. I don't know if you ever traveled through Wisconsin twenty-five or thirty years ago, as I did when I was a child. But I can tell you, the mere idea of finding Sheboyganites in the home of the Jaycees Bratwurst Days, partaking of such entertainment as karaoke over a bowl of Mabo Tofu, is enough to double my eyelids on a cold day. Of course, during the 1960s, there were only about six thousand plus Asians living in the entire state. Today, the population is sizable enough that some Wisconsin towns have an Asian gang problem. Here in Sheboygan, I find the moniker "Asian Diciples" (sic) scrawled along the main street underpass.

Most of the Hmong refugees were brought to Wisconsin towns like Eau Claire and Wausau by church sponsors. They were welcomed in small numbers, but as children were born and relatives arrived, some of the locals began to have second thoughts. I wonder what the reaction has been in Sheboygan. Mr. Ma is an irrepressible town booster—a Chinese-American Babbit for the nineties—and he puts a positive spin on race relations here. The town already has a long immigrant history, Germans, Slovenians, and Greeks among them, and also European Jews. The comic Jackie Mason is a native, and his father was a rabbi. But as I leave town I pass the Hebrew cemetery, which is now gated and locked. Vandals have taken to desecrating the graves.

I continue my trip north through Minnesota, bypassing Minneapolis to get to Duluth in time for St. Patrick's Day. Duluth, by the way, is where Geno Paulucci launched his Chung King food empire. In a converted factory building owned by Mr. Paulucci, I meet a Hmong woman named Pang-ku Yang. She sews high-school varsity jackets and athletic wear in a small garment shop, along with a half dozen other Laotian women. I wonder if they understand the significance of the varsity versus junior varsity letters, or the rituals behind the cheerleading skirts and the numbered jerseys they stitch together.

At home in the Harbor View housing project on the northside of town,

Pang-ku shows me a suitcase full of clothes that constitute the entirety of her possessions from home. Only the festival headdress, which she made herself, still fits. Pang-ku also brings out a pile of quilts hand sewn by herself and her sister. There are small pieces embroidered with idyllic scenes of farm animals and country life. The biggest one is epic in size and in the tale it tells. The entire history of the family's journey from the hills of Laos to Minnesota is woven into yards of cotton. The story begins in November of 1978, on the night of their baby daughter's funeral. As relatives gathered for the burial, a cousin showed up to warn Pang-ku's husband that North Vietnamese soldiers were on their way to the village to kill him. He had been a soldier for eleven years, since the age of fifteen, fighting the CIA's secret war in Laos. Mr. Yang fled to Thailand, and after a month, returned to help Pang-ku and the three remaining children escape.

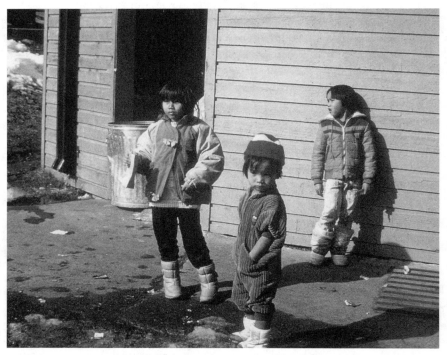

Pang-ku had never seen snow before arriving in Minnesota,
but her granddaughter, Maya, has known it all her life.
Photo credit: Quynh Thai

For a time, Mr. Yang had a part-time job at the Mama Sera spaghetti sauce factory.
Photo credit: Quynh Thai

When we escape, the older, they know, because we teach them. That if you yell or you cry even out loud, then everybody must be, got killed. And they, they afraid to and they quiet. But, they small, they don't know and they crying.
Photo credit: Quynh Thai

Quilts like Pang-ku's are now a popular item at crafts fairs wherever there are Laotian refugee communities. They generally depict happy scenes of the life the Hmong left behind, rather than the ravages of war. For those who know, the dissonance between their distant past, before the war, and their lives since then can be read between the lines of thread. But most buyers and collectors probably do not comprehend the symbolism or meaning woven into the quilts.

In the Thailand refugee camps, even the men learned to sew the quilts. It was the only work available, and it ameliorated the boredom. The Yang family has been in the United States since 1980, and has spent most of their years here on welfare. Mr. Yang is trained only as a soldier and subsistence farmer, and so has little in the way of transferable skills for the American workplace. But Pang-ku can sew, and her piecework earnings go a long way toward supporting the couple and the four sons and granddaughter who still live at home.

Pang-ku has been married before, to another man who was a Hmong soldier and who was killed during the war. She has lost four children in all, and many more family members. Three of her living sons were born in Laos and a Thailand refugee camp, and are named Ping, Chu, and Ong. The two born here in the United States are named Tom and Jerry. Tom, who wears a safety pin on his shoe for style, reads me a story he wrote for school called "Magic Tree." "In a clearing in a forest you find a magic tree. To have cash, you have to say please. Then the cash comes out like a machine. It never gets run over because it's a magic tree. Its leaves are always green. The first kid was John. He wished he could have money. He had a penny. These kids came out and said, 'Can I have your penny?' And they took it and ran away. John said, 'They could have said please.' And cash came out from the tree."

The Yangs first lived in Minneapolis, in a housing project on the poor side of town. On the night George Bush was elected president, in November 1988, three men broke into their apartment, threatening the family and yelling what Pang-ku could only make out to be "Where's Cholo? Where's Cholo?" Mr. Yang managed to shoot one of the robbers in the leg, which earned the Yangs a feature story on the evening news the next day. Ten years to the month after Mr. Yang was forced to leave his village in Laos, the family decided to pick up and move to the safer environs of Duluth.

The West

When my family moved to California in 1966, we ended up in a town that had a large Japanese-American community and more cousins alone than the entire nonwhite population of Mount Prospect. Since then, I have always associated the West Coast as something of an Asian-American homeland, where familiar food and relations are plentiful. As I drive through the West, I remember that white supremacists have a similar idea. The states of Idaho, Montana, Wyoming, Oregon, and Washington are considered the "white homeland" of the Aryan Congress.

I drive through the Mount Hood area of Oregon, the home of the Yasui family. Min Yasui was the crusading Japanese-American lawyer and plaintiff in the infamous Corum Nobus case. Although I have never been here before, it is a place I remember well from the documentary *Family Gathering*, made by his filmmaker niece, Lise Yasui. Spectacular country that can become as ugly and bigoted a place as one would find anywhere on the map. On the edge of the Mount Hood Wilderness Area, near the towns of Orient and Boring, I pass through Sandy, Oregon. At one time, it was the home of Patrick Purdy, a drifter and mass murderer. One day in January 1985, Purdy dressed in camouflage gear and, during recess, shot up an elementary school in Stockton, California. Five Cambodian and Vietnamese children were killed, and many more were injured. Afterward, local law enforcement denied the shooting was a hate crime, but Asian Americans all over the country assumed it was one of the more tragic examples of escalating anti-Asian violence. Had he gone to trial, the question of a racial motive would have certainly been the focus of the proceedings. But Purdy killed himself outside a classroom after he finished spraying the playground.

Victor Wong describes the Asian as being "the face of the enemy" in the popular American imagination. It is as if Bataan, Kaesong, and Da Nang are etched across our faces. This fact was never more clear to Asian Americans of my generation than during the Vietnam War. Like many others, I was weaned and raised on a steady diet of television. But the Vietnam War provided the first sustained, public picture of Asians that I had ever experienced in my lifetime. The first time something close to my own image had ever reflected back at me. The war came to symbolize the penultimate in anti-Asian racism. Agitation against the war, or any form of U.S. military action in the Third World for that matter, was central to the principles of our political identity.

And so I am intrigued when I arrive in Seattle and meet Michael Park, a progressive twenty-one-year-old militant activist, rap singer, cultural nationalist, and Marine recruit. Michael, aka Psycho Mike M.C., performs rap with his brother Rafael, a junior Tae Kwon Do champion who himself is also known as the Golden M.C. Their stage name is, aptly, the Seoul Brothers.

Yo, here's a taste of something delicious / And by the way it's also nutritious / Not made for the ears of a child / But for the ladies to go buck wild / You see, the rhyme is like Kentucky Fried Chicken / So get with me, huh, I'm finger-licking . . . (from "Taste of Honey," by Rafael Park, aka the Golden M.C.).

I first learned about the Park brothers in a local Asian-American newspaper, the *International Examiner,* and was attracted to their story because they are rappers. The Seoul Brothers name didn't hurt either. But it was their multiple identities that intrigued me the most: college students, singers, activists, one an up-and-coming martial artist and future lawyer, the other an aspiring journalist and Marine reservist. Both defiant youths and good Korean sons at the same time. They have promised their mother that they will marry Korean women.

Contrary to conventional wisdom, Michael and Rafael are rebellious because of their upbringing, not in spite of it. The two brothers were born in South Korea, but were raised in an integrated neighborhood on the northside of Seattle. Their mother, a deeply religious woman, was a nurse in Korea. Their father is trained as a political scientist, but has devoted most of his twenty years in America to helping out other Korean immigrants, often for little or no pay. The boys recall the years of living in a tiny apartment, which had modest furnishings but seven telephones. Mr. Park wanted to make sure people could always get through to him if they needed him.

Mr. and Mrs. Park were not happy that Michael had joined the Marine reserves, and they had quite a scare when the Persian Gulf War broke out in 1991. In fact, the couple left Korea because of compulsory military service. Mrs. Park remembers, "When I was a child in the fourth grade, the Korean War started. That's why I understand how tragic a war can be. At that time my third brother died. He was in his second year of college when he died. The People's Army took him away and that's why I don't like soldiers. I hate war." Mr. Park himself had been stationed in the demilitarized zone as a student conscript. As a youth, he was a staunch backer of the war who felt the South Korean dictatorship was necessary for stability in the region. Today, Mr. Park, like his wife, is a pacifist and firm believer in democratic freedoms. While I was there, he sat down with his sons to watch a videotaped speech of the Nation of Islam leader, Louis Farrakhan, and then engaged them in a friendly debate over his ideology.

Mr. Park reminded me of my own father. He was a Goldwater man in 1964, and was a hawk for most of the Vietnam War. Today he spends his retirement time volunteering for progressive organizations, and recently traveled to Sacramento with my mother to march in solidarity with the United Farm Workers. I am not sure when or how my father began to change. There were fiery debates over the Vietnam War, but they were debates nonetheless. I remember when a Japanese exchange student witnessed one such skirmish. In a traditional Asian household, the youngest daughter would certainly have no place challenging the patriarch over any issue. But my parents, like the Parks, and like Victor, sought dual ground in the best of both cultures.

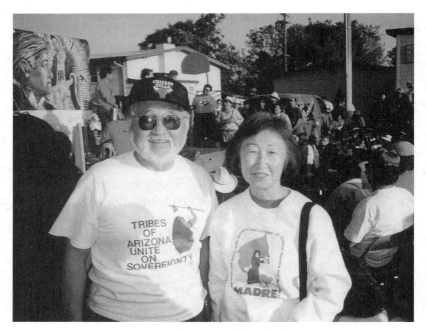

With my parents, still on the road.

When I was young, I always looked at my life as being too marginal even to discuss. Like Mike and Rafael, I landed in a racially integrated neighborhood and became a child of multiple worlds—Asian, black, white, brown—not simply the dual cultures we conventionally ascribe to the Asian-American experience. But that experience always seemed too singular, too weird to be an American story—too singular to be worthy of any telling beyond private memories. The Park brothers are supremely at home with the mixed bag of cultural influences that shape them. They are not distinguished by their level of assimilation, in the way we used to look at Americanization—conforming to a homogeneous norm. America seems to have caught up with the experience of young people like the Parks. In the making of *Fortune Cookies,* I set out to find who the Asian American is. Looking back at the Burtanog sisters of New Orleans, the Kochiyamas, Pang-ku, the Parks, even Mr. Choi, I realize the cumulation of stories speaks loudly of America itself. The question is no longer, "How do people become Americans?" but rather, "How has America become its people?"

List of Completed Works by Renee Tajima

Fortune Cookies: In Search of Asian America (working title). Producer/director/writer. Projected completion, 1995, feature-length color film, sound. Cross-country road trip in a rollicking search for the Asian-American identity. Commissioned by the Corporation for Public Broadcasting and coproduced by Quynh Thai.

Declarations: All Men Are Created Equal? Senior producer. 1993, 1-hour color video, sound. Public affairs special featuring television essays on equality by legal activist and author Derrick Bell, writer Beverly Donofrio, conservative free enterprise activist Robert Woodson, and education activist Demetrio Rodriguez. Directed segment "The Ballad of Demetrio Rodriguez" about his twenty-five-year struggle for public school equality in Texas. Produced for PBS.

Jennifer's in Jail. Director/writer. 1992, 1-hour color video, sound. Documentary about teenage girls in trouble with the law, focusing on Asian girl gangs, homeless, street kids in Hollywood, and incarcerated teenagers. Produced for Lifetime Television.

Special Olympics International. Director/writer. 1991, 10 minutes, color film, sound. Chronicle of rock musician Bob Seger's visit to Kathmandu for the Nepal National Games of the Special Olympics, the sporting event for athletes with mental retardation. Produced for ABC.

The Best Hotel on Skid Row. Producer/director/writer. 1990, 47 minutes, color film, sound. Documentary narrated by writer Charles Bukowski, profiles the denizens of a Skid Row singles hotel in downtown Los Angeles. Produced for Home Box Office, and premiered at the Cannes Film Festival.

What the Americans Really Think of the Japanese (*Americajin no Tainichi-kanjo no Tatamae to Honne*). Producer/director/writer. 1990, 90 minutes, color video, sound. (Japanese with no subtitles.) Documentary special on American attitudes toward Japan during the height of trade tensions between the two countries. Produced for Fujisankei.

Yellow Tale Blues. Executive producer/director. 1990, 30 minutes, color film, sound. Documentary explores the conflict between media myth and the reality of Asians in America. Features profiles of the families of filmmakers Renee Tajima and Christine Choy.

Monkey King Looks West. Producer/writer. 1989, 42 minutes, color film, sound. Documentary about the tales behind and within the Chinese Opera in America, focuses on three classically trained, immigrant opera performers who work day jobs as a butcher, an Atlantic City tour guide, and a Chinatown arts administrator.

Who Killed Vincent Chin? Producer/director. 1988, 82 minutes, color film, sound. Academy Award-nominated film in the Best Feature Documentary category, and winner of the Peabody Award and Dupont-Columbia Award. Documents the controversy over the beating death of a Chinese American in Detroit, Vincent Chin, by a Chrysler autoworker and the subsequent civil rights prosecution. Produced for PBS.

Haitian Corner. Producer. 1987, 75 minutes, color film, sound. Dramatic feature film, directed by Raoul Peck. Story of a Haitian poet living in self-exile in Brooklyn, New York. Winner of the Grand Prize at Festival du Cinéma "Images Caribes," and premiered at the Berlin International Film Festival. Produced for ZDF-Germany.

Permanent Wave. Producer. 1986, 20 minutes, color film, sound. Dramatic short film directed by Christine Choy as a part of the American Film Institute Women Directors Workshop, about a day in the life of a beauty shop. Stars Anna Marie Horsford and Lauren Tom.

Grenada. Producer/director. 1979, 14 minutes, color video, sound. Chronicle of the first anniversary of the New Jewel Movement in the Caribbean nation of Grenada, features interviews with former Prime Minister Maurice Bishop. Produced for the Harvard Forum.

PART IV

Multi-Capitalism

CHAPTER EIGHTEEN

Multiculturalism and Flexibility

Some New Directions in Global Capitalism

RICHARD P. APPELBAUM

Marx is dead, buried, all but forgotten. The headlong global rush to embrace capitalism, with (as Marx might have said) all its warts and pimples, has left only Cuba and North Korea as the standard-bearers of state-sponsored versions of socialism. Perhaps, if we stretch the definition of socialism a bit, we might include Myanmar. Vietnam? No way. With the Clinton administration ready to finally inter the last traces of MIA remains, Vietnam is poised to become a vast factory of low-wage, highly-skilled labor for American firms. China has already moved well down the capitalist road, and its southern Guangdong province is the fastest-growing economic region in the world—perhaps in world history. In China, in fact, both local and foreign capitalists have the best (or worst) of both worlds: the heavily subsidized and virtually captive workforce characteristic of what used to be called socialism, combined with a cowboy capitalist labor regime based on piecework, zero job security, and prohibitions against antimanagement organization.

But wait! Is Marx really to be relegated to the scrap heap of modernist history, displaced by a decentered postmodern global economy in which the seductions of capitalism and the global assembly line have rendered class struggle all but moot? Have science, technology, and information replaced labor-intensive factory production as the basis of global wealth? Are we truly entering a postindustrial world in which the labor theory of value has been superseded, with ordinary workers increasingly replaced by what U.S. labor secretary Robert Reich calls "symbolic analysts," people who work with their heads rather than their hands?

I think the news of Marx's death is premature. I say this not only as a realist who suspects that the Russian people may be having second thoughts about the virtues of unbridled capitalism, but also as a scholar who remains convinced that Marxist theory continues to have relevance for understanding the nature and limits of global capitalism. Moreover, these observations have implications for the future of multiculturalism; for as capitalism reasserts itself on a global scale, race, ethnicity, and gender are occupying a central role in the restructuring of capitalist relations.

The following theoretical observations grow out of a long-term study of changes in global capitalism. Alongside the explosion of low-wage factory jobs in what were once peripheral countries has come the reperipheralization of the core—the coming home of sweatshops to take advantage of the home market and cheap immigrant labor. Consider the fact that the only manufacturing industry in the United States that experienced a growth in employment in 1991 was the apparel industry, one that depends increasingly on a subminimum wage workforce from Mexico, Central America, and Southeast Asia. What does it mean that Los Angeles alone employs some 120,000 workers in five thousand sweatshops that are for the most part owned by ethnic minorities?[1]

Global capitalism has meant the feminization of labor worldwide, and the ethnicizing of labor on the home front. Class differences are overlaid with differences based on race and ethnicity in a highly volatile multiculturalism predicated on exploitation rather than mutual understanding. This essay is an attempt to reinsert a bit of forgotten Marxist materialism into the discourse of multiculturalism. It is organized into three theoretical moments, divided by two historical interludes, and followed by some reflections on capitalism and multiculturalism in both Los Angeles and the world capitalist economy. It is accompanied by a brief visual travelogue (see chapter 20) that will take us to apparel factories in Los Angeles, Hong Kong, China, Macau, and Vietnam.

Theory 1: Marx's Theory of Industrial Capitalism

In volume 1 of *Capital* Marx elaborates on his theory of capitalist production.[2] Drawing on the labor theory of value, Marx distinguishes between constant capital, variable capital, and surplus value as constitutive of the value of individual commodities as well as commodities in the aggregate (the wealth of nations). To briefly summarize his distinction, constant capital represents sunk investment in machinery and equipment, a fruit of past or congealed labor that comprises the principal means of producing wealth in capitalist society. Marx terms this form of capital "constant" because its value is given once in use; it can create no additional value on its own. Constant capital represents a fixed cost that must be paid off whether or not it is actually productively employed. To introduce a distinction that will become of central importance in the ensuing discussion, capital costs are essentially inflexible; once machines are bought they must be paid for whether they are running twenty-four hours a day or idled by labor strife or a sluggish economy.

Variable capital represents the cost of living labor, as indicated by the wage bill. In Marx's view, this is a form of "capital" because, under the capitalist mode of production, workers are equivalent to machines, objects to be used up in production in the most efficient ways possible. By this Marx means that workers are treated as appendages to the machines they operate, their labor power to be scientifically reorganized and managed until all conscious and self-controlling aspects have been rationalized away. Marx regards this quasi-human form of capital as "variable" because unlike constant capital, its value can vary according to the degree of exploitation: variable capital is capable of creating new value, in the form of variable amounts of surplus value, which are then appropriated by the capitalist. Furthermore, it is useful to see variable capital as varying in yet another way, which Marx elaborates in his analysis of the dynamics of capitalist production: workers, unlike machines, can be hired and fired to suit the momentary needs of production. Living labor can be broken down into nearly infinitesimal increments, enhancing the capitalist's flexibility in responding to changing market conditions. Workers can be hired or fired; they can be paid by the piece or the hour, according to the needs of the moment.

Surplus value is, of course, the difference between the value produced and the value of the capital (both constant and variable) required to produce it. Drawing on the labor theory of value, Marx argues that since only productive labor can make machinery, provide the raw materials required to quench its hunger, and then set it in motion to produce commodities, surplus value represents the unpaid labor extracted by the capitalist. Surplus value results from inequitable social relationships, which permit one class of people to exploit the labor of another. Among other things, it is the source of the capitalist's profit, which is what keeps the capitalist in business. When surplus value is threatened, by pressures from either rising capital costs or declining sales, the capitalist goes out of business. The story of the development of capitalism is the story of the struggle between labor and capital over the allocation of these costs of production.

Labor, then, provides capitalists with infinite flexibility, although of course labor's part in class struggle is to seek to reduce that flexibility by speaking with one voice, thereby taking on the "lumpy" character of constant capital. If all workers are treated as one, they are then equivalent to a single machine, a constant cost that must be incurred regardless of the needs of the capitalist. Marx predicts that capitalists will resist these efforts on the part of variable capital to simulate the power of constant capital through technological innovations that render such simulations moot: replacing them with actual machines. In Marx's terms, over time constant capital replaces variable capital, leading to a long-term rise in the ratio between the two (what Marx termed capital's "organic composition"). Marx recognized that built-in structural pressures for automation would result from both price competition between capitalists, which dictates a strategy of reducing unit costs through raising productivity, and class struggle, which dictates a parallel need to control living labor by substituting more tractable machinery.

Although Marx couldn't fully anticipate the end point of this process, it is clear that he foresaw the possibility of the fully robotic factory with continuously running machinery operated by a relative handful of highly trained engineers and technicians. The mixed consequences of this long-term tendency toward automation were also anticipated by Marx. On the one hand, automation would reduce costs and increase the amount of surplus that could be extracted from a diminishing workforce, while disciplining the remaining workers by threatening to render them superfluous. On the other hand, automation would lead to an increasing concentration of capital as enterprises became ever larger, fewer, and more capital-intensive. While this concentration would increase the power of gigantic monopolies, it would also increase their vulnerability, since vast amounts of capital would be tied up in machinery that must be kept running constantly in order to turn a profit. Labor actions could prove increasingly strategic in this regard, since a well-placed strike could send shock waves through the entire economy. Furthermore, the growing army of workers displaced by machines are a poor market for the goods those machines were churning out, leading to chronic and growing problems of overproduction and underconsumption. Devastating labor stoppages and economic stagnation were two of the prices capital would eventually pay for automation.

Interlude 1: The Transition to Postindustrial Capitalism

In the past twenty years, since Intel's 1971 invention of the microchip, capitalism has gone truly global. Communication and information technology has made it possible to coordinate most activities with a virtual disregard for time and space. The global assembly line has emerged, on which no country can leave its exclusive stamp. From cars to clothing to electronics, the hands that produce our goods and services reveal the exploitative side of multiculturalism: they are hands of color, of women, of impoverished Third World peoples driven by hardship and hunger to labor in the global factory.

The theories of the transition to a postindustrial world order have recognized the emerging global nature of capitalism. These theories, which have emerged in response to the rapidly shifting conditions of global production, have successively emphasized dependency,[3] the possibility of dependent development,[4] the new international division of labor,[5] and the world capitalist system.[6] Common to all of these theories is the recognition that capital is increasingly footloose on a global scale—that in their search for profits, transnational businesses have emerged that have a truly global reach.

Yet in different ways all of these theories share a number of assumptions that reflect the paradigm of industrial society out of which they grow, rather than a new framework based on a postindustrial world order. First, in varying degrees they all assume that the nation-state remains sovereign. One consequence of this assumption, for example, is an analysis of the class system reproduced at the global level, resulting in a world system of upper- (core), lower- (peripheral), and middle-class (semiperipheral) nations, with surplus flowing up and exploitation flowing down. Second, they all assume that physical labor remains the principal source of the wealth of nations. What drives the global economy, in the view of most of these theorists, is the search for cheap labor to run the global assembly line.

Theory 2: The Theory of Postindustrial Capitalism:
Karl Marx Meets Robert Reich

In the *Grundrisse*, his 1857-58 notebooks that were to become the foundation of volume 1 of *Capital*, Marx advanced the notion that in the final stages of capitalism, science and knowledge would replace labor as the source of value in production:

> The tendency of capital is thus to give a scientific character to production, reducing direct labor to a simple element in this process. . . . The production

process has ceased to be a labor process in the sense that labor is no longer the unity dominating and transcending it.

Direct labor and its quantity cease to be the determining element in production and thus in the creation of use value. It is reduced quantitatively to a smaller proportion, just as qualitatively it is reduced to an indispensable but subordinate role as compared with scientific labor in general. . . .

Labor does not seem anymore to be an essential part of the process of production. The human factor is reduced to watching and supervising the production process.

Invention then becomes a branch of business.[7]

Thus, in what must rate as one of the most prescient passages on the future of industrial society written at the time of its birth, Marx anticipates the postindustrial theorists. From Secretary of Labor Robert Reich to Harvard business economist Michael Porter,[8] from the post-Fordist Marxist geographers to Daniel Bell,[9] all seem agreed: we are entering a period in which information itself, rather than the physical production of goods, holds the key to wealth.

Using the terminology if not the assumptions of the original labor theory of value, economists, sociologists, and social geographers from left to right agree that "value-added" results increasingly from the application of knowledge, and not from the hands that make the goods. Reich, for example, in his postmodern rereading of Adam Smith, argues that the wealth of the twenty-first-century nation will be found in the work of its citizens, with work redefined in purely symbolic terms. This is the labor theory of value turned on its head: intellectual rather than physical labor holds the key to success in the global economy. Invention, design, marketing, retailing, networking, and other forms of "symbolic analysis" are the true source of value in the postindustrial world.

Needless to say, Marx and Reich drew opposite conclusions from these anticipated futures. In Marx's view in the *Grundrisse*, to the extent that the logic of capitalist development rendered labor superfluous, capitalism's ideological nature would be revealed for all to see: why should workers continue to slave away at meaningless, poorly paid, and increasingly unnecessary jobs, enriching a small group of capitalists and their professional-managerial entourage?[10] If machines could do the work, so be it; all that remained was to shatter the system of oppressive social relations that kept one class perpetually in thrall to another.

Reich, on the other hand, envisions a postindustrial utopia populated entirely by capitalists and members of the professional-managerial class, symbolic analysts all. In Reich's "can-do" world of people who use their minds to make things happen, there are no workers to be found—at least not in those nations that invest sufficiently in their most valuable resource, their people. Woe be unto the nation that fails to so invest, however, since that nation's semiskilled and unskilled workers are competing with an infinitely substitutable global workforce, one that will drag its wages down to a global level. Reich never makes entirely clear whether or not he believes that the United States, to take one national example, could in fact develop a workforce of one hundred million or so symbolic analysts who would be effectively insulated from the potential loss of their jobs through global competition. But it does seem clear that he is not overly concerned about the hands that will eventually wind up doing the detail labor, particularly if they are found half a world away.

Let us take one set of such hands—an actual case study of a woman who labors in one of Nike's six Korean-run Indonesian shoe factories. Sadisah (the pseudonym provided by *Harper's Magazine*, which first told the tale) earns about fourteen cents an hour, raking in just under forty dollars each month by laboring sixty-plus-hour workweeks manufacturing athletic shoes.[11] The shoes she makes sell for about eighty dollars a pair, of which her value-added contribution is a full eleven cents. There are various types of arithmetic that can be performed on these data. For example, it is easy to compute that it would take Sadisah two months to earn enough money to buy back the shoes she makes, although it is unclear where she would find the time for cross-training at the local athletic club. An even more interesting calculation is that Sadisah would only have to work an estimated 44,492 years to earn the $20 million multiyear endorsement fee Michael Jordan commanded before his short-lived retirement from professional basketball. It should be pointed out in this regard that Nike's 1991 profits reached $287 million on $3 billion in sales, a figure that is of course calculated after Michael Jordan and all of Nike's designers, advertising agencies, marketing services, managers, and owners have taken their cut.

This is a handsome rate of return, and reveals the "rational kernel" underlying Reich's reasoning: Michael Jordan's value-added alone is estimated at 10 percent of Nike's sales, roughly equivalent to the company's total annual profit. From a strictly capitalist viewpoint, his $20 million fee was a bargain, perhaps even more so than Sadisah's eleven cents. After all, there is only one Michael Jordan, and there are probably a billion or so Sadisahs around the globe, all hungry and available for work. Although it is unclear whether or not Michael Jordan truly qualifies as a symbolic analyst, there can be no question that he is a potent symbol to millions of consumers.

Nike's highly paid in-house ad agency, which constructed one of the most effective ad campaigns in history around this particular symbol, performs the very sort of symbolic analysis that Reich believes will fuel the global economy of the future.

Interlude 2: Globalizing and Localizing Forces in Global Capitalism

As capitalism embarks on its information-driven postindustrial phase, its contours are shaped by forces that simultaneously result in the spatial disaggregation of production on a global scale as well as the localization of production in tightly integrated economic regions. The former, centrifugal forces are driven by the search for cheap and controllable labor and are abetted by modern information technology. Bar scanners, electronic mail, telephones, fax machines—all permit a global coordination of just-in-time production and delivery systems.

The latter, centripetal forces are driven by the advantages that continue to accrue to spatial concentration of production in dense metropolitan industrial districts. Even in this high-technology age of information, there is no substitute for a hands-on approach to integrated design, marketing, retailing, buying, financing, and even production. It is hard to put several heads together to come up with a new design or advertising campaign or marketing plan if the heads are spread out around the globe. At the manufacturing level, the printed circuit must be inspected to determine if it meets company standards; the fabric must be felt to know if the garment will hang properly. Other things being equal, it is still better to have the company headquarters, research and development teams, factories, and principal customers close to one another. Labor costs are only one consideration among many in the changing geography of global capitalism.

Perhaps virtual reality simulations will eventually do away with time and space altogether, finally enabling quality-control officers or designers or company presidents to beam themselves aboard wherever they think they are really needed. But for the present time, face-to-face relations still confer quick turnaround and flexibility. When the presence of low-cost Third World labor is found in core country metropolitan areas, capital finds the best of both worlds: it needn't go too far from home to find cheap labor. Such "global cities" as Los Angeles, New York, London, and Tokyo combine core and periphery in a single centrally located region, constituting a form of black hole that swallows up the otherwise globalizing networks of postindustrial capitalism.[12]

Theory 3: Flexibility, Subcontracting, and Contradictions

Let us try to bring some of these ideas together by drawing on several theoretical frameworks that seem to be grappling with a common set of issues.

First, an increasingly globalized economic dispersion has occurred through the creation of global commodity chains, "network[s] of labor and production processes whose end result is a finished commodity."[13] These commodity chains consist of such pivotal points in the production process as raw materials extraction and processing, production and manufacturing, export, retailing, financing, marketing, and design—the entire spectrum of activities required to make a commodity.[14] While commodity chains are conceptualized as being dispersed over time and space, they must eventually "touch down" at different times and in different places, with different impacts on different locales. Commodity chain analysis shifts the framework for analyzing production; manufacturing is conceptualized as a dynamic process among interconnected firms, rather than as a static property of nations or nation-based corporations.

Commodity chains are particularly likely to be highly dispersed in such labor-intensive, cost-sensitive, retailer-driven production as apparel, athletic shoes, electronic assembly, toys, dolls, and so forth.[15] The companies that fabricate such commodities are truly manufacturers without factories, who source production through globally distributed subcontracting arrangements. Production is typically done in low-wage areas, from Indonesia to Los Angeles. In commodity chain analysis, core, periphery, and surplus value extraction are not conceptualized as attributes of nations, but as aspects of the commodity chain itself. There are core and peripheral activities; where each touches down, it will leave its stamp on the economic region. In the Reichian world of the information-based economy, core activities are those that require symbolic analysis, while peripheral activities are those that require physical labor. Often, contrary to Reich's utopian vision, they occur side by side in the same industrial district. Factory production may have been key to surplus value extraction and hence capitalist development during the phase of industrial capitalism, but in the postindustrial world this is no longer necessarily the case. Sadisah's factory may never induct her into the aristocracy of labor, nor will Indonesia's export processing zones necessarily ever elevate that country into core or even semiperipheral global status.

Second, it is clear that economic concentration in industrial districts continues to benefit capitalist production, as has been recognized since Alfred Marshall.[16] Industrial districts consist of dense concentrations of economic actors, who rely on one another to get the job done. They consist of elaborate subcontracting arrangements, often based on a handshake, and are characterized by speed, trust, and quick lines of communication. "Networks of trust" are typically mediated by intense familistic and ethnic ties; as one of the leading figures in the Los Angeles apparel industry explains it, "We're an information business."[17] Such "transaction-intensive networks" confer the flexibility required for efficiency and competitive advantage in a global economy.

It will be useful at this point to distinguish two meanings of "flexibility." The first meaning takes us back to our original discussion of Marx: flexibility entails the creation of truly variable capital through global subcontracting.[18] Labor can be taken on and cast off according to the momentary requirements of the marketplace. Surplus can be realized in one place, such as a Los Angeles design studio or marketing firm, while labor exploitation can occur in another—in the factory down the street or across the Pacific Ocean.

Since manufacturers subcontract labor rather than own their own factories, they are no longer legally responsible for wages, factory conditions, or the exploitation of labor; as the production manager for a major U.S. apparel manufacturer put it, "I'm not the sheriff."[19] Thus, costs and risks can be externalized: there is no danger of strikes closing down one's factory or idling one's machines, since one can always switch to more hospitable contractors elsewhere. Manufacturers no longer need worry about local or national health, safety, or labor regulations; they can always find a new subcontractor in a different state or a different country. Worries about health insurance, lawsuits, workers' compensation, and the other evils of class struggle can similarly be externalized. There is not even any serious danger of rising wages: somewhere in the world there is a factory where the price is right. Flexibility thus defines a contemporary moment in the class struggle, a means acquired by capitalists to once again render labor a truly variable form of capital just as it seemed to be gaining some measure of constancy.

This first, organizational form of flexibility is made possible by a second, more technological form: flexibility as the ability to respond instantly to changes in market conditions. During the industrial phase of capitalism, businesses relied on vertical integration to achieve quick response. Organizationally, it typically made sense for large firms to own or otherwise directly control as many forward and backward linkages as possible, from raw materials extraction to final sales. Because communications technology was rudimentary, only such internalized control and coordination seemed to afford the possibility of avoiding bottlenecks as well as intermediate layers of surplus value extraction.

In the postindustrial phase, however, a high degree of coordination can be achieved through advanced information technology without the need for vertical ownership or management. One American clothing giant, the Gap, can deploy more than five hundred factories around the globe, none of which it owns. When a shopper buys a Gap shirt at the local mall outlet, information about the purchase is scanned into a computer at the point of sale, where it joins a stream of thousands of other sales in a centralized computer in Hong Kong. There, the Gap's overseas buying office analyzes the pattern of sales, placing its orders with factories from Egypt to Hong Kong, from the Philippines to Mauritius. In the words of James Cunningham, the Gap Far East's Vice President for Offshore Sourcing, "the best retailers will be the ones who respond the quickest, the best . . . the time between cash register and factory shipment is shorter."[20] The Gap is an example of a buyer-centered commodity chain, a firm that is organized around retailing and sales rather than internalized sources of supply.[21] It is typical of many labor-intensive industries, from clothing to electronic assembly. I believe it is the organizational form of the future, one that will increasingly come to characterize all forms of production.

The growth of subcontracting is abetted by the recent acceleration of information technology, which has made possible just-in-time delivery, long-distance coordination and control, and a radical disaggregation of the commodity chain. The firm of the future will avoid investing in large amounts of constant capital and the workers to set it in motion. In the postindustrial world, "lean and mean" are the watchwords.[22] In the words of management guru Tom Peters associate Jim Kouzes, "contract out everything but your soul—what you do better than everybody else."[23] For many businesses it is better to have a small in-house design office, advertising agency, and perhaps retail outlet, and subcontract for everything else.

If modern information technology provides the means, subcontracting provides the organizational vehicle for a truly postmodern form of lean, mean capitalism in which only the profit centers remain in-house. Depending on the size of the firm, its organizational resources, and the nature of its business, subcontracting networks can extend down the street, throughout the metropolitan area, or around the world. An estimated thirty million Americans today work at subcontracted jobs, including temporary workers, part-timers, independent subcontractors, and other forms of contingent workers. One out of five nonmilitary workers put in fewer than thirty-five hours a week. It is estimated that as many as a third of U.S. workers fall into this category today, a number that may reach half by the end of the century, approaching the percentage in Japan.[24] Manpower, Inc., the world's largest temporary employment agency, handles more workers each day than General Motors or IBM. Manpower and similar agencies now handle 1.5 million workers, three times as many as a decade ago.[25]

Thus, thanks to modern technology, capitalism has the best of both worlds—it can globalize and/or localize to maximize its flexibility in both senses of the word. It can obtain organizational flexibility from subcontracting, reducing labor to truly variable capital, maximizing surplus extraction while minimizing costs and risks. And it can attain the technological flexibility needed to respond quickly to market changes, while retaining complete control over the labor process.

As with all structural contradictions of capitalism, this postindustrial resolution of the problems of labor's growing power during the industrial phase carries with it its own complications. I will mention two in passing, before turning in greater detail to a third that bears directly on the question of multiculturalism.

First, while subcontracting solves capital's growing problem of internalized labor costs, it also multiplies layers of profit centers. Every layer of subcontracting must have its cut in order to stay in business. During global expansionary times this may not pose a problem for capital, but during global recessionary times such as the present there is a severe profit squeeze. Kouzes's "soul of the business" may find itself acting in a very unsoulful manner, mercilessly cutting the prices it pays to its vendors, who in turn do the same to their own subcontractors, and so on down the line. Smaller subcontractors may be severely hurt, and workers will ultimately bear the brunt of the cost cutting. With each layer marching to the orders of the layer above it, and each layer taking its own cut, there is less and less left over for the people whose labor ultimately makes the goods. The only difference between exploitation in the industrial and postindustrial age is that during the latter, the soulful managers at the head of the line are spared the sight of the workers, who are now somebody else's problem.

Second, it should be obvious that the purpose of subcontracting (like all capitalist relations) is to cut costs to the capitalist. As I have indicated, subcontracting is specifically intended to chasten labor, destroying the once-proud "aristocracy of labor" in core countries by rendering it competitive with a low-paid global workforce. To the extent that this strategy is successful, Marx's problem of underconsumption once again rears its head, although now on a global scale. The so-called global economic recession, which currently plagues Japan and Germany as well as the United States, is in fact largely the result of this organizational restructuring of capitalism. The long boom in the global economy of the 1960s through the mid-1980s, during which time the four Asian dragons and other newly industrializing countries came of age, actually marked the undermining of the very global economic order that had made such "economic miracles" possible.[26] The Pacific shift was based in large part on the growing buying power of European and American workers, which it eventually undermined. Indonesian women workers, earning thirty-five dollars a month from Nike, are hardly a viable market for Air Jordans—nor are garment workers in Los Angeles, whose subminimum wages are in part repatriated to their families in Mexico or El Salvador or Guatemala.

The New Multiculture of Capitalism: The Case of Los Angeles

The third contradiction of postindustrial capitalism, which I will illustrate with the example of the Los Angeles apparel industry, is that it has promoted the ethnicization of capitalism on a global scale. As capitalism becomes a multitiered machine of many subcontracting arrangements, the faces and hands at the different levels differ in color from one another.

Beginning a generation ago, high and rising costs in the unionized apparel industry of the northeastern United States began to drive factories out of the region, first to the south, then to Mexico and the Caribbean, to Asia, to the world—and today back home to Los Angeles, where an abundance of impoverished immigrants from Mexico and Central America render long-distance subcontracting in search of cheap labor less necessary. This is not the place to explain the reasons for this reperipheralization of the core, which has to do with the failed economies in Mexico and Central America, as well as civil warfare and repressive governments in Guatemala and El Salvador. (Our own involvement in these causes is less well understood, particularly our support—through international lending organizations—of austerity programs that have driven wages down and contributed to the enormous cross-border wage disparities.)[27]

In Los Angeles county there are an estimated 125,000 garment workers laboring in some five thousand factories.[28] As many as a quarter of the workers are undocumented immigrants, and an unknown (but probably larger) percentage of the factories are unlicensed. Los Angeles today accounts for nearly a tenth of total U.S. employment in apparel.[29] The city's spatially concentrated downtown garment district—as well as numerous other similar concentrations spread throughout Los Angeles, Orange, and San Bernardino counties—confers multiple synergies for garment manufacturing.

Downtown Los Angeles provides a combination of working conditions associated with peripheral country status and postindustrial core country opulence, one that affords a disturbing vision of the emerging "global city" of the twenty-first century. On one side of the downtown divide—flanked by man-made barriers (the Harbor and Hollywood Freeways) that reinforce the existing hilly topography—lies the business, financial, governmental, and cultural heart of Los Angeles. Here one finds the city's centers of culture— the Music Center, the Dorothy Chandler Pavilion, the Mark Taper Forum. Just south of the Hollywood Freeway lie the principal federal, state, and local government agencies, including city hall, the central police station, and the courthouse. The corporate headquarters of the *Los Angeles Times* are found here, as are the towering spires of the major banks and financial institutions of the Pacific Rim economy: First Interstate World, ARCO Plaza (now Bank of America), Union Bank Square, Wells-Fargo, Home Savings, Citicorp, the World Trade Center, and the Pacific Stock Exchange. For the small part of the Pacific Rim economy that constitutes the garment industry, many of these institutions help provide capital, accounting, and other financial services. Nearby are the hotels, malls, and plazas of the Bunker Hill redevelopment project, "one of the largest postwar urban designs in North America."[30] "Little Tokyo" is found on the eastern fringe of this upscale portion of downtown; Chinatown is just across the Hollywood Freeway. All in all, one can locate some two dozen government buildings, an even greater number of banks, cultural institutions, and trade centers of various sorts, and nearly as many first-class hotels catering to the business traveler. The visual image is one of towering steel and glass, gerbil-like pedestrian walkways set several floors above street level, and integrated parking plazas that remove any need for ground-level pedestrian traffic. This antipedestrian downtown design was far from accidental, but rather was intentionally constructed so as to prevent any danger of human spillover from the surrounding impoverished slums and factory districts into the citadels of global capitalism.

As one moves south and east of Bunker Hill, this small area of capital and the symbolic analysts who serve it quickly gives way to the teem and dirt of the garment district, where one finds the hands that make the goods. The modern California Apparel Mart, at the corner of Los Angeles and 9th Streets, symbolizes the transition. In a neighborhood filled with factories, discount clothing stores, and the enormous open-air "knock off" apparel bazaar at Santee Alley, this thirteen-story structure, which claims its own zipcode, houses the showrooms of some fifteen hundred manufacturers, including some of the most celebrated labels in the fashion business. A few blocks east of the California Mart lies the Fashion Institute of Design and Merchandising, training the future designers and marketers of the "California look," while providing interns for the local apparel manufacturers.

The garment district for the most part is characterized by low, eight- to twelve-story buildings, mainly constructed during the 1930s, and many in need of repair. These buildings house the small factories (average size: sixteen workers) that produce the "California look."[31] A contractor may occupy an entire floor, or share the floor with others; a building may house as many as a dozen or more different sewing factories, all using the same bathroom. Not far from the sewing factories are a handful of buying offices that shop wholesale for the country's principal retailers. Here also are found yarn factories, fabric providers, and related fabric services; the flower, produce, and jewelry marts; sewing schools; immigration services, lawyers, and others serving or living off of the largely immigrant workforce.

The apparel industry in Los Angeles is spatially concentrated and ethnically stratified in a way that reveals the push-pull forces at work in the global economy. The industry has grown in Los Angeles because the concentration of industry-related professional, managerial, financial, and technical services, design and manufacturing capability, and a low-wage immigrant workforce—in the heart of the world's largest apparel market—has for many manufacturers overcome the attractiveness of yet-cheaper labor at a greater distance. Local production also enables manufacturers to avoid quotas and tariffs, which add especially to production costs outside the Mexico-Central America-Caribbean Basin region. (This region benefits from special programs designed to pay duties only on the value added in production, which, because of the low labor costs, is typically minimal.) Finally, local production enjoys the flexibility that results from subcontracting, in a system of labor control that divides the industry along ethnic lines.

The principal profits in the industry are realized by those who design the clothing, the firms that provide necessary financial and legal services, and those engaged in its sales. These include the manufacturers (more correctly designers, since they seldom engage in actual manufacturing of final products); bankers and accountants who specialize in apparel-related financing; the factors who buy up the retail accounts receivable from the manufacturers, freeing up money for fabric purchases; and retailers and retail buying offices. This upper stratum of the industry is almost entirely white, largely but not exclusively male, and disproportionately Jewish. It goes back to the turn of the century, when shepherding and apparel manufacturing began in Los Angeles. Union Bank, which continues to finance apparel manufacturers, was founded at that time as a repository for funds generated by the fledgling industry. Wealth generated in large part by the industry's founders gave rise to two of Los Angeles's principal hospitals, City of Hope and Cedars-Sinai. Family, friendship, and religious community ties that originated at that time continue into the present.

But the original founders of the industry have been largely supplanted by immigrants, first from New York City, then from the Middle East, and most recently from Asia. The apparel manufacturing community still remains relatively small and largely known to one another. Its core members—those longtime Angelinos, as well as East Coast transplants from one or two generations ago—honor one another at charitable fund-raisers, sit on the same boards, and belong to the same civic organizations and commissions. The interlopers—Middle Eastern Jews and Koreans—are less well integrated into the community. Such dense networks contribute to a Marshallian industrial district where apparel is "in the air." Here a deal is easily made over lunch at the outside patio of the California Mart, a design is readily imitated from among the thousands of wholesale lines on display within a few city blocks. Competition and personal rivalries complement a strongly shared culture, fostering an unending spin-off of fashion ideas and marketing strategies.

The other half of the local industry is concerned with the fabrication of clothing. The thousands of small factories are run mainly by small immigrant entrepreneurs, many of whom are barely a rung on the ladder above the workers they exploit. Turnover is estimated at 50 percent or more a year, as immigrants from Mexico, Guatemala, El Salvador, Korea, Taiwan, Hong Kong, and South Korea scramble for a toehold in the apparel economy. The factory owners constitute a layer between manufacturer and worker, often a layer of yellow skin between white and brown. The workers are almost entirely immigrants, predominantly female (although increasingly male), and, to an unknown extent, undocumented. Because manufacturers subcontract to factory owners they have until recently been treated as legally exempt from factory violations, so long as they employ licensed contractors; because contractors are small, economically unstable, and can easily procure fictitious licenses, they are virtually impossible to hold accountable.

The result is an industry where no one is likely to be held responsible for labor abuses—where there are no sheriffs. It is an industry ready-made for exploitation along lines of race and ethnicity, in which a white manufacturer might place an order to a struggling Korean contractor, who employs a Latino workforce that can neither understand his language nor fathom his culture. Such a situation is ripe for racial and ethnic resentment, an explosive situation in an already explosive city.

Conclusion: Race, Ethnicity, and Gender in Global Capitalism

Capitalism has always reinforced class divisions with divisions based on race, ethnicity, gender, and other forms of ascription. In any system based to a large degree on the exploitation of one group of people by another, such distinctions provide a useful basis for justifying inequality. Not only does this foster a "divide-and-conquer" ideology among those who otherwise might find common cause, but it also helps to foster a standard of exploitation based on what is accorded the least common denominator—whichever group finds itself at the bottom of the economic heap.

Since modern industrial capitalism originated in northern Europe, its racialization until recently has tended to divide along white and nonwhite lines. Today, with Japan a global capitalist player and the emerging Asian dragons (including China) in hot pursuit, we can expect this historically fundamental racialization to be overlaid by new and innovative forms. The Japanese are well known for their racial attitudes and corresponding practices toward Japanese-born Koreans, for example, while Koreans have themselves acquired a well-deserved reputation for their own brand of racialized economic exploitation in Central America and Los Angeles.[32] No racial or ethnic group is exempt from the possibility of developing its own brand of racism as a rationalization for its class practices. Racism preceded capitalism, and will likely survive it. But capitalism benefits from racism, and so gives it a particular focus and direction depending on the circumstances.

Capitalism may often appear to be color-blind. If African-American superstar athletes can sell athletic shoes, they will be elevated into the upper tier of the class structure by shoe companies. If Latinos constitute a growing market for goods, then goods will be produced and sold for Latinos. Yet capitalism continues to reinforce racial and ethnic divisions, albeit in different ways and on a global scale. What has occurred is a scrambling of the racial topography. The black-white made-in-America model of racialization is supplanted by a rainbow constellation of exploitative race relations, reinforcing class divisions with often virulent differences across racial and ethnic lines.

In the United States, where several decades of legislation and judicial decisions have outlawed most forms of overt discrimination, only those truly at the margins remain completely unprotected: newly arrived (and undocumented) immigrants, and inner-city African-American males. The former provide the local battalions of the reserve army of the global proletariat, while the latter are simply sacrificed, the frontline casualties of global economic restructuring joined with a national policy of economic triage. In both cases, racism and sexism play key justificatory roles; but the causes are at root economic. Within the American production system, race, ethnicity, and gender continue to serve class divisions. As I have sought to show in the example of the Los Angeles garment industry, one encounters a rainbow coalition of conflicting interests: Asians against Latinos, whites against people of color, documented against undocumented workers.

Globally, the lowest stratum of the class structure is comprised disproportionately of women, rural immigrants to urban areas and export processing zones, and racial and ethnic minorities as defined in a particular country. Although exploitation of these groups undoubtedly preceded their incorporation into the global economy, it has now taken on new forms, designed to keep their wage demands low and their interests divided. It is perhaps a telling irony that while the most egregious types of exploitation are formally illegal in the United States, American businesses continue to profit from such exploitation elsewhere in the world, where even the effort to struggle against exploitation is often ruthlessly suppressed.

Flexibilization and subcontracting facilitate these global patterns of exploitation, since not even paternalistic loyalties or corporatist leanings are permitted to detract from the hard-nosed pursuit of profit in the fast-moving information age. If businesses today are counseled to retain only their soul, will that soul include people whose color or gender differs from that of the few remaining soulful managers? It seems that as capitalism moves into its information-driven stage, it will find new and creative ways to reproduce its old racial, ethnic, and gender differences on a global scale.

Notes

1. Richard P. Appelbaum and Edna Bonacich, *A Tale of Two Cities: The Garment Industry in Los Angeles* (Los Angeles: Report to the Haynes Foundation, 1993).

2. Karl Marx, *Capital,* vol. 1: *A Critique of Political Economy* (New York: International Publishers, 1967 [1867]).

3. Samir Amin, *Accumulation on a World Scale* (New York: Monthly Review Press, 1974); A. Emmanuel, *Unequal Exchange: A Study of the Imperialism of Trade* (New York: Monthly Review Press, 1972); and Andre Gunder Frank, *Latin America: Underdevelopment or Revolution?* (New York: Monthly Review Press, 1969), *World Accumulation: 1492–1789* (New York: Monthly

Review Press, 1978), and *Dependent Accumulation and Underdevelopment* (London: Macmillan, 1979).

4. Fernando H. Cardoso and Enzo Faletto, *Dependency and Development in Latin America* (Berkeley: University of California Press, 1979); Peter Evans, *Dependent Development* (Princeton, N.J.: Princeton University Press, 1979); Tom Gold, "Dependent Development in Taiwan" (Ph.D. diss., Harvard University, 1981); Hyun-Chin Lim, *Dependent Development in Korea, 1963–1979* (Seoul, South Korea: Seoul National University Press, 1985).

5. Folker Frobel, Jurgen Heinrichs, and O. Krege, *The New International Division of Labor: Structural Unemployment in Industrialized Countries and Industrialization in Developing Countries* (Cambridge: Cambridge University Press, 1980), and "The Current Development of the World Economy: Reproduction of Labour and Accumulation of Capital on a World Scale," *Review* 5:4 (1982): 507–55; Dieter Ernst, *Innovation, Industrial Structure and Global Competition: The Changing Economics of Internationalization* (New York: Campus Verlag, 1987), and *The New International Division of Labour, Technology and Underdevelopment: Consequences for the Third World* (New York: Campus Verlag, 1980); and A. Lipietz, "New Tendencies in the International Division of Labor: Regimes of Capital Accumulation and Modes of Regulation," in *International Capitalism and Industrial Restructuring*, ed. R. Peet (Boston: Allen and Unwin, 1986).

6. Immanuel Wallerstein, *The Modern World-System* (New York: Academic Press, 1974), *The Capitalist World Economy* (Cambridge: Cambridge University Press, 1979), and *The Modern World-System II* (New York: Academic Press, 1980); and Terence K. Hopkins and Immanuel Wallerstein, "Commodity Chains in the World Economy Prior to 1800," *Review* 10:1 (1986): 157–70.

7. Karl Marx, *Grundrisse*, trans. Martin Nicolaus (New York: Vintage Books, 1978 [1857–58]), 375–80.

8. Robert Reich, *The Work of Nations* (New York: Alfred A. Knopf, 1991); Michael E. Porter, "The Competitive Advantage of Nations," *Harvard Business Review* (March–April 1990): 73–93, and *The Competitive Advantage of Nations* (New York: Free Press, 1990).

9. Allen J. Scott, "Flexible Production Systems and Regional Development," *International Journal of Urban and Regional Research* 12 (1988): 171–86; Allen J. Scott and Michael Storper, eds., *Production, Work, and Territory: The Geographical Anatomy of Industrial Capitalism* (Boston: Allen and Unwin, 1986); Michael Storper and Richard Walker, *The Capitalist Imperative: Territory, Technology, and Industrial Growth* (New York: Basil Blackwell, 1989); Michael Storper and S. Christopherson, "Flexible Specialization and Regional Industrial Agglomeration: The Case of the U.S. Motion Picture Industry," *Annals of the Association of American Geographers* 77 (1987): 104–17; Daniel Bell, *The Coming Crisis of Post-Industrial Society: A Venture in Social Forecasting* (New York: Basic Books, 1973), and "The Third Technological Revolution and its Possible Socioeconomic Consequences," *Dissent* (spring 1989): 164–76.

10. Barbara Ehrenreich and John Ehrenreich, "The Professional Managerial Class," in *Between Labor and Capital*, ed. Pat Walker (Boston: South End Press, 1979).

11. Jeffrey Ballinger, "The New Free Trade Hell: Nike's Profits Jump on the Back of Asian Workers," *Harper's* (August 1992): 46–47.

12. Saskia Sassen, *The Global City: New York, London, Tokyo* (Princeton, N.J.: Princeton University Press, 1991).

13. Hopkins and Wallerstein, "Commodity Chains in the World Economy Prior to 1800," 159.

14. See the essays in Gary Gereffi and Miguel Korzeniewicz, *Commodity Chains and Global Capitalism* (Westport, Conn.: Greenwood Press, 1994).

15. Gary Gereffi, "The Organization of Buyer-Driven Global Commodity Chains: How U.S. Retailers Shape Overseas Production Networks," in ibid., 95–122.

16. Scott, "Flexible Production Systems and Regional Development"; Scott and Storper, *Production, Work, and Territory*; Storper and Walker, *The Capitalist Imperative*; Storper and

Christopherson, "Flexible Specialization and Regional Industrial Agglomeration"; Porter, "The Competitive Advantage of Nations"; Michael J. Piore and Charles Sabel, *The Second Industrial Divide: Possibilities for Prosperity* (New York: Basic Books, 1984).

17. Sidney Morse, personal interview, 28 October 1992. Morse was the largest owner and director (in 1992) of the California Mart. (Two years later the mart was foreclosed and is currently under new ownership.)

18. Jeffrey Pfeffer and James M. Baron, "Taking the Workers Back Out: Recent Trends in the Structuring of Employment," *Research in Organizational Behavior* 10 (1988): 257–303.

19. Mitch Glass, personal interview, 14 August 1991. Glass was the vice president of production, Cherokee Corporation.

20. James Cunningham, personal interview, 28 November 1991. Cunningham was the Vice President for Offshore Sourcing, the Gap Far East, Hong Kong.

21. Gereffi, "The Organization of Buyer-Driven Global Commodity Chains."

22. Tom Peters, *Liberation Management: Necessary Disorganization for the Nanosecond Nineties* (New York: Alfred A. Knopf, 1992).

23. James M. Kouzes, *The Challenge of Leadership: How to Get Extraordinary Things Done in Organizations* (San Francisco: Jossey-Bass Publishers, 1987).

24. Robert Rosenblatt, "Benefits Studied for Part-Time Workers," *Los Angeles Times*, 16 June 1993: D14; Lance Morrow, "The Temping of America," *Time,* 29 March 1993: 40–41; Marco Orru, Gary G. Hamilton, and Mariko Suzuki, "Patterns of Inter-Firm Control in Japanese Business," *Organization Studies* 10 (1989): 549–74; and Michael Gerlach, *Alliance Capitalism: The Strategic Organization of Japanese Business* (Berkeley: University of California Press, 1992).

25. Janice Castro, "Disposable Workers," *Time,* 29 March 1993: 43–47.

26. Jeffrey Henderson and Richard Appelbaum, "Situating the State in the Asian Development Process," in *States and Development in the Asian Pacific Rim,* ed. Richard Appelbaum and Jeffrey Henderson (Newbury Park, Calif.: Sage Publications, 1992).

27. See Richard Rothstein, "Continental Drift: NAFTA and Its Aftershocks," *American Prospect* 12 (winter 1993): 68–84.

28. For a more detailed elaboration of these points, see Appelbaum and Bonacich, *A Tale of Two Cities,* and Bonacich in this volume.

29. Edna Bonacich and Patricia Hanneman, "A Statistical Portrait of the Los Angeles Garment Industry," unpublished manuscript (1991).

30. Mike Davis, *City of Quartz: Excavating the Future of Los Angeles* (London and New York: Verso, 1990), 229.

31. See Bonacich and Hanneman, "A Statistical Portrait of the Los Angeles Garment Industry."

32. Kurt Peterson, *The Maquiladora Revolution in Guatemala* (New Haven: Yale Law School, Orville H. Schell Jr. Center for International Human Rights, Occasional Paper Series 2, 1992; Appelbaum and Bonacich, *A Tale of Two Cities*; Gregg Scott, "Achieving Dignity and Embracing Hope: Daily Battles for Justice in the Los Angeles Garment Industry" (Santa Barbara, Calif.: UCSB Department of Sociology, Report to the Haynes Foundation, 1993).

CHAPTER NINETEEN

The Class Question in Global Capitalism
The Case of the Los Angeles Garment Industry[1]

EDNA BONACICH

The proponents of multiculturalism claim to address the issues of race, class, and gender, but in practice class often falls out of the picture. Multiculturalism's critique is aimed not only at "mainstream" academic discourse, but also at Marxism, which is seen as a Eurocentric, male-dominated approach to society. Marxism is accused of ignoring the peculiar experiences of women and people of color (including women of color in both categories), who have often been cut out of the "proletariat." By placing the proletariat at the center of its analysis of class struggle, Marxism tends to ignore the important struggles for social change engaged in by women and people of color.

Although bringing in the experiences and struggles of women and people of color as a central focus of attention is obviously a very important corrective to a narrowly conceived Marxism, I am concerned that sometimes too much of what Marxism has to offer gets thrown out. For instance, in shifting away from an emphasis on "shop-floor struggles," sometimes the importance of those struggles gets completely disregarded.

More important, the attack on Marxism is often framed as an attack on "structuralism," that is, a structural analysis of society that ignores the cultural component of experiences and struggles. A useful corrective has been introduced here, but again, I fear that some authors take it to extremes, disregarding social structure entirely in their shift toward emphasizing issues of culture, identity, and difference. (I acknowledge that there are some authors who study working women and people of color, including their shop-floor struggles, but their emphasis tends to be on "giving voice" to the workers rather than on analyzing the larger systems of oppression in which they find themselves.)

What happens too often, in my observation, is that "class" gets treated as a kind of cultural identity. A person is "working-class" because she came from a working-class background and is familiar with a working-class life-style. This enables university women to consider themselves to be working-class, even though they earn professional salaries and enjoy the advantages of being middle-class. The idea of class as a system of exploitation that is life-threatening to working people has fallen by the wayside. Instead, it has become another component of cultural identity, along with race and gender.

This transformation of class enables proponents of multiculturalism to feel comfortable about carrying on their debates within the confines of the university, since they can claim that race, class, and gender differences are all represented there. It is true that race and gender differences are present on university campuses, providing a rich milieu for challenging the university's Eurocentric and male-centered traditions. But the working-class is absent among the academic debaters (though not from the university as an institution in its employment of secretaries, janitors, food-service workers, etc.).

My hope in this short paper is to reintroduce the importance not only of class and class struggle, but of a Marxist structural analysis of the system. I do this by examining the garment industry in Los Angeles. Here we see the exploitative character of capitalism, and how it is being transformed and increased by globalization. Issues of race and gender are, of course, important for workers in this industry, but not so much as loci of identity and culture as ways in which their exploitation as workers is organized. In other words, race and gender are used by the capitalist class for the more effective exploitation of labor.

As I see it, racism grew out of the imperialist expansion of Europe. It was the ideology that accompanied Europe's colonial domination of the rest of the world. Imperialism and colonialism created a racially divided working class in which the colonized were relegated to various forms of coerced labor or were kept dependent on linked, noncapitalist economies. These relations were replicated in the United States when peoples of color were either conquered in the Americas or brought, under various degrees of coercion, into the country as workers. Although state-sanctioned racism has ended, racism continues to be replicated and is still of considerable use to the capitalist class in maintaining an especially disadvantaged sector of the working class. Thus, I am not saying that class is more important than race (or gender), but rather, that we must recognize the ways in which gender and race are intensely important elements of the system of class exploitation. In shunting aside the class dimension of race and gender, students of multiculturalism blind themselves to one of the most important engines of race and gender oppression.

The globalization of capitalism is making class relations more difficult to disentangle, a factor that may play a part in disregarding them. The lines of exploitation have become complex and obscure, not only at a global level, but even at a local level. For the remainder of this paper I examine class relations in the Los Angeles garment industry. I consider the question of fighting back: what is being done and what can be done to counter the power of capital? I end by considering what this says about the limitations of multiculturalism.

Class Relations in the Los Angeles Garment Industry

The Los Angeles garment industry is hierarchically organized. Workers are typically employed in small contracting shops, and the contractors appear to be their main exploiters. In reality, contractors work for manufacturers, who design and engineer clothing production, who purchase the textiles, and who wholesale the finished goods. Manufacturers merely contract out part of the labor, namely, the sewing and sometimes the cutting. In a sense, contractors serve as "labor contractors."

Garment manufacturers can contract out the sewing and cutting both locally and abroad. They are encouraged by certain U.S. government policies to contract in Mexico, Central America, and the Caribbean. Still, thousands of contracting shops exist in the United States, employing immigrant workers primarily from Asia and Latin America. The workers are mainly women, though a significant proportion is men. In Los Angeles the workers are frequently undocumented.

Contractors are also typically immigrants, with the majority from Asia. They are immigrant entrepreneurs, in fierce competition with each other. Manufacturers take advantage of the competition and are able to drive prices down to the bare minimum. The contracting system enables manufacturers to squeeze contractors and then claim they have no responsibility for conditions in the contracting shops because the contractors are "independent" businesses.

Despite their power in relation to contractors, manufacturers are generally powerless in relation to retailers, who in turn exercise control over them and take advantage of the competition among them. Clothing is typically not produced unless a retailer has placed an order. Manufacturers show their samples to retailers' representatives who choose whether or not to order them, at which point the clothing is put into production.

Retailing in the United States has undergone major restructuring in recent years, as stores have consolidated into giant chains, and huge discounters (like Wal-Mart) and specialty stores (like the Gap and the Limited) have emerged to challenge the traditional department stores. Not only do retailers have tremendous economic clout in relation to manufacturers, but they also have gone into garment manufacturing themselves. They produce clothing under their own "private labels" both locally and overseas, putting increasing pressure on manufacturers, whose market is shrinking.

The effect of this hierarchy, combined with international competition (which is partially generated by segments of U.S. capital that are producing clothing abroad), is to place extreme pressure on the workers. Los Angeles garment workers typically labor under onerous conditions. They often are paid less than minimum wage, are not paid overtime, and suffer from severe job insecurity as their employers go in and out of business. Child labor is sometimes found, and illegal homework is rampant.

Garment workers in Los Angeles are clearly "exploited," but by whom? Class relations are obscured by the hierarchy of contractors, manufacturers, and retailers, and are even more obscured by the many adjunct actors who participate in the industry. The industry resembles the food chain, with bigger fish eating fish that are a little smaller than them, and on down the line. How can class struggle be conducted under these circumstances, and against whom?

Another way to phrase the question is to consider where the surplus goes, because the definitive character of "exploitation" is the appropriation of the surplus generated by the labor of other people. In the Los Angeles garment industry surplus is extracted in two basic ways: by the classic system of returns to the ownership of private property in the form of profit, rent, and interest; and by the high salaries garnered by professionals and managers.

To give a couple of examples: among retailers, in 1991 the Gap, an apparel specialty store chain, made profits of $258.4 million, and its chief executive officer, Donald Fisher, received a salary of $2.48 million. Among the top sixty-three publicly held apparel retail chains, the average company earnings in 1993 were $92.35 million, and the average salary of their CEOs was $904,900.[2] Real-estate owners include, among others, the owners of the buildings where the contracting shops are located. Among them is Jack Needleman, owner of the Anjac buildings in the Los Angeles garment district, who is said to be worth at least $250 million.

High salaries go not only to direct employees of the industry, but also to adjunct professionals such as accountants, lawyers, and advertisers. For example, we visited two apparel CPAS, one of whom has an office in Santa Monica's Water Garden, which has a man-made lake and multiple fountains, and the other in a downtown office building with an indoor waterfall. These buildings are like temples to capital. We did not ask them how much they make, but it is clear that they are doing very well. The owners of the buildings they are in also collect rent, which ultimately comes from the industry.

We have been discovering that there is a power elite in the Los Angeles apparel industry—that is, the higher echelons tend to know each other and mix together. Their primary form of mixing seems to be through charitable organizations. They support such charities as Cedars-Sinai Hospital, the City of Hope, the United Jewish Fund, and Israel Bonds. They hold fund-raising dinners, where they get together and honor one of their members. People who sit on the boards of these organizations, and who attend their functions, include both owners of capital (e.g., the California Mart owners, big manufacturers, real-estate owners) and managers and professionals (e.g., bankers, accountants, buying officials, lawyers, retail managers, and top managers in large manufacturing firms). The distinction between capitalist and professional/manager seems unimportant at the social level.

The extraction of surplus is supported by ideology and the state. Ideological support is necessary because the tremendous differences in life circumstances between themselves and the workers must give the wealthy pause. How can they justify their tremendous privilege? They hold various beliefs to support themselves: This is an industry where anyone can rise. It is entrepreneurial. The workers, too, will be able to avail themselves of the opportunities the industry offers. Some claim that they themselves worked their way up from the bottom. They see garment work as an entry-level job. Workers will not have to stay there.

Part of their ideology is tinged with racism. Workers are seen as "primitive" people who do not even know how to use a toilet. Employers claim they are teaching the workers basic skills for living in a "civilized" society.

They believe strongly in the fact that there is a "free market," and that everyone is doing what they choose to be doing. The workers would not be doing these jobs if they did not want them. As one powerful manufacturer said: "No one is putting a gun to their heads." In other words, the employers accept inequality as a product of free choice and fail to acknowledge that there is any power or coercion exercised in the system. And they believe that inequality will "work itself out" through upward mobility.

Finally, their charitable activities help them to assuage their guilt. They see themselves as "giving something back" because they were among the lucky ones who made it in the system. They fail to recognize that their good fortune is predicated on the impoverishment of others.

The role of the state is complex. On the one hand, numerous protections for workers are built into the law, including the payment of minimum wage and overtime, the banning of child labor and homework, health and safety regulations, protections for the right to organize independent unions, anti-discrimination laws, and unemployment insurance. These kinds of laws are in the interests not only of workers, but of capitalists who want to prevent undercutting by other capitalists. In the apparel industry it is not untypical for a contractor to approach a manufacturer and offer to sew the goods for 10 percent less than what the manufacturer is paying, no matter what the price. The setting of minimal standards aims at preventing such deals.

In practice, however, these provisions are not enforced. The inspection agencies are woefully underfunded and understaffed and barely make a dent in preventing wholesale violations of the law. When the union has pushed for joint liability legislation to hold manufacturers responsible for conditions in their contracting shops, Republican governors have vetoed the bills. The National Labor Relations Act, protecting the right to form unions, is completely ineffective in this industry, as employers openly fire workers who show any desire to unionize. By the time a case works its way through the cumbersome bureaucracy, the shop will have closed, moved, changed its name, or taken other evasive action.

Apart from weak enforcement of protective laws, the state supports surplus extraction in three other major ways. It does so through immigration law, which creates an especially rightless group of workers who are subject to intimidation. It does so through the encouragement of capital flight to countries where labor standards are lower and where unions are suppressed, thereby increasing the profits of U.S. businesses. Most important, it does so by supporting the rights of private property, that is, the rights of owners of capital to garnish the socially generated surplus simply because of their ownership.

Fighting Back[3]

It is my impression, based on doing volunteer work with the International Ladies Garment Workers Union (ILG) in Los Angeles, that workers in this industry generally feel exploited. No doubt some feel grateful to be working at all, and to have a toehold in the United States. Others may also feel terrified of engaging in any struggle against their employers for fear of losing their jobs or, worse, being deported. Nevertheless, the potential for militancy on the part of immigrant garment workers is high, in my opinion.

Not only have garment workers participated in militant strikes, but immigrant workers in similar low-wage industries in Los Angeles have also shown their militancy. Sometimes they have won important victories, as in the Justice for Janitors campaign in Century City, which was able to overcome the contracting out of janitorial services by forcing the building owners to get their contractors to accept the union. Another extraordinary struggle was waged by drywallers, who were able, despite the fact that the workers were widely dispersed over several counties and hundreds of miles, to gain a union contract in an industry that had drastically reduced their wages and benefits. The Hotel Employees and Restaurant Employees (HERE) has shown its ability to make important gains against a set of union-busting hotel owners. They are currently (mid-1994) engaged in a campaign to organize several major downtown hotels at the same time, along with a parallel campaign to organize the hotels along Century Boulevard that serve the airport (LAX).

These movements show that Los Angeles's immigrant workers are ready to struggle for justice and respect. I do not want to minimize the effort that is required in organizing these workers; their commitment to unionization is not automatic. But the potential is certainly there. Consciousness is not the major stumbling block. Workers do not buy the dominant ideology that they are not oppressed. They feel their oppression intensely and have no illusions about it.

If the problem of fighting back does not lie in the workers themselves, where does it lie? It lies primarily in the problem of finding a winning strategy. The problem is that capital has developed new tools with which to crush labor. What was assumed to be an accommodation between capital and labor during the period when Keynesianism reigned has broken down. Now employers who used to accept unions as an inevitable, and even useful, part of the industrial landscape, have joined in a declaration of war to destroy the unions in this country (and everywhere else).

The processes we have been describing, including globalization and con- tracting out, are part of the effort to destroy worker self-organization and empowerment. Add to them the gutting of the National Labor Relations Board (NLRB) as a small corrective in the imbalance of power and the in- ability of Congress to pass a law prohibiting striker replacement. The class struggle is not dead; rather, the capitalist class is waging it with intensified fury.

Thus, the problem becomes, how does one develop a successful strategy in the face of this onslaught? Workers can be very militant, but their move- ments can be crushed, sometimes brutally. The dilemma is to find a way to fight and *win*. Fighting back occurs all the time, of course, both in everyday actions on the shop floor and in more visible mobilizations, such as marches and strikes. But these actions can often end in defeat and demoralization. Militancy can turn into resignation and despair unless a winning strategy can be developed.

As I have suggested, some unions working with immigrant workers in Los Angeles are beginning to put together campaigns that are showing signs of success. The strategic elements of these struggles include the following features:

First, the unions recognize that organizing solely at the contracting level will not work. Even if one succeeds in organizing such a shop, it will quickly go out of business because manufacturers will cease to send work to such a shop. It is thus necessary to organize larger groups of shops at the same time—for example, all the contractors of a single manufacturer, all the man- ufacturer-contractor complexes in a particular sector of the industry, or all the manufacturer-contractor complexes in a particular geographic location. Another approach involves including the retailer in the campaign, either as a direct producer of private label goods or as the recipient of sweatshop pro- duction. The inclusion of retailers enables the coupling of worker action with consumer boycott.

A second element in the new strategic thinking is the need to develop strong community support for one's campaigns. This includes two types of "community." First, the workers need the strong support of their own com- munities, including, importantly, their ethnic communities. Thus the move- ment for worker empowerment must join with other community-based movements, including movements for better housing, health care, environ- mental safety, and so forth. High on the list for Los Angeles workers is the movement for immigrant rights. The unions need to link with these other movements, as well as to demonstrate the importance of decent wages and working conditions to the general well-being of the ethnic communities that make up Los Angeles.

The second "community" whose support the workers need includes all those forces that are sympathetic to immigrant workers' struggles and can be mobilized on their behalf. These include political, religious, academic, consumer, and other groups that recognize the exploitation that is occurring and will lend their considerable social power in support of these struggles. For example, these forces can express their outrage against police efforts to crush strikes and demonstrations, and ensure that egregious antiworker tactics cannot be deployed by the capitalist class. They can exert pressure on political as well as economic actors by participating in demonstrations, by voting, by boycotting, by writing letters and articles for the press, and by making it clear to the hierarchy of employers that they are being watched. The "community," in this sense, can be an important moral force for checking the class struggle being waged by employers.

The moral case of garment workers (and of other workers in similarly exploitative industries) is certainly compelling. Their case is similar to that of the civil rights movement. A horrible injustice is being committed, but those who hold the reins of power, who live in considerable affluence, and who also control all the mass media of communication have no intention of allowing the system they have created to be challenged. A major battle must be waged to get the public to see the injustice and the necessity for supporting workers' movements. It is only when such a climate of public opinion has been created that a brutal crushing can be staved off.

A third strategic consideration concerns the unions themselves. There is a need for considerable internal reform on the part of unions. The demography of the workforce has changed dramatically, and the leadership of some unions has been very slow to reflect these changes. Some unions also became complacent during the postwar years, focusing on retaining the membership they had, and not bothering with organizing the unorganized. Unions need to change their orientation; some of them are.

For example, HERE Local 11 has a Latina president, Maria Elena Durazo, who brings to the union leadership not only a different demographic configuration, but also strategic development. Local 11 has broken down the distinction between representing existing members and organizing new members. All organizers represent, and all representatives organize. Existing members are active in recruiting new members and helping in the organizing struggle. By helping fellow workers put pressure on employers, the workers who have yet to win a contract are made individually less vulnerable. Meanwhile, workers who already have a contract know that their own contract will only improve if they can bring more of their industry under the union's control.

Another change that some unions are making is to give up on the NLRB as a defender of workers' rights to organize. Not only was the NLRB packed with pro-employer forces under the Reagan and Bush administrations, but it is also especially ineffective as a tool for organizing the kinds of industries that employ immigrant workers in Los Angeles today. The tremendous instability of employment connected with the contracting system makes drawn-out elections almost useless, let alone the fact that employers are able to avoid signing a contract even when an election has been won by a union. Even the filing of charges against employers for blatantly illegal practices is time-consuming, costly, and rarely assured of victory.

Consequently, unions are turning toward more direct action against employers, attempting to get them to come to the bargaining table without having to suffer through an extended legal procedure. This tactic is associated with greater militancy on the part of workers, as they take to the streets and make it impossible for employers to conduct business as usual.

The ILG has been pursuing some of this new strategic thinking by opening Garment Workers' Justice Centers. These centers enable workers to become associate members of the union and participate in the building of a mass workers' movement that will be able to put broad pressure on the industry as a whole. Meanwhile, Justice Center members engage in political demonstrations and help put pressure on one another's shops to deal with important grievances.

It is noteworthy that most of the recent union successes in Los Angeles have been in industries that are less likely to suffer the extreme mobility of the garment industry: janitorial services, hotels, construction. The garment industry, and manufacturing in general, faces the added threat that firms will leave if they are faced with the prospect of unionizing.

This challenge has limits, however. No doubt some of the apparel industry that has not already left will leave in response to NAFTA, and worse, should the latest GATT agreement be signed into law. However, certainly part of the industry will not leave, whatever threats it makes. The need for a quick turn, especially in the fashion sector of the industry, makes overseas production inefficient. Some of the industry is likely to remain regardless. More important, the threat of leaving creates local political contradictions that cannot be ignored. City, state, and federal governments cannot simply let all U.S. industry move abroad. They have to deal with the contradiction this implies for the well-being of society. Although crushing the local labor movement is one of their options, it is not one that is compatible with the democratic traditions of our country, and raises an important moral backlash that will have to be dealt with.

Ultimately, the U.S. labor movement will have to link forces with workers overseas. Tentative steps are being taken in this direction, especially with Mexican workers. The ILG is starting to treat the production systems of manufacturers, which they liken to an octopus, as simply having longer tentacles that stretch across borders. The principles involved in organizing such a structure do not change dramatically just because of its transnational nature. Of course there are special problems connected to the social and political situations in different countries. Still, the potential for cross-border actions is going to rise.

Another approach to organizing in the manufacturing industries of Los Angeles is a new project named LAMAP, the Los Angeles Manufacturing Action Project. Conceived by Peter Olney, who has worked for the ILG, the Furniture Workers, and Justice for Janitors, this project plans to develop a broad movement of immigrant workers who live and work in the multiple manufacturing shops that stretch south from downtown Los Angeles to the harbor along the Alameda Corridor. These industries have all suffered "restructuring" akin to that in the garment industry, including increased contracting out, the destruction of unions, and declining wages and working conditions. All rely heavily on immigrant workers. The goal of LAMAP is to create a coalition of relevant unions that will work together, building a movement that crosses traditional industry lines and is rooted in the community from which all the industries draw.

I do not want to suggest that these struggles are easy to wage. The power of capital is formidable. Employers are able to hire high-priced union-busting lawyers. They are often able to get the state to do their bidding. On the other hand, many immigrant workers are disenfranchised because they are undocumented and disqualified from voting, because they have not yet been able to gain citizenship, or because, even if they are citizens, they face institutional racism in the whole electoral system. Now these workers face a concerted campaign against them in a rising hysteria about immigration. They are being blamed for multiple social ills that they surely do not have the power to create; unfortunately, too many in the U.S. public are prepared to point blame downward as opposed to upward, where the real power lies.

Nevertheless, as I have tried to show, there are signs of movement. New ideas are bursting out all over, and some of them are being put into action.

Keep your eyes on Los Angeles: it may be the first place seriously to challenge the new hegemony that capital has achieved.

Conclusion

Let me relate this back to the issue of multiculturalism. Clearly class struggle is not dead. Even if the workers were completely passive, the capitalist class would be waging the class struggle fiercely. It is determined to cut the cost of labor, which it treats as merely a "cost of production," and not as living human beings.

Gender and race/ethnicity play important roles in the way the class struggle is being waged by capital. Employers do not shy away from using the historical oppression of women and oppressed racial/ethnic groups to their profitable advantage. They structure the workforce to take maximum advantage of divisions, legal disabilities, and any other edges they can gain. They seek out the point of least resistance anywhere it can be found in the world.

Workers must organize themselves and their communities around issues of race and gender oppression, as well as around strictly work-related issues. The best of the unions recognize this clearly and are moving ahead on a broad agenda that could be described as "multicultural." I remain disturbed, however, by some of the tendencies within the multicultural movement to disregard the importance of union struggles, and instead to focus exclusively on identity-based movements and identity politics. Feminism and nationalism, while important components of any working-class movement, sometimes seem to ignore or dismiss the importance of developing strong workers' movements and fighting against capitalism. The "enemy" gets defined as all men or all whites, while the class differentiation among gender and racial/ethnic groups is downplayed. Moreover, the class character of the advocates of this kind of multiculturalism is not critically examined.

I think it is important to acknowledge our own role in the system of oppression. We in the university are, of course, part of the professional-managerial stratum, taking out part of the social surplus through our relatively high salaries. Even when we try to align ourselves with the oppressed, we are still part of a system of exploitation and among the beneficiaries of it. If we are serious about abolishing the oppression of people like the garment workers, we need to consider our class's relationship to that oppression. Not only do we need to fight against the abuses of capital, but also to reclaim for the working class the expertise and control exercised by the professional-managerial stratum. We should be the servants of the working class, not its masters.

In sum, the goal (as I see it) is not to assert the equal importance of one's culture and gender within the nation's (and world's) capitalist institutions, but to overthrow capitalist rule, though surely with complete sensitivity to the special oppression and needs of women and people of color (including, of course, women of color). Too often, the advocates of multiculturalism lose sight of this goal. For this reason, multiculturalism can be co-opted by capitalist institutions, who see it as a nonthreatening movement. On the other hand, when we pursue class struggle, and fight for the end of the (white) capitalist system of expropriation of the social surplus based on ownership of private property, you can be sure that the opposition by the ruling class will be relentless and without accommodation.

The Marxist issues are as alive as they ever were in the experiences of garment workers in Los Angeles today. Perhaps we lose sight of them in the university because they are so difficult to deal with. It is easier to escape into issues of culture and identity and forget about the seemingly intractable problems of intense social, economic, and political inequality. Whether we look at it or not, the class question of global capitalism is utterly central to the lives of millions of people. We must be prepared to fight.

Notes

1. The research on which this paper is based is being developed by Richard Appelbaum and myself as a book manuscript that focuses on the apparel industry in Los Angeles. For my previous work on the apparel industry, see Edna Bonacich, Lucie Cheng, Norma Chinchilla, Nora Hamilton, and Paul Ong, eds., *Global Production: The Apparel Industry in the Pacific Rim* (Philadelphia: Temple University Press, 1994).

2. *Women's Wear Daily*, 7 July 1994: 5.

3. Many of the ideas presented in this section come from lengthy discussions with David Young of the International Ladies Garment Workers Union. I am also learning a great deal from serving on the community core group of Hotel Employees and Restaurant Employees Local 11, and on the core group of the Los Angeles Manufacturing Action Project.

CHAPTER TWENTY

Travelogue

The Garment Industry in Los Angeles and East Asia

RICHARD P. APPELBAUM AND GREGG SCOTT

Every story is a traveling story.
Michel de Certeau, *The Practice of Everyday Life*

What follows is a traveling story about the garment industry in the Pacific Rim, based on conversations and interviews with workers, managers, owners, and corporate executives. Our story begins in Los Angeles, where the explosion of apparel production signals the rebirth of old-time industrial manufacturing at a new time of postindustrial decline (see chapter 18). Our travels will take us to Hong Kong, South China, Macau, and Vietnam, and combine recollections from two visits.[1] Along the way we will encounter young women workers, low wages and long workweeks, and well-known American labels. We will find modern, open factories in Vietnam, and dingy, cramped workshops in Los Angeles. We shall see the industry that served as industrialization's original midwife performing much the same role in Asia two and a half centuries later.

Los Angeles

Louis Lujan's factory, just west of downtown Los Angeles. At the time of our July 1991 interview, Louis's hundred sewing machines were largely idle; his declining business supported fewer than fifty workers, mainly women from El Salvador and Mexico. Crammed into twelve thousand square feet of floor space (which cost him four thousand dollars a month), Louis was plagued by falling prices, growing competition from Asia and Mexico, workers' compensation claims, and two equipment thefts in a single year. Louis's thirty-seven years in the business had left him discouraged and disillusioned.

Louis's west downtown factory had been making clothing for more than a decade. Because of the intensity of competition among Los Angeles contractors, Louis told us he would "do anything" when it came to small-volume garment production, regardless of the nature of the task. His production output ranged from women's skirts to men's "jam" shorts, the latter a popular item among devotees of the widely exported Southern California beachwear look. Louis was also attempting to branch out into nonapparel manufacturing—for example, he had recently designed a combination seat cushion and beverage carrying case dubbed "cush 'n pak," which he hoped would appeal to sports fans and college students. He wondered aloud if our university store might be interested in placing an order.

Although Louis once priced his services on the basis of actual production costs, today he must take whatever the manufacturer offers. According to Louis, the commodity chain has a simple structure: the retailer sets the price for the manufacturer-designer, who in turn sets the price for the contractor, who must make the garment for whatever is offered. For example, Louis shows us a garment that retails for $32–$34. The retailer pays the manufacturer $15.75; the manufacturer pays Louis $3.50. Louis has only one place left to squeeze: the workers who produced the garment. The five who shared in its labor also share the $1.25 that remains after Louis takes his cut, which must cover all of his expenses as well as profits.

As far as Louis knows, despite their harsh conditions, not one of his workers has ever been involved with the union; in his candid opinion, "the union has no balls left." Louis himself may be running on borrowed time, unless "cush 'n pak" somehow manages to catch the public imagination. We have not yet seen it in any university store.

ABC Fashions, South Central Los Angeles. In this tiny shop, fifteen workers make garments ranging from women's skirts to children's beachwear. The physical working conditions are squalid; poor lighting, inadequate ventilation, unsanitary rest rooms, and a scarcity of "free space" for eating and resting are characteristics shared with many of the estimated five thousand factories in Los Angeles County.

Yet six of the workers we spoke with said that the physical environment only minimally affected their feelings about working at ABC. Rodolfo, the owner, migrated from El Salvador to Los Angeles in the early 1970s. He is reportedly generous, responsive, and sympathetic to the challenges facing Latino immigrant workers. Unlike many other contractors, Rodolfo claims to never pay less than the minimum wage; productive workers can earn much more. A few employees informed us that Rodolfo also offers interest-free loans to workers who are trying to assist family members in their migration to the United States. Because the owner's pleasant demeanor and overall "goodness" outweigh the unpleasant conditions that characterize the work setting, the workers in this factory said they feel a great deal of personal loyalty.

ABC Fashions carries three primary contracts, each of which was initiated informally with no more than a handshake binding the two parties. The sportswear made in Rodolfo's factory will retail in major discount department stores (like J. C. Penney and Mervyn's) for between $15 and $40 per item. Yet Rodolfo shares little of this return, and the price he pays for his economic marginality is an inability to compete for more lucrative contracts that require the special machinery (for example, sewing machines for denim) that he cannot afford. Rodolfo reports that contracts are harder and harder to come by, since his decision to pay minimum wage was rapidly pricing him out of the market. At the time of this writing (October 1994),

Rodolfo was trying to sell the factory to his wife's nephew. He hopes to stay on as production manager, a position that will afford him many of the same benefits he now enjoys, but without the associated anxieties of ownership.

Hong Kong

A nine-hour flight takes us to Hong Kong, a soon-to-be-former British colony and booming city-state on the southern tip of China. Asian-manufactured clothing making the return trip will require a bit longer, about two weeks in the truck-size "containers" that stack the decks of the enormous container ships that serve as the arteries of the world economy today. The transpacific flow has made Hong Kong the world's largest port, followed by Singapore; the combined ports of Los Angeles and Long Beach rank third. U.S.-Asian trade reached $361 billion by 1993; $144 billion in cargo passed through Los Angeles alone.

Hong Kong will become part of China in 1997, an inevitability whose economic significance is largely downplayed by local businesspeople. (The potential loss of political freedoms has been of somewhat greater concern, particularly since China crushed the Tiananmen uprising in 1989.) Hong Kong is an entrepreneur's paradise—a bastion of capitalist free enterprise whose towering high-rise apartments and offices are home to some of the world's most prosperous and powerful families. It is also a city of numerous low-wage workers, their ranks swollen by immigrants from nearby China. Yet despite its evident inequalities, Hong Kong unquestionably boasts a rising economic tide that carries most ships, not only the yachts of the business elites but the junks of many working people as well. It is for this reason that the garment industry is sunsetting in Hong Kong, even as it is sunrising to the east in Los Angeles.

Although the Hong Kong garment industry employs an estimated two hundred thousand people in nine thousand establishments, rising wages and land costs are driving labor-intensive industries north to China. Hong Kong is converting from a factory-based workhouse to a service economy of brokers and buyers, multinational corporate and financial headquarters, producer services and entrepreneurs. The enormous wage differentials between Hong Kong and China (garment workers earn $600–$800 a month in Hong Kong, $30–$50 a month just one hundred miles to the north) have had much the same effect as those between the U.S. and Mexico. Cross-border subcontracting in apparel is reinforced by the Out-Processing Arrangement, which permits Hong Kong firms to sew part of a garment in China, so long as the final sewing is done in Hong Kong factories (and therefore exported under Hong Kong quota).

Unlike the United States, Hong Kong has no mandated minimum wage, no employment security, no pensions, and no unemployment compensation. Furthermore, there is no legal right to collective bargaining; even in a fully unionized factory, the employer is under no obligation to comply with the union's demands, a situation that has recently led to wildcat strikes. Finally, there is no equal opportunity law here, so women cannot challenge their situation on the basis of sex discrimination.

Like Los Angeles, Hong Kong lacks a strong labor movement. Most unions in Hong Kong are nonoppositional; only the federation of Independent Trade Unions—and its affiliate, the Clothing Industry Workers General Union—can truly claim autonomy from governmental influence. But oppositional unions lack appeal to young, hip workers. According to labor activist and scholar Trini Leung, unions just cannot seem to shake their old-fashioned "frumpy" image: "We need a postmodern unionism to combat postmodern capitalism," she half-seriously jokes. In Leung's view, women should comprise the core of such a union. Given women's prevalence in the low-wage workforce, it is hard to contest her reasoning.

Unimix Industrial Centre, Hong Kong. A short ride on the Star Ferry brings us from Hong Kong island's sparkling waterfront office high-rises and seemingly endless shopping emporiums to their exact counterparts on the city's mainland in Kowloon. Another fifteen minutes in an air-conditioned taxi brings us to the San Po Kong industrial district, its run-down buildings teeming with factories and tiny workers' apartments. The Unimix Industrial Centre is largely owned by Wing Tai, a Cheng family multinational corporation with a billion dollars of commercial, manufacturing, and real-estate interests throughout East Asia. (PCH, an Orange County-based, all-American active sportswear company originally known for its surf look, is one Wing Tai spinoff.)

Unimix's giant factory, the largest under a single roof in Hong Kong, makes both woven and knit apparel. In 1991, when the accompanying photograph was taken, its products bore some of the best-known European and North American labels, including Calvin Klein, the Chelsey Group, Horne Brothers (UK), the Burton Group, Structure, British Home Stores, Marks and Spencer, Yves St. Laurent, Perry Ellis, Nino Cerrutti, the Gap—a moderately pricey clientele that could still afford Hong Kong's rising labor costs. Yet although the Unimix factory once boasted three thousand workers, by 1991 the number had declined to two thousand, and currently stands at around fifteen hundred. As Paul Tsang, Unimix's general manager, explained it, with wages running at roughly US$3 per hour and rents at US$1.10 a square foot, floor space was more profitably used for offices than sewing machines. Workers could always be picked up in China.

The Unimix factory is clean, well lit, and modern, although its vast expanses of sewing machines—all operating at full throttle—contribute to a nerve-racking din whose only barrier appears to be the ubiquitous portable radio with headphones. We see machines that display the fabrics for visual inspection, as well as computerized CAD-CAM machines creating the patterns for cutting. Paul's running narrative could easily be a page taken from Frederick Winslow Taylor: "This is where the brains are. We de-skill— we separate the planning from the actual execution, saving us money." Harry Braverman could not have put it more accurately.[2]

We are told that men do the standing work, women the sitting work. We see mostly the latter. The workers are mainly young women, many Chinese immigrants, most lacking the skills, education, and class background to get jobs as multilingual secretaries in multinational offices.

China

From the crowded terminal adjacent to the Prince Hotel in Kowloon we catch a modern, air-conditioned bus that fights the heavy traffic in Hong Kong's New Territories, China's New Economic Zone, and eventually China.

We are joined by Victor Leung, an assistant production manager for Wing Tai Garment International, whose job it is to oversee production at Wing Tai's FuWah factory in Dongguan, China. We are joined by a busload of businessmen, all of whom seem to own cellular telephones that ring constantly and operate seamlessly on both sides of the border.

The three-plus-hour trip takes us through a landscape that is hard to fathom and harder still to describe. The terrain—less than two decades ago dominated by rice paddies and sleepy agricultural towns—is now wall-to-wall high-rise: factories, dormitories, apartments, offices. Cities of a million people seemingly sprout up overnight, connected by a growing and already overtaxed system of superhighways. We are traversing southern Guangdong Province between Hong Kong and Guangzhou, the fastest-growing economic region in the world today, perhaps ever. We are truly on the capitalist road, one never subjected to an environmental impact statement.

We stop for lunch after arriving in the Dongguan Hillside Hotel, which features a miniature artificial waterfall cascading down an exterior landscaped wall. We eat in the non-Chinese restaurant upstairs, rather than the Chinese one downstairs, a preference of our host. Among other things, Victor discusses the virtues of fast-food restaurants, now a popular feature of efficiency-minded Hong Kong. Victor argues that McDonald's offerings are healthier than Chinese food, a somewhat surreal assertion that seems to fit nicely with our Chinese travel thus far.

FuWah Garment Factory, Dongguan, People's Republic of China. FuWah's principal client is a highly critical Japanese manufacturer, who is concerned with what he perceives as the factory's low-quality work. Victor, as Wing Tai's overseer for the factory, has the unhappy task of mediating between the workers, his production staff, and the eight Japanese quality control inspectors. More specifically, his job is to get the factory itself to adopt the "Japanese method" of quality control, which involves a time-consuming, detailed, systematic inspection of every garment that is produced.

FuWah employs nearly two hundred sewing-machine operators and an equal number of workers who do trimming, cutting, bagging, shipping, and other activities. Most of the workers are young and female. The machinery used here is less automated than what we saw at Unimix, and therefore more labor-intensive. But then, the Japanese client requires hand-stitched waistbands on its jeans, and labor is cheap.

The young female workforce generally comes from outlying regions of China. The women—girls, really—labor from 8:00 A.M. to 8:00 P.M., with an hour off for lunch and another hour for dinner; this goes down as eight hours on their time cards. They work seven days a week, and after work they sleep in company dormitories behind the factory, which we are not permitted to visit. They eat company food, for which they contribute a nominal amount. They are paid by the piece, with rates reportedly adjusted downward if pushed upward by rising productivity. Pay ranges from US$26 to $52 a month. They get a month off to go home during Chinese New Year, and a sizable bonus (US$13) if they return. Among other things, they are producing jeans that bear the suggestive label "Gapstar," whose exterior leather patch announces "authentic denim, European reference, built with the spirit of America."

Not so long ago, labor was protected in communist China: workers were permanently attached to a work unit, which provided them with a job, health care, a place to live, and script to buy food. But now there is a mixed system. A "free" labor market has been introduced, and the girls work by "choice," which gives them a much higher degree of independence than ever before. But they can also be fired, in which case they find themselves without any of the old protections.

Working conditions in the FuWah factory seem harsh to us. Only recently, for example, were workers permitted to have a cup of water or tea at their work station, provided that they did not soil the garments they were sewing. It is extremely hot in south China, and this would hardly seem to be a luxury. Unlike workers in other factories we have visited, the girls here do not smile at us as we pass through the factory.

Macau

Macau, a Portuguese colony, is a city-state like Hong Kong. It lies fifty miles distant, across the wide expanse of water where the Pearl River reaches the South China Sea. The journey is accomplished in less than an hour by hovercraft, a jet-powered ferry boat that skirts commuters between the two colonies. As we approach Macau, we are struck by its similarity to Hong Kong; albeit scaled down. In both places the skylines are dominated by high-rise offices and apartments; in both places, the Bank of China is the predominant feature. Macau itself sounds like a vast construction site, as it builds and rebuilds itself.

We were encouraged to visit Macau by U.S. Customs special agent Thomas Gray, whose territory includes Hong Kong and Taiwan as well. Macau, he pointed out, imports a large number of workers from China under a special work permit program. The program was originally intended to stem the illegal production of Macau garments in China, by bringing the Chinese workers to Macau instead. These workers—again, mainly young women from the rural hinterlands—earn far less than the native workers with whom they labor, and they get no benefits. They are recruited by contracting agents, to whom they pay 10 percent of their wages for housing. They agree to work for a specified period of time, usually two years, a term of indenture that is virtually assured by the fact that they surrender their passports to the agent when they arrive in Macau. As he packed his bags for a return trip to the United States, special agent Gray characterized these immigrant workers as "two-year subcontracted slaves."

Wintex Garment Factory, Macau. Located on the ninth floor of the Fok Tai Industrial Building on Macau's Estrada Marginal, Wintex is in a bustling industrial district where brand-new high-rise workers' apartments are replacing shanties and slums. Wintex is owned and run by Eulalia Cheong and her husband, K. L. Mok. She used to run a small import-export business; he was an architect. Their combined skills are evident in the open, airy design of the factory: immaculate rooms with colorful red ceiling fans, white and black wire bins at each work station to keep materials off the floor, strong neon lighting. Most of the clothing sells in the European Community, although some American labels are found here as well. Their sweaters wholesale for twenty dollars, and retail for at least twice that amount in U.S. department stores. We pass a bench where Esprit logos are being silk-screened onto T-shirts.

According to Mr. Mok, there is a labor shortage in Macau's apparel industry, which has led him to import Chinese workers under the above-mentioned contracting agreements. He tells us, however, that his Chinese workers make the same as the locals, about US$500–$600 monthly, except during a brief initial probationary period during which they earn half that amount. Contrary to what are apparently prevailing stereotypes in Macau, he reports that his immigrant workers are neither dumb, lazy, nor unmotivated. They certainly seem to us to be working very hard. Almost all the very young women we encounter working at sewing machines are from China (those at knitting machines tend to be from Macau). Workers live in the nearby high-rise flats, and frequently go home for their ninety-minute lunch break. Sewers are paid by the piece, and are allowed occasional breaks, such as fifteen minutes for tea or coffee in the afternoon, taken at a tea table. Ms. Cheong explains that they "set down the rules from day one with the workers, so they wouldn't establish bad habits," and that "this made for harmony and understanding later on."

Mr. Mok reports little labor turnover, and the factory is running at full capacity. As we pass a small Buddhist shrine constructed for his workers, he tells us they are like a closely knit family, that he pays them 10 to 15 percent more than the prevailing rate, and that he throws twice-yearly banquets for everyone. We come across a woman working on an overlock sewing machine; her productivity is such that she reportedly earns as much as US$800 per month. Wintex's decor would seem to resemble a trendy office more than a factory. The noise level is low, and workers focus on their machines but do not seem cut off from one another—perhaps because, since the portable radios with headphones appear to be absent, they are able to engage in conversation. The mood seems friendly, and we walk through to smiles.

Vietnam

We return to Hong Kong, and are soon aboard a Cathay Pacific 747 bound for Vietnam. The plane is filled not only with businessmen, but with a number of Vietnamese who are visiting their homeland for the first time after years of exile in Europe or North America. We speak with one man who is anxiously awaiting a reunion with parents he hasn't seen since he fled Vietnam in 1975. At that time he had only the army uniform on his back and a small bag containing a few possessions. Although he spoke no English, like hundreds of thousands of his compatriots he wound up in southern California. Today he is a successful Silicon Valley engineer.

The drama of flying to Ho Chi Minh City (still Saigon to its residents) is heightened by the presence of a large screen in the front of the passenger cabin, on which an emormous image of Indochina is being projected. In a style reminiscent of the original Indiana Jones movie, our route somehow traces its way forward on the map, snaking southward and then westward, rapidly closing in on Ho Chi Minh City. Our excitement mounts as lush jungle gives way to rice paddies and then the city itself, symbol of so much that decentered the United States a quarter century ago.

Hiep, a Vietnamese-born American from Orange County, meets us at the airport with his Vietnamese cousin Bao. Incongruously, Hiep speaks English with a flawless Baltimore accent. Today he is passing as a local, however, having returned to the country in hopes of making his fortune in the import-export business now that the United States plans to lift its long-standing trade embargo. Bao, who speaks almost no English, is an accomplished pianist specializing in European classical music. He lives marginally, barely making a living doing odd jobs and giving piano lessons.

Soon after checking into the Korean-owned Festival Hotel a couple of miles from the city center, we find ourselves on the back of Hiep's and Bao's motor scooters headed downtown. Although it is a sultry evening, the broad, French-designed boulevards are alive with countless living and moving parts. Thousands of bicycles, motor scooters, and occasional trucks converge at intersections long bereft of traffic signals or any other form of traffic control. Like a living organism, surging lanes of traffic somehow merge, cross one another, continue onward. The energy is palpable: a city of young people on the move, anxious to make a buck, hopeful that their former ally will once again establish full economic relations and provide markets for their factories and products.

Vietnam's apparel industry has a long history, although in the recent past state-owned factories produced millions of virtually identical garments for soldiers and workers in the former Soviet bloc, a manufacturer's dream where styles never changed and markets were perfectly predictable. Today, in its quest to become globally competitive, the industry is rapidly privatizing in order to better court foreign capital and clients.

Legamex State Factory, Ho Chi Minh City, Vietnam. One such rapidly privatizing factory is Legamex, a state-owned complex of six factories whose modern sewing equipment includes six computerized embroidery machines. At the time of our 1993 visit, Legamex was raising capital to privatize from a variety of sources, including Habitex of Belgium (its main apparel customer), the German DEG Bank, and the Hong Kong-based Chiap Hua Company. For Legamex, privatization means diversification as well—not only into other products and markets, but also into commercial real-estate investment, piggybacking on partner Chiap Hua's current ventures. They already hold a share in the "Villa Project," a planned urban development in which they hold a 30 percent stake; a shopping center is also being considered.

Legamex accounted for a tenth of Vietnam's clothing exports in 1990, thanks to the labor of six to eight thousand people working two shifts in the company's eight adjoining factories. Its annual sales were about $25 million—a modest figure by American standards, perhaps, but a small fortune in a country where the average annual income is less than US$500.

Ms. Nguyen Thi Son, Legamex director, reports that her family had been in the textile-apparel business for generations before her original factories came under state control. After a stint as vice-director of the State Trading Company, she took over Legamex when it was founded in 1987. Her twenty-three-year-old daughter, Nguyen Du Hong Van, heads the production planning department, where productivity graphs and time-motion charts adorn the walls. Although the rest of management is largely male, more than three-quarters of the workers are young Vietnamese women. Director Son was quoted in the September–October 1992 issue of *Vietnam Today* as attributing the dearth of women in top management positions to the fact that women must do all the housework even when employed outside the home, a fact that limits their professional mobility.

Legamex's main product consists of expensive Patagonia-style jackets, which sell in the European Community for US$250–$300. Workers average forty-eight hours during a six-day week, although Sunday overtime work (reportedly compensated) is not unusual. They are provided with one meal a day, mainly to keep them from leaving for their nearby flats. Within the factory is a worker canteen, educational facilities for the employees' children, and training programs for workers who wish to advance their knowledge and position within the company.

The average pay for workers is US$35–$40 monthly, and we are told that skilled workers can make as much as US$70. Managers, according to Ly Chanh Dao, the regional director of the Import and Export Department, do not make much more, although that will change with privatization.

Even before the United States formally lifted the trade embargo against Vietnam, well-known American manufacturers had been visiting the Legamex factory, eager to court business in a country where high-quality work can be had for a low price. Nor is this entirely a one-way street: director Son had already planned a trip to New York City to study the American market. As we conclude our interview, Mr. Dao inquires how he might come to the United States to study management—and asks me to send him some "critical path software for time motion study" (IBM compatible). If nearly two decades of communism have made an impact in what was once called South Vietnam, it is not evident in the Legamex factory complex.

Daewoo's Vietnam factories, Ho Chi Minh City, Vietnam. Daewoo is one of Korea's *chaebols*, the large conglomerates that dominate the Korean economy. Shinsung Tongsang Company Ltd., one of Daewoo's many holdings, recently decided to test the waters of Vietnamese apparel manufacturing, and dispatched Mr. Dong-Hyun Park to see if local factories could be brought up to Korean quality and productivity standards.

Mr. Park and his driver pick us up at the Festival Hotel shortly after noon, and devote the remainder of the day to braving the kinds of traffic jams that can only occur when nothing whatsoever interferes with the free flow of humans, vehicular traffic, and animals. As Mr. Park drives us to Daewoo's three factories on the outskirts of Ho Chi Minh City, he candidly admits that he is not entirely happy about this assignment. Vietnam is truly a hardship post by his standards, and even the country club atmosphere of Ah Phu Village—an expatriate residential enclave with tennis courts and other amenities—cannot shield him from the hot, tropical weather and harsh conditions of life. Mr. Park's attitude might be colored by the impending birth of his first child, for which his wife planned to relocate home to Korea for at least six months.

Daewoo has been in Ho Chi Minh City for the past year and a half, attracted by the low cost and relatively high quality of labor. Yet productivity is low—perhaps half of Korean standards—so it is a mixed blessing. Moreover, given the extremely low salaries of government officials, bribery is regarded as a routine cost of doing business, adding (for example) US$100 to the cost of every twenty-foot container that leaves the country.

Two of Daewoo's factories work under subcontract; the third is a joint venture with the Vietnamese government. Daewoo's factories primarily manufacture highly standardized polo shirts for the Japanese and European markets. All of the fabric is imported, largely from Daewoo's Korean textile mills. When we ask Mr. Park if Korea plans to open textile plants in Vietnam, he pauses thoughtfully, laughs, and then says "no comment."

Two of Daewoo's factories are newly constructed, their remote suburban location reflecting the much lower land costs. Their location, however, requires a long daily commute for Mr. Park, compounded by the fact that he must frequently return home during the day to place his telephone calls and faxes. (Long-awaited phone lines have not yet been installed.) The Vietnamese government provides the building and facilities; Daewoo the sewing machines, which revert to Vietnam in four years. The first factory we visit is a large, clean, open cinder-block and corrugated steel structure, with bright fluorescent lights hanging low over each work station. We remove our shoes and don slippers as we enter.

Mr. Park tells us that workers are paid "Korean-style"—by the month, not the piece; wages are pegged to a target level of output, based on a forty-eight-hour workweek. Almost all the sewers are young women. If workers exceed their quota, they get a bonus; if not, they work overtime. Monthly pay begins at US$20, but once workers get up to speed—say, in six months—they may earn US$35–$40. Although productivity is only 30 percent of target in this factory, the two full-time Korean technicians on the premises are there to assure that it triples within half a year.

Some three hundred to four hundred people labor in a single open room, using the characteristic Korean assembly-line process rather than the more common bundle method (in which each worker receives a bundle of cut fabric, performs the same operation on each piece, reties the bundle, and passes it to the next worker). Each worker completes a detailed operation, such as a pocket attachment, and passes the changed garment ahead for the next enhancement. The four production lines run the length of the factory, each spitting out 550 pieces each day. There are productivity norm signs along each line, to encourage workers to meet their long-term goal of fifteen hundred pieces. The noise is loud and the heat oppressive as the women labor under the watchful eyes of ten quality-control inspectors.

Conclusion

The apparel industry is rapidly globalizing. In the early 1960s, global apparel exports barely totaled $2 billion; today they have surpassed the $100 billion mark. Five Asian countries—China, Hong Kong, South Korea, Japan, and Taiwan—account for more than a third of the world's apparel exports; Hong Kong alone accounts for an eighth. The United States, in parallel fashion, has become the world's leading apparel importer; in most categories, from a quarter to a half of all the clothing we wear is made outside of the country.

During the coming decade, Hong Kong and Japan will diminish in importance as apparel exporters, relative to such low-wage giants as China, Vietnam, and the many other nations around the world where poverty and hardship drive young women from the countryside to cities in search of work. Their labor, arguably, will help their nations to industrialize—just as it did in Hong Kong, South Korea, Taiwan, and Singapore a generation ago. At the same time, their working conditions will be harsh, their wages low, and their rights nonexistent. They will be competing with their American immigrant counterparts on the global labor market, a fact that will push apparel wages downward in the United States, contribute to sweatshop working conditions, and make it difficult for unions to organize workers.

It is more than ironic that postindustrial society has brought in its wake a reindustrialization on a global scale. Today's globe-trotters often marvel at the similarities they encounter in once "exotic" places: from Hyatts to hamburgers, the world of the traveler looks increasingly the same no matter where one is. This similarity also holds true of the workplace, where First and Third World appear to be merging—at least for those whose physical labor produces the goods we consume.

Notes

1. The trips were made by Richard Appelbaum in November–December 1991 and April-May 1993. Unless anonymity was specifically requested by the interviewees, we have used their personal and business names.

2. Taylor was the father of "scientific management" at the turn of the century; his approach—calling for workers' de-skilling and separation from any vestige of control over the labor process—is critically analyzed in Harry Braverman's classic work, *Labor and Monopoly Capital: The Deregulation of Work in the Twentieth Century* (New York: Monthly Review Press, 1976).

CHAPTER TWENTY-ONE

Unified Capital and the Subject of Value

PAUL SMITH

The Frankfurt School—notably Horkheimer, it could be said—used to insist that fascism was a form of state capitalism and that the racism and anti-Semitism that marked the years of National Socialism could be understood only by way of that fact; that is, racism as such should not be treated as essential, but as a specifiable set of social relations under capitalism. Expressing a different but related view, Malcolm X once remarked, "You can't have capitalism without racism."[1]

In Britain in the 1980s the Thatcher government, in its attempts to construct the proper "English" subject to be the agent of its born-again laissez-faire capitalism, continually came a cropper on the question of race—particularly with its infamous definition of all nonwhites as "black." And the last few years in newly unified Germany have seen the emergence of various virulent strands of racism and xenophobia accompany the extension of the free-market system to the former German Democratic Republic (GDR).

The temptation for many right now—especially since the collapse of "actually existing socialism" and in the laboratory of the New World Order—is to attempt to combat racism in and of itself, as if it could be properly viewed, analyzed, and understood apart from its overdetermined relations to many other elements in the social. For instance, the tendency in Germany, in the wake of the unification of East and West, has been to think of the current anti-Semitism, xenophobia, and racism of a generalized stripe as something essential to German national culture; that is, the recent and ongoing social struggles around race, nationality, and ethnicity there are often explained as some kind of "return of the repressed" in Germany's collective unconscious, some kind of historical struggle over the soul of the nation and its fate or destiny. The links between the present moment and the 1930s are posited by way of an almost mystical conception of the German psyche, rather than by any reference to the history of the changes in capitalist formations that call up and deploy the forces of racism and so on.

It seems to me that, if we are to look on multiculturalism as a force or as an ideology that can seriously combat racism (or indeed, any of the other ways of construing otherness within the capitalist cultures of the North), then it will be necessary to think of it very much in terms of its specific historical and ideological relation to capitalism's condition at any given juncture and in any given culture or set of cultures. This is not to suggest that racism does not exist outside the parameters of capitalism, but rather to attempt to talk of racism as one available component (even a necessary and necessarily available component) of capitalist structure. The case of Germany is especially interesting in the present discussions of multiculturalism because of the way in which a certain (and perhaps rather unexpected) opportunity for economic unification under capitalism has been accompanied by the increased need for what we might call a "uniculturalism" in the newly unified nation. In the German context, that is, I think we can see rather clearly how the effort of capitalism to unify itself (an effort, I would argue, that is being played out across the whole of the North in the early 1990s) entails the construction of particular kinds of subjects and ideologies to serve its ends; the process—or the history—of such constructions seems to me important for any multiculturalist project to take note of.

One might look, then, with some profit at some of the events and cultural phenomena that follow upon the collapse of the Berlin Wall and the subsequent unification of Germany—a process that led to a number of crucial political-economic effects. My starting point, however, is not quite those events themselves, but rather some particular representations of them. I begin with two in particular, both texts that in their own way were best-sellers in Germany immediately after unification: one from the left, Elmar Altvater's *Future of the Market;* and one from the mainstream of economic commentary, Gerlinde Sinn and Hans-Werner Sinn's *Jumpstart: The Economic Unification of Germany.*[2]

It is remarkable that both from the left (Altvater) and from the middle right (Sinn and Sinn) the diagnosis of the collapse of actually existing socialism in the Eastern bloc, and particularly in the former GDR, rests on a common claim: namely, that in the communist bloc some kind of debilitating relationship had been established between, on the one hand, economic structuration and, on the other, the processes of civic life. For Altvater the problem is that civic and political culture had not been allowed to develop in such a way as to allow subjects to participate in decision-making processes; in other words, while certain levels of equality and of participation had been the norm (had even been required) in the GDR's economic life, the GDR itself was profoundly undemocratic. Altvater's assumption is that the GDR effectively mishandled the question of people's political desire by keeping it disjunct from issues of their economic survival and well-being. The political and the economic, in other words, were disjunctive.

For Sinn and Sinn the problem with actually existing socialism had been precisely the absolute collusion between the suppression of people's political desire and the eradication of what they understand as their fundamental economic nature. That nature apparently consists in what they call economic motivation and the desire to "do better" in materialistic terms. Actually existing socialism had established a civic and political system that was exactly designed to suppress the fundamental nature of the subject—its "natural" economic desire—by refusing to provide "incentives" for the subject's motivations. Such a close alliance of the political and the economic was predestined to fail, they claim: "Communist ideology, unlike that of Christianity, assumes that people are fundamentally good; but unfortunately they are not—they are fundamentally selfish. An economic system based on wishful thinking rather than on a realistic view of human nature cannot hope to succeed" (Sinn and Sinn, *Jumpstart*, 3). Thus Sinn and Sinn trot out the most hackneyed and untheorized notions of the subject as (paradoxical) accompaniment to their insistence on the "iron laws of economics." Altvater's diagnosis, predicated less on the appetite of the subject and more on its needs, is thereby perhaps more pertinent than the "human nature" discourse of Sinn and Sinn. But even there it is remarkable that the subject remains almost entirely *presumed*. In their divergence these two approaches share a lack of theorization of the subject even as they both register a problem with the relationship established in actually existing socialism between the political subject and the economic subject.

One difference between them, however, is that while Sinn and Sinn quite wrongly regard actually existing socialism as "Marxism in action," Altvater more realistically thinks of it as the Frankfurt School did—that is, as a particular form of state capitalism. For him, therefore, its development depended on (but also finally collapsed because of) a factitious separation of the political and economic realms. Indeed, like the Frankfurt School's descriptions of that older form of state capitalism, National Socialism, Altvater's version suggests that the totalitarianism of actually existing socialism is best seen as an extension of the logic of capitalism itself as it tries to keep the political and the economic apart—in other words, that there is a direct correlation between the intensity of the attempt to keep the political and the economic separate and the need for repressive state control.

These two texts, in their similarity and difference, then, provide two fundamental problematics. First, there is the issue of the relation between the political and the economic, where the supposed logic of the market dictates the necessity of a disjuncture between the two. And second, there is the issue of the nature of the subject. As regards the latter issue, it should be pointed out that the assumptions about—or the presumptions of—the subject that are to be found in Sinn and Sinn are more or less standard and normative within the field of economics; that is, more elaborate or theorized descriptions of the subject are scarce in the works of economists who by and large depend on this presumptive, "commonsense" version of a subject defined almost exclusively as a function of some kind of original appetitive desire. Mainstream economists almost never bother to go beyond this notion of the subject, although, on the left, some economists have recently begun to think of the constitution of subjectivity as germane to their understanding of economic processes. For instance, Jack Amariglio and Antonio Callari have proposed that capitalism works for the preparation of an "individual" who might be (1) endowed with an ultimately self-interested rationality, (2) convinced of the principle of equality, and (3) dedicated to the concept of private property.[3]

Obviously a lot more needs to be said about this "subject of capitalism," especially since Amariglio and Callari necessarily confine their remarks to delineating its epiphenomenal characteristics without addressing the complex (and largely cultural) processes of subject construction that might enable such characteristics to appear and to function as normative (to seem, that is, somehow "natural"). But Amariglio and Callari do help us grasp the importance of thinking about the factitious nature of the subject that is assumed and presumed in economic theory. One suggestive elaboration of their work would be to begin to define their "subject of capitalism" and its characteristics more specifically and historically in terms of capitalism's various processes of extracting surplus value. Indeed, one might be tempted to think of this subject as the "subject of value"—the requisite subject, that is, for specifiable regimes and modes of value production.

It is of course over and against such a "subject of value"—or in dialectical arrangement with it—that capitalism also construes various orders of otherness. The present essay is drawn from a larger project, called "Bearing North," in which I attempt to show how capitalism's current effort to unify itself in the North has entailed—and continues to provoke—a culturally gradated structure of otherness; that is, for the unification of capitalism to occur, there must exist not simply an equal and opposite kind of other for the subject of value, but a series of others. For instance, the national, racial, or ethnic composition of otherness is a variable; and at the same time the subject of value is implicitly masculine, so it has always a gender dimension. However, it is a characteristic of the supposedly universal logic of market capitalism that it can produce only a partial or imperfect socialization of its preferred subjects. Thus, even as a unifying capitalism profers and presumes both its subject of value and a deployed structure of otherness, actual agents knowingly and unknowingly resist those proferrings and presumptions. The current mode of capitalist unification in the North can be generalized as one where it has become increasingly necessary to *legislate* the "subject of value" (as in, for instance, the British government's attempts to criminalize propertyless subjects) and thus consolidate such a subject as a norm.[4]

With those thoughts or those themes in mind, let me return to the political and economic effects of German unification. These feature for the GDR what even mainstream economists have understood as "one of the worst and sharpest depressions in European history. . . . It continues unabated."[5] And for the new Germany what begins is the latest phase in what is often taken to be a chronic struggle over the stakes and forms of an authentic German culture, and along with this a whole series of disturbances and often violent rearrangements in the civic life of the newly unified nation. The cultural context would tend to demonstrate that the issue of race that has so spectacularly reemerged from and for German history is directly a function or symptom of a massive shift in the organization of the means of production (the economic unification of the two states). In that light I would suggest that the logic of unification or integration needs to be understood as an overdetermined construction of economic, civic, and ideological, as well as cultural, elements.

Something of a methodological watchword here can be suggested by recalling Adorno's admonitions to Benjamin during their exchange over the latter's work on Baudelaire: Adorno accuses Benjamin of explaining cultural forms merely by positivistic reference to "adjacent" social events and processes; and Adorno suggests that "materialist determination of cultural traits is only possible if it is mediated through the total social process."[6] No one would suggest—except perhaps Adorno himself—that the preferred schema of materialist determination would be an easy task to construe. But it can be said that the necessarily overdetermined condition of the "total social process" simply does not lend itself to the predominantly positivistic frames and paradigms of the methodologies of the current social sciences. Thus I begin by narrativizing some part of the particular crisis in capitalism and its cultures that is attendant upon the economic unification of the two Germanys. I want to take a first cue from Marx, who (in the course of a discussion admittedly somewhat oblique to my own) considers the role of overproduction in the emergence of capitalist crisis; he posits a definition of crisis that I think is generally applicable: "Crisis is nothing but the forcible assertion of the unity of phases of production which have become independent from each other."[7]

Now, in the United States and Europe economists have regularly suggested that both the economic promise and the political problems of German unification reside in the joining of West German capital with East German labor: "Capital is scarce in East Germany, but skilled labour (and labour that can quickly become skilled) is abundant," say Sinn and Sinn (*Jumpstart*, 43). Another commentator suggests that "Economic integration can be interpreted as the addition of qualified labour . . . and an obsolete capital stock to the West German economy."[8] And in the same vein (but with more sanctimony and with at least a hint of an old-fashioned colonialist voice) Birgit Breuel, head of the Treuhand (about which I'll speak in a moment) enumerates the virtues of this new labor force to which West German capital will be added: "They work hard and loyally . . . they have high intelligence and are well-trained, but they are not at all used to modern machinery."[9]

Capital and labor, then, are taken in my account as the two "phases" of the production process that had been kept apart and I suggest that their recent integration in the unification process is in fact the *origin of an imposed crisis*—the forcible assertion of the unity of separate phases of production. The crisis of unification will thus offer lessons about the cultural and civic mediation of capital's fundamental needs and the practices it designs to meet those needs. As the North struggles to unify itself, German unification can suggest some of the formations and consequences of capital's deep and complex imperatives; among these will be the necessary re-formations of social relations in terms of gender and race, not to mention class, in a situation where crisis at the economic level entails a reshaping of what I've called the structure of otherness. The particular reshapings can be understood as both the consequence of and the necessary condition of a major and enforced shift in the economic system. It might also be worth bearing in mind here one of Altvater's asides, to the effect that indeed "crisis symptoms in the capitalist West have been pushed into the background by the dissolution of the actually existing socialist societies" (*The Future of the Market*, 18); that is, and as always, the symptoms of capitalist crisis are played out at levels other than the economic, and to ideological effect.

My work has been using as point of entry into all this another event, in March 1990, before unification proper: the founding of an institution called the Treuhandanstalt. The Treuhand was established by the Federal Republic with the connivance of the transitional GDR Modrow government and immediately became the biggest holding company in the world (with an impeccable sense of taste, it was housed in the former Luftwaffe building in Berlin). Nominally, the Treuhand was a joint stock association given control of the privatization of the old GDR industrial Kombinate—220 of them broken up into about 8,000 smaller concerns, some of which have since themselves been broken down into hundreds of small enterprises and either privatized by Treuhand or put out of business altogether. By August 1992 Treuhand had sold off about 6,000 companies, and had over 2,000 remaining under its care. About a year later, and because of its habit of breaking up companies into smaller units, Treuhand still had about 2,000 companies, but had privatized a total of 8,422, and liquidated a further 2,578. By the time it closed its doors at the end of 1994, it had disposed of all but about a hundred concerns.[10]

The founding of the company occurred even before monetary unification in July 1990, but it got into full operation in August 1990 when Detlev Rohwedder, former head of Hoesch steel, took over as head. Part of his task was to turn around the company's reputation of being an uncontrolled operation beset by various scandals of influence peddling and favoritism. But Rohwedder did not last long as head of the Treuhand, and thereby hangs one strand of my tale of German unification. Rohwedder was assassinated in April 1991 by the Red Army Faction. The Red Army Faction is known in CIA documents as "the fourth generation of the Bader-Meinhof gang" and had been relatively active in 1991 (including its firebombing of a Treuhand office just before Rohwedder's killing). The activity of the Red Army Faction is one part of the narrative that I can't elaborate here. Suffice it to say that the terrorist murder of Rohwedder can be understood as one particular registra-

tion or symptom of civic and cultural reaction to the economic effort of integration. Both before and immediately after unification, the RAF was active
in opposition to what it called "reactionary Great Germany and Western
European plans to suppress and exploit people here and in the third world,"
and it justified Rohwedder's murder as ridding the world of another "imperialist beast."[11] The Red Army Faction has woven its activities into the civic
and cultural consciousness of the new Germany and has in a sense provoked
new terrorist activities (such as those of the recent organization of leftist
radical groups in Autonomen, but also of various right-wing groups).

Rohwedder's position at Treuhand was taken over by Birgit Breuel, who
remained its head for the life of the Treuhand; its role in effecting the crisis
of unification was conducted mostly under the leadership of Breuel. She is
—not surprisingly—a confirmed believer in the free market and has described herself as a committed Friedmanite. In 1991, attendant upon the
opening of a Treuhand office in New York, Breuel submitted to numerous
interviews and laid out for the U.S. business community some of the problems associated with the Treuhand's task of privatization and with unification in general. Interpreting Breuel's statements on that occasion, it would
seem that the problems of the Treuhand in the processes of unification
boiled down to three in particular.

First, there was a problem with persuading Ossis of the proper principles
of private property. For instance, Breuel complained about the simple-
mindedness of those East Germans who assumed that property nationalized by the GDR could be simply returned to them; a further difficulty arose
when the Treuhand offered mere pecuniary compensation for such property
claims.

Second, the Treuhand became willy-nilly an active agency in the carrying
out of labor policy. Directed by the political concerns of the government, the
Treuhand was compelled to impose various conditions and restrictions on
potential investors and buyers so as to ensure continued employment in the
old GDR businesses.

Third, a whole series of practical and philosophical difficulties arose simply because of the imposition of a system of value production on a people
that had historically not shared or been part of that system. The forced assertion of the unity of West German capital and East German labor entails
literally the devaluation of the former GDR economy. In other words, as the
Treuhand swept away the value system of a defeated economy, it often proposed the notion that the East German economy was essentially *without
value*. The assumption here—an assumption shared by many other econo-

mists, whether consciously or not—suggests that only capitalism can produce value. The notion is clearly an absurdity: any economic system, however vilified it might be, or however undesirable it actually is, produces value, defined through the particular form of its expropriation of labor.

At any rate, each of these problems or sets of problems meant that the Treuhand was forced to play a double role in the unification process. Contradicting the Treuhand's own official view of the efficacy of the automatic economic mechanisms of the free-market system (the regime of what Sinn and Sinn call the "iron laws of economics"), the Treuhand *also* became a political and ideological apparatus; that is, the familiar free-market theory, with its doctrinaire opposition between market and planned economies, subverted itself in the practice of the Treuhand. One way in which this contradiction was played out is in the question—much debated by economists, the Treuhand, and the government—as to whether there should be investment and restructuring of GDR industries before their sale. The restructuring option—a de facto planning and thus a subversion of undisturbed market forces—was, for example, the tactic favored by the Thatcher government when it undertook privatization of nationalized industries in Britain in the 1980s. And this is effectively the option the Treuhand was forced to adopt by a government concerned with the political and civic consequences of wholesale privatization. As Breuel ruefully admits, "The social aspect enters into every decision we make."[12]

My point here is that the Treuhand was fully a political entity even while it offered itself as a benign conduit for the easy operation of the economic principles of the free-market system. Indeed, the Treuhand was designed to usher in a properly unpoliticized or depoliticized vision of the market. In that sense it was a contradictory and even embarrassing phenomenon—the embarrassment appears when Breuel says that "we want to make ourselves superfluous as soon as possible."[13] Indeed, one way of focusing on this double role of the Treuhand is to contrast it to another such trust company, the National Trust in Britain, which buys and owns (in order to preserve) private land for the nation. Patrick Wright has said of the National Trust that it "has provided the state with a way out of the conflict between public interest and private property. The two are now negotiated but at a displaced level: as a registered company, the Trust holds property privately, and yet it does so in what it also works to establish as the national and public interest."[14] The Treuhand negotiated the same contradictory role and with the same ideological concern for some putative "public interest." Its goal, however—distinct from the conservation function of the National Trust—was precisely to disappear, to finally have the public and national interest both expressed and realized in the fait accompli of total privatization. Breuel again: "We will cushion East German workers, but eventually the logic of the free market must change their very existences."[15] Clearly, as Breuel's remark promises, the much-vaunted rationality of the free market reaches its goal of magical and objective self-regulation through the interpellation of subjects fit for or apt for a set of economic forces that themselves must be manipulated. The denial of the linkage between the political and the economic is played out across the bodies of subjects that must be pulled into the right place.

The selling off of the assets of the GDR, in what Treuhand itself described as "the sale of the century," is an event of huge significance at the political-economic level, even if only because it is the most extensive privatization program ever conducted (exceeding by far the post-Allende privatization in Chile, and on a different scale and of a different nature than anything in the new republics of the former Soviet Union). But, notably, it is not simply an attempt to convert a planned economy to a market one; it is rather a process whereby a planned economy is colonized and integrated into a market one. As such, the unification of the two Germanys might be (and has been) seen as the very *Aufhebung* of the historical dialectic of socialism and capitalism! More modestly and realistically, the unification is undoubtedly of interest as the locus for the application of a principle that abounds in political and economic thinking in the North: the principle that the market system is inherently different from and, obviously, superior to planned economies.

The confidence of this principle can be seen quite clearly in the discourses that have surrounded the economic unification in the United States and in Europe. To take stock of some of this, I've been looking at three different registers of economic discourse: business and trade journals, academic economics, and the documents of policy groups and think tanks such as the Brookings Institute or institutions like the World Bank or the International Monetary Fund. I won't be discussing here the trade and business journals—journals such as *Mergers and Acquisitions, Journal of Business Strategy,* or *International Management,* which throughout 1991 were stuffed with articles with titles like "A Buyer's Guide to East Germany's Company Bazaar." Nor will I discuss one of the most influential—if controversial— policy discussions carried out in the United States at the Brookings Institute by the Berkeley economists Akerlof, Rose, Yellen, and Hessenius; or the way the Brookings Institute functions thereby as a component of American involvement in the attempt to unify the capitalist North.[16]

As far as the academic economic discourse is concerned, one of the most remarkable contributions I found is by Horst Siebert in the *European Economic Review*. It is one of the few that overtly attack what it calls the "political economy of integration" for its being a compromised confusion of a market economy and a planned economy. Looking ahead to the prospects for successful integration, Siebert stresses the necessity of depoliticizing the market and delineates the proper nature of the "subject of value": "Moving from a centrally planned economy with government ownership of the means of production to a market economy will increase economic efficiency. This is because the motivation of people will change. . . . Economic decisions will be delegated to the market and will thus be depoliticized" (Siebert, "The Integration of Germany," 598–99).

Siebert thus exhibits the same kind of faith in people's motivation—the whole capitalist notion of incentive—as quoted earlier from Sinn and Sinn, and, like Breuel, he insists on the necessary divorce of politics and the market. His position is repeated in a different way by Lawrence Brainerd, a consultant for the IMF, who claims that success in unification depends on the conversion of East Germans to the necessity of putting themselves at risk. This, it appears to him, is the essential difference between market economy and planned economy: in the latter subjects are not agents; capitalism, by contrast, works through the construction of subjects who come to see themselves as "responsible"—and responsible because they "naturally" protect their own stake in private property.[17]

Siebert, for his part, elaborates on the necessary depoliticization of the market that will restructure and reorganize the GDR economy into something more efficient. This is to be done by "eliminating the production of intermediate inputs that can be provided more cheaply by markets, by discarding repair departments and by giving up social services like Kindergarten." Siebert's fear, throughout his whole analysis, is that "there is a definite risk that the political process will dominate the privatization." Already, he suggests, the process of currency unification in the two Germanys "had not relied on market forces" and thence had led to a weakening of the prospects for increased ex-GDR efficiency (Siebert, "The Integration of Germany," 600–601).

The combination of this view of the subject of value and a fear of the politicization of market forces can be taken as an indication not only of the immense but fundamental ideological task that market capitalism sets itself to undertake, but also of the contradictions embedded within that system. Despite the compromises, the fears, and the contradictions, none of these economic discourses will ultimately demur from Birgit Breuel's final words on the subject of economic integration: "Privatization is the best restructuring."[18] Indeed, like the nineteenth-century economists whom Marx derides in *Capital*, it is the habit of contemporary bourgeois economists to denounce "every conscious attempt to control and regulate the process of production socially as an inroad upon such sacred things as the rights of property, freedom, and the self-determining genius of the individual capitalist," while at the same time undertaking exactly the social control and regulation of the economic process.[19] The obfuscatory claims about the "naturalness" of a capitalist notion of value and about the "nature" of the subject are taken as givens (here, perhaps, as the right of the victor) and emerge, as I say, in the form of an incredible insistence on the part of economists that the GDR economy was essentially valueless and that it did not serve the interests and needs of a normative human subject, the subject of value.

In the former GDR, women were prime beneficiaries of a whole array of state provisions and civic privileges of the sort that still cannot be guaranteed to women in most democracies in the North. These seem to have been intended to persuade women to reconcile their active role in the GDR economy with their presumed role in reproduction and the family. But restructuring has massively displaced women from the workforce, and consequently has allowed the removal of the rights and benefits they received under the communist system. This is not to suggest that the condition of women in the GDR was altogether satisfactory; certainly they were encouraged as workers and had legal equality in civic society, but at the same time their additional role as mothers was not only installed into legal and constitutional discourse but was also culturally mythologized—and this despite the fact that, as Barbara Einhorn has shown, no conception of the private sphere was encouraged for women in the GDR.[20] But perhaps it can be suggested that women have now reverted to an even less satisfactory role in the new unified economy; there they are returned from the civic to the private while traditional ideas of motherhood and femininity are reinstalled as the "family values" of the private sphere that has become theirs to safeguard and nurture. Thus, in the economic conditions of the new, and in the ideological climate, there has been a diminution of women's citizenship and their economic status. But, as Einhorn has also remarked, many women right now are embracing their new condition "as welcome respite from the rigours of the double or triple burden to which they were subjected by state socialism" (ibid., 7). To put this another way, the new economy, bringing with it the capitalist definition of the subject of value, sees East German women as precisely *not* that subject. If one definition of the subject of value is that it be endowed with an ultimately self-interested rationality, women are now returned to the traditional nonself-interested roles of reproduction, child rearing, and homemaking. If another definition is that the subject of value be convinced of the principle of equality, women have had to explicitly abandon the equalities bestowed by the GDR state constitution. If a third is that the subject be dedicated to the concept and system of private property, women have little or no role to play in that system. In the same way as capitalist unification declares the GDR economy "valueless," GDR women cannot be constituted as the proper subject of value.

In the transition toward a unified Germany, perhaps the most remarkable symptoms of capitalism's provision of the subject of value arise around issues of race. Before unification, West Germany's economic system had been highly reliant upon low-paid foreign "guest workers," economic and political refugees from many parts of the world. The opening up to West German capital of a new, cheap labor force in the shape of the Ossis immediately meant (to put the matter crudely) that the existing cheap labor became economically superfluous. More important, perhaps, it facilitated the revival of the slogan "Germany for the Germans"; now that the Ossis could be seen as a properly German source of labor, the economically unified new nation might be able to unify its culture too. Thus, one of the immediate consequences of unification was the debacle in 1991 and 1992 surrounding guest workers and asylum seekers.

The issue first arose in earnest, one might say, in the spring of 1991 when thousands of Poles arrived in eastern Germany, an event that provoked so-called neo-Nazi forces into the open to protest and presaged a "long hot summer ahead."[21] The influx of foreign workers and asylum seekers (from countries such as Romania, Armenia, Turkey, Vietnam, Yugoslavia, Bulgaria) resulted in about a quarter of a million requests for asylum during the first part of 1992. The ensuing debates led not only to the Kohl government's extreme tightening of Germany's asylum provisions (with the connivance of the Social Democratic Party, it should be said), but also to the reporting of over two and a half thousand incidents of racist and xenophobic violence in 1992. Those reported incidents are generally believed to be only the tip of the iceberg, and in any case were serious enough that they included seventeen homicides.

In that context, it's hardly a surprise that, as an Infas Research Institute survey showed in September 1992, 51 percent of Germans believed that the slogan "Germany for the Germans" was "largely justified."[22] Of course, the particular political-economic nature of racism and xenophobia is likely to be differently constructed in the two different halves of the country: it might be surmised, at least, that Ossi racism is in part a resistance to the effects of unification, whereas in the West it is by and large a way of embracing unification. In both sides of the country, however, the problem of racism and xenophobia has continued right up to the moment of writing in 1995. The state's attempts to deal with such an alarming situation have only tended to sustain the proposition that racism and xenophobia, seen as entirely political and not as economic issues, are symptoms of the effort to construe the proper subject of value. The tightening of asylum rules, for instance, was clearly legislation intended to stabilize the population as a population of white Germans and provided, furthermore, the opportunity to demonize nonwhites, blaming the victim. Helmut Kohl's concession at the time to the effect that he could understand popular concern over a massive influx of asylum seekers sets the same tone, refusing to acknowledge that such "popular concern" was a symptom rather than a cause of his government's policies.[23] The unwillingness of the government even to name the problem as a problem of racism reached its acme in one sense when a 1993 report ascribed the social violence experienced simply to the temporary difficulties of people in both halves of the country (especially young people) in coming to terms with new situations. The report carefully skirts most of the salient economic circumstances of the new racism, preferring to see the issue either as political or as part of Germany's "bad conscience" about its past. At the same time, the implication is that the improper subjects who perpetrate violence should not be tolerated (not "cushioned," perhaps, to adopt Breuel's language quoted earlier in relation to Ossi workers) for long in the drive toward a common cultural identity in the two Germanys.[24]

With these briefly elaborated examples (which should be understood only as parts of a draft of a longer and less gestural essay) I am simply suggesting that the forcible assertion of the unity of Germany provokes crisis, or takes the deliberate risk of civic and cultural disturbance, in the interests of the directives of capitalism itself. The alarming symptoms in civic and cultural life are not only varied and overdetermined in and of themselves, but are also inextricably part of the economic crisis. The cultural and civic formations of what we might call a desired *uniculturalism* are intimately tied to the nature of this capitalist crisis. And since, as Marx insists, crisis is a moment at which the contradictions of what he calls "the bourgeois economy" of capitalism are paramount, any struggle against "uniculturalism" is bound to uncover at some point and at some level exactly those contradictions. What we can perhaps see in the German context is a playing out of some of the fundamental contradictions of capitalism and a display of the logics of late twentieth-century capital. Even though the collapse of actually existing socialism in other places has led to a set of quite different scenarios (most of which tend toward the chaotic rather than the unified, as in the former Yugoslavia), the German situation can be taken as a pure instance or a model by dint of the fact that there is indeed this forcible assertion of unity—this forcible assertion that is quite specifically controlled and managed by actually existing capitalism. Now, in that process we can glimpse the way in which the economic realm is articulated with the civic and the cultural; equally we can see the forging of a double-headed effort first to produce the appropriate subject of value, and second to deny or simply elide the connectedness of the political and economic realms. From such propositions it would not be hard to conclude that any effective political, civic, or cultural strategy produced by multiculturalism will be struggling not just against a reluctance of white culture to "integrate" racially or ethnically "diverse" cultures, but equally—perhaps more thoroughly—against a set of formations and ideologies that are crucial to capitalism's development and its current effort to unify itself in the North.

Notes

Some citations have been taken from electronic versions of newspaper and magazine reports, and in those cases I do not cite page numbers.

1. Quoted in Manning Marable, *Race Reform and Rebellion: The Second Reconstruction in Black America, 1945–1990,* 2d ed. (Jackson: University Press of Mississippi, 1991), 90.

2. Elmar Altvater, *The Future of the Market* (London: Verso, 1994); Gerlinde Sinn and Hans-Werner Sinn, *Jumpstart: The Economic Unification of Germany* (Cambridge: MIT Press, 1994).

3. Jack Amariglio and Antonio Callari, "Marxian Value Theory and the Problem of the Subject," *Rethinking Marxism* 2:3 (fall 1989): 1–30.

4. For the notion of the presumption of the subject, see my *Discerning the Subject* (Minneapolis: University of Minnesota Press, 1988). The use of the term "to profer" is explained in my *Clint Eastwood: A Cultural Production* (Minneapolis: University of Minnesota Press, 1993), xvi.

5. George A. Akerlof, Andrew K. Rose, Janet L. Yellen, and Helga Hessenius, "East Germany in from the Cold: The Economic Aftermath of Currency Union," *Brookings Papers on Economic Activity* 1 (1991): 1.

6. Fredric Jameson, ed., *Aesthetics and Politics* (London: New Left Books, 1977), 129.

7. Karl Marx, "Crisis Theory," in *The Marx/Engels Reader,* ed. Robert Tucker (New York: W. W. Norton, 1978), 448.

8. Horst Siebert, "The Integration of Germany: Real Economic Adjustment," *European Economic Review* 35 (1991): 592.

9. *Washington Post,* 1 August 1991.

10. Figures for 1992 and 1993 quoted from United Press International, 25 September 1992

and 23 May 1993, respectively. The following passage (from the *Economist*, 24 December 1994), reporting on the closure of Treuhand in 1994, is interesting for the way that it replicates the assumption that the GDR economy was valueless at the moment of unification, but also because it succinctly relays some of the contradictions of the Treuhand's project: "In 1990 the Treuhand was the world's biggest holding company, with 12,370 businesses from coal pits to a down-at-heel Berlin horse track. Since then, all but 100 or so have been sold or liquidated. A gaggle of smaller agencies remains, mainly to enforce contracts, manage the few companies left and dispose of the Treuhand's property portfolio. The big companies went mainly to western German or other European investors which were in the same industry; many smaller ones were bought by their managers. The Treuhand leaves behind a flourishing economy (eastern Germany grew by around 9% in 1994) and thousands of firms with at least a chance of surviving in the world market.

"Yet the cost was high. More than six out of ten of the 4m people Treuhand firms once employed have been sacked. What is left of East German industry is dominated by western owners. In its early days the Treuhand thought it would raise DM6000 billion ($370 billion) from privatisation; instead, it will raise about a tenth of that amount and hand the state a debt of DM270 billion. After a string of scandals, the federal auditor has assailed the Treuhand for exercising lax controls. According to a poll published recently in *Süddeutsche Zeitung*, a Munich-based newspaper, 91% of eastern Germans have a low opinion of it."

11. *Newsweek*, 15 April 1991; *Independent*, 3 April 1991.

12. *Christian Science Monitor*, 12 November 1991.

13. Ibid.

14. Patrick Wright, *On Living in an Old Country* (London: Verso, 1985), 52.

15. Breuel, quoted by InterPress Service, 24 February 1992.

16. See Akerlof et al., "East Germany in from the Cold," 1–105. Yellen's recent elevation to the Federal Reserve Board by the Clinton administration gives an idea of the influence of this group of economists.

17. Lawrence Brainerd, quoted in *IMF Survey*, 7 January 1991: 11–12.

18. Quoted in *International Herald Tribune*, 2 April 1994.

19. Karl Marx, *Capital*, vol 1: *A Critique of Political Economy* (New York: Vintage Books, 1977), 477.

20. Barbara Einhorn, *Cinderella Goes to Market* (London: Verso, 1994), 23.

21. *Daily Telegraph*, 13 April 1991.

22. Infas Survey Report, quoted by United Press International, 11 September 1992.

23. Quoted by United Press International, 9 September 1992.

24. See *Dossier on Xenophobia in Germany*, Germany Foreign Press Office, January 1993. Angelina Peralva, in her contribution to the book *Racisme et xénophobie en Europe* (Paris: La Découverte, 1994) has a more optimistic reading of this report (159–212). It does appear that the Kohl government has been more willing in 1994 and 1995 to crack down on right-wing groups.

CHAPTER TWENTY-TWO

Living on the Edge

Everyday Lives of Poor Chicano/Mexicano Families

PATRICIA ZAVELLA

The growth of multiculturalism in the U.S. academy has been fueled, in part, by the development of respective fields of study on those originally excluded from the canon—people of color, women, and gays and lesbians. Afro-American Studies, Asian-American Studies, Chicano Studies, Feminist Studies, Queer Studies, Puerto Rican Studies, and their respective variant titles (as well as departments and research institutes on white ethnics) were initiated within the context of the social movements of the late sixties and early seventies. Led by so-called radicals, there was debate over the inattention to social problems—poverty, racism, the Vietnam War, sexism, homophobia—by the social sciences and how academic work seemed out of touch with the profound contradictions existing in society. The impetus for change had come from the Great Society legislation, the civil rights movements—especially in providing access to educational institutions—and the nationalist, counterculture, feminist, and gay movements. Often led by students, faculty, and staff who engaged in strikes, fasts, and demonstrations demanding new programs, we in Ethnic Studies embarked on a concerted effort to make intellectual work "relevant," to analyze the pressing problems in our communities. The generation of knowledge itself—the construction of paradigms, the very research questions asked, and by whom—were all seen as reflections of power and privilege.[1]

Once established as academic programs or departments, the initial work of scholars working within Ethnic Studies often was to critique the then dominant theories, which, as was fashionable at the time, looked for internal cultural explanations of the social problems experienced by Chicanos.[2] Highly influenced by Marxism, early critics made challenges to structural functionalism and its variant, cultural determinism, with their ahistorical disregard for the structural bases of the oppression of people of color.[3] Within Chicano Studies, many of us saw our work as asserting the importance of race in theorizing about the Chicano experience—which meant framing and contextualizing the structural basis of racial inequality. With this project at hand, a generation of scholars began looking at history to understand how contemporary patterns of institutional racism and sexism were set in motion in historically specific ways.[4]

Now, in the early nineties, as the numbers of homeless and people experiencing poverty increase in the wake of the Reagan-Bush economic policies, the field of poverty studies has burgeoned once again. As during previous times when cultural analyses held sway, there are theoretical approaches to studying poverty that hold up the importance of internal cultural features of the poor. In studies that have been largely outside of Ethnic Studies discourse and placed within mainstream academic venues, the culture of the poor—particularly their values and behaviors—is being emphasized over structure and power. I will argue that such an approach limits our understanding of those currently living in poverty, particularly women and immigrants from Latin America.

Poverty Studies in the Nineties

Do "strong family values" determine how Mexicans adapt to living in poverty? Some researchers argue that in contrast to poor Blacks, Mexicans are more "stable" because poor Mexicans are more likely to live in nuclear families; because teenage pregnancy is a source of opprobrium, so if girls get pregnant, young men are pressured to marry and form nuclear households; and because extended family ties are important and, for cultural reasons, the main source of support for poor people.

Richard Taub argues that poor Mexicans in Chicago have very strong values about work, which include appreciating those who have two jobs, having women do industrial homework to increase their income or make crafts or garments at home to sell for extra income, and realizing that for women, hard work includes being responsible for housework after a day on the job.

Moreover, Mexicans (presumably immigrants, although he does not specify) expect men to be breadwinners, but also realize that men will be tired and often drink after work, and may engage in extramarital affairs.[5] The African Americans that he interviewed, on the other hand, specify that they resent being asked to perform work when it's not part of their job description, are critical of exploitative working conditions, and angry about the lack of promotions. Clearly, Taub is comparing two populations in different structural positions (immigrants and a subordinated racial group) and arguing that they have different cultural values. They may indeed have divergent value systems, but that can only be ascertained if they are asked the same questions, which does not seem to have been done. Part of Taub's evidence is that within a four-block area within a Mexican barrio in Chicago where he did ethnographic research, there were fifteen bridal shops, bakeries, caterers, and florists who specialized in weddings, but there is no such proliferation in Black neighborhoods. When he interviewed people, they agreed that a couple *should* get married when the woman gets pregnant.[6] With this data, Taub concludes that Mexican Americans have an intense commitment to the marital bond and to work, whereas Blacks do not, presumably because of cultural differences between the two populations. The implicit conclusion is that if Blacks just had different attitudes, they would have better lives.

Taub's and others' work falls within the dominant theoretical approach about the "urban underclass" that has become prominent in the social sciences. The term itself was coined by journalists and there is debate about who constitutes the underclass.[7] Probably the most influential formulation is that of William J. Wilson, a self-avowed liberal who aims to counteract conservative formulations that emphasize individual attributes within a culture of poverty.[8] Wilson focuses on the poor located in urban ghettos, who, because of severe racial segregation, are predominantly Black. He argues that because of restructuring in the economy with plant closures and deindustrialization in rust belt cities, Black men in the inner cities face chronic joblessness. With the departure of industry from major cities and the rise of the service sector, the remaining jobs provide low pay and few possibilities for promotion. Without the ability to support their families, fewer couples get married when women become pregnant. Accompanying the movement of capital out of the inner city came the flight of the Black middle class to the suburbs, followed by the exodus of stable working-class Blacks. Closely associated with the remaining socially isolated, impoverished neighborhoods are "concentration effects," where the sense of community is replaced by social disorganization. Those who remain in the inner city form an urban "underclass," made up of mainly poor single mothers—particularly teenage mothers—who rear children isolated from mainstream norms and behavior, and unemployed men.

Although Wilson claims he "draw[s] attention to the structural cleavage separating ghetto residents from other members of society and to the severe constraints and limited opportunities that shape their daily lives,"[9] he and other underclass theorists focus on the behavior and deduced values of the poor.[10] Thus, to understand high Black male unemployment, researchers do not interview employers about their perceptions of Black men, but unemployed men themselves, who then get cast as young men not developing a strong "work ethic" and losing their sense of masculine "honor"—valor, respect, appearance, and independence—which is rooted in Southern aristocratic tradition.[11] Rather than interrogating a firm's relocation policies about uprooting work sites or suburban tax benefits for relocating factories out of rust belt cities into the sun belt (or abroad), the inner cities are portrayed as bleak social spaces, where men "hang out" on the streets, engage in drug use to numb their feelings of powerlessness, and resort to crime to provide some income. Without discussion of the cutbacks in funding for agencies providing birth control and the controversy over parental consent for abortions for teenagers, adolescent females are presented as objectified and as being duped into sex with young men and then ending up on welfare.[12] Instead of documenting those programs that aim to involve ghetto parents in schools or offer innovative curricula, children are seen as having few "positive role models" with the departure of bourgeois Blacks. The influence of grassroots or community-based organizations—which address issues ranging from stopping gang violence to providing education regarding sexually transmitted diseases—is left unrecognized, without analysis of these groups' abilities to affect local policies or provide resources for the poor. Members of the urban underclass are portrayed as having lost all human agency or ability to contest the problematic features of poor neighborhoods, and similar dysfunctional attributes of wealthy or middle-class neighborhoods (such as drug use or the rise of white teenage pregnancies) are ignored, implying that social problems are exclusive to ghettos.

Embedded in the underclass approach are moral judgments about women's sexuality and men's work ethics. "Shiftless" men and "welfare queens," the putative models of individuals who are out of control, underlie much of the discussion of "family values" in relation to poverty. This view sees socialization, particularly the inculcation of the work ethic and of values about controlling one's sexuality, as taking place within families (or occasionally churches), where women and men are taught "proper" behavior and encouraged to marry.[13] The assumption is that if women would just control their sexuality, they would not be in the predicament of having illegitimate children and being pushed into dependency on the state. Moreover, this view assumes that if men would only hustle for stable jobs and form conventional households of nuclear families, they would not fall into poverty.

The ideological nature of this argument can be seen in the conservative media harangues that use underclass imagery to denounce the poor. In almost the same breath, media pundits bemoan the culture of poverty among welfare recipients and worry whether the "brown hordes" of Mexican and Central American immigrants, with their high fertility rates, will soon deplete American jobs and social services.[14] Recurrent pummeling of the immigrant poor also comes from state officials. California governor Pete Wilson's attacks on immigrants and welfare cheats, and the 1994 California initiative that would "Save Our State" from immigrant inundation, are part of a long history of blaming immigrants for the structural dislocations that plague this country. The cultural trope "Just say no" has taken on a political meaning far beyond Nancy Reagan's original slogan against drug use, as Blacks and Latinos are advised to change their behavior.[15] The influence of the media on people's behavior can be seen in the debate between Vice President Dan Quayle and the fictional television character Murphy Brown. The U.S. Census Bureau reports that about three hundred thousand births were unreported, apparently the result of parents lying to surveyors and either not admitting they had a child or claiming they were married when they were not. It took months before the Census Bureau was able to verify this underreporting through other sources, and the bureau attributes this "glitch" to the Quayle-Brown debate.[16]

The focus on value orientations and the behavior of the poor is problematic in several respects. The most obvious is that for these underclass theorists, poverty gets collapsed into family structure. They ignore the high number of families that include at least one employed adult, the so-called working poor. In 1991, 28 percent of Latino families, 22 percent of white families, and 12 percent of Black families below the poverty level had at least one adult who worked full-time during the whole year.[17] Clearly, finding the right mate will not preclude being poor. Focusing on family values ignores the fact that not all poor people engage in dysfunctional behavior or have weak family values.[18]

Moreover, socialization about marriage and sex also takes place in peer groups, in schools, and, especially for youths living in poverty, "on the streets,"[19] and lack of access to family planning may have more impact regarding bearing children out of wedlock than do women's desires. The assumption that pregnant teenagers would be better off within the bounds of marriage is belied by the high divorce and separation rates of young couples and by domestic violence rates that increase when men feel pressured through job loss or the increase of responsibilities beyond their means to meet them. This view also ignores the relationships that poor unwed fathers do have with their children, including the labor and other resources provided by his kin,[20] and it ignores the women who, despite strong family values, are abandoned by men who migrate in search of work.

The portrayal of inner city men is problematic, ignoring the intense activities for "getting paid," which range from finding legitimate employment to eventually moving into real jobs after brief experiences with street crime in neighborhoods where opportunities are few.[21]

This perspective on families of the poor also assumes that single women with children are heterosexual and would want to marry men, when some single mothers prefer to have sexual relationships and rear children with other women. It is difficult to estimate the number of women who are in these circumstances. A significant number of lesbians are experiencing their own "baby boom" and should be considered in the discussion of single parents. It is now clear that lesbian mothers often experience poverty, and must construct their own support systems and communities,[22] and some autobiographical writings illustrate the social isolation of lesbians from their extended families.[23] Like their heterosexual counterparts, lesbian single parents will suffer from "welfare reform" that is based on assumptions that the real problem is women's lack of conformity with "family values" and then pushes them off social programs and into the nexus of support networks.

With its jump cut to values and behaviors of the poor, the underclass perspective replicates the flawed "culture of poverty" argument of previous eras.[24] Yet the underclass framework has set the terms of debate in studies on Chicanos and Latinos living in poverty. Wilson himself suggested that "Hispanics" would show a steady increase in joblessness, crime, teenage pregnancies, female-headed families, and welfare dependency that characterize the underclass, while his followers simply lump Blacks and "Hispanics" together.[25] They ignore the scholars who show that the demographic profile of poor Chicanos is varied and does not match that of the "underclass," even those who live in the most poverty-stricken neighborhoods.[26] More important, an underclass perspective ignores the regional political-economic conditions that produce poverty. Wilson apparently has disavowed the term "underclass," yet his conservative followers use the politically charged image of welfare cheats to argue for policies that would push women into the labor force or training programs with limited child care to support their children before they are left without social benefits, and denigrates those who resist this path. Thus it becomes critical for us to provide alternatives to the "poverty of discourse about poverty."[27]

Latinos in Poverty

Indeed, Latinos have high and growing poverty rates. In California, approximately 22 percent of Latino families lived in poverty in 1992, compared to 22 percent of Blacks, 18 percent of Asians, and 7 percent of Anglo families.[28] Like their counterparts in different racial categories, households of Latina single mothers and their children are more likely to be poor.[29] Pérez and Martínez state that "the relationship between gender and poverty is critical to the discussion of Latino poverty, because almost one-half of all Hispanic poor families (45.7%) are maintained by a woman."[30] It behooves us to pay attention to the dynamics—economic, political, or cultural—that push increasing numbers of Latinas into single parenthood and that make supporting their children very difficult.

Female-headed households are a critical component of Latino poverty, but they are only one part of the story. When Latino men and women are included in the same national sample, we find consistent differences, with women generally having higher incidences of poverty, lower incomes, lower-paying jobs, higher unemployment rates, and higher incidences of domestic violence, all of which push them into dire living conditions.[31] In their random survey of Latinos in California, Hayes-Bautista and his colleagues found that the poverty rates among a sample of predominantly immigrants remained significant even by those of the third generation born in the United States, and that women consistently had higher poverty rates than men within each generation.[32] Clearly, large numbers of Latinos do not escape the bottom of the social structure and find the American dream by moving out of poverty.

Table 1. Latino poverty rates by generation and gender

	First generation		Second generation		Third generation	
	Male	Female	Male	Female	Male	Female
Poverty rate	34%	43%	27%	36%	20%	35%

Perhaps because of assumptions that Mexicans are culturally distinct, researchers, in their rush to focus on family values, often ignore the structural changes that Wilson points out. Some researchers of the Chicano/Latino population have used the logic of the underclass model to argue its inverse—that poor Latinos have "good" values and behavior. Their evidence for this conclusion is often inferences made from people's statements on surveys. For example, Testa and Krogh found that Mexicans had strong cultural norms against premarital sexual relations and that they initiated sex later than Blacks; therefore Mexicans' "higher levels of conventional marriage compared to blacks would appear to be related to slightly longer delays in the initiation of sexual activity."[33] But, of course, having sex and getting married are entirely different things.

Others find sociodemographic patterns and ask questions about family values, then leap to the conclusion that values determine behavior. Hayes-Bautista and his colleagues conducted a large random survey of Latinos in California. They found that Latino males have high labor force participation rates, and, despite consistently high unemployment rates, do not leave the labor force as "discouraged workers." Compared to Blacks and whites, Latinos receive the lowest amount of cash derived from income-transfer programs such as Social Security, welfare, and unemployment and other social programs.[34] Latinos in their sample are more likely to form nuclear households than Anglos, Blacks, or Asians.[35] Hayes-Bautista and his colleagues conclude that since Latinos have large families, they are "quite committed to fulfilling their parental roles and assuming familial obligations," and when Latinos agreed that extended kin are important, they were seen as "imbued with rich family values."[36]

These findings are very useful, but their interpretations are ahistorical and provide no context for making sense of their data.[37] They ignore the fact that undocumented immigrants are not eligible for welfare (Aid to Families with Dependent Children), food stamps, Social Security, unemployment compensation, or supplemental security income, despite their paying state and federal income taxes and state sales taxes.[38] Many immigrants avoid social services because they can jeopardize their amnesty status; they fear that applying for benefits will lead to deportation.[39] Moreover, Latinos have had a disproportionately higher increase in the percentage of families headed by women during the 1980s.[40] Hayes-Bautista and his colleagues also ignore the forces that created a decline of nuclear families in all groups over the past decades (e.g., Asians had immigration restrictions on women, so nuclear households have been impossible for some). They also do not take into consideration the structural changes occurring in California, including the flight of manufacturing in historically Black neighborhoods, or employers' discrimination against Blacks and Asians, which may have more to do with higher Latino employment than their own values.[41] In their zeal to refute the underclass model for Latinos, these researchers imply that Blacks or other groups do not have strong family values or a work ethic, and, ironically, they ultimately reinforce the model itself.

It is important to note that the high official rate of intact nuclear families among Mexicans masks the fluidity of family life and can be misleading. Indeed, recent ethnographic research shows that the "intact" nuclear family among Mexican immigrants can range from fictitious common-law marriages where "husbands" are in name only and women are very independent, often providing the sole economic support for the household, to cases where the women occasionally reside in Mexico, or where they cannot leave abusive marriages.[42] Other "intact" Mexican families include farmworker women who, because of employment discrimination in the United States and indigenous cultural norms rooted in Mexico, only migrate with male sponsorship and thus are pressured into remaining with their spouses.[43]

Nuclear families also include undocumented immigrant women and female "conditional residents"—those allowed to remain in the United States provided they stay wedded to their citizen or legal permanent resident spouses—who are at particular risk for spousal abuse once they settle in the United States.[44] These women sometimes find themselves married to men who use the threat of deportation as a weapon in the abuse of their wives. These men experience the conditions that often push men to abuse—high unemployment, layoffs, or low income, exacerbated by alcohol or drug use—and stresses associated with migration itself, such as anxiety about family members left at home, thefts from "old-timers" in new locales, or crowded living conditions.[45] The number of immigrant women coerced into remaining with abusive spouses is difficult to estimate, but various reports suggest that the population of abused immigrant women is disproportionately large. Data from a random sample survey of undocumented Latinas in the Washington, D.C., metropolitan area indicates that 60 percent report that they are battered by their spouses; agencies that provide resources to victims of domestic violence report that extremely high percentages of their clients are conditional residents.[46] The women forming this "hidden population," as it is being labeled, are often economically, linguistically, and psychologically dependent on their spouses. Like their fellow battered women who are citizens, women conditional residents are likely to experience a severe decline in resources if they leave their batterer spouses.[47] Furthermore, immigrant women migrate from Latin American countries not only to flee economic misery and political repression, but to *escape* domestic violence, sexual assault, or incest, often at the hands of their own partners or relatives.[48] Unfortunately, "strong family values" are often missing from Latino families as well.

The idea that Latinos have "good, stable nuclear families" says more about the discourse about poverty than about the conditions in the United States and Latin America under which migrants live. Moreover, it is not simply the type of data that is crucial. Some critics suggest that the shortcomings of underclass theory stem in part from the "difficulties inherent in using census data to measure a complex social reality."[49] As we have seen, underclass theory can be supported with ethnographic, census, or survey data. We could dismiss this as being faulty research, but there is an underlying ideological message: Mexicans are becoming the new "model minority," and our "good values" are being pitted against Blacks and others in poverty.[50] This kind of thinking is insidious and must be challenged.

We must be careful not to cast our analyses as value judgments (in this case positive ones), for this puts us in an analytic black hole: Mexicans' or Latinos' "rich" values are derived from their culture—and we are back full circle to cultural determinism. This perspective begs the question: if Latinos have such upstanding values and "stable" families, why are they disproportionately poor even by the third generation? Moreover, the policy implications of this thinking are benign neglect—just leave them alone because they're good citizens, or keep those policies that support positive values. What about those poor Latinos and Latinas who do use welfare and other social services? Do we condemn them as having dysfunctional values and unstable families? What about those who need social services but avoid applying because of language barriers or their fear of being deported?

Clearly we need an alternative perspective, one that analyzes the history of placement of groups in the local political economy, that provides some context for understanding differences between immigrants and U.S.-born Latinos, Asians, and Blacks who generally are concentrated in low-wage jobs, have few benefits or opportunities for occupational mobility, and in some cases are being displaced by technology or runaway shops. We need comparative historical analyses of the processes that concentrate certain populations in or push them out of particular sectors of the economy.

Regional Analyses

The current economic situation is one of structural change, in which fragmentation of the labor process, global integration of production sites and markets, and permanent layoffs of white- and blue-collar workers in the United States are part of the strategies for firms to remain competitive. The effects of these changes in late-capitalist enterprises, however, have been different for particular racial populations or regions. Mercer L. Sullivan states, "Despite the fact that economic restructuring has occurred nationally, its effects have not been uniform. Both African Americans and Latino Americans have suffered disproportionately from economic restructuring, but there are significant differences among minority communities in how they have been affected and how they have responded."[51]

To understand these processes, we must move to perspectives that capture the heterogeneity of Latinos, while noting common structural experiences. Each Latino group has its own history in different regions of the country, where particular structural processes—conquest and subordination, waves of migration and settlement, the specific nature of industrialization and urbanization, and discrimination toward racialized others—have produced particular configurations of segregation and economic vulnerability as lived experience. This segregation can be seen in Latino participation in regional labor markets, in settlement and housing patterns, in migrant streams as people move in search of work and community, and in particular groups' participation in regional or local politics. The case studies in Moore and Pinderhughes, Morales and Bonilla, and others demonstrate that the causes of Latino marginality in one sector of the economy may not be replicated in other regions.[52]

Once we focus on regions, I believe that we need to socially locate people, that is, examine groups' social makeup, including their entrance into the United States. Obviously, Cubans who were welcomed as political refugees into an ethnic enclave with established small-business owners had a different experience than undocumented Mexican migrant laborers in the same region.[53] For each region we need to understand whether there are significant numbers of citizens versus undocumented immigrants, note the gender composition and labor market opportunities of migrants and settlers, and pay attention to salient features of race relations, including discrimination against those with distinct racial features, and how their meaning changes over time. We should take note of other bases of internal differentiation, including generation, age, language use, or sexual orientation.[54] Juan Vicente

Palerm argues, for example, that immigrant farmworkers in California are increasingly diverse, and over the decade of the 1980s through the early 1990s, at least five types developed: "old, middle, new, recent," and a collection of specialized workers who follow specific crops (e.g., *los lechugueros*), who are regular sojourners from Mexico.[55] Examining the experiences of subcategories of Latinos should illuminate how some people are restricted to marginal sectors of the economy while others can experience some mobility in the labor market.

Moreover, looking at fine-scaled internal differences leads to more nuanced understandings of how Latinos' experiences reshape structural processes. For example, even among the most economically vulnerable immigrants there are differences based on time of migration. Immigrants who arrived a decade ago find different labor market opportunities than do more recent immigrants.[56] Mexican immigrants often establish "niches" within particular industries or occupations (say, citrus picking or as busboys) that contrast with American-born Mexican Americans, and may preclude the entrance of succeeding cohorts of Mexican immigrants.[57] Leslie Salzinger shows how Central American women immigrants, through the formation of work cooperatives that help "professionalize" domestic work, influence the creation of an upper tier of the housekeepers' labor market with better pay and working conditions.[58] Thus it is important to examine in detail how immigrants, U.S.-born Chicanos, and other Latinos are integrated into a regional economy, and the implications for their being forced into poverty. Paying attention to the bases of the heterogeneity of Latinos, while grounding this in structural changes, will provide a historicized analysis.

Besides regional analyses with attention to gender differences, households should be an important unit of analysis for understanding Latinos living in poverty. Even though Latinos have varied placement in labor markets, racial differences, different migration histories, and so on, they have similar patterns of using extended kin as sources of social support—for finding resources such as jobs, housing, training, or day care and for getting emotional support. Thus it is important to understand how Latino households are structured, how household structure changes in concert with different economic circumstances, whether households function in a similar manner in all Latino groups, and whether particular types of households are more vulnerable to being poor. Rather than posing a polarized analysis showing that Blacks are different from Latinos, I suggest that we examine particular regions to understand whether and how Latinos and Blacks have had different experiences of segregation (in housing and in the labor market), discrimination, and poverty. Then we can move on to an examination of how these structural forces are experienced in daily life and how the participants perceive their circumstances and manage the daily travail of being poor.

Poor Chicano and Mexicano Households

Carlos G. Vélez-Ibáñez and James B. Greenberg's work on "binational" Mexican families provides a good point of departure for understanding intrafamilial dynamics within poverty-stricken Chicano populations and how these families adapt to poverty.[59] They find that Mexicans living in conditions of poverty form "household clusters," networks of households that revolve around a nuclear family of grandparents or another key relative, with other kin and their households forming "peripheral" households. These household clusters contain "funds of knowledge," ranging from skills related to car repair to how to heal illnesses without resorting to doctors to information about dealing with social services. These funds of knowledge, transmitted through "thick" social relations with kin, enable Mexicans to share the burden and cope with poverty. Key features of household clusters include the exchange of goods and services, and ritual celebrations, where knowledge is shared. Vélez-Ibáñez and Greenberg argue that the economic and political context of the border facilitates the establishment of these households, and in the case of Tucson, Mexican households span the U.S.-Mexico border. Their work confirms others' findings that Chicanos are "familistic," that is, that they place a high value on living close to relatives (more so than Anglos), that kin are an important source of resources and social exchange, that Chicanos often migrate with the help of kin, and that they believe extended family members are the best source of emotional support.[60]

Palerm also argues that a significant portion (13 percent) of his sample of Mexican farmworker families constitutes "binational" families—those who maintain occupied homes on both sides of the U.S.-Mexico border:

> Families settled on the U.S. side of the border continue to provide a bridgehead for both new immigrants and seasonal migrants from Mexico. In fact, a large proportion of the seasonal migrants . . . were temporarily contained within the household structure of U.S.-settled families. Settled family members, moreover, continue to return to their home communities in Mexico, not only to visit kin and friends, but also to oversee farms and businesses owned there. Wage remittances to Mexico continue to characterize the behavior of the California-based farm workers; they not only assist and support family members living in Mexico, but also pay for home and farm improvements and invest in local businesses.[61]

These families often find that their kin networks in Mexico can provide greater emotional and material support than those in the United States, especially for women.[62]

How do Mexican immigrant or binational households differ from those that include U.S.-born Mexican Americans? Hurtado and her colleagues found that there are important differences between first-generation immigrants (born in Mexico) and second-generation (born in the United States but parents born in Mexico) and third-generation (born in the United States and parents born in the United States) Chicanos.[63] Those from the first generation are more likely to value living close to relatives than those of the second or third generation. Keefe and Padilla, on the other hand, find that in the Santa Barbara region this familistic behavior *increases* by the third generation because Chicanos have more relatives living in the area than Mexicans of the first generation.[64] Clearly, the role of extended kin in providing support to low-income Chicanos and Mexicanos is important, but needs further analysis.

Poverty in Albuquerque

Phillip B. Gonzáles argues that the historical causes of poverty in Albuquerque stem from the incorporation of rural Hispano villages, whose inhabitants were made vulnerable to labor market restructuring in a peripheral economy. Albuquerque went through four major restructuring phases beginning in the late nineteenth century: the city shifted from an obscure frontier outpost to the state's commercial center with the construction of the railroad; World War II fueled the development of regional air bases and weapons development and atomic research facilities, which became major employers; the Cold War saw the expansion of military-related manufacturing; and, beginning in the late sixties, there was an expansion of manufacturing primarily based on electronics and garment industries. During each of these phases, the Mexican-American population experienced neighborhood poverty in different ways. In the first phase, rural villages with their traditional cooperative labor practices were incorporated into the city of Albuquerque. Between 1941 and 1960, Mexican Americans from other southwestern states and from Mexico settled in the village areas. Beginning in the 1960s, the Mexican-American population continued to disperse throughout the city, even into neighborhoods long reserved for whites. Albuquerque was never a large settlement area for Mexican immigrants, primarily because of the lack of major industry. Only during the late 1980s did a significant number of Mexican immigrants begin to settle in Chicano barrios. Gonzáles argues that during each historical period, in different neighborhoods of the city, restructuring meant different experiences of poverty for Mexican Americans.[65]

In researching Albuquerque's electronics and apparel industrialization, my colleagues and I found that the location of production facilities within a primarily service economy and the recession of the early 1980s set up contradictory forces.[66] Relying on a gender division of labor already in place throughout the wage and skill hierarchy of the electronics and apparel industries worldwide, managers hired women to fill the large number of assembly jobs that were created as part of each new plant's production process. Mainly because managers of Albuquerque's electronics and apparel factories employed women who had high-school education or even some vocational training from the local community college, immigrant women did not form a large part of the labor force. Mexican-American women made up a greater proportion of the high-school-educated labor force in Albuquerque, and were recruited to these jobs in higher numbers than Anglo, Black, or Indian women. In a deliberately antiunion strategy, managers of these factories paid higher than minimum wages—our informants averaged between five and six dollars an hour—and provided good benefits that included medical insurance, maternity leaves, paid holidays, and, in some cases, profit sharing. We found that women's work in these factories brought important changes in family life as women became coproviders, mainstay providers, or, in the case of single parents, sole economic providers for their families.[67]

At the same time that women were recruited to electronics and apparel jobs in Albuquerque, jobs in mining, the oil industry, construction, and transportation were declining or subject to seasonal layoff. Thus men were increasingly economically vulnerable as unemployment rose during 1982 and 1983, and Hispanic men had higher unemployment rates than white men. Thus Hispana women had moved a step up within the working class, while sometimes their own spouses had skidded down. Those families fortunate enough to have women working in electronics or apparel industries, then, were low-income, since they relied on women's wages for family support. Yet these families were above the poverty level, and, with the women's excellent job benefits (particularly medical insurance), experienced some economic stability.

There are indications that the phenomenon of increased male dislocation in the economy may now be more widespread than in the 1982–83 recession when we did our research. In one recent survey of national unemployment rates, Latino males had higher rates than females.[68] Unfortunately, the restructuring of the economy often means that industries expand in one area of the globe only to contract in another. These gendered dynamics, where women are able to secure stable industrial jobs (albeit low-paying) while men are subject to high unemployment, are found along both sides of the U.S.-Mexico border.[69]

I will discuss the experiences of one woman from our Albuquerque study who was the exception to the rule, in the sense that she was the only female Mexican immigrant we interviewed. Upon migrating to Albuquerque, Marta Astorga was able to secure a job in an apparel factory. Her experiences illustrate the links between poverty and political economy, the importance of kin as support networks, the perceived differences between Mexican immigrants and Chicanos, and the dangers of jumping to conclusions about cultural values.

The Case Study

A mestiza born in Durango, Mexico, forty-one-year-old Marta Astorga was a single head of family with three children, ages ten, eight, and six. Like so many other unskilled men in Albuquerque's economy, her husband could not find steady employment until he moved to another city. Marta was a sewing operator at a large nonunion factory in Albuquerque that was highly segregated by race/ethnicity and gender. She estimated that 97 percent of her coworkers were women, and the majority were Chicanas. Because of Reagan's recession, Marta had been working short weeks, sometimes able to get only twelve hours of work a week to support her family. Moreover, she claimed that there was discrimination, so that operators who were the "favorites" of the supervisor—that is, Mexican-American women—would get the better jobs.

Five months before our interview, Marta was forced out of the labor force because of her many problems at work: her machine kept breaking, causing her to lose wages and slow up the production line for others; her eyes became inflamed from the dust and chemicals, which further slowed her pace; and her supervisor was not supportive. After several written warnings, Marta was pressured to quit. She believed that if she had spoken English well, she might have been able to keep her job. Hesitantly, she observed: "Lots of times they don't give the heavier work to the Chicanas because they know that the Chicanas will cry and they don't want to do the heavier work.

And the Mexicans that don't understand much, so as not to argue and lose time, do not protest against it as much." She did not state the obvious—that immigrants would be more vulnerable in a depressed labor market, so they did not contest the discrimination. Marta had not adjusted to her new unemployed status and called herself "a housewife, I think." She seemed somewhat disconcerted when describing her circumstances, almost as if she couldn't believe how things had become so bad.

Marta's family is the product of the economic restructuring and demographic changes of the 1980s. She and eventually many of her extended kin migrated to Albuquerque from Juárez, Mexico, in search of work, to "better" themselves. Initially Marta claimed she had immigrated with a visa and that she felt free to occasionally visit her mother, four siblings, and their families on the other side of the border. Yet when I tried to ask about the circumstances of her immigration, she became tense and did not want to discuss it in detail, implying that she might have come "without papers" or that her visa had lapsed. She believed that her factory job was good because it had provided health benefits and, when working full-time, enough wages to support her children and to bring out a sister, who then provided day care while Marta worked.

After losing her factory job, Marta's search for another job was unsuccessful in Albuquerque's depressed labor market. To support her three children, she was working one or two days a week cleaning house for a wealthy Anglo family, earning wages of $30–$60. Her ex-spouse sent money about four times a year, with each payment averaging about $150. Marta survived by budgeting her income scrupulously, making clothes for her children and some for herself. And, she observed, "We eat lots of beans." She was behind on her rent, had no insurance of any kind, and was struggling to pay off her medical and dental bills. She rented a tiny house on the edge of town from her employers, who did not press her for the back rent.

Marta's ex-spouse would return for occasional visits of a few days or a few months. Marta knew that he was living with another woman in a nearby state and had "several families," but did not know his address or how many children he had. She was very angry with him but made it a point to say she was not separated or divorced. Marta spoke wistfully of the early days of their marriage, when she had been happy, and would not represent herself as a single woman.

Marta epitomized traditional family values: she believed that men should support the family, that men should earn more than women, that women should stay home with the children when they are little, and that she missed some of the best experiences of her children's early development because she was away from them while working. She had contested this traditional configuration somewhat. When she was married, Marta performed a double day—doing housework and child care after her long day of wage work—and she believed that this was an "injustice." Her contestation, however, had remained repressed. Unlike other single parents in our study who had children to support, Marta, without a steady job, was not ready to denounce her children's father.

Marta did not receive welfare or even food stamps, nor, because she had "quit," any unemployment benefits. Besides her meager wages from domestic work, Marta relied on seven siblings living in Albuquerque who provided occasional gifts of food or clothing for the children. Her kin, especially her sisters and sisters-in-law, also provided emotional support and were the source of weekend socializing and entertainment, as well as frequent phone calls.

Despite her bleak situation, Marta was no demoralized victim. She hoped to return to the regular labor market for the higher wages and medical benefits it offered and realized that working boosted her self-esteem: "Since I started working, that's when I found out that I can be useful and that I can fend for my own self. That I shouldn't let myself be mistreated by other persons, that I should feel worthwhile for my own self. I feel more confident, and I have learned so much. It was so hard, but I learned." She found the hardest part of her life "being alone," raising her children and trying to make ends meet without a spouse. Ever practical, Marta looked blank when I asked what the government could do to help families like hers. She apparently did not see government aid as an option for her because of her legal status. Her former company, however, was another story: "They [the managers] could switch all the people who have been working there for too many years to jobs that are not as hard, especially for older people. They aren't useless. It's simply that they've been on the job for too long. But they're tired now. It's impossible to keep on going so much, especially in a place like that. It's very hard." Nevertheless, Marta hoped to leave the informal sector and was looking for another factory job because of the higher pay: "I have to keep looking for work."

Marta Astorga indeed lived on the edge and struggled to make ends meet with very few resources. The culture of her daily life was one of isolation and fear of freely seeking institutional support because of language barriers and her unclear legal status. Although she did not live in a binational household herself, she was integrated into a household cluster and maintained close contact with kin in Mexico who apparently did. Marta was managing with the help of emotional support from and material exchange with her kin, who spanned both sides of the border. Despite her strong family values, she was unable to find a good job that would bring her household out of poverty.

Conclusion

Marta Astorga's life is similar to the lives of thousands of women on both sides of the U.S.-Mexico border who struggle to support their children with very few labor market options. These women endure the transcultural process of men leaving and establishing new households when they cannot find work; they must create nurturing social relations for themselves and their children. In many ways, Marta's life is the product of economic restructuring and demographic changes that Wilson deems as important. Like thousands of other immigrant women, she had migrated north in search of work, then experienced economic dislocation when her spouse could not find a job in the secondary labor market and she lost her own job in recessionary conditions. The informal economy, with its extremely low pay and lack of benefits, except for those provided through the paternalism of her employers, was her only recourse. Marta is also like the respondents in Hayes-Bautista's survey—someone who has "strong family values," avoids social services, and makes sure that her children are educated. Yet she is neither welfare queen nor model minority. Marta's "traditional values" include deference to her wealthy Anglo benefactors, repression of her anger toward her ex-spouse, and reliance on self and kin rather than on institutional support, such as job-training opportunities, or even food stamps. With these kinds of material changes, Marta could have supported her children and perhaps even eventually fulfilled her desire for a nuclear family by reuniting with her spouse on the basis of her steady employment.

In the current debate over the causes of poverty and the "underclass," there is no public policy advocate for Marta Astorga and other immigrant families in similar circumstances.[70] Moreover, in their rush to denigrate the values and behaviors of female single parents, underclass theorists have not fully contextualized the experiences of all types of poor people or considered why some women end up in single-parent households despite strongly supporting family values.

Clearly, poor Mexicans like Marta Astorga present a challenge to academics who now realize that our multicultural society includes many different types of families, households, cultures, and experiences. As we attempt to understand the "new immigrants" and their relations with already settled populations of varied cultural expressions, it is critical that we not fall into the American bog of family ideology, based on myths of the homogeneous nuclear family as the norm. Poor people have always lived flexible lives, migrating in search of work, living with extended kin, taking in boarders, doubling up with friends when they become homeless or need temporary help. The nuclear family of breadwinner pop and cookie-baking mom does not even typify white middle-class families. In refuting the underclass model, we must present careful analyses of local political economies, of how some groups have found labor market niches and others have been marginalized. In short, institutional discrimination and exclusion based on race, ethnicity, class, and gender—not family values—explain the persistence of poverty and create the context for how Mexicans adapt to being poor. Just as the underclass model has been problematic for understanding Blacks in poverty, we rush to cultural models about Latinos in poverty at our peril. Structural and cultural analyses of international *and* local levels will be necessary to understand Mexicans who are poor.

Notes

Thanks to Gloria Cuadraz, Micaela di Leonardo, Avery Gordon, Ramón Gutiérrez, Aída Hurtado, Josie Méndez Negrete, Christopher Newfield, Melvin Oliver, Adolph Reed Jr., Denise Segura, and Lynet Uttal for their helpful critical comments on different versions of this paper. Conversations with Felipe Gonzáles also helped in formulating this analysis.

1. See Raymond V. Padilla, "Chicano Studies at the University of California, Berkeley: En Busca del Campus y la Comunidad" (Ph.D. diss., University of California, Berkeley, 1975); Carlos Munoz, "The Quest for Paradigm: The Development of Chicano Studies and Intellectuals," in *History, Culture and Society: Chicano Studies in the 1980s,* ed. Mario T. García et al. (Ypsilanti, Mich.: Bilingual Press, 1983).

2. For an overview of how these political contestations affected theories pertaining to race, see Michael Omi and Howard Winant, *Racial Formation in the United States: From the 1960s to the 1980s* (New York and London: Routledge, 1986).

3. Estevan T. Flores, "The Mexican-Origin People in the United States and Marxist Thought in Chicano Studies," in *The Left Academy: Marxist Scholarship on American Campuses,* vol. 3, ed. Bertell Ollman and Edward Vernoff (New York: McGraw-Hill, 1986), 103–38.

4. For a full discussion of the paradigm shift in the social sciences within Chicano Studies, see Tomas Almaguer, "Ideological Distortions in Recent Chicano Historiography: The Internal Colonial Model and Chicano Historical Interpretation," *Aztlán* 18: 1 (1989): 7–28. See also Patricia Zavella, *Women's Work and Chicano Families: Cannery Workers of the Santa Clara Valley* (Ithaca, N.Y.: Cornell University Press, 1987), 6–11.

5. Taub fails to describe any background information about his informants, to indicate when he is referring to Mexican immigrants or informants born in the United States, or to specify how many individuals he has interviewed. He does indicate that he is unsure how representative his sample is for Mexicans in Chicago. See Richard Taub, "Differing Conceptions of Honor and Orientations toward Work and Marriage among Low-Income African-Americans

and Mexican-Americans" (paper presented at the Chicago Urban Poverty and Family Life Conference, University of Chicago, 23 August 1991).

6. See also Mark Testa and Marilyn Krogh, "Nonmarital Parenthood, Male Joblessness and AFDC Participation in Inner-City Chicago" (final report prepared for the Assistant Secretary for Planning and Evaluation, November 1990).

7. For an excellent genealogy of the term and how it has become popularized, see Adolph Reed Jr., "The Underclass as Myth and Symbol: The Poverty of Discourse about Poverty," *Radical America* 24 (January 1992): 21–40.

8. William Julius Wilson, *The Truly Disadvantaged: The Inner City, the Underclass, and Public Policy* (Chicago: University of Chicago Press, 1987). A MacArthur prize fellow, Wilson heads the Center for the Study of Urban Inequality at the University of Chicago.

9. William Julius Wilson, "The Underclass: Issues, Perspectives, and Public Policy," in *The Ghetto Underclass: Social Science Perspectives*, ed. William Julius Wilson (Newbury Park, Calif.: Sage Publications, 1993), 1–24, 2.

10. Some of the debate over the underclass can be found in Michael B. Katz, ed., *The "Underclass" Debate: Views from History* (Princeton, N.J.: Princeton University Press, 1993), and Bill E. Lawson, ed., *The Underclass Question* (Philadelphia: Temple University Press, 1992).

11. Testa and Krogh, "Nonmarital Parenthood"; Taub, "Differing Conceptions of Honor."

12. With the authority provided by using the ethnographic present and ignoring variability, Elijah Anderson validates the political rallying cry for "personal responsibility" by presenting young men's quest for "getting over" and the logic of young women's "irresponsibility" as consuming mothers. See Elijah Anderson, *Street Wise: Race, Class and Change in an Urban Community* (Chicago: University of Chicago Press, 1990), 112–37.

13. L. B. Schorr, *Within Our Reach: Breaking the Cycle of Disadvantage* (New York: Anchor Press, 1988); Wilson, *The Truly Disadvantaged*.

14. For one example of this hysteria, see Michael Meyer, "Los Angeles 2010: A Latino Subcontinent," *Newsweek*, 9 November 1992: 32–33.

15. The "True Love Waits" campaign launched in 1993 by the Southern Baptist Convention sex-education program hoped that up to five hundred thousand teenagers would sign covenants vowing to remain chaste until marriage. See David Briggs, "No Sex Till Marriage, Teens Vow: Campaign Hopes to Sign up 500,000," *San Jose Mercury News*, 24 September 1993.

16. See "Family Values Skewed Census Data: Political Debate Left 300,000 Births Unreported, Government Survey Says," *San Jose Mercury News*, 3 January 1994.

17. Sonia M. Pérez and Deirdre Martínez, *State of Hispanic America 1993: Toward a Latino Anti-Poverty Agenda* (Washington, D.C.: National Council of La Raza Report, 1993), iii (figures rounded).

18. Rina Benmayor, Rosa M. Torruelas, and Ana L. Juarbe present a wonderful ethnographic study about Puerto Rican women welfare recipients who enroll in a literacy program and then, through writing about family life, experience gratifying changes in how they perceive themselves and their neighborhoods. See "Responses to Poverty among Puerto Rican Women: Identity, Community and Cultural Citizenship" (Report to the Joint Committee for Public Policy Research on Contemporary Hispanic Issues of the Inter-University Program for Latino Research and the Social Science Research Council, 1992).

19. Diego Vigil, *Barrio Gangs: Street Life and Identity in Southern California* (Austin: University of Texas Press, 1988); Joan W. Moore, *Going Down to the Barrio: Homeboys and Homegirls in Change* (Philadelphia: Temple University Press, 1991).

20. Carol Stack, *All Our Kin: Strategies for Survival in a Black Community* (New York: Harper Colophon Books, 1974).

21. Mercer L. Sullivan, *"Getting Paid": Youth Crime and Work in the Inner City* (Ithaca, N.Y.: Cornell University Press, 1989).

22. Ellen Lewin, *Lesbian Mothers: Accounts of Gender in American Culture* (Ithaca, N.Y.: Cornell University Press, 1993).

23. Gloria Anzaldúa, *Borderlands/La Frontera: The New Mestiza* (San Francisco: Spinsters/Aunt Lute, 1987); Cherríe Moraga, *Loving in the War Years, lo que nunca pasó por sus labios* (Boston: South End Press, 1983).

24. For very early formulations, see Daniel Patrick Moynihan, *The Negro Family: The Case for National Action* (Washington, D.C.: U.S. Department of Labor, 1965); Oscar Lewis, *La Vida: A Puerto Rican Family in the Culture of Poverty—San Juan and New York* (New York: Vintage Books, 1965); and William Madsen, *Mexican Americans of South Texas* (New York: Holt, Rinehart, and Winston, 1964). For critiques, see Adolph Reed Jr., "Equality: Why We Can't Wait," *Nation*, 9 December 1991: 733–37; Adolph Reed Jr., "The Underclass as Myth and Symbol"; Douglas S. Massey, "Latinos, Poverty, and the Underclass: A New Agenda for Research" (Social Science Research Council-commissioned paper, 1992); Stack, *All Our Kin*; Charles A. Valentine, *Culture and Poverty: Critique and Counter-Proposals* (Chicago: University of Chicago Press, 1968).

25. Wilson, *The Truly Disadvantaged*, 35; Schorr, *Within Our Reach*, 17.

26. David E. Hayes-Bautista et al., *No Longer a Minority: Latinos and Social Policy in California* (UCLA: Chicano Studies Research Center, 1992); Joan Moore, "An Assessment of Hispanic Poverty: Is There a Hispanic Underclass?" (Working Paper, Tomás Rivera Center, 1988); Refugio I. Rochin and Adela de la Torre, "Economic Deprivation of Hispanics" (Working Paper, Tomás Rivera Center, 1989); Fernando M. Treviño et al., "The Feminization of Poverty among Hispanic Households" (Working Paper, Tomás Rivera Center, 1988).

27. Reed, "The Underclass as Myth and Symbol," 21.

28. Hayes-Bautista et al., *No Longer a Minority*, 13.

29. Diana Pearce, "Women, Work, and Welfare: The Feminization of Poverty," in *Working Women and Families*, ed. Karen Wolk Feinstein (Beverly Hills, Calif.: Sage Publications, 1979), 103–24; Treviño et al., "The Feminization of Poverty among Hispanic Households."

30. Pérez and Martínez, *State of Hispanic America 1993*, 12.

31. Ibid., 12–15.

32. Hayes-Bautista et al., *No Longer a Minority*. These researchers surveyed 1,086 Latinos, of whom 84 percent were of Mexican origin and 15 percent from other Latin American countries. They use "Latino" to refer to the entire sample. See also Aída Hurtado et al., *Redefining California: Latino Social Engagement in a Multicultural Society* (UCLA: Chicano Studies Research Center, 1992), 7 and 53.

33. Testa and Krogh, "Nonmarital Parenthood," 99.

34. Hayes-Bautista et al., *No Longer a Minority*, 166; also see Testa and Krogh, "Nonmarital Parenthood," 83.

35. By 1980, 47 percent of Latinos formed nuclear households, compared to 38 percent for Asians, 25 percent for Anglos, and 22 percent for Blacks. See Hayes-Bautista et al., *No Longer a Minority*, 19.

36. Ibid., 17. I am not contesting the finding that Latinos are more likely than whites or Blacks to reside in intact nuclear families or less likely to use social services. Rather, I am questioning the interpretation of those findings. Hayes-Bautista writes: "In spite of such *socially responsible* behavior in both the public and private spheres, Latinos are the most likely of any group to live in poverty" (ibid., xi; emphasis mine). This implies that groups other than Latinos living in poverty do not have socially responsible behavior, and it implies that the behavior of the poor themselves, rather than the behavior of and decisions by employers, teachers, or government officials, leads to poverty. For a review of the literature on Latino families, see Aída Hurtado, "Variations, Combinations, and Evolutions: Latino Families in the United States," in *Latino Families: Developing a Paradigm for Research, Practice, and Policy*, ed. R. E. Zambrana and M. Baca Zinn (Thousand Oaks, Calif.: Sage Publications, in press).

37. In another project, Franklin J. James compared seven census tracts in Denver with poverty rates exceeding 40 percent to understand "the possible roles of concentration effects, job market conditions and other factors in producing poverty and deprivation among neighborhood residents" ("Persistent Urban Poverty and the Underclass: A Perspective Based on the Hispanic Experience" [paper prepared for a conference on persistent poverty convened at Trinity University, San Antonio, by the Tomás Rivera Center, 8 April 1988], 18).

38. The only public services that undocumented immigrants can receive are emergency medical care, prenatal care, and K–12 education. See Estevan T. Flores, "Research on Undocumented Immigrants and Public Policy: A Study of the Texas School Case," *International Migration Review* 18:3 (1984): 505–23.

39. Immigrants whose status was legalized under the 1986 amnesty program are disqualified from Aid to Families with Dependent Children or Medi-Cal for five years after obtaining legal, permanent residency.

40. The overall percentage of families headed by females was highest for Blacks, at 47.7 percent, followed by 29.3 percent for Hispanics and 17. 4 percent for whites. However, between 1980 and 1985, the *increase* in female-headed families was 50.7 percent for Hispanics, followed by 22.6 percent for whites and 14.2 percent for Blacks. It appears that Latinos and whites are catching up to the high rates of Black single parents, regardless of their values. See U.S. Bureau of the Census, *Current Population Report,* Series P–60, cited in James, "Persistent Urban Poverty and the Underclass," table 12.

41. Melvin L. Oliver, James H. Johnson Jr., and Walter C. Farrell Jr., "Anatomy of a Rebellion: A Political-Economic Analysis," in *Reading Rodney King, Reading Urban Uprising,* ed. Robert Gooding-Williams (New York: Routledge, 1993), 117–41.

42. Julie Goodson-Lawes, "Changes in Feminine Authority and Control with Migration: The Case of One Family from Mexico," *Urban Anthropology,* Special Issue on Latino Ethnography 22: 3–4 (1993): 277–89; Adelaida Del Castillo, "Negotiating the Structure and Cultural Meaning of Sex/Gender Systems: Mexico City's Women-Centered Domestic Groups," *Urban Anthropology,* Special Issue on Latino Ethnography 22:3–4 (1993): 237–58. For descriptions of domestic violence in a migrant Mexican-American family, see Fran Leeper Bus, ed., *Forged under the Sun/Forjada bajo el sol: The Life of María Elena Lucas* (Ann Arbor: University of Michigan Press, 1993).

43. Alicia Chavira-Prado did research on Tarascan Indian migrants from Mexico who engaged in chain migration between Cherán, in the state of Michoacán in Mexico, and Cobden, in southern Illinois. See Alicia Chavira-Prado, "Work, Health, and the Family: Gender Structure and Women's Status in a Mexican Undocumented Migrant Population," *Human Organization* (spring 1992): 53–64; Alicia Chavira-Prado, "The Female Undocumented Experience" (paper presented at the Association of Latina and Latino Anthropologists-sponsored session, "*Rompiendo Barreras de Género*: Social Constructions of Gender in U.S. Latino Communities," American Anthropological Association Annual Meetings, San Francisco, November 1992).

44. Michelle J. Anderson, "A License to Abuse: The Impact of Conditional Status on Female Immigrants," *Yale Law Journal* 102:6 (1993): 1401–30.

45. For a discussion of these problems, see Ramón "Tianguis" Pérez and Dick J. Reavis, trans., *Diary of an Undocumented Immigrant* (Houston: Arte Público Press, 1991).

46. Anderson, "A License to Abuse," 1403.

47. Legislation has been proposed that would allow female conditional residents to file their own applications for status as permanent residents. As of September 1994, such legislation has not passed. See Carolyn Jung, "Enduring Abuse to Get Legal Residency: Immigrant Women Hostages to Husbands," *San Jose Mercury News,* 3 January 1994: 1.

48. Lourdes Arguelles and Anne Rivero, "Violence, Migration, and Compassionate Practice: Conversations with Some Women We Think We Know," *Urban Anthropology,* Special Issue on

Latino Ethnography 22:3–4 (1993): 259–76; Rosalía Solórzano-Torres, "Female Mexican Immigrants in San Diego County," in *Women on the U.S.-Mexico Border: Responses to Change*, ed. Vicki L. Ruiz and Susan Tiano (Boston: Allen and Unwin, 1987), 41–60.

49. Joan Moore and Raquel Pinderhughes, eds., *In the Barrios: Latinos and the Underclass Debate* (New York: Russell Sage Foundation, 1993), xv.

50. In an otherwise careful critique of underclass theory, Moore and Pinderhughes observe: "By contrast with [William Julius] Wilson's portrayal of the decay of the black family and other institutions, Latino institutions were generally viable" (ibid., xvi).

51. Mercer L. Sullivan, "Puerto Ricans in Sunset Park, Brooklyn: Poverty amidst Ethnic and Economic Diversity," in *In the Barrios*, 1–26, 3.

52. Moore and Pinderhughes, *In the Barrios;* Rebecca Morales and Frank Bonilla, eds., *Latinos in a Changing U.S. Economy: Comparative Perspectives on Growing Inequality* (Newbury Park, Calif.: Sage Publications, 1993). See also Louise Lamphere, ed., *Structuring Diversity: Ethnographic Perspectives on the New Immigration* (Chicago: University of Chicago Press, 1992); Louise Lamphere, Patricia Zavella, Felipe Gonzáles, and Peter B. Evans, *Sunbelt Working Mothers: Reconciling Family and Factory* (Ithaca, N.Y.: Cornell University Press, 1993); and Robert Lee Maril, *Poorest of Americans: The Mexican-Americans of the Lower Rio Grande Valley of Texas* (Notre Dame: University of Notre Dame Press, 1989). For two excellent case studies of racial differences in Los Angeles and the multiracial rebellion following the acquittal of Rodney King's assailants, see Melvin L. Oliver, James H. Johnson Jr., and Walter C. Farrell Jr., "Anatomy of a Rebellion," and Manuel Pastor Jr., *Latinos and the Los Angeles Uprising: The Economic Context* (Claremont, Calif.: Tomás Rivera Center, 1993).

53. Alejandro Portes and Robert L. Bach, *Latin Journey: Cuban and Mexican Immigrants in the United States* (Berkeley: University of California Press, 1985).

54. Patricia Zavella, "Reflections on Diversity among Chicanas," *Frontiers, a Journal of Women's Studies* 13:2 (1991): 73–85.

55. Juan Vicente Palerm, "Farm Labor Needs and Farm Workers in California, 1970–1989" (Report for the State Employment Development Department, U.S. Department of Labor, 1991), 5.

56. Leo R. Chávez, *Shadowed Lives: Undocumented Immigrants in American Society* (New York: Harcourt Brace Jovanovich, 1991).

57. Wayne Cornelius, "Mexican Immigrants in the San Francisco Bay Area: A Summary of Current Knowledge" (Research Report Series 40, San Diego: University of California, Center for U.S.-Mexican Studies, 1982).

58. Leslie Salzinger, "A Maid by Any Other Name: The Transformation of 'Dirty Work' by Central American Immigrants," in *Ethnography Unbound: Power and Resistance in the Modern Metropolis*, ed. Michael Burawoy et al. (Berkeley: University of California Press, 1991), 139–60.

59. Carlos G. Vélez-Ibañez and James B. Greenberg, "Formation and Transformation of Funds of Knowledge among U.S.-Mexican Households," *Anthropology and Education Quarterly* 23:4 (1992): 313–34. See also Carlos G. Vélez-Ibañez, "Ritual Cycles of Exchange: The Process of Cultural Creation and Management in the U.S. Borderlands," in *Celebrations of Identity: Multiple Voices in American Ritual Performance*, ed. Pamela R. Frese (Westport, Conn.: Bergin and Garvey, 1993), 119–43.

60. M. Jean Gilbert, "Extended Family Integration among Second-Generation Mexican-Americans," in *Family and Mental Health in the Mexican American Community*, ed. J. Manuel Carlos and Susan E. Keefe, monograph no. 7 (Los Angeles: Spanish-Speaking Mental Health Research Center, 1978), 25–48; Hurtado et al., *Redefining California;* Susan Emley Keefe, "Urbanization, Acculturation, and Extended Family Ties: Mexican Americans in Cities," *American Ethnologist* (spring 1979): 349–65; Susan Emley Keefe, "Real and Ideal Extended Familism among Mexican Americans and Anglo Americans: On the Meaning of 'Close' Family Ties," *Human Or-*

ganization 43:1 (1984): 65–70; Susan E. Keefe, Amado M. Padilla, and Manuel L. Carlos, "The Mexican American Extended Family as an Emotional Support System," in *Family and Mental Health in the Mexican-American Community,* 49–68; Susan E. Keefe and Amado M. Padilla, *Chicano Ethnicity* (Albuquerque: University of New Mexico Press, 1987); Joan Moore, "Mexican Americans and Cities: A Study in Migration and the Use of Formal Resources," *International Migration Review* 5:3 (1971): 292–308.

61. Palerm, "Farm Labor Needs and Farm Workers in California," 89.

62. Goodson-Lawes, "Changes in Feminine Authority and Control with Migration."

63. Hurtado et al., *Redefining California,* 20.

64. Keefe and Padilla, *Chicano Ethnicity.*

65. Phillip B. Gonzáles, "Historical Poverty, Restructuring Effects, and Integrative Ties: Mexican American Neighborhoods in a Peripheral Sunbelt Economy," in *In the Barrios,* 149–72.

66. Lamphere, Zavella, Gonzáles, and Evans, *Sunbelt Working Mothers.*

67. Coproviders earned wages nearly equal to those of their spouses, while mainstay providers were the primary breadwinners in their families. We also have a category of secondary providers, which includes wives who earn less than their spouses.

68. Pérez and Martínez, *State of Hispanic America 1993.*

69. María Patricia Fernández-Kelly, *For We Are Sold, I and My People: Women and Industry in Mexico's Frontier* (Albany: State University of New York Press, 1983); Vicki L. Ruiz and Susan Tiano, eds., *Women on the U.S.-Mexico Border: Responses to Change* (Boston: Allen and Unwin, 1987).

70. The National Council of La Raza suggests policy interventions such as equalizing educational outcomes for Latinos, ending housing and labor market discrimination against Latinos, making work "more rewarding" through increased minimum wage levels or better benefits, or increasing entitlement programs. See Pérez and Martínez, *State of Hispanic America 1993.*

PART V

Multiculturalism and the Production of Culture

CHAPTER TWENTY-THREE

Machine Talk

STEVE FAGIN

As with many of the presenters at the conference, I have the problem of condensing a much longer piece—in my case, a two-hour video, *The Machine That Killed Bad People*. The tape endures this fate in its own unique style, which, as is the California manner, I will "share" with you.

First of all, people get the wrong impression when seeing a segment of the tape. They presume "Oh yes, I've seen a bit. I'm sure if I saw the whole piece all of this mishmash would be a seamless coherence." No such luck. The piece works in a fragmentary style, trying to emulate the way television constructs meaning through fragmentation. The viewer is held together, or in the language of theory "is constructed," in the manner in which the caramel holds the chocolate and peanuts together in a Snickers bar, only then to bind the same elements to your teeth. Second, the order of the fragments works as a complex chain of commands. One opens the mind like one cracks a safe: three to the right, two to the left, five backward, spin the dial, and "Open Sesame!"—the mind is open to suggestion. TV functions this way, opening up the phatic, dysfunctional channels of our minds.

It is this need for ordering that insists that the piece be two hours long. Most independent videos range from 3 to 11 minutes long, in order to deal with the normal exhibition context of the art gallery or museum. I truly see the piece as being as short as I could make it. I often boast that it's like Roger

Bannister when he just broke the four-minute mile saying 3 minutes, 59.4 seconds: my tape is not 2 hours, it's 1 hour, 59 minutes, 42 seconds.

I should also point out that the piece is experimental, and by this I mean it's working on a question, exploring options. I see this as the responsibility of the independent arts. I must confess that this type of work is best when it comes out of a character affliction, not an ambition. One should never start off trying to be experimental; it ends up being kitsch like Dalí. One should be like Raymond Roussel, an artist I've done a piece on, trying only to make "the most popular piece in the world," or be like Victor Hugo, or, in my case, Steven Spielberg, ending up shocked at people's incredulity.

A lot has happened since the piece's inception with the overthrow of the Marcos dictatorship in February 1986. As it was happening, I thought, "What an extraordinary event I am watching!" The exclamation heralds the crossing of a great historical divide: the transition from Chicago 1968 and the truly narcissistic baby boomer motto "The whole world is watching." I remember "watching" in Istanbul (pass the opium, please!) with about as much social engagement as I could muster, seeing friends of mine being beaten. The space traversed from Chicago to Manila lurches from empathy to interactivity. As my piece was being completed in 1989, the 1986 overthrow of the Marcoses (what's called the Edsa Revolution in the Philippines, the first revolution to be named after a traffic jam) was beginning to be perceived as the prototypical TV revolution on an international scale. The event was being reconstructed as the pilot episode for the second-most popular show of that season, *From China to Ceausescu,* with Ted Koppel as the series host. Only the Simpsons were more popular.

As a prelude to showing my piece, and to bring you back to those thrilling days of yesteryear, I will give you a series of suggestions on how one might have watched some of the telehistorical events that have occurred between now, November 1992, and the completion of the piece in December 1989, challenging the baby boomer conceit that all events should be watched as if we were still in 1968 (even though I must concede my own nostalgia for opium in Istanbul).

I should make it very clear that I think the only history worth watching occurs on cable television, with Ted Turner emerging as a twenty-first-century Herodotus. I hold this to be immutable. I'll start with the most recent event, the presidential election, surfing stations. C-Span was definitely the station of choice, with Ross Perot dancing like Henry Fonda in *My Darling Clementine* into a visual sunset. Patsy Cline's song "Crazy" plays the whole time as people come in and out of frame, such a romantic gesture—

but the gesture goes on and on, durational TV turning the charming into a repetition compulsion. I start off humming along to Patsy Cline's "Crazy" and end up trapped in a labyrinthine chase film. Patsy Cline has been transformed into Joseph Lewis, no longer "crazy about you" but just plain "gun crazy." I begin to wish C-Span would have commercials. I need to go to the restroom.

The campaign itself, having taken so long (sort of like an academic job interview), had to be watched on different stations at different times of day. In the morning, with coffee, the networks, but as an amendment to my prohibition against anything but cable news I say, like Lot leaving Sodom, "Listen, but don't turn to watch." The insipid patter of *Good Morning America* gives a bottom beat worthy of the brilliant Cuban bassist Cachao. In the afternoon one had to be mobile, catching the syndicated shows: *Oprah, Donahue, Geraldo.* At night, the Arkansas Ornette Coleman Bill Clinton knew that it was either Arsenio on Fox or Rome itself, CNN. Even Bush figured this out, appearing on *Larry King Live* the Friday prior to the election.

Our next step backward comes to rest on Hurricane Andrew. Of course one would have watched the Weather Channel, but against the grain of its intention, without channel surfing. The Weather Channel, which I believe to be the most-watched cable station, is viewed on the average for thirty seconds per hit. The network's pacing assumes this and so they want people to switch the station. I must admit I watch this station only seasonally, in the winter, when living in California encourages my sadistic side to enjoy the Michelin snow reports from the East.

It is from the Weather Channel that I draw my model of history—much different from the Marxist dialectic (easterly winds) being assumed by many of the presenters in this conference. In my model of history, one is dominated by a bunch of gadgets, predictions that try to predict through means more folkloric than scientific. Once the storm is sighted and named, the process becomes a bit more ritualistic. If people have ever been involved in a hurricane, the response of people is quite the opposite of what I would have assumed. No one panics. Instead, people's lives become meticulous. Maps, tracking devices, shortwave radios, inch by inch, step by step, but then the hurricane hits and all becomes unpredictable. It stops, starts, jumps, and one just rides it out. I do think history works like this. We can know something is going to break, all the circumstances are right, but we cannot assume effects, only opportunities. Systems will hover off the coast, the Holy Roman Empire can last on the verge of collapse for five hundred years, gradually losing its holiness, its Romanness, its empireness, until all at once, it collapses into chaos, a black hole.

Likewise, dictatorships like Ceausescu's or Marcos's can hold on to power in their last stages for such a long period of time that it becomes a managerial style in itself. Capricious and erratic, but with the logic of the last-stages-style of management. When things crack, like a hurricane hitting land, everything becomes unpredictable. Where is the power going to turn next? It is this moment in history, the contact with land, that I am interested in engaging. Looking for a northwest passage but feeling like I'm going over Niagara Falls in a barrel.

Next event, the Rodney King uprising. This was best watched on local cable. Again, since I'm in southern California, I was able to watch the local Los Angeles stations. Now, this event was a beautiful study of dissonance being recuperated. During this type of brought-to-you-live event, one becomes painfully aware of the training of the local newscasters. All they know how to narrate is a five-alarm fire. Regardless of the origin and direction of the event, it eventually seeps to this level. At first, everything is a bit off: the wrong person is being interviewed, dark figures are running in and out of the frame, passers-by are contradicting the on-the-spot reporter. It is very interesting to observe how, over time, they turn it into one of the few stories they have been trained to tell, and when the eleven o'clock news comes on, it's all so comfy. Another fire story. Logo, then traffic copter view of "raging flames," cut to center frame, well-lit summary of damage to retailers, and finally talk to an eyewitness for fifteen seconds, the camera cutting before they even make eye contact with the camera. The coverage from eight to eleven, however—what a difference! Random camera movements, people competing to tell different types of stories, and the newscaster groping for a lead. It's truly extraordinary to watch it tilt and turn, a couch-potato game of pinball unraveling before your sour cream cherry-flavored bag of chips.

The Persian Gulf War. As stupid as it might sound, the only place on my eighty-three-channel TV set I could find people of color being slaughtered for no apparent reason was on ESPN. The Buffalo Bills were killing "the grey and black." The Raiders were being slaughtered. The Bills were using their "hurry-up" offense, the score was around 60 to 3 after a quarter, and I switched back to CNN to the TV moment of the war that first Saturday, before live coverage was thereafter quarantined. An oral virus was sweeping the airwaves, much more lethal than anything the Iraqis would ever release. It was during the coverage of a Scud attack, the camera frantically scanning the sky in a manner much more disorienting than anything from Michael Snow's experimental film *La*

Région Centrale. The newscaster, trying to talk through a gas mask, is looking like a character from a Soviet constructivist play, with costumes by Rodchenko. Bobbi Battista, hysterically shrieking into her knocked-askew-by-the-gas mask earplug that they had overheard from Dan Rather's assistant that there was a gas attack. This roller-coaster ride of rumor and disinformation is circulating like an oral tear-gas attack, the best experimental theater I've seen in years. It was like a new installment of a Wooster Theater Group performance. This was the last day this type of coverage appeared on the network. There were no more live Scud broadcasts after that.

The last events leading back to my tape are the TV revolutions of 1989: Berlin, Prague, Budapest, modeled after the Edsa Revolution in the Philippines. I must concede this was the last great moment of the major networks, watching before bed, horizontally, between one's toes. I'm sure that there has been some type of study that has shown that Ted Koppel's hair really looks sexy when seen between one's toes. The thing I most remember about this coverage was the radical time difference among the performers. It was always daytime for the people on screen during *Nightline,* or they were about to have breakfast, being awakened in the middle of the night. Truly, these events took place in a hybrid time more like a dream than waking life.

To the piece itself, *The Machine That Killed Bad People.* The piece grew out of an epiphany, which, like all wisdoms of that genre, is now on the verge of becoming a cliché. While watching the overthrow of the Marcoses it became apparent that there was no longer a conceptual separation among event, televising, and watching; the spatial separation had been imploded and now constituted a single complex multispatial/multitemporal event. During the Gulf War, many "well-meaning" people voiced their horror over the observation of this style of event: earth-shattering spectacle, televised, controlled by rumor and the intimacy of the frame. Television had revealed its disposition: a wanton creature not good for modern dance or *Masterpiece Theatre*, good only for assassinations, touchdowns, revolutions, and earthquakes. These are hypertraumas and dramas of the present tense.

Unlike these well-meaning people, I was not appalled by this observation. It seemed a squandered sentiment, as useful as being appalled by a thunderstorm. Instead of critiquing this mode of television, I wanted to study its scale and force and see if I could learn to ride, then change, its course. I saw the format as powerful and I wanted to figure out how to use it and alter the effect, keep the intensity but change the meaning. Too many papers in this conference have talked of resistance to spectacle, putting the cross in front of the vampire, or simply watching from the outside and saying "I told you so" over and over again, a rosary-stroking gesture that is often called critique. So I jumped in and tried to create a network of my own, trying to cross Bertolt Brecht with Ted Turner; I couldn't do any more harm than efforts to convert spring wheat into winter wheat: no one was going to starve to death because of my less than noble experiment. I wanted to tangle with this postmodern octopus, the CNN-ification of the planet.

Before showing some of the tape I would like to talk a bit about the different responses I've had to the piece among the Filipino communities. I've had basically two diametrically opposed responses. When I've shown it to intellectuals who were raised in the Philippines, the response has been intensely supportive. There is an appreciation of the piece's effort to acknowledge a complex Filipino identity, where there is no essential Filipino waiting to be released from imprisonment in First World pop culture. The brilliance of Filipino intellectuals is their ability to perform their identity not by some form of raw expressivity, but through subtle toning: irony, self-deprecation, and black humor allow them to resolve the seeming paradox of both embracing and liberating themselves from U.S. popular culture. Are Filipinos neocolonialized? "Yes, then no" or "No, then yes," depending on the individual. So these sophisticates have been a source of great support for my piece. On the other hand, when the piece has been viewed by young Filipino-

American college students, they have been disappointed or even angered. Why all the emphasis on Filipino involvement with U.S. culture? Where are the pure Filipino values they wish to embrace? I try to indicate to them that the piece is about the extraordinary twists and turns of this involvement, what's called the special relation that is the Filipino-U.S. liaison.

With regard to the formal strategies of the piece, the inspiration lies in work done in the 1930s. If one figure were to be singled out it would be the Portuguese-American novelist John Dos Passos, and his magnum opus *U.S.A.* In Dos Passos, the newspaper was seen as the complex site of how people construct their narrative relation to events through a patchwork quilt of visually simultaneous, self-canceling stories. Just look at the formal richness of a newspaper page: pictures, large and small typeface, stories all over the place, obituaries juxtaposed with statistics about the comparative literacy in developing nations. What an experimental form in terms of its grammar, though the semantics are reductive and most often conservative. The form encourages the opening up of the imagination and then its contraction. This is the issue that interested me. I wanted to transform this type of experimentation done in the thirties to the narrative image-site of the present: cable television. I worked off of cable television formatting, trying to take advantage of its grammatical resourcefulness, the way things are told and how they're juxtaposed, and redress the semantic redundancy and conservativeness. If an image-grammarian were to study my piece in the twenty-third century, it would be perceived as typical.

I'm going to show parts from all four sections of the piece and then take questions. I'll take the questions à la Donahue, and have someone go around the audience with a mike. It's that time of late afternoon when our appetite for truth has shifted: we no longer crave soap opera but the syndicated talk show. Our midday meal is dominated by melodrama, high tea by confession.

The following is excerpted from the script of *The Machine That Killed Bad People*:

Manila, December 7, 1972
Thousands watched on live television as she was carried off, her beige terno soaked in blood. Dr. Robert Chase, a hand expert from Stanford University flown in to consult, said he believed the First Lady survived due to her expertise at ping-pong. "She threw her arm up and danced back when he came forward, and that was part of her ping-pong capability."

It was in Leyte that she, Imelda Romualdez Marcos, had first heard of

Europe. Brought by her widowed father to live in the family home, already nearly falling down. Her nun half sister told her the story of the opera singer Maria Malibran. As a little girl, her father, a famous tenor, had forced Maria to sing in the role of Desdemona in Rossini's *Othello*. This would be her debut. Her father told her that if she didn't sing perfectly he would strangle her to death. The critical scene of the opera occurred, his hand on Maria's throat. She couldn't tell if it was Desdemona being strangled to death by her jealous husband, or her own father trying to kill her. She sang perfectly.

Ten years later, Maria, now the most famous soprano in Europe, learns that she has but a few months left to live. She has only one request. Before she dies she wishes to play the lead in *Othello*.

Imelda arose, the morning after the assassination attempt, in the manner of the hysteric who, after a hectic day of being beaten, tortured, and defeated by her symptoms, awakes refreshed.

She had dreamed of mermaids, but this image was replaced by a more troubled one. Huge stones took shape before her, carved with strange etchings. It was a temple and a tomb, a royal tomb. A white vapor rose up from one of the pillars. It took the shape of a queen, a miracle of beauty. The woman smiled at Imelda and took her hand. Her hand slipped from the beautiful vision's grasp. Imelda tried to shout; she heard loud voices calling to her. At this moment she rejoined the living.

Later in the day, still watching the events broadcast in an endless loop on the television, she remained puzzled. Why had Ver's security, standing by, not rushed to her rescue? Ver politely explained that his men had wished to remain out of camera range, to give her center stage.

It was the custom in the Romualdez household to gather in the sala after supper for an evening of music. Don Vicente played the piano, one daughter played violin, and Imelda sang. After the Americans had retaken Leyte, several would gather to hear this pure voice soar over the accompaniment of the piano and violin. Eventually this was brought to the attention of Irving Berlin, touring the liberated South.

Although her range of songs was more distinguished, from the Abelardo Kundimans to selections from *The Desert Song*, Imelda sang to Berlin "You Are My Sunshine." She had been told this was the anthem of the American liberation. Despite Berlin's praises, Imelda decided not to pursue a singing career.

The tragedy of the twenty-first of August.

Marcos's trusted watchdog, General Fabian Ver, still lying on his back, his aides thinking him sound asleep, listened to their squelched laughter as they still told that joke. "No, you have it the wrong way 'round. Galman first committed suicide, then murdered Aquino."

They laughed.

All that remained on the tarmac to mark the bodies were thinly drawn chalk outlines, Ninoy's partially obscured by a muddied footprint. The body of Galman had been hastily removed, his blood both still wet and dried.

Eighteen bullets had pierced the body, entering both front to back and back to front. The Aquino corpse had but one bullet hole through the back of the neck. He had worn the same body armor as the American president.

General Ver turned onto his belly. He had dreamed of a battle, lasting not even a minute. Suspended in midair, their knives flashing. The slash in midair made thrice the damage as the one on the ground. He thought, "In the air they are angels, on the ground, merely fowl."

He returned.

The saving grace of the assassination was that it had been so perfectly bungled. He imagined the American ambassador saying, "Surely the work of amateurs." He would nod and mumble not even a word, but the letters N.P.A.

Cockfights.

The half-sleep reminded Ver of blue grass.

Kentucky.

Trained in torture, by experts, he bristled at their taunts. "Nothing but barbarism," they would say. He would smirk and remind them that "the cock had lost to the eagle by one vote when THEIR republic had selected its national symbol."

As he lay there, eyes fixed on the ceiling, he lost control. The Romans had derisively called cockfighting the Greek diversion.

The laughter had subsided.

His aides, fallen silent, turned toward him to listen, and he overheard his own voice saying into thin air, "Cocks are birds, it is us that have brought them down to earth."

This letter, dated December 17, 1951, was recently discovered quite by accident in an attic in Detroit, Michigan. At this time it would be best to withhold the author's name. We can, however, tell you a bit about him. He was Oliver North's hero and after his tour of duty in the Philippines he went on to Vietnam and finally Central America.

It has been said about him—no, about a character in a novel based on him—that he was determined to do good. Not to any individual, but to a country, a continent, a world.

Well, here's the letter.

Dear Dad,

Thanks so much for your letter dated October 13. Sorry to be so slow to respond but things take so long here, and I was off in the jungles of Luzon. But even there I heard that the Yankees had won the World Series; most everyone here, even the Flips, root for the Yanks. It didn't surprise me that the Yanks had won—what else is new?—but I was shocked to find out they had beaten the Giants. What the heck happened to the Dodgers? Well, your letter really filled me in on that. I must confess I took a certain unsavory pleasure in the way you described the excruciating details. I, like you, wondered why Dresson had put Branca in, after the Giants had murdered him all year and Thomson himself had hit a homer off him in game one. My favorite part of your letter, even more than the overpunctuated rendition of Russ Hodges saying over and over again, "The Giants win the pennant, the Giants win the pennant, the Giants win the pennant." Did it really need four exclamation points each time? Was the postgame interview with Dresson, him saying, without any punctuation in his voice, "I called the bull pen and they said Erskine just bounced a curve, Roc ain't ready, and Branca's throwing hard." He would have been better off consulting a numerologist. How can you put someone in, with the pennant on the line, who's wearing a big fat thirteen all over their back? Well, at least that turncoat Durocher lost the series.

As to some of your questions, yes, I'm still playing the harmonica and no, I don't like the Europeans any better; they seem so tired and cynical. They don't seem to see the importance of all this: oppression, communism, atheism . . . To them it seems like a mah-jongg game. I think they just come over to our officers' club because they think it's safe from the hand grenades. They are so easily amused, eating fried chicken and taking drugs. It's really true, the fate of the world is in our hands and we just have to round the Filipinos into shape. My advertising experience comes in handy and this seems to be the terrain that we can turn this thing around on. Magsaysay is a bit stupid, but at least he listened and does what we tell him. And the song I wrote, "Mambo, Mambo Magsaysay," is all the rage.

Sometimes this war makes me feel like a kid again back in Detroit. Often it's games and pranks that work. I concocted this eye of God scheme, borrowing it from the Egyptians—a little ancient history never hurt. We would, in the middle of the night, paint these evil eyes on the houses of suspected Huks. It would really scare the Huk out of them. Also, we have thought of a rather clever use of aircraft. We broadcast from the other side of the clouds, over loudspeakers, telling the natives not to feed the Huks. This voice of God seems to work better than the Voice of America.

Well, I guess by the time you receive this letter it will be a white Christmas. Here in the jungle, it's just green and more green. But at least it's a Christian country. They really carry on about Christmas. It seems to start up a week after the Fourth of July, reach full throttle Labor Day, and a crescendo level from Thanksgiving to Christmas Eve. It sure is festive, a bit too festive, almost pagan. Now I understand what McKinley meant when he said we had to Christianize them.

Wait till next year.

Your loving son

P.S.: Tell Mom to send some of her cookies; the desserts here are just too sweet. Also, around here you can't find any serious reading—only novels, plays, and poetry—so send me something, anything. I trust you.

Question and Answer

SF: I'll leave out the spectacular climax for another time, because time is up. That's the trouble with dealing with a two-hour piece in this context, so if we could have the lights, I'll try to expand or relate to something by taking questions. There's a mike that's supposed to come around.

R: I'd first like to introduce myself. I'm Rachel and I left the Philippines in 1984, right after Aquino left, uh, was assassinated. Again, the diaspora of Filipinos coming to the United States at that time trying to escape the economy, whatever we were afraid of, but the feeling that I got from this is, sort of, in between outrage. I'm angered because there is no narration.

SF: In fact, there's nothing but narration. The whole piece is governed by a series of stories. There's simply not a box narration. I mean, the most hideous narration in the world is actually NPR, and when I was talking about TV, the one thing I neglected to say is that the one channel I never look to for knowledge is PBS. On National Public Radio they say, "This person is going to say this," and then they say it. Instead, there's basically this cluster of different stories told over images, some of which I pull in one way, some of which overlap in other ways. Others contain others which resist. There's nothing but versions of narration. There's simply not a metanarration. The piece is an effort to take a cluster of discourses in narrations on many different levels and see if they could be juggled for politics. I suggest that politics should not be a universal, metadiscursive clarity but rather a constructed, rough-edged relation to differences.

V: I have to question who you're targeting as an audience because I don't know much about the Philippines, except for what I've read in the newspaper and then some stuff in journal magazines. If you're trying to target a general audience, which I assume that everyone is in here, I don't think that the message that you're trying to convey is coherently put together. It's very mumbo-jumbled and, frankly, I feel like it's very disorganized and I'm disappointed. I didn't get a lot out of it. Can you sort of explain this on a more general level and not use, like, artistic or whatever training that is behind the video? Because I don't understand.

SF: I think the point of this type of piece is really to say that to assume that there's a passive audience that you're supposed to target like some position on the dartboard is a mistake. I think the effort of experimental work is to try to construct a type of experimental text that raises types of questions in ways that enable people to open up to be able to organize information in different ways and, as I said before, the effort of the piece is to deal with the complexity without reducing it and still produce direction. The point with this type of work is to move away from some universal notion of video as a medium addressing an already existing monolithic audience. It's a question of expertise, I think, and not elitism, education and not arrogance, and a logic on another level as opposed to mumbo-jumbo.

List of Completed Works by Steve Fagin

Virtual Play: The Double Direct Monkey Wrench in Black's Machinery (1984)
An 80-minute video on Lou Andreas-Salomé.

The Amazing Voyage of Gustave Flaubert and Raymond Roussel (1986)
A 75-minute video on Flaubert and Roussel.

The Machine That Killed Bad People (1990)
A 120-minute video on the overthrow of the Marcos dictatorship in the Philippines.

Zero Degrees Latitude (1993)
A 60-minute video concerning the impact of North American evangelism in Ecuador.

All works available through Drift Distribution in New York and Video Data Bank in Chicago.

CHAPTER TWENTY-FOUR

"It's All Wrong, but It's All Right"

Creative Misunderstandings in Intercultural Communication

GEORGE LIPSITZ

Popular culture provides opportunities for escaping the parochialisms and prejudices of our personal worlds, for expanding our experience and under-standing by seeing the world through the eyes of others. But popular culture can also trap us in its own mystifications and misrepresentations, building our investment and engagement in fictions that hide the conditions of their own production—the contexts of power, hate, hurt, and fear that give rise to seemingly neutral cultural texts. Gender, ethnicity, and race often serve as devices for building dramatic tension or supplying texture and meaning to cultural texts, but these representations can serve both progressive and reactionary purposes.

In its most utopian moments, popular culture offers a promise of recon-ciliation to groups divided by differences in power, opportunity, and experi-ence. Commercial culture puts people from diverse backgrounds in contact with one another, creating contrasts that can call attention to existing social divisions as well as to the potential for eventual unity and community. But intercultural communication in popular culture can also create new sources of misunderstanding, misreading, and misappropriation that exacerbate rather than remedy social divisions.

Intercultural communication, like all communication, involves some measure of miscommunication. We can never really know how the world looks or sounds through the eyes and ears of others; we use metaphors to convey our experiences because of the impossibility of communicating our experiences to someone else directly. As scholars from many disciplines have argued in recent years, the inevitability of representation always involves the need for metaphors that make direct, unmediated, and perfect communication impossible. But although we can never know the exact dimensions, resonances, or consequences of any act of communication, we nonetheless have to make choices about cultural messages by analyzing their impact on our understanding of the world and our ability to act in it.

Critics of commercial culture often condemn the properties of mass media that encourage consumers to expropriate cultural creations for inappropriate purposes. Long ago, Walter Benjamin noted how the mechanisms of mass production ripped cultural practices from the sites and circumstances that gave them meaning, marketing them as mere novelties for uncomprehending consumers. Certainly these propensities account for the seamy history of exploitation and appropriation of folk cultures around the world by the culture industry, for the ways in which forms of expression connected to concrete social issues in particular places have circulated around the globe stripped of their local meanings.

On the other hand, many of these commodities have drawn the investment and engagement of consumers because their moral and political messages have gained even more power when applied to a new situation. Certainly the role of reggae music from Jamaica in articulating the aspirations of the African diaspora and the appeal of "magic realist" literature by Central American writers for European and American postmodern readers stem in part from the moral and political power of Caribbean and Central American strategies of signification and grammars of opposition to explain new realities for audiences encountering an increasingly cosmopolitan world. Even when listeners and readers have been ignorant of the exact original and local meanings of reggae or magic realism, they have often displayed advanced understanding about how they could use resonances of an "unfamiliar" culture to "defamiliarize" their own culture and then "refamiliarize" themselves and others with it on the basis of the new knowledge and critical perspectives made possible by cultural contrast.

The complexities of intercultural communication in popular culture compel us to look carefully at what might at first appear to be misunderstandings and mistakes. People who appear to be "mistaken" about another culture sometimes really know things that cannot be represented easily because their knowledge is illegitimate by existing standards and paradigms.

Especially on issues of identity involving nation, race, gender, sexuality, and class, "mistaken" ideas often contain important insights. Without minimizing the very real dangers of cross-cultural appropriations and misunderstandings, we must nonetheless be open to the kinds of knowing hidden within some "incorrect" perceptions.

Intercultural communication has been a foundational reality for North Americans for four hundred years. European exploration and settlement entailed the conquest, enslavement, and genocide of peoples of color, and vicious racial stereotypes in popular culture about Indians, Mexicans, Asians, and Blacks have functioned to obscure historical crimes and turn guilt and repression into entertainment and ideological domination. On the other hand, grassroots panethnic alliances have often given rise to popular culture products that present a utopian picture of potential interracial and interethnic cooperation. Culture in the United States has always been intercultural, and we can learn a great deal about both the promise and the peril of cross-cultural dialogue by exploring the cultural questions that have confronted specific cultural consumers and producers in our history.

Consider, for example, the case of eight-year-old Veronica Bennett (later Ronnie Spector of the vocal group the Ronettes) singing for her family in a flat in Spanish Harlem on a Sunday afternoon in 1951. One of her uncles put an electrician's light in a Maxwell House coffee can to make a "spotlight," and her father moved the coffee table to the middle of the room to make a "stage." Bennett recalls:

> That light seemed to focus all the warmth in the room on me as I belted out Hank Williams's "Jambalaya" in my eight-year-old voice. "Jambaylie, cold fish pie, diddly gumbo," I sang, with no idea what the words meant or if I even had them right. But when I looked around the room and saw all my aunts and uncles smiling and tapping their feet to keep time, I knew I must have been doing something right. In the middle of the song I stopped singing and improvised a little yodel. I was trying to imitate what all the cowboy singers used to do. And that was the beginning of the "whoa-oh-oh-oh-oh-ohs" that would become my trademark as a singer.[1]

Bennett mangled Hank Williams's lyrics in her rendition, changing "crawfish pie" into "cold fish pie" and substituting "diddly gumbo" for "filé gumbo." Her admission that she didn't know and didn't care what the words meant seems to provide strong support for critics concerned about the distracted and incomplete reception of intercultural messages in popular culture. Certainly, few people would imagine the maximally competent audience for Hank Williams's country-and-western song to be Ronnie Bennett's interracial family in Spanish Harlem. But further investigation reveals some interesting dimensions to Bennett's choices in singing this song.

Ronnie Bennett grew up as the daughter of an African-American/Native American mother and a Euro-American father. Her mother's sister Susu married a Puerto Rican, making Ronnie's cousin Nedra a mixture of African American, Native-American, and Puerto Rican ancestry. This extended family lived in a neighborhood that "had Chinese laundries, Spanish restaurants, and black grocery stores." At school, Black children teased Veronica about her light skin, calling her "skinny yellow horse" and yelling "Hey, half-breed, get your ass back to the reservation."[2] She later recalled:

> The blacks never really accepted me as one of them. The white kids knew I wasn't white. And the Spanish kids didn't talk to me because I didn't speak Spanish. I had a little identity crisis when I hit puberty. I remember I used to sit in front of the mirror, trying to decide just what I was. Let's see now, I'd think. I've got white eyes, but these are black lips. My ears—are they white ears or black ears?[3]

Bennett appropriated "Jambalaya" from Hank Williams, who was no stranger to the kinds of cultural questions that confronted Veronica Bennett. Williams grew up in a white working-class family, but received his first vocal training and guitar lessons from black street singers Big Day (Connie McKee) and Tee Tot (Rufus Payne). Williams habitually described himself as "part Indian," and his band, the Drifting Cowboys, included a Native American and a Mexican American. He wrote "Jambalaya" by taking the melody from the Cajun song "Grand Texas" and adding to it English lyrics that he thought sounded Cajun.[4]

So when the African-American, Native American, and Euro-American Ronnie Bennett sang "Jambalaya" for her Puerto Rican, African-American, Native American, and Euro-American family, she was imitating a version of a Cajun song written and recorded by an Anglo-American singer who thought of himself as a Native American trained by African Americans, and who played in a band with a Mexican American and a Native American. The "whoa-oh-oh-oh-oh-ohs" that Bennett took from "cowboy singers" and that became her trademark vocal signature as the lead singer of the Ronettes, came from Euro-American efforts to imitate the African-American musical sensibility expressed through changes in pitch and use of "impure" tones. [5]

Ronnie Spector may not have known the correct words to "Jambalaya," but her attraction to it reflected more than a simple misunderstanding. It functioned efficiently to evoke the kind of mixed subject position in music that Bennett had experienced her whole life. From one perspective, her rendition of the song might seem ignorant or incompetent, but from another it can be interpreted as an uninterrogated and perhaps unexpected form of intelligence and competence in finding a song that turned cultural contradictions into a creative expression of cultural hybridity.

Similarly creative "misunderstandings" about popular culture pervade an important scene in Cheech Marin's film *Born in East L.A.* An Immigration and Naturalization Service officer questions Marin's character, Rudy, to see if he is a U.S. citizen or an undocumented alien. Rudy protests that he was "born in East L.A.," so the officer tests his familiarity with U.S. culture, asking him the name of the president of the United States. Flustered by the question, Rudy replies, "That's easy, that dude that used to be on *Death Valley Days*—John Wayne." Rudy's failure to identify Ronald Reagan marks him as "incompetent" in his civic knowledge. But, of course, his conflation of Ronald Reagan with John Wayne reveals a larger truth: that Reagan's masculinist and paternalist politics and image "played" John Wayne for the American public.

In another scene in *Born in East L.A.*, Rudy attempts to teach some Mexican conjunto musicians "the most famous rock-and-roll song ever." He starts to play "Twist and Shout," but the other musicians hear the chord progressions and start singing "La Bamba." Rudy gets exasperated by their "incorrect" response, but the similarity between the two songs teaches the audience (if not the characters in the film) that Chicano identity is already sedimented within what might seem like a uniformly Anglo U.S. popular culture. In a film devoted to exploring the heterogeneous and composite nature of Chicano identity, it is appropriate that Rudy identifies "Twist and Shout," a song written for a Black singing group by Jewish songwriters who admired and attempted to copy Puerto Rican dance music, as his own, while missing its similarity to Mexican music. After the band shares "Twist and Shout" and "La Bamba," Rudy introduces them to other music that reveals the composite and dialogic nature of Chicano culture—a version of Jimi Hendrix's "Purple Haze," where they bill themselves, in an interlingual pun, as "Rudy and His New Huevos Rancheros," and "Roll Out the Barrel," a Czech song that Rudy sings in German (which he learned in the military) but whose polka form brings to the surface the similarities (and interactions) between German/Czech and Mexicano music in the United States.[6]

Wayne Wang employs similar strategies of creative misunderstanding in his film *Chan Is Missing.* While searching for Chan, cabdriver Joe tries to draw on his cultural roots by "thinking Chinese," while Joe's nephew and partner Steve is more "American" in his approach. But neither approach succeeds in understanding Chan, who is not only Chinese, but also likes to dance to mariachi music at the Manila Town Senior Center. Chan is Chinese, Chinese-American, and intercultural; no one narrative, however perfectly understood, can contain or explain him.

Japanese-American poet Lawson Fusao Inada presents another creative misunderstanding in his prose poem "Fresno," where he reflects upon the Asian-American, Armenian-American, and Mexican-American neighborhood in which he was raised. Inada talks about African-American music as the glue that held together these diverse groups. He remembers that for young people in Fresno Black music was the "lingua franca" that "enfranchised" and "conferred citizenship" on those who proved knowledgeable about it.[7]

On the surface, Inada's identification seems disastrously incorrect; how could identification with America's most disenfranchised group confer cultural citizenship on immigrants and their children? But taken less literally, his poem illumines a greater truth, what Albert Murray calls the "inescapably mulatto" nature of American culture. The Black music that Inada and his classmates regarded as quintessentially "American" was and continues to be one of the nation's great achievements, even if the credentialing institutions of society fail to recognize it as such.

Another kind of music offers an important insight in Oscar Zeta Acosta's *Autobiography of a Brown Buffalo*. The author wonders why the song "A Whiter Shade of Pale" holds such portent for him as he becomes more deeply involved in Chicano activism during the late 1960s. He hears it again and again on the radio, and it seems to speak directly to him. "The song moves me deeply. It reminds me of Luther's 'A Mighty Fortress Is Our God,'" he writes.[8]

Acosta never explains the importance of "A Whiter Shade of Pale," but in his confusion he leaves some clues. Of course, one possible connection comes from the song's psychedelic imagery and the massive quantities of hallucinogenic drugs that Acosta's book suggests he was taking. But "A Whiter Shade of Pale" also combines European forms—the melody is from Johann Sebastian Bach's "Air" from his Orchestral Suite No. 3 in D Major—with African-American styles (the soul ballad tradition exemplified in the singing of Sam Cooke) in a way that resonates with Acosta's presentation of Chicano identity as a mysterious and always surprising entity forged from dialogue between Euro-American, Afro-American, Spanish, Indian, and Chicano sensibilities. Acosta's references to "A Mighty Fortress Is Our God" also contain musical accuracy since many of the devices employed to build a sense of majesty in "A Whiter Shade of Pale" appear frequently in Lutheran hymns. Acosta is not simply "confused" or "incompetent" about "A Whiter Shade of Pale," but rather his confusion brings to the surface things that he knows but cannot articulate except through his identification with the song.

Ethiopian-American film scholar Teshome Gabriel offers an example of yet another kind of creative misunderstanding in a story about an African friend of his who grew up believing that Pete Seeger was Black. Gabriel's friend knew that the folksinger participated in the civil rights movement, that he sang freedom songs, and that he included Paul Robeson among his personal friends. When the African's view of Seeger's ethnicity got him involved in an argument after he came to the United States, his adversary showed him a picture of Seeger that clearly showed him to be white. But the African remained adamant. "I know that Pete Seeger is Black," he replied. "Why should I change my mind just because I see his face?" In this instance, blackness becomes a political position, something determined more by culture than by color. Although the African is factually wrong about the meaning of Seeger's identity within the context of U.S. culture, his "misunderstanding" also contains at least a strategic grain of truth.[9]

One can well understand how these kinds of "misunderstandings" allow people of color to see "families of resemblance" that reframe their separate experiences as similar, although not identical. But what about the danger of misunderstandings incorporated into Euro-American appropriation of the cultures of aggrieved populations? For example, Jefferson Starship's Marty Balin told an interviewer in 1983 that "I grew up with the beat era; when I was twelve years old, I'd go down to the clubs and watch John Coltrane and Miles Davis. I didn't know what I was doing, but I could feel something happening."[10]

Balin's recognition that he didn't know what he was doing seems to confirm the views of critics who stress the limits of reception and the barriers to intercultural communication. Part of what Balin didn't know at the age of twelve was the way that his experiences as a listener had been influenced by the history of Euro-American appropriation, colonization, orientalism, and primitivism. But, given the segregated nature of U.S. society, the censoring apparatuses of the culture industry and the state, and the systematic miseducation carried on by institutions of instruction, something else had to be happening in Balin's response to jazz at the same time. His sense that "something was happening" may also have been a recognition of the inadequacy of his existing language to know exactly how and why Coltrane and Davis affected him, how their music broke through the walls erected to keep them unknown to him, and how subversive their thinking might be to the culture in which he was raised. At the very least, it provided him with the inspiration to do more looking and listening, to see music as a potential site for the kinds of exciting and profound changes in human relations that Balin helped along in his capacity as a member of one of the leading bands of the 1960s counterculture.

Just as artists and audiences have been influenced positively by "creative mistakes," so too have artistic products themselves been enhanced by imperfect cultural exchanges. Artists from aggrieved communities have often profited from less than perfect knowledge about the exclusionary rules devised from within other cultures. Their "ignorance" of the intentions of others to exclude them has often served as an impetus to creativity; not knowing they were supposed to fail enabled them to succeed. Los Angeles Chicano artist Harry Gamboa Jr. remembers learning about art museums only after he had been painting for years. His inspirations and models came mainly from comic books, neighborhood graffiti, advertising, and prints used on calendars. When he discovered that museums exhibited "art," he took his drawings to the curator of the most prestigious local museum. They were rejected on the spot. Later, Gamboa went through more conventional channels, but got the same result. "We tried to get our work inside the museum, just like all the other Chicano artists in town," he recalls in reference to the origins of the guerrilla art group "Los Four." Gamboa and his friends found the art museum uninterested in their work, "so one night, we went over there and spray painted our names on the outside of the building. We felt that if we couldn't get inside, we would just sign the museum, and it would be our piece."[11]

Gamboa and Los Four titled their tagging of the museum "Pie in De-Face," and their action generated enthusiastic support among community artists and audiences because it articulated accumulated resentments about exclusion from the establishment definition of "culture." This action succeeded, at least in part, because from the start Gamboa "failed" to learn the lesson his society was trying to teach him—that "art" didn't include him. By remaining "ignorant," he positioned himself perfectly to challenge rather than accept that judgment.

Technical "misunderstandings" can also often be productive for artists. In the 1920s, Bix Beiderbecke could make changes on the trumpet and cornet that no one else could master because he taught himself the instruments and learned all the "wrong" fingerings. The way he fingered the instrument would have been a detriment to skillful playing for most music written within the Western symphonic tradition, but within jazz it enabled Beiderbecke to perform maneuvers that came easily to him but that seemed highly skilled to most other artists and to audiences. Similarly, Black jazz musicians in turn-of-the-century New Orleans often confounded classically trained musicians who tried to play with them because they played in so many "hard keys." They had no self-conscious intention of playing "difficult" music, but, like Beiderbecke, they were self-taught, and the black keys on the piano felt easier to play because they were physically farther apart on the keyboard. Consequently, they developed a style of playing in keys like F sharp, making extensive use of what other musicians had been taught to ignore or to treat as forbiddingly difficult. But these keys were only "hard" to those whose training started them in the key of C and others more commonly employed in the Western classical tradition.[12]

Charlie Parker's "mistakes" proved equally instructive. When he entered his first "cutting contest" (a bandstand battle where musicians tried to out-play each other), Parker didn't know about playing in key and was laughed off the stage. He took his saxophone with him to the Lake of the Ozarks, where he spent an entire summer teaching himself to play in every key—an education that better-schooled musicians might see as wasteful for someone in a dance band, where three or four keys were usually all that was required. But the ability Parker developed gave him exceptional resources as a musician, which he explored more fully in his years as a leader in bebop composing and playing. In a similar fashion, Roeland Roy Byrd, known professionally as Professor Longhair, used to confound nightclub owners by insisting on an upright piano rather than a grand piano. Most musicians considered the grand to be the superior instrument, but Longhair liked to kick the baseboard of the piano to help create the polyrhythms that made his playing so exceptional. His choice of instruments certainly added to the delight of his audiences, if not to that of club owners and their insurance companies when they discovered the damage that his kicks did to these instruments.

By calling attention to these creative mistakes, I am not dismissing the serious consequences of cultural appropriation and exploitation. Neither am I claiming that all or any people have perfect competence in decoding the materials they encounter through popular culture. I am not saying that it is better not to know than to know. We still need cultural studies scholarship that is grounded in history, that is ideologically attuned to understanding the limits of any one artist's or audience's subjectivity. But I do want to argue that people may know a lot even if they don't know the history of the literature they like or the names of the notes they play and hear, and that their imperfections as consumers of intercultural communication do not necessarily render them oblivious to effects of power or to the resonances of hate, hurt, and fear in the cultural creations they enjoy. People are more curious, more ingenious, and more intersubjective than their roles as consumers and citizens acknowledge or allow. Consequently, they often fashion fused subjectivities that incorporate diverse messages about who they are. Often, they make mistakes and they distort what they see and hear. Sometimes they do violence to others by stealing stories and appropriating ideas. But they also display a remarkable ability to find or invent the cultural symbols that they need.

It is important to document the harm done by uncomprehending appropriations of cultural creations, to face squarely the consequences of mistakes in the reception, representation, and reproduction of cultural images, sounds, and ideas. But the biggest mistake of all would be to underestimate how creatively people struggle, how hard they work, and how much they find out about things that people in power never intended for them to know.

Notes

I would like to thank Susan McClary, Rob Walser, Michael Omi, Janet Walker, Avery F. Gordon, and Christopher Newfield for their comments and criticisms of earlier drafts of this essay.

1. Ronnie Spector (with Vince Waldron), *Be My Baby: How I Survived Mascara, Miniskirts, and Madness or My Life as a Fabulous Ronette* (New York: Harper Perennial, 1990), 5.

2. Ibid., 1–2.

3. Ibid., 10.

4. Richard Leppert and George Lipsitz, "Everybody's Lonesome for Somebody: Age, Gender, and the Body in the Music of Hank Williams," *Popular Music* 9:3 (October 1990).

5. Spector describes her vocal maneuver as a "yodel," but while it gestures toward the yodeling tradition, it doesn't involve the full form as expressed in the music of yodelers like Elton Britt or Eddie Arnold. Instead, it involves the changes in pitch, impure tones, and instrumentalized-sounding vocals that cowboy singers appropriated from African-American music.

6. See Rosa Linda Fregoso, "Born in East L.A.," *Cultural Studies* 4:3 (October 1990).

7. Lawson Fusao Inada, "Fresno," American Studies Association meetings, Costa Mesa, California, 8 November 1992. Author's notes.

8. Oscar Zeta Acosta, *The Autobiography of a Brown Buffalo* (New York: Vintage Books, 1989), 35.

9. Teshome Gabriel, "Every Individual Is a Crowd," presentation at the University of California, San Diego, 12 April 1991.

10. Marty Balin, "Starship Interview," *Trouser Press* (March 1983).

11. "Interview with Harry Gamboa, Jr.," in *Murals: Sparc's Southern California Chicano Mural Documentation Project* (Santa Barbara: University of California, Santa Barbara Library, Special Collections, n.d.), 1.

12. Burton Peretti, *The Creation of Jazz* (Urbana: University of Illinois Press, 1992), 102, 104. Irving Berlin also never learned to read music and preferred to use these hard keys while composing at the piano.

CHAPTER TWENTY-FIVE

Imagining Los Angeles in the Production of Multiculturalism

LISA LOWE

Ridley Scott's science-fiction thriller film *Blade Runner* (1982) portrays Los Angeles in the year 2019 as a ruined, deteriorating city in postindustrial decay, a grand slum plagued by decaying garbage, dirt, ethnic ghettos, and radioactive rain. In composing this dystopic setting, the film represents L.A. as a pastiche of Third World, and particularly Asiatic, settlements: the storefronts are marked by neon Chinese ideograms, the streets filled with Chinese, Latino, Egyptian, and Cambodian faces. Everyone is talking "city-speak," which the blade runner Deckard's voice-over narration describes as "a mishmash of Japanese, Spanish, German, French, what-have-you . . . I knew the lingo." Overlooking the city is a "Japanese simulacrum," a huge advertisement that alternates the image of a seductive Japanese woman's face and a Coca-Cola sign, a portentous emblem of future Japanese economic hegemony in the "city of angels."[1] The portrait of L.A. as a metropolis congested with poor Asian, Latino, African, and Arab immigrants projects the future of the First World *as* the Third World. In *Blade Runner*'s version of the twenty-first century, it is no longer necessary to travel out to see "the world"; "the world" has come, and now inhabits, indeed possesses, Los Angeles. At the same time, the film's predominant intrigue—a narrative in which the blade runner Deckard serves the law by hunting down replicants, but ultimately, in fleeing with his replicant lover Rachel, subverts the law that would maintain the dominance of humans over androids—thematizes and critically opposes the very erasure of differences (the indistinguishability of machines and human beings, of species, race, and economic status) performed by the film's collapse of racial and economic difference in the representation of L.A. as ethnic ghetto. In other words, *Blade Runner*'s representation of a Third World invasion of L.A. does not perform a univocal homogenizing of difference, conflict, and otherness, but rather this representation is somewhat contested; the construction of Los Angeles as multicultural dystopia is put into question by the narrative in which Deckard comes to identify with the plight of the subordinated replicants, no longer seeking to kill them, but rather wishing to provide for their escape.

Against *Blade Runner*'s gloomy threat of multiculturalism, I wish to pose a more celebratory, but no less problematic, vision of Los Angeles as multicultural metropolis: the city represented in the September 1990 Los Angeles Festival of the Arts. For sixteen days, the festival represented the city as benevolent host to 550 performance events by artists and performers from twenty-one countries of Asia, the Pacific, and Latin America; as with *Blade Runner*, it may not be possible to constitute the festival as a univocal object. Part of the multiplicity of the festival-object is due to the sheer plenitude of performances, the uniqueness of the geography, the impossibility of having been at all sites, in all neighborhoods, at all times. My comments about the festival are directed more at a multiplicity produced by the variety of competing narratives that structured the presentation of events; among the different narratives vying for authority in the festival, I briefly address four, which I term, for convenience, the narratives of authenticity, genealogy, heterogeneity, and opposition. These narratives overlap and conflict, and I propose that it may not serve our inquiry to attempt to reconcile the narratives, or to determine one as dominant; rather, it seems that it is at the sites of conflict and antagonism between these different narratives that we find the most interesting, and most suggestive, moments in the production of multiculturalism.

I will be arguing that although film and festival representations register the increase of immigrant, racial, and ethnic populations in Los Angeles, both images of multiculturalism are problematic; neither topos reckons with the material differentiations of heterogeneous and unequal racial, ethnic, and immigrant communities in Los Angeles (or to extend our scope, in the state of California, where demographers declare that we are nearing a time in which more than 50 percent of the population will be Asian, Latino, African-American, and other "minority" populations). To the degree that multiculturalism claims to register the increasing diversity of populations, it precisely obscures the ways in which that aesthetic representation is not an analogue for the material positions, means, or resources of those populations; this is not so much a question of posing the figural against the literal, or the metaphorical against an essentialized notion of the "real," as it is a revelation of an undialectical confusion of historically differentiated spheres.[2] Although the concept of multiculturalism registers the pressures that demographic increases of immigrant, racial, and ethnic populations bring to all spheres, these pressures are registered only partially and inadequately in aesthetic representations; the production of multiculturalism instead diffuses the demands of material differentiation through the homogenization, aestheticization, and incorporation of signifiers of ethnic differences. Multiculturalism levels the important differences and contradictions within and among racial and ethnic minority groups according to the discourse of pluralism that asserts that American culture is a democratic terrain to which every variety of constituency has equal access and in which all are represented, while simultaneously masking the existence of exclusions by recuperating dissent, conflict, and otherness through the promise of inclusion.[3] Multiculturalism is central to the maintenance of a consensus that permits the present hegemony, a hegemony that relies on a premature reconciliation of contradiction and on persistent distractions away from the incommensurability of different spheres.[4] In this sense, the production of multiculturalism at once "forgets"—and in this forgetting, exacerbates—a contradiction between the concentration of capital within a dominant class group and the unattended conditions of a working class increasingly comprised of heterogeneous immigrant, racial, and ethnic groups.[5]

Both *Blade Runner*'s and the L.A. Festival's images of multiculturalism are, in a sense, driven by the increased presence of Third World people in Los Angeles; yet where *Blade Runner* produces a dystopic image of a decaying city engulfed, taken over by, Asians, Africans, and Latinos, the L.A. Festival presented the city as an aestheticized utopia of Third World artists. Multiculturalism in the L.A. Festival is represented as a polyvocal symphony of cultures; it is as if the festival's importing of selected "world" artists serves to "innoculate" L.A. against unmanaged "alien" invasions of the sort imagined by Scott's *Blade Runner*. A narrative of authenticity stressed the role of the city as a "curator" whose task was the salvaging and protection of pure cultural objects threatened with extinction in their native lands; this narrative identified originary places and moments of authentic culture (such as the Mayan, Chinese, or Aboriginal), located outside of the city, both temporally and geographically "other" to the contemporary "fallen" milieu of Los Angeles. This narrative of authenticity surrounded, for example, the presentation of the Kun Opera, exiled from communist China and protected by the city; or the Court Performers from the Yogyakarta Palace of Java, whose performance was described as "the first time a Javanese court ensemble ... and this range of repertoire, has been seen outside Indonesia"; or the Balinese gamelan players, Maori haka war dancers, and Ecuadoran folk musicians, which the festival described as "resisting the disintegration of their culture in the face of rapidly accelerating westernization of their Pacific homelands." In this sense, "Los Angeles" was constituted as the Western curator/ethnographer who no longer needed to venture out to meet the exotic tribes, because these cultures could now all be brought to Los Angeles.

At the same time that these authentic cultures were constituted as distant and beyond the local sites of Los Angeles, a concomitant genealogical narrative tied L.A. to the ancient Chinese, Mayans, and Aborigines. The program stated, for example: "Seen side by side, a new reality comes clear—that many of the ideas, traditions, and practices of our colleagues are shared by the artists living and working in Los Angeles today ... the Festival celebrates humanity and the cycles of life: the remembrance of *our* ancestors, *our* hopes for the future." Yet, in conflating Third World artists and the general population of the city, the precise relationship between Okinawan dance and Black gospel music, for example, was "fudged," glossed over. The festival's staging of theater, dance, and music performances from Thailand, China, Japan, Australia, the Philippines, Indonesia, Mexico, Central America, Chile, Panama—adjacent to work by artists from within the city of Los Angeles itself—also enunciated to some extent this genealogical narrative pronouncing the identity and continuity of "global" and "local" cultures. The festival program read:

> 1990. We've arrived at the last decade of our century and it's a new world out there. With 85 languages spoken in the L.A. school system, it turns out that most of that new world is alive and living right here in this city. . . . We are living on the verge of the "Pacific Century." . . .
>
> This is a festival of new stories for a new America existing in a new world. . . . It's a delightful opportunity for Los Angelenos to travel to places where they don't usually go, to feel the presence of the multiple cultures that co-exist in our sprawling city. . . . After all, who owns culture?

Built upon the notion of connecting traditional non-Western cultural performance with the contemporary residents of Los Angeles, the city became a living museum; the Chicano/Latino, Chinese, Japanese, African-American,

Thai, and Korean neighborhoods were opened up as locations for the performances by artists from Mexico, China, Japan, Africa, Thailand, and Korea. These connections foregrounded new contrasts, invented new hierarchies, suggested new cultural mixtures and constellations. And as the final question "After all, who owns culture?" implies, the juxtapositions were aimed at thematizing the shift in hegemonic rule of Western art and culture toward a newly invented syncretism of "Pacific culture." However, the production of multiculturalism as a *representation* of a changing cultural hegemony must be distinguished from shifts in the existing hegemony itself; the synthetic production of multiculturalism unravels, and may be best contested, at the moments when the contradiction between the representational economy of ethnic signifiers on the one hand, and the material economy of resources and means on the other, becomes unavoidably clear. That is, what the claim to "new stories for a new America" made dangerously invisible is that to most African Americans, Asians, or Latinos living and working in Los Angeles today, on the other 349 days of the year it may be very clear indeed *who* "owns" culture: it is pronounced in the official language all must learn to speak; it is declared if you can't afford to buy the garments that you are employed to sew; it is evident if your call to 911 fails to bring emergency assistance to your neighborhood.

Antagonistic to the narratives of authenticity and genealogy—both of which we might say are developmental narratives that depend on notions of continuity, progression, and conversion—was a concurrent narrative of heterogeneity, whose formal characteristic was juxtaposition, pronounced in apparently random contrasts between the ancient and the postmodern, the arts of the street and the arts of the theater, "high" and "low," the Latin and the Asian, the developing worlds and the overdeveloped worlds. A collection of events at Griffith Park one weekend, for example, featured twenty different acts on five simultaneous stage locations in the park: Cambodian singers, Flamenco dancers, Japanese puppet theater, mariachi bands, a Balinese children's choir—all performed at once. In relying on the structure of heterogeneous juxtaposition, this narrative tended to erase the history of each performance, by leveling the nonequivalent statuses of each particular form, genre, and cultural location. Afro-Brazilian dancers, zydeco bands, performances of Aboriginal myths and legends, and Hawaiian hula were all accorded the same relative importance. "Los Angeles" was represented as a postmodern multicultural cornucopia, an international patchwork quilt; while the means of representation were the very uneven, unassimilable differences among these diverse acts, the important signified was a notion of Los Angeles as multicultural spectacle. In the process, each performance tradition was equated with every other, and its meaning leveled and generalized to a common denominator whose significance was the exotic, colorful advertisement of Los Angeles. Despite tensions between the narratives of authenticity, genealogy, and heterogeneity, all of these narratives may risk, in different ways, erasing and occluding the "material" geographies of L.A.; neither topos reckons with the practical relationships between heterogeneous and economically unequal racial, ethnic, and immigrant communities in Los Angeles, a city that is already the home to more people of Mexican descent than any other city outside Mexico, more Koreans than any other city outside Asia, and more Filipinos than any city outside the Philippines. There is a tendency, to varying degrees, to level the important distinctions and contradictions within and among racial and ethnic minority groups according to a pluralism that effectively continues to privilege the centrality of dominant culture. As Hal Foster argues, pluralism promotes a form of tolerance that leaves the status quo unthreatened; the margins are absorbed into the center, the heterogeneous is domesticated into the homogeneous.[6] It is pluralism's leveling of the material, and not simply aesthetic unevennesses of racial, ethnic, and immigrant cultures, as well as its erasure of exclusions, that I believe risks the depoliticization of multiculturalism. In this sense, it is the productive conflict and irresolution between pluralist and antipluralist narratives that mark, in my view, the most interesting moments of the festival.

Thus, while the aestheticizing and pluralizing tendencies of these narratives are problematic, it also seems clear that none of these narratives monolithically "colonizes" the radically nonequivalent populations and locales each seeks to include and represent; in this sense, the leveling of Asians, Latinos, and African Americans (each itself a contradictory grouping, crossed by differences of language, generation, class, national origin, gender, religion) is also at certain moments challenged by important pressures from resisting, or oppositional, narratives. The oppositional narrative made some use of the juxtapositions from the narrative of heterogeneity, but in the oppositional narrative, the contrasts were inflected differently; attention was drawn to the inequalities between cultural objects by attaching, when possible, the object to some cultural context of production and reception, thereby making the history of the object explicit. For example, narratives of resistance were made possible in the staging of the Thai Likay performers at the Wat Thai Temple in North Hollywood, or in the placement of the African Marketplace near West Central L.A.; that is, these stagings generated interesting connections between cultural performance and local communities and geography. In this way, a Black American community was attached to African cultural forms in a relationship that was not based on identity, but that was not entirely discontinuous either. In addition, disparate communities were introduced to one another—for example, relationships were articulated between the Thai and gay communities in North Hollywood. Where the narrative of heterogeneity could have juxtaposed and equalized the Korean shaman with mariachi bands, an oppositional narrative worked to attach the Korean shaman to the Korean-American community by staging his arrival in a Korean-American strip mall, suggesting a degree of dialectical relationship between object and community. Yet, ironically, while shamanism has an important history in Korea, many Korean Americans in Los Angeles are Christian, a disjunction occluded by the narrative of heterogeneity.

The eruption of riots in Los Angeles in 1992 following the verdict that freed four white policemen accused of beating a Black man, Rodney King, is a most vivid example of the contradiction between multiculturalism as the representation of the liberal state and the material poverty and disenfranchisement that are the conditions of those represented. Although the U.S. media consistently attempted to construct the riots as a racial conflict between Blacks and Koreans, the looters enraged by the King verdict were not only Blacks, but also Chicanos, Latinos, and working-class whites; all violently objected to the denial of brutally racialized economic stratification. I wish to locate a radical critique of multiculturalism in the 1993 documentary film Sa-I-Gu by Christine Choy, Elaine Kim, and Dai Sil Kim-Gibson, which deals with those events.[7] The film powerfully disrupts a developmental, genealogical narrative that assimilates an ethnic immigrant into the capitalist economy. The very different articulations of the Korean immigrant and Korean-American speakers contradict a notion of the homogeneous authenticity of immigrant groups. Thus, the film radically challenges the liberal myth of pluralist inclusion, both on the level of the speakers' testimonies and in terms of the interrupted, particularist form of the film itself.

Sa-I-Gu collects together heterogeneous interviews with Korean immigrant and Korean-American women speaking about the Los Angeles crisis in the aftermath of the King verdict.[8] The film is not a narrative, but a series of clips of Korean immigrant workers, shopkeepers, owners of grocery stores, liquor and convenience stores, laundries—women who speak about their losses and their disillusionment. Their testimonies are contradictory, unsynthetic, unhomogeneous. They speak about the lack of support from the Los Angeles Police Department and the National Guard during the uprisings. They speak about the shock of working long hours in order to eke out a living. They speak about losing sons, husbands, livelihoods, and opportunities. The film opens with an interview with the mother of Edward Jae Song Lee; Lee was shot and died during the crisis when he was mistaken by a store owner for a looter. Her testimony focuses on mourning the loss of her son, as well as her disillusionment with the promises of capitalism, inclusion, and protection by police or government. She says: "At the time, I thought it was one man who shot my son. But if I think broadly, it is not just an individual matter. Something is drastically wrong." Another woman interviewed states: "I would like to express my feeling about this after the riot. Right now I'm angry at everybody. Or on contrary, I'm angry at myself. Because I don't know to whom to where I should be angry at them. I am totally confused, totally confused." The statements of both of these women articulate the desire to grasp an explanation of the convergence of racism and capitalism, as much as their "confusion" attests to the unavailability of this convergence. Indeed, the Los Angeles crisis, in which Korean Americans became the recipients of violent anger that might well have been "better" directed at white capital in other parts of the intensely spatially segregated city, illustrates precisely how a society can mask the interlocking dominations of racism, patriarchy, and capitalism, not only by ideologically constructing multicultural inclusion, but by separating and dividing its objects—as Black youth, as Korean shopkeeper, as Chicana single mother. It is this isolation of objects that contributes to the fragmentation of social life in the advanced capitalist USA, and this isolation likewise contributes to the fragmentation of political organization against the interlocking dominations. The statement of "confusion" at not knowing where to focus blame implies a desire for an explanation for the convergences of dominations; at the same time, it articulates the difficulty of apprehending or seizing more than a fragment of that convergence. If structured domination and oppositional responses to it remain unavailable to groups and individuals, then domination functions and persists precisely through the unavailability of this structure. Multiculturalism is one ideological representation of the liberal imperialist state that enacts that unavailability. In the film *Sa-I-Gu* a powerful particularism—particular griefs, losses, and anger—demystifies multiculturalist inclusion and moves us toward an interrogation of the convergence of dominations of which multiculturalism is the ideological expression and resolution. *Sa-I-Gu* is a radical objection to multiculturalism and a forceful testimony about the conjunction of capitalism with racism and patriarchy in Los Angeles.

Let me conclude by stressing the importance of oppositional narratives and practices, and by foregrounding their conflicts with the narratives of authenticity, genealogy, and heterogeneity, conflicts that build pressure against the pluralist tendencies of a produced multiculturalism. If we do not stress these oppositions, the geographies and histories of immigrant settlement in Los Angeles are dangerously obscured, segregation of neighborhoods is masked as spatial contiguity, and racial and class violence between groups is aestheticized in a multicultural juxtaposition of ethnic images. Without these tensions, multiculturalism fails to come to grips with the material inequalities and strata of a city like Los Angeles: the separations, unevennesses of opportunity due to different groups' histories of labor, racism, and poverty.[9] The narratives of multiculturalism that do not make these connections, or that do not make space for oppositional critiques, risk denuding racial and ethnic groups of their specificity. Subject to the leveling operations of both postmodern pastiche and pluralism, African, Asian, and Latino cultures become all equally other, are metaphorized as all equally different, all whole without contradiction. These narratives, which suppress tension and opposition, suggest that we have already achieved multiculturalism, that we know what it is, that it is defined simply by the coexistence and juxtaposition of greater numbers of diverse groups; these narratives allow us to ignore the profound and urgent gaps, the inequalities and conflicts, among racial, ethnic, and immigrant groups; they let us off the hook. The suggestion that multicultural discourses might ultimately emphasize, rather than domesticate, the productive irresolution, opposition, and conflict of these various narratives is neither a call for chaos nor a return to traditional Western notions of art and high culture. It is rather an assertion that it may be through contradiction that we begin to address the systemic inequalities built into cultural institutions, economies, and geographies, and through conflict that we call attention to the process through which these inequalities are obscured by pluralist multiculturalism.

Notes

1. See Giuliana Bruno, "Ramble City: Postmodernism and *Blade Runner*," *October* 42 (summer 1987): 61–74.

2. On the relationship between aesthetic culture and material economy, see David Lloyd, "Analogies of the Aesthetic: The Politics of Culture and the Limits of Materialist Aesthetics," *New Formations* (spring 1990): 109–26.

3. On the logic of pluralism in critical discourse, see Ellen Rooney, *Seductive Reasoning: Pluralism as the Problematic of Contemporary Literary Theory* (Ithaca, N.Y.: Cornell University Press, 1989).

4. Gramsci distinguishes hegemony from the violent imposition of rule and elaborates it as the process through which a particular group gains consent to determine the political, cultural, and ideological character of a state; pluralism elicits the consent of racial and ethnic groups

through the promise of equal participation and equal citizenship. See Antonio Gramsci, *Selections from the Prison Notebooks*, ed. and trans. Quintin Hoare and Geoffrey Nowell Smith (New York: International Publishers, 1971). However, Gramsci defines hegemony as always existing within the context of pressures from subaltern groups, pressures that can be articulated into counterhegemonic formations. For further discussion of how Gramsci's concept of hegemony also includes within it the possible challenges by emergent groups, see Stuart Hall, "Gramsci's Relevance for the Study of Race and Ethnicity," *Journal of Communication Inquiry* 10 (summer 1986); Radha Radhakrishnan's discussion of the Rainbow Coalition in "Towards an Effective Intellectual: Foucault or Gramsci?" in *Intellectuals*, ed. Bruce Robbins (Minneapolis: University of Minnesota Press, 1990); and Chantal Mouffe, "Hegemony and New Political Subjects: Toward a New Concept of Democracy," in *Marxism and the Interpretation of Culture*, ed. Cary Nelson and Lawrence Grossberg (Urbana and Chicago: University of Illinois Press, 1988).

5. The description of the "forgetting" of differentiated spheres recalls Horkheimer and Adorno's analysis of the "culture industry": "the idea of 'fully exploiting' available technical resources and the facilities for aesthetic mass consumption is part of the economic system which refuses to exploit resources to abolish hunger" (Max Horkheimer and Theodor Adorno, *The Dialectic of Enlightenment*, trans. John Cumming [New York: Seabury Press, 1972], 139). Benjamin comments also on the production of aesthetic culture as distraction: "Distraction as provided by art presents a covert control of the extent to which new tasks have become soluble by apperception. Since, moreover, individuals are tempted to avoid such tasks, art will tackle the most difficult and most important ones where it is able to mobilize the masses.... The public is an examiner, but an absent-minded one" (Walter Benjamin, "The Work of Art in the Age of Mechanical Reproduction," in *Illuminations*, trans. Harry Zohn [New York: Schocken, 1969], 240–41). However, for Horkheimer and Adorno, the analysis of the "forgetting" of historical differentiation is part of a critique of mass culture as deception and its undermining of society's emancipatory potential, whereas for Benjamin, technology and mass culture do not in themselves lead to deception or appropriation, but can also be means, as with Brecht, of initiating political action (in this, it might be said that Benjamin portends postmodernism's "antiaesthetic" celebration of mass culture, technology, and the crisis of representation, as means of calling attention to the end of the autonomous aesthetic object, a critique of official representations and narratives, and the possibility of destructuring the order of representation; see Hal Foster on a "postmodernism of resistance" in the introduction to *The Anti-Aesthetic: Essays on Postmodern Culture* [Port Townsend, Wash.: Bay Press, 1983]). For a very persuasive discussion of the ideological and utopian functions of mass culture, see Fredric Jameson, "Reification and Utopia in Mass Culture," *Social Text* 1:1 (1979): 130–48.

6. Hal Foster, "The Problem of Pluralism," *Art in America* (January 1982): 9–15.

7. *Sa-I-Gu*, produced by Christine Choy, Elaine Kim, and Dai Sil Kim-Gibson, Cross Current Media (1993); distributed by National Asian American Telecommunications Association, 346 Ninth Street, 2d floor, San Francisco, CA 94103.

8. *Sa-I-Gu*, meaning "4.29" or April 29 (the date of the Rodney King verdicts), alludes to the history of Korean nationalism, by putting the 1992 attack on Korean Americans in the context of other Korean nationalist struggles. Elaine Kim writes in "Home Is Where the Han Is," in *Reading Rodney King, Reading Urban Uprisings*, ed. Robert Gooding-Williams (New York: Routledge, 1993): "Situated as we are on the border between those who have and those who have not, between predominantly Anglo and mostly African American and Latino communities, from our current interstitial position in the American discourse of race, many Korean Americans have trouble calling what happened in Los Angeles an 'uprising.' At the same time, we cannot quite say it was a 'riot.' So some of us have taken to calling it *sa-i-ku*, April 29, after the manner of naming other events in Korean history—3.1 (*sam-il*) for March 1, 1919, when massive protests against Japanese colonial rule began in Korea; 6.25 (*yook-i-o*), or June 25, 1950, when the

Korean War began; and 4.19 (*sa-il-ku*), or April 19, 1960, when the first student movement in the world to overthrow a government began in South Korea. The ironic similarity between 4.19 and 4.29 does not escape most Korean Americans" (216). I wish to stress that Korean-American na-tionalism in the aftermath of the L.A. crisis is not a direct transference of Korean nationalism but a discontinuous rearticulation of it that includes the crucial consideration of the racialization of Korean immigrants in the United States as workers of color. For a powerful discussion situating the racialization of racial, ethnic, and immigrant groups in the United States in the ne-gotiation between dominant institutional constructions of race and the political struggles of social movements, see Michael Omi and Howard Winant, *Racial Formation in the United States: From the 1960s to the 1980s* (New York and London: Routledge, 1986).

9. See Mike Davis, *City of Quartz: Excavating the Future in Los Angeles* (London and New York: Verso, 1990); George Lipsitz, *Time Passages: Collective Memory and American Popular Culture* (Minneapolis: University of Minnesota Press, 1990). Davis's and Lipsitz's works attach the different histories of racial and ethnic communities to neighborhoods, urban history, labor movements, and community practices, and to popular cultural forms such as rap, rock and roll, low-riding, or graffiti.

CHAPTER TWENTY-SIX

A Style Nobody Can Deal With

Politics, Style, and the Postindustrial City in Hip Hop

TRICIA ROSE

Multiculturalism—no doubt a complex and contested term—often refers to a process of incorporation of marginal groups' contributions into a mainstream or dominant culture. In this context, multiculturalism is pressed into service to highlight and legitimize the contributions of "others" to invisible yet omnipresent cultures of whiteness. Hence, multiculturalist efforts include revisions to the overwhelmingly white male author-based literary canon to include writers and oral masters of color and women, and rewritings of Christopher Columbus that transform him into an agent of imperialism rather than a heroic discoverer. In other words, the "multi" in "multicultural" frequently refers to multiple "others" knocking on a central gate of power.

Although these efforts have been important in challenging cultural and intellectual hierarchies, there are other modes of cultural dialogue that are not as easily seen from this vantage point. In the cases of contemporary popular culture and the diverse communities of young people who create, consume, and propel it, multicultural exchanges develop in several ways, most notably via day-to-day cross-cultural contacts, identification with mass-mediated images, similar cultural traditions, and shared lived experiences of oppression. In this sort of multiculturalism, a variety of groups are engaged in feisty and congenial dialogues that focus not only on resisting and/or critiquing dominant institutions, but also on developing forms that grow out of intercultural exchanges.

Hip hop continues to be a rich space for the development and exploration of these interactions. Most heavily (but not exclusively) shaped by multiple sources of Afro-diasporic cultural influences and the postindustrial urban New York terrain, hip hop emerges in the mid-to-late 1970s as a form of cultural affirmation and resistance. Puerto Rican, Dominican, and Cuban immigrants—whose musical and cultural traditions have strong ties to the Afro-diaspora—along with other Carribean Afro-diasporic cultures, such as Jamaicans and Haitians, were especially important actors in the multicultural development of hip hop. No doubt these "multiple others" are knocking at a central gate, but they are also hard at work in communication with each other, building cultural bridges and new identities that affirm and transform cultural traditions in new environments not only for purposes of staking societal claims, but also for pleasure and regeneration.

Life on the margins of postindustrial urban America is inscribed in hip hop style, sound, lyrics, and thematics.[1] Emerging from the intersection of lack and desire in the postindustrial city, hip hop manages the painful contradictions of social alienation and prophetic imagination. Hip hop is an Afro-diasporic cultural form that attempts to negotiate the experiences of marginalization, brutally truncated opportunity, and oppression within the cultural imperatives of African-American and Caribbean history, identity, and community. It is the tension between the cultural fractures produced by postindustrial oppression and the binding ties of black cultural expressivity that sets the critical frame for the development of hip hop.[2]

Worked out on the rusting urban core as a playground, hip hop transforms stray technological parts intended for cultural and industrial trash heaps into sources of pleasure and power. These transformations have become a basis for digital imagination all over the world. Its earliest practitioners came of age at the tail end of the Great Society, in the twilight of America's short-lived federal commitment to black civil rights and during the predawn of the Reagan-Bush era.[3] In hip hop, these abandoned parts, people, and social institutions were welded and then spliced together, not only as sources of survival but as sources of pleasure.

Hip hop replicates and reimagines the experiences of urban life and symbolically appropriates urban space through sampling, attitude, dance, style, and sound effects. Talk of subways, crews and posses, urban noise, economic stagnation, static, and crossed signals leap out of hip hop lyrics, sounds and themes. Graffiti artists spray-painted murals and (name)"tags" on trains, trucks, and playgrounds, claiming territories and inscribing their otherwise contained identities on public property.[4] Early breakdancers' elaborate technologically inspired street-corner dances involving head spins on concrete sidewalks made the streets theater-friendly and served as makeshift youth centers. The dancers' electric robotic mimicry and identity-transforming characterizations foreshadowed the fluid and shocking effect of morphing, a visual effect made famous in *Terminator 2*. DJs who initiated spontaneous street parties by attaching customized, makeshift turntables and speakers to streetlight electrical sources revised the use of central thoroughfares, made "open-air" community centers in neighborhoods where there were none. Rappers seized and used microphones as if amplification was a life-giving source. Hip hop gives voice to the tensions and contradictions in the public urban landscape during a period of substantial transformation in New York and attempts to seize the shifting urban terrain, to make it work on behalf of the dispossessed.

Hip hop's attempts to negotiate new economic and technological conditions as well as new patterns of race, class, and gender oppression in urban America by appropriating subway facades, public streets, language, style, and sampling technology are only part of the story. Hip hop music and culture also rely on a variety of Afro-Caribbean and Afro-American musical, oral, visual, and dance forms and practices in the face of a larger society that rarely recognizes the Afro-diasporic significance of such practices. It is, in fact, the dynamic and often contentious relationship between the two—larger social and political forces and black cultural priorities—that centrally shapes and defines hip hop.

The tensions and contradictions shaping hip hop culture can confound efforts at interpretation by even the most skilled critics and observers. Some analysts see hip hop as a quintessentially postmodern practice, while others view it as a present-day successor to premodern oral traditions. Some celebrate its critique of consumer capitalism, while others condemn it for its complicity with commercialism. To one enthusiastic group of critics, hip hop combines elements of speech and song, of dance and display, to call into being through performance new identities and subject positions. Yet to another equally vociferous group, hip hop merely displays in phantasmagorical form the cultural logic of late capitalism. I intend to demonstrate the importance of locating hip hop culture within the context of deindustrialization and to show how hip hop's primary properties of flow, layering, and rupture simultaneously reflect and contest the social roles open to urban inner-city youth at the end of the twentieth century.

In an attempt to rescue rap from its identity as postindustrial commercial product and situate it in the history of respected black cultural practices, many historical accounts of rap consider it a direct extension of African-American oral, poetic, and protest traditions, to which it is clearly and substantially indebted. This accounting, which builds important bridges between rap's use of boasting, signifying, preaching, and earlier related black oral traditions, produces multiple problematic effects. First, it reconstructs rap music as a singular oral poetic form that appears to have developed autonomously (e.g., outside hip hop culture) in the 1970s. Quite to the contrary, rap is one cultural element within the larger social movement of hip hop. Second, it substantially marginalizes the significance of rap as *music*. Rap's musical elements and its use of music technology are a crucial aspect of the use and development of the form and are absolutely critical to the evolution of hip hop generally. Finally, and most directly important for this discussion, it renders invisible the crucial role of the postindustrial city on the shape and direction of rap and hip hop and makes it difficult to trace the way hip hop revises and extends Afro-diasporic practices using postindustrial urban materials. Hip hop's styles and themes share striking similarities with many past and contiguous Afro-diasporic musical and cultural expressions; these themes and styles, for the most part, are revised and reinterpreted using contemporary cultural and technological elements. Hip hop's central forms—graffiti, breakdancing, and rap music—developed, in relation to one another, within Afro-diasporic cultural priorities, and in relation to larger postindustrial social forces and institutions.

What are some of the defining aesthetic and stylistic characteristics of hip hop? What is it about the postindustrial city generally and the social and political terrain in the 1970s in New York City specifically that contributes to the emergence and early reception of hip hop? Even as today's rappers revise and redirect rap music, most understand themselves as working out of a tradition of style, attitude, and form that has critical and primary roots in New York City in the 1970s. Substantial postindustrial shifts in economic conditions, access to housing, demographics, and communication networks were crucial to the formation of the conditions that nurtured the cultural hybrids and sociopolitical tenor of hip hop's lyrics and music.

The Urban Context

Postindustrial conditions in urban centers across America reflect a complex set of global forces that continue to shape the contemporary urban metropolis. The growth of multinational telecommunications networks, global economic competition, a major technological revolution, the formation of new international divisions of labor, the increasing power of finance relative to production, and new migration patterns from Third World industrializing nations have all contributed to the economic and social restructuring of urban America. These global forces have had direct and sustained impact on urban job opportunity structures, have exacerbated long-standing racial and gender-based forms of discrimination, and have contributed to increasing multinational corporate control of market conditions and national economic health.[5] Large-scale restructuring of the workplace and job market had its effects upon most facets of everyday life. It has placed additional pressures on local community-based networks of communication and whittled down already limited prospects for social mobility.

In the 1970s, cities across the country were gradually losing federal funding for social services, information service corporations were beginning to replace industrial factories, and corporate developers were buying up real estate to be converted into luxury housing, leaving working-class residents with limited affordable housing, a shrinking job market, and diminishing social services. The poorest neighborhoods and the least powerful groups were the least protected and had the smallest safety nets. By the 1980s, the privileged elites displayed unabashed greed as their strategies to reclaim and rebuild downtown business and tourist zones with municipal and federal subsidies exacerbated the already widening gap between classes and races.

Given New York's status as hub city for international capital and information services, it is not surprising that these larger structural changes and their effects were quickly and intensely felt in New York.[6] As John Mollenkopf notes, "during the 1970s, the U.S. system of cities crossed a watershed. New York led other old, industrial metropolitan areas into population and employment decline."[7] The federal funds that might have offset this process had been diminishing throughout the 1970s. In 1975, President Ford's unequivocal veto to requests for a federal bailout to prevent New York from filing for bankruptcy made New York a national symbol for the fate of older cities under his administration. The New York *Daily News*'s legendary headline "Ford to New York: Drop Dead" captured the substance and temperament of Ford's veto and sent a sharp message to cities around the country.[8]

Virtually bankrupt and in a critical state of disrepair, New York City and State administrators finally negotiated a federal loan, albeit one that accompanied an elaborate package of service cuts and carried harsh repayment terms. These dramatic social-service cuts were felt most severely in New York's poorest areas and were part of a larger trend in unequal wealth distribution and were accompanied by a housing crisis that continued well into the 1980s. Between 1978 and 1986, the people in the bottom 20 percent of the income scale experienced an absolute decline in income while the top 20 percent experienced most of the economic growth. Blacks and Hispanics disproportionately occupied this bottom fifth. During this same period, 30 percent of New York's Hispanic households (for Puerto Ricans it is 40 percent) and 25 percent of black households lived at or below the poverty line. Since this period, low-income housing has continued to disappear and blacks and Hispanics are still much more likely to live in overcrowded, dilapidated, and seriously undermaintained spaces.[9] It is not surprising that these serious trends have contributed to New York's large and chronically homeless population.

In addition to housing problems, New York and many large urban centers faced other major economic and demographic forces that have sustained and exacerbated significant structural inequalities. Although urban America has always been socially and economically divided, these divisions have taken on a new dimension. At the same time that racial succession and immigration patterns were reshaping the city's population and labor force, shifts in the occupational structure away from a high-wage, high-employment economy grounded in manufacturing, trucking, warehousing, and wholesale trade and toward a low-wage, low-employment economy geared toward producer services generated new forms of inequality. Earlier divisions in the city were predominantly ethnic and economic. "New York," Mollenkopf concludes, "has been transformed from a relatively well-off white blue-collar city into a more economically divided, multi-racial white-collar city." This "disorganized periphery" of civil service and manufacturing workers contributes to the consolidation of power among white-collar professional corporate managers, creating the massive inequalities in New York.[10]

The commercial imperatives of corporate America have also undermined the process of transmitting and sharing local knowledge in the urban metropolis. Ben Bagdigian's study *The Media Monopoly* reveals that monopolistic tendencies in commercial enterprises seriously constrain access to a diverse flow of information. For example, urban renewal relocation efforts not only dispersed central-city populations to the suburbs, they also replaced the commerce of the street with the needs of the metropolitan market. Advertisers geared newspaper articles and television broadcasts toward the purchasing power of suburban buyers, creating a dual "crisis of representation" in terms of whose lives and images were represented physically in the paper and whose interests got represented in the corridors of power.[11] These media outlet and advertising shifts have been accompanied by a massive telecommunications revolution in the information processing industry. Once the domain of the government, information processing and communication technology now lie at the heart of corporate America. As a result of government deregulation in communications via the breakup of AT&T in 1982, communications industries have consolidated and internationalized. Today, telecommunications industries are global data transmittal corporations with significant control over radio, television, cable, telephone, computer, and other electronic transmittal systems. Telecommunication expansion coupled with corporate consolidation has dismantled local community networks and has irrevocably changed the means and character of communication.[12] Since the mid-1980s, these expansions and consolidations have been accompanied by a tidal wave of widely available communications products, which have revolutionized business and personal communications. Facsimile machines, satellite-networked beepers, cordless phones, electronic mail networks, cable television expansions, VCRs, compact discs, video cameras and games, and personal computers have dramatically transformed the speed and character of speech and written and visual communication.

Postindustrial conditions had a profound effect on black and Hispanic communities. Shrinking federal funds and affordable housing, shifts in the occupational structure away from blue-collar manufacturing and toward corporate and information services, along with frayed local communication patterns, meant that new immigrant populations and the city's poorest residents paid the highest price for deindustrialization and economic restructuring. These communities are more susceptible to slumlords, redevelopers, toxic waste dumps, drug rehabilitation centers, violent criminals, redlining, and inadequate city services and transportation. This also meant that the city's ethnic- and working-class-based forms of community aid and support were growing increasingly less effective against these new conditions.

In the case of the South Bronx, which has been frequently dubbed the "home of hip-hop culture," these larger postindustrial conditions were exacerbated by disruptions considered to be an "unexpected side effect" of a larger, politically motivated "urban renewal" project. In the early 1970s, this renewal (*sic*) project involved massive relocations of economically fragile people of color from different areas in New York City into parts of the South Bronx. Subsequent ethnic and racial transition in the South Bronx was not a gradual process that might have allowed already taxed social and cultural institutions to respond self-protectively; instead it was a brutal process of community destruction and relocation executed by municipal officials and under the direction of legendary city planner Robert Moses.

Between the late 1930s and the late 1960s Moses executed a number of public-works projects, highways, parks, and housing projects that significantly reshaped the profile of New York City. In 1959, city, state, and federal authorities began the implementation of his planned Cross-Bronx Expressway, which would cut directly through the center of the most heavily populated working-class areas in the Bronx. Although he could have modified his route slightly to bypass densely populated working-class ethnic residential communities, he elected a path that required the demolition of hundreds of residential and commercial buildings. In addition, throughout the 1960s and early 1970s, some sixty thousand Bronx homes were razed. Designating these old blue-collar housing units as "slums," Moses's Title I Slum Clearance program forced the relocation of 170,000 people.[13] These "slums" were in fact densely populated stable neighborhoods, comprised mostly of working- and lower-middle-class Jews, but they also contained solid Italian, German, Irish, and black neighborhoods. Although the neighborhoods under attack had a substantial Jewish population, black and Puerto Rican residents were disproportionately affected. Thirty-seven percent of the relocated residents were nonwhite. This, coupled with the subsequent "white flight," devastated kin networks and neighborhood services. Between the late 1960s and mid-1970s, the vacancy rates in the southern section of the Bronx skyrocketed. Some nervous landlords sold their property as quickly as possible, often to professional slumlords; others torched their buildings to collect insurance payments. Both strategies accelerated the flight of white tenants into northern sections of the Bronx and into Westchester. Equally anxious shopkeepers sold their shops and established businesses elsewhere. The city administration, touting Moses's expressway as a sign of progress and modernization, was unwilling to admit the devastation that had occurred. Like many of his public-works projects, Moses's Cross-Bronx Expressway supported the interests of the upper classes against the interests of the poor and intensified the development of the vast economic and social inequalities that characterize contemporary New York. The newly "relocated" black and Hispanic residents in the South Bronx were left with few city resources, fragmented leadership, and limited political power.

The disastrous effects of these city policies went relatively unnoticed in the media until 1977, when two critical events fixed New York and the South Bronx as national symbols of ruin and isolation. During the summer of 1977 an extensive power outage "blacked out" New York and hundreds of stores were looted and vandalized. The poorest neighborhoods (the South Bronx, Bedford-Stuyvesant, Brownsville, and Crown Heights areas in Brooklyn, the Jamaica area in Queens, and Harlem), where most of the looting took place, were depicted by the city's media organs as lawless zones where crime is sanctioned and chaos bubbles just below the surface. The 1965 blackout, according to the *New York Times,* was "peaceful by contrast," suggesting that the blackout that took place during America's most racially tumultuous decade was no match for the despair and frustration articulated in the blackout of the summer of 1977.[14] The 1977 blackout and the looting that accompanied it seemed to raise the federal stakes in maintaining urban social order. Three months later, President Carter made his "sobering" historic motorcade visit through the South Bronx to "survey the devastation of the last five years," and announced an unspecified "commitment to cities." (Not to their inhabitants?) In the national imagination, the South Bronx became the primary "symbol of America's woes."[15]

Following this lead, images of abandoned buildings in the South Bronx became central popular cultural icons. Negative local color in popular film exploited the devastation facing the residents of the South Bronx and used their communities as a backdrop for social ruin and barbarism. As Michael Ventura astutely notes, these popular depictions (and, I would add, the news coverage as well) rendered silent the people who struggled with and maintained life under difficult conditions: "In roughly six hours of footage—*Fort Apache, Wolfen* and *Koyaanisqatsi*—we haven't been introduced to one soul who actually lives in the South Bronx. We haven't heard one voice speaking its own language. We've merely watched a symbol of ruin: the South Bronx [as] last act before the end of the world."[16] Depictions of black and Hispanic neighborhoods were drained of life, energy, and vitality. The message was loud and clear: to be stuck here was to be lost. And yet, while these visions of loss and futility became defining characteristics, the youngest generation of South Bronx exiles was building creative and aggressive outlets for expression and identification. The new ethnic groups who made the South Bronx their home in the 1970s began building their own cultural networks, ones that would prove to be resilient and responsive in the age of high technology.

North American blacks, Jamaicans, Puerto Ricans, and other Caribbean people with roots in other postcolonial contexts reshaped their cultural identities and expressions in a hostile, technologically sophisticated, multi-ethnic, urban terrain. While city leaders and the popular press had literally and figuratively condemned the South Bronx neighborhoods and their inhabitants, its youngest black and Hispanic residents answered back.

Hip Hop

Hip hop culture emerged as a source of alternative identity formation and social status for youth in a community whose older local support institutions had been all but demolished along with large sectors of its built environment. Alternative local identities were forged in fashions, language, street names, and most importantly, in the establishment of neighborhood crews or posses. Many hip hop fans, artists, musicians, and dancers continue to belong to an elaborate system of crews or posses. The crew, a local source of identity, group affiliation, and support, appears in virtually all rap lyrics and cassette dedications, music video performances, and media interviews with artists. Identity in hip hop is deeply rooted in the specific, the local experience, and in one's attachment to and status in a local group or alternative family. These crews are new kinds of families forged with intercultural bonds, which, like the social formation of gangs, provide insulation and support in a complex and unyielding environment and may, in fact, contribute to the community-building networks that serve as the basis for new social movements.

The postindustrial city, which provided the context for creative development among hip hop's earliest innovators, shaped their cultural terrain, access to space, materials, and education. Although graffiti artists' work was significantly aided by advances in spray-paint technology, they used the urban transit system as their canvas. Rappers and DJs disseminated their work by copying it on tape-dubbing equipment and playing it on powerful, portable "ghetto blasters." At a time when budget cuts in school music programs drastically reduced access to traditional forms of instrumentation and composition, inner-city youth increasingly relied on recorded sound. Breakdancers used their bodies to mimic "transformers" and other futuristic robots in symbolic street battles. Early Puerto Rican, Afro-Caribbean, and black American hip hop artists transformed obsolete vocational skills from marginal occupations into the raw materials for creativity and resistance. Many of them were "trained" for jobs in fields that were shrinking or that no longer existed. Graffiti writer Futura graduated from a trade school specializing in the printing industry. But, since most of the jobs for which he was being trained had already been computerized, he found himself working at McDonald's after graduation. Similarly, African-American DJ Red Alert (who also has family from the Caribbean) reviewed blueprints for a drafting company until computer automation rendered that job obsolete. Jamaican DJ Kool Herc attended Alfred E. Smith auto mechanic trade school, while African-American Grand Master Flash learned how to repair electronic equipment at Samuel Gompers vocational high school. (One could say Flash "fixed them alright.") Salt N Pepa (both with family roots in the West Indies) worked as phone telemarketing representatives at Sears while considering nursing school. Puerto Rican breakdancer Crazy Legs began breakdancing largely because his single mother couldn't afford Little League baseball fees.[17] All of these artists found themselves positioned with few resources in marginal economic circumstances, but each of them found ways to become famous as entertainers by appropriating the most advanced technologies and emerging cultural forms. Hip hop artists used the tools of obsolete industrial technology to traverse contemporary crossroads of lack and desire in urban Afro-diasporic communities.

Stylistic continuities were sustained by internal cross-fertilization between rapping, breakdancing, and graffiti writing. Some writers, such as black American Phase 2, Haitian Jean-Michel Basquiat, Futura, and black American Fab Five Freddy, produced rap records. Other writers drew murals that celebrated favorite rap songs (e.g., Futura's mural *The Breaks* was a whole car mural that paid homage to Kurtis Blow's rap of the same name). Breakdancers, DJs, and rappers wore graffiti-painted jackets and T-shirts. DJ Kool Herc was a graffiti writer and dancer before he began playing records. Hip hop events featured breakdancers, rappers, and DJs as triple-bill entertainment. Graffiti writers drew murals for DJs' stage platforms and designed posters and flyers to advertise hip hop events. Breakdancer Crazy Legs, founding member of the Rock Steady Crew, describes the communal atmosphere between writers, rappers, and breakers in the formative years of hip hop: "Summing it up, basically going to a jam back then was [about] watching people drink, [break]dance, compare graffiti art in their black books. These jams were thrown by the [hip hop] DJ. . . . it was about piecing while a jam was going on."[18] Of course, sharing ideas and styles is not always a peaceful process. Hip hop is very competitive and confrontational; it fosters both resistance to and preparation for a hostile world that denies and denigrates young people of color. Breakdancers often fought other breakdance crews out of jealousy, writers sometimes destroyed murals, and rapper and DJ battles could break out in fights. Hip hop remains a never-ending battle for status, prestige, and group adoration that is always in formation, always contested, and never fully achieved. Competitions among and cross-fertilization between breaking, graffiti writing, and rap music were fueled by shared local experiences and social position and similarities in approaches to sound, motion, communication, and style among hip hop's Afro-diasporic communities.

As in many African and Afro-diasporic cultural forms, hip hop's prolific self-naming is a form of reinvention and self-definition.[19] Rappers, DJs, graffiti artists, and breakdancers all take on hip hop names and identities that speak to their roles, personal characteristics, expertise, or "claim to fame." DJ names often fuse technology with mastery and style: DJ Cut Creator, Jazzy Jeff, Spindarella, Terminator X Assault Technician, Wiz, and Grand Master Flash. Many rappers have nicknames that suggest street smarts, coolness, power, and supremacy: L. L. Cool J (Ladies Love Cool James), Kool Moe Dee, Queen Latifah, Dougie Fresh (and the Get Fresh Crew), D-Nice, Hurricane Gloria, Guru, MC Lyte, EPMD (Erick and Parrish Making Dollars), Ice-T, Ice Cube, Kid-N-Play, Boss, Eazy-E, King Sun, and Sir Mix-A Lot. Other names serve as self-mocking tags or critique society, such as Too Short, The Fat Boys, S1Ws (Security of the First World), The Lench Mob, NWA (Niggas With Attitude), and Special Ed. The hip hop identities for breakdancers like Crazy Legs, Wiggles, Frosty Freeze, Boogaloo Shrimp, and Headspin highlight their status as experts known for special moves. Taking on new names and identities offered "prestige from below" in the face of limited legitimate access to forms of status attainment.

In addition to the centrality of alternative naming, identity, and group affiliation, rappers, DJs, graffiti writers and breakdancers claim turf and gain local status by developing new styles. As Dick Hebdige's study on punk illustrates, style can be used as a gesture of refusal, or as a form of oblique challenge to structures of domination.[20] Hip hop artists use style as a form of identity formation that plays on class distinctions and hierarchies by using commodities to claim the cultural terrain. Clothing and consumption rituals testify to the power of consumption as a means of cultural expression. Hip hop fashion is an especially rich example of this sort of appropriation/critique via style. Exceptionally large "chunk" gold and diamond jewelry (usually "fake") mocks yet affirms the gold fetish in Western trade; "fake" Gucci and other designer emblems, which are cut up and patch-stitched to jackets, pants, hats, wallets, and sneakers in custom shops, work as a form of sartorial warfare (especially when "fake" Gucci-covered b-boys and b-girls brush past Fifth Avenue ladies adorned by the "real thing"). Hip hop's late 1980s fashion rage—the large plastic (alarm?) clock worn around the neck over leisure/sweat suits—suggested a number of contradictory tensions between work, time, and leisure. Early 1990s trends—oversized pants and urban warrior outer apparel, as in "hoodies," "snooties," "tims," and "triple fat" goose-down coats—make clear the severity of the urban storms to be weathered and the saturation of disposable goods in the crafting of cultural expressions.[21] As an alternative means of status formation, hip hop style forges local identities for teenagers who understand their limited access to traditional avenues of social status. Fab Five Freddy, an early rapper and graffiti writer, explains the link between style and identity in hip hop and its significance for gaining local status:

> You make a new style. That's what life on the street is all about. What's at stake is honor and position on the street. That's what makes it so important, that's what makes it feel so good—that pressure on you to be the best. Or to try to be the best. To develop a new style nobody can deal with. [22]

Styles "nobody can deal with" in graffiti, breaking, and rap music not only boost status and elevate black and Hispanic youth identities, they also articulate several shared approaches to sound and motion that are found in the Afro-diaspora. As black filmmaker and cultural critic Arthur Jafa has pointed out, stylistic continuities between breaking, graffiti style, rapping, and musical construction seem to center around three concepts: *flow, layering,* and *ruptures in line.*[23] In hip hop, visual, physical, musical, and lyrical lines are set in motion, broken abruptly with sharp, angular breaks, and yet sustain motion and energy through fluidity and flow. In graffiti, long winding, sweeping, and curving letters are broken and camouflaged by sudden breaks in line. Sharp, angular, broken letters are written in extreme italics, suggesting forward or backward motion. Letters are double and triple shadowed in such a way as to illustrate energy forces radiating from the center— suggesting circular motion—and yet the scripted words move horizontally. Breakdancing moves highlight flow, layering, and ruptures in line. Popping and locking are moves in which the joints are snapped abruptly into angular positions. And, yet, these snapping movements take place in one joint after the preceding one—creating a semiliquid effect that moves the energy toward the fingertip or toe. In fact, two dancers may pass the popping energy force back and forth between each other via finger-to-finger contact, setting off a new wave. In this pattern, the line is a series of angular breaks and yet sustains energy and motion through flow. Breakers double each other's moves (like line shadowing or layering in graffiti), intertwine their bodies into elaborate shapes, transforming the body into a new entity (like camouflage in graffiti's wild style), and then, one body part at a time, revert to a relaxed state. Abrupt, fractured, yet graceful footwork leaves the eye one step behind the motion, creating a time-lapse effect that not only mimics graffiti's use of line shadowing, but also creates spatial links between the moves that give the foot series flow and fluidity.[24]

The music and vocal rapping in rap music also privileges flow, layering, and ruptures in line. Rappers speak of flow explicitly in lyrics, referring to an ability to move easily and powerfully through complex lyrics, as well as of the flow in the music.[25] The flow and motion of the initial bass or drum line in rap music is abruptly ruptured by scratching (a process that highlights as it breaks the flow of the base rhythm) or the rhythmic flow is interrupted by other musical passages. Rappers alternately stutter and race through passages, always moving within the beat or in response to it, often using the music as a partner in rhyme. These verbal moves highlight lyrical flow and points of rupture. Rappers layer meaning by using the same word to signify a variety of actions and objects; they call out to the DJ to "lay down a beat," which it is expected will be interrupted, ruptured. DJs layer sounds literally one on top of the other, creating a dialogue between sampled sounds and words.

What is the significance of flow, layering, and rupture as demonstrated on the body and in hip hop's lyrical, musical, and visual works? Interpreting these concepts theoretically, it can be argued that they create and sustain rhythmic motion, continuity, and circularity via flow; accumulate, reinforce, and embellish this continuity through layering; and manage threats to these narratives by building in ruptures that highlight the continuity as they momentarily challenge it. These effects at the level of style and aesthetics suggest affirmative ways in which profound social dislocation and rupture can be managed and perhaps contested in the cultural arena. Let us imagine these hip hop principles as a blueprint for social resistance and affirmation: create sustaining narratives, accumulate them, layer, embellish, and transform them. But also be prepared for rupture, find pleasure in it, in fact, *plan on* social rupture. When these ruptures occur, use them in creative ways that will prepare you for a future in which survival will demand a sudden shift in ground tactics.

While accumulation, flow, circularity, and planned ruptures exist across a wide range of Afro-diasporic cultural forms, they do not take place outside of capitalist commercial constraints. Hip hop's explicit focus on consumption has frequently been mischaracterized as a movement *into* the commodity market (e.g., hip hop is no longer "authentically" black if it is for sale). Instead, hip hop's moment(s) of "incorporation" are a shift in the already existing relationship hip hop has always had to the commodity system. For example, the hip hop DJ frequently produces, amplifies, and revises already recorded sounds; rappers prefer high-end microphones; and both invest serious dollars for the speakers that can produce the "phattest" beats. Graffiti murals, breakdancing moves, and rap lyrics often appropriate and sometimes critique verbal and visual elements and physical movements from popular commercial culture, especially television, comic books, and karate movies. If anything, black style through hip hop has contributed to the continued blackening of mainstream popular culture. The contexts for creation in hip hop are never fully outside or in opposition to commodities; they involve struggles over public space and access to commodified materials, equipment, and products. It is a common misperception among hip hop artists and cultural critics that during the early days, hip hop was motivated by pleasure rather than profit, as if the two were incompatible. Yet, it would be naive to think that breakdancers, rappers, DJs, and writers were never interested in monetary compensation for their work. The problem was not that they were uniformly uninterested in profit; rather, many of the earliest practitioners were unaware that they could profit from their pleasure. Once this link was made, hip hop artists began marketing themselves wholeheartedly. Just as graffiti writers hitched rides on the subways and used its power to distribute their tags, rappers "hijacked" the market for their own purposes, riding the currents that were already out there, not just for wealth but for empowerment. During the late 1970s and early 1980s, the market for hip hop was still based inside New York's black and Hispanic communities. So, although there is an element of truth to this common perception, what is more important about the shift in hip hop's orientation is not its movement from precommodity to commodity but the shift in control over the scope and direction of the profit-making process, out of the hands of local black and Hispanic entrepreneurs and into the hands of larger white-owned, multinational businesses. And, most important, although black cultural imperatives are obviously deeply affected by commodification, these imperatives are not in direct opposition to the market, nor are they "irrelevant" to the shape of market-produced goods and practices.

Hebdige's work on the British punk movement identifies this shift as the moment of incorporation or recuperation by dominant culture and perceives it to be a critical element in the dynamics of the struggle over the meaning(s) of popular expression. "The process of recuperation," Hebdige argues, "takes two characteristic forms . . . one of conversion of subcultural signs (dress, music, etc.) into mass-produced objects and the 'labelling' and redefinition of deviant behavior by dominant groups—the police, media and judiciary." Hebdige astutely points out, however, that communication in a subordinate cultural form, even prior to the point of recuperation, usually takes place via commodities, "even if the meanings attached to those commodities are purposefully distorted or overthrown." And so, he concludes, "it is very difficult to sustain any absolute distinction between commercial exploitation on the one hand and creativity/originality on the other."[26]

Hebdige's observations regarding the process of incorporation and the tension between commercial exploitation and creativity as articulated in British punk is quite relevant to hip hop. Hip hop has always been articulated via commodities and engaged in the revision of meanings attached to them. Conversely, hip hop signs and meanings are converted and behaviors relabeled by dominant institutions. Graffiti, rap, and breakdancing are fundamentally transformed as they move into new relations with dominant cultural institutions.[27] In 1996, rap music is one of the most heavily traded popular commodities in the market, and yet it still defies total corporate control over the music, its local use, and its incorporation at the level of stable or exposed meanings.

These transformations and hybrids reflect the initial spirit of rap and hip hop as an experimental and collective space where contemporary issues and ancestral forces are worked through simultaneously. Hybrids in rap's subject matter, not unlike its use of musical collage, and the influx of new, regional, and ethnic styles have not yet displaced the three points of stylistic continuity to which I referred earlier; approaches to flow, ruptures in line, and layering can still be found in the vast majority of rap's lyrical and musical construction. The same is true of the critiques of the postindustrial urban American context and the cultural and social conditions it has produced. Today, the South Bronx and South Central are poorer and more economically marginalized than they were ten years ago.

Hip hop emerges from complex cultural exchanges and larger social and political conditions of disillusionment and alienation. Graffiti and rap were especially aggressive public displays of counterpresence and voice. Each asserted the right to write[28]—to inscribe one's identity on an environment that seemed Teflon-resistant to its young people of color, an environment that made legitimate avenues for material and social participation inaccessible. In this context, hip hop produced a number of double effects. First, themes in rap and graffiti articulated free play and unchecked public displays, and yet the settings for these expressions always suggested existing confinement.[29] Second, like the consciousness-raising sessions in the early stages of the women's movement and the black power movement of the 1960s and 1970s, hip hop produced internal and external dialogues that affirmed the experiences and identities of the participants and at the same time offered critiques of larger society that were directed to both the hip hop community and society in general.

Out of a broader discursive climate in which the perspectives and experiences of younger Hispanics, Afro-Caribbeans, and African Americans had been provided little social space, hip hop developed as part of a cross-cultural communication network. Trains carried graffiti tags through the five boroughs; flyers posted in black and Hispanic neighborhoods brought teenagers from all over New York to parks and clubs in the Bronx, and eventually to events throughout the metropolitan area; and, characteristic of communication in the age of high-tech telecommunications, stories with cultural and narrative resonance continued to spread at a rapid pace. It was not long before similarly marginalized black and Hispanic communities in other cities picked up on the tenor and energy in New York hip hop. Boom boxes in Roxbury and Compton blasted copies of hip hop mix tapes made on high-speed portable dubbing equipment by cousins from Flatbush Avenue in Brooklyn. The explosion of local and national cable programming of music videos spread hip hop dance steps, clothing, and slang across the country faster than brush fire. Within a decade, Los Angeles County (especially Compton), Oakland, Detroit, Chicago, Houston, Atlanta, Miami, Newark and Trenton, Roxbury, and Philadelphia had developed local hip hop scenes that linked (among other things) various regional postindustrial urban experiences of alienation, unemployment, police harassment, and social and economic isolation to their local and specific experience via hip hop's language, style, and attitude.[30] Regional, and increasingly national, differences and syndications in hip hop have been solidifying and will continue to do so. In some cases these differences are established by references to local streets and events, neighborhoods and leisure activities, preferences for dance steps, clothing, musical samples, and vocal accents. At the same time, cross-regional syndicates of rappers, writers, and dancers fortify hip hop's communal vocabulary. In every region, hip hop articulates a sense of entitlement and takes pleasure in aggressive insubordination. Like Chicago and Mississippi blues, these emerging regional hip hop identities affirm the specificity and local character of cultural forms as well as the larger stylistic forces that define hip hop and Afro-diasporic cultures.

Developing a style nobody can deal with—a style that cannot be easily understood or erased, a style that has the reflexivity to create counter-dominant narratives against a mobile and shifting enemy—may be one of the most effective ways to fortify communities of resistance and simultaneously reserve the right to communal pleasure. With few economic assets and abundant cultural and aesthetic resources, Afro-diasporic youth have designated the street as the arena for competition and style as the prestige-awarding event. In the postindustrial urban context of dwindling low-income housing, a trickle of meaningless jobs for young people, mounting police brutality, and increasingly draconian depictions of young inner-city residents, hip hop style *is* black urban renewal.

Notes

This essay is adapted from Tricia Rose, *Black Noise: Rap Music and Black Culture in Contemporary America* (Middletown, Conn.: Wesleyan University Press, 1994).

1. I have adopted Mollenkopf and Castells's use of the term "postindustrial" as a means of characterizing the economic restructuring that has taken place in urban America over the past twenty-five years. By defining the contemporary period in urban economies as postindustrial, Mollenkopf and Castells are not suggesting that manufacturing output has disappeared, nor are they adopting Daniel Bell's formulation that "knowledge has somehow replaced capital as the organizing principle of the economy." Rather, Mollenkopf and Castells claim that their use of postindustrial "captures a crucial aspect of how large cities are being transformed: employment has shifted massively away from manufacturing toward corporate, public and nonprofit services; occupations have similarly shifted from manual workers to managers, professionals, secretaries and service workers" (John Mollenkopf and Manuel Castells, eds., *Dual City: Restructuring New York* [New York: Russel Sage Foundation, 1991], 6). Similarly, these new postindustrial realities entailing the rapid movement of capital, images, and populations across the globe have also been referred to as "post-Fordism " and "flexible accumulation." See David Harvey, *Social Justice and the City* (Oxford: Basil Blackwell, 1988). For an elaboration of Bell's initial use of the term, see Daniel Bell, *The Coming of Post-Industrial Society* (New York: Basic Books, 1973).

2. My arguments regarding Afro-diasporic cultural formations in hip hop are relevant to African-American culture as well as Afro-diasporic cultures in the English- and Spanish-speaking Caribbean, each of which has prominent and significant African-derived cultural elements. While rap music, particularly early rap, is dominated by English-speaking blacks, graffiti and breakdancing were heavily shaped and practiced by Puerto Rican, Dominican, and other Spanish-speaking Caribbean communities that have substantial Afro-diasporic elements. (The emergence of Chicano rappers takes place in the late 1980s in Los Angeles.) Consequently, my references to Spanish-speaking Caribbean communities should in no way be considered inconsistent with my larger Afro-diasporic claims. Substantial work has illuminated the continued significance of African cultural elements to cultural production in both Spanish- and English-speaking nations in the Caribbean. For examples, see Herbert S. Klein, *African Slavery in Latin America and the Caribbean* (New York: Oxford University Press, 1986); Ivan G. Van Sertima,

They Came before Columbus (New York: Random House, 1976); and Robert Farris Thompson, *Flash of the Spirit* (New York: Random House, 1983).

3. See Allen J. Matusow, *The Unraveling of America: A History of Liberalism in the 1960s* (New York: Harper and Row, 1984).

4. In hip hop, the train serves both as means of interneighborhood communication and as a source of creative inspiration. Big Daddy Kane says that he writes his best lyrics on the subway or train on the way to producer Marly Marl's house. See Barry Michael Cooper, "Raw Like Sushi," *Spin* (March 1988): 28. Similarly, Chuck D claims that he loves to drive, that he would have been a driver if his rapping career hadn't worked out. See Robert Christgau and Greg Tate, "Chuck D All over the Map," *Village Voice*, Rock 'n' Roll Quarterly 4:3 (fall 1991).

5. See John H. Mollenkopf, *The Contested City* (Princeton, N.J.: Princeton University Press, 1983), especially pp. 12–46, for a discussion of larger twentieth-century transformations in U.S. cities throughout the 1970s and into the early 1980s. See also Mollenkopf and Castells, *Dual City*; Michael Peter Smith and Joe R. Feagin, eds., *The Capitalist City: Global Restructuring and Community Politics* (London: Basil Blackwell, 1987); Michael Peter Smith, ed., *Cities in Transformation: Class, Capital and the State* (Beverly Hills, Calif.: Sage Publications, 1984); and Saskia Sassen, *The Mobility of Labor and Capital: A Study in International Investment and Labor Flow* (Cambridge: Cambridge University Press, 1988).

6. I am not suggesting that New York is typical of all urban areas, nor that regional differences are insignificant. However, the broad transformations under discussion here have been felt in all major U.S. cities, particularly New York and Los Angeles—hip hop's second major hub city—and critically frame the transitions that, in part, contributed to hip hop's emergence. In the mid-1980s, very similar postindustrial changes in job opportunities and social services in the Watts and Compton areas of Los Angeles became the impetus for Los Angeles's gangsta rappers. As Robin Kelley notes: "The generation who came of age in the 1980s was the product of devastating structural changes in the urban economy that date back at least to the late 1960s. While the city as a whole experienced unprecedented growth, the communities of Watts and Compton faced increased economic displacement, factory closures, and an unprecedented deepening of poverty. . . . Developers and city and county government helped the suburbanization process along by cutting back expenditures for parks, recreation, and affordable housing in inner city communities" (Robin D. G. Kelley, "Kickin' Reality, Kickin' Ballistics," in *Race Rebels: Politics and the Black Working Class* [New York: Free Press, 1994], 192). See also Mike Davis, *City of Quartz: Excavating the Future of Los Angeles* (London and New York: Verso, 1990).

7. Mollenkopf, *The Contested City*, 213.

8. Frank Van Riper, "Ford to New York: Drop Dead," *Daily News*, 30 October 1975: 1.

9. Philip Weitzman, "'Worlds Apart': Housing, Race/Ethnicity and Income in New York City," Community Service Society of New York (CSS) (1989). See also Terry J. Rosenberg, "Poverty in New York City: 1980–1985," CSS (1987); Robert Neuwirth, "Housing after Koch," *Village Voice*, 7 November 1989: 22–24.

10. Mollenkopf and Castells, *Dual City*, 9. See also Parts II and III of the collection, which deal specifically and in greater detail with the forces of transformation, gender, and the new occupational strata.

11. Ben Bagdigian, *The Media Monopoly* (Boston: Beacon Press, 1987). Despite trends toward the centralization of news and media sources and the fact that larger corporate media outfits have proven unable to serve diverse ethnic and racial groups, a recent study on New York's media structure in the 1980s suggests that a wide range of alternative media sources serve New York's ethnic communities. However, the study also shows that black New Yorkers have been less successful in sustaining alternative media channels. See Mitchell Moss and Sarah Ludwig, "The Structure of the Media," in Mollenkopf and Castells, *Dual City*, 245–65.

12. See Tom Forester, *High-Tech Society* (Cambridge: MIT Press, 1988), and Herbert

Schiller, *Culture, Inc.: The Corporate Takeover of Public Expression* (New York: Oxford University Press, 1989).

13. Similar strategies for urban renewal via "slum clearance" demolition took place in a number of major metropolises in the late 1960s and 1970s. See Mollenkopf, *The Contested City*, especially chapter 4, which describes similar processes in Boston and San Francisco.

14. Robert D. McFadden, "Power Failure Blacks Out New York; Thousands Trapped in Subways; Looters and Vandals Hit Some Areas," *New York Times*, 14 July 1977: A1; Lawrence Van Gelder, "State Troopers Sent into City as Crime Rises," *New York Times*, 14 July 1977: A1; Charlayne Hunter-Gault, "When Poverty Is Part of Life, Looting Is Not Condemned," *New York Times*, 15 July 1977: A4; Selwyn Raab, "Ravage Continues Far into Day; Gunfire and Bottles Beset Police," *New York Times*, 15 July 1977: A1; "Social Overload," *New York Times*, editorial, 22 July 1977: A22.

15. Lee Dembart, "Carter Takes 'Sobering' Trip to South Bronx," *New York Times*, 6 October 1977: A1; Richard Severo, "Bronx a Symbol of America's Woes" *New York Times*, 6 October 1977: B18; Joseph P. Fried, "The South Bronx USA: What Carter Saw In New York City Is a Symbol of Complex Social Forces on a Nationwide Scale," *New York Times*, 7 October 1977: A22.

16. Michael Ventura, *Shadow Dancing in the USA* (Los Angeles: J. P. Tarcher Press, 1986), 186. Other popular films from the late 1970s and early 1980s that followed suit included *1990: The Bronx Warriors* and *Escape from New York*. This construction of the dangerous ghetto is central to Tom Wolfe's 1989 best-seller and the subsequent film *Bonfire of the Vanities*. In it, the South Bronx is constructed as an abandoned, lawless territory from the perspective of substantially more privileged white outsiders.

17. Interviews by the author with all artists named except Futura, whose printing trade school experience was cited in Steve Hager, *Hip Hop: The Illustrated History of Breakdancing, Rap Music, and Graffiti* (New York: St. Martin's Press, 1984), 24. These artist interviews were conducted for my book on rap music entitled *Black Noise*.

18. Interview by the author with Crazy Legs, November 1991. "Piecing" means drawing a mural or masterpiece.

19. See Henry Louis Gates Jr., *The Signifying Monkey: A Theory of African-American Literary Criticism* (New York and Oxford: Oxford University Press, 1988). Gates's suggestion that naming be "drawn upon as a metaphor for black intertextuality" is especially useful in hip hop where naming and intertextuality are critical strategies for creative production (see pp. 55, 87).

20. Dick Hebdige, *Subculture: The Meaning of Style* (London: Methuen, 1979). See especially pp. 17–19, 84–89.

21. "Hoodies" are hooded jackets or shirts, "snooties" are skullcaps, and "tims" are Timberland brand boots.

22. Nelson George et al., eds., *Fresh: Hip Hop Don't Stop* (New York: Random House, 1985), 111.

23. Although I had isolated some general points of aesthetic continuity between hip hop's forms, I did not identify these three crucial organizing terms. I am grateful to Arthur Jafa, who shared and discussed the logic of these defining characteristics with me in conversation. He is not, of course, responsible for any inadequacies in my use of them here.

24. For a brilliant example of these moves among recent hip-hop dances, see *Reckin' Shop in Brooklyn*, directed by Diane Martel (Epoch Films, 1992).

25. Some examples of explicit attention to flow are exhibited in Queen Latifah's "Ladies First": "Some think that we can't flow, stereotypes they got to go"; Big Daddy Kane's "Raw": "Intro I start to go, my rhymes will flow so"; and Digital Underground's "Sons of the P": "Release your mind and let your instincts flow, release your mind and let the funk flow" (later, they refer to themselves as the "sons of the flow").

26. Hebdige, *Subculture*, 94–95.

27. Published in 1979, Hebdige's *Subculture* concludes at the point of dominant British culture's initial attempts at incorporating punk. My project examines the points of incorporation and responses that come after the initial moment of incorporation to which Hebdige's study is devoted.

28. See Duncan Smith, "The Truth of Graffiti," *Art & Text* 17: 84–90.

29. For example, Kurtis Blow's "The Breaks" (1980) was both about the seeming inevitability and hardships of unemployment and mounting financial debt and the sheer pleasure of "breaking it up and down," of dancing and breaking free of social and psychological constrictions. Regardless of subject matter, elaborate graffiti tags on train facades always suggest that the power and presence of the image is possible only if the writer has escaped capture.

30. See Bob Mack, "Hip-Hop Map of America," *Spin,* June 1990.

Annotated Bibliography

DARRYL B. DICKSON-CARR

As the myriad essays in this volume have demonstrated, the concept we know as "multiculturalism" has many different interpretations and manifestations. Its place in the evolution of global economics and politics is widely debated; as a result, information about how and where we may find examples of multiculturalism is relatively easy to find. On the other hand, discussions of the *origins* of multiculturalism are much less common. Where such discussions are found, scholars of race and ethnicity are locked in debate over where and when multiculturalism first found a foothold in sociopolitical consciousness. I refer the reader to the Introduction to this volume for one history of the concept.

This bibliography does not attempt to cover the entire history of the term multiculturalism or its antecedents and variants. That effort would require a bibliography easily several times the size of this one, and could only serve to overwhelm the reader with confusing choices. Rather, this bibliography surveys a selection of the more prescient and salient documents that explore the basic (and occasionally far more complicated) terms of the debate on multiculturalism and its social purposes. The categories that divide the bibliography are designed to touch upon those areas in American culture where different understandings of multiculturalism have been contested and (to one degree or another) implemented. Furthermore, the texts listed offer a sampling of some of the most common places where different brands of multiculturalism (ranging from corporate "diversity management" training to educational guidelines) are currently found and have been found over the last twenty-five years.

What becomes readily apparent as one surveys the resources listed here is that most discussants of multiculturalism or racial and ethnic matters are making serious attempts to achieve a semblance of social justice, whether that justice be achieved in the political, social, or economic arenas, or at least to make living and working communities appear more egalitarian. In the vast majority of these cases, the authors of a given book or article view *education* as the key to sociopolitical equity for a given racial or ethnic group. This education may take the form of education in the public school system, a university education, or a (re)orientation with the needs of racial/ethnic employees and business partners in the workplace.

Since education is the basic key to multiculturalism's success or failure in the public domain, it might be expected that the most abundant category for materials on multiculturalism is "Multiculturalism in Primary and Secondary Education." This is the area where ideas and discussions of multiculturalisms caused the least anguish and produced the most extensive work. Many of these works are direct or distant descendants of the integration-oriented civil rights era, during which, at least initially, the most pressing issue for politicians and educators was intelligent enforcement of school desegregation. As the civil rights movement became more complicated, however, educators began to perceive that inequities in schools and educational quality were the result not only of segregation but also of prejudices that teachers and administrators may have held against students of color and of the absence of a school system where people of color could have control of their own schools. The latter turned out to be a more radical notion of restructuring the school system, but the former has been served very well by the articles listed here, in which authors frequently demonstrate the many ways that educators have been biased against their constituencies and suggest methods for overcoming or correcting those biases.

As physical desegregation became a slightly more tangible reality in American schools, educators (particularly educators of color) began to reassess the means of making children from disenfranchised racial groups as well as their white counterparts feel more comfortable with one another and with their peers' histories, since the lessons in children's formative years regarding racial, ethnic, and other social matters are probably the most thoroughly entrenched. The period extending from the early 1970s through the mid-1980s saw a wealth of books and articles on multicultural education that attempted to encourage the changes in education already noted; in recent years (when the debate on multiculturalism has escalated) this wealth has become a veritable flurry. The reader, however, should be aware that most of the work on multicultural education seeks the common end of providing an education sensitive to the cultural situation of children of color. More often than not, differences occur in the strategy for attaining an egalitarian educational system rather than in the general goal itself. This does not mean, though, that it is not necessary to read a variety of texts to understand what needs to be set in motion for multiculturalism to succeed; not all of the strategies mentioned earlier are equally applicable to all parts of the populace, and most could use the supplementary views of alternative texts. In fact, the wisest reading strategy would be to pick texts from different periods (for example, one from the early 1970s, one from later in the decade, one from the early 1980s, and so on), inasmuch as it is helpful to review approaches that may have been discarded in favor of less controversial ideas.

Of further note should be the fact that even multicultural education at the public school level has come under fire in recent years, though not nearly to the degree that its cousin at the college level has. The idea of revising the manner in which colleges teach and hire (and, by extension, *who* they teach and hire and *what* they teach, as well as *how* they teach it) is one of never-ending debate, but the racial portion of this debate began to simmer in the late 1960s (especially at such campuses as Berkeley, the University of California, Santa Barbara, and Howard), when students and professors (many of color) registered some of the first demands for Black Studies and Chicano/Latino Studies departments and courses. Such demands had enormous implications, since the country's universities are generally considered training grounds and test labs for ideas that could affect the rest of the nation. Appropriately, then, the category of "Multiculturalism in Higher Education" signals a tenuous link between the topics of primary education and the others, inasmuch as it covers teaching methods, policy, educational opportunities, and hiring at the university level. A few of the authors that have worked on multiculturalism in primary schools have contributed to discussions of university policy and pedagogy (most notably Donna M. Gollnick). But by and large, the scholars writing about these areas tend not to exchange ideas. Perhaps one reason for this separation of resources is that the most sincere and widespread concern for making American institutions reflect the composition and needs of all levels of the nation's population has reached the university primarily within the last decade. In that time, educators have made penetrating observations and studies of the university environment and its potential for enacting multicultural policies. Central to the incorporation of multiculturalism into university policies and practices is the issue of affirmative action in all its permutations. Although most of the texts under the higher education rubric touch upon this issue along the way, it is one that needs further exploration, since affirmative action is perhaps the most divisive (and therefore the most crucial) component in the multiculturalism debate occurring within academia's halls.

In fact, multiculturalism-oriented policies in American universities have provided more grist for the antimulticulturalism mill than they have at any other societal level. It should come as no surprise, then, that most of the entries under "The Multiculturalism Debates" focus on the university. These articles or essays represent the more staunchly rhetorical, and (in some cases) even demagogic, voices concerned with American racial matters, especially those that emerged within the last decade in the forefront of the debates. We have culled most of these articles and books from the more "mainstream" portion of the mass media, such as newsmagazines or the more popular academic journals. Within these publications, the multiculturalism debate has engendered the most widespread attention (or notoriety), to say nothing of generating considerable heat. A substantial number of these polemics, however, are in want of serious historical scholarship, whether they be for or against multiculturalism. A curious facet of the debate waged in the popular press is an unsettling tendency for antimulticultural critics to lump multiculturalism in the same camp with Afrocentrism or other ethnocentric theories, even if those theories have demonstrated a marked aversion to being truly multicultural (that is, to looking at history from multiracial points of view). Not unlike the resistance to the physical integration of African Americans into the mainstream university environment, the antimulticulturalism approach in the polemics marks a stubborn and often poorly thought-out resistance to, even a backlash against, the integration of ideas fostered by African Americans. This trend is especially problematic insofar as the American public is led to believe that the work of Afrocentrists, whether right or wrong, is synonymous with multiculturalism, and this frequently leads to a rejection of multiculturalism at all levels of society, including primary and secondary education. These articles and their authors will probably continue to produce the most controversial statements and wield the greatest influence on public opinion as scholars continue to debate multiculturalism.

A less discussed, though no less essential, area of the multiculturalism phenomenon is "Multiculturalism in the Corporate World." One of the central demands of virtually all social protest movements, such as those that preceded and emerged from the activism of the 1960s, has been for jobs, or equal access to jobs, for oppressed groups. As the social, racial, and class dynamics of both the United States and the world in the 1960s transformed into those of the 1970s and 1980s, private corporations began to adjust their business policies to accommodate some of the demands and needs of a racially shifting labor pool, one that began to include significantly more African, Asian, and Latino Americans. Given the reluctance of the American workforce to include these groups in everyday operations, corporations were forced, whether by the government or from within, to make greater efforts to cope with a slightly more diverse workforce. These coping mechanisms, however, were and are not necessarily intended to be more inclusive corporate policies; rather, many of them are intended to defuse conflicts within the workforce, to enforce an artificial peace. Additionally, "diversity management" texts generally do not provide much more than cursory histories of corporate multiculturalism. Rather, they tend to act as instructional "textbooks" for implementing specific management methods. And pursuant to those goals, numerous authors (many of whom are full-time consultants) have produced volumes that explain these methods in incredible detail for managers of all levels in order to make their intra- and interbusiness relations run more smoothly through cultural awareness. Notable authors in this vein include Farid Elashmawi, Pierre Casse, and Muriel James. Of further note should be the recent publication dates of these authors' works. "Diversity management" is a relatively young development under the multiculturalism rubric, one that has yet to be extensively interrogated and explored.

On the other hand, the topic of "Multiculturalism in the Humanities," not unlike "The Multiculturalism Debates," has been extensively mined by academics. Given the fact that the focus of pro- and antimulticulturalism discourse has been on considerations of canonicity in literature, curriculum, and program structures in the university and of the infusion of divergent politics into everyday life on the American campus, it makes sense that those academic disciplines most apt to call for and extend these discourses should produce numerous texts on multiculturalism. Most of the works placed under this category fill considerable numbers of pages discussing, undermining, and revising the notion of multiculturalism or complicated issues of race tangential to the current debate. Very few, however, engage the logistical issues of *pedagogy* with the kind of rigor that Betty E. M. Ch'maj's

Multicultural America does. The predominant trend, instead, is to review the past and current policies and politics of integrating different definitions and practices of multiculturalism into the classroom. Henry Louis Gates Jr.'s collection of essays reviewing the controversy over canonicity offers a fair summary of the pedagogical issues on the American campus, while Reginald Martin's interview of author and scholar Ishmael Reed provides an insight into a definition of multiculturalism in the early 1980s. Additionally, the entire January–February 1992 issue of *Change* magazine includes some of the most insightful and practical histories and applications of multicultural pedagogy produced since the controversy around the term arose. Many scholars in this category have formulated their perspectives from different kinds of race theory, which, instead of discussing what multiculturalism might mean or how it might be practiced in general, revolve around *specific* racial and/or ethnic groups and question the very idea of "race" and its history as a social and political concept. Unfortunately, many serious race theorists (and the articles we have culled from them) are ensconced in ethnic or racial studies departments (and journals or presses), such as Black/African-American Studies, Asian-American Studies, or Chicano/Latino Studies programs and departments, which may prevent their work from receiving its due notice from the rest of the scholarly community. Additionally, many of these volumes have been produced within the last few years. This phenomenon is partially attributable to the fact that scholars of race and ethnicity have only recently begun to discuss the relation of racial histories to the concept of multiculturalism.

"Multiculturalism in Society and Public Policy," while a relatively short list, is as important as the education-oriented areas. Here, the majority of texts center on how federal, state, and local agencies and institutions might be able to address the problems that are endemic to particular racial or ethnic groups in the United States. Legislative bodies, welfare systems, the legal profession, and other forms of public social organization find themselves increasingly burdened with demands to accommodate the needs of different social or racial groups that cannot be covered through "blanket" measures. The reaction to this demand takes the form of increased study of the economic and political conditions that lead to certain groups' difficulties with navigating bureaucratic institutions. Such texts as Clausen and Bermingham's *Pluralism, Racism, and Public Policy* or Michael Omi and Howard Winant's *Racial Formation in the United States* help to delimit some of the general issues facing public policymakers. The remainder of the texts in this area, however, tackle more specific institutions and problems, the selection of which shall be left to the reader.

As the reader begins to pick and choose among these numerous rubrics, s/he will notice that the tone of the arguments, as well as the intentions of the proponents and opponents of multiculturalism, shift considerably between areas. For example, the sorts of issues at stake in implementing multiculturalism at the university level tend to be much more complex, or at least more acrimonious, than those at the primary educational level. This is not to say that one is somehow less important than the other by virtue of being less fraught. But whereas the primary and secondary levels are often concerned with pedagogical methods that accommodate a diverse general populace, the college and university levels are often concerned with diminishing resources, whether financial, cultural, ideological, or otherwise, for which a few impassioned groups must continually struggle. One of the principal concerns of corporate multiculturalism, on the other hand, is maintaining control of a potentially and practically volatile workforce.

So when, therefore, we encounter the term multiculturalism at any point in general public discourse or within these texts, we must force ourselves to consider the social realm in which the term appears. To transfer the same sorts of sociopolitical considerations from one area where they have full validity to another could prove to be disastrous and confusing. Although it is simultaneously true that some common ground exists between the various areas, such as the calls for education or affirmative action mentioned earlier, the relationships between each become more complicated beyond these few common points. Only by undertaking thorough and particularistic inquiries into the many uses of the concept and practice of multiculturalism could we discern to what degree it not only is working but *could* work with our support.

I. The Multiculturalism Debates

Adams, Willi Paul. "U.S. Fears of Multiculturalism are Unfounded." *Public Affairs Report* 32:2 (1991).

"An American Culture." *National Review* 43 (1991): 18.

Asante, Molefi Kete. *The Afrocentric Idea.* Philadelphia: Temple University Press, 1987.

———. *Afrocentricity: The Theory of Social Change.* Buffalo, N.Y.: Amulefi, 1980.

———. "Multiculturalism: An Exchange." *American Scholar* 60 (spring 1991): 267–72.

Auster, Lawrence. "The Forbidden Topic." *National Review* 44 (1992): 42–44. This article draws links between multiculturalism and immigration.

Brustein, Robert. "The Use and Abuse of Multiculturalism." *New Republic* 205 (1991): 31–34.

Contention: Debates in Society, Culture and Science 1:3 (1992).

Decter, Midge. "E Pluribus Nihil: Multiculturalism and Black Children." *Commentary* 92 (1991): 25–29.

Draper, Roger. "P.C. Pipe Dreams." *New Leader* 75 (1992): 16–17.

D'Souza, Dinesh. "Multiculturalism 101: Great Books of the Non-Western World." *Policy Review* 56 (1991): 22–30.

Erickson, Peter. "What Multiculturalism Means." *Transition: An International Review* 55 (1991): 105–14.

Fraser, Laura. "The Tyranny of the Media Correct." *San Francisco Bay Guardian* (17 April 1991).

Gates, Henry Louis, Jr. *Loose Canons: Notes on the Culture Wars.* New York: Oxford University Press, 1992.

Hacker, Andrew. "Multiculturalism and Its Discontents." *Black Scholar* 24:1 (1994): 16–17.

———. *Two Nations: Black, White, Separate, Hostile, Unequal.* New York: Scribner's, 1992.

Hughes, Robert. "The Fraying of America." *Time* 139:3 (February 1992): 44–49.

Jay, Gregory. "Liberalism and Multiculturalism." *Democratic Culture* 2:1 (1993): 10.

Jones, Malcolm. "It's a Not So Small World." *Newsweek* 118:9 (September 1991): 64–65.

Leo, John. "The Words of the Culture War." *U.S. News & World Report* 111 (28 October 1991): 31.

Marable, Manning. *Black America: Multicultural Democracy in the Age of Clarence Thomas, David Duke and the L.A. Uprisings.* Westfield, N.J.: Open Media, 1992.

Maudlin, Michael G. "Now That's Multicultural!" *Christianity Today* 36 (13 January 1992): 15.

Nelson, Cary. "Canon Fodder: An Evening with William Bennett, Lynne Cheney, and Dinesh D'Souza." *Works and Days: Essays in the Socio-Historical Dimensions of Literature and the Arts* 9:2 (1991): 39–54.

Plagens, Peter. "Multiculturalism or Bust, Gang." *Newsweek* 116 (24 September 1990): 68–69.

Ravitch, Diane. "Multiculturalism." *American Scholar* 59 (summer 1990): 337–54.

———. "Multiculturalism: An Exchange." *American Scholar* 60 (spring 1991): 267–76.

———. "Multiculturalism or Cultural Separatism: The Choice Is Ours." *New Perspectives Quarterly* 8 (fall 1991): 79.

Royal, Robert. *1492 and All That: Political Manipulations of History.* Washington, D.C.: Ethics and Public Policy Center, 1992.

Schlesinger, Arthur M., Jr. *The Disuniting of America.* The Larger Agenda Series. Knoxville, Tenn.: Whittle Direct Books, 1991.

———. "Multiculturalism or Cultural Separatism: The Choice Is Ours." *New Perspectives Quarterly* 8 (fall 1991): 79.

Siegel, Frederick F. "The Cult of Multiculturalism." *New Republic* 204 (18 February 1991): 34ff.

Stimpson, Catharine R. "Multiculturalism: A Big Word at the Presses." *New York Times Book Review* 96 (22 September 1991): 1ff.

Terkel, Studs. *Race: How Blacks and Whites Think and Feel about the American Obsession.* New York: Anchor Press, 1992.

Trachtenberg, Stephen. "Multiculturalism Can Be Taught Only by Multicultural People." *Phi Delta Kappan* 71 (April 1990): 610–11.

Walljasper, Jay. "Multiculturalism and Me." *Utne Reader* (November–December 1991): 154–55.

Willie, Charles Vert. "Multiculturalism Bashing: A Review of Magazine Coverage." *Change* 24 (January–February 1992): 70–73. The entire issue of *Change* (a magazine for educators) from which this article emerges is an excellent source for discussions of multiculturalism in education. It covers many of the primary points of the debates for any educator who is attempting to get a grasp of the current (that is, as of early 1992) political and logistical facets at all educational levels. This is *not*, however, an entirely pro-multiculturalism issue. Willie's article, unfortunately, does not live up to the title, if one is expecting a review of *all* recent magazine coverage. Instead, this article summarizes other articles that appeared in the *New Republic*'s 18 February 1991 special issue on multiculturalism. Willie picks out a few of the more problematic antimulticulturalism articles and discusses their considerable leaps of logic and lack of proof. Interestingly, Willie is pretty polemical himself, especially at the end of the article, when he makes a very rough transition from his discussion of multiculturalism to political correctness.

II. Multiculturalism in Operation

A. In the Arts and Museums

Adams, Robert McCormick. "The Central Challenge for Museums Today May Be to Find Ways to Address the Increasing Diversity of Our Society." *Smithsonian* 23 (April 1992): 13–14.

Bamberger, Joan. "Reclaiming Traditions: A Symposium on Craft Revivals Points to the Multiculturalism of Today." *American Craft* 51 (August–September 1991): 74–77.

Cembalest, Robin. "Goodbye, Columbus?" *Art News* 90 (October 1991): 104–9.

Chong, Ping. "Notes for 'Mumbling and Digressions: Some Thoughts on Being an Artist, Being an American, Being a Witness. . . .'" *MELUS* 16:3 (1989): 62–67.

Ciani, Kyle Emily. "The Machado Quilt: A Study in Multi-Cultural Folk Art." *Uncoverings: Research Papers of the American Quilt Study Group* 12 (1991): 190–207.

Clinton, Michelle T., Sesshu Foster, and Naomi Quinonez, eds. *Invocation L.A.: Urban Multicultural Poetry.* Albuquerque, N.M.: West End Press, 1989.

Foster, Sesshu. "Fresh Harvest: New Multicultural Poetry by and about Workers." *Northwest Review* 28:2 (1990): 146–54.

Galinsky, Karl. *Classical and Modern Interactions: Postmodern Architecture, Multiculturalism, Decline, and Other Issues.* Austin: University of Texas Press, 1992.

Gibbins, John Joseph. "The American Theatre's Attempts to Achieve Multiculturalism on Stage through Non-Traditional Casting." Ph.D. diss., Northwestern University, 1992.

Glidden, Robert. "Finding the Balance." *Design for Arts in Education* 91 (May–June 1990): 2–13.

King, Edith W. "Using Museums for More Effective Teaching of Ethnic Relations." *Teaching Sociology* 20:2 (1992): 114–20.

La Duke, Betty. *Women Artists: Multi-Cultural Visions.* Trenton, N.J.: Red Sea Press, 1992.

Lippard, Lucy R. *Mixed Blessings: New Art in a Multicultural America.* New York: Pantheon Books, 1990.

Mason, Rachel. *Art Education and Multiculturalism.* London and New York: Croom Helm, 1988.

Multicultural Focus: An Exhibition of Photography for the Los Angeles Bicentennial: Municipal Art Gallery, Barnsdall Park, January 27–February 22, 1981. Santa Monica, Calif.: The Center, 1981.

Rodriguez, Fred. "Cultural Pluralism and the Arts: Designing Multicultural Materials for Music Educators." *Design for Arts in Education* 86 (March–April 1985): 38–42.

Rodriguez, Luis J. "Living on the Hyphen: Multicultural Diversity in the Arts." *Mid-American Review* 12:1 (1991): 3–7.

Sacramento Metropolitan Arts Commission. *New and Emerging Organizations Pilot Program: Phase I, Technical Assistance to Multi-Cultural Groups, 1987.* Sacramento, Calif.: Sacramento Metropolitan Arts Commission, 1987.

Schuman, Jo Miles. *Art from Many Hands: Multicultural Art Projects for Home and School.* Englewood Cliffs, N.J.: Prentice Hall, 1981.

B. In Primary and Secondary Education

Adler, Sol. *Multicultural Communication Skills in the Classroom.* Boston: Allyn and Bacon, 1993.

Alderson, Brian. "Lone Voices in the Crowd: The Limits of Multiculturalism." In *Cross-Culturalism in Children's Literature: Selected Papers from the Children's Literature Association, Carle-*

ton University, Ottawa, Canada, ed. Susan R. Gannon and Ruth Anne Thompson. New York: Pace University Press, 1988. 5–10.

American Association of Colleges for Teacher Education, Commission on Multicultural Education. *Directory of Multicultural Education Programs in Teacher Education Institutions in the United States, 1978.* Washington, D.C.: Accreditation Standards for Multicultural Teacher Education Project, AACTE, 1978.

The American Tapestry: Educating a Nation: A Guide to Infusing Multiculturalism into American Education. Alexandria, Va.: National Association of State Boards of Education, 1991.

Arora, R. K., and C. G. Duncan. *Multicultural Education: Towards Good Practice.* London and Boston: Routledge and Kegan Paul, 1986.

Au, Kathryn Hu-Pei. *Literacy Instruction in Multicultural Settings.* Fort Worth, Tex.: Harcourt Brace Jovanovich, 1993.

Bagley, Christopher. "Cultural Diversity, Migration, and Cognitive Styles: A Study of British, Japanese, Jamaican, and Indian Children." In Verma and Bagley, 217–46.

Baker, Gwendolyn C. *Planning and Organizing for Multicultural Instruction.* Reading, Mass.: Addison-Wesley, 1983.

Banfield, Beryle. *Black Focus on Multicultural Education: How to Develop an Anti-Racist, Anti-Sexist Curriculum.* New York: E. W. Blyden Press, 1979.

Banks, James A., and Cherry A. McGee Banks, eds. *Multicultural Education: Issues and Perspectives.* 2d ed. Boston: Allyn and Bacon, 1993.

Banks, James A., and James Lynch, eds. *Multicultural Education in Western Societies.* New York: Praeger, 1986.

Baptiste, H. Prentice, Jr. *Multicultural Education: A Synopsis.* 2d ed. Washington, D.C.: University Press of America, 1979.

Baptiste, H. Prentice, Jr., and Mira Lanier Baptiste, eds. *Developing the Multicultural Process in Classroom Instruction: Competencies for Teachers.* Washington, D.C.: University Press of America, 1979.

Bennett, Christine I. *Comprehensive Multicultural Education: Theory and Practice.* Boston: Allyn and Bacon, 1986.

Bodnar, John E., Vandra Masemann, and Ray C. Rist. *Multicultural Education: Perspectives for the 1980s.* Buffalo, N.Y.: Department of Social Foundations and Comparative Education Center, Faculty of Educational Studies, State University of New York at Buffalo, 1981.

Boyer, James. *Multicultural Education: From Product to Process.* New York: ERIC Clearinghouse on Urban Education, Institute for Urban and Minority Education, Teachers College, Columbia University, 1983.

Broadbent, John. *Assessment in a Multicultural Society: Community Languages at 16+: A Discussion Document.* York, England: Longman for Schools Council, 1983.

Brown, Daphne M. *Mother Tongue to English: The Young Child in the Multicultural School.* Cambridge, England, and New York: Cambridge University Press, 1979.

Bull, Barry L., Royal T. Fruehling, and Virgie Chatterey. *The Ethics of Multicultural and Bilingual Education.* New York: Teachers College Press, 1992.

California Association of School Librarians, Human Relations Committee. *Words Like Freedom: A Multi-Cultural Bibliography.* Burlingame: California Association of School Librarians, 1975.

California State Department of Education, Bureau of Intergroup Relations. *Guide for Multicultural Education: Content and Context.* Sacramento: California State Department of Education, 1977.

California State Department of Education, Office of Intergroup Relations. *Planning for Multicultural Education as a Part of School Improvement.* Sacramento: California State Department of Education, 1979.

Caliguri, Joseph P., Jack P. Krueger, and Young Pai. *An Annotated Bibliographical Guide to the Literature on Bilingualism and Multicultural Education.* Kansas City: School of Education, University of Missouri, 1980.

Cardenas, Jose Angel. *Multicultural Education: An Annotated Bibliography.* San Antonio, Tex.: Intercultural Development Research Association, 1976.

Chace, William M. "The Real Challenge of Multiculturalism." *Education Digest* 56 (May 1991): 34–36.

Chambers, Joanna Fountain. *Hey, Miss! You Got a Book for Me? A Model Multicultural Resource Collection Annotated Bibliography.* 2d ed., rev. and expanded. Austin, Tex.: Austin Bilingual Language Editions, 1981.

Cohen, David, and Monroe D. Cohen, eds. *Louis Armstrong Middle School (East Elmhurst, N.Y.) Resources for Valuing Diversity: The Louis Armstrong Middle School (I.S. 227Q) Multicultural Collection.* East Elmhurst, N.Y.: Louis Armstrong Middle School, 1990.

Colangelo, Nicholas, Dick Dustin, and Cecelia H. Foxley. *The Human Relations Experience: Exercises in Multicultural, Nonsexist Education.* Monterey, Calif.: Brooks/Cole Publishing Company, 1982.

———, eds. *Multicultural Nonsexist Education: A Human Relations Approach.* 2d ed. Dubuque, Iowa: Kendall/Hunt Publishing Company, 1985.

Cross, Dolores E., Gwendolyn C. Baker, and Lindley J. Stiles, eds. *Teaching in a Multicultural Society: Perspectives and Professional Strategies.* New York: Free Press, 1977. This anthology is divided into three parts, all devoted to arguing for multicultural education, but each with a different emphasis. The first contains essays that provide histories of and arguments for cultural diversity in general, and is eventually linked to the need for multicultural education, the focus of the second section. The third section outlines strategies for implementing the proposals of the second section. Three essays are particularly intriguing and informative: Meyer Weinberg's "A Historical Framework for Multicultural Education," James Deslonde's "You Know the Rules! Myths about Desegregation," and Asa Hilliard's "Intellectual Strengths of Minority Children," all of which argue for changes in teacher attitudes as precursors for improved education.

Current, Richard N. "The 'New Ethnicity' and American History: Wisconsin as a Test Case." *History Teacher* 15:1 (1981): 43–50.

Diaz, Carlos, ed. *Multicultural Education for the 21st Century.* Washington, D.C.: NEA Professional Library, National Education Association, 1992.

Diversity in Teacher Education: New Expectations. San Francisco: Jossey-Bass Publishers, 1992.

Everstz, Linda Cathryn. "Textbooks in a Multicultural Society: A Look at the 1990 Social Studies Textbook Adoption in the State of California." Ph.D. diss., University of California, 1992.

Ferguson, Henry. *Manual for Multicultural and Ethnic Studies: A Survival Manual for the Innovative Leader.* Thompson, Conn.: InterCultural Press, 1977.

———. *Manual for Multicultural Education.* 2d ed. Thompson, Conn.: InterCultural Press, 1987.

"Focus: Multiculturalism in Education." *Education Digest* 57 (December 1991): 3–16.

Forbes, Jack D. *The Education of the Culturally Different: A Multi-Cultural Approach.* Berkeley: Far Laboratory for Educational Research and Development, 1968.

Fradd, Sandra H. *Foundations of Multicultural Education.* Gainesville: Department of Special Education, University of Florida; Washington, D.C.: U.S. Department of Education, Office of Educational Research and Improvement, Educational Resources Information Center, 1990.

Gibson, Margaret Alison. "Approaches to Multicultural Education in the United States: Some Concepts and Assumptions." *Anthropology and Education Quarterly* 15:1 (1984): 94–120.

Gold, Milton J., Carl A. Grant, and Harry N. Rivlin, eds. *In Praise of Diversity: A Resource Book for Multicultural Education*. Washington, D.C.: Teacher Corps, 1977.

Gollnick, Donna M. *Profile of the Multicultural/Bilingual Education Activities of Professional and Related Education Organizations*. Washington, D.C.: American Association of Colleges for Teacher Education, 1978.

Gollnick, Donna M., and Philip C. Chinn. *Multicultural Education in a Pluralistic Society*. 3d ed. Columbus, Ohio: Merrill Publishing Company, 1990.

————, eds. *Multiculturalism in Contemporary Education. Viewpoints in Teaching and Learning* 56:1. Bloomington: School of Education, Indiana University, 1980.

Gomez, Gloria. *An Introductory Guide to Bilingual-Bicultural/Multicultural Education: Beyond Tacos, Eggrolls and Grits*. Dubuque, Iowa: Kendall/Hunt Publishing Company, 1982.

Grant, Carl A., ed. *Multicultural Education: Commitments, Issues, and Applications*. Prepared by the Association for Supervision and Curriculum Development, Multicultural Education Commission. Washington, D.C.: Association for Supervision and Curriculum Development, 1977. This volume is one of several that emerged just as the popular understandings of both cultural pluralism and multiculturalism were changing in the 1970s. As a manifesto calling for necessary changes in the educational system, it rejects the notion that multicultural education should reify a "dominant school culture." Rather, Grant sees an awareness of cultural pluralism's benefits as the direct antecedent to implementing a truly multicultural educational system. Most of the short essays included in the volume follow this basic philosophy, and tend to be written by scholars of color exploring such issues as funding, racial justice, stereotypes, and sexism in education.

————. *Sifting and Winnowing: An Exploration of the Relationship between Multi-Cultural Education and CBTE* [Competency-Based Teacher Education]. Madison: Teacher Corps Associates, University of Wisconsin, 1975.

Grant, Carl A., and Christine E. Sleeter. *Turning on Learning: Five Approaches for Multicultural Teaching Plans for Race, Class, Gender, and Disability*. Columbus, Ohio: Merrill Publishing Company, 1989.

Grant, Gloria, ed. *In Praise of Diversity: Multicultural Classroom Applications*. Omaha: Teacher Corps, Center for Urban Education, University of Nebraska, 1977.

Hallman, Clemens L. *Implications of Psychological Research for Assessment and Instruction of the Culturally Different: Bilingual Multicultural Education Training Project for School Psychologists and Guidance Counselors*. Gainesville: University of Florida Press, 1983.

Hallman, Clemens L., Antonette Capaz, and David Capaz. *Value Orientations of Vietnamese Culture: Bilingual Multicultural Education Training Project for School Psychologists and Guidance Counselors*. Gainesville: University of Florida Press, 1983.

Heid, Camilla A., ed. *Multicultural Education: Knowledge and Perceptions*. Bloomington: Indiana University, Center for Urban and Multicultural Education; Washington, D.C.: U.S. Department of Education, Office of Educational Research and Improvement, Educational Resources Information Center, 1988.

Hernandez, Hilda. *Multicultural Education: A Teacher's Guide to Content and Process*. Columbus, Ohio: Merrill Publishing Company, 1989.

Hill, Patrick J. "Multi-Culturalism: The Crucial Philosophical and Organizational Issues." *Change* 23:4 (1991): 38–47.

Hymowitz, Kay S. "Self-Esteem and Multiculturalism in the Public Schools." *Dissent* 39:1 (1992): 23–29.

Johnson, Lauri, and Sally Smith. *Dealing with Diversity through Multicultural Fiction: Library-Classroom Partnerships*. Chicago: American Library Association, 1993.

Kalantzis, Mary, and Bill Cope. "Pluralism and Equitability: Multicultural Curriculum Strategies for Schools." *Curriculum and Teaching* 4:1 (1989): 3–20.

Kendall, Frances E. *Diversity in the Classroom: A Multicultural Approach to the Education of Young Children*. New York: Teachers College Press, 1983.

Kohl, Herbert. "The Politically Correct Bypass Multiculturalism and the Public Schools." *Social Policy* 22:1 (1991): 33–40.

Kruse, Ginny Moore, and Kathleen T. Horning, with Merri V. Lindgren. *Multicultural Literature for Children and Young Adults: A Selected Listing of Books, 1980-1990, by and about People of Color*. 3d ed. Madison: Wisconsin Department of Public Instruction, 1991.

Kwak, Kyunghwa. "Second Language Learning in a Multicultural Society: A Comparison between the Learning of a Dominant Language and a Heritage Language." Ph.D. diss., Queens University, 1992.

Lambert, Wallace E., and Donald M. Taylor. "Assimilation versus Multiculturalism: The Views of Urban Americans." *Sociological Forum* 3:1 (1988): 72–88.

Lawless, Ken. *Harvesting the Harvesters. Book 10: Cooling Down the Melting Pot: Bilingualism and Multiculturalism*. Potsdam, N.Y.: MENTOR, Potsdam College, 1986.

Levine, Arthur, and Jeannette Cureton. "The Quiet Revolution: Eleven Facts about Multiculturalism and the Curriculum." *Change* 23:4 (1991): 24–29. This easily accessible article lays out the basic issues at stake in the multiculturalism debates. It offers an excellent starting point for those interested in discovering how multiculturalism is impacting or will impact education at all levels of the educational system.

Levy, Berlowitz Ruth. "Interpreting in Multicultural Settings." In *Interpreting—Yesterday, Today and Tomorrow,* ed. David Bowen and Margareta Bowen. Binghamton: State University of New York Press, 1990. 117–21.

Linskie, Rosella, and Howard Rosenberg. *A Handbook for Multicultural Studies in Elementary Schools*. San Francisco: R & E Research Associates, 1978. This book is an elementary teacher's guide for devising exercises that will incorporate the experiences and knowledge of ethnic/racial students into everyday classroom life. It includes illustrations, examples, and detailed, clear instructions.

Lipsky, William E., ed. *Planning for Multicultural Education: A Workshop Report*. Los Angeles: Curriculum Inquiry Center, University of California, 1977.

Love, Roni Lerner. "Motivating Teachers: An Individualized Approach to Implementing a Multicultural Curriculum." Ph.D. diss., University of California, Irvine, 1977.

Lynch, James. *Education for Citizenship in a Multicultural Society*. London and New York: Cassell, 1992.

———. *The Multicultural Curriculum*. London: Batsford Academic and Educational, 1983.

———. *Multicultural Education in a Global Society*. London: Falmer Press, 1989.

———. *Multicultural Education: Principles and Practice*. London and Boston: Routledge and Kegan Paul, 1986.

MacGregor, Molly Murphy. *National Women's History Week: A Multi-Cultural Infusion Model*. Santa Rosa, Calif.: National Women's History Week Project, 1985.

Male, George A., et al. "Policy Issues in the Education of Minorities: A Worldwide View." *Education and Urban Society* 18:4 (1986): 395–499. This special issue of *Education and Urban Society* is a collection of essays on the education of minorities in different countries around the world. There are no articles that deal exclusively with the United States, but the separate articles on Canada, the United Kingdom, and Australia are extremely useful for comparative purposes.

Manna, Anthony L., and Carolyn S. Brodie, eds. *Many Faces, Many Voices: Multicultural Literary Experiences for Youth: The Virginia Hamilton Conference*. Fort Atkinson, Wis.: Highsmith Press, 1992.

McCarthy, Cameron. "Multicultural Approaches to Racial Inequality in the United States." *Curriculum and Teaching* 5:1–2 (1990): 25–35.

————. "Multicultural Education, Minority Identities, Textbooks, and the Challenge of Curriculum Reform." *Journal of Education* 172:2 (1990): 118–29.

McCarthy, Cameron, and Warren Crichlow. *Race, Identity, and Representation in Education.* New York: Routledge, 1993.

McDiarmid, G. Williamson. *What to Do about Difference? A Study of Multicultural Education for Teacher Trainees in the Los Angeles Unified School District.* East Lansing, Mich.: National Center for Research on Teacher Education; Washington, D.C.: U.S. Department of Education, Office of Educational Research and Improvement, Educational Resources Information Center, 1990.

McKenna, Francis R. "The Myth of Multiculturalism and the Reality of the American Indian in Contemporary America." *Journal of American Indian Education* 21:1 (1981): 1–9.

Michigan Department of Education. *Position Statement on Multicultural Education.* Lansing: Michigan Department of Education, 1979.

Milton Van Brunt, Vida L., ed. *Black Students in a Multicultural Setting: Implications for Teacher Effectiveness.* Madison: Teacher Corps Associates, University of Wisconsin-Madison, 1979.

Modgil, Sohan, et al., eds. *Multicultural Education: The Interminable Debate.* London and Philadelphia: Falmer Press, 1986.

Montero, Martha, ed. *Bilingual Education Teacher Handbook: Language Issues in Multicultural Settings.* Cambridge, Mass.: Evaluation, Dissemination and Assessment Center for Bilingual Education, 1982.

————. *Bilingual Education Teacher Handbook: Strategies for the Design of Multicultural Curriculum.* Cambridge, Mass.: National Assessment and Dissemination Center, 1979.

Multicultural Education Center, College of Education, University of Arizona. *The Cultural Literacy Laboratory: A New Dimension in Multicultural Teacher Education.* Tucson: University of Arizona Press, 1973.

Multicultural Education: The Interdisciplinary Approach: A Summary of Conference Proceedings, April 1–3, 1976, San Diego, April 29–May 1, 1976, Oakland. Sacramento: California State Department of Education, 1977.

Multicultural Education Resource Guide: African Americans, Asian Americans, Hispanic Americans, and Native Americans. Lansing: Michigan State Board of Education, 1990.

Multicultural Teacher Education. Washington, D.C.: Commission on Multicultural Education, American Association of Colleges for Teacher Education, 1980.

National Study of School Evaluation, Multicultural/Multiracial Project. *Evaluation Guidelines for Multicultural/Multiracial Education, Designed Primarily for Secondary Schools.* Arlington, Va.: National Study of School Evaluation, 1973.

Nichols, Margaret S. *Multicultural Educational Materials in the Areas of Black, Mexican-American, American Indian, and Oriental Cultures: Supplement, November 1970, to Bibliography of a Demonstration Collection Assembled by Margaret S. Nichols for All Ages and Reading Abilities.* Stanford, Calif.: Multicultural Collection, Stanford University, 1970.

————. *Multicultural Materials: A Selective Bibliography of Adult Materials concerning Human Relations and the History, Culture, and Current Social Issues of Black, Chicano, Asian American, and Native American Peoples.* Rev. expanded ed. Stanford, Calif.: Multicultural Resources, 1974.

————. *Preliminary Edition Bibliography of Multicultural Materials for Educators: A Selective Listing of Materials concerning the History, Culture, and Current Problems of Racial and Ethnic Minorities in California.* Sacramento: California State Department of Education, 1973.

Nichols, Margaret S., and Margaret N. O'Neill. *Multicultural Bibliography for Preschool through Second Grade: In the Areas of Black, Spanish-Speaking, Asian American, and Native American Cultures.* Stanford, Calif.: Multicultural Resources, 1972.

Nieto, Sonia. *Affirming Diversity: The Sociopolitical Context of Multicultural Education.* New York and London: Longman, 1992. Nieto provides a compelling argument for implementing multicultural education at the primary and secondary school levels. Part of her argument rests on case studies of individual students that demonstrate the importance of well-informed and well-trained *teachers* in making multicultural education work. Nieto also includes a superb bibliography on multicultural education.

Pasternak, Michael G. *Helping Kids Learn Multi-Cultural Concepts: A Handbook of Strategies.* Champaign, Ill.: Research Press, 1979.

Pedersen, Paul. *A Handbook for Developing Multicultural Awareness.* Alexandria, Va.: American Association for Counseling and Development, 1988.

Perry, Theresa, and James W. Fraser, eds. *Freedom's Plow: Teaching in the Multicultural Classroom.* New York: Routledge, 1993.

Peters, Abe, ed. *Building the Bridges: Report of the National Conference on Multicultural Education, November 11–14, 1981, Winnipeg, Manitoba.* Regina, Sask.: L. A. Weigl Educational Associates, 1982.

Pizzillo, Joseph J., Jr. *Intercultural Studies: Schooling in Diversity.* Dubuque, Iowa: Kendall/Hunt Publishing Company, 1983.

Pusch, Margaret D., ed. *Multicultural Education: A Cross-Cultural Training Approach.* La Grange Park, Ill.: Intercultural Network, 1979.

Ramsey, Patricia G. *Teaching and Learning in a Diverse World: Multicultural Education for Young Children.* New York: Teachers College, Columbia University, 1987.

Ramsey, Patricia G., Edwina Battle Vold, and Leslie R. Williams. *Multicultural Education: A Source Book.* New York and London: Garland Publishing, 1989.

Redburn, Dennis B., and Charles Payne, eds. *Multicultural Education Clinic Papers: Proceedings of the Association of Teacher Educators Spring Clinic, 1975.* ATE National Multicultural Education Clinic, Ball State University, 1975. Muncie, Ind.: Ball State University, 1976.

Reyhner, Jon, ed. *Teaching the Indian Child: A Bilingual/Multicultural Approach.* 2d ed. Billings: Eastern Montana College, 1988.

Richardson, Richard C., and Louis W. Bender. *Fostering Minority Access and Achievement in Higher Education: The Role of Urban Community Colleges and Universities.* San Francisco: Jossey-Bass Publishers, 1987.

Rizvi, Fazal. *Ethnicity, Class and Multicultural Education.* Victoria, B.C.: Deakin University, 1986.

Rodriguez, Fred. *Education in a Multicultural Society.* Washington, D.C.: University Press of America, 1983. Rodriguez's text compares the different models upon which socialization between different racial and ethnic groups has been based. Its primary project is to map out ways to get American children (and by extension, American adults) to *value* cultural pluralism, not simply tolerate it. This book is especially significant inasmuch as it provides relatively clear, concise definitions of *what* "multicultural education" is (and is not) before it launches into its history of interethnic/racial relations.

———. *Mainstreaming a Multicultural Concept into Teacher Education: Guidelines for Teacher Trainers.* Saratoga, Calif.: R&E Publishers, 1983.

Simonson, Rick, and Scott Walker, eds. *Multi-Cultural Literacy.* Saint Paul, Minn.: Graywolf Press, 1988.

Sims, William E., and Bernice Bass de Martinez, eds. *Perspectives in Multicultural Education.* Washington, D.C.: University Press of America, 1981.

Sleeter, Christine E. *Empowerment through Multicultural Education.* Albany: State University of New York Press, 1991.

———. *Keepers of the American Dream: A Study of Staff Development and Multicultural Education.* London and Washington, D.C.: Falmer Press, 1992.

Sleeter, Christine E., and Carl A. Grant. *Making Choices for Multicultural Education: Five Approaches to Race, Class, and Gender.* Columbus, Ohio: Merrill Publishing Company, 1988.

Smoler, Fredric Paul. "What Should We Teach Our Children about American History?" *American Heritage* 43 (February–March 1992): 7, 45–52.

Trueba, Henry T., and Carol Barnett-Mizrahi. *Bilingual Multicultural Education.* Rowley, Mass.: Newbury House Publishers, 1979.

———. *Bilingual Multicultural Education and the Professional: From Theory to Practice.* Rowley, Mass.: Newbury House Publishers, 1979.

Verma, Gajendra K., "Multiculturalism and Education: Prelude to Practice." In Verma and Bagley, 57–77.

Verma, Gajendra K., and Christopher Bagley, eds. *Race Relations and Cultural Differences: Educational and Interpersonal Perspectives.* New York: St. Martin's Press, 1984.

Vold, Edwina Battle, ed. *Multicultural Education in Early Childhood Classrooms.* Washington, D.C.: NEA Professional Library, 1992.

Williams, Byron, et al. *Manual for Evaluating Content of Classroom Instructional Materials for Bilingual-Multicultural Education.* San Diego: Institute for Cultural Pluralism, School of Education, San Diego State University, 1977.

Wurzel, Jaime S., ed. *Toward Multiculturalism: A Reader in Multicultural Education.* Yarmouth, Maine: Intercultural Press, 1988.

C. In Higher Education

Auletta, Gale S., and Terry Jones, eds. "The Inclusive University: Multicultural Perspectives in Higher Education." *American Behavioral Scientist* 34 (1990).

Berman, Paul, ed. *Debating P.C.: The Controversy over Political Correctness on College Campuses.* New York: Laurel, 1992.

"A *Black Scholar* Special: Student Strikes: 1968–69." *Black Scholar* 1:3–4 (1970): 65–75.

Bunzel, John H. *Race Relations on Campus: Stanford Students Speak.* Stanford, Calif.: The Portable Stanford, 1992.

Butler, Johnnella, and Betty Schmitz. "Ethnic Studies, Women's Studies, and Multiculturalism." *Change* 24:3 (1991): 36–41.

Cahn, Steven M., ed. *Affirmative Action and the University: A Philosophical Inquiry.* Philadelphia: Temple University Press, 1993. This edition of scholarly papers on affirmative action does an excellent job of demarcating the most important philosophical issues surrounding university hiring and manages to cover many of the same issues pertinent to the multiculturalism debates.

Cotera, Martha, comp.; Nella Cunningham, ed. *Multicultural Women's Sourcebook: Materials Guide for Use in Women's Studies and Bilingual/Multicultural Programs.* Austin, Tex.: Women's Educational Equity Act Program, U.S. Department of Education, 1982.

"Cracking the Cultural Consensus." *Society* 29 (November–December 1991): 5–44.

Davis, Lenwood G. *A Bibliographical Guide to Black Studies Programs in the United States: An Annotated Bibliography.* Westport, Conn.: Greenwood Press, 1985.

Duster, Troy. "They're Taking Over!" *Mother Jones* 16 (September–October 1991): 30–33.

Erickson, Peter. "Rather Than Reject a Common Culture, Multiculturalism Advocates a More Complicated Route by Which to Achieve It." *Chronicle of Higher Education* 37:41 (1991): B1–B3.

Gollnick, Donna M., Frank H. Klassen, and Joost Yff. *Multicultural Education and Ethnic Studies in the United States: An Analysis and Annotated Bibliography of Selected ERIC Documents.* Washington, D.C.: American Association of Colleges for Teacher Education, 1976.

Harris, Robert L. *Three Essays: Black Studies in the United States.* New York: Ford Foundation, 1990.

Hassenger, Robert. "True Multiculturalism." *Commonweal* 119 (10 April 1992): 10–11.

Hawkins, John N. *Asian American Studies and Asian Studies: Interrelationships.* Los Angeles: Asian Pacific American Research Seminars, Asian American Studies Center, UCLA, 1980.

Hwang, David Henry. "Evolving a Multicultural Tradition." *MELUS* 16:3 (1989): 16–19.

Kelley, Don Philip. "Course of Study Outline in Multi-Cultural Studies." Ph.D diss., University of California, Irvine, 1976.

Kolenda, Konstatin. "E Pluribus Unum." *Humanist* 51 (September–October 1991): 40ff.

Loo, Chalsa M., and Garry Rolison. "Alienation of Ethnic Minority Students at a Predominantly White University." *Journal of Higher Education* 57:1 (1986): 58–77.

Nakanishi, Don T. *Asian American Studies and the Changing University.* Berkeley: National Association for Asian and Pacific American Education, 1980.

Nordquist, Joan, ed. *The Multicultural Education Debate in the University: A Bibliography: A Bibliographic Series.* Santa Cruz, Calif.: Reference and Research Services, 1992.

Olivas, Michael A. "Financial Aid Packaging Policies: Access and Ideology." *Journal of Higher Education* 56:4 (1985): 462–75.

Reflections on Political Correctness: A Collection of Student Papers on Multiculturalism, Speech Codes and "The Canon." Santa Cruz: University of California, Santa Cruz, 1992.

Richardson, Richard C., Jr., and Elizabeth Fisk Skinner. *Achieving Quality and Diversity: Universities in a Multicultural Society.* New York: American Council on Education: Macmillan; Toronto: Collier Macmillan Canada; New York: Maxwell Macmillan International, 1991.

Robbins, Bruce. "Othering the Academy: Professionalism and Multiculturalism." *Social Research* 58:2 (1991): 355–72.

Schoem, David, et al. *Multicultural Teaching in the University.* New York: Praeger, 1993. This anthology is perhaps the most cogent offering that attempts to do what the many early texts on multiculturalism in primary education have already accomplished: address the disparate areas in the contemporary American university where different forms of multiculturalism are needed, and *create strategies* for implementing them, as both policies and pedagogies. Of particular interest is David Schoem's essay on training teaching assistants to understand multiculturalism, as well as the definition of multiculturalism used here, which is not restricted to ethnicity and race; it also includes sexuality, which is a relatively new and welcome addition to the dialogue on making the university multicultural.

Smith, M. G. "Ethnicity and Ethnic Groups in America: The View from Harvard." *Ethnic and Racial Studies* 5:1 (1982): 1–22.

Stanford University Committee on Minority Issues. *Building a Multiracial, Multicultural University Community: Final Report of the University Committee on Minority Issues.* Stanford, Calif.: Stanford University, 1989.

Thomas, Gail E. *Black Students in Higher Education: Conditions and Experiences in the 1970s.* Contributions to the Study of Education, no. 1. Westport, Conn.: Greenwood Press, 1981. Thomas's book is intended both to review the history of the increased access for Black students in higher education and to assess the experiences, programs, and problems that either contributed to, continued, or eroded the barriers to college in the 1970s. This volume is similar to the revised California Master Plan for education, insofar as it determines which methods of qualifying, admitting, and retaining Black students are destined for success or failure. A wide range of educational scholars contributed to this volume, including Charles V. Willie and Ada M. Fisher.

UCLA Chicano Studies Center. *Chicano Studies Center, Growth and Development, 1969 to 1975: A Summary Statement.* Los Angeles: The Center, 1975.

Washburn, David E. *Ethnic Studies: Bilingual/Bicultural Education and Multicultural Teacher Education in the United States: A Directory of Higher Education Programs and Personnel.* Miami: Inquiry International, 1979.

What It Is: Multicultural Dorm Yearbook, 1975–1976, Merrill College, University of California. Santa Cruz, Calif.: n.p., 1976.

Williams, Patricia J. "Blockbusting the Canon." *Ms.* 2:22 (September–October 1991): 59–63.

Yarbrough, Larry. "Three Questions for the Multiculturalism Debate." *Change* 24:3 (1991): 64–69.

D. In the Corporate World

Alster, Judith, Theresa Brothers, and Holly Gallo, eds. *In Diversity Is Strength: Capitalizing on the New Work Force.* New York: Conference Board, 1992.

Betances, Samuel. "Diversity: Multiculturalism in Education and Business." *Vocational Educational Journal* 66:8 (1991): 22–23.

Casse, Pierre. *Training for the Multicultural Manager: A Practical and Cross-Cultural Approach to the Management of People.* Photographs by M. L. Bussaty. Washington, D.C.: Society for Intercultural Education, Training, and Research, 1982.

Coleman, Troy. "Managing Diversity at Work: The New American Dilemma." *Public Management* 72:9 (1990): 2–4.

Copeland, Lennie. "Learning to Manage a Multicultural Workforce." *Western City* 65 (1989).

Crabtree, Kristen M., and Ann Morrison. *A Practical Guide to Diversity Literature.* La Jolla, Calif.: Center for Creative Leadership, 1992.

Cross, Elsie. "Issues of Diversity." In *Sunrise Seminars,* vol. 2, ed. D. Vails-Weber and J. Potts. National Training Laboratories Institute for Behavioral Sciences, 1991.

"Cultural Diversity." *Working Woman* 16 (January 1991): 45ff.

Elashmawi, Farid, and Philip R. Harris. *Multicultural Management: New Skills for Global Success.* Houston: Gulf Publications, 1993.

Fine, Marlene Gail. "Cultural Diversity in the Workplace." *Public Personnel Management* 19:3 (1990): 305–19.

Friesen, John W. *When Cultures Clash: Case Studies in Multiculturalism.* Calgary, Alta.: Detselig Enterprises, 1985.

Gamst, Frederick. "Industrial Ethnological Perspectives on the Development and Characteristics of the Study of Organizational Cultures." *Studies in Third World Societies* 42 (1990).

Henderson, George. *Cultural Diversity in the Workplace: Issues and Strategies.* Westport, Conn.: Quorum Books, 1994.

Jackson, Susan E., et al., eds. *Diversity in the Workplace: Human Resources Initiatives.* Professional Practice Series. New York: Guilford Press, 1992.

James, Muriel. *The Better Boss in Multicultural Organizations: Guide to Success Using Transactional Analysis.* Walnut Creek, Calif.: Marshall Publishing, 1991.

Jamieson, David. *Managing Workforce 2000: Gaining the Diversity Advantage.* San Francisco: Jossey-Bass Publishers, 1991.

Johnson, William B., and Arnold H. Packer. *Workforce 2000: Work and Workers for the 21st Century.* Indianapolis: Hudson Institute, 1987.

Kauffman, L. A. "The Diversity Game." *Village Voice* (31 August 1993): 29–33.

Kessler, Lorence L. *Managing Diversity in an Equal Opportunity Workplace: A Primer for Today's Manager.* Washington, D.C.: National Foundation for the Study of Employment Policy, 1990.

Kliment, Stephen A. "Managing Diversity." *Architectural Record* 179 (February 1991): 11.

Leo, John. "The 'Us' versus 'Them' Industry." *U.S. News & World Report* 111 (16 December 1991): 42.

Mabry, Marcus. "Past Tokenism." *Newsweek* 115 (14 May 1990): 37ff.

———. "Pin a Label on a Manager—and Watch What Happens." *Newsweek* 115 (14 May 1990): 43.

March, Robert M. *Working for a Japanese Company: Managing Relationships in a Multicultural Organization.* Tokyo and New York: Kodansha International, 1992.

Nelton, Sharon. "A Tougher Challenge for Family Firms." *Nation's Business* 79 (June 1991): 65.

Reich, Robert. *The Work of Nations.* New York: Vintage Books, 1992.

Samuelson, Robert. "The Multicultural Corporation." *Washington Post* 112 (23 August 1989): A27.

Sowell, Thomas. "Cultural Diversity: A World View." *American Enterprise* 2:3 (1991): 44–55.

———. *Race and Economics.* New York: David McKay, 1975.

Strategic Plan for Human Resources Management. Washington, D.C.: U.S. Department of the Interior, ca. 1991.

Thiederman, Sondra B. *Bridging Cultural Barriers for Corporate Success: How to Manage the Multicultural Work Force.* Lexington, Mass.: Lexington Books, 1991.

———. *Profiting in America's Multicultural Marketplace: How to Do Business across Cultural Lines.* New York: Lexington Books; Toronto: Maxwell Macmillan Canada; New York: Maxwell Macmillan International, 1991.

Thomas, R. Roosevelt, Jr. *Beyond Race and Gender: Unleashing the Power of Your Total Work Force by Managing Diversity.* New York: American Management Association, 1991.

———. "From Affirmative Action to Affirming Diversity." *Harvard Business Review* (March–April 1990): 107–17.

Walton, Sally J. *Cultural Diversity in the Workplace.* Business Skills Express Series. Burr Ridge, Ill.: Irwin Professional Publications/Mirror Press, 1994.

White, J. P. "Diversity's Champion." *Los Angeles Times Magazine* 111 (9 August 1992): 14ff.

E. In the Humanities

Anderson, James M. "The Development and Conceptualization of Ethnic Studies in Michigan." *Ethnic Forum* 1:2 (1981): 23–28.

Barnes, A. E. "Blaspheming like Brute Beasts: Multiculturalism from an Historical Perspective." *Contention: Debates in Society, Culture and Science* 1:3 (1992): 37–58. Barnes argues that multiculturalism as we know it today, contrary to the views of Diane Ravitch and John Searle, was the initial condition of the "West" and became recessive only when northern Europe asserted its own cultural superiority to other regions on the basis of race. Cultural unity was historically an effect of a Northern supremacist project. Minority scholars, he concludes, should avoid the "romanticism" that infects these European nationalist projects.

Bernal, Martin. *Black Athena: The Afroasiatic Roots of Western Civilization.* New Brunswick, N.J.: Rutgers University Press, 1987. Bernal's most famous work, like Henry Louis Gates's below, is not a guidebook to multiculturalism itself, but it is perhaps the most widely discussed example of the sort of scholarly revisionism that has fueled antimulticulturalist critics (albeit some of the best scholarship), inasmuch as Bernal calls rather passively accepted accounts of ancient history into serious question with elaborately detailed research.

Braided Lives: An Anthology of Multicultural American Writing. St. Paul, Minn.: Minnesota Humanities Commission: Minnesota Council of Teachers of English, 1991.

Buenker, John D., and Lorman A. Ratner, eds. *Multiculturalism in the United States: A Comparative Guide to Acculturation and Ethnicity.* Westport, Conn.: Greenwood Press, 1992. Buenker and Ratner have collected essays discussing the histories of and processes through which American ethnic/racial groups have (or haven't) become assimilated into the American mainstream. Strangely enough, the editors omit several important racial/ethnic groups (which the editors admit is problematic). All of the essays, however, are written by scholars from the groups in question. The collection's purpose is to map out those cultural spaces that are particular groups' exclusive property and, conversely, where those same groups have acquiesced to the mainstream's demand that they sacrifice their ethnicity.

Burke, Ronald K., ed. *American Public Discourse: A Multicultural Perspective.* Lanham, Md.: University Press of America, 1992.

Cadzow, John. "The Growth of Ethnic Studies: The Kent State University Experience." *Ethnic Forum* 1:1 (1980): 25–27.

Carby, Hazel V. *Multicultural Fictions.* Birmingham: Centre for Contemporary Cultural Studies, University of Birmingham, 1979.

Chicago Cultural Studies Group. "Critical Multiculturalism." *Critical Inquiry* 18:3 (1992): 530–55.

Ch'maj, Betty E. M., ed. *Multicultural America: A Resource Book for Teachers of Humanities and American Studies: Syllabi, Essays, Projects, Bibliography.* Lanham, Md.: University Press of America, 1993.

Daniels, Lee A. "Diversity, Correctness, and Campus Life: A Closer Look." *Change* 23:5 (1991): 16–20.

Dasenbrock, Reed Way. "Intelligibility and Meaningfulness in Multicultural Literature in English." *PMLA* 102:1 (1987): 10–19.

Dennis, John. *O, Promised Land: A Multi-Cultural Reader.* Rowley, Mass.: Newbury House, 1982.

Dent, Gina, ed. *Black Popular Culture.* Seattle: Bay Press, 1992. Some articles compare and contrast Black popular culture with multiculturalism.

Devy, Ganesh N. "The Multicultural Context of Indian Literature in English." In *Creativity in the New Literatures in English: Cross/Cultures,* ed. Geoffrey V. Davis and Jelinek H. Maes. Amsterdam: Rodopi, 1990. 345–53.

DuBois, Ellen Carol, and Vicki L. Ruiz, eds. *Unequal Sisters: A Multicultural Reader in U.S. Women's History.* New York: Routledge, 1990.

Durham, Carolyn A. *The Contexture of Feminism: Marie Cardinal and Multicultural Literacy.* Urbana: University of Illinois Press, 1992.

Gates, Henry Louis, Jr. *Loose Canons: Notes on the Culture Wars.* Oxford: Oxford University Press, 1992.

———. *The Signifying Monkey: A Theory of African-American Literary Criticism.* New York and Oxford: Oxford University Press, 1988. Although Gates's magnum opus of African-American literary theory does not necessarily deal with multiculturalism per se, it operates under a related premise: we must reckon the history of a people through the internal logic of their culture in order to understand their achievements. This book has been elevated in the public mind as a symbol of what multiculturalism is doing or should do.

Geyer, Michael. "Multiculturalism and the Politics of General Education." *Critical Inquiry* 19: (1993): 499–533.

Glazer, Nathan. "In Defense of Multiculturalism." *New Republic* 205 (2 September 1991): 18ff.

Gunew, Sneja. "Postmodern Tensions: Reading for (Multi)Cultural Difference." *Meanjin* 49:1 (1990): 21–33.

Hull, Gloria T., Patricia Bell Scott, and Barbara Smith, eds. *All the Women Are White, All the Blacks Are Men, but Some of Us Are Brave: Black Women's Studies.* Old Westbury, N.Y.: Feminist Press, 1982.

Hunter, James Davison. *Culture Wars: The Struggle to Define America.* New York: Basic Books, 1991.

Kafka, Phillipa. "A Multicultural Introduction to Literature." In *Practicing Theory in Introductory College Literature Courses,* ed. David B. Downing. Urbana, Ill.: National Council of Teachers of English, 1991. 179–86.

———. "Another Round of Canon Fire: Feminist and Multi-Ethnic Theory in the American Literature Survey." *MELUS* 16:2 (1989): 31–49.

Lippert, Paul. "The Semantics of Multiculturalism." *ETC.: A Review of General Semantics* 48 (1991–92): 363–74.

Martin, Reginald. "An Interview with Ishmael Reed." *Review of Contemporary Fiction* 4:2 (1984): 176–87.

Miller, Wayne Charles. "Toward a New Literary History of the United States." *MELUS* 11:1 (1984): 5–25.

Moraga, Cherríe, and Gloria Anzaldúa, eds. *This Bridge Called My Back: Writings by Radical Women of Color*. Watertown, Mass.: Persephone Press, 1981.

Morton, Carlos. "Celebrating 500 Years of Mestizaje." *MELUS* 16:3 (1989): 20–22.

Nandan, Satendra, ed. ACLALS *Triennial Conference (5th: 1981: University of the South Pacific) Language and Literature in Multicultural Contexts*. Suva, Fiji: University of the South Pacific; Mysore, India: Association for Commonwealth Language and Literature Studies, 1983.

Pap, Michael. "NESA and the Status of Ethnic Studies in America." *Ethnic Forum* 1:1 (1980): 25–27.

Payne, James Robert. *Multicultural Autobiography: American Lives*. Knoxville: University of Tennessee Press, 1992.

Redding, Jay Saunders. "The Negro in American History: As Scholar, as Subject." In *The Past before Us: Contemporary Historical Writing in the United States*, ed. Michael Kammen. Ithaca, N.Y.: Cornell University Press, 1980. 292–307.

Rico, Barbara Roche, and Sandra Mano. *American Mosaic: Multicultural Readings in Context*. Boston: Houghton Mifflin, 1991.

Rose, Marilyn Gaddis. "The Multinational Curriculum: (Why We Need One and) What to Translate for It." In *New Literary Continents: Selected Papers of the Fifth NDEA Seminar on Foreign Area Studies Sponsored by the School of International Affairs, Columbia University, and Council on National Literatures*, ed. Anne Paolucci. Whitestone, N.Y.: Griffon House, 1984. 49–55.

San Juan, E., Jr. "Multiculturalism vs. Hegemony: Ethnic Studies, Asian Americans, and U.S. Racial Politics." *Massachusetts Review: A Quarterly of Literature, the Arts and Public Affairs* 32:3 (1991): 467–78.

Schmidt, Peter. "Introduction to Williams' 'Letter to an Australian Editor' (1946): Williams' Manifesto for Multiculturalism." *William Carlos Williams Review* 17:2 (1991): 4–12.

Sowell, Thomas. "A World View of Cultural Diversity." *Society* 29 (November–December 1991): 37–44.

———. "What 'Cultural Diversity' Means." *Wilson Quarterly* 16 (spring 1992): 16.

Taylor, Charles. *Multiculturalism and "The Politics of Recognition": An Essay*. Princeton, N.J.: Princeton University Press, 1992.

———, ed. *Guide to Multicultural Resources*. Madison, Wis.: Praxis Publications, 1989.

West, Cornel. *Beyond Eurocentrism and Multiculturalism*. Monroe, Maine: Common Courage Press, 1993.

Wolf, Bryan. "Firing the Canon: Introduction." *American Literary History* 3:4 (1991): 707–52.

Yarmolinsky, Adam. "Loose Canons: Multiculturalism and Humanities." *Change* 24:3 (1991): 6–9.

F. In Society and Public Policy

Abilock, Debbie. *A Database of Resources for Developing Multicultural Library Collections. HyperCard Conversion by Ray Olszewski*. California Bay Area Independent School Libraries, 1992.

Aguero, Kathleen, ed. *Daily Fare: Essays from the Multicultural Experience*. Athens: University of Georgia Press, 1993.

Allan, Lyle. "A Selective Annotated Bibliography of Multiculturalism." *Social Alternatives* 3:3 (1983): 65–72. This bibliography concerns itself primarily with definitions and policies and practices of multiculturalism in Australia, with a few resources from New Zealand and Canada. Only the last section of the bibliography is devoted to overseas materials, including the United States. All of these resources, however, including the comparative insight that studies of multiculturalism in Canada and New Zealand contain, may prove useful in studies of multiculturalism as a global concept.

Appleton, Nicholas. *Multiculturalism and the Courts.* Bilingual Education Paper Series vol. 2, no. 4. Los Angeles: National Dissemination and Assessment Center, 1978.

Auster, Lawrence. *The Path to National Suicide: An Essay on Immigration and Multiculturalism.* Monterey, Va.: American Immigration Control Foundation, 1990.

Barkan, Elliott R. "Haven, Heaven, and Hell: America and Its Ethnic Minorities, 1945–1980." *Journal of American Ethnic History* 2:2 (1983): 83–92.

Bibliography on Multicultural Drug Abuse Prevention Issues. Rockville, Md.: U.S. Department of Health and Human Services, Public Health Service, Alcohol, Drug Abuse, and Mental Health Administration; National Institute on Drug Abuse, Division of Prevention and Treatment Development, Prevention Branch, 1981.

Bozeman, Adda Bruemmer. *The Future of Law in a Multicultural World.* Princeton, N.J.: Princeton University Press, 1971.

Braham, Peter, Ali Rattansi, and Richard Skellington, eds. *Racism and Antiracism: Inequalities, Opportunities and Policies.* London: Sage Publications, 1992.

Brooks, Roy L. *Rethinking the American Race Problem.* Berkeley and Los Angeles: University of California Press, 1990.

California Department of Mental Health, Citizens Advisory Council. *Multi-Cultural Issues in Mental Health Services: Strategies Towards Equity: Report.* Sacramento: State of California, Health and Welfare Agency, Department of Mental Health, Citizens Advisory Council, 1979.

California Ethnic Services Task Force. *Multicultural/Multilingual Resources: A Vendor Directory.* Inglewood, Calif.: California Ethnic Services Task Force, 1979.

California Legislature Joint Committee for Review of the Master Plan for Higher Education. *California Faces . . . California's Future: Education for Citizenship in a Multicultural Democracy.* M. Brian Murphy et al., consultants. Sacramento: California Legislature, 1988. This report is arguably the most thorough attempt to enact a policy of multicultural education in the United States, insofar as it actually includes wording for possible legislative bills (some of which have been proposed and passed). But its most intriguing features are a detailed and devastating analysis of California's economy, the status of the state's higher educational system, and current race relations (as of 1989), and a forceful, compelling argument that multiculturalism in education is both inevitable and desperately needed. It also fascinatingly documents what multiculturalism meant immediately before it became a highly controversial term.

Center for Policy Development. *Adrift in a Sea of Change: California's Public Libraries Struggle to Meet the Information Needs of Multicultural Communities.* Sacramento: Distributed by California State Library Foundation, 1990.

Clausen, Edwin G., and Jack Bermingham, eds. *Pluralism, Racism, and Public Policy: The Search for Equality.* Boston: G. K. Hall and Company, 1981. Clausen and Bermingham provide an overview of pluralism, circa 1980. The book is divided into three sections: the first reviews forms of inequality in America and how these forms have affected the United States' relations with other nations; the second offers suggestions for promoting pluralism in the schools; the third is devoted to sharp criticisms of pluralism and other purportedly antiracist agendas (especially those promoted by mainstream American liberalism). Some prominent authors in the volume are Douglas W. Lee, Maulana Ron Karenga, and Sucheng Chan.

Cohen, Neil A., ed. *Child Welfare: A Multicultural Focus.* Boston: Allyn and Bacon, 1992.

Community Education and Multiculturalism: Immigrant/Refugee Needs and Cultural Awareness. Washington, D.C.: U.S. Conference of Mayors, 1982.

Cox, David R. *Welfare Practice in a Multicultural Society.* Englewood Cliffs, N.J.: Prentice Hall, 1989.

Dana, Richard Henry. *Multicultural Assessment Perspectives for Professional Psychology.* Boston: Allyn and Bacon, 1993.

Dillard, John M. *Multicultural Counseling: Toward Ethnic and Cultural Relevance in Human Encounters.* Chicago: Nelson-Hall, 1983.

Eggington, Everett. "Ethnic Identification and Perception of Racial Harmony." *Urban Review* 12:3 (1980): 149–61.

Espiritu, Yen Le. *Asian American Panethnicity: Bridging Institutions and Identities.* Philadelphia: Temple University Press, 1992.

Feuer, Lewis Samuel. "From Pluralism to Multiculturalism." *Society* 29 (November–December 1991): 19–22.

Fishman, Joshua A. "Toward Multilingualism as an International Desideratum in Government." *Annual Review of Applied Linguistics* 6 (1985): 2–9.

Frideres, James S. *Multiculturalism and Intergroup Relations.* Contributions in Sociology no. 75. New York: Greenwood Press, 1989.

Furness, Anne-Marie. "Development of Local Services and Community Action on Behalf of Multiculturalism." *Social Work Papers* 17 (1983): 15–25.

Glazer, Nathan, and Daniel Moynihan, eds. *Ethnicity: Theory and Experience.* Cambridge: Harvard University Press, 1975.

Gollnich, Donna M., assistant project director, Frank H. Klassen, project director. *State Legislation, Provisions and Practices Related to Multicultural Education.* Washington, D.C.: Accreditation Standards for Multicultural Teacher Education Project, American Association of Colleges for Teacher Education, 1978.

Gordon, Milton M., ed. *America as a Multicultural Society. Annals of the American Academy of Political and Social Science* 454. Philadelphia: American Academy of Political and Social Science, 1981.

———. *Assimilation in American Life: The Role of Race, Religion, and National Origins.* New York: Oxford University Press, 1964.

Haddock, Mable, and Chiquita Mullins Lee. "Whose Multiculturalism? PBS, the Public, and Privilege." *Afterimage* 21:1 (1993): 17–20.

Horowitz, Tamara. "The Positive Legacy of Positivism." *Critical Quarterly* 33:1 (1991): 88–92.

Hurtado, Aída, et al. *Redefining California: Latino Social Engagement in a Multicultural Society.* Los Angeles: Chicano Studies Research Center, University of California, Los Angeles, 1992.

Jackson, Bailey W., and Evangelina Holvino. *Multicultural Organization Development.* Ann Arbor: University of Michigan Press, 1988.

Katz, Judith H. *Facing the Challenge of Diversity and Multiculturalism.* PCMA working paper, no. 13. Ann Arbor: Center for Research on Social Organization, University of Michigan, 1988.

Kukathas, Chandran. "Are There Any Cultural Rights?" *Political Theory* 20:1 (1992): 105–39.

Lambert, Wallace E. *Coping with Cultural and Racial Diversity in Urban America.* New York: Praeger, 1990.

Lenz, Gynter. *Crisis of Modernity: Recent Critical Theories of Culture and Society in the United States and West Germany.* Boulder, Colo.: Westview Press, 1986.

Lerda, Valeria Gennaro. *From "Melting Pot" to Multiculturalism: The Evolution of Ethnic Relations in the United States and Canada.* Biblioteca di cultura (Bulzoni Editore) 418. Rome: Bulzoni Editore, 1990.

Locke, Don C. *Increasing Multicultural Understanding: A Comprehensive Model.* Multicultural Aspects of Counseling Series. Newbury Park, Calif.: Sage Publications, 1992. Locke's book is aimed primarily at counselors and educators. It summarizes the common cultural experiences of most of the major American ethnic and/or racial groups in order for these professionals to respond sensitively to the concerns of their patients and students. Locke manages to carefully cover a smart array of groups and their historical experiences and concerns. Additionally, he wisely and continuously places caveats in his text to remind the reader that his models of understanding are not meant to cover all individuals in each group.

Lovrich, Nicholas P., Jr. "Continuity and Change in American Ethnic Politics." *Social Science Journal* 18:1 (1981): 107–13.

Magnarella, Paul J. "Justice in a Culturally Pluralistic Society: The Cultural Defense on Trial." *Journal of Ethnic Studies* 19:3 (1990): 65–84.

Messolonghites, Louisa. *Multicultural Perspectives on Drug Abuse and Its Prevention: A Resource Book.* Rockville, Md.: U.S. Department of Health, Education, and Welfare, Public Health Service, Alcohol, Drug Abuse, and Mental Health Administration, National Institute on Drug Abuse, Division of Research Development, Prevention Branch, 1979.

Mississippi Governor's Multi-Cultural Advisory Council. *Report of the Governor's Multi-Cultural Advisory Council.* Jackson: Mississippi Governor's Multi-Cultural Advisory Council, 1979.

Morgan, Gordon D. *America without Ethnicity.* Port Washington, N.Y.: Kennikat Press, 1981.

Multicultural Education and the American Indian. Los Angeles: American Indian Studies Center, University of California, 1979.

Norgren, Jill. *American Cultural Pluralism and Law.* New York: Praeger, 1988.

Peterson, William, Michael Novak, and Philip Gleason. *Concepts of Ethnicity.* Cambridge: Belknamp Press of Harvard University Press, 1982.

Pisano, Jane Gallagher. "After the Riots: Multiculturalism in Los Angeles." *National Civic Review* 81:3 (summer–fall 1992).

Smedley, Audrey. *Race in North America: Origin and Evolution of a Worldview.* Boulder, Colo.: Westview Press, 1993.

Smith, David E., et al., eds. *A Multicultural View of Drug Abuse: Proceedings of the National Drug Abuse Conference, 1977.* Cambridge: Schenkman Publishing Company, 1978.

Smolicz, J. J. "Cultural Alternatives in Plural Societies: Separatism or Multiculturalism?" *Journal of Intercultural Studies* 4:3 (1983): 47–68.

Takaki, Ronald. *A Different Mirror: A History of Multicultural America.* Boston: Little, Brown, 1993.

Toure, Kwame (formerly Stokely Carmichael), and Charles V. Hamilton. *Black Power: The Politics of Liberation in America.* New York: Random House, 1967. This book's reissue includes afterwords by Hamilton and Toure that describe Black Power as a "reformism" that failed. Some lessons for current-day multiculturalism may lie herein.

Trager, Oliver. *America's Minorities and the Multicultural Debate.* New York: Facts on File, 1992.

Triandis, Harry C. "The Future of Pluralism." *Journal of Social Issues* 32:4 (1976): 179–208.

Trueba, Henry T. *Healing Multicultural America: Mexican Immigrants Rise to Power in Rural California.* Washington, D.C.: Falmer Press, 1993.

Tumin, Melvin M., and Walter Plotch, eds. *Pluralism in a Democratic Society.* Praeger Special Studies in U.S. Economic, Social, and Political Issues. New York: Praeger, 1977. Intended to aid in curriculum reform in American schools, *Pluralism* is a volume for the "history teacher who wishes to introduce ethnic studies into the classroom" so that s/he may "deal with each ethnic group in the United States without twisting history totally out of context" (from the Foreword). The editors have divided the book into three sections: (1) "A Search for Definition" (cultural pluralism and the social scene); (2) "Psychological Background" (how acceptance or rejection of cultural pluralism is acculturated in the United States); (3) "Curriculum Development" (implications of cultural pluralism for curriculum reform). Most of the articles have extensive charts, tables, and graphs to help support their claims.

Wiebe, Robert H. *The Segmented Society: An Introduction to the Meaning of America.* New York: Oxford University Press, 1975. This book is a brief (200 pp.) history of the influx and subsequent mixing (or lack thereof) of the different ethnic and racial groups in the United States. As such, it "identifies three distinctive social systems" (one lasting until 1790, one from 1830 to 1890, and one from 1920 to 1975) that established policies circumscribing American ethnic and racial groups. Wiebe outlines the subtle differences between various types of race-centered socialization and traces their link to what we now call multiculturalisms.

Contributors

Norma Alarcón is associate professor of Chicano studies and ethnic studies at the University of California, Berkeley. She is the editor and publisher of Third Woman Press, and has published numerous essays and articles on Chicano literature and Chicana feminism. A leading feminist theorist, Alarcón has written a book on the Mexican feminist novelist and poet Rosario Castellanos, and has translated into Spanish the classic book, *This Bridge Called My Back*.

Richard P. Appelbaum is professor of sociology and director of the Center for Global Studies at the University of California, Santa Barbara. He is the author of *Karl Marx*, numerous articles and books on housing and urban policy, and the editor, with Jeffrey Henderson, of *States and Development in the Pacific Rim*. He is currently conducting research on global contracting in the garment industry, looking at the changing geography of capitalist production and its impact on labor.

Edna Bonacich is professor of sociology and ethnic studies at the University of California, Riverside. She is the author of *The Economic Basis of Ethnic Solidarity: Small Business in the Japanese Community* (with John Modell) and *Immigrant Entrepreneurs: Koreans in Los Angeles, 1965-1982* (with Ivan Light), and the coeditor of *Labor Immigration under Capitalism: Asian Workers in the U.S. before World War II* (with Lucie Cheng), *Global Production:*

The Apparel Industry in the Pacific Rim (with Lucie Cheng, Norma Chinchilla, Nora Hamilton, and Paul Org), and *The New Asian Immigration in Los Angeles and Global Restructuring* (with Paul Org and Lucie Cheng).

Wendy Brown is professor of women's studies and legal studies at the University of California, Santa Cruz. She is the author of *Manhood and Politics: A Feminist Reading in Political Theory* and *States of Injury: Essays on Power and Freedom in Late Modernity.*

Antonia I. Castañeda is assistant professor of history at the University of Texas at Austin. Her research focuses on mestizas in colonial California, on women of color in the nineteenth-century Spanish/Mexican/U.S. borderlands, on Chicana/o history, and on Chicana feminisms. In addition to her book-length manuscript entitled *Indias, Españolas, Mestizas, Mulatas, Coyotas, Lobas, y Chinas in Colonial California: The Gendered, Racial and Sexual Politics of Colonialism,* her current projects include an annotated bilingual edition, with a critical introduction, of nineteenth-century California narratives and a social history of Tejana farmworkers in Washington State.

Angie Chabram-Dernersesian is associate professor of Chicana/o literature at the University of California, Davis, where she teaches Chicana/o studies. She has authored articles in the areas of Chicana/o studies, criticism, and ethnography and is coeditor, with Rosa Linda Fregoso, of a special volume of *Cultural Studies* on Chicana/o cultural representation, which includes her essay "Chicana/o Studies as Oppositional Ethnography."

Jon Cruz is assistant professor of sociology at the University of California, Santa Barbara. He has written on historical aspects of African-American music, Filipino Americans, and conservative populism. He is completing a book on elite appropriations of black music in the nineteenth century and is coeditor of *Viewing, Reading, Listening: Audiences and Cultural Reception.*

Angela Y. Davis is professor of History of Consciousness at the University of California, Santa Cruz, where she was recently appointed Presidential Chair in African American and Feminist Studies. Her articles and essays have appeared in numerous journals and anthologies, both scholarly and popular. She is an internationally recognized writer, scholar, lecturer, and activist and the author of several books, including *Angela Davis: An Autobiography; Women, Race and Class;* and a forthcoming volume on black women's music and social consciousness. She currently is conducting research on incarcerated women, racism in the U.S. criminal justice system, and alternatives to jails and prisons.

Darryl B. Dickson-Carr is assistant professor of English at Florida State University. His dissertation, "Black Satire: The Revision of an Art Form in

Twentieth-Century America," studies the history of satire by African-American authors.

Steve Fagin has produced four video epics and has contributed phototext pieces to such publications as *Social Text, Documents,* and *Breakthroughs.* His work has been extensively theorized in *Artforum, Camera Obscura,* and *October* as well as in several critical books. In 1994 a major retrospective of his work was held at the Museum of Modern Art in New York. A book on his work is forthcoming. He teaches at the University of California, San Diego.

Rosa Linda Fregoso is the author of *The Bronze Screen: Chicana and Chicano Film Culture* (University of Minnesota Press) and coeditor with Norma Iglesias of *Mirades de Mujeres* (forthcoming). Fregoso has published on film, cultural studies, and feminism in numerous anthologies and journals, including *Cultural Studies, Theory and Society, Cineaste,* and *Journal of Communication.* She is an associate professor of women's studies at the University of California, Davis.

Avery F. Gordon is assistant professor of sociology at the University of California, Santa Barbara. She is the coeditor of *Body Politics* (with Michael Ryan) and the author of *Ghostly Matters* (forthcoming from the University of Minnesota Press) and several articles on knowledge, gender, and race.

Neil Gotanda has written and lectured extensively on issues of race and legal ideology. His current work uses legal materials to explore questions of racial ideology, immigration, and Asian Pacific Americans. Educated at Stanford, Berkeley, and Harvard, he is professor of constitutional law at Western State University College of Law in Fullerton, California, and resides in West Los Angeles.

Ramón Gutiérrez is professor of history and chair of the Department of Ethnic Studies at the University of California, San Diego. Recipient of the prestigious MacArthur Foundation award, Gutiérrez is the author of *When Jesus Came, the Corn Mothers Went Away: Marriage, Sexuality, and Power in New Mexico, 1500-1846,* as well as numerous articles on Chicano history.

Cynthia Hamilton is the director of African and African-American studies at the University of Rhode Island. She has been an active participant in community affairs and a contributor to many journals and newsletters, and has produced news and commentary programs for public radio on the topics of civil liberties, culture, and politics.

M. Annette Jaimes Guerrero was a visiting professor in American Indian studies at Arizona State University in 1994–95. During the summer of 1995 she was a field researcher in a Native Researchers Cancer Control Training

Program at the University of New Mexico Health Sciences Center with the University of Arizona. In fall 1995 she joins the faculty of the San Francisco State University Women's Studies program.

George Lipsitz is professor of ethnic studies at the University of California, San Diego. A pioneer in the field of cultural studies, Lipsitz is the author of *Dangerous Crossroads*; *A Rainbow at Midnight*; *Time Passages: Collective Memory and American Popular Culture*; *Sidewalks of St. Louis*; *A Life in the Struggle: Ivory Perry and the Culture of Opposition*; and *Class and Culture in Cold War America*.

Lisa Lowe teaches comparative literature at the University of California, San Diego. She is the author of *Critical Terrains: French and British Orientalisms* (1991) and a book on Asian-American cultural production (forthcoming).

Wahneema Lubiano teaches in the Department of English and the Program in African-American Studies at Princeton University. She is the author of numerous articles on African-American women writers and on African-American popular culture and theory, including "Black Ladies, Welfare Queens, and State Minstrels: Ideological War by Narrative Means" in *Racing Justice, En-Gendering Power: The Anita Hill-Clarence Thomas Controversy and the Construction of Reality*, edited by Toni Morrison.

Christopher Newfield is associate professor of English at the University of California, Santa Barbara. He is the author of *The Emerson Effect: Individualism and Submission in America* and of articles on nineteenth-century American culture and contemporary society and culture. He has edited *After Political Correctness: The Humanities and Society in the 1990s* with Ron Strickland.

Michael Omi is currently associate professor of ethnic studies and chair of the Asian American Studies Program at the University of California, Berkeley. He writes about racial theory and politics, and is the coauthor, with Howard Winant, of *Racial Formation in the United States: From the 1960s to the 1990s*.

Lourdes Portillo is a filmmaker living in the Bay Area. Her most recent film is *The Devil Never Sleeps*. Her other films include *Las Madres: The Mothers of the Plaza de Mayo* and *La Ofrenda: The Day of the Dead*.

Cedric J. Robinson is chair of the Department of Black Studies and professor of political science at the University of California, Santa Barbara. Robinson is the author of *Terms of Order*, the pathbreaking *Black Marxism: The Making of the Black Radical Tradition*, and numerous articles on U.S., African, and Caribbean political thought, Western social theory, film, and the press. His most recent work is *The Anthropology of Marxism*. He is also an editor of the journal *Race and Class*, and the producer of *Third World News Review*, a local television program.

Tricia Rose is assistant professor of Africana studies and history at New York University. She is the author of *Black Noise: Rap Music and Black Culture in Contemporary America* and coeditor, with Andrew Ross, of *Microphone Fiends: Youth Music and Youth Culture*.

Gregg Scott is a Ph.D. candidate in the Department of Sociology at the University of California, Santa Barbara. He is currently doing fieldwork in Los Angeles for his dissertation, which is entitled "Globalization, Multiculturalism, and the Fashioning of Resistance: A Historical-Sociological Ethnography of Class Struggle in the Los Angeles Apparel Industry."

Paul Smith is professor of English at George Mason University. He is the editor, with Alice Jardine, of *Men in Feminism*, and, with Lisa Frank, of *Madonnarama*. He is the author of *Pound Revised, Discerning the Subject* (University of Minnesota Press) and most recently *Clint Eastwood: A Cultural Production* (University of Minnesota Press). His next book, *Bearing North: Essays in Cultural Studies*, is forthcoming, as is an edited collection of essays, *Boys: Culture and Masculinity*. He recently published a collection of translations from Jean Louis Schefer, *The Enigmatic Body*.

Renee Tajima is an Academy Award-nominated filmmaker who lives in Los Angeles and New York City. She is the director of the powerful documentary *Who Killed Vincent Chin?*, *The Best Hotel on Skid Row*, and *Jennifer's in Jail*. She is a commentator for National Public Radio's *Crossroads* series and has been a film critic for the *Village Voice*, associate editor of the *Independent Film & Video Monthly*, and editor of *Bridge: Asian American Perspectives*. Her most recent film-in-progress, to be broadcast on PBS, is entitled *Fortune Cookies: In Search of Asian America* (working title) and explores the search for Asian America.

Patricia Zavella is professor of community studies at the University of California, Santa Cruz. She is the author of *Women's Work and Chicano Families: Cannery Workers of the Santa Clara Valley* and *Sunbelt Working Mothers: Reconciling Family and Factory*, coauthored with Louise Lamphere, Felipe Gonzáles, and Peter B. Evans. She is currently researching poverty in Santa Clara County, comparing how Mexican immigrants, Chicanos, and whites adapt to the local labor market, and how economics and cultural notions about gender and sexuality affect the formation of poor households.

Index

COMPILED BY MARTIN L. WHITE